THE LANCELOT-GRAIL
READER

GARLAND REFERENCE LIBRARY OF THE HUMANITIES
VOLUME 1770

THE LANCELOT-GRAIL READER

SELECTIONS FROM THE MEDIEVAL FRENCH ARTHURIAN CYCLE

EDITED BY

NORRIS J. LACY

GARLAND PUBLISHING, INC.
A MEMBER OF THE TAYLOR & FRANCIS GROUP
NEW YORK & LONDON
2000

Published in 2000 by
Garland Publishing, Inc.
A member of the Taylor & Francis Group
29 West 35th Street
New York, NY 10001

10   9   8   7   6   5   4

Library of Congress Cataloging-in-Publication Data

Lancelot (Prose Cycle) .   English.   Selections.
    The Lancelot-Grail reader : selections from the medieval French
Arthurian cycle / Norris J. Lacy, editor.
        p.   cm.   —   (Garland reference library of the humanities ;
2162)
    Includes bibliographical references.
    ISBN 0-8153-3419-2 (alk. paper)
    1. Lancelot (Legendary character)—Romances.   2. French prose
literature—To 1500—Translations into English.   3. Arthurian
romances.   I. Lacy, Norris J.   II. Title   III. Series.
PQ1489.L2E56   2000   99-39114
843' . 1—dc21   CIP

Contents

Introduction

NORRIS J. LACY

The legend of King Arthur has its roots in the fifth or sixth century, following the Roman withdrawal from Britain around A.D. 410. Not long after that time, stories began to circulate concerning the exploits of a hero and leader to whom the name "Arthur" would eventually be attached. Although it is clear that there was never a "King Arthur" corresponding to the legendary figure known to modern readers, there may very well have been a real model, or multiple models, for the king. But whether he lived or not, the tales about him captured the popular imagination and grew into one of the great and enduring legends of all time.

Early references to Arthur, however, were mostly limited to lists of battles or isolated anecdotes about his accomplishments. Only in the twelfth century was he endowed with a full biography and finally established as a king and not merely a warrior. That fictional biography was part of Geoffrey of Monmouth's Latin chronicle entitled *Historia regum Britanniae* ("History of the Kings of Britain"), written around 1136. Geoffrey presents many of the Arthurian motifs now familiar to us: Arthur's conception and birth, his wars, his marriage to Guenevere, his eventual wounding and departure for Avalon.

Other familiar Arthurian subjects were introduced by French authors who wrote in the decades following Geoffrey. For example, Wace, a French adapter of Geoffrey's work, first wrote of the Round Table in 1155. However, the most important of these writers—indeed, one of the half-dozen most important of all Arthurian authors—is Chrétien de Troyes, who composed five Arthurian romances late in the century (ca. 1170–90). It was Chrétien who introduced the Grail and Camelot into world literature, and it was also he who first presented a young French knight named Lancelot, who quickly became both a favored knight of the Round Table and the lover of Arthur's queen, Guenevere.

The Grail is at the center of Chrétien's final and unfinished romance, *Perceval or The Story of the Grail.* There the Grail is a wondrous and mysterious dish or platter, and although it is once described as a "holy object," it is not the Holy Grail as we now think of it. But soon after, another writer of romance, Robert de Boron, took up the Grail theme and, in effect, reinvented it after scripture. Robert's identification is explicit: the Holy Grail was the vessel of the Last Supper, later given to Joseph of Arimathea, who used it to collect Christ's blood following the Crucifixion.

Early in the thirteenth century, the Arthurian world (including Merlin, the Round Table, and Camelot), the intriguing love story of Lancelot and Guenevere, and the quest for the holy and elusive Grail—these and other themes and motifs coalesced in the remarkable Arthurian cycle of romances known variously as the Lancelot-Grail, the Prose *Lancelot,* the Vulgate Cycle of Arthurian Romance, or occasionally the Pseudo-Map Cycle.[1]

The Vulgate Cycle

The full cycle comprises five romances, although comparatively few of the manuscripts preserve all five. Three of the romances, probably composed within a decade or so after 1215, form the core of the Vulgate. The first of those is *Lancelot,* often identified as the *Lancelot* Proper to distinguish it clearly from the cycle within which it often stands.[2] This is a huge, sprawling romance, its dimensions indicated by the fact that Alexandre Micha's critical edition of it required nine volumes.[3] Although the romance recounts many of Arthur's wars and adventures, its primary subject, as the title indicates, is Lancelot. In this romance we read of Lancelot's infancy, his upbringing by the Lady of the Lake (whose power comes from both Merlin and the Devil), and his introduction at court. We also follow his subsequent chivalric adventures, which include numerous instances of imprisonment, wounds, and deceptions. A significant portion of the romance is devoted to Galehaut, the knight who arranges for Lancelot's first amorous rendezvous with the queen. Other knights whose adventures are traced in some detail in the *Lancelot* are Gauvain (Gawain), Hector, and Bors, the last of whom begins here his emer-

---

[1]The last derives from the cycle's attribution, within the text itself, to Walter Map. The attribution is false: Walter had died before the romances were composed.

[2]Some manuscripts of the *Lancelot* Proper do not include the preparations for and predictions of Galahad's coming. Consequently, many scholars, most notably Elspeth Kennedy (see bibliography), have concluded that there also existed a shorter noncyclic *Lancelot,* which in many of its parts was virtually identical to the cyclic version but which was intended to stand as an independent composition.

[3]More precisely, eight volumes of text and a volume of indices. For his edition, see the bibliography following this introduction.

gence as one of the elect who, along with Perceval and Galahad, will achieve considerable success in the Grail Quest.

That quest is recounted in the following romance, entitled *La Queste del saint Graal* ("The Quest for the Holy Grail"); it offers an account of the quest by Arthur's knights and its ultimate accomplishment by Galahad. At the beginning of the work, knights vow that they will seek the Holy Grail for "as long as it is necessary." Readers may initially be surprised to note that Arthur is far from enthusiastic about the quest; instead, he is angry and depressed about the prospect, for he immediately understands that, although the quest may unite his knights in a common purpose, that purpose does not—except negatively—involve Camelot or the Round Table society itself. Indeed, as Arthur realizes, the Grail both draws knights away from his court and, owing to the dangers inherent in the quest, ensures that many of them will not return.

But those dangers are not simply a matter of physical separation and peril, for the *Queste* constitutes an actual and sometimes explicit repudiation of the Round Table. In this romance, traditional chivalric values are supplanted by an ideal of "celestial chivalry," which is both a religious ideal and an extraordinarily rigorous moral standard that precludes from final success in the Grail Quest not only those who have sinned but even those who have ever been *tempted* to sin. Although there is a hierarchy of failure, with some knights eliminated early and others (Bors and Perceval) permitted entry to the Grail Castle with Galahad, it is only the last who, owing to the absolute purity that makes him a Christ-figure, can achieve the ultimate Grail vision.

The reexamination of both chivalry and love continues in the final romance in the chronology of Arthur's reign. *La Mort le roi Artu* (or *La Mort Artu,* "The Death of King Arthur") is the cycle's epilogue, and it starkly presents the story of an impoverished post-Quest Round Table, now bereft of many of its best knights. In this romance, we are told that no more adventures are available to Arthur's knights. Consequently, their chivalric activity is initially limited to sport, that is, to a series of tournaments that Arthur organizes in a desperate effort to maintain their martial skills. Later, those skills are used, tragically, in what the narrator and several of his characters call "the war that will have no end," a struggle that will pit Lancelot against Gauvain and Arthur and will eventually destroy Camelot.

The seeds of that destruction were sown long before, and primary among its causes, along with Mordred's treachery, is the love of Lancelot and Guenevere. Lancelot had vowed during the Grail Quest to renounce his relationship with the queen, but at the very beginning of the *Mort Artu* we are told that they immediately lapse again into sin and that, moreover, they are so careless and indiscreet that soon their behavior is revealed. And once revealed, their love provokes a cataclysm that leaves few alive.

At the end, Arthur, gravely wounded by his illegitimate son, Mordred, is taken away in a boat by several women, including his half-sister Morgan le

Fay. Yet this text does not hold out the promise, familiar to us from other accounts, that Arthur will survive and will return in the hour of Britain's greatest need. Indeed, three days later, Arthur's tomb is discovered. The light that illuminated the world for "one brief shining hour," as T.H. White would later put it, has been extinguished.

No sooner were these first three romances composed than other authors added *L'Estoire del saint Grail* ("The History of the Holy Grail") and *Merlin*. Though written later, these two stand before the three others in terms of their chronological schema, and they thus provide a retrospective introduction to the cycle. The *Estoire* foreshadows the *Queste,* even duplicating many of its events but presenting those duplications as predictions. It also traces the "prehistory" of the Grail back to the time of Joseph of Arimathea, to whom the Holy Vessel was entrusted, as well as Joseph's son, Josephus (the first Christian bishop) and his descendants. Eventually, the Grail is placed in a castle and guarded in anticipation of the coming of the chosen Grail knight.

The *Merlin* romance and a narrative continuation known as the *Suite-Vulgate* ("Vulgate [or Merlin] Continuation") give an account of the magician's life. They emphasize his role in Arthur's conception, when Merlin's powers transform Uther Pendragon into the likeness of Igerne's husband and thereby enable Uther to lie with her. *Merlin* also dramatizes the test of the sword in the stone and the young man's accession to the throne. Although magic plays an important role in this romance's exposition, its central subjects are political and military in nature, with Merlin serving as the king's advisor. However, the author also emphasizes religious or mystical symbolism, informing us, for example, that the Round Table is a replica of the Grail Table, which was itself modeled after the Table of the Last Supper. The *Suite* also links this romance to the *Lancelot* by recounting the birth of Lancelot, as well as Arthur's marriage to Guenevere.

Authorship

Scholars have been unable to identify the author or authors of the romances, although a number of hypotheses have been advanced. Jean Frappier suggested that the cycle had an "architect," someone who planned at least the *Lancelot-Queste-Mort* group and who may well have written part of it. The notion of a single plan is based in part on the existence, throughout the romances, of an elaborate system of cross-references, foreshadowings and predictions, and recapitulations and recalls. That the narrative attitudes toward some subjects, and especially toward what is customarily if misleadingly called "courtly love," differ from one romance to another may well reflect an attempt to make the cycle into an exploration of, or a dialogue on, those subjects. The *Lancelot* and *Queste* authors clearly contradict each other in their treatment of courtly love. The former offers at least a muted endorsement of the love of Lancelot and Guenevere, a love that seems both to inspire and to ennoble Lancelot. The *Queste,* on the other hand, is uncompromisingly hostile toward such love, which is seen as not only frivolous but as sinful and pernicious.

The *Mort Artu* maintains, in modified form, that hostility toward the relationship of Lancelot and Guenevere, and it does not shrink from tracing the consequences of a love already roundly condemned in the preceding romance. However, the narrator of the final volume evinces less interest in moral judgment than in the social and political implications of actions. The love affair that Lancelot and Guenevere resume, with far more passion than discretion, proves destructive, and what is destroyed is nothing less than the Arthurian world. Yet, ruinous though that love may be, its consequences merely accelerate and complete a process of decline and decay begun much earlier. The *Queste* has imposed an implicit death sentence on chivalry, Camelot, and Arthur himself; the *Mort Artu* carries out the sentence.

Composition

Whether the Vulgate had one or several authors, the construction of the cycle is extraordinary. Compositions of this length and complexity, often following as they did the progress of large numbers of knights whose adventures take them in many directions, required a way to maintain clearly the multiple story lines. Part of the solution in the Vulgate was a sophisticated technique called *entrelacement* or structural interlace. The foreshadowings and recalls already mentioned are an element of this method. It consists, to oversimplify drastically, of the regular suspension of one story line to pick up one or more others; when those are in turn suspended, the text may take up another narrative or return to the original one to elaborate it further, again dropping it one or several times before tying it up with others. Within these multiple and intercut narrative lines, the authors maintain a remarkably precise and consistent chronology.

Although a very brief description of interlace inevitably makes it sound elementary and obvious, it is anything but that. The effect, as Eugene Vinaver long ago pointed out, is less that of a mosaic, with interlocking pieces set next to one another, than that of a tapestry, with its narrative threads interwoven in such a way that ". . . a single cut across it, made at any point, would unravel it all."[4] As Vinaver notes, a theme is introduced, only to disappear, to reappear, and to be ". . . abandoned again, but it keeps recurring, while in the intervals other themes rise to the surface, each broken up into comparatively short

---

[4]Eugene Vinaver, *Form and Meaning in Medieval Romance,* Modern Humanities Research Committee (Leeds: Maney, 1966), p. 10.

fragments, all carefully interwoven with one another, entwined, latticed, knotted or plaited like the themes in a Romanesque ornament caught in a constant movement of endless complexity" (*Form and Meaning,* p. 17).

To complicate matters further, the precise nature and uses of interlace vary from romance to romance within the cycle, and toward the middle of the last one, *La Mort le Roi Artu,* it largely disappears, yielding to a straightforward narrative method that emphasizes direct cause-and-effect relationships, as the cycle hurtles toward its conclusion and the destruction of the Round Table society and of the Arthurian world.

The Post-Vulgate Cycle

Not long after the Vulgate Cycle was composed (or perhaps even as it was being concluded), it was modified to produce another, related, cycle. The latter is known variously as the Post-Vulgate Cycle, the Post-Vulgate *Romance of the Grail,* or the Pseudo-Robert de Boron.[5] It has not survived whole, and many portions of it are known only through fragmentary translations into Spanish or Portuguese. However, scholars have largely reconstructed it from the fragments.[6]

There is reason to believe that this cycle may be the work of a single author or adapter. From the Vulgate Cycle he apparently simply borrowed the *Merlin,* and perhaps the *Estoire* as well, with little change. Those narratives are followed by a transitional section known as the *Suite du Merlin* ("The *Merlin* Continuation"). There is no *Lancelot* romance per se, but there is a greatly expanded Post-Vulgate *Queste del saint Graal,* followed by a truncated *Mort Artu.* There is a concomitant shift of focus and interest: no longer is the downfall of the Arthurian world traceable in large part to Lancelot's and Guenevere's love. Instead, it results principally from Arthur's own sin when he engaged in an incestuous relationship with his sister and engendered Mordred.

A major impetus for future action is the Dolorous Stroke (or Dolorous Blow), a lance blow by Balin that strikes King Pellehan through the thighs. The result is the Waste Land, the withering and ruin of the land, whose health is tied to that of its king.[7] Thus, Merlin ". . . found trees down and grain destroyed and all things laid waste, as if lightning had struck in each place. . . . He found half the people in the villages dead, both bourgeois and knights, and

---

[5]As the Vulgate misleadingly identifies its author as Walter Map, so does the Post-Vulgate contain a spurious attribution to Robert de Boron. Robert was in fact the author of a Grail romance or of a trilogy that may well have served as the model for the later prose reworkings, but he did not compose the Post-Vulgate.

[6]Most notable among those scholars is Fanni Bogdanow. See bibliography.

[7]This theme is the subject of T.S. Eliot's 1922 poem "The Waste Land," though his direct inspiration was from Jessie Weston's 1913 *From Ritual to Romance.*

he found laborers dead in the fields. . . . He found the kingdom of Listinois so totally destroyed that it was later called by everyone the Kingdom of Waste Land . . ." (Asher, IV, 214).

The function of the Grail quest in the Post-Vulgate is to repair the damage done by the Dolorous Stroke. When the quest has been completed, Galahad is able to heal Pellehan. Soon after, Galahad is made king of Sarras, the land to which the Grail returns; he dies a year later, and the Grail is taken up into heaven.

The *Post-Vulgate Death of Arthur* reflects some of the events of its Vulgate counterpart but is reduced to about one-eighth the length of the earlier romance. Near the end, the author adds a provocative detail: when Arthur's grave is found, it is empty except for his helmet. The text does not promise his return, but unlike the Vulgate *Mort Artu,* it is careful not to close off that possibility. In the Post-Vulgate, Arthur is proclaimed a "mysterious king, whose death no man shall know." A cycle dominated by a sense of mystery thus closes by evoking the greatest mystery of all—Arthur's fate.

About This Book

Between 1993 and 1996, a team of nine translators produced full and annotated translations of both cycles in five large volumes. The present book is drawn from that work. We have chosen neither to condense the entire translation nor to offer numerous short excerpts from the Vulgate Cycle. Instead, we have reproduced fewer and longer selections, chosen from among the most significant episodes of the original.[8]

In the case of the Post-Vulgate, we offer only a small sampling of episodes, even though these are important and exceedingly fascinating romances that are far more than a reworking of the Vulgate.[9]

The excerpts reprinted here are connected by narrative summaries provided by the editor. Those summaries, italicized and enclosed within square brackets, are designed to be as brief as possible, and much essential or

---

[8]Owing to the length of the Lancelot-Grail Cycle—about six times longer than the present volume—we have had to eliminate a great deal of fascinating material. That includes battle scenes and tournaments, often narrated at great length and in extraordinary detail by the authors. Our deleting those scenes in large numbers does not indicate that we consider them unimportant; on the contrary, it is apparent that medieval audiences savored and appreciated them. However, such sequences, far more than most other material from the cycle, can be cut without disrupting the narrative coherence of the text.

[9]Though not contained in our excerpts, an example of the differences between the Vulgate and the Post-Vulgate is the latter's inclusion of Tristan, Iseut, and her husband, King Mark, in the Arthurian pantheon. This cycle, therefore, along with the French *Prose Tristan* of about the same time, represents the final fusion of the Tristan legend with that of Arthur. Originally, they had been independent narratives.

fascinating material is omitted; only enough is retained to permit the reader to grasp the connection between passages and to follow the major narrative lines of the cycles.[10] In some cases, a few sentences of summary may represent a page or less of the original; elsewhere they may replace several chapters. (Wherever short passages are omitted without summary, that omission is indicated by ellipsis marks enclosed in square brackets: [. . .].) Those who may want more information are directed to the full translation or to the fuller chapter summaries printed in Volume V (pp. 315–80) of that translation.

One of the unfortunate but unavoidable consequences of this approach is the partial loss of the interlacing technique that weaves together the diverse narrative threads. Although the technique and effect of interlace have been described briefly in this introduction, only a reading of the full texts can convey the richness of the cycles' material and the complexity of their design.

We have retained few of the notes that accompanied our original translation. The majority of those notes concerned such technical matters as variant manuscript readings and translation problems. Others clarified the elaborate references (to characters or events) that are a part of the interlace technique. In the latter case, those notes remain if the material to which a passage refers to is included in this volume.

However, some of the original notes referred to material we have excised here. For example, when Gawain is asked for news of Lancelot (in *Lancelot,* Chapter 43), he replies that "I haven't seen him since he was victorious in the tournament at Penning Castle"—but that tournament is not a part of our excerpts. Similar examples occur frequently, and statements such as "Lancelot came to the castle where he had earlier fought a battle" or "This was the same maiden who had liberated Lancelot" may refer to a character or event that the reader has not encountered before. Rather than clutter the text with cumbersome explanatory notes about what is *not* here—an approach we found awkward and distracting—we have chosen simply to forewarn the reader in the introduction. We generally identify allusions to excluded material only when the text would be otherwise incomprehensible.[11]

The present volume retains the chapter structure of our original, but we have renumbered chapters consecutively. The following list identifies the

---

[10]On occasion we have departed from our original translation in very small ways, such as the addition of a proper name to clarify a pronoun reference; in those instances we have not inserted brackets.

[11]It should be added that, on occasion, the text itself, using its customary formulas "as the story has told" or "as the story will tell," refers to events that are not included in the cycle as we have it. Either the events in question were never composed or they existed in the original but were dropped from subsequent manuscript copies. Such inconsistencies are however comparatively rare, considering the length and narrative complexity of the cycle.

chapters of the full translation to which the present ones correspond. (For example, in *The History of the Holy Grail*, Chapters 1 through 8 of this volume reproduce all or parts of Chapters 1, 2, 4, 7, 8, 30, 34, and 40 of the five-volume translation.)

The History of the Holy Grail, trans. Carol J. Chase: Chapters 1–2, 4, 7–8, 30, 34.

The Story of Merlin, trans. Rupert T. Pickens: Chapters 1, 3–5, 20, 25, 27–29, 37, 42, 57, 59–60.

Lancelot, multiple translators: Samuel N. Rosenberg, Chapters 9, 21–22, 24, 40, 46; Carleton W. Carroll, 52, 58, 59, 69–71; Samuel Rosenberg, 72, 74–75, 80, 95, 101, 105–06; Roberta L. Krueger, 107–14, 120–21, 137, 140; William W. Kibler, 149–50, 154, 156–57; Carleton W. Carroll, 159, 169, 171, 176–79.

The Quest for the Holy Grail, trans. E. Jane Burns: Chapters 1–5, 7, 9–10, 15, 20–22, 63–67, 69–72, 80–85.

The Death of Arthur, trans. Norris J. Lacy: Chapters 1, 5, 11–12, 21–25.

In Appendix, excerpts from *The Post-Vulgate Cycle,* trans. Martha Asher: Chapters 20, 75, 148; 1, 85, 97, 147; 37; 1, 7, 11, 13, 66, 158. (Because our intent is to offer from the Post-Vulgate a few subjects that are either lacking from the Vulgate or developed differently here, these excerpts are grouped thematically rather than arranged chronologically.)

We wish to renew the acknowledgments in the original translations and to add to them our gratitude to Derek Morr, for invaluable computer assistance, and to Kristi Long and James Morgan of Garland Publishing.

Selected Bibliography

Translation

Lacy, Norris J., ed. *Lancelot-Grail: The Old French Arthurian Vulgate and Post-Vulgate in Translation,* 5 vols. New York: Garland, 1993–96. [This is the translation excerpted in the present volume. For more information about the cycles, see the introduction by E. Jane Burns (I, xv–xxxii). In IV, 163–66, Martha Asher offers additional introductory and bibliographical material concerning the Post-Vulgate. Full summaries of all the material are also presented in vol. V.]

Editions Of The Medieval Texts

The following titles are the critical editions from which we translated. Readers wishing to locate material in those editions can do so by consulting the full translation cited above; the first footnote in each chapter of the translation is a reference to the corresponding pages of the edition.

Ponceau, Jean-Paul, ed. *L'Estoire del Saint Graal.* Doctoral dissertation (Paris), 1989.
Bogdanow, Fanni. *La Version Post-Vulgate de la "Queste del saint Graal" et de la "Mort Artu."* 3 vols. Paris: SATF, 1991.
Frappier, Jean, ed. *La Mort le Roi Artu.* 3rd ed. Geneva: Droz, 1964.
Kennedy, Elspeth, ed. *Lancelot do Lac: The Non-Cyclic Old French Prose Romance.* 2 vols. Oxford: Clarendon, 1980.
Micha, Alexandre, ed. *Lancelot: Roman en prose du XIIIe siècle.* 9 vols. Geneva: Droz, 1978–83.
———, ed. *Merlin: Roman du XIIIe siècle.* Geneva: Droz, 1979.
Pauphilet, Albert, ed. *La Queste del saint Graal.* Paris: Champion, 1921.
Sommer, H. Oskar, ed. *The Vulgate Version of the Arthurian Romances.* 7 vols. Washington, DC: The Carnegie Institute, 1908–16.

Selected Studies

Baumgartner, Emmanuèle. *La Queste del saint Graal*. Paris: Champion, 1979.

Bogdanow, Fanni. *The Romance of the Grail: A Study of the Structure and Genesis of a Thirteenth Century Arthurian Prose Romance*. Manchester: University of Manchester Press, 1966.

————. "The *Suite du Merlin* and the Post-Vulgate *Roman du Graal*. In Roger Sherman Loomis, ed., *Arthurian Literature in the Middle Ages: A Collaborative History*. Oxford: Clarendon, 1959, 1974. Pp. 325–35.

Burns, E. Jane. *Arthurian Fictions: Rereading the Vulgate Cycle*. Columbus: Ohio State University Press, 1985.

Frappier, Jean. "The Vulgate Cycle." In Roger Sherman Loomis, ed., *Arthurian Literature in the Middle Ages: A Collaborative History*. Oxford: Clarendon, 1959, 1974. Pp. 295–318.

Kennedy, Elspeth. *Lancelot and the Grail: A Study of the Prose Lancelot*. Oxford: Clarendon Press, 1986.

Kibler, William W., ed. *The Lancelot-Grail Cycle: Text and Transformations*. Austin: University of Texas Press, 1994.

Leupin, Alexandre. *Le Graal et la littérature*. Lausanne: L'Age d'Homme, 1982.

Lot, Ferdinand. *Etude sur le Lancelot en prose*. 1918; Paris: Champion, 1954.

Micha, Alexandre. *Essais sur le cycle du Lancelot-Graal*. Geneva: Droz, 1987.

————. "The Vulgate *Merlin*." In Roger Sherman Loomis, ed., *Arthurian Literature in the Middle Ages: A Collaborative History*. Oxford: Clarendon, 1959, 1974. Pp. 319–24.

The Lancelot-Grail Cycle

The History of the Holy Grail

TRANSLATED BY CAROL J. CHASE

1. Prologue.

The one who, by order of the Great Master, is setting in writing the high and noble story of the Grail first sends greetings to all those men and women who believe in the glorious Holy Trinity, that is, the Father and the Son and the Holy Spirit—the Father, who creates and gives life to all things; the Son, who delivers all those who believe in Him from perpetual pain and brings them to the high joy without end; the Holy Spirit, who sanctifies and purifies good things.

The name of the writer of this story is not divulged at the beginning. However, the words that will be said herein will permit you to know a great deal about his name, his life, and his ancestry. But he does not wish to reveal his name at the beginning, for three reasons. First, if he gave his name and said that through him God had revealed such a noble and lofty story as that of the Grail, the foundation of all stories, the treacherous and envious might interpret it as boastfulness. The second reason is that someone who knows him might hear his name, and thus might prize the story less, because it had been written down by such a humble person—for he holds himself to be the most humble and despised person ever created. The third reason is that if there were anything improper in the story, through either the omissions or the naïveté of writers who later transmit it from one place to another, all the blame would be placed on him. For there are now in our times more mouths that recount evil than good, and a man is blamed more for doing a single bad deed than he is praised for one hundred good ones. For these three reasons he does not wish his name to be completely revealed, even though no matter how much he may wish to cover it up and hide it, it will be better known than he would like. However, he will clearly reveal how the high history of the Holy Grail was confided to him and when, and who gave it to him.

Seven hundred seventeen years after the Passion of Jesus Christ it happened that I, the most sinful of all sinners, was lying in a small hut, at the hour called the vigil of the night. The place where I was lying, as God knows (who knows all thoughts), was far away and remote. And I can say this much: it was in a wilder place than there is in all of fair Britain. Nevertheless, it was very delightful and pleasant, for when Our Lord wants to work His way in one of His Christians, He has soon prepared him so that all the things the world despises please him, and all those the world prizes annoy him. That night, I was lying down as you have heard—it was the night between Maundy Thursday and Good Friday—and may it please Our Lord, I had done the matins[1] ser-

---

[1]Times of day in the Middle Ages were based on the canonical hours laid out in the rule of St. Benedict. Since these hours were regulated by the sun, the exact time varied according to locality and season, but the following approximations can be given: prime, or first hour, was at sunrise; tierce fell at mid-morning (about 9:00 A.M.); sext, at midday; nones, at mid-afternoon (about 3:00 P.M.); vespers, at sunset; complin was at about 9:00 P.M.; matins, at midnight; and lauds, at about 3:00 A.M.

vice called Tenebrae.[2] And then there came over me a great desire to sleep, so I began to doze in my bed where I lay.

Hardly had I begun to doze when I heard a voice that called me three times by name and said, "Wake up and listen: three things are the same as one, and one is the same as three; one can do as much as the three, and they are naturally none other than one." At these words I awoke and looked around me and saw such brightness that nothing so great could issue from any earthly light. After that I saw a man standing in front of me, so handsome and charming that his beauty could not be described by any mortal man's tongue. And when I saw him, I was so awed that I did not know what on earth to say or do.

He looked at me and said, "Did you understand anything at all of the words I spoke to you?"

Trembling, I answered him, "My Lord, I am not at all certain."

He spoke again. "I have brought knowledge about the Trinity." He said this because I had been in doubt about how the Trinity could have three persons and yet only one deity and only one power. Nor had my faith ever allowed of doubts on any other point but this. Then He said to me, "Do you know who I am yet?"

And I replied, "My Lord, my eyes are mortal and thus do not have the power to look directly at the Light of all Lights, nor does my mouth have the strength to say what would confound all sinning tongues."

He leaned down toward me and blew upon my face, and then it seemed to me that my eyes were one hundred times clearer than ever before, and I felt in my mouth a great marvel of tongues. And He said to me, "Do you know who I am yet?"

When I opened my mouth to answer, I saw a fiery brand leap from my body, just like burning flames. I was so terribly afraid when I saw it that I could not say a word. And when He saw my fright, He said, "Be not afraid, for the fountain of all certainty is here before you, and be assured that I have come here to teach you the truth about everything you question, for I hold the true teachings concerning all doubts. I am He through whom all good knowledge is learned, for I am the Great Master through whom all earthly masters know all the good they have learned; yet masters are they not, for none can be master except Him who has all knowledge. I am the Master to whom Nicodemus said, 'Master, we know that you came from God.'[3] I am He about whom the Scripture said, 'All knowledge comes from God Our Lord and is with Him and always has been since before the beginning of time.'[4] Because I am the perfect Teacher, He who is the fountain of all knowledge, I have come to

---

[2] The office of matins and lauds sung on the last three days of Holy Week.
[3] See John III, 2.
[4] See the Apocrypha, Ecclesiasticus, I, 1. Reference given by Ponceau.

you, for I want to teach you about all the things that puzzle you; thus I will make you certain and wise about something about which no mortal man was ever certain, and through you, it will be plain and clear to all those who ever hear it told."

At these words He took me by the right hand and put in it a small book no longer or wider than the palm of a man's hand. As I held the book, He said to me, "Do you want to know what I have given you?" I replied that I would very much like to know, and He said, "This is the book in which you will find greater marvels than any mortal heart could conceive. Nor will you ever have any doubts that will not be set straight by this book. Inside are My secrets, which I Myself put there with My own hand, that no man might see if he be not purged beforehand by confession and by three days of fasting with bread and water; and after that he must speak in such a way that he speaks the language of the heart and not that of the mouth. For these secrets cannot be named by any mortal tongue, lest all the four elements be disturbed: it will rain blood, and there will be other marvels; the air will be troubled, the earth will shake visibly, and water will change its color. All this will happen by the power of the words that are written in this book.

"And there is more: any man who looks often inside this little book, as one should, will win the two greatest joys that exist: joy of the soul and joy of the body. For there is no mortal man, no matter how distressed, if he can see inside sincerely, as he should, whose heart will not be delivered at that moment of all anguish and filled with all the joys a mortal heart can have, so pleasant and delightful are the words within; this is the joy of the body. And on the other hand, his soul will be gradually illuminated by spiritual love, so that if he desires earthly things, it will be to put them to work for his Creator; nor will anyone who has held and seen this little book one time die a sudden death, no matter what sin he has committed in this life. This is the joy of the soul."

When He had said this, a voice cried out like a trumpet; then came such a loud noise from on high that it seemed to me that all the firmament had fallen and that the earth had plunged into an abyss; and if the light had been very bright before, it was one hundred times brighter then, for I was so overcome by it that I thought I had lost my sight. And so I fell to the ground as if in a faint. After quite some time, I regained my senses and opened my eyes, but I saw nothing living around me, nor did I know what to think about what I had seen; rather I would have considered it all to be a dream, had I not found the little book in my hand, just as the Great Master had given it to me.

I arose at once, very happy and joyful and, holding all the while the little book with both hands, I fell into prayers, until God brought the day, which I had been longing for. When it was light enough for me to make out the letters, I began to read. At the beginning I found a title that said: "This is the beginning of your lineage." When I saw this, I was very happy, for there was nothing on earth I desired so much as hearing about my lineage. After I had looked at it so long that the hour of prime had passed, it seemed to me that I had read nothing, since so much remained to be read. For I saw there so many words that I was completely baffled how they could be amassed in such a little book, since it seemed to be no larger than the palm of a man's hand. I marveled so much that I myself would have doubted even as I looked at it, if it had not been given to me by the One who can put a great many words in a small place, and who can fill a large place with very little. Thus I looked at the book until about the hour of tierce, till I had learned a great part of my lineage.

There I saw the names and lives of so many valorous men that I hardly dare say or acknowledge that I am descended from them. For when I saw their good lives and the great travails that they had suffered on earth for their Creator, I could not imagine how I could better my life in order that it be worthy of being remembered with theirs. Nor did it seem that I was a man compared with them, but a mere imitation of a man and a disgrace. I dwelled on these thoughts for a long time, but returned finally to the book and read to the end of my lineage. Then I found a title that said: "The book of the Holy Grail begins here." When I had read until past noon and it was probably the hour of nones, I found another that said: "This is the beginning of the fears." I began to read what came after this, seeing things that were terribly fearsome and frightful, and God knows I saw them with great fear, nor would I ever have dared to continue if He by whose commandment all living things are moved had not directed me to do so. After having seen a number of marvelous things, I found the fourth title, which said: "This is the beginning of the marvels." And then I began to think very hard.

As I was thinking, a ray like burning fire descended from the sky and came before my eyes, as loud as thunder. It seemed very much like a flash of lightning, except that the light lasted longer and was brighter and more fearsome. And it descended before me so suddenly that my eyes flashed in my head, and it seemed to me that my brain was stunned, so that I fell to the ground in a dead faint. But the daze did not last very long; as it pleased Our Lord, it passed, and then I lifted my head, opened my eyes, and saw that all the firmament was turning dark and that the sun was losing all its brightness, so that it was as dark as a deep winter night. And when this darkness had lasted long enough for someone to go one hundred steps, it pleased God to end it.

Then it began to grow bright, little by little, so that the sun returned in its former brightness. And now in the place where I was, there descended a scent so sweet and pleasing that if all the spices in the world were compared with it, I do not think they would render the thousandth part of its sweetness or pleasing perfume. Then I heard around me such a sweet song of praise that all the instruments and all the melodies one could hear on earth would be nothing compared with it, for there were so many voices that I do not think anything mortal could ever count the number. And it seemed to be so near that if these were visible things, I could have touched them with my hand; but no matter how much I looked, I could not see even one of all those who were singing. I was able to hear that their song praised Our Lord and that it always ended with: "May honor, glory, power, and force forever be with the destroyers of death and the restorers of eternal life." I understood this refrain of praise, but I could not understand the rest of the song. But above all, it was sweet and pleasing to hear. After they had thus sung, there rang out on high a great marvel of I know not what instruments resembling small bells, and when they ceased ringing the voices started again.

They sang this way seven times, and when it came to the eighth time, they broke off their song so suddenly that it appeared that they had fallen into an abyss. Then it seemed to me that the wings of all the birds in the air flew past me. Once the song had stopped, so did the wonderful fragrance I had smelled for a long time, which had pleased me so much that I would never have sought to be otherwise than I was, as long as it pleased Our Lord.

Thus it ceased. I began to think intently about the marvel I had heard for so long. And then came a voice from on high that said to me, "Stop thinking, get up, and go return to God what you owe Him, for it is certainly time." At these words, I got up, looked around me, and saw that it was already past the hour of nones. Seeing this, I marveled at how quickly the day had gone by, for I thought it was still matins, so much had the reading of the little book pleased me. Upon arising, I put it in such a place that it was always before my eyes. After that I sang my hours, the way they are to be said on that day. And when I had said them, I began the sweet and pious service of the death of Jesus Christ, for on this day did He truly die. Because of this, His body is not symbolically sacrificed on this day, for when the truth comes forward, its figuration must be set aside. On all the other days, the Sacrament is celebrated as a sign that He was sacrificed for us, but on the day that He was truly crucified—this day, Good Friday—it is not, for there is no sign, since the day has come when He was truly crucified.

When, with God's help, I had finished the service up to the point where the priest performs the three parts of the Sacrament, and I was about to receive my Savior, an angel came before me, took me by both hands, and said, "These three parts are forbidden to you, until I have shown you clearly why you have used only one substance and assured you about all these things." At these words, I was raised on high, not in body but in spirit, and I was carried to one of the most delightful places that man has ever seen, to my knowledge, for no matter how much joy any heart could think of, or any tongue could speak of, or any ear could hear of, one hundred thousand times as much would be found there. And if I said that this was in the third heaven, where Saint Paul was carried by the Holy Spirit, perhaps I would be telling the truth;

but it would soon be considered boastfulness and lies. Yet I will say this much: there I was shown what Saint Paul says no tongue of mortal man should reveal. After I had looked at the marvels for a long time, which were more numerous than any mouth could say, the angel called me and said, "Have you ever seen such great marvels?" I replied that I never thought anything so great could exist, and the angel told me he would show me a greater thing yet.

Then he took me and led me to another level, which was a hundred times clearer than glass and so preciously colored that no man could describe with certainty the color, so artful and astonishing it was. There he showed me the power of the Trinity, for I saw the division of the Father and the Son and the Holy Spirit so that I could distinguish one person from another; and I saw clearly how these three persons belong to one substance and one deity and one power. Nevertheless, if I said that I saw the three persons divided one from the other, may neither the envious nor the traitorous reproach me, they who serve only to accuse and blame others. Nor may they say to me that I have spoken against the authority of Saint John the great Evangelist, for he said that no man ever saw the Father or can see Him,[5] and I agree with him. All those who have heard this do not know that when he spoke, he meant mortal men, for as long as the soul is in the body, man is mortal. And it is only the flesh that dies, but once man has shed his body, then he is spiritual, and once he is spiritual, he can certainly see spiritual things. Therefore, you can admit that Saint John meant that no mortal man can see the majesty of the Father.

While I was intent on these great marvels and curious to see them, something rang out just like a crack of thunder, and it seemed to me that all the firmament shook. At once so many celestial beings came that the number was countless. As I looked, all of them fell backwards around the Majesty, as if they had all fallen in a faint. When I saw this, I was terribly afraid, and the angel took me and led me back whence he had taken me. But before he put my spirit in my body, he asked, "Have you seen great marvels?" I said they were so great that if anyone were permitted to recount them to people on earth, no man, no matter how saintly or close to God, would be believed. Above all, no mortal heart could have the courage or the strength to maintain it, nor tongue to tell it. And he said to me, "Are you certain yet about the things you questioned so much?" I answered that there was no man on earth so disbelieving that, if he wished to listen to me with good will, I could not make him understand the points of the Trinity, because I had seen and learned them.

Then he said to me, "Now I will put you whence I took you, and then you

---

[5]See John I. 18.

will receive your Savior more certainly than you did before, for you should not receive a guest you do not know. And if you have seen great marvels, you will find some in this little book that you will not hold to be any less marvelous; but you will not look at it again before you have celebrated the Resurrection of Jesus Christ your Savior." Thereupon, he put my spirit back in my body, and I felt just like someone who has slept and who awakens; and I thought I would see the angel, but he had gone. I looked and saw my Savior—the Eucharist—before me as it was when the angel carried me away; I took it, received it, and took communion with good will and great devotion.

When the service was over, I took the little book and placed it in a small chest where the box containing the host was kept. After that I locked the chest tightly with a key, as I wanted to protect it, and I knew no better place to put it, for it was a very beautiful and pure spot. When I left the chapel, I saw that it was already so late that it was getting dark; I entered my little house and ate such food as Our Lord had given me. Thus I spent this day and the next, until the day of the Resurrection of the Savior came. And when it pleased Him that I perform the service of the day, which is as holy as Our Savior, who sanctified the day, I entered with certainty and ran immediately to the book to see the holy words, for they were so sweet and pleasant to hear that they made me forget all the hunger of the body. But when I opened the chest where I had put the book, I did not find it. This made me so upset that I did not know how to contain myself, and I fully believed that I would never be happy again. So I began to think how it could have been taken from this place, for I had found it closed the way I had left it, and I had taken the key.

While I was thinking about this, I heard a voice say to me, "Why are you so astonished, and what do you fear? Do not marvel if the book has been removed without the chest having been opened. In such a way did Jesus Christ leave the sepulcher without moving the stone. But be comforted, and go eat, for before you see the book, you must undergo great difficulties." When I heard this, I considered myself well rewarded.

[*A voice commanded the narrator to leave to accomplish a task. During his travels, the power of the book was used to cast out a devil. After he returned, a vision came to him.*]

The Great Master came before me dressed in the same clothes as the first time and said, "On the first workday of the week that begins tomorrow, you are to begin copying the book I gave you elsewhere, in order to finish it before Ascension, for it will no longer be seen on earth once the time comes that marks My ascent to heaven. You will find all the things you need to write in the cupboard behind your altar. Do not be afraid of the fact that you have never done such work, for no work can be badly done that is undertaken for Me." Then He left.

In the morning, after arising, I went to the cupboard to see if my vision was true, and found all the things a writer needs. Once Sunday had passed, and I had sung Mass on Monday, I took the little book and the parchment and began to write straightaway. It was the second Monday after Easter, and the writing began with the story of the Crucifixion of Jesus Christ, as you will hear, and I will begin in this way.

2. Joseph of Arimathea Lays Christ's Body in a Sepulcher and Is Imprisoned.

On the day that the Savior of the world suffered death—which confounded our death and restored eternal life to us—there were still very few people who believed in Him: only the glorious Virgin, His sweet mother, and His disciples, who at this time were called His brothers. And though there were others who believed in Him, they were few, so that when the Scripture says He prayed, "Dear Father, if it can be, let Me not undergo this Passion,"[6] He was distressed not so much about the body's anguish as about the fact that He saw His death had not yet redeemed anyone, and that He had not won anyone over by His death other than the thief who asked for mercy on the cross. Because of this, the Scripture says, "I am just like the one who sought the stubble remaining in the field after harvest," that is to say, by His death He had redeemed only the thief, who was nothing compared to the other people, as the stubble is nothing compared to the other grain.

Nevertheless, there were already many who had begun to believe, but they did not dare do it openly because they were afraid of the Jews. Of all the secret believers, the holy writing of the Grail speaks of a noble knight who lived at that time, whose name was Joseph of Arimathea. Arimathea was a city in the land of Ramathaim, beyond the river Jordan, and the text says it belonged to Elcan, Samuel's father. In this city Joseph was born, but he had come to Jerusalem seven full years before Jesus Christ was crucified. He was very pious, gentle, and devout and had converted to Jesus Christ's faith, but he did not dare show it, for the Jews would have killed him. Joseph possessed all the good qualities that mortal man can, for he loved and feared God and was pious and gracious toward his fellow men. He honored and revered those above him and was peaceable and amicable toward his relatives. He neither wronged nor harmed those beneath him and was full of compassion for those who suffer. Such were his good qualities. The first psalm of the Psalter speaks of him when it says, "Happy is the man who does not agree with or follow the advice of the wicked and who does not wish to follow the road sinners take."

---

[6]See Matthew XXVI, 39 and 42; Mark XIV, 36; and Luke XXII, 42.

This man Joseph was in Jerusalem with his wife and a son named Josephus, not the one the Scripture relies upon so often as a witness, but another one who was no less lettered. This Josephus brought his father's lineage across the sea to fair Britain, which is now called England, crossing without oars or a tiller, and with no other sail than the length of material in his undertunic, as the story attests farther along.

When the day came that Jesus was put on the cross, Joseph, who had placed all his love in Him, was very sorrowful. And he thought he would willingly glorify and honor all the things that had belonged to Him, for the text says that "no adversity can divide loyal love."[7] When Joseph saw on the cross the One whom he believed to be the Son of God and the Savior of the world, he was neither frightened nor led to lose his faith because of seeing Him die, but waited for His holy Resurrection, believing in it with certainty. And because he could not see Him alive, he thought he would do what he could to obtain some of the things He had touched while He was alive.

So he went to the house where Jesus had held the Last Supper, where He ate the Paschal lamb with His disciples. Upon arriving, Joseph asked to see the place where He had eaten. He was shown a room set up for dining, on the top floor of the house. There Joseph found the dish[8] from which the Son of God and two others had eaten, before He gave the twelve disciples His flesh and blood to take in communion. Very pleased, Joseph took the dish to his house and put it in an honored and beautiful place.

When Joseph learned that the Savior of the world was dead and that those who had found Him dead intended to break His thighs just as they did to other thieves, he did not want to wait until the cruel and traitorous men who did not believe in Him took Him down from the cross with their vile and filthy hands. So he went to Pilate, whose liege knight he was, for he had been in his service for seven whole years. When he came before Pilate, he beseeched him, as a reward for all the services he had done, to grant him a gift that would cost him very little. And Pilate, who liked him and his service very much, agreed, for he owed him much greater riches than he had requested. Joseph asked for Jesus's body, and Pilate gave it to him, not knowing what he was giving him, for he thought he was giving the body of a poor fisherman, while he was actually giving him the Giver of all great gifts and the Resurrection of all flesh created in human form. This was the richest gift any mortal man ever gave. But because Pilate was not aware of what he was giving, it should be called a humiliation rather than a gift, for if he had believed in the great glory and power of the One whose body he was giving, he would not

---

[7]Perhaps a reference to Proverbs XVII, 17.
[8]The dish was in fact a bowl (*escuele*); both words will be used henceforth. Medieval people usually ate from a bowl, which two people shared.

have taken all the riches and power in the world in exchange. Once it was granted to him, Joseph, who knew very well the great glory of the gift, was very joyful, and he considered himself to be well rewarded, much more so than Pilate considered himself to have rewarded him.

Upon reaching the cross where He still hung, Joseph began to weep very tenderly because of the great pain He had suffered. After he had taken Him down, sighing and weeping bitterly, he laid Him in a sepulcher he had had cut out of the rock, where he himself was to be put at his death. Then he went to his house to seek the bowl. Returning to the body, he used it to gather as much of the blood that dripped out as he could. Then he brought the dish back to his house. Since then, through this dish God has performed many miracles in the Promised Land and many other lands.

After putting the bowl in the purest place he knew of, Joseph took the richest cloth and returned to the sepulcher, where he wrapped the body of his Lord as richly and honorably as he could. Once he had done this, he laid it in the sepulcher and put a very big and heavy rock at the entrance, because he did not want anyone to enter the place where so noble a thing lay as the body of the Son of God.

But when the Jews saw that Joseph had taken down from the cross the One whom they had sentenced to death and damned, and that he had buried Him so nobly, they were very angry and said that it was right that Joseph pay for what he had done against God and their faith. So they decided to seize him at night as soon as he had fallen asleep and take him to a place where he would never be heard of again. All of them agreed upon this plan.

That night, once people were asleep, they set out, and one of them knocked on the door. When it was opened, they all entered at once and seized Joseph, who was sound asleep, and led him a good seven leagues away from Jerusalem to a stronghold belonging to the bishop Caiaphas. This house was in a big marsh, and it had a hollow pillar which seemed to be solid. Inside this pillar was the most hideous and filthy prison ever seen. Nor would any man ever have realized it was there, had he not been told about it beforehand, so subtly crafted was it. After they had led Joseph out of Jerusalem, he was turned over to two of them who had sworn that no one would ever hear news of him from them. They took him to the prison and forbade the jailer to give him anything to eat other than a piece of bread and a cup of water. They immediately returned to Jerusalem, arriving before daybreak, where they heard a great tumult and lamentation for Joseph, who was gone.

When Pilate found out about it, he was very sorrowful. He did not know what to do, for he strongly suspected that the Jews had done this at the prompting of the Master of their faith. Thus he did not know what to do. And when the Sunday came when Jesus was risen, and the guards had told the Jews how they had lost Him, they said they would make Joseph pay dearly for their loss. Thus Caiaphas sent a message to the jailer, to give him nothing to eat and to let him die of hunger. But the Lord, for whom the Jews sought his death, did not intend to abandon him in his affliction; rather He rewarded him one hundred times over for his service. For once His body had left the sepulcher, He came to Joseph in prison, bringing the holy dish Joseph had hidden in his house, with the blood in it that he had gathered, to provide him comfort and company. Seeing this made Joseph very joyful, and then he truly knew this was God. Thus he did not regret his service but was so joyful that he did not care that he was in prison, since he had the comfort, life, and company of his Lord.

Thus the Savior of the world appeared to Joseph before anyone else and comforted him greatly. And He said He was certain that Joseph would not die in prison but would leave safe and sound; nor would he suffer pain or chagrin, for he would always be in His company. And when he left, all who saw him would consider it a miracle. After that he and his descendants would carry His name to foreign places. But it was not yet the time for him to leave; rather, Joseph would remain there until everyone believed him to be dead. And after his departure, His name would be glorified and praised, and many people would believe in Him.

Thus Joseph remained in prison so long that he was completely forgotten, and no one spoke of him anymore. His wife, who was still a young woman, remained behind, distraught, with her son Josephus, who was not yet a year and a half old on the day his father was imprisoned. The lady was often urged to remarry, but she said she would never have a carnal relationship with a man before she knew for certain the truth about her lord, whom she loved more than any other living thing. When the child came of age to marry, his relatives exhorted him to do so, but he was so in love with Jesus Christ because of his mother's guidance that he said he would never marry any other but Holy Church, for he believed in God and had been baptized by the hand of Saint James the Minor, who was bishop of Jerusalem for a long time after Jesus Christ's death.

Joseph remained in prison, as you have heard, until forty-two years had passed. And then Vespasian, the emperor of Rome, freed him, and you will hear how this came about. Joseph was in prison for forty-two years without ever leaving, nor was he ever given anything other to eat than bread and water, and very little of that, about every three days.

On the day that Jesus Christ was crucified, Tiberius Caesar was emperor of Rome, and he remained in power for ten more years. Afterwards reigned his nephew Gaius, who lived only one year. And then Claudius ruled the Roman empire for fourteen years; then Nero, who held the empire fourteen years. Following Nero, came Titus and his son, Vespasian, who was ill. In the third year of Titus's reign, Joseph was freed from prison. This is indeed forty-two years, counting from the Crucifixion of Our Lord Jesus Christ up to Joseph's liberation, and you will hear how he was freed.

3. Joseph and His Followers Depart;
Joseph Preaches Before Evalach in Sarras.

At this point the story says nothing more about Vespasian and begins telling about Joseph, who sent for all his relatives and friends. He began to teach them the faith just as Our Lord had commanded, and he preached to them about Jesus Christ until he converted a good seventy-five, some of whom had already been baptized but whose faith had grown cold. And those who had not been baptized immediately received baptism. Then Joseph and his followers left the city; and it was already past the hour of nones. Once he was beyond the city, Joseph took the road leading to the Euphrates, just as Our Lord had commanded. And when he arrived in Bethany, it began to grow dark.

Then his people said to him, "Dear lord, where shall we spend the night? If we pass this city, we won't find a place to lodge today."

And Joseph replied, "My lords, brothers and sisters, don't be afraid; God the all-powerful, for whose love we have all left our land, will help us so that neither lodging nor food will be lacking. But take care not to despair of His great mercy, for if you serve Him loyally, as a good Christian should, there is nothing your heart could conceive of in the morning that it would not receive before nightfall. Nor did He ever show so much love to our ancestors in the desert as He will show us, if we serve Him as the father should be served by his children. But if we serve Him like stepsons, as our fathers did in the desert, He will not act toward us as a father but as a stepfather, for He will not help us but will fail us when our need is greatest."

Thereupon Joseph left off speaking, and they traveled until they arrived at a wood called the Wood of the Ambush, half a league from Bethany. It was called by that name because in this wood Herod the Tetrarch was ambushed when the Jews delivered him over to Areta, the king of Damascus, because Herod had abandoned Areta's daughter when he took his brother Philip's daughter as wife.

When they reached this wood, Our Lord called Joseph: "Joseph, I am your God, your Savior, your Defender. I am He who delivered your ancestors from the hand of Pharaoh with signs and portents. I had them cross the Red Sea on dry ground and led them to the desert where their hearts had everything they desired. There they angered Me in various ways, at the Water of the Quarrel and by the calf they made to worship.[9] Nevertheless, I helped them and defended them against everyone, so that I put their enemies under their feet.[10] Despite all this, they neither remembered nor acknowledged that I had done good things for them, nor did they serve Me. Rather, in the end they re-

---

[9]See Exodus XVII and XXXII.
[10]See Psalms CX. 1 and Matthew XXII. 44.

warded Me cruelly by damning Me on the wooden cross. But even if the fathers served Me ill, I will not hate the sons, for I want them to repent of their sins, and I care not about death. Because I want you to confer My mercy on the sons of the evil fathers, I have chosen you to carry My name and My faith throughout foreign lands. And you will be the leader of a greater multitude than you think. Through you, they will have My love and My help. And if they wish to consider Me as Father and Lord, they will profit and advance. Now go to your people, and have them take lodging in this wood, and they will have all the food and everything they want, each in his lodging. Before you leave this wood, you shall make an ark for My bowl, and you shall say your prayers in order to have the love of your Lord God. And when you wish to speak to Me, open the ark, wherever you may be, so that only you and your son Josephus see the bowl. Now go and prepare your people and do as I have commanded."

Thereupon Joseph left and came to his people. He had them prepare lodgings in the wood with branches and leaves. After that, they went to pray. And when they returned from prayers, each one found in his hut what he desired to eat. They ate and drank as much as they pleased, and they were more comfortable that night, at their meal and sleeping on the grass, than they had ever been before. In the morning Joseph had the ark made, just as Our Lord had commanded; inside it he put the Savior's dish. After all the people had prayed before the ark, they left the wood and set out on their way, traveling until they arrived at a city called Sarras, between Babylon[11] and Salamander.

From this city came the first Saracens. Those who say that the Saracens are named after Abraham's first wife are not to be believed, for this was falsely invented, nor does it seem reasonable. It is not unknown that Sarah was a Jew, and her son Isaac was a Jew, as were all those who were Isaac's issue. Because the greatest part is considered to represent the whole, and since Jews descended from Sarah, it does not seem reasonable that the Saracens took their name from her. But they were called Saracens after this city named Sarras, because this was the first city where they became certain of what they worshiped. And in this city was founded and established the sect that the Saracens maintained until the coming of Mohammed, who was sent to save them, though he damned himself first, and them afterwards, by his gluttony. Before the founding of the sect, the people of Sarras had no faith, but worshiped everything that pleased them, so that what they worshiped one day was not worshiped the next. But then they established the worship of the sun and the moon and the other planets.

On the eleventh day after leaving Jerusalem, Joseph came to this city with his followers. Upon their arrival at the city's entrance, Our Lord called

---

[11]Babylon is the name by which Cairo was generally known during the Middle Ages.

him and said, "Joseph, you shall go into the city and preach My name, and baptize all those who receive the faith, in the name of the Father, the Son, and the Holy Spirit."

Joseph then replied, "Lord, how will I know how to preach so well, I who have never undertaken such a thing?"

And Our Lord said to him, "Fear not about this, for you have only to open your mouth, and I will put into it a great abundance of words. Nor will you ever find any man, no matter how valiant or learned, who can resist the words I will deliver from your mouth. And I will make you like My apostles, through the miracles and prodigies that I will perform through your hands. But take care that your faith does not become cold, for as long as you are a true believer, anything you dare to ask for will be granted in your need. Now go and think about doing my work, so that you may be paid as a loyal servant. And whatever menace you may receive, be not afraid, for I will watch over you and defend you, wherever you may go."

Joseph left at once and entered the city with his followers. When the inhabitants of the city saw so many people together—for they numbered at least seventy-five—and saw that they were barefoot, they began to wonder who these people were. Joseph and his disciples did not stop until they came before the Temple of the Sun, the most beautiful temple in the city. The Saracens honored and revered it more than all the others, because it was a temple to the sun, the noblest of all the planets. At the entrance to this temple there was a very high, beautiful chamber that had been built and established for the peers of the city to hold their courts of justice and business assemblies. This room was called the Seat of Judgment.

Joseph and the seventy-five I told you about who were in his group entered this room. They were followed by a large number of the Saracens, who marveled at their strangeness, having never seen such unusual people. Upon entering the room, Joseph found a large number of Saracens, including the lord of the city himself, who was called Evalach the Unknown. He was called the Unknown because no man knew in what country he was born, nor where he came from; nor had they ever had news from anyone who had seen or heard of him in the land. But he was so valiant that through his feats of chivalry he had conquered all the land up to the border of Egypt. And he was still very valiant and courageous, but he was so old that he could not endure the effort of bearing arms. Thus he was no longer as feared or dreaded as he had been in his youth. Rather, the Egyptians were warring against him and had already won a good part of his land that bordered on theirs. No more than three days earlier, they had defeated him in battle, routing him from the battlefield. Because of this, he had sent for all the wise men in his domain, for he wanted to ask their advice about how he might avenge the shame the Egyptians had done to him.

At this point, Joseph arrived and heard them discussing the king's defeat and misfortune. After hearing the truth of the matter, he rejoiced, for he thought that the time had come for his words to be heard and put to work, because of the great need King Evalach had of Our Lord's help. So he began to thank Our Lord, his Creator, for bringing him there at such a favorable moment. The king had spoken to all his noblemen, and was unable to find help. Rather, they had all failed him, saying they would never again combat the Egyptians, for the latter were far more numerous, and thus only misfortune could befall them. And this was clear, they said, for things had already gone so badly that they did not think it was possible to recoup. As you can hear, they all failed him, urging him to seek peace with the Egyptians, if he could, for they themselves dared not undertake war.

This frightened the king so much that he did not know what to say. Then Joseph came before him; seeing him so sad, pale, and pensive, he said, "Evalach, do not be so afraid, for if you believe my advice, you will have joy and victory over your enemies, and glory that will never end."

When Evalach heard this, he looked at him haughtily and said, "Who are you who can give me victory over my enemies and eternal joy?"

To these words Joseph responded, "By my faith, King Evalach, I did not promise that I would give you victory or eternal joy. But I tell you that if you believe me, you will have victory and joy without end, through the gift and the grace of the One who is powerful over all things."

[*After urging Evalach to destroy his idols, Joseph preached to him of biblical history and in particular of the Virgin Birth, Christ's life, and Christianity's redemptive powers.*]

4. Josephus's Investiture.

The story says that in the morning, as soon as Joseph saw dawn appear, he and his people arose and came to worship before the ark. When they were all kneeling before it, they heard a loud noise from above; at the same time they felt the earth tremble forcibly beneath them. The place where they were lodged and were worshiping was a palace, called the Spiritual Palace. Daniel the prophet had given it this name, when he returned from battle with King Nebuchadnezzar, who had captured him along with other Jews and taken him to Babylon. As he returned, Daniel went through this city; when he came to the palace, he saw Hebrew letters written on the door in charcoal that said this palace was spiritual. It was the custom to use this name; it never changed, and as long as the palace stands it will be called spiritual. But before Joseph stayed there the people of the city had never known or heard why it was called this, and then they learned how and for what reason.

Immediately after the ground had trembled beneath the Christians who were praying in the palace, just as you have heard, the Holy Spirit descended before each one of them, in the semblance of a flash of fire. They looked at one another, marveling, and saw the flash of fire enter each other's mouth. None of them said a word; rather they thought they were all bewitched because of the fire they saw entering their bodies. Thus they remained awhile without saying a word, so afraid were they, until something came through there just like a soft and gentle breeze, giving off such a wonderful fragrance that it seemed to them they were amidst all the good spices in the world.

After the arrival of this good wind, they heard a voice speak aloud to them, just as you will be able to hear, saying, "Listen to Me, My new sons, I am God, your Lord and your heavenly Father, who has fought for you and won you against all the world through My flesh, which I suffered to be broken in order to redeem you, and through My blood, which I was willing to shed. Because I have shown you such great love as to redeem you with My flesh and blood, which no earthly father would ever have done for his son, you owe Me, it would seem, greater love than any earthly son has ever given his father. Now listen therefore to what God your Lord and Father will say to you.

"Listen to this, Christians, you who are the new people of the True Crucified One. I have loved you so much and held you so dear that I have put in you My Holy Spirit, which for love of you I sent to earth, from on high where it was in the glory of My dear Father, who will never die. I have granted you higher honor and nobility than your ancestors in the desert, where for forty years I gave them everything their hearts desired. But I have satisfied you more than them, for I have given you My Holy Spirit, which I never gave them. Take care therefore not to fall into their wickedness, for I did only good to them and they did only evil. Though they honored Me with their mouths, they never loved Me with their hearts. And in the end they made this clear, for when I came to summon them to My great feast and to the great joy of the wedding I wanted to celebrate between Me and Holy Church, they did not deign to come, nor did they ever wish to acknowledge Me, who had done only good to them. Because I came among them humbly, they said that I was not their God. And they had such great contempt for the fact that I dared to tell them I was their God that they seized Me then like a thief in hiding and broke My flesh and pierced My limbs and My body. In return for the great honors I had done them, they rewarded Me with spite and disdain, and for the sweet drinks I had given them in the desert, they gave Me on the cross the vilest and most agonizing drink they could find. After all this, they gave Me death, though I had given them earthly life and promised them eternal life. Thus I found them, to whom I had always been a gentle Father, to be through and through cruel and terrible stepsons.

"Take care not to resemble that cruel lineage, for it is your duty to change your ways from those of your former life. If you act toward Me as My loyal sons, I will act toward you as your loyal and gracious Father, and I will do more for you than I did for My prophets who served Me in the past with good hearts and minds. If they had My Holy Spirit with them, you too will have it. And you will have yet another thing, for you will have My body in your company every day, just as I was bodily on earth with My apostles who loved Me greatly. Now hold firmly to your faith, for I will watch over you and guide you wherever you may go, with the difference that I was seen on earth, but now you will no longer see Me in such a semblance.

"Now come forward, Josephus, My servant, for you are worthy of being a minister, and of having such a high thing in your keeping as the flesh and blood of your Savior. I have tested you and found you to be purer and cleaner of all natural sins than any mortal flesh could conceive. Because I know you and what you are better than you do yourself—for I know you to be untouched by greed, free of pride, and pure of all wickedness, without any share in lust and filled with chastity—because of this I wish you to receive from My hand the greatest dignity any mortal man can have. None other will receive it from My hand; rather, henceforth those who have it will receive it from you."

Thereupon Josephus stepped forward, trembling and fearful. He began to shake and weep very hard and thank his Creator, who called him to receive such a great honor, which in his opinion no mortal man could be worthy of or deserve through anything he had ever done, unless God alone granted it through His grace. When he came up to the ark, Our Lord said to him, "Open the door, and be not afraid of what you will see."

In dread and fear Josephus opened the door of the ark. Upon doing so, he saw a man dressed in a robe a hundred times redder and more hideous than fiery lightning, and whose feet, hands, and face were exactly the same. Around this man were five angels all dressed in the same kind of robe and with the same appearance. Each of them had six wings that seemed to be made of burning fire, and each held in his left hand a bloody sword. The first held in his right hand a large bloody cross, but it was impossible to tell of what wood it was made. And the second held in his right hand three bloody nails, from which red blood still seemed to be dripping. The third angel held in his right hand a lance whose iron tip and wooden shaft were likewise covered with blood up to the point where the angel grasped it. The fourth angel held right before the face of the red man a sponge that was also thoroughly tinted with blood. And the fifth angel held in his hand a kind of whip, which was all bloody and seemed to be made of twisted wands tied together.

Each one of these angels held a scroll with writing that said, These are the arms by which the judge who is here vanquished and overcame death. And the man around whom the angels were standing had white letters in Hebrew written in the middle of his forehead that said, In this semblance I will come to judge all things on the cruel and terrible day. This is what the writing said. And it seemed that red bloody dew flowed from his feet and hands all the way down to the ground.

It seemed to Josephus that the ark was four times wider than it had been before, for the man he saw was inside as well as the five angels. He was so astonished at the marvel he saw that he did not know what to say, so he bent his head toward the ground and began to think very intently. As he pondered with bowed head, the voice called him. He looked up and saw the man crucified on the cross that the angel held; the nails he had seen held by the other angel were on the man's feet and hands, while the sponge was pressed against His chin, and he seemed to be a man who was surely in the anguish of death.

After that Josephus saw that the lance he had seen in the hand of the third angel was embedded in the side of the crucified man; down the handle dripped a stream composed neither completely of blood nor of water, and yet it seemed to be of blood. Under the feet of the crucified man he saw the bowl that his father Joseph had placed in the ark; it seemed to him that the blood from the feet of the crucified man was dripping into this bowl, and that it was already nearly full. It appeared to Josephus that it was about to run over and that the blood would spill. Then it seemed to him that the man was about to fall to the ground; that the two arms had already slipped from the nails, so that the body was falling, with the head down. Seeing this, he tried to run forward to lift Him up. But when he was about to step inside the ark, he saw the five angels with their swords at the entrance of the door. Three of them held the points of the swords out against his coming, while the other two lifted theirs on high and made as if to strike him. Despite this, he still tried to go past, so much did he desire to raise up Him who he believed was his God and his Savior. But when he tried to put the other foot inside, he could not, but was obliged to stop, for he was held so strongly from behind by his arms that he could not go forward. He looked and saw that two angels were holding him, each with one hand, while with the other hand one held an ampulla, and the other, a censer and a box.

When his father Joseph saw him look back, he was astonished that he had been so long at the door of the ark without saying or doing more and wondered what he could have been looking at so long. And then Joseph rose from where he was in prayer and went toward his son.

When Josephus saw him nearby, he put out his hand and began to cry, "Ah, good father Joseph, do not touch me, lest you take me away from the great glory where I am, for I am so illumined with spiritual revelations that I am no longer on earth."

Hearing these words, Joseph was so full of anguish and so eager to see this marvel that he paid no attention to any warning, but fell on his knees before the door of the ark and looked. Inside the ark he saw a small altar covered with white cloths; on top of all of them was a splendid red cloth, which was as beautiful as satin. On this red cloth, at one end of the altar, Joseph saw three nails dripping with blood and a bloody lance-tip. At the other end was the dish he had brought; and in the middle of the altar, there was a splendid gold vessel, in the form of a chalice with a gold cover on top. He could not see the cover very well, nor what was on it, for it was covered with a white cloth so that only the front was visible. Beyond the altar he saw a very beautiful hand holding a completely red cross, but he did not see the person to whom the hand belonged. And before the altar he saw two hands holding two candles, but he did not see the body to which the hands belonged.

While he was looking inside, he listened and heard the door of a room fly open. He turned his eyes toward the room and saw two angels come forth, one of whom held a stoup full of water, and the other an aspergillum in his right hand. After these two came two others carrying in their hands two large gold vessels just like basins. Around their necks they had two beautiful stoles like none any mortal man had ever possessed. Once the two had come out of the room, three others came after them, carrying three gold censers shining with rich precious stones so that they seemed to be on fire. And with the other hand each one held a box full of incense and myrrh and many other precious spices, which gave off such a sweet scent that the house seemed to be filled with the sweetest fragrance any man had ever smelled.

Next, he saw another one come forth with writing on his forehead, saying, I am called the power of the supreme Lord. This one carried over his hands a cloth as green as emeralds. And under this cloth was the holy dish. To the right of this angel there was another one carrying a book of Gospels. Such a rich and beautiful book would never have been seen by the eyes of any earthly man, if this one did not exist. And on the left there was an angel carrying a sword whose pommel was gold and whose hilt was silver, while the entire blade was as red as a flame of burning fire. Once these three had come forth, behind them came three others carrying three burning candles, which were of all the colors that mortal tongue could name. After that Joseph looked and saw Jesus Christ come forth in the same form as He had appeared to him in the jail where he had been imprisoned, when He left the sepulcher in body and in spirit on the day of the Resurrection.

In this semblance Joseph saw Him come forth, except that now He had put on the vestments that a priest must wear when he intends to celebrate the Sacrament of Our Lord. And the first angel, who was carrying the aspergillum, dipped into the water and went along sprinkling it on the Christians who were there. None of them saw the one who was sprinkling the water, except Joseph and his son Josephus. These two saw him clearly.

Then Joseph took his son by the hand and said to him, "Dear son, do you know yet who this man is who leads such a beautiful retinue with him and who walks in such honor?"

And Josephus replied, "Dear father, I know truly that this is the One about whom David said in a verse in the Psalter, that God ordered His angels to watch over Him wherever He might go; no man could be served and honored by angels as He is."[12]

---

[12]See Psalm LXXXXI. 11.

At that moment the entire group passed before them. It went all around the interior of the palace, and everywhere it went, the angel sprinkled water from the aspergillum. When it came to the ark, all of them knelt before Jesus Christ, and then before the ark. After going around the entire interior of the house, the group returned to the ark.

Then Our Lord called Josephus. And Josephus responded, "Lord, here is Your servant ready to do Your will."

And Our Lord said to him, "Do you know what the water that you have seen sprinkled here symbolizes? It is the purification of the places the evil spirit has frequented, for this house has always been the devil's lodging. It must therefore be purified and cleansed before My service can be performed here. And yet it was cleansed and purified as soon as the Holy Spirit, which I sent to you, descended. But I have sprinkled it with this water because I want you to do likewise in all the places where My name is to be called and My service performed."

And Josephus said to Him, "Lord, how can the water purify if it is not purified beforehand?"

"You will bless the water of purification and the water of baptism in the same way," said Our Lord, "by making over it the sign of the great redemption, that is, the sign of the true cross, and you will say that this shall be in the name of the Father and the Son and the Holy Spirit. And for him who believes in the power of this benediction, no evil spirit will ever reside in a place where this water is sprinkled, because all the devil fears is hearing the conjuration of the Holy Trinity and seeing the sign of the cross. That is how his power was destroyed, and that is why I am teaching it to you and telling you to act in this way.

"Henceforth," said Our Lord to Josephus, "I want you to receive the honor I promised you, that is the sacrament of My flesh and blood. And all My people will see it openly, for I want them to bear witness before kings and counts that they have seen the holy unction I have placed on you in order to establish you as sovereign pastor, after Me, to watch over My new sheep, that is, the sovereign bishop to keep My New Law, Christianity. Just as Moses, My new servant, was minister and leader of the sons of Israel, through the power I gave him, in the same way you will be the guardian of this people, for they will learn from your mouth how they should serve Me, and how to maintain the New Law and keep to My faith."

Then Our Lord took Josephus by the right hand and pulled him close to Him, so that all the Christians there saw clearly His appearance and the angels who were around Him. Then a white-haired man came before the ark, wearing on his shoulders the richest vestments any earthly man had ever worn. After him came forth another who was marvelously handsome and young, carrying a crosier in one hand and in the other a pure white miter. The crosier was also white, while the handle was red. After these two had come forth, they dressed Josephus in all these vestments: first the sandals, and then the other things a bishop should have. Once he was dressed, they sat him on a throne that was ready there through the will of Our Lord, who wanted to make him comfortable in every way.

This throne was so noble that no man who saw it could say for sure of what it could be made. All those who made splendid things, many of whom later came to see it, said that in all the world there were no rich stones like those in the throne. And those who see it now say the same thing, for it has never left the city, but has been kept as a relic since Josephus left. Nor has any man ever sat in it since then without dying upon standing up, or without being wounded before standing up. And later a wonderful miracle occurred, when the city was taken by a Saracen king who was making war on the land. After finding the throne and seeing it to be so splendid, he said that he prized it more than the entire city and that he would take it to Egypt, the land where he was king. There he would sit on it every day that he wore his crown. But when he tried to carry it away, he was not able to, for neither he nor any man could move it from the place where it was. And he said that he would sit on it anyway, even if he could not carry it away. As soon as he was seated, Our Lord took such great vengeance that both of his eyes flew out of his head. Thus Our Lord showed that this was not a throne or chair for any mortal man except for the one for whom He had prepared it. And He performed many other miracles there that the story does not speak about here, but will when the time and place come, farther along.[13]

When Josephus was seated on the throne, all the angels came before him. And Our Lord anointed and consecrated him in the way a bishop should be, so that all the people saw it clearly. The unction with which he was anointed was taken from the ampulla the angel was carrying—the angel who had taken him and held him by the shoulders when he tried to enter the ark, as you heard about earlier. And with this same unction were anointed all the kings from the time Christianity came to England until the time of Pendragon, who was King Arthur's father. Nor do those who recount the adventures know very well why he was called Pendragon, for it is well known that he was given the name Uther in baptism, but the chronicle of this book will tell farther on very clearly why he was called this, and how this unction was lost when he was about to be crowned.[14]

Once Josephus was anointed and consecrated, just as you have heard,

---

[13]Despite this announcement, the throne is mentioned only once more, briefly.

[14]The origin of Uther Pendragon's name is explained in the *Merlin*, in a portion of the text summarized at the beginning of our Chapter 2. At the beginning of the battle in which Uther's brother, Pendragon, lost his life, a vision of a fire-breathing dragon appeared in the sky. Merlin later explained that the dragon symbolized Pendragon's death and Uther's survival, whereupon Uther added his brother's name to his own.

Our Lord put the crosier in his hand and the miter on his head. And on his finger He put a ring no mortal man could imitate, nor could he describe the power of the stone. Once He had prepared all these things, as you have heard, He called him and said, "Josephus, I have consecrated and anointed you as a bishop, in such dignity as you and My other people who are here have seen. Now I will tell you what these vestments you have put on mean, for no one should wear them if he does not do what the meaning requires. This shoe you have put on means that you must take no step in vain; you should keep your feet from taking the way of wrongdoing, but should go praying, preaching, and helping the helpless—this is the way you must make your feet work, for I want you to keep to the Scripture, which says, 'Blessed is the man who does not follow the advice of the wicked and who does not take his feet where the traitorous and the sinful go and who does not sit on the throne of destruction, but puts his will and strength into accomplishing the commandments of the law of Our Lord, keeping all his thoughts on this night and day.'[15] Your feet should walk in this way, for they should not take any step in vain.

"Next I will tell you about the other vestments. The one you have put on over your tunic symbolizes chastity, for this is a virtue through which the soul, when it leaves the body, departs white and clean and pure, thus harmonizing with all the good things of the soul, that is, with all the qualities it contains. Thus, you must first have chastity inside you, in order to make of it the foundation on which to establish all the other virtues. The other vestment on top of it, which is just as white, symbolizes virginity. Just as virginity cannot be in any place unless chastity be in its company, likewise no priest should put this one on top before putting on the one underneath. This other vestment, which covers the head, symbolizes humility, which is contrary to pride, for pride always goes proudly, with its head raised, but humility goes gently and softly, with head bent. The priest should go this way, in great humility, with head bent.

[*He then explained that the green symbolized patience and that the white symbolized justice. Furthermore, the armband signified abstinence; the neckband, obedience; the crosier, vengeance and mercy; the ring, marriage to Holy Church; and the hat, confession.*]

"Now you are anointed and consecrated, and I have given you the order and rank of bishop to teach My people and honor My New Law. I want you to watch over their souls. I will ask you about any I lose through your failings and lay the blame on you, on the great and terrible day when I take vengeance and do justice for every misdeed, when everything hidden in the heart is

---

[15]See Psalm I. 1–2.

revealed. And if I find you to be a loyal servant of this small new people, whose souls I entrust to you, I will give you a domain a hundred times better, just as the Gospel promises those who leave their property for My love.[16] Because I commend these souls to you and make you their shepherd, I want you to be their spiritual guard. And I am confiding to Joseph the care of the body, for I want him to provide and dispense those things the body needs. Now come forward, and you will celebrate the sacrament of My flesh and My blood, so that all My people will see it clearly."

Thereupon Our Lord led Josephus up to the ark so that all the people saw him enter it. And they all saw it grow and become larger so that all were comfortably inside. And they saw the angels come and go before the door. There Josephus celebrated the first sacrament ever done this people, but it was completed very quickly, for he said only these words, which Jesus Christ said to his disciples at the Last Supper: "Take this and eat it; this is My flesh, which for you and many other people will be delivered over to agony and torment." Likewise, he said about the wine, "Take this and drink it all, for this is the blood of My New Law, My very own, which will be shed for you, in remission of your sins."[17] These words were said by Josephus over the bread he found prepared on the paten covering the chalice; and the bread immediately became flesh, and the wine, blood. Then Josephus saw clearly that he was holding between his two hands a body just like that of a child, and it seemed to him that the blood he saw in the chalice had fallen from the child's body. Seeing this frightened him so much that he did not know what to do. So he remained silent and began to sigh and weep in great anguish because of his great fear.

Then Our Lord said to him, "You must break apart what you are holding so that there are three pieces."

Josephus replied, "Oh, Lord, have mercy on your servant, for my heart could not bear to break apart such a beautiful figure."

And Our Lord said to him, "If you do not obey My commandment, you will have no part in My heritage."

Then Josephus took the body and, putting the head to one side, broke it off from the trunk as easily as if the flesh of the child were cooked like meat when it has been forgotten on the fire; next, fearfully, he broke the rest into two parts. As he began to separate the parts, all the angels before the altar fell to their knees on the ground. They remained there until Our Lord spoke and said to Josephus, "What are you waiting for? Take what is before you and eat it, for this is your salvation." When Josephus heard Him, he knelt and beat his chest and cried for mercy, weeping about all his sins.

---

[16]See Matthew XIX, 29, and Mark XX, 30.
[17]See Matthew XXVI, 26; Mark XIV, 22; Luke XXII, 19; First Corinthians XI, 23.

When he stood up again, all he saw before him on the paten was a piece in the semblance of bread. He took it, raised it on high, and after giving thanks to his Creator, opened his mouth to put it inside. He looked and saw that it was still an entire body. When he started to pull it back, he could not, for he felt that it was being put inside his mouth before he could close it. After he had eaten it, it seemed to him that all the sweet and delectable things one's tongue could name had entered his body. Next he received part of the holy consecrated drink that was in the chalice. Once he had done this, he saw an angel take the paten and the chalice and put them both on the holy dish, one on top of the other. On the paten he saw several pieces that looked like bread. After the angel had taken the dish, another one came and raised the paten on high along with what was on top of it, and carried it with both hands outside of the ark. And the third angel took the chalice and carried it away in the same way after him, while the one carrying the holy dish was last of all.

When all three of them had left the ark, so that all the people saw them, a voice spoke and said, "My small people, newly reborn in spiritual birth, I send you your salvation, that is, My body that suffered physical birth and death for you. Now take care therefore that you have true faith to receive and eat such a lofty thing, for if you believe perfectly that this is your Savior, you will receive it to the everlasting salvation of the soul. And if you do not believe it completely, you will receive it to the everlasting damnation of the soul and the body. He who eats of My body and drinks of My blood and is not worthy of it, will eat and drink his destruction. Nor can anyone be worthy of it if he is not a true believer. Now take care therefore that you believe it."

Then the angel who was carrying the paten came before Joseph, who knelt and received with joined hands his Savior in visible form, as did each of the others, for it seemed to each one that when the piece in the semblance of bread was put in his mouth, he saw a completely formed child enter his mouth. After they had all received the sacrament, the three angels went back inside the ark and put the vessels they were carrying on the altar.

Then Our Lord called Josephus and said, "Josephus, you shall serve Me in this way every day from now on, you and all those whom you invest with the order of priest and bishop. And if you ordain a priest, you will put your hand on his head and make the sign of the cross in the name of the Trinity. But to consecrate a bishop, you must do everything I did to you, for a bishop should be above a priest. And all those who are invested with this honor will have the same power to condemn and absolve as My apostles had on earth. Henceforth you shall establish a bishop in each city where My name is received through your word, and he shall be anointed with this holy unction, as shall all the kings who come to My faith through you. Now the time is approaching when King Evalach will turn from the wrong road of the idols to faith in the glorious Trinity, for the knights are nearby who are coming to seek Joseph to explain to him a great marvel that I showed him last night in a vision. Take off your vestments, and you and Joseph shall go together, and you shall make him certain of all the things he will ask you. Be not afraid if you see all the good clerks of their faith come against you, for you shall vanquish all of them, so that they will not be able to contest your words. And I will give you such good grace in the eyes of King Evalach that you will tell him part of what is to come, through the power of My Spirit. And all those who have received or who will receive My Spirit will have the power to chase forth the bad spirits wherever they appear."

Thereupon Josephus went to take off his vestments, leaving them all in the ark on the altar. Then he called one of his first cousins who was in the group, whose name was Lucan. Josephus assigned him to guard the ark, day and night. In our time this custom is still maintained in the high churches, for the one who guards all the treasure of the church is called the treasurer. At that time it had never been done, but then Josephus invested Lucan, just as you have heard; nor was Lucan chosen because he was his cousin, but because he knew him to be more religious than any of the others.

5. Josephus Preaches Before Evalach.

At that point the king's messenger came and told Joseph that the king was sending for him. Joseph and his son went before him; upon leaving the palace, they crossed themselves and commanded the others to pray that God, who is the guide of those who have lost their way, might lead King Evalach to the way of truth. When they came before the king, he ordered them to be seated. And he told Joseph to prove to him what he had said about the Father and the Son and the Holy Spirit—how they could be three persons and only one God; and how the maiden had given birth without damaging her maidenhead; and how the Son could be conceived without carnal relations between a man and a woman.

When the king had said this, Joseph stood up and said the same words he had said earlier, and in this very way proved it. After he had spoken, a clerk stood up, who was held to be the wisest and the most instructed in their faith. He spoke against Joseph, saying he said nothing, "for if the Father and the Son and the Holy Spirit were only one God, none of the three was a complete, perfect God, or else the persons of the Son and of the Holy Spirit had no part in God. And if they were both completely divine, there would therefore be three deities. No one could reasonably dispute this, for any man who did could not reasonably prove or establish as truth that one of the three persons was a complete deity in itself, once either of the others was mentioned. If it were said that the Holy Spirit was a perfect, complete God, and that the three were only one deity, it would be clear that one was worth as much as the three. Thus it is true that the two are nothing when the third is honored; because the two persons lose their power through the third, everyone can clearly see and recognize that none of the three is a perfect and complete deity."

After the man had spoken so harshly against the Trinity, Joseph was very fearful about defending and proving it. He did not know how to answer right away to show that what the other had said was wrong, for it did not please Our Lord.

At once Josephus stood up and, speaking loudly enough for everyone to hear him clearly, said to the king, "King, listen to what I will tell you. This is sent to you by the God of Israel, the Creator of all things. He says to you, 'Because you have brought your false advocates against My faith, I have decided to take such great vengeance on you that before the third day has passed, you shall fall into such great misfortune that you will not believe any living creature could keep you from losing all earthly honor first and then your life.' God will punish you this way because you do not want to accept the faith in His glorious name; rather you have scorned and spurned the demonstration He made last night of His secrets and miracles, which He revealed to you in a vision. Because of this, the God of the Christians sends you this message through the mouth of His servant who is speaking to you: He will give your mortal enemy glory and honor and victory over you for three days and three nights. Your power will be unable to sustain against him, nor will you dare await the man who has always been unable to confront you in force until now, when he will defeat you through the betrayal of your counselors, who have gone over to him because of his great gifts.

"Thus the God of the Christians will show you that no creature can survive who is not prepared to follow His commandment, nor will you ever recover the great honor you are beginning to lose, unless you recover it through His help. If you consider me to be a liar about this thing, you will soon hear news by which you will know that Our Lord has shown me something about your adventures. You can be sure that Tholomer the Fugitive, who is king of Babylonia, has prepared his entire army and is moving against you very rapidly. The God of the Christians also says, 'I will deliver the Unknown King into the hands of the terrible Egyptians, because he fled from Me and did not recognize Me. He who has always fled will pursue the one who has always pursued him and will lead him to the fear of death, for I want to make him recognize that I alone am the King of Kings and the Fortress of all peoples.'"

Then Josephus turned to the man who had spoken so harshly against the Trinity and said, "Listen, you who have been against and spoken against the Trinity and the holy belief in the Christian God; now hear what He tells you through His servant who is speaking to you. 'You,' He says, 'who are My creature, and who should obey My commandments everywhere, have condemned My faith and dishonored My name. Because I want you to know that you have spoken against the One who has power over you and all things, I will make you feel My earthly justice strike, so that you will suffer from it. And the others will take warning from what happens to you, for you have always had earthly knowledge, but you have never wished to know the spiritual, nor could you ever see it. And if you ever wished to speak of it, you would not be able to speak the truth. Because you have been mute and blind in spiritual knowledge, to which you should address all your words and clear sight, I will show you that earthly knowledge is powerless against the spiritual. In the sight of everyone here, I will take away from you earthly speech and sight, for My Spirit is of such power that it will cause good speakers to become mute and the clear-sighted to go blind; and it will cause the mute to speak well and the blind to see clearly.'"

As soon as Josephus had said this, his interlocutor lost the power of speech. When he wished to speak, he felt in his mouth a hand holding his tongue, but he could not see it. He stood up in order to make a better attempt to speak, but as soon as he had risen, he could see nothing. Feeling this, he began to bellow so loudly that he could be heard clearly as far away as one could shoot an arrow. And it seemed to everyone who heard him that it was a bull. When the others saw this marvel, they were very wrathful. They all rushed upon Josephus and would have torn him to pieces as best they could, but King Evalach jumped to his feet and, taking a naked sword, swore by the power of Jove that he would have all those who put their hands on him massacred and put to death. For they would have betrayed him if they had murdered Josephus under his safe-conduct, had he not protected him against them.

Thus a tumult was raised throughout the entire hall. The king called Josephus and asked him who he was. Josephus came forward and told him he was the son of Joseph. The king said to him that he spoke well and truthfully about many things. Then he asked how he had taken away the power of speech and sight from the man who had spoken against him. And Josephus replied that it was not he who had taken away his power of speech, but the Christian God, against whom he had spoken. It was He who had taken away his power of speech and his sight, "for this is the God whose word can never be changed by anyone. As He commands, so it must be."

"What!" said Evalach, "Is it true then that Tholomer the Fugitive will lead me up to the fear of death and have power over me for three days and three nights?"

"Certainly," said Josephus, "it is true, and there is no living man who can change this."

The king asked him how he could know this.

"Then you have not heard," said Josephus, "how the Spirit of the Christian God is so powerful that it causes the mute to speak and the blind to see clearly? That is, all those who have had no instruction will know all the power of the Scripture through the grace of the Holy Spirit."

"By my faith," said the king, "if it comes about as you have related, I would rather be dead than alive, but I cannot believe any of it. Nevertheless, if I saw one of your predictions come true, I would believe you better."

"King," said Josephus, "when you see this happen to you, you will believe me."

"Can I avoid it?" asked the king.

"Yes, certainly," said Josephus, "but in only one way."

"And what is that?" said the king.

"I will tell you," said Josephus. "If you receive Jesus Christ's faith, and if you believe in it perfectly from the time you receive it, you will have help and deliverance. But you can be sure that whatever the mouth may say, if the heart is not in it, you will not be delivered, for God is not someone who can be tricked or deceived by appearances. Rather, He is of such deep wisdom that He knows everyone's thoughts and sees everything hidden in the heart."

Then the king asked his name, and he said he was called Josephus. And the king said, "Josephus, tell me whether the man who lost his speech and sight will ever recover them."

"King," said Josephus, "have him taken before the gods in whom you believe, and you will hear what they reply about the healing and the battle."

The king had him taken to the temple, and he himself went as well, with Josephus and his father. The pagan priests made an offering at the altar of Apollo, whom they called the god of wisdom, and asked the image above the altar how the man could be cured of his infirmity, or whether he would ever be cured. But no matter what they asked the idol, they could never get a word out of it. The king came forward and asked it what would be the outcome of the war, but he could not get an answer, any more than the others. And the devil, who was in the statue of Mars, whom they called the god of war, began to cry out, "Foolish people, what are you trying to do? There is a Christian among you, who has so bound Apollo through the commandment of Jesus Christ his God that he has no power to respond, nor will any god, wherever he may be, dare or be able to give a response once he has exorcized him."

As soon as the devil had said this, he began to cry out so loudly that it seemed to everyone in the temple that he was in a burning fire. And he said to Josephus, "Bishop of Jesus Christ, leave off what you are saying, for you are causing me to burn, and I will flee from here and go where you command." Thus the devil who was in Mars's image cried out, because of the exorcism Josephus had performed, for the latter so constrained and punished him that he left the image, in the sight of everyone in the temple. He knocked the statue to the ground and broke it into small pieces. Once he had done that, he took a very large golden eagle from the altar to the Sun and hit the image of Apollo with it in the face so forcefully that he broke the nose and the right arm. Then he went past all the idols of the temple, striking each one with the eagle until he had broken a limb.

The people were very frightened by this, for they saw the marvels the eagle was doing, but they could not see who was holding it, and this was the thing that scared them the most. Then the king called Josephus and asked him what this could be that was breaking the images in this way. Josephus replied that he should go ask at Mars's altar. The king went there and wished to sacrifice, but Josephus would not let him. Rather, he told him that if he made such a sacrifice, he would die a sudden death. When the king asked for a response at the altar, the devil said he dared not speak to him because of Josephus. The king asked him if he had such great power over the gods, and the devil said that none of them could speak in front of him if he did not give them leave. The king beseeched Josephus to give him leave to speak, which Josephus did.

The devil said to the king, "King, do you want to know why he has such great power? He has two angels with him who guide him and protect him everywhere he goes; one of them holds a naked sword, and the other a cross. These two held me so tightly, by his command, that they made me break these images, just as you see. Nor will any of them ever be able to give an answer wherever this man may be, because of the power that has been given to him by Jesus Christ, his God."

Next the king asked him if the man who had lost his eyesight and speech would ever regain his health. And the devil replied, "King, if he recovers, it will not be through our power, for we have none. He must be healed by the One whose commandment brought him the trouble. If not, he will never be cured."

[*Evalach (renamed Mordrain) and others were later converted. An angel wounded Josephus in the thigh with a lance, and Nascien (Mordrain's brother-in-law) was blinded by looking into the Grail. Both were healed by angels. Later, Nascien boarded a strange ship, in which were a bed, a crown, and a sword. The ship had been built by Solomon to let the chosen knight know that his coming was known long in advance. The sword was that of King David. A portico at the end of the bed was made from trees grown from a branch that Eve had plucked from the Tree of Knowledge. Nascien was lost and sought by others, while he and his wife sought news of Joseph of Arimathea. Nascien had several dreams about his lineage, especially about his descendants Lancelot and Galahad.*]

6. Josephus and Some of His Followers Cross the Sea Without a Ship and Arrive in England.

Now the story says that when Joseph left Sarras, he wandered with his companions for many days, going where chance took them, until they crossed the river Euphrates and many lands. Many people stopped them and tried to hold them prisoners because they were Christians. But whenever they were imprisoned, Our Lord delivered them and freed them from all earthly subjection.

One night during the winter they lay in a wood, in lodges they had made themselves, after having eaten food in as much abundance as their hearts dared to conceive or their mouths describe. That night Joseph was next to his wife, a good lady in God's and the world's eyes, and praised by everyone who knew her. And then there descended a voice that said to Joseph, "The High Master, at whose order you left your country with the large group you took with you, makes this command: tonight you are to know your wife carnally. May such seed issue that will keep and maintain the land that is promised to you. And when this child, who will be a male, is born, he shall be called Galahad.[18] Thus the Arbiter of all things commands."

To this, Joseph replied, "I am ready to do His command, but I am old and so frail that I don't know how this can be, except that He has said it."

"Fear not, Joseph," said the voice. "for thus it is to be, since the High Master wishes it." Then it became silent and said no more.

That night Joseph knew his wife and fathered Galahad, who was later such a worthy man that one should certainly recall his deeds and the nobility of his life in the hearing of all worthy men, so that the wicked will abandon their folly, and worthy men, who hold the order of chivalry, may better themselves toward the world and God.

Every day they prayed before the Holy Vessel before eating anything, praying to Our Lord to guide them safely to the land that had been promised to them. They wandered until Our Lord guided them to the sea, arriving just as night fell, on a Saturday evening. When they reached the sea, they found neither ship nor galley by which they might cross. They were terribly afraid of remaining there. So they began to weep bitterly and cry for mercy to Our Lord, praying in tears that, in His sweet pity, He would come to succor and help them in this need, for they were in greater need than they had ever been since leaving their country. Then they went to Josephus, their bishop, and began to cry for mercy, weeping very softly, saying, "My lord, what shall we do? We must remain on this side, for we have neither ship nor galley with us to take us across. For God's sake, tell us if we will remain on this side, or whether we will cross over, and if this is the land that is promised to us and our descendants, where we are to spend the rest of our lives and do Our Lord's service."

Seeing their fear, Josephus took heartfelt pity on them, because they had departed from their country, leaving their lands and riches and beautiful households, and besides, most of them were his relatives. Then he said to them, "Dear lords and ladies, do not be afraid before you know why. I tell you that He who has been your guide until now will lead us across in safety, but He will not take all of you, and I will tell you why.

"When you departed from your countries, leaving your lands and the

---

[18]Not the same Galahad who would later achieve the Grail quest; however, the birth of the latter (the son of Lancelot) was earlier prophesied in *The History of the Holy Grail.*

comforts of this world for the love of the sovereign Crucified One, you promised to serve Him as sons should serve their father, that is to say that henceforth you would keep yourselves from sinning, whatever you might have done before. And He promised to give you whatever your heart conceived and to deliver you from the hands of all those who wished to harm you. It seems to me He has kept His promise, for since then you have never asked for anything that He did not immediately give you, and many times since then you were held prisoner by many a prince from whom He delivered you. Thus He has indeed repaid your promise.

"But you have badly repaid Him, for when He spoke to you at the entrance of the Wood of the Ambush, each of you vowed to hold to chastity and keep his flesh pure until he had permission to hold his wife. You know very well that you made this promise. Now look how you have acted. You have kept your promise so well that many are in vile and filthy lust, while others are already so cool and indifferent to doing well that many regret leaving their country. Thus some are sullied with regret and others with lust, because of what they did and because in their hearts they forgot what they had promised.

"But whatever they have done, truly, the others, whose bodies and hearts still belong to Our Lord, and are still as hot and burning with the fire of the Holy Spirit and the ardor of charity as they were in the beginning, and who have since then kept their flesh pure and held to chastity, as they had promised—these will truly cross without a ship and without oars, and they will be held up by the sea, that is, the world, because they have in them neither dirt nor filth nor stain nor baseness. These people will cross without a ship, for their faith and belief and great purity will carry them across.

"And you who have fallen into sin, and who have not watched over yourselves as well as you should have, will have ships and galleys, and you will follow us. Do you know why Our Lord does not want us to separate? He does not want the death of a sinner. Rather, He wants him to live and better himself and to recognize and return to the straight path of truth. I have told you this so that you might recognize your folly, once you have confessed the fact that you have erred toward Our Lord, and no longer remain in it, whatever you may have done in the past."

When those who felt guilty of the sins of which they were accused heard this speech, they drew back from Josephus and began to carry on the greatest and most wondrous lamentations that you will ever hear, calling themselves miserable, wretched, and unhappy. This group could have numbered four hundred sixty. And the others, who had not committed the sins they were accused of, approached Josephus, knelt before him, and said, "My lord, how can it be that we will cross without ships or galleys, while our companions won't cross with us?" And he said that they would see. In this group there were some one hundred fifty by count, and most of them were Josephus's relatives.

The night was quiet and serene, and the sea beautiful and peaceful, without a storm. The moon shone very brightly, and the weather was pleasant, just like in April, and this was the Saturday before the Resurrection of Our Lord. Josephus came to his father, kissed him, and said, "Follow me." And then he went to those before him and kissed them all, one after another, saying to each one what he had said to his father.

He was about to step into the sea when a voice said to him, "Josephus, do not enter thus, but put those who watch over and carry the Holy Vessel in front. Then remove your under-tunic[19] from your back, and tell your father to put his foot on the length that extends to the knee; after that, call all those you have kissed and have each one do likewise. If they have indeed done what they promised their Savior, they will all be able to stand on the length of cloth, and it will suffice for all. But those who have not kept their promise will not be able to stay there. This cloth will be ship and galley and will carry them across this sea before day breaks."

Josephus did what the voice told him: he called the men carrying the Holy Vessel and had them enter the sea, saying, "Go with assurance, for the power of the Holy Vessel will guide you."

Fearlessly, they entered the water at once and began to walk on top just as if they were on flat ground, carrying with them the Holy Vessel called the Grail. When Josephus saw that they had all set out in this way, he removed his under-tunic from his back and put on his robe, telling his father to step onto the length of cloth. He was already on top of the sea, having spread his under-tunic on the water just as if it were land. Joseph came forward and stepped onto it. He called another relative, whose name was Bron, and who already had twelve handsome, grown children. When he called him, the latter stood on the length of cloth of the tunic, just as Joseph had. Then Josephus called all the one hundred fifty, and as each one stepped on the length of cloth, it grew and became bigger, just as the High Master willed it.

An evident miracle occurred, so that all one hundred fifty stood on the length of cloth of the under-tunic except two whom Our Lord did not consider fit for His service, as they should have been. One was the father of the other, and the father was called Simeon. When these two tried to set foot on the length of cloth, after having entered the water, they sank like a piece of lead. Upon seeing this, Joseph, who knew very well who they were, said, "You acted badly by deceiving us. Now it is indeed clear how little faith you have."

Once they had sunk to the bottom of the water, they struggled because

---

[19]The principal medieval undergarment was the "chemise," worn by both men and women. On the male it came about to the knees. Though one was not considered improperly attired in only a "chemise," a tunic or robe was usually worn over it; that is why we have chosen the word "under-tunic."

they were afraid of dying and therefore had to reach shore. Those who had remained behind ran to help them, grabbing them and pulling them to land.

And Josephus, who was holding his under-tunic by the sleeves, began to go forward, pulling it after him across the water. They had all commended themselves to Our Lord, putting themselves in His hands and in His command and placing themselves and all their hope in Him. Everything went so well for them that before daybreak they had arrived in Great Britain and saw the land and the country that was completely peopled with Saracens and unbelievers.

After their arrival, once Josephus had put his under-tunic back on, they all knelt on the seashore and began to thank Our Lord and praise Him greatly for having shown them such a wonderful sign of pity that night. And Josephus, who had gone aside a little from the others, began to pray to Our Lord, asking Him in tears, in His sweet pity, to lead those who had remained behind safely to the place where they had arrived.

As soon as he had made this request, a voice replied, saying, "Josephus, your request has been heard, for those you want to see will arrive soon. And you can be sure, truly, that this land where you have come is promised to your descendants, who are to increase and to fill the country with people more fitting than those who are there now. Take care henceforth to be strong and ardent in preaching Jesus Christ's name and the truth of the Gospel everywhere you go. Continue as long as you can, for you can be sure that no matter how much you hurry, you must suffer before the Christian faith is spread throughout this land. Now stand up, and do as I have told you."

After hearing this, Josephus stood up, looked toward the heavens, and said, "Lord, your servant is here, ready to do what you command." Then he turned toward his father and his relatives and said, "My lords, I have wonderful news for you. This is the land that is promised to us and our descendants. It is therefore fitting that it be planted with new trees: since unbelief and false religion are firmly held here, it is fitting that Jesus Christ's faith, which is good and right for eternal life, be planted and raised and rooted here, and that the Saracen faith, which is cultivated and upheld here, be removed."

Those who were before Josephus responded, "My lord, our hearts and bodies are prepared to do what you command. We are ready to die or live in order to glorify the faith of the True Crucified One. Command, and we will obey your commandments to the best of our ability."

He said he would not command anything before he had certain news about their companions who had remained on the other side of the sea. But with that the story leaves off speaking about Josephus and his companions and returns to Nascien, in order to bring his story to an end.

[*Nascien, along with Josephus's followers, arrived in Britain. Amid miracles and visions, the Christians won a great victory over the Saracens, but they continued to suffer trials and betrayals.*]

7. Moses Sits at the Grail Table; Bron's Son Alan Is Named Future Guardian of the Grail.

When Josephus saw that King Mordrain had become a monk and that Nascien intended to stay with the duke, he left Galafort with his relatives, to preach and announce the truth of the Gospel. After they had left Galafort, taking leave of Nascien, the queen, and the other knights, they wandered far and wide throughout foreign countries, until they came to a city called Camelot. It was the richest of the Saracen cities in Great Britain, and it was so important that the pagan kings were crowned there, and its mosque was larger and taller than in any other city.

At the time when the Christians came to Camelot, its lord and king was the cruelest man in the world, and his name was Agrestes. When Josephus came to the city and began to preach the name of the High Lord, there were only unbelievers in all the country around Camelot. That day, as it pleased Our Lord, it happened through Josephus's words that one thousand fifty Saracens converted and turned to the Christian faith, abandoning the evil belief they had held before.

[*King Agrestes, witnessing these conversions, decided to pretend to convert, then, once Josephus was gone, make his people reject Christianity. He did so, martyring twelve companions left behind by Josephus.*]

The people sent a messenger to Josephus, telling him what had happened and asking him to come as soon as he could, for they needed him greatly. Hearing this made him very unhappy, and he came to them in tears. He had the bodies of the twelve martyrs taken from before the cross and buried in a chapel. Then he ordered the cross washed. It was blackened with blood, for it is well known that blood gets blacker and blacker as the days go by. However, God worked a great miracle here, for the stone of the cross did not change color, but remained black in memory of the blood that was shed there. For this reason those who knew the truth about it called it the Black Cross, and this name never changed until King Arthur's reign, at the time when the adventures of the Grail were brought to an end.

Once the bodies of the worthy men who had been martyred in this way were buried, Josephus ordered the pagan temples that had been built in the city of Camelot knocked down, the idols burned, and all the edifices of the pagan religion completely destroyed. In the middle of the city he had the Church of Saint Stephen the Martyr built. Then, seeing that the people in the country had calmed down and returned to the Christian faith, he left the city.

After he had traveled for about two days, he and all his followers reached a large knoll called the Giant's Knoll. It was a Friday, and that day Bron was sitting next to Josephus at the table of the Holy Grail. Between them, at the very middle of the table, there was easily enough space to put a man's chair.

When Peter, a relative of Josephus, saw this empty space, he said to Josephus, "My lord, why don't you call someone to sit there? There are so many worthy men crowded together at this table eating in discomfort. It seems to me that it would be a good thing if you called one of them, for the empty space is of no benefit to us."

"Peter, my good friend," said Josephus, "this place is to stay empty. No one may sit here who is not worthier than all others. It is not for nothing that it's empty: it serves as an important symbol, for you should understand that it symbolizes the place where Jesus Christ sat at the holy table on the day of the Last Supper when He ate with His disciples. This place is empty because it awaits its master, Jesus Christ, or someone He will send. That is why I don't want anyone to sit here now."

Those at the table, and especially the ones in mortal sin, considered these words proud and presumptuous. Once they had eaten, some said that Josephus was only telling a tall tale and a lie, "for doubtless one can sit in this seat as surely and as easily as in any other place, without greater danger." Twenty-four people were at this discussion, all from the land of Jerusalem, and the two who had said the most were called Simeon and Moses. These two said to the others, "My lords, what do you think about your bishop and what he said today at the table about the empty place? Does it seem to you that he is telling the truth—that anyone who sat there would be doing a foolish thing and that it is forbidden to all except the one Our Lord will send?"

"Certainly," said the others, "we believe it is more of a lie than the truth, but it isn't fitting for us to reproach him with everything he tells us. Nevertheless, we would like to have someone sit there, for then we would be sure whether he told us the truth."

"In God's name," said Moses, "if you want to ask him to let me sit there, I will do so tomorrow and take the risk. I believe I have served Our Lord so well since leaving our country that I don't think I need to worry."

"In God's name," said the others, "we will gladly ask him, if you swear you will sit there."

And he swore it.

Then they came to Josephus and said, "My lord, there is an empty place at your table, which amazes us. And we have found among us a religious man, leading a holy life, who is worthy of sitting there. We beseech you, my lord, for God's sake and for your honor and his, to let him sit there."

Josephus asked who this was who was worthy of sitting in the place where he did not dare sit.

And they replied, "My lord, it's Moses, your relative and ours."

"My God," said Josephus, "he already stayed behind with his father when we crossed the sea. They could not follow us, but remained with the others who had sinned against their Creator. And now you tell me he is such a

worthy man that he wants to sit in this place? Certainly, it's hard to believe
you, except that Our Lord quickly makes a worthy man out of a sinner."

"My lord," said they, "whatever you say, we know he is such a worthy
man that it is fitting for him to sit there. Therefore, we implore you to allow it
in order to learn whether God will grant him this honor."

He replied that he would be pleased if Moses were such that it would
please Our Lord for him to sit there. "But I don't believe he is. And yet I will
let him sit there, since you wish it."

They thanked him, returned to Moses, and told him he had permission to
sit in the empty seat. And he said they could therefore be sure he would sit
there. That night things were left at that and were discussed no more.

The next day, at the hour of prime, when they were sitting at the table of
the Holy Grail, they came to Moses and said, "Moses, now you may go sit
where you said yesterday that you would, for you have permission." And he
said he would do so in that case. He went where Josephus and Bron were sitting, pretending to be so humble and full of piety that it was a wonder. And he
seemed to be a very worthy man.

When Josephus saw Moses coming, he said, "Moses, don't sit here unless you are worthy of it, for otherwise you can be sure you will regret it.
Don't think this place was prepared for a sinner, for it is the symbol of the
place where Our Lord sat on the day of the Last Supper. Therefore, don't sit
here unless you are the worthiest man of us all, for I believe this will lead to
the destruction of your body and eternal torment for your soul."

When Moses heard this, he was very frightened, and yet he replied, "My
lord, I believe I'm worthy of sitting there and that Our Lord will not be angry."

"Come forward, then," said Josephus, "and sit down, for if you are what
you should be, it will soon be made clear."

Then Moses came forward and sat between Josephus and Bron. But he
had not been there long when those at the table saw seven hands come down
from the heavens, all of them burning and in flames. They could not see the
bodies the hands belonged to, but they could see that they were casting fire
and flames onto Moses so that he caught fire and began to burn as brightly as
if he were a dry bush. Once he had caught fire and was burning fiercely, they
saw the hands take him and raise him from where he was sitting and carry
him through the air to a large and remarkable forest nearby. When those sitting at the table saw this, they were all very frightened.

They all began to talk about it and said to Josephus, "Oh, my lord, now
we know indeed that you were telling us the truth about this seat. Those who
advised him to sit there in spite of your having forbidden it sinned and did
evil. For God's sake, tell us, if you know, where he was taken and whether he
has been saved or has perished."

"You will be certain about this in time," said Josephus, "for I will show
you the place where he has been put, so that you will be able to see him

clearly. Then you will know whether he is comfortable or not. After that I will tell you whether he has perished or been saved."

After these words no one asked him anything more, for they were very frightened by what they had seen.

Once they had eaten, Bron said to Josephus, "My lord, give me your advice about something I'm going to ask."

"Tell me what it is," Josephus replied.

"I have twelve sons, all close relatives of yours. I beseech you to send for all of them. Once they have come before you, ask them how they intend to act from now on and whether they will marry or not."

"I will certainly do this," said Josephus.

Then he sent for all of Bron's children. When they had come before him, Josephus took them aside, far from the others, and asked each one what kind of person he wanted to be and whether he wished to marry. Eleven said they would marry, just as the rest of their line had done. The twelfth did not accept this, but stated forcefully that he would never have a wife and would remain a virgin all the days of his life and serve the Holy Vessel called the Grail as long as he had life in his body. The twelfth of Bron's children chose to keep holy virginity and to serve the Holy Vessel, while the others all chose to have a wife.

When Josephus saw the son who had vowed to keep virginity and serve the Holy Vessel, he began to embrace him and kiss him, rejoicing more than anyone in the world. And he said to the eleven who had asked for wives, "You will have what you have requested, for I will find brides for all of you. May God grant that you keep yourselves as true as one should in marriage. And you," he said to the twelfth, "have requested two things: to remain a virgin and to be a minister of the Holy Vessel. I grant you the one, and Lord God grants you the other. May He grant that you be a virgin all the days of your life, in mind and in deed, so that your flesh might not be sullied by the sin of lust. May God give you this, my dear friend, for I gladly grant that you be a minister of Holy Church and of the Holy Vessel. Because you have chosen such a high thing as virginity, I grant that after me, you be invested with the guardianship of the Holy Vessel you have requested, so that you will be its guardian after my death. And when you have passed from this world, the one you give it to and his descendants will be its lords. The grace of the Holy Vessel will be so important that if their lands are ever devastated, they will receive food in abundance as long as they live. I give you this gift, dear friend, because of the high gift you have requested."

The boy knelt before Josephus and, in tears, thanked him. And Josephus invested him with the Holy Vessel after his death. Then he did for the other brothers what he had promised, for he saw that they were all married well, as they wished.

After taking care of Bron's children in this manner, Josephus began to wander through Great Britain with his followers, as chance led him. Not a day passed without his group growing by twenty or thirty men who followed him, barefoot and in humble pilgrim's woolens, leaving their riches and inheritance in order to keep him company. Nor did he go anywhere without converting a great number of people to the Christian faith and taking them away from unbelief, for his words were so powerful and full of ardor, through the grace and power of the Holy Spirit which was at work in him, that he found hardly anyone so unbelieving that he was not easily converted once he heard Josephus. As a result, his group increased daily.

One day it happened that they came to an uncultivated and barren land where they could not easily find food. Do not think that everyone in Josephus's group lived from the grace of the Holy Vessel; but some did—those who were worthy men leading good lives. And the others, who were in mortal sin and lust, and who did not want to mend their ways, despite any prayers or sermons, did not live from it, but from what they found or what people gave them.

The day they entered this wasteland I have mentioned to you, it happened that they descended into a deep, wide valley. In the middle they found a large pond; at the far end there was a small boat and a fishing net. When they reached the pond, they sat down to rest, and some of them took their robes off because it was hot.

Then the Holy Vessel was brought out, and Josephus and his ministers began the service they offered every day. Those in the company who were worthy men, leading good lives and those who were not ordained for this service stepped forward a little and said their prayers, asking Our Lord in His sweet pity to lead them safely wherever they might go and to send them enough grace to sustain their bodies. That day the Christian ministers served the Holy Vessel humbly.

After doing this as they should, they sat down in the middle of the field, and some began to spread tablecloths, while others lay folded cloths on the grass, for they wanted to eat at the dinner hour, and they had no other tables. Once they were ready to eat, Peter, one of Josephus's relatives, carried the Holy Grail before the ranks. It happened that at the coming of the Holy Vessel all the tablecloths where the religious worthy men sat were covered with the most beautiful food a mortal heart could conceive. But where the sinners were sitting, no one could see any sign of the grace of the Holy Grail. Rather, that time the sinners had nothing to eat.

After the others had eaten and stood up, the sinners came to Josephus and began to say, "Oh, my lord, what will we do? If you don't help us, we will be destroyed, for the grace of the Holy Vessel did not give us food as it used to. Therefore, you must take care of us, if you don't want us to die of hunger."

Hearing this, Josephus replied, "My lords, it grieves me that things are so. Now your faith is apparent: you have abandoned God, and He has abandoned you. As long as you were good sons, He was a good Father, for as long as you served Him loyally, He gave generously whatever you needed. But now you have begun to serve Him like stepsons, and He will give you food like a stepfather. So you can clearly see that no good comes from abandoning Him, for if you still held to Him, you would still have whatever your hearts conceived. And yet, because I see you are so unfortunate, I will advise you as best I can. I would not do this if I saw you had something to eat nearby."

Then Josephus called Bron's twelfth son, the one he had chosen to be a minister of the Holy Grail; and this child was called Alan the Fat. Do not think this was the Alan who was descended from Celidoine's line,[20] for he was never a king, nor did he ever wear a crown, while the other was a king who wore a crown and held beautiful, rich lands. When Alan came before him, Josephus said in the presence of everyone there, "Alan, you who will be one of the most gracious of our lineage, as I believe, go to the pond and get in the little boat; throw the net you will find there into the water and catch a fish, which these people will live on tonight, for they need it."

The child did as Josephus commanded. He went to the water, got in the little boat, took the net, and threw it in the water and dragged it to shore. When he got there, those who were waiting looked in the net and found only one fish, though it was undoubtedly a large one. They told him to go after more, for this one would not suffice for a tenth of those who had had no food. Josephus said he would not go back, and he ordered the fish taken out and cooked. Once it was cooked, he ordered those who had not eaten to sit down. They did so, for they needed to eat. Then Josephus said to Alan, "Alan, take this fish and make three parts. Put two of them at the two ends of the table, and the third in the middle. And pray to Our Lord to show you in His sweet pity—not as a favor to you, but through His grace—how generous He is toward you and how gracious He will be to you once you are entrusted with the Holy Vessel."

Then Alan began to weep very tenderly, and he came before the Holy Vessel, where he remained in prayer for a long time. After completing his prayer, he did what Josephus had ordered, dividing the fish into three parts and putting them in three places. As soon as he had done so, Our Lord worked such a beautiful miracle for him that, in honor of the child and as a sign of the goodness that was to be in him, He multiplied the fish until all those who had had no food were filled as if all the good things in the world had been set out in abundance. And after everyone had eaten, what was left over was greater than the original fish.

Because of the great plenty they had had from the gift of the fish Alan had caught, they gave him a name that was never abandoned, for they called

---

[20] Celidione is Nascien's son.

him the Rich Fisherman. Thereafter he was called more often by that name than by his right name. And in his honor and because of that day's grace, all those who were invested with the Holy Vessel were called Rich Fishermen. Without a doubt all those who were invested by him had more grace in the world than he did, for all were crowned kings, whereas he was not. But in remembrance of this, the pond was henceforth called Alan's Pond. And this adventure brought such great joy to those to whom it happened that I could recount none greater.

While they were talking about this, Joseph said to his son Josephus, "The desire has come over me to leave you and go where chance will lead me. My desire to do this is so strong that I think some good will come of it. You can be sure I will come back to you as quickly as I can, for once I have left you, I will want to see you again soon."

[*Josephus traveled around for fifteen years, converting people to Christianity. Eventually, just a day before his death, he came to the abbey where King Mordrain lived. Josephus used his own blood to make a cross on the shield that Mordrain had used in battle against Tholomer. The shield was not to be used until Galahad came for it.*]

8. The Holy Vessel Is Passed on to Alan.

Now the story says that when Josephus saw he was about to die and that his payment of the natural debt could not be postponed, he saw Alan before him, weeping night and day. This troubled him, and he asked, "Alan, why are you crying?"

"My lord," he said, "I am crying like the sheep that should grieve when it is left without a shepherd. The wolf can easily attack and strangle it. My lord, I am saying all this because of you, who are a shepherd, while I am your sheep. You are going away now and leaving me alone. Who will watch over me? Who will be my shepherd from now on?"

"God will watch over you and be a good and loyal shepherd—not a bad one, who leaves his sheep in a dangerous place," said Josephus. "He is a true shepherd who, in order to bring the sheep back from exile, let His body be delivered over to death. This shepherd, my dear friend, will protect you from the wolf, for He takes care of you so that the enemy cannot lay a hand on you."

Then he had the Holy Vessel brought before him and said to Alan, "Alan, I entrust you with this, as Jesus Christ entrusted my father. When you pass from this world, you can invest the person you wish. And henceforth they will be entrusted with it in this kingdom, and you will be the one who will invest them."

Alan took the Vessel, very happy and joyful about the gift he had received. As soon as Josephus died, Alan left Galafort, taking with him his brothers, who were all married except one called Joshua. He was not yet married, and he was one of the good knights in the world, and he was the one whom Alan loved the most of all his brothers. When Alan left Galafort, his relatives began to ask where he was going. "Certainly," he said, "I don't know, except where God and chance take me."

[*Alan journeyed to the kingdom of the Land Beyond, where he converted the inhabitants.*]

After the kingdom of the Land Beyond was thus converted in this way to Our Lord, the king said to Alan, "My dear Alan, I ask you for God's sake to do something for me."

"My lord," said Alan, "tell me, and if I can, I will do it."

"Alan, my dear friend, I am asking you to leave the Holy Vessel, with which you are entrusted, here forever. You can be sure that if it pleases you to do so, in its honor I will build the most splendid and best-situated stronghold possible. And I will do even more for love of you, something that should honor you, for I will give my daughter to your brother Joshua as his wife and leave him all my land, crowning him during your lifetime, with the agreement that this vessel will stay in this land."

Alan said he would be pleased for it to remain, for it was his intent to entrust Joshua with it after his death. The king had his daughter brought at once and gave her to Joshua and invested him with all his land. Then the king had a beautiful stronghold built above rapid-running water. He had many sumptuous palaces and large houses built, as well as a manor as splendid as any that existed. Once it was finished and prepared, they found on one of the gates a miraculous inscription in Chaldean saying, THIS CASTLE SHOULD BE CALLED CORBENIC. And in that language "Corbenic" means "place for the Holy Vessel." When they saw the name in writing, they said it did not please Our Lord that it be called by any other name, so they called it that right away. And they had people come at once to inhabit the castle. Once this was done, they brought the Holy Vessel and put it in a high room next to the main palace.

The Sunday after the Vessel was brought to the palace, the king ordered the wedding celebrated between his daughter and Joshua. This was done, and the people of the country did homage to Joshua. He was crowned that day in Corbenic Castle and married King Alphasan's daughter. That day everyone who ate was filled with the grace of the Holy Vessel, so that there was no one who did not have whatever he could describe to eat. That night Joshua and his wife lay in a room below and conceived Aminadap, who was king after Joshua and held the kingdom of the Land Beyond.

That night King Alphasan slept in the main palace; in the middle a very beautiful, sumptuous bed was made up. During the night, around midnight, he awoke, and looking before him, saw the Holy Vessel sitting on a silver table; in front of it was a man he did not know, who looked like a priest when he is saying Mass. Around him there seemed to be more than a thousand voices, giving thanks to Our Lord. He did not see the bodies from which the voices came, and yet he heard around him the noise of feathers and beating of wings as loudly as if all the birds in the world were there.

Once the song of praise was over and the Holy Vessel was carried back into the room it had come from, a man who seemed to be enveloped in flames came to King Alphasan and said, "King, no man should lie in this palace— neither you nor anyone else—for scarcely could any man, through a good life, be worthy of remaining in the place where the Holy Vessel was honored as you saw. You did a very foolhardy thing in coming to sleep here; Our Lord wants vengeance taken."

Then he released a lance he was holding and struck the king through both thighs so that the lance appeared on the other side. And he said to the king, "Now may others refrain from staying in the Palace of Adventures, for they can be sure that anyone who stays here will die or leave in shame, unless he is definitely a good knight."

Then he pulled his lance out and left at once. The king fainted from the pain and lay the rest of the night in such distress that he thought he was certainly going to die before day came.

The next day, when the lords came to the palace and saw the king so badly wounded, they were more than a little frightened, and they asked him how this had happened. He told them, "Ah, for God's sake, don't ask me to talk, but take me quickly out of this palace, for the place is so praiseworthy because of the Holy Vessel's presence that no knight should stay here, especially at night, when the Holy Vessel is brought in. You can be sure that the palace has a nobler name than any I have ever seen."

They asked him what its name was, and he said it was the Palace of Adventures, because greater adventures and marvels would happen there than anywhere in the world. Thus the king taught the name of the palace to those who did not know it before. And henceforth it was always called this. Because of the adventure that befell the king, many knights came and stayed there at night, but none stayed who was not found dead in the morning, until Arthur's nephew Gawain came. He did not die, and yet he was so shamed and injured that he would not have wished to undergo this in return for all the kingdom of Logres.[21]

King Alphasan lived ten days after being wounded, sick and unable to be healed. He and Alan passed away on the same day and were buried next to each other in the Church of Notre Dame at Corbenic. Thus the Holy Grail remained in Corbenic Castle.

---

[21]For the realization of this prediction, see *Lancelot*, Chapter 31.

King Joshua ruled his land with a firm hand. After him reigned his son Aminadap, who married one of the daughters of Luce, the king of Great Britain. This young man and woman had a son named King Carcelois, a valiant and brave knight and a worthy man in God's and the world's eyes. King Carcelois fathered King Manuel, and he fathered King Lambor. They were all kings and held land and were called the Rich Fishermen.

This Lambor was a good knight who loved God so much that it was believed there was no more worthy man than he in all of Great Britain, either in a religious house or any other place. He had a neighbor called Varlan, a rich king whose lands bordered on his. He was a Saracen recently converted to Christianity, and the two were at war against one another with all of their forces.

One day it happened that King Lambor and King Varlan had assembled their men above the seashore, and a great and wondrous battle had begun between them. In it King Varlan was defeated, and all his men were killed, so that he fled alone toward the seashore. When he reached shore, he found a ship that had just landed. This ship was the most beautiful and sumptuous he had ever seen or ever would see in all his life. [. . .]

When it reached shore, the king jumped into the ship. After looking at the sword [that he found there], he drew it from the scabbard and turned back. Finding King Lambor in his path, he struck him on the helmet. The sword was so sharp that it split the king from the top of his helmet, through the horse, right down to the ground. This was the first blow of the sword in Great Britain.[22] There resulted such great persecutions to both kingdoms—the kingdom of the Land Beyond and that of the land of Wales—to avenge King Lambor, whom God loved so much, that for a long time afterwards the lands that should have been cultivated were not. Nor did wheat, oats, or anything else grow, nor did the trees bear fruit, nor were any fish to be found in the waters except very little ones. And for this reason, the land of the two kingdoms was called the Waste Land.

When Varlan saw that the sword cut so well, he decided to go back and take the scabbard. So he returned to the ship and put the sword into the scabbard. As soon as he had done so, he fell dead before the bed. All those who saw this then said that he died because he had drawn the sword. [. . .] Through this adventure that I have told you, the two kingdoms that bordered on each other were completely devastated and destroyed.

After King Lambor, his son Pellehan reigned, who was wounded in both thighs in a battle in Rome. Because of the wound he received in this battle,

---

[22]This blow corresponds to what will elsewhere be called the Dolorous Stroke. In Malory, for example, Balin wounds Pellam with the spear of Longinus, resulting in the infertility of the Waste Land.

everyone who knew him called him henceforth the Maimed King, since this wound could not be healed until Galahad, the very good knight, came to visit him. And then without fail he healed it.

From Pellehan descended a king named Pelles, a very handsome, brave knight, and a worthy man. The latter had a daughter whose beauty surpassed that of all the women who ever lived in Great Britain, except Queen Guenevere, King Arthur's wife. With this young woman, who was so beautiful and noble, Lancelot fathered Galahad, the good knight who brought the adventures of Great Britain to an end.[23] Although he was conceived in sin, Our Lord did not consider this, but rather the high branch of worthy men from whom he was descended, and his good life, and the good purpose he had in life. So He granted him in His graciousness so much grace that he brought to an end all the adventures the other knights had failed in or were unable to finish.

[*Nascien and his wife died, as did King Mordrain's wife. Mordrain had the shield with the cross brought to an abbey where it would stay until Galahad took it.*]

---

[23]Galahad's conception is described in the *Lancelot*, Chapter 33.

The Story of Merlin

TRANSLATED BY RUPERT T. PICKENS

1. Merlin's Conception and Childhood Deeds.

In this part the story says that the devil grew very angry after Our Lord had gone to Hell and freed Adam and Eve and as many others as He pleased, so that when the devils saw it they were very much afraid and they were greatly astounded by it.

So they met and said, "Who is this who so overwhelms us that no power we have can stop Him from doing whatever He pleases? We did not believe that any man born of woman could fail to belong to us, yet He overwhelms us! How can He have been born? For we have not seen in Him any leanings for earthly delights such as we have seen in all other people."

Another devil then answered them and said, "He has been able to harm us because we thought that we could overcome Him. Remember, the prophets said that the Son of God would come to earth to save sinners, descendants of Eve and Adam, as many as He pleased. And we went and took those who said this and tormented them more than the others. Yet, it seemed that our torture did not hurt them, rather they brought solace to the other sinners by telling them that the One who would deliver them would come down to earth.

"What the prophets said has now happened, and He has taken from us all those we had won for ourselves, so that we cannot lay claim to any of them, and He has also taken away all the others with such might that we cannot understand it. Don't you know that He washes them in water in His own name and that they are baptized in that water in the name of the Father and the Son and the Holy Ghost? By this we should know that we have lost them, and we have no power over them until they come back to us through their own deeds. So our strength fails, for He has taken it from us. What's more, He has left ministers on earth who will go on saving souls, so long as they do not do our works, if they are willing to repent and give up our works and do what their teachers command. This is how they are utterly lost to us.

"He has indeed provided spiritual substance who came down to earth to save humankind and lowered Himself to be born of a woman and suffer the torments of the world. He came without our knowledge and not through the fleshly lust of a man or a woman, though we saw Him and assailed Him in every way we could. When we had put Him to the test and seen that we could not find any of our works in Him, He was willing to die to save human creatures. He loved them greatly indeed, since He wanted to undergo such great suffering to have them for Himself and take them from us.

"And we must work very hard to get them back, so that He will not have taken anything from us that is ours by right, and we must trick Him and work our way so that they cannot find their way back or even speak with those through whom they might have forgiveness."

Then they all said together, "We have lost everything, since He can forgive sins until the end of humankind, if He can find people doing His works, whereby they are His. And even though they do our works all the time, they will be lost to us if they repent. Thus, we have lost everything!"

Then they began talking all at the same time and said, "The ones who have hurt us most are those who tell the news of His coming down to earth: they are the ones through whom the great harm has come to us. The more they said it, the more we tortured them, so it seems that He came all the more quickly to help them and to save them from the torments we worked on them. But how can *we* have someone who might speak out and tell about our aims, our deeds, and our ways of life—who might have the power, like us, to know things done and said and past? If we had someone who had that power and who knew those things, and if he were on earth with other folk, then he could help us trick them just as the prophets who were with us tricked us, those who told us what we did not believe could happen. And he could also foretell things that were to come about and be said soon and far in the future, so that he would be believed by everybody. Anyone who can bring about such a thing will have worked wonders!"

Then one of them said, "I don't have the power to conceive or to cause a woman to conceive. But if I had that power, I would do it well! For I know of a woman who gladly does everything I want. And there is among us," he went on, "one who can take on the likeness of a man and lie with a woman, so long as he does it as secretly as he can." They undertook to engender a man who would teach the others. The devils were mad for thinking that Our Lord did not know this plan.

[*The devil caused the deaths of a young woman's father, mother, and sister and then led her to live a sinful life. A priest persuaded her to mend her ways, and she did so for a time, after which an argument with her remaining sister made her forgot the priest's teachings.*]

This one devil had the power to lie with a woman and get her with child. Then he was all ready, and he lay with her carnally as she slept, and she conceived. After this had been done, the young woman awoke. As she was awakening, she remembered the wise priest, so she crossed herself and said, "Holy Lady Mary, what has happened to me? I feel so much worse than when I went to bed. Fair, glorious Mother of God, pray your dear Son to keep my soul and defend my body from torment and from the might of the devil."

Then she got up and began looking for the one who had done this thing to her, for she thought she could find him. She ran to the door of the room, but found it locked; she looked everywhere in her room, but found no one. It was then that she understood that she had been tricked by a devil. She began wailing, softly calling out to Our Lord and entreating him not to allow anyone to shame her in this world.

Night went by and day came. As soon as it was light, the devil took the younger sister away, for she had done well in what he had brought her there to do. When she and the young men had gone, the elder sister came out of her room in great distress. She called her manservant and told him to bring two women. As soon as they had come, she left and made her way until she found her confessor.

When he saw her he said to her, "You are in trouble, for I see that you are very frightened."

"Sir," she told him, "something has happened to me that has never happened to any other woman. I come to you so that you'll tell me what to do, for you have said to me that people cannot commit such a great sin that, if they confess it and repent of it and do whatever their confessor tells them, it will not be forgiven. Sir," she went on, "I have sinned, and you should know that I've been ensnared by a devil."

Then she told him how her sister came to the house, how she grew angry with her, how she and the young men beat her, how she went to her room burning with wrath and closed the door against her, and how, because of her great anger and the distress she felt, she forgot to cross herself "and all the commands you gave me as well. When I awoke I found myself shamed and deflowered. My room was closed as fast as when I locked it myself, and I did not find a soul there, so I do not know who did this to me. Sir, I have been betrayed, and I beg you, have pity. If my body suffers torment, please pray for my soul so that it will not be lost." [. . .]

He blessed her with the sign of the cross and commended her to God, and she set out on the way back to her house. And she led a very good and simple life. When the devil saw that he had lost her—and he did not see that she was behaving otherwise than she always had—he became very angry.

So she was until the seed she bore in her body could no longer be hidden. She grew so big that the other women noticed it and stared at her belly. They asked her if she was with child and who the man was that had done it to her. She answered, "May God bring me into joy, but I don't know and I never knew."

They said to her, "Have so many men lain with you that you don't know which one to accuse?"

But she answered, "May it not please God that I give birth to the child if ever to my knowledge anything happened to me that should bring me to this."

When they heard this they crossed themselves and said, "Dear friend, that could not be, nor did that ever happen to you or anyone else. Perhaps you love the man who did this to you so much, as much as or more than you love yourself, so that you're not willing to name him. But what a shame for you that, as soon as the judges learn about it, you will have to die!"

When she heard that she would have to die because of it, she was filled with great dread, and she said, "God save my soul, but I never saw or knew the one who has done this to me."

The women laughed at her and thought she was crazy, and they said, "What a shame about your lovely homestead, its good land and fine buildings, for it will soon be lost."

When she heard this she was greatly frightened, and she went off to her confessor and told him what the women had said to her. The good man saw that she was pregnant with a living child, and he was quite amazed. "Dear sister," he said to her, "have you faithfully kept the penance I imposed on you?"

"Yes, sir," she answered, "and I have done nothing wrong."

"And did this wonder ever happen to you more than one time?"

She answered no, and he was astounded and wrote down the hour and the night just as she had told to him, and he said that she had to be quite sure about it: "And when the child who is in you is born, I am bound to know if you have lied to me. And I have strong faith in God that, if it is just as you have told me, you will not have to fear death. But you will have reason to be afraid when the judges find out, for they will arrest you just to have your buildings and your good land, yet they will say that they are bringing you to justice. And when you have been arrested, let me know and I will come to comfort you and help you if I can. God will help you: He will be with you if things are as you say."

Then he said, "Go home and don't worry; lead a good life, for a good life helps bring people to a good end."

So the young woman went back home that night and lived very quietly until the judges came to the region. And when they found out what had happened to her, they sent men to her house to get her; they arrested her and took her away with them. As soon as she was taken prisoner, she sent for the same good priest who had always counseled her; and when he found out about her, he came to her as fast as he could.

When he had come there, they called for him, and he found that the judges had already had the young woman brought before them. The good man gave them the young woman's testimony, and he said that she did not believe she needed to fear anyone. But the judges said to him, "Do you think a woman can become pregnant and have a child without lying with a man?"

The good man answered, "I won't tell you everything I know about it, but I can certainly tell you this: if you will believe me, you won't bring her to justice until she has had the child. It would not be right or just otherwise: the child has not deserved death, since it did not commit the sin, and the child has done nothing wrong in the sins of the mother."

The judges answered, "We will do as you advise."

And the good man said, "If you follow my advice, you will keep her well guarded and locked in a tower where she cannot do anything foolish. Lock two women up with her to help her give birth when she needs it, and don't let them out either. My advice is to leave her there until she has the child and until the child can eat by itself and ask for what it needs. And then, if you are bent on doing something more, do what you please. If you have faith in me, you will do as I advise; if you want to do otherwise, I can't do any more about it."

And the judges answered, "It seems to us that what you say is right."

Everything they did just as the good man had set it forth. They put the young woman in a very strong stone house and had all the doorways walled up. And they locked up two women with her, the most skilled they could find for doing what had to be done. High up they left one window open through which they could pull up whatever they needed. When the good man saw this, he spoke to the young woman through the window and said to her, "When your child is born, have it baptized as soon as you can. And when you are put outside, the judges will want to try you, so send for me."

So she stayed a long time in the tower. The judges took care of everything she needed and had it brought to her. She was inside there so long that at last she had her child as it pleased God. And when he was born, he unavoidably had the power and the mind of a devil, and the cunning, because he was sired by one.

But the devil had behaved most unwisely, for Our Lord had bought true repentance with His death. The devil had ensnared the young woman through deceit and trickery while she was asleep. As soon as she felt that she had been beguiled, she confessed and cried out for mercy where she ought. And when she cried out, she put herself under the mercy and the commandments of the Lord God and Holy Church. This is why God did not want the child to lose, because of the devil, anything that belonged to him; rather He allowed the child to have what was his by right. Therefore, He bestowed on him the devils' art of knowing things that are done, said, and past—all this he knew. And Our Lord, who is all-knowing, knew, by the mother's repentance, by her good confession, by the cleansing of confession, and by the true repentance He knew to be in her heart, that she had not wanted or willed what had happened to her. By the power of the baptism with which the child was washed in the font, Our Lord willed that the sin of the mother should not harm him. And He also gave him the sense and the power to know the future.

This is the reason why he knew the things that were done, said, and past: he inherited this from the devil. Moreover, he knew things that were to come; Our Lord willed that he should know things contrary to those he knew from the other side. Now he could turn to whichever side he wanted, for if he wished, he could give the devils their due, or else His to God just as well.

Thus was he born. And when the women had received him, they were all deeply frightened, for they saw that he was hairier than they had ever seen any other child. After they had shown him to his mother she crossed herself and said, "This child frightens me very much."

And the other women said, "And we are so afraid of him that we can scarcely hold him."

She said to them, "Send him down and have him baptized."

They asked her, "What do you want him named?"

And she answered, "The same as my father's name."

Then they put him into a basket and sent him down with a rope, then they gave orders to have him baptized: "Let him bear the name of his grandfather on his mother's side; that good man was called Merlin by his father."

Thus the child was baptized and named Merlin after his grandfather. He was then given to his mother to be nursed, for no other woman dared do so. His mother nursed him until he was nine months old. The women who were with her told her many times that they were quite amazed that the child, who was so hairy, was only nine months old, yet he looked as if he was two years old or more.

[*At eighteen months, Merlin began to talk and was thought a devil. His mother was condemned to death. Merlin used his gifts to reveal secrets and predict events. He also explained his own origin and nature.*]

"I want you to know and believe that I am the son of a devil who ensnared my mother. Know also that one kind of devil is called incubi, and they live in the air. God allowed me to have their intelligence and their memory, so I know things that are done, said, and past; this is how I know what your mother has done. And Our Lord has permitted and wills me to have this in my memory because of my mother's goodness. And because of her holy and true repentance, the penance that this worthy man imposed on her, and the commands of Holy Church which she believed, God has given me such power that I know the things that are to come." [. . .]

[*Merlin asked that these things be told to Blaise, his mother's confessor. Soon Merlin decided to have Blaise record in writing what the former would tell him.*]

Merlin began to recount the love between Jesus Christ and Joseph of Arimathea, just as it had been, and to tell about Joseph and his offspring and those people who had the vessel called the Grail and all their accomplishments, just as they had been, about Alan and his companions, how he left his father's house, how Petrus had departed, how Joseph disposed of his vessel, and how he died. Afterward he told him about the devils, how they had gathered together because they had lost the power they had enjoyed over humanity before, and he told him how the prophets had done them harm and how, for this reason, they had conspired to make a man. "And they said they would make me. You heard all about it and you learned from my mother and other people about their deeds and tricks—and then the foolishness they are all so full of, for they have lost me and every other advantage."

Thus did Merlin set out the plan for the work that he ordered Blaise to undertake. And Blaise was amazed at the wonders that Merlin told, but they seemed to be nonetheless true and good and beautiful, so he devoted himself to writing them down, so much so that one day Merlin said to Blaise, "You must suffer a great deal for this undertaking, and I will suffer more than you."

And he asked him how that was.

"People will come from the west to seek me out. And those who will come to find me will have promised their lord that they would kill me and bring him my blood. But when they see me and hear me, they won't want to kill me. But when I go away with them, you will go to the place where the people are who possess the holy cup, the Grail. Forever thereafter, your work and your book will be told about, and your book will be gladly heard everywhere. But it will not have authority, because you cannot be among the apostles, who never put anything down in writing about Our Lord that they had not seen or heard, and you do not put down what you have seen or heard except as I tell you to. And just as I will remain obscure except concerning those things wherein I wish to reveal myself, so will your book remain hidden. In a short while it will come about that no one will thank you for it, and you will take it away with you when I go off with those who are to come for me.

"You will go to Western parts, and the book of Joseph will be put together with yours. And when you have fulfilled your task, and when you are, as you should be, in the company of the Grail, then your book will be joined to Joseph's book, and everything will have been proved true concerning my labors and yours, and God will bless it if it pleases Him. And those who hear it will pray to Our Lord on our behalf. And when the two books are put together, there will be one beautiful book, and the two will be one and the same thing, except that I cannot say or recount the intimate words between Jesus Christ and Joseph.

"In England there had not yet been a Christian king, and about those who had come before, I do not care to tell anything except what has bearing on this story."

2. Uther Pendragon and the Round Table; The Perilous Seat.

[*Merlin repeatedly amazed others with his gifts. He also served as a military advisor to Uther and his brother Pendragon in their war against Vortigern. He predicted the death of one of the brothers in battle; Pendragon died, and Uther, known henceforth as Uther Pendragon, became king.*]

So Merlin stayed for a long time: he was King Uther Pendragon's chief adviser, and the king confided in him. At last, a long time later, Merlin called Uther Pendragon and said to him, "Why don't you do more for your brother Pendragon, who lies on the Plain of Salisbury?"

And he answered, "What do you want me to do with him? I will do whatever you advise me to do."

And Merlin said, "You swore to do as I wish, and I promise you that we will build something that will be seen as long as this world lasts. Do as you have promised, and I will keep my word."

And Uther Pendragon answered, "Tell me what I can do and I will very gladly do it."

And he said to him, "Now learn how to do something that no one has ever known before, and it will be spoken of ever hereafter."

Uther Pendragon answered, "I will do so very gladly."

"Now send someone for great stones that are in Ireland, and send along two boats in which to bring them, and they will not be able to bring so many back that I cannot set them all up. And I will go to show them which ones I want so they can bring them back."

And the king said that he would very gladly send them there, and he sent a great many boats. And when they got there, Merlin showed them some great stones, long and wide. And he said to them, "Here are the stones we came to find."

When they saw them, they thought it was all madness, and said that all together they could hardly turn one of them over, "and we will never put such stones on our boats at sea."

And Merlin said, "If you don't wish to do this, then you have come for nothing."

They turned about and went back to the king and told him the wonder Merlin had ordered them to perform, which they knew no man on earth could do. And the king said to them, "Now wait until he comes."

When Merlin came, the king told him the story his men had brought back to him. And Merlin answered, "Since they have all let me down, I will do what I have promised all by myself."

Then by the power of magic he had the stones brought from Ireland which are still in the burial ground at Salisbury.[1] And when they had come, the king went to see them and took many of his people to see the wonder of the stones. When they saw them, they said that all of them together could not move one of them, and they wondered at how he got them there, for no one had seen it or heard about it. And Merlin said that someone should set them upright, for they would be more beautiful standing straight up than lying down.

And the king answered that no man could do that but God, "unless you did it."

And Merlin said to him, "Now you go away and I will set them up, and I will have fulfilled my pledge to Pendragon; otherwise, I would have begun something for his sake that can never be brought to an end."

So Merlin stood the stones up. They are still in the burial ground at Salisbury and will be there as long as the world lasts. And so this work was over,

---

[1]The reference, clearly, is to Stonehenge.

and Merlin came back to King Uther Pendragon; he served him a great deal and loved him. A long time had gone by since he had come to understand in whom he had put his love, and he knew that he would believe him in everything he said.

One day it happened that Merlin came to the king and said to him privately, "I must talk to you about the highest secrets I know. For I see that all this land is yours; you are firmly in command of it as lord, and no one could rule it better. It is because I love you that I want to tell you something. Don't you remember that Hengist would have killed you if it hadn't been for me? Thus it seems to me that you ought well to believe me and love me."

Uther Pendragon answered, "There is nothing that you would say that I would not believe and do all in my power to bring about."

"Sir, if you do this, it will all be for your own good, for I will teach you something that will hardly distress you, and you could never do anything whereby you might so easily have the love of God."

And the king answered, "As surely as you say it, if it can be done by any man, I will do it."

Then Merlin said, "What I will tell you will be a very strange thing to you, and I bid you, keep it hidden and do not say it to your courtiers or your knights, for I mean for all the worth and honor and thanks to be yours."

And the king said that he would never talk about it except through him alone.

He then said to the king, "Sir, you must take it as truth that I know everything that is past, gone by, and spoken, and I want you to know that this skill came to me from a devil. Sir, Our Lord, who is powerful over all things, has given me the intelligence and the knowledge to recognize and to know things that are to come. And thanks to that sovereign power, the devils lost me, for I will never, God willing, be subject to their will. Sir, now do you know where my power to do the things I do comes from?

"I will tell you what I know Our Lord wants you to do. And when you know it, be sure to honor Him according to His will. Sir, you must believe that Our Lord came to earth to save the world and that He sat down at the Last Supper and said to His disciples, 'There is one of you who will betray me.' Sir, everything was true just as He said, and the one who did Him wrong left His fellowship, just as He said he would.

"Sir, after this it happened that Our Lord suffered death for our sake. And a knight[2] asked to take Him down from the cross, and He was given to him in place of his wages. Sir, this hired soldier loved Our Lord very much, for he wanted Him and agreed to have Him given to him. Sir, His disciples bore many hardships and many fearsome things afterwards. And it happened a

---

[2]That is, Joseph of Arimathea.

long time after Our Lord was raised from the dead that the knight was in a wilderness along with some of his kin and a great many others who had gone along after him. Sir, a very great famine overcame them, and they complained to the knight, who was their leader. And he prayed to Our Lord to give them a sign telling them why He wanted them to suffer this trial.

"Our Lord ordered him to make a table in the name of the table that was at the Last Supper and to put a cup he had on that table after he had covered it with a white cloth, and he was to cover the vessel fully as well. Sir, Jesus Christ gave that cup to him, and with this cup He divided the fellowship of the good from the wicked. And, sir, anyone who could sit at that table could fulfill his heart's desires in every way.

"Sir, at that table there was always an empty seat that stood for the place where Judas sat at the Last Supper when he understood what Our Lord was saying on his account and he left the fellowship of Jesus Christ. And his seat was left empty until Our Lord put another man there to take his place to bring the count to twelve. And the empty seat at the new table stands for that place. Thus these two tables are very much alike, and Our Lord perfects men's hearts at the second table. And they call the cup, from which they have that grace, the Grail.

"If you will believe me, you will set up the third table[3] in the name of the Trinity, and by these three tables will the Trinity be signified in its three Persons, the Father, the Son, and the Holy Ghost. I promise you that if you do this, great good will come to you from it and great honor to your soul and your body, and in your time will happen things that will utterly amaze you. If you will do this, I will help you, and I promise you that if you do, it will be one of the most talked about things ever. For Our Lord has indeed granted grace to those who will know how to speak well of it. And I tell you also that this cup and the people who keep it have drawn westward, by the will of Jesus Christ, to these parts. And even those who do not know where the cup is have come here, and Our Lord, who brings good things to pass, led them. If you believe me, you will do what I advise you to do about these things. If you do this, and if you will believe me, you will be very glad indeed."

Thus spoke Merlin to Uther Pendragon, and the king was very glad about it. And he answered, "I do not want Our Lord to lose, because of me, any part of the thing that must be done according to His will. Indeed, I want you to know that I love Him. I put it all onto you, and I will do anything you order me to do, if I can."

So King Uther Pendragon put the whole burden onto Merlin, who was very glad to bear it. And Merlin said, "Sir, now look to the place where you would like most to do what you must."

---

[3]It is not explicit until much later that the third table is the Round Table.

And the king answered, "I want it to be done where you would most like it done, where you know it can best be done according to the will of Jesus Christ."

Merlin replied, "We will do it at Carduel in Wales, so have your people gather there to meet you on Whitsunday, and you will be ready to give out great gifts and to be of good cheer. And I will go before you and have the table built, and you will give me silver and men who will do what I order them to do. And when you get there and your people are gathered, I will pick out the ones who are to stay there."

As Merlin set it out the king ordered it done, and he sent word throughout his kingdom that he would hold his court at Whitsuntide at Carduel in Wales, and all knights and all ladies were to be there to meet him. This is what the king made known everywhere. Merlin went off and had the table built and everything done there that needed to be done. And so it was until the week before Whitsunday, when the king came to Carduel.

And when he had got there, he asked Merlin how he had fared, and he answered, "Very well."

So the people gathered that Whitsuntide at Carduel, a great many knights and ladies and other folk.

Then the king said to Merlin, "Which ones will you choose to have sit at that table?"

And he said, "Tomorrow you will see happen what you never thought you would see. For I will seat there the worthiest men in your kingdom, and never, once they have sat there, will they want to leave this place to go back to their lands and domains. Then you will see for yourself who the worthiest are."

And the king answered, "That I will very gladly do."

And the next day Merlin did just as he had said. It was Whitsunday, and Merlin chose fifty knights, and he bade them, and had others do likewise, to sit at that table and eat the food that was there, and they did so very willingly. And then Merlin, who was full of powerful craft, went among them and called to the king, when they had sat down, and showed him the empty seat. Many others saw it, but they did not know what it meant or why it was empty, except for the king and Merlin. When he had done this, Merlin told the king to go take his seat. And the king said that he would not sit until he had served all who were at the table, and when he had done this he went to sit down. So they were for a whole week, and during the season of that feast the king gave away much wealth and many lovely jewels to ladies and unmarried gentlewomen.

And when it came time for leave-taking, the king went to his worthy companions and asked them how they were. And they answered him, "We have no wish ever to leave here, and we want always to be at this table at the hour of terce, so we will have our wives and children come to this town. And so we will live here at our lord's pleasure, for this is what our hearts tell us to do."

The king asked, "Do you all feel this way?"

And they all said, "Yes indeed! And yet we wonder at how this can be. For many of us have no bonds with any among us; others have not seen each other before, and few of us were friends before. And now we all love each other as much as a son should love his father, or more, and it does not seem to us that we will ever be parted unless it is by death."

When the king heard them speak in this way, he took it for a very great wonder, as did all those who heard it. And the king was most glad and ordered everyone in the town to love, believe, and honor them just as they would his own self. And so Uther Pendragon founded that table in his own time.

Then he came to Merlin and said to him, after the crowds had gone, "You told me the truth indeed, and now I really believe that Our Lord wills this table to be founded, but I wonder at the empty seat. I would like you please to tell me, if you know, who is the one that will sit there."

And Merlin answered, "I can tell you only that the place will not be taken in your time, and the one who will sit there has not yet been conceived. The one who will take that seat must fulfill the adventures of the Grail. This will not be in your time, but in the time of the king who will rule after you. And I bid you, hold all your gatherings and all your high courts in this town, and I ask you please to stay here and hold your court here three times every year."

And the king told him that he would gladly do this, and Merlin said to the king, "Sir, I will go away, and you will not see me again for a very long time."

The king asked him where he was going. "Then you will not be in this town for all the feast days I will keep here?"

And he answered, "I will not. I do not want them to believe what they will see happening, for I want no one to say that I have brought about what will happen."

So Merlin left Uther Pendragon and came into Northumberland to Blaise, and he told him these things, the founding of that table and many other things which you will hear in his book. And so Merlin stayed more than two years, when he did not go to court.

[*There were those who asked about the empty seat at the table, and there were those who insisted on sitting there, agreeing only to wait until Whitsunday.*]

The king went off to Carduel and took a great crowd with him. And the ones who came to try the seat spread the word everywhere that Merlin was dead and that peasants had killed him in a wood where they said they had found him behaving like a wild man. And they told the story so often and had it repeated so much that the king himself believed it, because Merlin had taken so long to come and seemed not to care about the test for the seat. And when the evening before Whitsunday came, the man who wanted to try the place came forward.

He was a highborn and very wealthy man, and he said to the king, "Sir, we must try the seat."

And the king answered, "Who is the one to do it?"

"No one but I will sit there," he said.

Then he came to the table where the fifty worthy men were sitting, and he said to them, "I come to sit with you to share your fellowship."

And these men did not answer a single word, but bore themselves in a kindly way and watched what he wanted to do. And the king was there with a great crowd of people gathered about.

The man went forward to the place, moved in between two of the gentlemen, and sat down. He had just the time to put his thighs onto the seat when he melted away just like a ball of lead, and was lost from sight right before everyone, so that they did not know what had become of him. And when they saw that he had thus perished, everyone else wanted to sit in the place. But the king ordered the worthy gentlemen to stand up, so that after they had got up from the table no one would know which was the place, and they all rose straightway.

The sorrow in the court was great, and the court was utterly distraught by this wonder. The king was more aghast than anyone else, and he thought he had been made a fool of. He said for all to hear that Merlin had plainly told him before that no one should take that seat, and that that man did not want to believe him; the king himself had forbidden it, but the man would not give up just for that—so did the king explain himself.

And when, two weeks later, Merlin came to court, and after the king had been told that he was there, the king was most happy and went out to greet him. As soon as Merlin saw the king, he said that he had behaved most unwisely about the place, for he had allowed someone to sit there. And the king said to him, "He tricked me."

"So has it happened to many who mean to trick others and trick themselves instead," said Merlin. "You know this because he spread the word that peasants had killed me."

The king said, "It is true that he said so."

And Merlin said to him, "You ought now to have learned your lesson not to try the seat anymore, and I warn you that if you do, you could be badly hurt. For the place and the table have great meaning; they are very high and most worthy, and they will bring great good to those who are in this kingdom."

The king asked him please to tell him what had happened to the man who sat at the place, "for I am awestruck."

And Merlin answered, "It is not your place to ask, and it would be worthless to you even if you knew. Think instead about those who still sit at the table and how to keep up in the most honorable way you can what you have started. Come hold all your high feasts and joyful celebrations in this town in honor of this table. For you know without doubt, thanks to the test you have seen, how worthy it is, for you cannot honor it too much. So I will leave you. Be careful to do just as I have told you."

The king said that he would very willingly do so.

3. Uther's Love for Ygraine; Arthur's Conception and Birth.

So the king and Merlin parted company. And when the king knew that Merlin was gone, he ordered handsome buildings and houses to be built in the town, for he would henceforth hold his courts and his other gatherings there. And he sent word throughout all his land that all in his kingdom should know that he would be in Carduel on all feast days, such as Christmas, Whitsunday, and All Saints, and they should come there without being summoned again. So for a long time the king by custom held all his courts in Carduel.

At length the king happened, one certain time, to wish to call his barons together, and, for the honor and love of him, he wanted them to bring their wives and noble vassals and knights. He had them summoned and sent his letters everywhere, and they did everything the king had asked. So there were a great many married and unwed ladies, and many knights.

I cannot begin to tell you who all the people at that court were. But I must tell you about those my source story speaks of one after the other. And I want you to know in truth that the duke of Tintagel was there and Ygraine his wife. And when he saw Ygraine, the king loved her deeply, but he did not show it, except that he more willingly looked at her than any of the other women. And she herself took note of it and knew in her heart that the king did indeed love her. When she fully understood this, she was slow in coming before him, and avoided it if she could, for she was very beautiful and utterly faithful to her husband. And the king, for love of her, but so that no one would take notice, sent jewels to all the ladies at the feast; he sent Ygraine some she was sure to like. She knew that he had sent them to all the ladies, and she did not want hers, but she dared not refuse them; instead she took them, and she knew in her heart that the king had given jewels to the other ladies only because of her, but she made no sign of this.

Thus King Uther Pendragon held his court, and every man was there with his wife, but he did it all for love of Ygraine, who had so overwhelmed him that he did not know what to do. The holiday court ended, but before the people left, the king entreated all his barons to be with him again on Whitsunday as they had been at that time, and he asked them to bring their wives as they had just done. And they all swore they would.

That was the end of it. And when the duke of Tintagel left court, the king rode along with him and did him great honors. The king then said to Ygraine, the duke's wife, that she was taking his heart away with her, but she did not show that she had understood him. So the duke went off and took leave of the king, as did his wife. The king stayed in Carduel and gladdened the worthy men of the table who were left behind, and he brought cheer to the table, but his heart belonged wholly to Ygraine, and he pined for her until Whitsuntide.

Then the barons gathered again and their wives too, and the king was very glad when he knew that Ygraine had come. At that feast he gave many gifts to the knights and ladies, and the king had the duke and Ygraine sit with him to eat. The king gave so many gifts and looked at her in such a way, that Ygraine knew in truth that he loved her, and she was sorely distressed; as all could see, she was deeply worried, but she dared not talk about it. So the king was very cheerful at the feast, and he took delight in his barons. But when the holiday was over, all wanted to go back to their lands and took their leave. And the king begged them to come back to court and bring their wives when he sent for them, and they said they would.

So the people in the court scattered, and all year the king bore the misery of his love for Ygraine. At the end of the year he could hide it no longer, and he told two of his closest friends about his distress and the agony he felt because of Ygraine.

And they said, "What do you want us to do about it?"

And the king asked them, "How could I be with her more often?"

They told him that if he went to the land where she was, he would be blamed because people would take note of it.

So he asked, "What advice will you give me?"

And they said to him, "The best advice we know is for you to call together a great court at Carduel. Send word to all who will come there that they must not leave for two full weeks, and everyone must come ready to stay for the two weeks. Tell all your barons to bring their wives. So you will have a long time to spend with Ygraine, and you can take delight in your love."

When the king heard this, it seemed to him that they were giving him good advice, so he did as they had told him. He sent word to his barons to be at Carduel on Whitsunday, to bring their wives, and to come all ready to stay two weeks. And they came there and brought their wives, just as the king had ordered.

On that Whitsunday the king was of a mind to wear his crown, so he did, and he had many handsome gifts bestowed on his barons and wherever else he thought it worthwhile. On the day the king gave the feast he spoke to one of his advisers, named Ulfin, whom he very much trusted, and he asked him what to do, for love of Ygraine was killing him and he could neither sleep nor rest. He was at his wits' end, for he thought he would die, and he would be utterly unable to live without some kind of help.

[*Ulfin spoke to Ygraine on Uther's behalf, but she informed her husband the duke of Uther's intentions, and the couple left Arthur's court and went to Tin-*

tagel. Uther and his army invaded the duke's land. Uther asked Merlin for advice concerning Ygraine.]

Then Merlin told the king, "You will have to go there very boldly, for she is a most honorable lady and very faithful to God and her husband. But soon you will see what power I have to deceive her. I will bestow on you the likeness of the duke, and it will be so good that all people there will take you for their lord. The duke has two knights who are closer to him, and to Ygraine as well, than anyone could be. One is called Bretel and the other Jordan. I will make Ulfin look like Jordan, and I will take Bretel's shape. I will have the gates opened for you, and thanks to these shapes, I will get you inside there to go to bed, along with Ulfin and myself. But you will have to leave there very early in the morning when Ulfin and I go out, for we will hear very strange news there. Get your army ready to leave your barons in charge, and give orders forbidding anyone to go toward the castle before we get back. And be careful to tell no one where you are going but the two of us who are here."

The king and Ulfin answered that they would do everything he ordered. Merlin made things ready for what he had to do.

And he said to them, "I will give you your new likenesses on the way."

And the king hurried to do as fast as he could what Merlin had ordered. When he had done, he came straight to Merlin and said to him, "I have done what I had to do. Now tend to your business."

Merlin said to him, "The only thing left to do is to leave."

They got on their horses and rode until they came to Tintagel.

Then Merlin said to the king, "Now wait here a little, and Ulfin and I will go over there."

He and Ulfin went to one side, separated, and went straight back to the king. Merlin brought a herb, and the king took it and rubbed himself with it; and after he put it on himself, he looked unmistakably just like the duke.

And Merlin said then, "Do you recall ever having seen Jordan?"

The king answered, "I know him very well."

And Merlin showed him Ulfin in the likeness of Jordan.

When Ulfin saw the king, he said, "Good Lord God! how can any man be changed to look like another?"

And the king asked him, "What do you think about me?"

Ulfin answered, "I recognize you as no one but the duke."

And the king told him that he looked just like Jordan. After they had spoken thus for a while, Merlin came, and it seemed to them that he was Bretel. So they talked together and waited until night came. Just after darkness began to fall, they came straight to the gate of Tintagel. Merlin, who looked just like Bretel, knocked at the gate, and the gatekeeper and those who guarded the gate came out to him.

And he said, "Open the gate. See, this is the duke coming!"

They opened the gate and saw clearly, so it seemed to them, Bretel, the duke, and Jordan, and they let them in. And Bretel forbade them to tell anyone that the duke had come.

Several of them ran to tell the duchess that the duke had come. And they rode until they came to the great hall, and they got down from their horses. Merlin told the king privately that he should behave like the duke, cheerfully. Then all three went up to the room where Ygraine was already lying in bed.

As fast as they could, they had their lord's boots taken off, and they put him to bed with Ygraine. This is how the good king called Arthur was conceived. The lady took great delight in the king, for she thought that he was surely her husband the duke, whom she loved very much, and they lay together until daylight the next morning.

Then news came to the town that the duke was dead and his castle taken. When the two companions, who had got up, heard the news, they went straight to their lord where he lay and said to him, "Sir, get up and go to your castle, for news has come to your people that you are dead."

And he jumped up and said, "It is no wonder they think so, for I left the castle and no one knew it."

Then he took leave of Ygraine and kissed her in plain sight of all who were there when he left. And the three of them went out of the castle as quickly as they could, and no one recognized them. When they were outside, they were very happy.

And Merlin came up to the king and said, "Sir, I have done all I promised you. Now be sure to keep the oath you swore to me."

The king answered, "You have made me far happier and served me far better than any man ever did another, and I will certainly hold to our bargain."

And Merlin said to him, "I am laying claim to my reward, and I want you to give it to me. You should know that you have fathered a male child in Ygraine: this is what you have given me, and you must not have him. Any power you have over him you have yielded to me. Have the hour and night you sired him written down, and you will know whether I am telling the truth."

"And I swear to you," said the king, "that I will do everything you have told me, and I surely owe it to you."

So they rode as far as a river, and Merlin had them wash in that river. After washing, they lost the shapes they had taken on, and they looked as they had at first.

[*Merlin advised the king to marry Ygraine; Uther agreed, and Ygraine, defenseless without the duke, accepted his offer.*]

The wedding of the king and Ygraine was on the thirtieth day after he had lain with her in her room.

And of the lady's elder daughter and King Lot were born Sir Gawain, Agravain, Guerrehet, Gaheriet, and Mordred. And King Neutres of Garlot took the other daughter, a bastard named Morgan. On the advice of his kinsmen, Neutres put her in a nunnery to learn to read and write, and she learned so much so well that she mastered the arts. She became wonderfully skilled in an art called astrology, and she worked hard all the time and knew a great deal about the healing arts. For her mastery of knowledge, people called her Morgan the Fay. The king behaved justly toward all the other children, and he loved all the duke's kinfolk.

So the king took Ygraine, and at length it showed that she was with child. The king lay one night beside her and put his hand on her belly. He asked her by whom she was pregnant, for she could not be carrying his child: since he had married her, he had not lain with her without having it written down; and she could not be pregnant by the duke, for she had not seen him since a long time before his death.

And as the king kept heaping guilt on her, she grew frightened and ashamed, so she said, weeping, "Sir, I cannot deny what you already know. For God's sake, please take pity on me, for I will tell you things that are amazing but true, if you promise me that you will not leave me."

The king said, "Speak confidently, for I will not leave you for anything you might say."

When she heard this she was greatly cheered, and she said to him, "Sir, I will tell you amazing things."

So she told him how a man had lain with her in her husband's shape, and he had brought two men with him who looked like the two men her husband most loved in all the world. "Thus he came into my room in front of all my liegemen, and he lay with me, but I thought certainly that he was my husband. That man fathered this child with whom I am pregnant, and I know for a fact that he was conceived on the very night my husband was killed. And when the news came to me the next morning, that man was still lying in my bed. He gave me to understand that he was my husband and that his men didn't know what had become of him, and he left right away."

When she had given her account, the king answered and said, "Dear friend, take care to hide this from every man and woman you can, for you would be shamed if anyone knew it. And I want you to know that this child you are carrying is neither yours nor mine by rights. Neither you nor I will have him, nor will we keep him near us. Rather I beg you to hand him over to the one I'll recommend you give him to, so that we will never hear of him again."

And she answered, "Sir, you may do what you will with me and all that is mine. I am at your beck and call."

The next morning the king came to Ulfin and reported to him all his and the queen's words.

When Ulfin had heard them, he said, "Now you can see clearly how honorable and faithful my lady is, for she did not dare lie to you even about such an upsetting matter. You have carried out very well what Merlin gave you to do, and he could not have it any other way."

So the king waited until the sixth month, when Merlin had promised him to come. And he did come, and he spoke to Ulfin in private and asked him to tell him about many things, and Ulfin told him the truth as he knew it. Then he came to the king, and the king told him how he had spoken with Ygraine, how Ulfin had negotiated the peace, and how he had accepted it.

And Merlin answered, "Ulfin has to a degree atoned for his sins in abetting your love-making. But I have not atoned for my sin in helping to deceive the lady about the child fathered in her womb and she does not know by whom."

The king answered, "You are so learned and so worthy that you will know how to atone for this."

And Merlin replied, "You will have to help me."

The king said that he would help him in any way he could. "And the child," said the king, "I will see that you have him."

And Merlin said, "In the nearby country there is one of the worthiest men in your kingdom, the best endowed with all good traits. He has a wife who has just given birth to a son, and she is very worthy and faithful. This good man is not at all wealthy, so I want you to send for him and tell him that you will give him of your own wealth if he and his wife swear on saints' relics that a child who will be brought to them will be nursed with the woman's very milk and raise him as their own, and to give their son over to another woman to be nursed."

The king answered, "I will do just as you have said."

Then Merlin took leave and went off to Blaise.

[*Arthur was born and given to Antor and his wife, who reared him faithfully. When Arthur was sixteen, Merlin informed Uther, who was grievously ill, that his son would succeed him and would perfect the Round Table. Uther then died, after which Merlin announced that a new king would be chosen on Christmas Day.*]

4. The Youth of King Arthur; The Sword in the Stone.

On Christmas Eve, all the clergy in the kingdom and all the barons of worth were gathered in Logres, for they had very well sent out the orders and done all else Merlin had told them to do. After they had all come, they lived very humbly and very uprightly, and they waited there for the midnight Mass, and they prayed Our Lord to give them an overlord who was worthy to uphold the religion of Christendom. But there were many men who said that they were mad to believe that Our Lord meant to choose their king.

As they were talking, they heard the bells ringing for the first Mass of the day, so they went to the service. And when they had all come together, a holy man from the countryside got ready to sing the Mass.

But before he began the service, he spoke to the people and said to them, "You are gathered here for three things that are for your welfare, and I'll tell you what they are: to save your souls, first and foremost; to bring honor to your lives; and to see the wonders and amazing displays of His might that Our Lord will bring about among you this day, if it is His will to give you a king and leader to safeguard and keep Holy Church and to uphold all folk. We are gathered here to choose a king, but we don't know which man would be best for our well-being, and we cannot know this by ourselves, so let us pray the King of Kings to show us His will as truly as He was born this day, and this each one of us will pray as best we know how."

They did just as the good man had asked them, and he went on to sing the Mass. And after he had sung as far as the offertory, certain people went to the open space outside the church. Dawn had broken, and they saw a huge stone in front of the church, and they could not tell what kind of rock it was. In the middle of the stone was an iron anvil at least half a foot high, and a sword was sticking through the middle of the anvil down into the rock.[4]

When those who had left the church saw it, they were amazed, so they ran to the archbishop and told him. When he had heard it, he took some holy water, went to the stone, and sprinkled it with the water. Then he leaned down and saw on the stone writing that was all of gold, and he read it. The writing said that the one who pulled this sword out would be king of the land by the choice of Jesus Christ. And when he had read the writing, he told the people. Then the stone was entrusted to ten worthy knights to be guarded, and everyone said that God had given them a great sign. And they went back inside the church to hear Mass, and they thanked Our Lord.

When the good man had come before the altar, he turned toward the people and said to them, "My dear lords, now you can see that there is something good among us, since by your prayers and entreaties Our Lord has given you a sign. And I beseech you, by all wonders that Our Lord has wrought on earth, that no one go against God's choice for any high rank or wealth that God may have endowed him with. For Our Lord who has given us a sign will show us the way to do the rest."

Then the worthy archbishop sang his Mass. And when he had sung all of it, they went to the stone, and each one asked the other who should try it first. Then they all agreed that no one would try it unless the ministers of Holy Church allowed it. With these words, there was a very great uproar, because the highest-born and wealthiest men who had the strength to do so said that

---

[4]This sword is not Excalibur. (The latter was originally Gawain's sword, later carried by Arthur.)

they would try it first. Many a word was then spoken that must not be remembered or set down.

And the archbishop spoke so loudly that they all could hear him, and said, "My lords, you are not so wise or so worthy as I thought. I want you to know this: that Our Lord, who knows and sees all these things, has chosen one man, but we do not know who he is. I can tell you for the truth that wealth and high rank and nobility will have nothing to do with it, but only the will of Jesus Christ. And I have such trust in Him that, if the one who is to draw the sword out were not yet born, it would never be drawn out until he was born and he himself drew it out."

The worthy nobles and the learned men were all of one mind that he spoke the truth, and they swore to abide by the agreement they had made with the bishop. And when he heard this, he was very glad, and he wept with feeling.

And he said to them, "I mean for you all to know that I will do my utmost to work according to the will of Jesus Christ for the welfare of Christendom, so that I will have no blame, God willing."

He then showed the people the great wonder that Our Lord had wrought for them as a sign that there would be a true election of a king, "for when Our Lord established law and order on the earth, He set them in the sword. The rule that was over the laity must come from a layman and must be by the sword, and the sword was, at the beginning of the three orders, entrusted to knighthood to safeguard Holy Church and uphold true law and order. And by this sword Our Lord has ordained for us this election.

"You can all be sure that He has kept in His sight the one He wills to rule. High-ranking men should not boast that the sword will be drawn out by wealth or pride, but the poor should not be upset if the highborn try it before they do, for it is fitting that the wealthy should go first. There is no one here who would not, if he knew how, choose the worthiest one among us to make him king."

They said all of one voice that they would agree to whatever he advised. The archbishop went on to sing a solemn Mass. After it was sung he chose two hundred and fifty of the worthiest gentlemen he knew of, and he had them try pulling the sword out, but it was all for nothing. When they had tried it, he then ordered the others to put themselves to the test.

Then they all tried it one after the other, but there was no one who could ever move that sword. They then entrusted ten worthy knights to guard it, and they were told to let anyone undertake the test who wanted to and to watch carefully to see the one who would draw the sword out. The sword held fast for a week, when all the barons went to High Mass on the Feast of the Circumcision. And the archbishop said to them, "My lords, I told you so: you would all in time come to try pulling the sword out. Now you can truly understand that no man will ever draw it out but the one whom Our Lord wills to be king."

And they all said that they would not leave the town before knowing on whom Our Lord wanted to bestow His grace.

When Mass had been sung, all the barons went to their lodgings to eat. After eating, the knights went jousting, as they usually did, outside the town, and many people went out to see the games. When the knights had fought for a long time, they gave their shields to their serving men and began to joust again. And they fought among themselves so hard that a free-for-all broke out, and everyone from the town, armed and unarmed, ran there.

Antor's son Kay, who had been knighted earlier, on All Saints' Day, called his brother Arthur and said to him, "Go get me my sword at our lodging."

Arthur was always willing to be helpful, so he answered, "Very gladly!"

He then spurred his horse and rode to their lodging. He looked for his brother's sword or another one, but he could not find any, because the lady of the house had hidden them all in her room and gone off to see the fighting with the other ladies. When Arthur saw that he could not find a sword, he turned back and went by the church where the stone was. The thought came to him that he had never tried the test, and if he could pull the sword out he would take it to his brother. So he came straight back, and, still on horseback, he took the sword by the hilt, drew it out, and covered it with the bottom of his tunic. But the men who were to guard the sword had run to the melee.

Kay ran up to meet his brother and asked him for his sword. He answered that he could not find it, but that he had brought him another, so he gave him the sword from the anvil. Kay asked him where he had found it, and he told him that it was the sword from the stone. Kay took it and hid it under his tunic, and went looking for his father.

When he found him, he said to him, "Sir, I will be king. Here is the sword from the stone."

When his father saw it, he was thunderstruck, and he asked him how he had got it. Kay answered that he had taken it out of the stone. When Antor heard this, he did not believe him, but said to him that he knew very well that he was lying about it. Then they both went to the church, and the lad followed after them.

Antor said to his son, "Dear son, don't lie to me. Tell me how you came to have this sword. If you lie to me, I'll know it and I will not love you for it."

And he answered, for he was very much ashamed, "I won't lie to you. My brother Arthur brought it to me when I told him to bring me mine, but I do not know how he got it."

When Antor heard this, he said to him, "Give it to me, for you have no right to it."

And Kay gave it to him. Antor looked around and saw Arthur. He called to him and said, "Come here, dear son. Take this sword and put it back where you took it."

He took it and put it into the anvil, and it held there just as fast as before.

Antor ordered his son Kay to take it, and he leaned down, but could not get it out. Then Antor went into the church and called both of them inside.

He took Arthur in his arms and said to him, "Sir, if I could see to it that you were king, what advantage would there be for me?"

And Arthur answered, "Sir, I cannot have that or any other worthwhile thing and not have you as my lord, for you are my father."

Antor answered him, "I am your father for having raised you, but in truth I do not know who sired you or who your mother was."

When Arthur heard the man he believed to be his father disown him as his son, he was grief-stricken and began to weep. And he said, "Dear Lord God, how shall I ever have anything when I am fatherless?"

Antor said to him, "Sir, you are not fatherless, for you must have been sired by a father. Now, dear sir, if Our Lord means you to have His grace, and if I help you become king, what advantage will there be for me?"

And Arthur said, "Sir, whatever you please."

Then Antor told him about the favor he had done for him and how he had raised him. He had his own son taken away from his mother and given to another woman to be nursed, while Arthur had his wife's milk. "Thus you should return the favor to me and my son, for never was a child reared more lovingly than I have reared you. So I entreat you, if God bestows this grace on you, and if I can help you out, please reward my son."

And Arthur said, "I beg you not to disown me as your son, for I would not know where else to go. And if God grants me this honor, I will give you anything you ask."

Antor said, "I will not ask you for any of your land. I ask only that my son Kay be your seneschal for as long as he lives and that he never lose his stewardship for anything he might do to any man or woman of your land or to you yourself. If he is wicked and foolish, you will have to bear with him, for his ways of thinking and behaving must have come to him from the peasant girl who nursed him. So that you might be reared properly, he lost his birthright. This is why you must humor him more than others. So I beg you, please give him what I ask."

Arthur said, "I very willingly grant you this."

Then they took him to the altar, and he swore that he would faithfully keep his word. And when he had so sworn, they came back out in front of the church. By then the melee had come to an end, and the barons came back to the church to hear vespers. Antor then called his friends and told them that Arthur had drawn the sword out, and they told the archbishop.

"Sir, this is one of my sons," said Antor. "He is not a knight, but he begs me to let him try the test of this sword. Please call the barons together."

And he did. Then they all gathered at the stone. And when they had come together, Antor ordered Arthur to take the sword and give it to the archbishop, and he did. And when the archbishop saw this, he took him in his arms and began to sing the *Te Deum* very loudly. Then they took him into the church.

The barons who had seen it were most upset and distraught, and they said it could not be that an upstart boy was their king. But the archbishop grew angry and said, "Our Lord knows better than we what everyone is!"

Antor and his kinsmen stood by Arthur, and the common folk did too, but the barons were against him. Then the archbishop made a bold speech. "If everyone in this world," he said, "wished to stand against this election and God alone wanted it to be, it would be. And I will show you what faith I have in God."

Then the archbishop said to Arthur, "Dear son, go put the sword back into the stone."

And he took it in plain sight of all, and after he had put it back, the archbishop spoke and said, "Never has a more perfect election been carried out or witnessed. Now go, my wealthy lords, and see if you can pull it out again."

And they went and tried the test one after the other, but they could not draw it out.

And the archbishop said, "Anyone who wants to go against the will of God is a madman. Now you understand the will of the Lord God!"

And they answered, "Sir, we do not go against His will, but it is very strange to us that a mere boy should be lord over us."

The archbishop said to them, "The One who chose him knows him better than we do and better than we know ourselves."

The barons begged the archbishop to leave the sword in the stone until Candlemas, when many others might try it who had not yet done so, and the archbishop allowed it. So the sword stayed there until Candlemas. Then the people were all gathered, and all who wanted underwent the test. When they had all tried it, the archbishop said, "It would be right for you to do the will of Jesus Christ. Go, dear son Arthur. If Our Lord wills you to be king and guardian of this people, show us."

And he went forward and pulled out the sword and gave it to the archbishop.

[*There were further delays, and Arthur was required to repeat his feat several times, but eventually he was judged fit to serve.*]

They then rose in a body and took Arthur in their arms and led him to the place where the kingly raiment was, and they attired him with it. And when he was dressed, the archbishop was ready to sing Mass.

And he said to him, "Arthur, go get the sword—the justice with which you will defend Holy Church and Christendom in every way as best you can."

Then the procession went to the stone. And when they had come there, the archbishop said, "Arthur, if you are willing to swear and promise all the saints that you will safeguard the rights of Holy Church, keep lawful order and peace in the land, give help to the defenseless as best you can, and uphold all rights, feudal obligations, and lawful rule, then step forward and take the sword with which Our Lord has shown that you are His elect."

When Arthur heard this, he wept for joy, and many others wept for him.

And he said, "As truly as God is Lord of all things, may He give me the strength and the might to do what is right and to uphold all the things that you have told me and I have heard."

He went down on his knees and took the sword in both his hands. He raised it out from the anvil as easily as if the sword had not been held fast by anything. He bore the sword upright in his hands, and they took him to the altar and set him down there. And when he was seated, they anointed him and crowned him and did everything that must be done to a king. And when he was crowned and the Mass sung, they all left the church; and when they looked, they did not see the stone, nor did they find out what had become of it.

This is how Arthur was made king, and he held the land and the kingdom of Logres in peace for a long time.[5]

[*However, some barons were jealous of Arthur, and the king made an alliance with King Ban and King Bors against their enemy Claudas; Ban and Bors swore fealty to Arthur. Together they defeated the invaders, but the wars continued. King Lot too fought the Saxons.*]

5. King Lot's Young Sons; Mordred's Parentage.

[. . .] It is also true that King Lot's wife was one of King Arthur's half-sisters, his mother's daughter. This lady gave birth to Gawainet, Agravain, Guerrehet, and Gaheriet, who were all King Lot's sons. Furthermore, she also bore Mordred, who was the offspring whom King Arthur fathered. And I will tell you how, for the history will be more worthwhile if I make you understand how Mordred was sired by him, for many people would find King Arthur less worthy because of it if they did not know the truth.

As it happened, when the barons of the kingdom of Logres were gathered at Carduel to choose a king after the death of Uther Pendragon, King Lot brought his wife with him, and many other barons had brought theirs as well. King Lot happened to have a very beautiful hall for himself and his household. Antor, his son Kay, and Arthur had a part of that very same house off by themselves, as far from the others as they could get. But when King Lot learned that Antor was a knight, he asked him to eat with him, and he had him sit at his own table with his son Kay, who was newly knighted. And King Lot had a room made up where he slept with his wife, while Antor slept in the hall

---

[5]The *Merlin* proper attributed to Robert de Boron ends at this point, where the so-called *Merlin* Continuation begins as a link to the *Prose Lancelot*.

with his son Kay. Arthur had set up his bed in a corner near the door to King Lot's room, for squires should sleep away from knights.

Arthur was a very handsome lad, and he was very clever. He had noticed everything about the lady. He had seen that she was beautiful and plump; he strongly desired her in his heart and loved her for it. But the lady did not heed this, for she was very faithful to her husband.

It happened that the barons had agreed to set a day when they would come to court, conferring together at Black Cross. And the night before he was to leave in the morning, King Lot told his household, as quietly as he could, to saddle their horses at midnight and to get their arms ready. They did as they were bidden, keeping what they did under wraps as best they could; the king did not even speak to his wife about it, but got up as quietly as he could at midnight so that she never knew what was happening. So the king went off to Black Cross, and his wife stayed behind all alone in her bed.

And Arthur, who had noticed that the king had gone away, got up and went to the lady's bed and lay down with her. And after he had got in bed with her, he turned his back to her, for he did not dare do anything else. And it so happened that the lady awoke and, still half asleep, turned toward him, for she truly thought that he was her husband, and she put her arms around him. When Arthur saw that she had embraced him, he understood that she had not noticed who he was, so he put his arms around her and lay with her fully, and the lady gave him much pleasure, and she did it willingly, for she thought that he was her husband. And this is how Mordred was conceived.

And when Arthur had done to the lady that which gave him such great delight, he did not have to wait a very long time before she went back to sleep. He went back to his own bed very quietly, so that no one realized what he had done until the next day, when he happened to tell it himself when he was serving the noonday meal, cutting meat on his knees. And the lady happened to say to him, "Get up, my dear young man; you have knelt long enough."

And he told her in a low voice that he could never deserve the good things she had done for him, and she asked him what that was all about. He told her that he would not say unless she swore to him that she would not tell anyone or try to find a way to cast blame on him or do anything harmful to him. She answered that no harm could come to her from that, and she very willingly swore to what he asked, for she had no reason to worry. And he told her how he had lain with her the night before, and the lady was deeply ashamed and blushed, but no one knew what their secret was. So that is how Arthur lay with his sister, and it never happened again, but the lady knew that she was with child by him.

When it was time for the child to be born, the news had spread through the country that the one who was Uther Pendragon's son would be king. And in her heart the lady loved him better for it than anyone could ever say, but she did not dare show it because of her husband King Lot, and the war between King Arthur and those of her country sorely distressed her.

[*Gawainet[6] learned from his mother that he was Arthur's nephew, and he and his brothers decided to go to Arthur's court to be knighted by the king. Saxons overran Arthur's land, and Gawainet and his brothers defeated them. The Knights of the Round Table supported King Leodagan against the Saxons, but Leodagan was captured. His daughter, Guenevere, admired Arthur and wondered about his identity.*]

6. The Two Gueneveres.

In truth, King Leodagan's wife was a very highborn lady of great beauty. When he had taken her from her father's house and married her, the lady took one of her maidens with her who was very beautiful. This maiden greatly loved the seneschal, so that at last he asked her to be his wife. The king liked her a great deal because she had served him wholeheartedly; she was faithful in her service, and the king gave her to him most willingly.

When the seneschal married her, she was sitting at table among the ladies eating. She was very richly adorned, and the king found her to be very beautiful; he fell so deeply in love with her that he could not get her out of his heart. Without any doubt, she was one of the most beautiful ladies in the world. But he put off doing anything about it right then. At length, one Saint John's Day, the king happened to have sent Cleodalis to ride against the Irish, who were waging war against him at that time. And the lady had stayed with the queen to keep her company, for they loved each other very deeply.

King Leodagan had fathered on his wife a little girl whose name was Guenevere, who later grew to be very beautiful. And King Leodagan's wife was a very good lady who lived a very holy life, and there were very few nights indeed when she did not get up and go to matins and listen to the service until after Mass. On the very night her daughter Guenevere had been

---

[6]Deleted here is a description of Gawain, including a curious fact to which the authors allude on several occasions, though with variations in the details: that Gawain's strength changed with the time of day. The present chapter tells us that "When he got up in the morning, he had the strength of the best knight in the world; by the time the hour of prime came, it had grown twofold; at terce, the same thing. At midday he went back to the strength he had at first, and at nones and all the nighttime hours, he always still had his first strength." The *Lancelot* (Chapter 32) informs us instead that "around noon he doubled his strength, which is why no one was able to conquer him in a sword fight, although there were many more skilled with lances." *The Death of Arthur* indicates that his strength increased until noon, at which time he was indomitable, and ebbed thereafter.

conceived, she went to matins and came to find the seneschal's wife, but she found her sleeping and did not want to awaken her, so she left her alone and went off to the church, which was nearby. And King Leodagan, who had for a long time yearned to lie with that lady, got up as soon as the queen had gone, put out the candles, then went to lie with the seneschal's wife.

When the lady felt him getting into bed with her, she asked him fearfully who he was. He said that it was he, and he told her to keep quiet: if she shouted a single word, he would kill her with his sharp sword, or if she thrashed about in the least. The lady defended herself with words as much as she could, but she did not dare speak out loud, so her arguments availed her very little. The king lay with her and fathered a daughter on her, and it was the very night his daughter was conceived by his wife.

And it happened that, when the queen had given birth, she found a little mark in the small of her daughter's back that looked like a king's crown. And as soon as she was born, the seneschal's wife began to scream from the pain in her belly, and she gave birth to a very beautiful daughter who looked like the queen's daughter, and no one could tell the one from the other but for the mark of the crown the queen's daughter had on her back. And each one was baptized Guenevere, and they were always nursed together. [. . .]

7. The Victorious Arthur Falls in Love with Guenevere.

[*The Saxons were routed, and during the ensuing celebration, Arthur and Guenevere were attracted to each other.*]

King Arthur was filled with great beauty, and the maiden stared at him and he at her. And she said softly to herself that a lady had reason to be very happy if such a good and handsome knight as he asked her for her love, and shame on her who refused him.

No sooner had the tables been set up than the food was ready, and the knights all sat down. But the knights of the Round Table sat side by side at a table off to themselves with the knights whom the king had engaged, and King Bors and King Ban seated Arthur between themselves, for they did him the highest honors they could. And King Leodagan took notice of who was sitting beside whom at that table, and in his heart he thought, from the honor they bore Arthur and the service they did him, that he was lord over them all, and he wondered mightily who he could be; he would have given anything to know who he was. "And may it please you now, Lord God," he said, "that he should wed my daughter! In truth, I would not have believed that such a young lad could have the worthy knighthood there is in him, and he could not have it at all unless he were a very highborn man indeed! And I might just as well believe that he is a spiritual being whom Our Lord has sent to me to fight for this kingdom and keep it safe, not for love of me, but to raise up

Christendom and Holy Church and keep them, and that is how they were able to leave this city against the gatekeeper's will." [. . .]

King Leodagan's daughter served King Arthur wine in her father's goblet, and King Arthur looked at her long and hard, and he very much liked what he saw before him. For she was the most beautiful woman in all Britain at that time, and she was endowed with a very fine body. On her head she wore a golden coronet with precious stones. Her face was clear and so naturally made up with white and red that she needed not more or less. Her shoulders were straight, and the skin lustrous, and her body was very well put together, for her waist was slender and her hips low, and they suited her wonderfully. Her feet were pale and well arched, her arms were long and rounded, and her hands were white and plump. Why should I go on telling you about the maiden's great beauty? If she was indeed beautiful, then she was endowed with even greater goodness, generosity, courtesy, sense, worthiness, sweetness, and nobility.

When King Arthur saw the maiden, who was of such great beauty, kneeling before him, he was very eager to look at her, first of all because her breasts were firm and hard like little apples, and her skin was whiter than new-fallen snow, and she was neither too plump nor too thin. And King Arthur so yearned for her that he lost himself in thought and stopped eating, and he turned his face away because he did not want the two kings or anyone else to notice anything. [. . .]

And Arthur loved and yearned for the daughter of King Leodagan, and he was daydreaming so about her that he forgot where he was; he very much wanted to have her as his wife and helpmeet, if he could. And the story says that she was the wisest woman in Great Britain, the fairest and best loved who was in that whole land, excepting only Elaine the Peerless, wife of Persides the Red of the Castle of Gazevilte and daughter of King Pelles of Listenois of the Castle of Corbenic; she was the niece of the Fisher King and the king ailing from his wounds. The first was called Alan of the Isle in Listenois. The second was ill and had been wounded with the Avenging Lance, which is why he was called the Maimed King, and he had been wounded through both his thighs; his right name was King Pellinor of Listenois. King Alan and Pellinor were brothers. The maiden I told you about was their niece and the daughter of King Pelles, who was the brother of the two I have just named for you. That maiden was the most beautiful woman who had ever been in any land, and the noblest, and she kept the Most Holy Grail until Galahad was conceived.

But now the story falls silent about her and says no more about her for a while, but you will be enlightened as to how it was taken away from her and why, and how the adventures of the Holy Grail drew to an end. [. . .]

[*The Saxon wars continued, with Gawainet and his brothers distinguishing themselves and steadily earning fame.*]

8. Merlin Meets Viviane and Teaches Her His Magic.

[*Merlin informed his master, Blaise, that the Saxons would soon be defeated and that he, Merlin, would help fulfill the adventures of the Holy Grail. He then met Viviane, a beautiful young woman who was the daughter of Dyonas.*]

Merlin made his way until he came to the Forest of Briosque. He took on the shape of a most handsome youth and drew near a spring that fed a pond, very beautiful and very clear, with sand that shone so brightly that it seemed to be of fine silver. Viviane often came to this spring to play and enjoy herself, and she was there on the very day that Merlin came. And when Merlin saw her, he looked at her for a long time before he said a word. And he said to himself that he would be most unwise to fall asleep in sin and lose his mind and his knowledge just to know the delights of a young lady, to shame her and to lose God.

After Merlin had long been deep in thought, he went forward and greeted her nevertheless. And when she saw him, she answered, like the well-bred girl she was, "May the Lord who knows all thoughts bestow on you the will and the heart to treat me well, and may He bestow on me as well the worth and honor that are my due."

When Merlin heard the maiden speak, he sat down at the edge of the spring and asked her who she was. She told him that she had been born in that country, the daughter of a vavasor there, "a noble man," she said, "who lives in this manor. And who are you, fair, dear friend?" asked the maiden.

"Lady," he said, "I am a wandering apprentice, seeking my master; he used to teach me my trade, which is most praiseworthy."

"And what trade is that?" she asked.

"In truth, lady," he said, "he has taught me so well that I could raise a castle right here and have a great many people take refuge inside and others fall upon it from without. And I could do something else just as well: I could walk across that pond without getting my feet wet. And I could make a river flow over there where no water has ever run before."

"Indeed," said the maiden, "this is a worthy trade! I would give a great deal to learn to do such fine tricks."

"To be sure, lady" he answered, "I know many others that are even better than these are and more delightful for entertaining highborn men. For no one could suggest any kind of trick that I couldn't do or continue doing as long as I like."

"In truth," said the young lady, "if you don't mind, I'd like to find out about your tricks, and I would swear to be your lady love and your friend forever, without any wrongdoing or baseness, for as long as I live."

"Indeed, lady," he said, "you seem to me so gentle and of such noble bearing that for your love I would show you a few of my tricks, on your oath that your love will be mine, for I ask you for nothing else."

She granted his wish without seeing or understanding his cunning. And Merlin went off and drew with a staff a ring in the middle of a heath; then he came back to the maiden and sat down again at the spring. But it was not long before the maiden looked and saw ladies, knights, maidens, and squires in great number coming out of the Forest of Briosque. They were holding hands and came singing and making merry as no one had ever seen, and tumblers, dancers, and musicians passed before the maiden and gathered all around the ring that Merlin had drawn. And after they had gone inside, there began such wonderful singing and dancing that no one could tell a fourth of the merriment there. And Merlin raised up a castle fair and strong, and beneath it an orchard with all the good smells in the world; the blossoms and fruit gave off such a sweet smell that it is wonderful to tell about. The maiden, who heard and saw all of this, was so astounded by the wonder she beheld and so happy looking at it that she was speechless; and she was so bewildered that she did not know what song they were singing unless they sang it again. Truly, love begins in happiness and ends in grief! Their merrymaking went on thus from the ninth hour until vespers; people heard the noise far away, and it was loud and clear and delightful to listen to. [. . .]

Then Merlin went to the maiden, took her by the hand, and said to her, "Lady, what do you think of this?"

"Dear friend," answered the maiden, "you have done enough to make me yours!"

"Lady," he said, "keep the promise you have made me."

"Of course I will, gladly," she said, "but you haven't yet taught me anything."

"So I'll tell you about my tricks," said Merlin, "and you'll write it all down, for you know your letters well enough, and I will teach you more wonders than any woman has ever known."

"What?" said the maiden. "How do you know that I can read and write?"

"Lady," he answered, "I know it for a fact, for my master has taught me so well that I know everything that everyone does."

"In truth," said the maiden, "this is by far the fairest learning I've heard about, and the most useful anywhere, and I would know it most gladly. And things that are yet to come," the maiden went on, "do you know anything about that?"

"Yes, of course, my fair friend," he said, "a great deal."

"For God's sake," said the maiden, "what do you go on looking for? In truth, you would put up with a great deal if you got some pleasure out of it!"

While the maiden and Merlin were talking together, the ladies and maidens gathered together and went off dancing toward the wood, along with the knights and squires. And when they got to the edge, they rushed in so fast that they did not know what might become of them. Indeed, the castle and everything had all faded into nothing, but the orchard stayed some time afterwards because of the maiden, who sweetly entreated Merlin. And the orchard was called "The Haven for Joy and Happiness." And when Merlin and the maiden had been together for a long time, Merlin said to her, "Fair maiden, I am going away, for I have much to do elsewhere."

"What?" said the maiden. "Fair dear friend, won't you teach me anything about your tricks?"

"Lady," said Merlin, "now don't be in a hurry, for you will know everything soon enough, and you will need a great deal of time and a long stay in the same place. Meanwhile, you have not yet given me any pledge of your love."

"Sir," she said, "what pledge would you have me give you? Tell me and I will do it."

"I want you to swear," he said, "that your love will be mine, and you along with it, to do whatever I wish whenever I will."

And the maiden thought awhile and then said, "Sir, I will do this if, afterwards, you swear to teach me everything I ask you, so that I will know how to do it."

He told her that that suited him. And the maiden pledged that she would keep her oath just as she had sworn, and he took her pledge. Then he taught her a trick that she worked many times afterwards, for he taught her how to make a river appear wherever she wished, and it stayed there as long as she wanted, and many other tricks the words of which she wrote down on parchment just as he told them, and she knew how to bring about many things. And after he had stayed until vespers, he commended her to God, and she him. But first, the maiden asked him when he would come back, and he told her the eve of St. John's Day. [. . .]

9. Arthur Betrothed to Guenevere.

[Merlin offered further military advice and told Arthur of the adventures that had occurred in his realm, the land of Logres. Then Merlin spoke to Leodagan of Arthur's need for a wife.]

"I will first tell you," said Merlin, "what we have come looking for. See here one of our young lords, a young man, and a very good knight, as you know. And you may know for a fact that he is a man of higher birth than you and higher in any other way, although you are crowned a king. But he does not have a wife betrothed to him, so we go about through the countryside seeking adventures until we find a highborn man who would give him his daughter as a wife."

"Oh, God have mercy!" said King Leodagan. "Why go on looking? I have the most beautiful daughter in this land, the most nobly behaved and the best taught anywhere! She could lack nothing in breeding or good lands. If it is to your liking, and his, I would give her to you. Take her as your mate and wife. I have no other heirs to bequeath my lands to but her."

And Merlin said that he would not turn him down, God willing, and the four companions thanked him heartily.

Then the king himself went to find his daughter, and he had her dressed and adorned the most beautifully and the most richly he could, and he led her by the hand into the room where the four companions were waiting for her. A great crowd of knights followed him in. All the knights of the Round Table were there, and the forty about whom the story has told you earlier, and other highborn men who had come to the army to help King Leodagan. And when the king and his daughter came into the hall, which was large and beautiful, the four companions came to meet him.

Then King Leodagan spoke so loudly that he was heard and understood by all, and he said, "Noble young lord, I do not know what name to call you by. Come forward and take my daughter as your betrothed, who is so lovely, wise, and courtly, and all the honor that she brings with her after my death, for I could not give her to one more worthy, as all the nobles here well know."

He stepped forward and gave Leodagan his thanks, and the king gave her to him with his right hand, and each pledged his assent to the other with very noble bearing. And the bishop of Carhaix, who had been sent for, blessed them with his right hand. Then the joy and merrymaking were as great as they could be.

Then Merlin came forward and spoke, and he said to the king, within hearing of all who were there, "Sir, wouldn't you very much like to know who we are and to whom you have given your daughter?"

And the king, who longed so much to know that he never thought he would find out very soon, answered that he would very much like to know.

"Now, may all who will hear it," said Merlin, "know that you have given your daughter to King Arthur of Britain, the son of Uther Pendragon, and you must swear faith to him, and all those of this kingdom who wish to do him honor must do so as well without delay. And then we will go all the more gladly and all the more confidently to fight the bearded king who means to take and hold this land, but it will go otherwise than he thinks. And you should know that these two worthy men here are brothers, and both have been crowned king. One is named King Ban of Benoic and the other King Bors of Gaunes, and they were born of the highest stock anyone knows. And the other companions are sons of kings and queens or earls or castellans."

When King Leodagan and the other barons heard that was King Arthur, they were happier than they ever had been. The companions of the Round Table were the first to come before him, and they swore faith to him, for they had long wished to do so, and afterwards came King Leodagan and then all his companions all together. Then the betrothal was celebrated, so grand that none had seen better, and more than anyone else, Guenevere was happy with her betrothed.

And that evening Merlin made himself known to the companions of the Round Table, but no others. When King Leodagan saw who he was, he said that God had granted him good fortune in this world to have given him the love and friendship of such a worthy man. "And above all else, dear Lord God," he said, "it does not bother me that you have made me your agent, since my daughter and my land are bound over to the worthiest man in the world."

Thus spoke King Leodagan, and they all went to sleep and rest. [. . .]

[*The war against Claudas continued. Gawain and his brothers were knighted. Merlin befriended Morgan and taught her some spells; he also spoke of Viviane to Blaise, who worried that she would betray Merlin. Arthur informed Leodagan that he would marry Guenevere a week later.*]

10. The False Guenevere.

[. . .] Now the story says that Guenevere, Cleodalis's stepdaughter, had very wealthy kinsmen on her mother's side, and they were very good knights. They hated King Leodagan for the great shame he had brought to Cleodalis because of his wife, whom he had kept for so long in spite of them all. As it happened, they were gathered together on the same evening Merlin came, and there were sixteen of them in all, and they were talking together of many things; but Cleodalis was not at this meeting, and he knew nothing about it. And they asked one another what they could do to hurt the king more and annoy him. They agreed at last that they would speak to the nurse of King Arthur's betrothed, and they would be so generous toward her that, on the night when Guenevere was to lie down with her husband, the old woman would put the seneschal's daughter with the king instead of her; and she would take Guenevere to play in the garden that evening, and "then we will seize her and take her to such a place that he will never hear news of her, nor will she be recognized, wherever she goes. Now let's go and talk the nurse into doing this, and when it is over we will be lords of the king and his kingdom."

Then they decided that seven of them would undertake the kidnapping, and they would have a boat ready where they would take her. After this planning, the traitors went their ways happy and cheerful because they thought that they had done very well, and they bought the boat and everything they needed. And they made the nurse such promises that she agreed to do what they wanted.

But as soon as they had reached their agreement, Merlin knew it. He went straight to Ulfin and Bretel and drew them aside by themselves, and he explained to them the treachery word for word just as they had plotted it; and when they heard it, they crossed themselves in wonder. Then they asked Merlin what they should do about it.

"I will gladly tell you this," said Merlin. "Tomorrow evening, after you have eaten your meal, put your armor on under your clothing, and go hide under an apple tree in the garden. They will come unarmed but for their swords, and they'll go to their lookout where they'll hide until it is time for the nurse to bring the queen to play. And be careful that you are ready to rescue her as soon as they have taken hold of her, for you will lose her very fast if they can get her into the boat."

"Sir," said the barons, "God willing, we will not lose her, since we know so much about it."

"Take care," said Merlin, "not to tell anyone that I have said this to you, for I would never love you."

"In truth," said the worthy gentlemen, "we would rather lose our birthright than say anything about it."

With that, the three friends went back into the hall, and they found that the knights wanted to leave, and they went straight to their lodgings to rest and sleep until daybreak the next morning. Then the barons and the knights got out of bed and gathered in the hall. And King Leodagan had his daughter dressed more richly than any king's daughter ever was, and she was of such great beauty that everyone stared at her in wonder. And King Ban took her on one side and King Bors on the other, and they led her to the church of St. Stephen. There was a great gathering of nobles there to walk along with her, and they all held hands and walked two by two. The first two were King Arthur and King Leodagan, the second two Sir Gawainet and Sir Yvain, and after them went Galescalain and Agravain, and next Dodinel and Guerrehet, and next Sagremor and Gaheriet, and next Kay the Seneschal and Kay of Estral, and after them came King Ban and King Bors, who were leading the young lady. She wore flowing robes: she had the richest cap that anyone had ever seen on her golden head, and she was dressed in a robe of beaten gold so long that it trailed more than a half-yard behind her, and it fit her so well that everyone was astounded by her great beauty. Next came Guenevere the stepdaughter of Cleodalis, who was wonderfully beautiful and comely, and she held Girflet and Lucan the Wine Steward by their hands. Next came the newly knighted two by two, and after them the companions of the Round Table, then the barons of the Kingdom of Carmelide, then the noble ladies of the country and the burghers. This is how they came to the church.

When they got there they found the archbishop of Brice, in the land of Logres, and Sir Amustan, Leodagan's good chaplain, and it is he who married King Arthur and Guenevere and blessed them. And the archbishop sang Mass, and great were the offerings of kings and high princes. And when the service was over, they went back to the great hall, where there was a great crowd of all kinds of singers. [. . .]

And Guenevere stayed behind in her room alone with her nurse. And that day the treachery was brought into play whereby she was to be taken prisoner and betrayed by the kinsmen of Guenevere, stepdaughter of Cleodalis the Seneschal; they had convinced the old woman, who was the nurse of Guenevere, King Arthur's wife, to grant them what they wanted. They said that they would wait for her in the garden beneath the great hall, and they would have the other Guenevere with them. After they had made their case, they went into the garden and hid under the trees; there were ten of them, but they were armed only with swords. They had the false Guenevere with them, and they stayed there for a long time until the barons had left and gone to their lodgings.

And the queen was undressed as though to go to bed. Then the old woman took her into the garden to make water. The traitors were lying in wait in the garden hidden beneath a grafted pear tree; when they saw her coming, they kept very still and crept toward the wall little by little. But Bretel and Ulfin had not forgotten what Merlin had told them. They were well armed beneath their clothing, and they had hidden crouched under the steps the queen was to take to go outside. They kept very still and were seen by no man or woman, and they likewise had their ears cocked to listen. After they had been there quite a long time, they saw the old woman who held the queen by the hand and was going straight to where the traitors were on the lookout. And when they saw that the queen had gone far from her room, they laid hands on her from all sides and handed the other Guenevere over to the old woman. And when the queen saw her, she understood clearly that she had been betrayed, and she prepared to scream, but they told her that if she uttered a single word, they would kill her—even if she made any sound at all. Then they drew their bare swords and left along the river that ran below the garden, where a boat they had come in was tied up. The garden was quite high above the river, and the only way they could get there was by a little path which was very hard to go up and down because of the rocks that were heavily strewn all over it. And if they could only have got into the boat, the queen would have been lost without hope of recovery.

[*Ulfin and Bretel attacked the traitors, killing most of them and rescuing the queen.*]

Then Ulfin and Bretel took the queen and led her away very frightened to her bedroom, and they told her not to be afraid anymore. Afterward they took the false Guenevere and led her off to their lodging, for they did not want anyone to find out about their secret.

Just as you have heard, the traitors were dealt with according to Merlin's advice, and the queen was rescued by the two worthy men. And as soon as they had left, Merlin knew it, and he came straight to King Leodagan and told him to send three of his young ladies to the queen's room to put her to bed. And the king asked him, "Why? Can't her nurse do it?"

And Merlin told him the whole truth just as it had happened. When the king heard it, he was deeply amazed about it, and he said that he could never rest until he had spoken to her. Then King Leodagan left and came straight to the bedroom where his daughter Guenevere was, and he took three young ladies with him to get her ready for bed. When she saw him, she began to weep mightily, and the king took her by the hand, drew her to one side, and spoke to her all alone. And she told him the truth just as it had happened, from beginning to end, and the king told her that she had nothing to fear, for she need worry no more. And the king ordered the three ladies to get her ready for bed, and they did as they were told; nor did King Leodagan want to leave the room before they had put her to bed. After that, he came to his daughter's bed, raised the cover, and turned it down until he saw the mark of the crown on her back. Then he knew indeed that she was his daughter, whom he had had by his wife. After that, he put the cover back over her and went out of the room without saying a word, and the ladies wondered why he had done that. [. . .]

Thus was Queen Guenevere to have been deceived by the traitors—by the ones because of whom she later had very great sorrow, which happened a long time afterwards, just as the story will relate it to you, if there is anyone to tell it to you. For the king lost her for a good three years, when he never had her with him. Galehaut, a wealthy prince in the kingdom of Sorelois, took her away for love of Lancelot. And the king kept the false Guenevere as his concubine until one day when, as it happened, he was taken ill. And this was because of Bertelay, a traitor who brought it about that King Arthur was unwilling to give her up for anyone's sake; in the end, everything on earth rotted. And the land and kingdom were under interdict for nearly three years, when no man's or woman's body was buried in consecrated ground except secretly and under threat of excommunication. And Our Lord allowed such hardship to befall them for the breech of faith in their sins, and they were sinful indeed.

[*Gawain defeated his father and forced him to swear fealty to Arthur. Then news spread of the Holy Grail, and the knights undertook the quest for the holy object.*]

11. The Children of Pelles; Galahad Predicted.

Here the story says that King Pelles had a son who was not a knight, although he was a good twenty-five years old, but he was wondrously well built in body and limb, and he was wonderfully handsome. When his father asked him when he wanted to become a knight, he answered that he would never be a knight before the best knight known in the world should give him arms and knight him.[7]

"Indeed, dear son," said King Pelles, "you will then have to wait a long time."

"I don't know what I'll do," said the lad, "but I'll yet serve him three years before he makes me a knight, so that I can learn about arms and fighting while I am with him. And do you know why I want to get to know him and find out from which prince he comes? He could very well be one to whom I'll show the way to come to these parts in order to fulfill the adventures of this country that will soon begin, so I've been told. I have said this to you yourself many times, for I would be most distraught not to see my uncle healed from the wounds he has through his thighs."[8]

"Dear son," said King Pelles, "he would never succeed in this if you showed him the way, for he must be of such knighthood and so given to adventure that he will come here by himself to ask about the Holy Grail, which my fair daughter has in her keeping. She is still only seven years old, but a child is to be fathered on her by the best knight known to anyone, and there must be three to fulfill the adventures; two must be virgins and the third chaste."

[*Pelles's son left for Arthur's court to become Gawain's squire. The Saxon wars continued, with most of the Saxons eventually slaughtered. Arthur then had to battle the Romans, who claimed Britain as their own. First, though, he had to fight a giant at Mont-Saint-Michel. Then his army defeated the Romans. Next, Arthur had to fight a great cat at the Lake of Lausanne, after which his army defeated the forces of Claudas.*]

12. Merlin's Imprisonment.

[. . .] Then Merlin wished to go see his master Blaise, and he would tell him what had happened, although he had not seen it all, and from there he would go see his lady Viviane, for the time he had set with her[9] was drawing near. So he came to King Arthur and told him that he had to leave. And the king and queen asked him most sweetly to come back soon, for he would be a great

---

[7]The text refers to *la colee,* a part of the knighting ceremony involving an embrace, a light blow with the hand, or the placing of the flat side of the sword blade on the shoulder of the new knight.

[8]The text reads *parmi ses cuisses,* "in the midst of his thighs." The expression, which originates in Chrétien de Troyes's *Li Contes del Graal* ("The Story of the Grail") in speaking of the Fisher King, doubtless indicates a sexual wound "between his thighs."

[9]That he would return to her in a year.

comfort to them and most welcome company, for the king loved him very much indeed, because he had helped him in times of great need, and thanks to him and his counsel Arthur had become a king. So the king said to him very affectionately, "Dear friend Merlin, you are going away. I will not keep you here against your will, but I'll be most unhappy until I see you again. For God's sake, hurry back!"

"Sir," said Merlin, "this is for the last time. Farewell, I commend you to God."

When the king heard him say that it was for the last time, he was dumb-founded. And Merlin left without another word, weeping, and he made his way until he came to Blaise, his master, who was very glad at his coming. He asked him what he had done since leaving him, and Merlin told him every-thing. Then he recounted word for word, all in order, all the things that had happened to King Arthur: about the giant he had killed, his battle with the Ro-mans, and how he had killed the cat. [. . .]

And when Merlin had told all these things and made an account of them, Blaise set them down in writing one after the other, all in order, and this is how we still know them. After Merlin had tarried there a week, he left and told Blaise that it was for the last time, for he was going to stay with his lady, and he would never have the power to leave her or to come and go as he wished.

When Blaise heard Merlin, he was filled with sorrow and heartache, and he said, "Since you cannot ever leave her, don't go!"

"I must go," said Merlin, "for I have sworn an oath to her. And I am so overwhelmed by love for her that I could not leave her. And I have shown her and taught her all the knowledge she has, and she will yet know more, for I cannot leave her."

Then Merlin went away from Blaise, and he made his way a short while until he came to his lady, who was very glad to see him, as he was to see her. And they tarried together for a long time.

And right away she asked him about a great many things he knew how to do, and he taught her so much that he was later taken for a fool—and he still is. And she remembered everything and put it down in writing, for she was good at clerkly learning and knew the seven arts.

When Merlin had taught his lady everything she could ask, she began wondering how she could keep him forever. And she began to wheedle Merlin more than she had ever done before, and she said to him, "Sir, there is still something I don't know that I would be very happy to know. And so I beseech you to teach me how I might keep a man imprisoned without a tower or walls or irons, but through wizardry, so that he could never get away but through me."

And when Merlin heard her, he shook his head and began to sigh. And when she saw that, she asked him why he was sighing.

"My lady," he said, "I'll tell you. I know full well what you are thinking, and I know that you want to keep me. And I am so overcome by love of you that I must do your will."

And when the young lady heard him, she put her arms about his neck and said that he had to belong to her, for she was his. "You know very well," she went on, "that the great love I feel for you has even made me leave my father and mother to hold you in my arms day and night. All my thoughts, all my longing are for you. Without you I have no joy or happiness; all my hopes are in you, and I can find happiness only in you. And since I love you and you love me, isn't it right that you should do my will and I yours?"

"Indeed, lady," said Merlin, "yes! Now tell me what you want."

"Sir," she said, "I want you to teach me how to make a very beautiful, proper place that I can make magic so strong that it cannot be undone. And we'll stay there, you and I, in joy and delight whenever we wish."

"Lady," answered Merlin, "I'll gladly do this for you."

"Sir," she said, "I don't want you to do it, but you will teach me how to do it and I'll do it," she went on, "more to my liking."

"I grant you this," said Merlin.

Then he began to explain it, and the lady wrote down everything he said. And when he had told her everything, she was very happy and loved him more and was more cheerful to him than she usually was. Then they tarried together for a long while, until one day came when they were walking hand in hand through the Forest of Broceliande looking for ways to find delight, and they came upon a beautiful bush, green and high, that was a hawthorn loaded with flowers. They sat down in its shade, and Merlin laid his head in the lady's lap, and she began to rub it until he fell asleep. And when the lady felt that he was sleeping, she got up carefully and with her wimple drew a circle all about Merlin and the bush, and she began to cast her spells. Then she sat down again beside him, took his head in her lap, and held him there until he awoke. And he looked about him, and it seemed to him that he was in the most beautiful tower in the world, and he found himself lying in the most beautiful bed he had ever lain in. Then he asked the young lady, "Lady, you have indeed tricked me if you do not stay with me, for no one but you has the power to undo this tower."

And she said to him, "Dear friend, I will come here often, and you will hold me in your arms and I you, and you will do forever whatever you please."

And she kept her oath to him faithfully, for few days or nights went by when she was not with him. Merlin never thereafter left the stronghold where his lady love had put him, but she came and went as she wished.

So the story falls silent right here about Merlin and his lady love, and it speaks about King Arthur.

The story says that from the time Merlin left King Arthur and told him that it was the last time he would see him, King Arthur was filled with sorrow and bewilderment, and he dwelt on the words Merlin had said to him. He waited for him in that state of mind for seven weeks or more, and when he saw that Merlin was not coming back, it was a marvel how sad and worried he was. And one day Sir Gawainet asked him what was wrong.

"In truth, dear nephew," answered the king, "I am brooding because I think I've lost Merlin, and he'll never come back to me, for he has stayed away longer than he used to. He said that it was for the last time, and I am afraid that he was telling the truth, for he never lied in anything he told me. God help me, I would rather have lost the city of Logres than him. I would like very much to know whether anyone can find him near or far, so I beg you, look for him, if you love me, until you find out the truth about him."

"My lord," said Sir Gawainet, "I am ready to do your will, and you will see me leave at once. And I swear to you on the oath I gave you the day you made me a knight that I will look for him a year and a day or until I have truthful news of him. A year from today you will have me back, God willing, and if he keeps me from death and prison, unless I have truthful news about him first."

The same oath was sworn by Sir Yvain, Sagremor, Agravain, Guerrehet, Gaheriet, and twenty-four knights in their company. [. . .] And they rode out of the city of Logres all together as King Arthur willed it, and they undertook their quest for Merlin. And when they were outside the city, they parted ways at a cross they found at the edge of a forest where the road forked into three branches. There they split into three bodies.

But with that the story falls silent from speaking about them. [. . .]

13. Gawain and Merlin.

[. . .] As it happened, Sir Gawainet was riding through the Forest of Broceliande. [. . .] All at once he heard a voice not very far away from him, and he turned toward the place where he had heard that voice. He looked up and down and saw nothing but a kind of smoke no thicker than a mist, and he could not go through it.

Then he heard a voice that said, "Sir Gawainet, do not despair, for everything will happen as it must happen."

And when Sir Gawainet heard the voice that had thus called him by his right name, he answered and said, "For God's sake, who is it that speaks to me?"

"What?" answered the voice. "Don't you recognize me? You used to know me well. This is what happens to something left and forgotten, and the proverb is true that the wise man says: if you leave the court, the court leaves you. And so it has been with me. While I frequented the court and served King Arthur and his barons, I was known and loved by you and the others. And because I have left the court and no longer know it, I am unknown by you and the others, but I shouldn't be, if only faith and loyalty reigned through the world!"

When Sir Gawainet heard the voice speaking these things to him, the thought came to him that it was Merlin. And so he answered at once, "Indeed, sir, in truth I ought to have recognized you, for I have heard you speak many times. And so I beg you, show yourself to me so that I might see you."

"Sir Gawainet," said Merlin, "you'll never see me, and I am very sorry, for I can do no more about it. And after you leave here, I'll never speak to you or to anyone else but my lady, for no one will ever have enough strength to break in here, whatever may happen, and I cannot get out, nor will I ever. For there is no tower in the world so strong as the one where I am locked away, and it is not of wood or iron or stone, but it is enclosed by nothing more than air through enchantment so strong that it cannot be undone at any time. I can't get out, and no one can get in except the lady who has made it and who keeps me company here when it pleases her, and she can come and go at will as she pleases."

"How can this be, dear friend Merlin?" asked Sir Gawainet. "So you are held prisoner in this way and cannot free yourself whatever you may do? And you can't come out to me? How can such a thing happen to overwhelm you, who are the wisest man in the world?"

"But I am the most foolish!" said Merlin. "For I was well aware of what would happen to me. And I was so foolish as to love someone else more than myself! And so I taught my lady how she might imprison me, and no one can ever free me!"

"In truth," said Sir Gawainet, "Merlin, I am bitterly sorry about this, and so will be my uncle King Arthur, who has sent men out through all lands in search of you!"

"Then he must bear it," answered Merlin, "for he'll never see me nor I him—this is how things have happened to work out—nor will any ever speak to me after you, and it would be useless to try. And even you, if you had not turned this way, would never have heard me speak. Now go back and greet King Arthur and my lady the queen and all the barons, and tell them all about me. And you will find the king at Carduel in Wales, and you'll see him there. And you will find all of your companions with whom you left. You will not be despondent about what has happened to you, for you will find the lady who did this to you in the forest where you met her before; but don't forget to greet her, for that would be a mad thing to do!"

"Sir," said Sir Gawainet, "I won't, God willing!"

"Then farewell, go with God," said Merlin, "and may He keep King Arthur and the kingdom of Logres and you and all the barons, for you are the best men there are in the whole world."

With that Sir Gawainet went away happy and sad—happy because Merlin had reassured him about what had happened to him, but sad because Merlin was lost to the world. And so he went his way and rode until he came to the sea, and he crossed over in all haste and took to the road to Carduel in Wales. [. . .]

14. The Birth of Lancelot and the Loss of Benoic.

The story says that after King Arthur had left King Ban of Benoic and his brother King Bors of Gaunes, the two brothers stayed in Benoic rejoicing with great gladness, and their wives, who were very beautiful and comely, were with them. And so it happened, as it pleased Our Lord, that King Ban and his wife had a son who was named Galahad in baptism, but his surname was Lancelot; he kept the name Lancelot all his life. He brought great joy and happiness to King Ban and his wife, the queen, and the queen loved him so much that she nursed him with her own milk.

And King Bors's wife had a son who was called Lionel, and he was handsome through and through, and twelve months later she had another named Bors. Afterwards these three youths won very great renown in the kingdom of Logres and throughout every land, and they became known for their deeds at arms.

Shortly after the younger of King Bors's two children was born, King Bors fell gravely ill, and he lay for a long time in the city of Gaunes. And King Ban, his brother, was filled with sorrow and heartache, for he could not be with him as he wished, because of a wicked and ruthless neighbor of his, whose land bordered his own. This was King Claudas of the Land Laid Waste, who was so angry and upset about his castle that King Arthur had had pulled down that he nearly went mad, and he could think of no one on whom to avenge himself but King Ban and King Bors, who bordered on his land, because they were King Arthur's men. So he made war on them, and he finally won over a prince of Rome, named Pontius Anthony, to help him. This prince came to him very willingly, because he hated King Arthur and all his men because of his love of the Emperor Lucius, whom they had killed. King Hoel of Nantes died in that dispute, and he had long waged war on King Claudas.

And, for their part, the Romans fought until they had Gaul under their sway, and they sent the men of Gaul and the Land Laid Waste, along with Pontius Anthony's men, against King Ban of Benoic, who defended himself with all his might, for he had a great heart and great skill at arms. [. . .] In the end, King Ban was so weakened from the loss of his men that he could not hold out against the Romans, and they beleaguered him and day by day took his castles and strongholds. And he could not get help from his brother, King Bors, who lay sick in his bed, from which he never got up.

What gave him the greatest distress was that Pontius Anthony had brought such a great number of men with him that they took his city of Benoic and all his land from him, and he had not one city or castle left that was his own except the castle of Trebe, where Queen Elaine was with Lancelot, her son, who still lay in his cradle. [. . .]

Here ends the Imprisonment of Merlin. God lead us all to a good end!

Lancelot

TRANSLATED BY CARLETON W. CARROLL,
WILLIAM W. KIBLER, ROBERTA L. KRUEGER,
AND SAMUEL N. ROSENBERG

Part I

TRANSLATED BY SAMUEL N. ROSENBERG

[*Claudas seized King Ban's land, imprisoned Lancelot's cousins Lionel and Bors, and plotted to wage war on Arthur. The Lady of the Lake kidnapped Lancelot, the infant son of Ban and Elaine.*]

1. Portrayal of Lancelot as a Boy.

At this point the story recounts that when Lancelot had been in the care of the Lady of the Lake for the three years you have heard about, he was so beautifully developed that everyone seeing him thought that he was a third again older than his real age. Along with being big for his age, he was better behaved and more intelligent and agile than a child of his age was expected to be. The Lady found a tutor who taught him how to behave like a man of good birth. Still, in the whole household there was no person apart from the young woman and a maidservant of hers who knew who he was, and so they all called him The Child, as the tale has already explained.

As soon as the boy could handle it, his tutor made him a bow of appropriate size and light arrows and taught him how to shoot at a target. Then, when he was ready, he had him shoot at little birds in the forest. As he grew bigger and stronger in body and limb, his bow and arrows also increased in size and he began to hunt hare and other small animals and large birds wherever he could find them. As soon as he could mount a horse, he was given a very fine one that was well equipped with reins and saddle and other things. He rode up and down around the Lake, never going very far; nor was he alone, but had the fine company of noble lads, both older and younger, and of men of high birth. He behaved so beautifully in their company that everyone who saw him thought that he was one of the noblest and most refined beings in the world. And, indeed, he was.

Chess and backgammon and all the games he saw he learned so easily that when he reached the age of training for knighthood, there was none left for anyone to teach him. He was, says the story, the handsomest lad in the world, with the most beautifully formed torso and limbs. Nor may the details of his face be overlooked; they need to be described for all people who like to hear about great beauty in a youth. He had a perfect complexion, neither too fair nor too dark, but a blend of the two; it might be called light brunet. His face glowed with such harmoniously measured natural ruddiness that it was obvious that God had combined the three tones: fair was not eclipsed or spoiled by dark nor dark by fair, but they were rather tempered by each other, and the ruddy overlay brightened the blend of the other tones with its own brightness, so that the face showed no inequality of colors but only a harmonious mixture of all three.

His mouth was small and well proportioned, the lips red and well shaped, and the teeth small, white, and compact. His chin was shapely, with a tiny cleft; the nose was moderately long, slightly hooked in the middle. His eyes were bright and smiling and full of delight as long as he was in a good mood, but when he was angry, they looked just like glowing coals and it seemed that drops of red blood stood out from his cheekbones. He would snort like an angry horse and clench and grind his teeth, and it seemed that the breath coming out of his mouth was all red; then he would shout like a trumpet in battle, and whatever he had his teeth in or was gripping in his hands he would pull to pieces. In short, when he was in a rage, he had no sense or awareness of anything else, and this became apparent on many an occasion. He had a high, becoming forehead, with dark, widely separated eyebrows; his fine hair was so purely blond and gleaming that throughout his early years no hair could ever have been of more beautiful color. But when he reached the age to bear arms—as you will hear—his hair changed from pure blond to auburn, and it was always curly and moderately light and very attractive.

There is no point in wondering about his neck. Even as the neck of a beautiful woman, it would have been very becoming and attractive, well proportioned to the shoulders and body, neither too thin nor too thick, neither overly long nor overly short. His shoulders were high and wide as they ought to be, and his chest was such that one so broad and full and well developed could not be found in any other body. No one could have found fault with any part of him, but people who saw him did agree that, if his chest had been a bit less fully developed, he would have been that much more attractive and appealing. Later on, the worthy Queen Guenevere, who had more to say on the subject than others, said that God had not given him a chest in any way too big or deep or expansive, for it suited his great heart, which would have burst had it not been lodged in a large enough enclosure. "And if I were God," she said, "I would not have made Lancelot any smaller or any bigger."

Such were his shoulders and his chest. His arms were long and straight, with just the right development of flesh and muscle around the bones. His

hands were just like a woman's, except that the fingers were slightly less delicate. As for his back and hips, you could not imagine better made in another
knight. His thighs and legs were straight, and his feet properly arched; and no
man ever stood more straight than he.

He sang marvelously well when he wanted to, but it was not often, as no
one ever showed so little cheerfulness without good grounds; but when he
had good reason to celebrate, he was more spirited and gay by far than anyone else could be. And he often said,[1] when he was full of joy, that there was
nothing his heart dared undertake that his body could not accomplish, so
much did he trust in the joy which let him meet many a great challenge with
success. But such self-confident words were taken the wrong way by many
people, who believed that he was speaking out of arrogance and boastfulness.
That was not the case, however, and he was rather expressing the great assurance that he found in the very source of his joy.

That was how Lancelot looked, and how his face and torso and limbs
were crafted. But qualities of the heart were firmly fixed in him as well, for he
was the dearest and the most good-natured of all comparable youths, yet he
knew too how to deal with men of ill will. No boy of such great generosity
had ever been seen: he gave to his companions as eagerly as he received. He
honored men of good birth with an open heart and undivided attention; and
no such-mannered youth had ever been seen, for he was never disagreeable to
anyone without a reason so good that no one could blame him for it. But
when he was angered by some wrong done to him, it was no easy thing to
calm him down. He was of such keen mind and sound judgment that, once he
had passed his tenth year, he hardly ever strayed from proper behavior. Still,
if he had a desire to do something which to his heart seemed good and reasonable, he was not easy to stop and he paid no heed to his tutor. [. . .]

[*Lionel and Bors were rescued and came to live with Lancelot at the Lake.
The wars against Claudas continued, and Arthur regretted that he had not
aided Ban.*]

2. The Lady of the Lake and Lancelot, Now Eighteen Years Old, Discuss the Meaning of Knighthood and Then Leave for King Arthur's Court at Camelot.

At this point, according to the story, Lancelot had been in the care of the Lady
of the Lake for a long time and had reached the age of eighteen. He was such
a handsome young man that it would have been pointless to seek a handsomer

---

[1]That is, once he had grown up and come to know the "joy" of love. The "very source
of his joy," a few lines below, is no doubt a reference to Guenevere.

anywhere in the world, and he was so bright and well behaved that there were never any grounds for blame or correction in anything he undertook. When he was eighteen years old, he was strikingly tall and robust, and the Lady bringing him up realized that it was now right and timely for him to enter the order of knighthood and that it would be sinful and grievous if she delayed it, for she had often cast lots to see what the future would bring and she knew very well that great honor was in store for him. If she had been able to delay the event, she would gladly have done so, since, with all the caring and motherly love that she had devoted to him, she would find it very hard to live without him. But if she were to forestall his entry into knighthood at the right age, she would be committing a mortal sin as great as treason, for she would be depriving him of something that he could not easily recover later on.

[Lancelot expressed the desire to become a knight.]

"I will describe the qualities it takes, then," said the Lady, "though not all of them, because I don't have the understanding to describe them all. Still, listen closely to what you hear, and make an honest judgment with your heart and mind, for however great your eagerness to be a knight, you must not let the eagerness stop you from thinking it out first of all. The truth is, man has been granted reason and understanding so that he can consider what is right before undertaking anything.

"Bear in mind, then, that knighthood was not established lightly or because knights were in the beginning nobler men or of higher birth than other men; indeed, all mankind is descended from a single father and mother! But when envy and covetousness began to grow in the world and might began to win out over right, at that time all people were still equal in rank and birth. But then came a time when the weak and the peaceable could no longer withstand or hold out against the strong, so they established over themselves champions and defenders who would protect them and uphold justice and drive back the strong who were wronging and oppressing them.

"This task of defense was conferred upon those men whom people commonly deemed the most worthy: men who were tall and strong and handsome and lithe, loyal and brave and bold, men who had all the virtues of heart and body. But knighthood was not given to them lightly or without a price; no, a heavy burden was placed on their shoulders. Do you know what it was? In the beginning, when the order of knighthood began, it was required of anyone who wanted to be a knight and was legitimately chosen that he be courteous and not base, gracious and not a scoundrel, compassionate toward the afflicted, generous and helpful to the needy, ready and able to foil thieves and murderers, an upright judge unswayed by love or hatred—love that might weigh against the right or hatred that might plead in favor of the wrong. A knight must not, out of fear of death, do anything that might bring him dishonor or even a hint of it, but must fear a shameful act more than death. Above all, knighthood was established to defend the Holy Church, for the Church cannot take up arms to avenge herself or return harm for harm; and this is why knights were created: to protect the one who turns the other cheek when the first has been hit. Know, too, that in the beginning, according to the Scriptures, no one but knights dared to mount a horse—a *cheval,* as they said—and that is why they were called horsemen, or *chevaliers.*

"But the arms that a knight, and no one but a knight, bears were not given to him groundlessly; indeed, there are good grounds for them, and they have great meaning.

"The shield that hangs from his neck and covers his chest signifies that, just as it protects him from blows, the knight must protect the Holy Church from all evildoers, whether thieves or unbelievers. If the Church is assailed or at risk of attack, the knight, as her son, is duty-bound to come forward and take the blows. He must be her champion and defender, for if a mother is beaten or insulted in front of her son and he does not avenge her, he should be denied his daily bread and locked out.

"The hauberk worn by a knight to protect all parts of his body signifies that the Holy Church is likewise to be enclosed and protected by the knight's defensiveness. He must be so keenly watchful and well prepared that no evil-doer will ever come up to the front door or the back door of the Church and not find the knight there, alert and all ready to bar his way.

"The helmet on the knight's head, which is the most visible part of his armor, signifies that he must likewise be visible to all people as the enemy of those who would harm or injure the Holy Church. He must be like a watch-tower, a sentinel's post that from all sides can be seen rising high above all other buildings to frighten off criminals and thieves.

"The lance that the knight carries, which is so long that it pierces his foe before he reaches him, signifies that, just as the solid wooden shaft and sharp steel head make unarmed people back away for fear of death, the knight must be so bold and brave and determined that fear of him will travel far and stop any thief or evildoer from daring to come near the Church. They will run away for fear of him, with no more power against him than unarmed people have against the sharp-steeled lance.

"The sword girded to the knight is sharp on both sides, and not without good reason. The sword, of all weapons, is the most honored and noble, and the one with the greatest worthiness, for it can harm the foe in three ways: it can be used head on, to stab to death, or sidewise, to cut to the right or to the left. The double edge signifies that the knight must be a soldier of Our Lord and His people. With one edge, the sword strikes those who are enemies of Our Lord and His people, and mock His faith. With the other, it has the task of taking vengeance on those who try to shatter human fellowship, that is, those that rob one another and those that kill one another. That is the power of the two edges; the point is rather different. The point signifies obedience, for everyone must obey the knight. And it signifies obedience on just grounds, for it stabs; and nothing, not even a loss of land or property, stabs a man's heart as cruelly as having to obey against his will. That is the significance of the sword.

"The horse that the knight sits on and that takes him wherever he needs to go signifies the common people, for the people must likewise bear the knight and attend to his needs. The people must search out and provide him with everything he requires to live honorably, so that he may protect and defend them night and day. The knight sits astride the common people, for, just as the knight spurs his horse and guides it toward the goal he chooses, he has the task of guiding the people according to his will and in legitimate subjection; indeed, the people are under him, and that is where they are meant to be.

"In that way you can see that the knight must be a lord over the people and a soldier of God, for he must protect and defend and safeguard the Holy Church, that is, the clergy, whose task it is to serve the Holy Church, and widows and orphans, and the tithes and alms instituted in the Church. Just as the people support him materially and secure for him whatever he needs, so the Holy Church is bound to support him spiritually and, through prayer and alms, secure his everlasting life, so that God may be his savior in the life to come just as he is the defender and protector of the Church on earth. Thus the task of meeting all his earthly needs falls to the people, and the Holy Church must attend to the needs of his soul.

"A knight must have two hearts, one hard and solid as a diamond and the other soft and yielding as hot wax. The one which is hard as a diamond must be set against the disloyal and the ruthless, for, just as the diamond cannot be reshaped by polishing, the knight must remain pitiless and cruel toward the wicked who abuse and trample on justice as much as they can. And just as soft, hot wax can be molded and shaped as one likes, people who are good and compassionate should be able to bring out all the knight's graciousness and kindness. But let him take care not to show his heart of wax to the wicked and the disloyal, for all the good he did for them would be an utter loss for him. The Scriptures tell us that a judge damns himself when he saves a guilty man from death and lets him go; and if, with a diamond-hard heart, he rages against good people whose only need is for mercy and pity, he loses his soul. For, according to the Scriptures, a man who loves disloyalty and wickedness hates his own soul; and God himself says in the Gospels that what one does for the needy one does for oneself.

"Whoever is ambitious to become a knight needs to have all these traits. And whoever is not willing to behave as I have explained would do well to keep away from knighthood, for if he strays from the right path, he is shamed first of all in the eyes of the world and then in the eyes of God. The day he enters the order of knighthood, he vows to God that he will behave according to the teachings of the man who dubs him a knight, and who is better able to explain it all," added the Lady, "than I am. If he then breaks his word to Our Lord God, he rightly loses all the honor that he was looking forward to in heaven. In the eyes of the world, he is also shamed with good reason, for the honorable men of this world cannot tolerate a man in their midst who has forsworn himself before his Creator. The youth who would be a knight must have the purest and most clean of hearts; if he has not, let him not set himself such a goal and aim so high, for it is better to go through all of life without being a knight than to be dishonored on earth and lost to God. Knighthood is a greater burden than people think! [. . .]

"You will soon be made a knight, though, by the worthiest man in the whole world, King Arthur himself. We will set out this very week, so that we can reach him no later than the Friday before Saint John's Day,[2] which falls on the Sunday following this one. That's very soon, but I want you to become a knight on the Feast of Saint John, with no further delay. Just as Saint John was the most laudable and meritorious man that a woman ever conceived through fleshly union, may God, who was born of a virgin in order to redeem His people, grant you likewise the gift of surpassing in knightly excellence all the knights living today. And much of your fate I know."

Thus the Lady of the Lake promised the boy that he would soon be a knight, and he could not have been more overjoyed.

"Now take care," she said, "that no one know about this, and I'll see to everything you need without drawing anyone's attention."

The Lady prepared what the boy needed; indeed, she had long ago put together for him the outfitting of a knight: a white hauberk that was both strong and light, a polished silver helmet of splendid beauty, a shield as gleaming white as snow with a beautiful raised center made of silver. She wanted him to have nothing that was not silver-white. She also had ready for him a sword that in many a place had been well tried out before becoming his (and once he had it, it went through more good tests); it was of just the right size, not heavy, and remarkably sharp. A spear was prepared for him with a short, thick, and rigid white shaft and a sharp, pointed tip of silvery iron. Along with that, the Lady had set aside for him a large, strong, swift horse of proven speed and daring, and it was pure white as fresh fallen snow. For the young man's knighting, she had had made clothes of white satin, a tunic and cloak, and the cloak was lined in ermine, so that he should have nothing that was not white, and the tunic was lined inside with white silk taffeta.

In this way the Lady prepared everything the young man needed for his knighting, and then she set out very early on the third day. It was a Tuesday, and the Feast of Saint John was coming only a week after the following Sun-

---

[2]The Feast (nativity) of John the Baptist, June 24.

day. The Lady took to the road and traveled to King Arthur's court in high style, for in her escort she had as many as forty riders all dressed in white and mounted on pure white horses. She was also accompanied by five hundred knights and her lover, who was a valiant and handsome man. The Lady also had with her three young ladies, the one who had suffered an injury for the sake of the children[3] and two others, and the three who more than deserved their place in the group, Lionel and Bors and Lambègue as well, and with them many other young men.

After much riding, they came to the sea and set sail, and they arrived in Great Britain on Sunday evening, at the port of Floudehueg. From there they rode with proper royal credentials to Camelot, where they were told King Arthur would be for the Feast. They traveled straight on until they came Thursday evening to a castle named Lawenor, some twenty-two English leagues from Camelot. The next day, the Lady set out very early in order to make the most of the morning, since the heat was great, and she rode through a forest that stretched as far as two English leagues from Camelot. She was remarkably withdrawn and downcast, for she was heartsore to think the lad was about to leave her, and she sighed and wept tender tears.

But now the story stops speaking of her for a moment and speaks of King Arthur.

3. Lancelot at Camelot: Queen Guenevere, Knighthood, and Departure for Nohaut.

[*The Lady of the Lake came to Camelot and asked Arthur to knight Lancelot. Then she advised Lancelot about chivalry.*]

She said to him, "My dear prince, you are about to leave me. I want you to know that you are not my son, but were born to one of the finest knights and most honorable men in the world and to one of the best and most beautiful ladies ever to have lived. You can't know any more about either father or mother right now, but soon you will know the whole truth. Take care to be as beautiful in your heart as you are in body and limb, for you have as much beauty as God could bestow on any child and it would be a great wrong if your prowess did not prove its equal. And take care to ask the king tomorrow evening to make you a knight. And once you have been knighted, don't delay a single night in his house, but start your travels through all lands in search of wonders and adventures, so that you can gain fame and renown. Never stop in

---

[3]This is Saraïde, who had earlier rescued Lionel and Bors; that event is not included in the present volume.

one place longer than you have to, and take care that you do all you can not to be surpassed by anyone in feats of chivalry. And if the king asks you who you are or what your name is or who I am, just say that you don't know, except that I am a lady and that I brought you up. I have likewise forbidden your squires to say anything more than that. But let me tell you this much before I leave: I want you to know that I meant no indignity in having you serve the two king's sons who have lived with you, for you are of no less noble birth than they and they are both first cousins to you. I have devoted to you all the love that can grow out of raising a child, and for that reason—in remembrance of you—I will keep them with me as long as I can. And when it's time for Lionel to become a knight, I'll still have Bors."

When Lancelot heard that the two boys were his cousins, he was wonderfully happy and said to the Lady, "How good of you to tell me this! I feel so much better now, relieved to know of your comfort and overjoyed for myself!"

At that, the Lady took a small ring from her finger and put it on the boy's finger, saying that it had the power to uncover and reveal all magic spells. Then she bade him farewell, kissed him very tenderly, and spoke these parting words: "My dear prince, I leave you with this teaching: the more you succeed in harsh and dangerous adventures, the more confident you will be of succeeding in others. And when now and then you find a challenge that, with all your God-given knightly skills, you cannot meet, remember that there is no man born who could do so in your place. I would say much more but can't. My heart is very heavy, and I find it hard to speak. Be on your way now, my good, fair, gracious prince. Sought after by all men and loved by all women more than any other knight, that's how you will be. I know."

Then she kissed his mouth, his cheeks, and his eyes with tenderness and turned away, so choked with sorrow that she could not utter another word. The boy was deeply moved, and his eyes filled with tears. He ran over to his two cousins, kissed Lionel first and then Bors, and said to Lionel, "Lionel, you mustn't feel overwhelmed or hopeless if your land is in the hands of Lord Claudas. More friends than you think will help you recover it."

[*Lancelot was brought before the king and queen.*]

The queen looked at him tenderly, and he looked at her, too, every time he could do so without being noticed. He wondered where all the beauty could come from that he saw in her, and beside hers the beauty of the Lady of the Lake or of any other woman he had ever seen lost all its value for him. Nor was he wrong to admire no other woman as he did the queen, for she was the sovereign of all women and the very font of beauty. But if he had known all the great worthiness that was hers, he would have gazed at her even more gladly, for it surpassed that of every other woman, rich or poor.

She asked Sir Yvain the young man's name, and he answered that he did not know it.

"And do you know," she said, "whose son he is or where he was born?"

"No, my lady," he said, "only that he is from Gaul, since he speaks the language the right way."

Thereupon the queen took the boy's hand and asked him where he was from. At her touch, he started as if suddenly awakened, and he was so taken with the thought of her that he did not know what she was saying. She noticed how flustered he was, and asked him a second time, "Tell me," she said, "where you're from."

He looked at her helplessly and said with a sigh that he did not know. She then asked him what his name was, and he answered that he did not know that, either. The queen realized right away that he was flustered and troubled, but she dared not think that it was because of her; and yet she did somewhat suspect so, which made her stop her questioning. Not wanting to worsen the boy's confusion, she rose from her seat and, in order to keep anyone from having the wrong idea or noticing what she suspected, said that he did not strike her as being a very sensible young man and that, whether wise or foolish, he was in any case ill bred.

"My lady," said Sir Yvain, "you and I don't really know what he is like; and it may be he's been forbidden to tell us his name or anything about himself."

She said that that might well be, but said it in a whisper, so that the boy did not hear it.

The queen went to her room. When the time for vespers came, Sir Yvain took the young man's hand and led him to the service. After vespers, the king, the queen, and their knights went behind the great hall into a lovely garden on the banks of the stream that ran by the king's dwelling. Sir Yvain took the young man there, too, and following them came a crowd of other youths who were to be knighted the next day. [. . .]

Then Sir Yvain took him to the great hall, where the tables were set up and covered with cloths, and they sat down to eat. Afterwards, Sir Yvain took the youth to his lodgings and, when darkness fell, led him to a church, where he kept vigil all through the night; not once through the night was he allowed to sleep. In the morning, Sir Yvain took him back to his quarters and told him to sleep until High Mass. Then he took him to the church with the king, for on the great feast days the king always heard Mass at the richest and most important church in the town he was in, and in any case he went to High Mass every day.

Just before they left for the church, the arms of all the youths who were about to be knighted were brought, and they armed themselves according to the custom of the time. Then the king gave each one the accolade, but he did not gird them with their swords until they would come back from the church.

After the accolades, they went to hear Mass all armed, as was the custom at that time.

[*A knight arrived with a message from the lady of Nohaut, who was in need of military aid; Lancelot asked and received Arthur's permission to offer his assistance to the lady.*]

"Good sir," said the young man to the knight, who was waiting for him, "start out by yourself; I'll catch up with you as soon as I've spoken to my lady the Queen." And to his squires he said, "And you, go with him and take all my equipment." Then in secret he told one of his squires to take his sword as well, for he was eager to owe his knighthood to a hand other than the king's.[4]

"My lord," said the knight who was waiting for him, "I'll go ahead as far as the woods and wait for you there."

"Yes, go," said the young man; "I'll follow you right away."

Thereupon the knight left, along with the young man's squires. Then, together with Sir Yvain, the young man went to court, passing through the great hall where the king and many of his fine knights were still lingering. The flap of the young man's hood of mail was hanging open, so that his face was exposed. He and Sir Yvain reached the queen's room. Seeing the queen, he did not hesitate but knelt before her and warmly gazed at her as long as he dared. But then embarrassment overcame him, and he suddenly lowered his eyes, while Sir Yvain said to the queen, "My lady, this is the young man you saw last evening, whom the king has knighted. He is here to take leave of you."

"Really?" said the queen. "Is he already on his way?"

"Yes, my lady," said Sir Yvain, "he is going to help the lady of Nohaut as the king's champion."

"Good God! Why is my lord allowing him to go?" [. . .]

"There's no doubt, my lady," said Sir Yvain, "that this is disturbing to my lord the king, but the young man asked it as a favor."

At that, everyone within earshot said, "That's the young man who freed the wounded knight! God, what a bold thing to do!"

"God!" said the ladies and the maidens who were there. "Look how handsome and elegant he is, and how well built! He must be a man of great prowess."

Then the queen took him by the hand and said, "Stand up, my dear sir; I don't know who you are. You are perhaps of nobler birth than I know; if I allow you to remain on your knees in front of me, that's not very proper of me, is it?"

---

[4]It must be remembered that Lancelot has not yet been through the final stage of knighting, the girding with the sword. It is this stage that will determine whose knight he is.

"Ah, my lady," he sighed, "first you must forgive me for behaving so brashly toward you."

"What brashness do you mean?" she said.

"My lady," he said, "I left here earlier without your leave."

"My dear friend," she said, "you are so young that you can only be forgiven for such a misdeed: of course I forgive you!"

"Thank you, my lady," he said. Then he added, "My lady, if it were agreeable to you, I would, wherever I might be, look upon myself," he said, "as your knight."

"Yes," she said, "go right ahead."

"My lady," he said, "now, with your leave, I will go."

"Goodbye," she said, "goodbye, my dear friend."

And he whispered to himself, "All my thanks, my lady, for letting me be that."

Then the queen took his hand to raise him, and he was thrilled to feel her bare hand touch his. He took leave of the ladies and maidens, and Sir Yvain led him back out through the great hall.

At his lodgings, he covered the young man's head and hands with armor and, as he was about to put on his sword, he exclaimed, "Good Lord, sir! But you're not a knight!"

"How's that?" said the youth.

"Simple," said Sir Yvain; "the king has not girded you with the sword! Let's go to him right now, and he'll do it!"

"My lord," said the other, "wait here a moment. I'll run after my squires to get the one they're carrying, because that's the only one I'd want the king to gird me with."

"I'll come with you," said Sir Yvain.

"No, my lord," he answered. "I'll dash after them as fast as my horse can go, and then I'll join you right back here."

He left, and Sir Yvain remained waiting. But the young man had no wish to come back, for his aim was to be knighted not by the king but by a certain other person, who he believed would benefit him more.

Sir Yvain waited for him for a long while; then, seeing that he was not coming back, he went straight to the king and said, "My lord, we have been tricked by the young man who has gone off to be Nohaut's champion."

"What do you mean?" said the king.

"Well," he said, "you didn't gird him with a sword." And he went on to tell the king how the young man was supposed to go fetch his sword and come right back.

The king was surprised and wondered why he had not come back, since Sir Yvain had told him that he was not yet a knight.

"Well," said Sir Gawain, "I think he is a nobleman of very high standing, and I am sure he was offended by the fact that my lord the king did not gird him with the sword before all the others. That's why he has gone away."

The queen said that that might well be true, and many of the knights agreed. But at this point the story stops speaking of the king and queen and their whole entourage, and turns to the young man on his way to rescue the lady of Nohaut.

[*Using a sword sent to him by the queen, Lancelot successfully defended the lady of Nohaut.*]

4. Lancelot, as the White Knight, Captures the Dolorous Guard and Learns His Identity.

[*Lancelot came to the castle of Dolorous Guard. Aided by wondrous shields sent to him by the Lady of the Lake, he overcame heavy odds and captured the castle.*]

He was then taken into an extraordinary graveyard which lay between the walls, and he was indeed surprised by what he saw. It was enclosed on all sides by closely battlemented walls, and on many of the crenels rested a helmeted knight's head, and at each of these there was a gravestone with words on it that said, HERE LIES SO-AND-SO AND UP THERE IS HIS HEAD. But at the crenels where there was no head the stones spelled out, HERE WILL LIE SO-AND-SO. And there followed the name of many a fine knight from King Arthur's land and elsewhere, the finest knights known.

In the middle of the graveyard lay a large slab of metal extraordinarily crafted in gold and stones and enamels, which bore words that said, THIS SLAB WILL NEVER BE RAISED BY HAND OR STRENGTH OF MAN, SAVE BY THE ONE WHO WILL WIN THIS WOEFUL CASTLE AND WHOSE NAME IS ENGRAVED UNDERNEATH. Many people, by force or with some machine, had tried to raise that slab in order to learn the name of the good knight; but the lord of the castle had put the greatest effort into it, in order to learn the name and try to have the man killed.

The knight, still fully armed, was led up to the slab, and he was shown the inscription, which thanks to his schooling he could easily read. When he had read it, he looked up and down the slab and saw that, even if it lay unencumbered in an open space, four of the strongest knights in the world would have more than enough trouble raising it from the shorter of the two ends. He then grasped the longer and swung the slab upward about a foot above his head.

Then he saw the words that said, HERE WILL LIE LANCELOT OF THE LAKE, SON OF KING BAN OF BENOIC. He let the slab down again, knowing that it was his own name that he had just seen.

He looked up at the damsel whom his Lady had sent, who had just seen the name as clearly as he had.

"What did you see?" she said.

"Nothing," he said.

"No, it was something," she said. "Tell me what it was."

"Don't, please!" he said.

"Do, please!" she answered. "I saw just what you saw."

And she whispered it in his ear, which upset him and made him beg her to say nothing about it to anyone.

"I won't," she said. "Have no fear."

With that, the people took him off to the great hall of the castle, one of the most beautiful in the world although it was small, and they relieved him of his armor and rejoiced over him. The great hall was the seat of the lord of the castle and was splendid with all the things that belonged in the court of a powerful, highborn man.

That is how the White Knight won the Dolorous Guard. The young lady stayed with him, making him remain there for a while so his many wounds and injuries could heal. But the people of the castle were very sorry that their previous lord had escaped. If he had been caught, he would have revealed all the secrets of the place; but now the people were afraid they would never be known, since they doubted that they could keep their new lord at home for forty days. If he stayed, then all the spells and all the strange happenings by day and night would come to an end; the fact was, no one ate or drank in safety, nor went to bed or rose. Thus the town was both glad and sorry, yet they welcomed their new lord with all the joy that was due.

But here the story stops speaking of him and takes another path instead, as you will hear.

[*Arthur and others came to Dolorous Guard, but Lancelot left and was wounded in a tourney. Gawain sought him far and wide.*]

5. Lancelot Returns to the Dolorous Guard and Puts an End to Its Enchantments.

[*A squire told Lancelot that the queen was prisoner in Dolorous Guard and that she could be freed only by the knight who would win the castle. Coming to the castle, Lancelot spoke with the squire:*]

"Where is my lady the queen?"

"I will take you to her, my lord," he said.

He went ahead and the knight followed, and they came into the great hall. The building stood atop a solid mass of rock whose outer face was hewn plumb, and the door by which they entered, the only way in, was made of iron so thick that nothing could break it down. The knight had taken off his helmet, but his ventail was still in place.

The young man gave him a handful of candles and said, "You go ahead and light the way, while I go back and close the door."

The knight thought that he was telling the truth, but he was not; indeed, he had betrayed him, for the queen was not there. The youth darted back and shut the door, and the knight, seeing himself entrapped, was thrown into sore distress, for he realized that he could not leave that place at will.

He remained there through the night. In the morning, a lady no longer very young came and spoke to him through a window. "Sir knight," she said, "you can see what the situation is: you cannot leave this place without agreeing to certain terms."

"What terms, my lady?" he said.

"You are the man who won the right to this castle. It was up to you to bring peace to the castle, but you suddenly disappeared instead."

"My lady," he said, "has my lady the queen been freed?"

"Yes," she said, "and you are here in her place. It is now time for you to release the castle from its magic spells."

"How can I do that?" he asked.

"If you swear to do your utmost in the Adventure of the Castle, you will be freed."

He agreed. Then relics were brought to the window, and the knight swore as the woman had stipulated; after that, the iron door was opened and he walked out. He was then brought a good meal, because he had had nothing to eat since the morning of the day before. Once he had eaten, they explained the Adventure to him, saying that he had either to stay in the castle for forty days or else go in search of the keys to the spells. He answered that he would rather go in search of the keys, if he knew where they were, but "let's be quick about this task," he said, "as I have much to do elsewhere."

They brought him his armor and, once he was armed, took him to the graveyard where the tombs were. From there they went into a chapel that stood on the side near the tower, and, when they were inside, they showed him the way down to an underground cellar and told him that the keys to the spells were down there. He crossed himself and started down, holding his shield up to protect his face and carrying his naked sword. He saw nothing but the doorway below and, beyond it, a great brightness. He reached the doorway and, as he did so, he heard a great noise all around him, but he crossed the threshold. Then it seemed to him that the whole cellar was about to cave in and that the whole earth was spinning. Hugging the wall, he went on as far as a doorway leading into a second room. When he reached it, he saw two statues of knights cast in copper, each holding a steel sword so big and so heavy that two men could barely have lifted it. They stood guard at the doorway and kept striking with their swords at such a pace that no one could pass through without being hit.

The knight was not frightened by them, but raised his shield above his head and plunged on through. One struck him a blow that sliced right through the shield and came down onto the right shoulder, cutting so fiercely through the mail of his hauberk that red blood started flowing down the whole length of his body and he fell face down onto the ground. But he jumped right back up and, picking up his shield and the sword, which had fallen, he held the shield over his head and never looked anywhere but straight ahead. He came to another doorway and there saw a large well, which was giving off a terrible stench and was also the source of all the noise that he had been hearing; it was at least seven feet across. The knight saw the black, fearsome well and then, on the far side, a man, whose face was black as ink and from whose mouth darted bluish flames: his eyes glowed like burning coals, and his teeth matched the rest. The man was holding an axe and, as the knight came near, he gripped it with both hands and raised it to defend himself. The knight did not see how he could very well move forward, for even if there had only been the well, it was a treacherous leap across for a heavily armed knight.

He put his sword back into the scabbard and, removing the shield from around his neck, grasped it by the inside straps with his right hand. Then he moved back as far as he could in the room and, running at top speed toward the well, he flung his shield forward and struck so hard at the face of the man with the axe that the shield broke apart, but the man remained on his feet. The knight then rushed at him with all the strength he had and smashed into him so hard that he would have tumbled into the well if he had not grabbed his attacker. But the man let the axe drop as the knight seized him by the throat with his strong, unyielding hands and forced him down onto the ground with no strength to get up. The knight dragged him over to the well by the throat and threw him in. Then he pulled his sword back out of the scabbard and suddenly saw in front of him a splendidly cast copper statue of a maiden who was holding the keys to the spells in her right hand. He took them, then went over to the copper pillar that stood in the middle of the room and read the words that he saw there: THE BIG KEY IS FOR THIS PILLAR AND THE SMALL ONE FOR THE PERILOUS CHEST.

The knight opened the pillar with the big key and, when he reached in for the chest, he listened for a moment and heard inside a din and cries so loud that the whole pillar shook. He crossed himself; then, as he went to unlock the chest, he noticed that thirty copper pipes rose out of it and from each pipe came a horrible voice, each one louder than the next; it was from these voices that came the castle's spells and wonders. He put the key into the chest and, as soon as he had opened it, a great whirlwind arose and such a great noise that it seemed to him that all the devils were part of it, as, in fact, they were.

He fell down in a faint and, once he had regained his senses, he took the key to the chest as well as the key to the pillar and went over to the well, but he found it filled in and dry. And as he looked about, he saw the pillar crumble down to the ground and saw the copper maiden and the two knights guarding the door collapse and shatter. He went outside with the keys and saw all the people of the castle coming toward him; and when he went into the grave-yard, he saw none of the graves and none of the helmets that used to be on the crenels.

Then the people showed him all the joy they felt, and he made an offering of the keys on the altar of the chapel. They all then led him to the great hall, and it would not be easy to describe the fuss that they made over him. They admitted, too, that they had sent a squire after him to report how the queen was being held captive in the castle, "because we thought that your great valor would make you take her place in prison." When he realized that the queen had not been there, he felt tricked; nevertheless, he was pleased with the outcome.

That night he stayed at the Dolorous Guard and the next morning took his leave, for he could be delayed no longer. And from that time on the castle was called the Joyous Guard.

Thus the knight took his leave and slowly made his way to the Tourna-ment, and the story tells nothing about what happened on the way, except that in the city where he had acquired his red shield he now acquired a white one with one black band, and this is the one he bore at the Tournament.

[*Gawain learned (and revealed) that the White Knight was Lancelot. Arthur had strange dreams presaging his own fall from power. Lancelot was en-tranced by the sight of Guenevere.*]

6. King Arthur Receives a Challenge from Galehaut.

Here the story tells that the king came out of the woods just before the hour of nones. That evening, when he was having supper, there came in an elderly knight of very honorable appearance. He was covered in armor except for his head and hands, and his sword was girded on.

He walked straight up to the king, did not greet him, but said right in front of his table, "King, I am sent to you by the most honorable man of his generation, Galehaut, the son of the Fair Giantess, with this message: that you should surrender your land to him or hold it in fee from him. If you are will-ing to be his liegeman, he will hold you dearer than all the kings that he has overcome."

"Good sir," said the king, "I have never held land in fee from anyone but God, and I will never hold land from your lord."

"I am very sorry to hear that," said the knight, "since you will now lose both your honor and your land."

"Nothing you say matters to me," said the king, "for, God willing, he will not have the power to take anything away from me."

"King Arthur," said the knight, "know, then, that my lord challenges you;

and in his name I tell you that within a month he will be in your land. And once he has come here, he will not go away until he has conquered all of it; moreover, he will take away your wife, Guenevere, whom he has heard praised above all other earthly women for her beauty and her virtues."

The king answered, "Sir knight, I have heard your threats and will not be frightened. Let each man do the best he can! Should your lord take my land away, I would be distressed; but he will never have the power to do it!"

Thereupon the knight turned to go; but when he reached the door of the great hall, he turned back toward the king and said, "Ah, God! what sorrow! what a misfortune!"

Then he mounted his horse and rode off with two other knights who had been waiting for him outside the door.

The king asked Sir Gawain, his nephew, if he had ever seen Galehaut, and he answered no, as did most of the knights present.

But Galegantin the Welshman, who had wandered through many lands, stepped forward and said, "My lord, I have seen Galehaut. He is a good half-foot taller than any other knight known, is better loved by his people than any other lord in the world, and has conquered more than anyone else of his age. He is young and unmarried, and those that have met him report that he is the noblest knight, the most gracious in the world and the most generous. But for all that," he went on, "I am not claiming to believe that he, or anyone else, could overpower you. If I thought that, then, so help me God, I'd rather be dead than alive!"

The king at that point put an end to all the talking and said that he wanted to go back to the woods the next morning. He called together those whom he wished and said that he would set out early, as soon as he had heard Mass.

In the morning, he set out once he had heard Mass and went off into the woods; and the story has nothing more to say about him right now.

Part II

TRANSLATED BY CARLETON W. CARROLL

7. The End of Galehaut's War with Arthur;
Lancelot and Guenevere's First Tryst.

[*Galehaut attacked Arthur. Lancelot had been imprisoned by the lady of Malehaut; now released, and wearing black armor, he was awaiting permission of the lady to enter the war between Galehaut and Arthur. After arduous battles, in which Gawain was injured, the lady of Malehaut spoke with Guenevere.*]

"My lady, do a good thing and send word to that knight that he should take part in the fighting for your sake, and show you which side he is on, ours or theirs. Then we shall know what he intends to do and whether there is any valor in him."

"Fair lady," said the queen, "I have many other things on my mind, for today my lord the king is in danger of losing all his land and all his honor. And my nephew is lying here in such a state as you can see, and I see so much misfortune that I no longer have any desire for great challenges or entertainments the way I used to, for I have much to occupy myself. But you may send him that message, as may these other ladies, if they wish."

"Indeed, my lady, I am all ready to do so, if someone else were willing to join me. If you will, send him word, and I'll gladly join in."

"My lady," said the queen, "I will not become involved in this. Send him a message, you and these other ladies, if you wish."

Then the lady of Malehaut said that if the other ladies wished to send him a message on their part, she would do so on hers. They all agreed to this.

The queen lent them one of her maidens to bear this message. The lady of Malehaut composed the message, and Sir Gawain added two of his lances and a squire to carry them. Then the lady said to the maiden, "My lady, you will go to that knight who is lost in thought, and tell him that all the ladies and maidens of King Arthur's household send him greetings, except for my lady the queen, and they send him this message and beseech him, if he ever expects to win wealth or honor in any place where any of them has authority or power, to perform such feats of arms today, for their sake, that they may be grateful to him. And give him these two lances which Sir Gawain sends him."

Then the maiden mounted upon a palfrey, and the squire followed her bearing the lances; they came to the knight, and the maiden delivered her message. When he heard Sir Gawain's name, he asked where he was, and the maiden said, "He is in that brattice, with many ladies and maidens."

Then he took leave of the maiden and told the squire to follow him. He looked at his legs and settled himself firmly in his stirrups, and it seemed to Sir Gawain, who was watching him, that he grew by half a foot. Then he looked toward the brattice and went spurring across the fields.

When Sir Gawain saw him go, he said to the queen, "My lady, my lady, behold the finest knight in the world, for I never saw any other bear arms so well as this one."

Then they all, ladies and maidens, ran to the windows and the battlements to watch him. He galloped off as hard and as fast as his horse could go, and saw to right and left much fine jousting and many fine melees, for a large portion of the lively young knights of King Arthur's court had already entered the field in order to perform feats of arms; and from Galehaut's army came now ten, now twenty, now thirty, now forty, now a hundred, in one place more and in another fewer. The Black Knight avoided all the melees and spurred to meet a large troop where there were fully one hundred knights. He plunged among them and struck one knight so violently that he bore both him and his horse to the ground, all in a heap. And when his lance failed him, he struck with the stump as long as it lasted, right down to the grip, and then he rushed back to his squire who bore the two lances, took one of them, threw himself back among them, and jousted so skillfully that all the others left off their jousting and fighting so as to watch him. He performed so many feats of arms with the three lances, as long as they lasted, that Sir Gawain swore that to his knowledge no other man could have done as much. As soon as all three lances were shattered, he came back beside the river, to the place where he had been before, and turned his face toward the brattice, with great tenderness in his gaze.

Sir Gawain spoke of this and said, "My lady, do you see that knight? You may be sure that he is the most valiant in the world. But you gravely erred by refusing to be named in the message that was sent to him. He may have taken it for pride on your part, for he clearly sees that the matter at hand concerns you more than it does all the others, and perhaps he thinks that you had little esteem for him, since you did not deign to ask him to fight for your sake."

"Upon my word," exclaimed the lady of Malehaut, "he is clearly showing us that he'll do no more for *us*. Now let anyone who wishes send him a message, for our challenge will accomplish no more today."

"My lady," said Sir Gawain to the queen, "do you think I was correct in what I said?"

"Dear nephew," she said, "what do you want me to do?"

"My lady, I'll tell you. He has much who has the services of a man of quality, for many things have been accomplished through the presence of a man of quality, which otherwise would have failed. So I'll tell you what to do. Send greetings to this man, and beseech him to take pity on the kingdom of Logres and the honor of my lord the king, which will be lost today unless God and he intervene. And if he expects ever to have joy or honor in any place where you have power, then let him today perform such feats of arms for your sake that you will be grateful to him, and let it appear by his deeds that he has come to the rescue of the king's honor and your own. And you may be sure, if this knight is willing to defend our cause, that my lord the king will not be defeated this day, whatever power Galehaut may have. And I'll send him ten lances with sharp heads and thick and sturdy shafts, with which you will see many a fine joust before the day is out, and I'll send him three of my finest horses, all covered with my arms. And be assured that if he does his best, he will make good use of all three."

Thus spoke Sir Gawain, and the queen readily granted him permission to send whatever message he wished in her name. And the lady of Malehaut was so happy at this that she was practically flying, for she thought she had attained all she had always sought.

Then Sir Gawain called the maiden who had carried the first message, and sent her to the pensive knight, wording the message as he had said it to the queen; then he called four of his squires and ordered three of them to take three of his horses to the knight, appropriately covered, and the fourth was to take ten of his strongest lances.

Then the maiden went to the knight and delivered the message from Sir Gawain and the queen and gave him the gifts. And the knight asked the maiden, "Where is my lady?"

"My lord," she said, "up in that brattice, with many ladies and maidens, and that's where Sir Gawain lies wounded. You may be sure that you'll be well observed."

And the knight said to her, "My lady, tell my lady the queen that it will be as she desires, and convey my thanks to Sir Gawain for his gift." Then he took the strongest of the lances that the squire carried and told them all to follow him.

The maiden took her leave, and returned and delivered the knight's messages to the queen and Sir Gawain. Then the lady of Malehaut began to smile very broadly.

[*The battle resumed and continued unabated. Lancelot, still described simply as the Black Knight, distinguished himself among all the knights. At nightfall, battle ceased. Galehaut invited Lancelot to spend the night in the former's camp. The next morning, Galehaut wanted Lancelot to stay longer; in exchange for his agreement, Lancelot requested a boon: that Galehaut eventually swear fealty to Arthur. A day later, the two knights, now fast friends, rejoined the battle; Arthur's forces were being defeated when Lancelot asked that his wish be granted. Galehaut surrendered to Arthur and was greatly honored. The queen asked Galehaut to bring the Black Knight to her. After some delay, Lancelot, still anonymous, came to the queen. She asked him a number of questions about his past accomplishments, and he answered truthfully.*]

"Aha," she said, "then I indeed know who you are: your name is Lancelot of the Lake."

Then he said nothing.

"In God's name," she said, "it does you no good to conceal it; this has long been known at court. Sir Gawain first revealed your name there."

Then she told him, just as Sir Gawain had done, of the third battle, when Sir Yvain said that the maiden had said, "This is the third one." Then she asked him why he had allowed the worst man in the world to lead him by the bridle.

"My lady, because I had power over neither my heart nor my body."

"Now tell me," she said, "were you ever at the battle?"

"Yes, my lady."

"And what sort of armor were you wearing?"

"My lady, it was completely red."

"Upon my word," she said, "you speak the truth. And at the most recent battle, why did you perform so many feats of arms?"

He began to sigh deeply, and the queen pressed him with questions, as though she clearly knew how things were with him. "Tell me confidently," she said, "how things are with you, for I'll never betray you. I know that you acted as you did for some lady; tell me who she is, by the allegiance you owe me."

"Ah, my lady, I see that I must tell you. My lady, it is you."

"I?" she asked.

"In truth, my lady."

"It was not for me that you splintered the three lances my maiden brought you, for I had not associated myself with the message."

"My lady," he said, "I did for them what I had to and for you what I could."

"Now tell me: all the things you have done, for whom did you do them?"

"For you, my lady."

"What? Do you love me so much?"

"My lady, I do not love myself or any other so much."

"And since when do you love me so much?"

"My lady, since the moment I was called a knight and yet was not one."[5]

"And by the allegiance you owe me, what is the source of this love you have placed in me?"

At these words the lady of Malehaut, who had kept her head lowered, made a point of clearing her throat and raised her head. He immediately recognized the sound, for he had heard it many times before. He looked at her, recognized her, and was so overcome with fear and anguish in his heart that he could not respond to what the queen had said. He began to sigh deeply, and the tears flowed from his eyes so abundantly that the samite he was wearing was wet down to the knees. And the more he looked at the lady of Malehaut, the more his heart was saddened.

The queen noticed this, and saw that he was looking most piteously in the direction of the ladies, and she said to him, "Tell me, where does this love come from that I am asking you about?"

He did his best to reply, and said, "My lady, from the moment I've just told you about."

"How then was that?"

"My lady, you yourself made it happen, by making me your friend, if your words did not lie to me."

"My friend?" she asked. "How was that?"

"My lady," he said, "I came before you, when I took my leave of my lord the king, fully armed but for my head and my hands, and I commended you to God and said that I was your knight in whatever place I might be. And you said that you wanted me to be your knight and your friend. Then I said, 'Goodbye, my lady,' and you said, 'Goodbye, my dear friend.'[6] Since then those words could never leave my heart; those were the words that made me a worthy knight, if I am one; never have I been so badly off that I did not remember those words. They comfort me in all my troubles; they have kept me from all evil and saved me from all dangers; those words satisfied me in all my hunger, and made me rich in my great poverty."

"My word," said the queen, "those were fortunate words, and God be praised for making me say them. But I didn't take them as seriously as you did, and I've said that to many a knight without a thought that went beyond the words. Your thought was not base in the least, but on the contrary generous and noble, and good has come to you thereby, for it has made a worthy knight of you. And yet it is now customary for knights to make a great show

---

[5]A reference, again, to the fact that Lancelot had gone through most of the knighting ceremony, but had not yet received the sword. The queen sends him a sword, at his request.

[6]See Chapter 3.

to many ladies of what they value little in their hearts. Your appearance tells me that you love one of those ladies there—I don't know which one—more than you love me, for you wept from fear, and you dare not look directly at them. I can tell that your thoughts are not of me as much as you pretend. Now by the faith you owe the person you love most, tell me which of the three you love so much."

"Ah, my lady, may God truly help me, none of them ever had my heart in her power."

"That will not avail you," said the queen; "you can conceal nothing, for I've seen many such things, and I can see that your heart is over there, even though your body is here."

She said this deliberately to see how she could make him ill at ease, for she was quite sure his thoughts of love were only for her; otherwise he would never have performed such feats for her, the day of the black armor, but she delighted in watching his discomfiture.

He was so full of anguish at this that he was near to fainting, but his fear concerning the ladies held him back. And the queen herself feared for him, seeing him change so; she grasped him by the shoulder, to keep him from falling, and called to Galehaut. The latter jumped up, ran to her, and saw that his companion was in such a sorry state that his heart was in turn filled with anguish, and he said, "Oh, my lady, tell me, for God's sake, what has happened to him."

And the queen told him what she had alleged.

"Ah, my lady," said Galehaut, "for God's sake, you might well take him from me through such violent emotion, and that would be a great wrong."

"Truly," she said, "it would indeed, but do *you* know why he performed so many feats of arms?"

"Indeed, my lady, I do not."

"My lord," she said, "if what he has told me is true, it was for me."

"My lady," he replied, "may God truly help me, you may well believe that, for just as he is more valiant than other men, so too is his heart truer than all others."

"You were very right to say he was an excellent knight," she said. "If you only knew what feats of arms he has performed, since he became a knight!"

Then she related all his knightly deeds, as he had told them to her, and said he had acknowledged that he had worn the red armor at the other battle, "and I must tell you that he did all that because of a single word." Then she told him, just as you have heard, what she had said.

"Ah, my lady," said Galehaut, "for God's sake and because of his great merit, have pity on him, just as I did for you what you asked."

"What pity," she said, "do you want me to show him?"

"My lady, you know that he loves you above all others, and has done more for you than any knight ever did for a woman. And be assured that the peace between my lord the king and me would never have been, had it not been for this knight and if he himself had not brought it about."

"Indeed," she said, "I know full well that he's done more for me than I could ever deserve, had he done no more than try to bring about the peace; there's nothing he could ask of me that I could honestly refuse. But he asks nothing of me and is instead sorrowful and downcast ever since he looked toward those ladies. I do not suspect him of feeling love for one of them, but he fears one of them may recognize him."

"My lady," said Galehaut, "it's not fitting to speak of this, but take pity on him, for he loves you more than himself; God help me, when he came I knew nothing of his thoughts except that he was afraid of being recognized, and he never revealed anything else to me."

"I'll take pity on him as you wish, for you have done what I asked of you, and I must do what you wish, but he asks nothing of me."

"My lady," said Galehaut, "surely he doesn't have the power to do so, for one cannot love what one doesn't fear. But *I* ask something of you on his behalf, though even if I didn't ask anything of you, you should nevertheless take steps to win him, for you could conquer no richer treasure."

"Truly," she said, "I know that well, and I'll do whatever you direct."

"My lady," said Galehaut, "many thanks; I ask that you give him your love, and that you take him as your knight forevermore, and become his loyal lady for all the days of your life, and you will have made him richer than if you had given him the whole world."

"In that case," she said, "I grant that he should be entirely mine and I entirely his, and that any breach or violation of our compact should be repaired by you."

"Thank you, my lady. But now there must be a preliminary pledge."

"Whatever you stipulate," said the queen, "I will do it."

"My lady," said Galehaut, "many thanks. Therefore, give him a kiss, in my presence, to mark the beginning of a true love."

"This is neither the time nor the place for kissing," she said. "Have no fear, I'm as eager for it as he is, but those ladies there are already wondering that we have done so much, and they would necessarily see it. And yet, if he wishes, I will most willingly give him a kiss."

Lancelot was so joyful and also so dismayed by this that all he could reply was, "Thank you, my lady."

"Ah, my lady," said Galehaut, "have no doubt about his wishes, for that's all he thinks of. And be assured that no one will know, for we will withdraw, the three of us, as if we were conferring together."

"Why should I need to be urged?" she asked. "I wish it more than you or he."

Then all three withdrew together, as if they were conferring. Seeing that the knight dared do no more, the queen took him by the chin and gave him a prolonged kiss in front of Galehaut, so that the lady of Malehaut knew that she was kissing him.

Then the queen, who was a most wise and worthy lady, began to speak: "Dear friend," she said to the knight, "I'm yours, because you have done so much, and this gives me great joy. Now take care that this be kept secret: this is necessary, for I'm one of the ladies in all the world about whom the greatest good has been said. If my reputation were to suffer because of you, it would be a base and ugly love. And I ask the same of you, Galehaut, who are so wise, for if harm came to me from this, it could only be because of you; but if it brings me benefit or joy, you will have bestowed it."

"My lady," said Galehaut, "*he* could do you no wrong, but I've merely done what you ordered me to do. Now you must hear a request from me, for I told you yesterday that you could soon do more for me than I for you."

"Speak confidently," she said, "for there's nothing you could request that I wouldn't do."

"Then you have accepted, my lady," he said, "to grant me his companionship."

"Indeed," she replied, "if you didn't have that, then you would have profited little by the great sacrifice you made for him."

Then she took the knight by the right hand and said, "Galehaut, I give you this knight forevermore, except for what I have previously had of him. And you," she said to the knight, "give your solemn word on this." And the knight did so. "Now do you know," she said to Galehaut, "whom I have given you?"

"My lady, I do not."

"I have given you Lancelot of the Lake, the son of King Ban of Benoic."

And in this way she revealed his identity to Galehaut, whose joy was the greatest he had ever known, for he had heard many rumors that this was Lancelot of the Lake and that he was the finest knight in the world, though landless, and he knew well that King Ban had been a very noble man.

Thus was the first tryst between Lancelot and the queen brought about by Galehaut.

[*Guenevere then arranged for Galehaut and the lady of Malehaut to become lovers. Lancelot left with Galehaut, and Gawain and others looked for him. Gawain fought in defense of the lady of Roestoc, and she came to tell Arthur of the victory and to learn the identify of her defender.*]

8. The Split Shield; Hector Sets Out in Quest of Gawain.

[. . .] At that point, an armed knight entered, accompanied by a beautiful maiden bearing a shield slung upside-down around her neck. The knight could not carry it, for his arm was broken between the hand and the elbow. He had fastened it as well as he could with splints, but between them he was in such pain from the bones knocking together that he was near to fainting. The knight dismounted in the middle of the courtyard; many helped him and the maiden.

When he had dismounted, the knight asked where the queen was, and there were many who told him, for all gathered around them to see the wounded knight and the maiden with the shield. When he had come before the queen, he greeted her first, "in the name of the knight who bears you more love than you bear him, and who sends you the message that you rendered him half a service which you might have made whole.[7] For this reason he wishes you to know that he owes you but a half-repayment, and that he will give it to you at the first opportunity."

Then the queen began to think and asked the knight who this was who sent her this message; he replied that he did not know, "but he ordered me to tell you this and he said that you knew him well."

And when the queen saw that he was injured, she asked him who had injured him. "Truly, my lady," he said, "the knight of whom I spoke unhorsed me so violently that I fell and broke my arm in the way that you see."

Next, the maiden who bore the shield spoke and said to the queen, "My lady, I bring you greetings from the wisest lady now alive, and the most beautiful I know of; she asks that you keep this shield for the love of her and of another, whom you love even more, and she sends you this message: that she knows more about your thoughts and shares them more than anyone else in the world, for she loves the same person you do. And be assured that if you keep this shield, it will cure you of the greatest sorrow you ever had and will give you your greatest joy."

"God help me," said the queen, "this shield is very much worth keeping; may the lady who sends it enjoy good fortune, and welcome to you who brought it. But for God's sake, who is that lady? Tell me, for I would be very glad to know her."

"My lady," she said, "I'll tell you what I can: she is called the Lady of the Lake."

When the queen heard this, she immediately knew who the lady was; she jumped up to embrace the maiden who had brought the shield, and welcomed her as joyfully as she could. Then the queen herself removed the shield from the maiden's neck, examined it closely, up and down, and saw that it was completely split, from the base right up to the top, and only the cross-piece of

---

[7]The knight is Gawain; the "half a service" is an allusion to an earlier scene, where Guenevere's instructions are less complete than they might have been.

the boss, which was both rich and beautiful, kept the two parts from falling apart; they were so far from one another that one could stick one's hand between them without touching either side.

On one of the parts of the shield there was a knight, as richly armed as the artist's skill could make him, except for his head; on the other half was the most beautiful lady ever portrayed. At the top they were so close that he had his arms around her neck, and they would have been kissing, had it not been for the split in the shield, and below they were as far from one another as they could be.

And the queen said to the maiden, "Truly, my lady, this shield would be very fine, were it not so badly split. Now tell me, in the name of the one you love most, what does it mean that it is so split, for it appears quite new, and tell me the truth of the knight and the lady who are painted upon it."

And the maiden replied, "My lady, this is a knight, the best presently alive, who asked for a lady's love, the worthiest presently alive, in my opinion. The knight was so successful, through both his love and his deeds, that the lady gave him her love. But so far there have been only kisses and embraces, as you see on this shield; when it comes to pass that their love is complete, then be assured that this shield, which you see so broken apart, will be whole again, and the two parts will hold together. Then you will be freed from the greatest sorrow that ever befell you, and you will experience the greatest joy you have ever known. But this won't happen until the best knight outside King Arthur's court has joined his household. And if I said he was the best both outside and inside, I wouldn't be lying, so much have I heard of him, for he has performed more feats of arms in a short time than any other."

The queen was delighted by this explanation, and she welcomed the maiden with much rejoicing, and in her heart she felt she knew who the knight might be.

[*Hector left to seek Gawain, and the latter, along with other knights, was looking for Lancelot. Hector met Gawain and fought him until each learned the other's identity.*]

9. The Lady of Roestoc Learns the Identity of Her Champion.

At this point the story relates that after Hector had left the court, the queen came back to the wounded knight and had his armor very carefully removed. This was very painful for him, for he fainted twice before the hauberk was taken from his back. The queen did all she could to make him comfortable. She had the shield that the maiden had brought hung in her chamber so that she saw it every day, for she greatly delighted in seeing it, and she never went anywhere without its being borne before her and hung in her chamber at all times, until it was again made whole through the adventure which this story will recount later.[8] And then the maiden who had brought it left, for the queen could retain her no longer.

Next the queen went to see Hector's lady, in order to comfort her, and as soon as the maiden saw the queen she said to her that she wished that she, the queen, might be as joyful because of the person she most loved, before she died, as she herself was because of him whom she loved more than any other living being. The queen was badly frightened by this, and later there came a time when the maiden would have given anything not to have said what she did, for not long thereafter she was as distressed as she had been joyful, or even more so.[9]

The day after Hector's departure, at the hour of tierce, the lady of Roestoc was ready to return to her land and had come to take leave of the king and the queen. At the queen's request the seneschal had left the wounded knight in her care, until he recovered, on condition that the knight would return to him after his recovery. The king and the queen had tried to retain the lady a while longer, but that could not be, for her sorrow was too great, and it distressed her to see more people. Thus she took leave of the king and the queen, but the queen and the lady of Malehaut persuaded the dwarf's niece to remain with them so that she would hear news of Hector, for news and tales of adventures reached the court every day, and she would find more solace and company there than elsewhere.

While the lady was taking her leave of the queen, there entered a squire, carrying a shield that was not completely whole, for both above and below the boss there were great holes made by lances, and at both top and bottom it had been cut and sliced and broken apart until there was not a third of it left, and yet enough of the colors remained that it was still clearly recognizable, and it was a golden field with a red lion. The squire asked for news of the lady of Roestoc; she and the queen were pointed out to him, and he dismounted and came to the chamber.

When the dwarf and the seneschal saw him enter, they said, "Look, my lady: upon my word, here is the shield of your knight, whom Hector has gone seeking." When she saw it, all her blood drained away and she sat down, unable to remain standing.

When the squire approached, there was not a member of the household who did not recognize him, and they ran to meet him and joyfully welcomed him. Then he asked which was the queen, and she was pointed out to him. The squire came before her, removed the shield, and knelt down. And the

---

[8]See Chapter 11.
[9]This may be an announcement of the queen's despair, when Lancelot is taken prisoner by the Saxons (Chapter 11) and when he goes mad (Chapter 12).

queen said, "Why, I believe I would be sure to recognize this shield, were it not in such poor condition."

"My lady," said the squire, "I bring you very good news of Sir Gawain, that he is hale and hearty." Then the queen would let him say no more, but took the shield and embraced and kissed it and rejoiced over it as she would have done over the knight who had borne it. [. . .]

10. Galehaut Takes Lancelot to the Lost Island.

Now the story tells that while Sir Gawain was fighting against the knight of the causeway, wounding him and making him admit defeat, and defeating the men-at-arms by his prowess, so that they no longer dared stir, a squire set out directly for Sorhaut, where Galehaut and his companion were staying in his dwellings outside the city. He told them that a knight had defeated the knight of the North Wales causeway and all the men-at-arms as well, but he did not know his name. When Galehaut heard this he was amazed and told his companion that a knight errant had defeated one of the best knights of his land, as well as ten men-at-arms.

Lancelot said he hoped God would grant that the knight would come their way.

"Why?" asked Galehaut.

"Because, my lord," he replied, "we're in prison[10] here and for a very long time have seen neither jousts nor knightly deeds, and our lives are wasting away. May God truly help me, if he comes here I'll fight with him!"

Galehaut began to laugh, and those who heard him said he had no wish for repose. Then Galehaut thought he would keep him from fighting, if he could. He had a fine dwelling place upon an island in the Ausurne; there was easily half a league of water on every side, and it was called the Lost Island because it was so surrounded by water and isolated. He thought he would take Lancelot there.

That evening one of his knights, named Elias of Ragres, asked to guard the causeway. He was a fine, bold knight, and Galehaut granted him this. Then that very night he took his companion to the Lost Island, and Elias went off to guard the causeway. There he met Sir Gawain, and Elias gave him a joyful welcome as soon as he knew who he was.

Sir Gawain asked him where Galehaut was, and he replied that he had no news of him.

"No? Isn't he in Sorhaut?"

"In truth," replied Elias, "he departed last night at midnight, and we don't know where he went."

---

[10]Lancelot's choice of words is surprising, since he and Galehaut had gone to Sorelois (Galehaut's kingdom) completely of their own free will.

Then Sir Gawain was greatly distressed, for he feared his quest would be prolonged.

In the morning Sir Gawain took his leave, and he and Hector departed, since there was a guard at the bridge. He told the wounded knight, who was still there, to swear that he would go to King Arthur's court, surrender himself to Queen Guenevere, and tell her that Hector had found him and that he would return to court as soon as he could, and that Hector would have returned, "if I hadn't retained him to accompany me. Now tell me your name," he added, "since you already know mine." And he said his name was Elinan of the Isles.

Then Elinan, in great discomfort, went to King Arthur's court and told the news. The king was very glad, and the queen had his wounds cared for. After that he was a member of King Arthur's household, for he was a very worthy knight.

When the queen learned that Hector had found Sir Gawain, she was delighted. Then she told his ladylove, who was overjoyed and greatly comforted, for no one had been able to make her laugh or play since he had gone away. But it grieved the king more than anyone else that Sir Gawain had not succeeded in his quest, because of the urgent nature of his mission, and he knew no way of bringing it to a successful conclusion without him.

11. Gawain and Hector Find Lancelot; The Battle of Saxon Rock.

[*Lancelot, on the Lost Island, was preoccupied and very distressed because he had had no news of the queen. Gawain and Hector found Lancelot, who was then reconciled with Gawain.*]

Two days later a maiden came to see Sir Gawain, and drew him aside. "My lord," she said, "I am sent to you by your brother Agravain, who sends you word that King Arthur is leaving for Scotland, where the Irish and the Saxons have entered; you are to go there and to send him word of how you have succeeded in your quest."

"Well," he replied, "thanks be to God. Now stay here for the rest of the day."

That night Sir Gawain begged Lancelot for his company, and he readily granted it and anything else he might wish. And Hector also became part of that company; all three of them swore to this because he was the queen's knight and eminently worthy. Afterwards Sir Gawain stated that he wished to stay there the whole week, "and in the morning each of us will have blood drawn from our right arm." Lancelot said that he had never been bled, but that he would do it for the love of Sir Gawain.

The next day they were bled, and Sir Gawain had the maiden take Lancelot's blood to his brother Agravain, who was completely cured as soon as he was anointed with it. And Galehaut had a shield made for Lancelot according to the queen's command, and he brought the shield to one of his knights. And Sir Gawain told them of the army that was going to meet the Saxons, for he thought they knew nothing of it, and he asked Galehaut and Lancelot to accompany them, and they agreed.

"But let us go," said Galehaut, "in such a way as not to be recognized; let's all bear unfamiliar arms." And the others agreed.

They stayed there the whole week. Then they set out to go join the battle, and they went along asking for news until they met the same maiden whom Sir Gawain and Hector had met, who had informed them about the Lost Island. They all greeted her, and she invoked God's blessing upon them.

"My lady," said Galehaut, "do you have any news of King Arthur?"

"Yes," she replied, "entirely reliable news, and I can tell you that you will get no news of him today or tomorrow except from me, but I won't reveal it for free."

"In truth," said Lancelot, "we will give you whatever you wish in exchange."

"Give me your solemn word," she said, "that, when I summon you, you will give me what I ask, even as much as a league of land from your domains."

"We will never fail you in this," they said, and all four of them gave her their word.

"The king is at Arestel, in Scotland, and as soon as you reach there, you'll find him laying siege to Saxon Rock, I believe."

Then she left, and they all commended her to God, as she did them. They spent their days in travel until they came to Arestel and found the king laying siege to the Rock, just as the maiden had said, and the Rock was so strong that those in it feared nothing except being starved. It had been secretly fortified at the time Vortigern married the daughter of Hengist the Saxon.[11] From there to Arestel was fully twelve Scottish leagues, and everything was destroyed between them, except for one castle in which there lived a maiden named Gamille. She knew more about enchantments than any other maiden in the land; she was very beautiful, and of Saxon lineage. She was as much in love with King Arthur as she could possibly be, but the king knew nothing of this.[12]

When the four knights reached the king's camp, Sir Gawain asked Lancelot, "What shall I do? I wouldn't dare enter King Arthur's court until I can bring reliable news of Lancelot, for I have sworn to this."

---

[11]The succeeding conversations contain a number of references to events deleted from the present volume. This reference is to *Merlin*; subsequent ones are to earlier portions of the *Lancelot*.

[12]This statement is totally at variance with what is related later in this chapter.

"My lord," said Galehaut, "if you please, let's leave that until after the battle, for you can surely wait until then to enter King Arthur's house. Then Lancelot will go wherever you wish."

Sir Gawain granted this request, and said there were still twenty knights on this quest. "And we all swore that we would be at King Arthur's first battle, if we were free to do so, and we made arrangements so as to be able to recognize one another. Now I'll go see whether I can find any of them, and then I'll come back to you."

"We'll wait for you," said Lancelot, "but take Hector with you."

"Indeed," said Galehaut, "and we'll set up our tent outside here, between the camp and Arestel, so that we won't be recognized. And whenever we leave the camp we'll do so by night, so that no one will know who we are." And all of them approved this.

Then Sir Gawain and Hector rode into the camp, and people looked at them with wonder, since they carried their shields with the inside outward. Sir Gawain found all his companions except for Sagremor, whose lady had detained him because she loved him so much she could not do without him. Nevertheless, he arrived before the battle was over. Then his companions asked him whether he had succeeded in any way, and he replied that he had everything he sought, "but I won't reveal my identity," he said, "until the battle is over." Then he told Sir Yvain that his companions should take lodging in groups of two or three, so as not to be noticed, "and I'll do likewise, with this knight, whom I cannot fail."

Then Kay asked him who he was.

"In truth," he replied, "this is the knight who unhorsed all four of you at the Spring of the Pine."

They were mightily puzzled by this, and Sir Yvain said that he would be a fine knight, if he stayed alive.

At that point they departed, and Sir Gawain said they were all to be together at the battle the next day. Then he went to where Galehaut had set up his tent, and this was at the edge of a wood, in a lovely spot, enclosed all around by a lofty palisade, which one entered through a little gate, for this was a garden belonging to one of the burghers of Arestel. There the tent was pitched, and there were easily ten squires, one of whom was Lionel, who was most worthy and judicious.

And every day King Arthur spoke to the maiden of the castle, begging her for her love, but she cared nothing for him, though she had so affected him that he loved her beyond all measure.

The battle took place the day after Sir Gawain's arrival. Lancelot bore the black shield with a diagonal white band, Galehaut bore the shield belonging to the King of the Hundred Knights, and Sir Gawain the shield of white and azure; it belonged to the best knight of Galehaut's household, named Galain, the duke of Ronnes. And Hector bore the white shield with the red band across it, which was the shield of Aguinier, one of Galehaut's companions. The king himself bore arms. They did battle with the Saxons and the Irish, but the king did not have many troops, so he had to acquit himself well. In fact, he did so better than ever before, and this was more for the maiden who was watching him from the Rock than for himself.

When the king himself had entered the fray, Sir Gawain and his twenty companions joined the battle, but Galehaut and Lancelot stayed behind so as not to be noticed. Then the two of them passed before the house where the queen was staying. She and the lady of Malehaut had climbed up to the battlements of the tower, and when the queen saw Lancelot, she said to the lady of Malehaut, "Do you recognize those two knights?"

Then the lady began to smile, for she readily recognized them, both by Lancelot's shield and by the pennoncel he had attached to his helmet, and this was the first distinguishing mark ever worn on a helmet in the time of King Arthur.

Then the two knights looked up, and saw what they most loved. Lancelot was so overcome that he nearly fell to the ground and had to hold onto the neck of his horse. Lionel was riding next to him, armed in a metal cap and a habergeon like a foot-soldier, and he rode with bowed head, so that no one would recognize him. But when he looked up, he recognized the queen, and she recognized him and had him summoned by a page. He dismounted, leaned the lances he was carrying against the base of the tower, and began to climb up. He met the queen upon the stair, and she said to him, "Be sure that the jousting takes place in front of here." Then she went back to the top of the tower, and he remounted his horse and spurred after his lord, carrying the lances. He told him what the queen had said, but Lancelot was so deeply lost in thought that he could only reply, "Let it be as my lady wishes."

Then they reached the scene of the battle and saw the field covered with fighting. Lancelot charged in and began so valiantly to perform feats of arms that all who saw it were astonished. Sir Gawain was fighting some way off, but it took little time before he heard of this, as someone told him a knight was performing marvels up ahead. He arrived with his companions, and they immediately drove the enemy forces back to their camp, inflicting many casualties.

When Lionel saw this, he advised Lancelot to get ready to do as he had been instructed. But he replied, "Go tell my lady that cannot be, unless I place myself on the other side; if that is what she wishes, I will bring them all before the tower." And Lionel went off to tell her.

As soon as she saw him, she descended. When he had delivered his message, she climbed back up and said that she did wish it, "but let him take care," she added, "as soon as he sees my cloak hanging from the battlements with the lining outwards, to come back from the other side, and if the king suffers any losses in the pursuit, let him be sure to make amends for them."

Lionel went back and delivered this message to Lancelot. And Galehaut called Sir Gawain and said, "My lord, I know how the king might capture the mightiest men from the other side: if we turned from there and led the king's forces right up to the edge of the water, without stopping, and if we then turned back, we could not fail to capture or kill them all."

Sir Gawain said he would do whatever Galehaut wished, "but how," he objected, "can I go against my uncle and my liege lord?"

"Why, it would be for his advantage," said Galehaut.

"In that case," replied Sir Gawain, "I would do it."

Then they turned toward the Saxons, twenty-three knights, all most worthy, including Galehaut. At once the king's forces had to fall back, since the other knights were against them, and they never stopped until they reached the edge of the water, where the tower was situated. But they did so calmly, and with scarcely any losses, for the enemy were intent upon pursuing them and believed they had won the day, and so they took no prisoners, but drove them into the water by force. The king's grief was so great that he was nearly out of his mind, and he bitterly lamented the absence of Sir Gawain and his companions.

Then Lancelot looked toward the tower and saw the queen's cloak hanging, lining outwards, and declared that now they had suffered enough. "Now at them!" he cried. Then they all turned about and charged full speed at the Saxons, cutting them off from behind, with a furious attack and a mighty shout. They were thrown into great confusion, believing themselves to be completely surrounded, and the king's men came back and met them.

But Lancelot and his company were at the rear, where he performed such marvels that the queen was quite amazed, for he was striving mightily to keep his adversaries near the tower. He and his companions were at the passage to the ford, for they all had to come back through there. So many were killed and unhorsed in the ford that the water was all dammed up. And the queen observed that all his hardships at the other battle were nothing compared to what he had endured here, and she was thoroughly puzzled as to who those knights with him were, who were acquitting themselves so well. Sir Gawain and Hector and all the others performed marvels, and no one could get in among them without being either killed or unhorsed; they all made such efforts in fighting for one another that it was a wonder to behold. And because they killed so many knights in the ford, it was from that day on called the Ford of Blood, and it will be forevermore.

Lancelot, along with his companions, took so many blows at the ford that his helmet was all split and dented, and the circlet hung down. So the queen called to one of her maidens and sent him a splendid helmet belonging to the king. "And tell him that I cannot watch this slaughter any longer and that he is to begin the pursuit, for I wish it."

The maiden took the helmet to him and gave him the queen's message;

he replied, "Many thanks!" Then he removed his helmet and laced on the new one, and withdrew a little, along with his companions. The Saxons crossed the ford and took flight, overcome by fear; their losses were too great, and they fled. Lancelot and his companions pursued them, and in the chase the king's men captured a knight named Aramont, the brother of Agleot, the Saxon king, and one of their best knights. And they captured fully two hundred other Saxons and Irishmen, all mighty lords, and killed some of the best. Three times during the pursuit, Lancelot helped King Arthur remount, for two of his horses were killed under him and the third fell and broke its neck. The king would have fared very badly had Lancelot not been there, for he was on his own, so intent were his men on pursuing their enemy and on taking prisoners.

That day the king's enemies were severely harried and driven back to their own camp. All day long the fierce fighting continued, until evening began to fall. Then Galehaut came to Sir Gawain and advised him to remain there until the forces withdrew, "and then we will leave." Sir Gawain agreed to this. Then he and Lancelot came before the tower. The queen came down; they both greeted her and she greeted them. She saw that Lancelot's arm was covered with blood up to the shoulder, and she feared he was mortally wounded. She asked them how they were, and they replied, "Well."

"And does your arm not pain you?"

"No, my lady."

"I wish to see it," she said.

She embraced Lancelot in his suit of armor, and the lady of Malehaut embraced Galehaut; the queen whispered to Lancelot that she would heal him before the next day, if he had no mortal wound, and he replied that he had no fear of death as long as she wished him well. Then she bade them mount, for she dared detain them no longer, and told Lionel she wished to speak to him. The two knights went off to their tents and removed their armor. It was already beginning to grow quite dark.

As he left the battle, the king passed below the Rock. The maiden said she wished to speak to him; he was very pleased and waited for her. She descended, came to him, and said, "My lord, you are the worthiest man alive, and you give me to understand that you love me above all women. I wish to test this, if you dare do one thing for me."

"There is nothing that I wouldn't do for you."

"I want you to come lie with me tonight in this tower."

"There is no obstacle," he replied, "if you promise I may do with you what a knight should do to his ladylove."

She promised him this, and he said he would come just as soon as he had seen his knights and dined with them.

"At the gate," she said, "you will find my messenger who will come to get you."

Then the king, full of joy, left her and returned to his knights, who saw him happier and more joyful than ever before. He sent word to the queen that she would not have him with her that night and that she should rejoice, since the battle had gone so well for him. She was not at all sorrowful about this.

That night Lionel came to the queen's residence, and she told him that Lancelot and Galehaut were both to come speak to her there that night, and she showed him by what route.

"My lady," he replied, "Sir Gawain and Hector are with them. How will they get away?"

When the queen heard this, she was delighted that they had found one another, "but this is not to prevent them from coming," she added, "and I'll tell you how. They will go to bed in the presence of Sir Gawain, and when they're sure that he's asleep, they will get up, and then the three of you will come here"—and she showed him a garden adjoining the bailey of the castle—"and we'll be outside the bailey. Tell them to come in full armor and on horseback."

Then Lionel went back and related what he had been told, and the two knights were overjoyed.

That night, when those in the king's tent had gone to bed, the king rose as quietly as he could, and he and his nephew Guerrehet, to whom he had revealed his plan, put on their armor, went to the gate of the castle, and found the messenger of his beloved. Then they accompanied him into the great fortress and found the maiden waiting for them. She gave them a fine welcome and had the king's and Guerrehet's armor removed. Then the king lay down with his ladylove in a splendid bed, and Guerrehet lay with a beautiful maiden in another room.

After the king had lain a long time with his ladylove and had his way with her, more than forty knights entered the tower, fully armed and with naked swords, and forced open the door to the room. The king jumped up as best he could, clad only in his breeches, and ran to his sword in order to defend himself. The knights were carrying many burning candles, and it was bright enough to see clearly. They told him not to defend himself, and he obeyed: since he had no armor, he saw that any defense would be to no avail, and he let himself be taken prisoner. And some ran into the other room and captured Guerrehet. Then they dressed both of them and imprisoned them in a fortified room where a single door was the only way in or out, and that door was made of iron.

So the king and Guerrehet were in prison. Galehaut and Lancelot arose from their beds; they had before them two squires, whom they ordered not to move so that, if the others awoke, they would take the two knights for squires. Then they came, fully armed, to the garden, and the squires lay down in their beds. The knights found the gate to the garden unlocked and went in. The camp was guarded only at the front, for at the rear, toward the garden, the water ran so deep that no one would have set foot there because of the muddy marsh. Once inside the garden, they closed the gate and went to the bailey; there they dismounted, found the two ladies waiting for them, and led their horses to a lean-to adjoining the bailey. And in all the bailey there were only the queen and her maidens; the other people were nearby, in a very large house, for she had deliberately cleared out the bailey.

When the two knights had removed their armor, they were led to two chambers, and each of them, very much in love, lay with his beloved, and they had all the joys that lovers can have. At midnight, the queen arose and went to the shield that the maiden from the Lake had brought her. In the darkness she felt it and found it completely whole, without a crack, and she was overjoyed, for now she was certain that she was better loved than any other woman.

In the morning, shortly before daybreak, the two knights arose and put on their armor in the queen's chamber. And the lady of Malehaut, who was very astute, looked at the shield by the light of the candles, saw that it was whole again, and said to the queen, "My lady, now we can see that the love is complete." Then she went to Lancelot and took him by the chin, and he was deeply ashamed because he had spent many days in her power and had always concealed his true feelings from her.

Then to rescue him the queen said, "My lady, if my father is a king, so too is his, and if I am worthy and fair, he is more so."

Then Galehaut asked what all this meant, and she related how the shield had been brought to her, that the Lady of the Lake had sent it, and that it had always been cracked until that time. For a long time they looked at it with wonder. And the lady of Malehaut remarked that just one thing kept the shield from being as it had been foretold,[13] and that was that Lancelot was not of the household of which he was to be.

Then the queen implored him to stay, if Sir Gawain asked him to do so, for she was so overwhelmed by him and by his love that she did not see how she could ever do without him. But she said this so softly that Galehaut did not hear it, for he would have been deeply saddened by it. Then they departed and arranged to come back the next night.

[*Gawain, Lancelot, Hector, and Galehaut were also captured (through a ruse). With Yvain leading the troops in Arthur's place, the battle against the Irish and Saxons began.*]

That day King Yder rode a horse he thought to be the finest in the world, and because he loved it so, he had it completely covered with iron before the

---

[13]By the Lady of the Lake, Chapter 8.

battle. And then he did something that was criticized at first, but for which he was subsequently praised; it had never been seen before but would henceforth be a thing to be done: he made a banner showing his coat of arms and said he wanted it carried where a banner could not go, and he felt his horse was so good that he wanted all those broken under attack to rally to him. The banner was very fine, for the field was white with broad red stripes and was made of cordovan and the stripes were made of scarlet cloth from England. And whatever people wore at that time, the horse-blankets were only of leather or of cloth—the stories bear witness to this—so that they would last longer.

The king's companions acquitted themselves very well that day, following the exhortation of Sir Yvain, for such a fine battle had never been fought without the presence of King Arthur, and there was not a single knight who did not perform many feats of arms. But whatever they did, it was nothing compared to the prowess of King Yder: he outdid everyone, on both sides, and because he had said that all were to rally to his troop, he endured so much that day that he was maimed for the rest of his life; from the moment he entered the fray he never removed his helmet from his head or retreated or fled from where he set his feet. And his horse was as fine as could be: it endured so much under him that it was wounded three times and its blanket was all cut to bits; it was so covered in blood, its own and that of others, that horse and rider were all crimson. On all sides men were crying that King Yder had carried the day. Mounted upon his horse, he prayed that God might sustain him in his undertaking without breaking faith or giving ground, and to let him die at the end, for he would never again have a day so fine or fair.

King Yder endured so much that day and performed so many feats of arms, he and the companions of King Arthur, that the Saxons were routed and turned their backs. Then began a great pursuit; their losses were heavy, and King Arthur's men pursued them furiously. Everyone marveled at King Yder's horse, for no beast that had run all day long ever ran as fast or as freely as that horse did in the pursuit. It lasted a long time, and many fell on each side. But it happened that King Yder rode over a fallen Saxon who was holding a naked sword, and he struck King Yder's horse and completely split open its belly. It ran on quite some way, but then collapsed under the king; Yder had lost much blood, and he remained unconscious on the ground. Queen Guenevere and the other ladies came running, and they themselves bore King Yder from the field. Everyone believed he was irretrievably lost. He was borne to the queen's chamber, and the world's noblest ladies wept and mourned for him.

The king's forces had pursued their enemy all the way to Malaguine, a mighty Saxon fortress, and they came back with many prisoners and had killed many of their foes. Then the army camped nearer the Rock than they had before, yet not very close, for the Rock was lofty, and they could not endure the arrows and bolts that rained down from above, nor could one besiege it from any side, for on the other side the marsh was so vast that nothing could enter it.

The army long remained camped before the Rock, and for a very long time the Saxons never dared attack the king's forces, but endeavored to send for troops throughout their domain. And the king's men came from every direction, for people everywhere knew that the king had been captured. So the army camped before the Rock and was on watch night and day: every day and every night, beneath the gate on the side toward the water, two hundred armed knights watched to see that they did not take away the king or his companions.

12. Lancelot's Madness and Cure; Defeat of the Saxons and Irish; Lancelot, Galehaut, and Hector Become Companions of the Round Table.

Now the story tells that Lancelot, in the Saxons' prison, was in such a state that no one could encourage him to eat or drink, and all day long he grieved so bitterly that no one could comfort him. His head was empty of thought, and a rage and a madness arose so violently in his head that no one could withstand him, and he had inflicted two or three wounds on every one of his companions. So the jailer took him and put him in a room by himself; he could see clearly that Lancelot was genuinely mad, and he felt great pity for his prisoner. Galehaut begged the jailer to put the two of them together, but he was unwilling to do so, saying that the madman would kill him.

"Don't let that concern you, my friend," he said, "for it would be better for him to kill me than to leave me." But the jailer was wicked, and he refused to cooperate.

Word spread until the lady of the Rock heard of this and went to see for herself; she asked the jailer who he was, and he replied that the others said he had not a penny's worth of land. "Oh, dear," she said, "then it would be a mortal sin if we didn't let him go. Open the lower gate for him."

That was the gate on the side toward King Arthur's men, in the slope of the Rock, just above the water. But there was another gate that was closed by enchantment, for there was nothing to close it except the air; all those who saw it thought one could enter there unhindered, but no one could enter except the people of the castle: they went in and out as often as they liked, by the power of the enchantment. Through this postern the people of the castle sallied forth to attack the army many times in rapid succession, and as soon as they could set foot back inside, they had nothing to fear from the whole army.

Galehaut heard the news that Lancelot had been freed, and his grief was so great that he was nearly out of his mind, and in such a state that he could neither eat nor drink. Lancelot returned to the camp, but everyone feared him and fled before him because of the wonders he had performed. At length he came before the queen's lodgings, and she was watching from the windows.

When she saw him, she fainted, for everyone was following him, as they do a man who is out of his mind. When she recovered from her faint, she told the lady of Malehaut, who was holding her in her arms, that she was about to die.

"My lady," she exclaimed, "what has happened to you?" And the queen told her. "Ah, my lady, for God's sake, we must hide him, for it may be that he is feigning madness in order to see us, and if he is really out of his mind, we will hold him until he is cured."

The queen sent her to him and then rushed into a room, for she feared she would faint because of him. But when she was there, she could not stay, but came back out in order to see him. The lady of Malehaut went to him and was about to take him by the hand, but he ran to get some stones to throw at her, and she began to scream. The queen cried out to him, and as soon as he heard her he sat down and put both hands before his eyes like one ashamed; he was unwilling to get up for anyone, and the lady of Malehaut dared not go forward. Then Queen Guenevere came out, took him by the hand, and ordered him to rise. He rose at once and she led him to an upper room. The ladies-in-waiting asked who he was, and some said he was one of the best knights in the world, but none could make him be calm except the queen. As soon as she ordered him to be calm, he no longer moved, and everyone marveled at her power over him. Then she sent for Lionel and he came, but he could do nothing: whenever he touched him, Lancelot attacked him, and so the queen did not leave his side.

So Lancelot stayed in that room and lay before the queen. Every night she had all candles and torches extinguished, because the light, she said, caused him great harm; then she shared her bed with him, and grieved so bitterly all night that it was a wonder how she could go on. And everyone believed it was actually for the king.

In this way the queen's grief and Lancelot's madness went on for a long time, until one day the Saxons attacked the camp and there was great fighting between the two sides. Lancelot, who had not slept for nine nights, was sleeping at last, and the queen was overjoyed. She rose as quietly as she could and saw the two armies joining in battle. She immediately fainted, and the lady of Malehaut again took her in her arms. When she had recovered from her faint, her friend blamed her severely, saying, "My lady, why do you torment yourself?"

"God help me," she replied, "I am right to do so, for I see everyone dead, and I must surely die afterward."

Then she grieved so bitterly that no one could comfort her or calm her down; she came back to Lancelot and fainted as soon as she saw him. When she had recovered, she said, "O flower of the world's knighthood, what a great pity that you're not as well as you were just a short while ago! How quickly this mortal combat would now be brought to an end!"

When he heard her lamenting his feats of arms, his jousting, and his swordsmanship, he leapt up and saw, hanging at the other end of the room, the shield that the maiden from the Lake had brought to the queen. He thrust out his hands and grabbed it, slung the guige round his neck and shoved his arm through the straps. In a bracket there was also a lance, old and sooty; he ran to it and grabbed it, then turned to a round stone pillar and struck it so violently with the lance that the head was completely shattered. When he had done this, he was so weak he could no longer stand, but fell down and lost consciousness. And when he recovered, he asked where he was, and they told him he was in the house of King Arthur and Queen Guenevere. When he heard this, he fainted again. And when he recovered, the queen asked him how he had felt that day; he replied by asking her where his lord and Sir Gawain were, and they told him they were imprisoned in the Rock.

"Oh God," he cried, "why am I not there too? It would be much better for me to die with them than here, since my lady is not here!"

Then the queen saw that he had regained his senses; she took him gently in her arms and said, "Dear friend, here I am."

He immediately opened his eyes, recognized her, and said, "My lady, now let her come whenever she likes, since you are here!" All the ladies wondered whom he was speaking of, and he said it was Death.

Then the queen said to him, "Dear friend, do you know me?"

"Yes, my lady."

"And do you know," she asked, "how you were imprisoned in the Rock?"

"My lady, the prison of the Rock was fatal to me, for I never ate or drank for as long as I was there."

And the ladies all began to weep.

"Dear friend," said the lady of Malehaut, "do you know me?"

"My lady, I know you very well, for you did me great harm and treated me with great honor."

Then all knew for certain that he was cured. They asked him how he felt and what pain he had had; he answered that he did not know, but that he could not stand up again, try as he might. Then he looked and saw the shield he bore and said, "Oh God, who put this shield on me? Take it off, for it torments me!"

They took it off, but as soon as they had done so, he jumped up and was as mad as before, and he ran off down the hall. When the queen saw this, she fainted and lay unconscious so long that all her ladies were badly frightened.

While the queen lay in her faint, a very tall and very beautiful lady arrived. She was dressed in silk as white as snow, and she was followed by other ladies, three knights, and some ten squires. The lady and her attendants went up to the queen's chambers. The queen had recovered from her faint and heard the noise of people saying "Welcome, my lady." She dried her eyes and went to meet her visitor, embraced her, and told her she was welcome. They sat down on a couch and began to converse together.

The doors to the great chamber were closed on Lancelot, and his attacks of madness resumed and he began to tear down the doors. No one was bold enough to open them to him. The visitor asked what was happening, and the queen sighed and was unable to keep the tears from welling in her eyes. She replied that this was a knight who deserved great pity, for he was one of the best knights in the world, but he had now fallen into such a great madness that no one could stand against him.

"Oh, my lady," she said, "open the door and let me see him."

"Oh, my lady," replied the queen, "he is now more violent than he ever was," and she told her how he had regained his senses not long before, and how he had gone mad again as soon as the shield had been removed from him.

"My lady," said the visitor, "have the door opened, for I would very much like to see him."

Then the queen had the door opened, and Lancelot was about to rush out but the lady took him by the hand and spoke to him, using the name she had used when she raised him in the lake, for this was she who had raised him in the lake, and she had called him "Fair Foundling." As soon as she had spoken this name, he stopped and was deeply ashamed. Then she asked for the shield, and it was brought to her. "Ah," she said, "dear friend, you have so distressed me that I have come from far away to deliver you." Then she placed the shield upon him; he accepted whatever she did, and as soon as she had placed the shield upon him, he regained his senses. Then she took him and made him lie down upon a couch; he recognized her and began to weep most bitterly, and the queen was sorely puzzled as to who she could be.

When he had regained his senses, he saw the shield upon him and he said, "Oh, my lady, remove this shield, for it torments me!"

"No, I won't," she replied, "nor will it be removed as long as I wish it to remain." Then she called one of her attendants and had her get a very precious ointment from one of her jewel cases. She took it and anointed him on both arms, both temples, his forehead, and on top of the skull. As soon as she had done that, he fell asleep.

The lady returned to the queen and told her, "My lady, I'll now be on my way and commend you to God. Take care that this knight is not awakened; let him sleep as long as he wishes. When he awakens by himself, let a bath be prepared and have him get into it; then he'll be completely cured. And see that he carries no other shield than this one, for as long as he can hold out in battle."

"Oh, my lady," said the queen, "tell me who you are, for I have the impression you're well acquainted with this knight, since you came from distant lands by long days' journeys in order to cure him."

"Indeed, my lady, I should be well acquainted with him, since I raised him in his great poverty, when he had lost his father and his mother. With God's help I raised him until he became a tall, handsome young man; then I brought him to court and persuaded King Arthur to make him a knight."

When the queen heard this, she ran to embrace her, saying, "Oh, my lady,

welcome! Now I believe I know who you are: you are the Lady of the Lake."
And she replied that this was true. "Dear friend," said the queen, "I beg you to
remain here awhile, to please me and in order to cure our knight, for I owe
you my love, and you are the lady I must most honor in all the world. Be assured that my love for you could be no greater, for you have rendered me the
greatest service possible by sending me that shield. I have tested it so thoroughly that I know that everything you said concerning it is true."

"My lady," said the Lady of the Lake, "be assured that you will see still
greater wonders concerning that shield than you have seen thus far, for I knew
in advance what has happened, and for that reason I sent it to you, knowing
full well that I could send it to no one else who would hold it so dear. And I
must tell you that because of the great prowess that was to manifest itself in
this knight, I raised him until he became a knight, tall and handsome as you
saw him at court. And he never knew who he was; rather I concealed his identity because of a knight whom I loved more than any man alive,[14] fearing that,
if he found out, he would get the wrong idea, and so I spread the word that the
young man was my nephew. And now when I have returned, I'll say that I
came to free King Arthur from prison; he *will* be freed within a week, and I
can tell you that this is the one who will free him. But see that he carries no
other shield than this one, for you'll find in it everything my maiden told you
when she brought it to you at Quimper-Corentin.[15]

"But I sent you one message through her that I later regretted and that
gave me great sorrow, and I feared it would distress you, for I said that I was
the lady who knew more about your thoughts and shared them most fully, for
I loved the same person you did.[16] But be assured that my love for him is only
that of a mother for her child, and I love you for his sake. Now I will be on my
way, but I'll tell you one thing, because my love for you is great. I beg you to
keep, to hold fast, and to love above all others him who loves you above all
others, and cast off all pride toward him, for he neither desires nor esteems
anything except you. The sins of the world cannot be pursued without folly,
but one defeats his folly who finds right and honor in it. And if you can find
folly in your loves, this folly is to be honored above all others, for you love
the lord and the flower of the whole world. You can boast that no woman was
ever able to do what you can do, for you are the companion of the worthiest
gentleman and the lady of the best knight in the world, and in your newfound
power you have gained much, for first you have won him, the flower of all
knights, and then you have won me, whatever I might be able to do.

"But now I must depart, for I can delay no longer. Be assured that the

---

[14]This knight was not mentioned when the Lady of the Lake took Lancelot to her
"aquatic" abode, but he was mentioned elsewhere, and once it will be said that she had
married this knight.

[15]See Chapter 8.

[16]This is a near echo of the maiden's speech in Chapter 8.

greatest power in the world draws me away, the power of love, for I love a knight who doesn't know where I am, though his brother came here with me. Yet I'm not afraid of his becoming angry with me as long as that is what I wish. But one must take great care not to distress the person one loves as much as oneself, for one is not truly loved who is not loved above all earthly things. And a person who is in love can have no joy except from the one he loves, and therefore one must love the person from whom all joy comes."

They spoke together at great length until vespers drew near, becoming well acquainted and offering each other their service, but at length the queen could no longer detain the lady. When she saw that such was the situation, the queen dared not further beseech her to stay; they commended each other to God, and the Lady of the Lake and her retinue mounted and departed. The queen was now happier than she had been for a long time; she returned to Lancelot and did not stir from his side until he awoke.

When he awoke he complained bitterly. She asked him how he felt, and he replied, "I am well, but I'm extremely weak and I don't know why." Until he was fully restored to health, she did not wish to tell him how he had been ill. The bath was prepared, and they placed him in it and did everything ladies can do for the comfort of a sick knight, until he recovered fully and regained his beauty and his strength.

Then they told him how he had been out of his mind and how no one but the queen could stand against him. "And the lady who raised you, the Lady of the Lake," said the queen, "was here, and had she not been, you would never have been cured."

He replied that he thought as much and that he had seen her, "but I thought I had dreamt it."

Then the queen began to smile broadly, and he was greatly taken aback and embarrassed, for he was now certain they had seen his disgraceful behavior, and he feared the person he most loved in all the world would love him less as a result. But there was no need, for she had no power to do so. When he lamented to her, she comforted and reassured him, saying, "Don't be concerned, dear friend, for—may God truly help me—you are more my master and more certain of me than I am of you, and so you should be, for I haven't taken this upon myself for the present alone, but for all the days that my soul remains within my body."

Now Lancelot was restored to health and had whatever he requested; he had his share of every joy a lover may have, and that is all the story reveals to you. He spent a week and a day in this fashion, and by then he was so handsome that it was a wonder to behold. And the queen was so in love with him that she did not see how she could ever live without seeing him. It grieved her to see him so impetuous and so courageous, for she did not see how she could go on living without him, if he ever left court: she would have preferred there to be a little less boldness and less prowess in him.

[The Irish and Saxons again attacked, and Lancelot, distinguishing himself in battle, repelled the enemy. Then he freed Arthur, Gawain, Hector, and Galehaut.]

So the Rock was captured, and the king and a great number of his men were inside. And Sir Gawain came forth from the tower and said to the king, "My lord, you will lose Lancelot, if you don't take care, for Galehaut will take him away as soon as he can; he is more jealous of him than any knight is of a young lady. But I'll tell you what to do: order the gate to be closed, so that no one can go out except with my permission, and make me swear to this, and Kay the Seneschal and Sir Yvain and my brother Guerrehet, and we will have such a company that no one will be able to get in or out."

Then the king came to Galehaut and took him by one hand and Lancelot by the other, led them to the great tower, and had them disarm; then they sat down upon a couch. The king then summoned Sir Gawain and had him swear the oath, and then Sir Yvain, Kay, and Guerrehet. When Galehaut heard this, he knew precisely why it was being done, and he gave a sigh of anguish from his heart. Then he said to Lancelot, "My dear companion, we have reached the point where I will lose you, for I know for certain that the king will ask you to remain in his household. And what shall I do, who have completely devoted my heart and soul to you?"

"Truly, my lord," said Lancelot, "I must love you more than any man in the world, and so I do, and, God willing, I'll never be a member of the king's household, if I'm not forced to do so. But how can I refuse anything my lady may command?"

"I would not force you to go that far," replied Galehaut, "for if she wills it, then so it must be without any opposition."

So the two of them spoke together. And the king resumed conversation with them, and they put on a show of greater joy than they felt in their hearts. The king sent for the queen, and she came most joyfully. When she entered the tower, each one jumped up to greet her, but she left all the others and threw her arms around Lancelot's neck and kissed him in front of all those present, because she wanted to deceive them all, that no one might suspect the truth of what was between them. No one saw this who did not the more esteem her, but Lancelot was deeply embarrassed. She said to him, "Sir knight, I don't know who you are; this grieves me, and I don't know what to offer you. For the love of my lord the king, and for my honor which you have today upheld, I grant you my love and myself, as a loyal lady must reward a loyal knight."

When the king heard her speak in this manner, he esteemed her highly because she had done so without specific instructions. Then in turn she rejoiced over Sir Gawain, Galehaut, and all the companions of the quest, for all had come except Sagremor. Many questions were asked about him, and Sir Gawain related how he had left him with a maiden with whom he was in love.

Afterward, the queen related how Lancelot had been cured of madness in her chambers, and how a lady called the Lady of the Lake had cured him.

"My lady," said the king, "do you know who this knight is?" She replied that she did not. "Then know that he is Lancelot of the Lake, he who carried the day in the two battles between Galehaut and me."

When the queen heard this, she pretended this was a source of great astonishment, and she crossed herself repeatedly. After this Sir Yvain related the wondrous feats of arms Lancelot had performed all that day. "My lord, my lord, we believed that not all the knights had come to the battle, and she sent him to us all alone, saying that she was sending us enough help to take the place of the two hundred knights who were at Arestel. In this my lady spoke the truth, for so help me God, if the two hundred had been there without him, we would never have accomplished what we have now accomplished, and never would the Saxons have been captured by the two hundred, the way they were by him alone."

"Upon my word," said the king, "he has performed more feats of arms in rescuing me than in all his other acts of prowess, for he captured such a castle as this, which was doing me more harm than all the other castles in the world, and I must love him above all men."

Next Hector came before the queen and said, "My lady, here is the object of my quest," indicating Sir Gawain. The queen thanked him and rejoiced over him, and Sir Yvain showed him great honor by relating how Hector had delivered Sagremor and himself from the prison of the King of the Hundred Knights and how he had defeated the seneschal. And Sir Gawain related how Hector had unhorsed Kay and Sagremor and Girflet and Sir Yvain at the Spring of the Pine. Then there were many who looked at him, for he was richly praised, and his ladylove was overjoyed above all the others.

Then the meal was prepared, and they sat down. When they had eaten, the king summoned the queen and in private said to her, "My lady, I wish to ask Lancelot to remain with me and to be a companion of the Round Table, for his great prowess has been amply demonstrated. So if he does not wish to stay for my sake, throw yourself at his feet."

"My lord," she replied, "he is pledged to Galehaut and is his companion, so it would be well that you beg Galehaut to allow it."

Then the king went to Galehaut and earnestly begged him to allow Lancelot to join his household and to remain with him as his lord and companion.

"Ah, my lord," said Galehaut, "I did all I could to help you in your time of need, and that is all I can do. God help me, I couldn't live without him; you would take my life from me." He said this because he did not believe the queen would blame him.

Then the king looked at her, and said, "My lady, beseech him."

She immediately threw herself upon her knees. When Lancelot saw her on her knees, his heart was deeply troubled; he did not wait for Galehaut's permission, but leapt up and said, "Ah, my lady, I will stay with my lord the king according to his pleasure and yours." And he raised her up.

"My lord," she said, "many thanks."

"My lord," said Galehaut, "you won't have him in this way! I prefer to be poor and happy instead of rich and miserable. Retain me with him, if ever I did anything that pleased you; you must do this for me and for him, for I must tell you that all the love I bear you comes to you because of him."

Then the king leapt to his feet, thanked him, and said that he did not retain them as his knights, but as his companions and his masters.

In this way the king retained Lancelot and Galehaut and then Hector as his companions, and in honor of the two of them the joy was so great in the king's household that greater joy could not be described. And the king declared that he wished to hold high court the next day in the Rock itself, to celebrate Lancelot: it was noble and splendid, and that was the seventh day preceding All Saints' Day, and every day of that week he wore his crown, and every day the court was larger and more splendid. On All Saints' Day the three knights were seated at the Round Table, and the scribes who recorded the deeds of the companions of King Arthur's household were summoned. There were four of them: the first was named Arodian of Cologne, the second Tantalides of Vercelli, the third Thomas of Toledo, and the fourth Sapient of Baghdad. These four wrote down all the feats of arms of King Arthur's companions, and otherwise their great deeds would never have been known. First of all they wrote down the adventures of Sir Gawain, because that was the beginning of the quest for Lancelot, and then those of Hector, because they formed a branch of that story, and then the adventures of all the other eighteen companions. All this was the story of Lancelot, and all these others were branches thereof. And the story of Lancelot formed a branch of the story of the Grail, when it was integrated into it.

The king and his company continued this rejoicing every day of the celebration, which lasted until two days beyond All Saints' Day, and then he left the Rock, leaving a contingent of guards behind, and set out at a leisurely pace on the journey back toward Britain. When the king reached Carlion, Galehaut took leave of him and begged him to let him take Lancelot with him to his homeland. Very reluctantly the king granted this, but the queen agreed, telling him that they would soon be in Advent. She succeeded in persuading the king, on condition that they solemnly promise to come to him on Christmas Day. He told them he would be staying in the city where he had knighted Lancelot.[17] In this way Galehaut and Lancelot departed and headed for their land. And the king and his company returned by easy stages to Britain.

---

[17] This was Camelot.

Part III

TRANSLATED BY SAMUEL N. ROSENBERG

13. The Nobility of Galehaut.

Now, riding away with his companion, Galehaut was both happy and unhappy: happy that he had his companion with him and unhappy that he had
become part of King Arthur's household, for he was sure that he would
thereby lose him forever. And he had given him his heart with a love greater
than loyal companionship alone could make a man feel for someone outside
his family. But no proof of this is needed here, for in the end, as our story will
go on to show, it was clear that the grief it caused him swept away all joy and
brought him death. But his death ought not be spoken of at this point, for the
death of such a worthy man as Galehaut is not a thing to bring up before its
time. And all the stories that speak of him agree that he was in every way the
most valiant of all great princes, after King Arthur, with whom no man living
in those years can be compared.

Nevertheless, the book of Tantalides of Vercelli, which speaks of Galehaut's exploits more than any other, claims that even King Arthur was not
more valiant by much and, if Galehaut had been able to live out a full life with
all the robust courage that he had when he went to war against King Arthur,
he would have outdone all those who themselves had outdone all others. He
himself confided as much to Lancelot, saying that when the war began, he
was set on conquering the world; and that was quite plain, as he was a knight
at the age of twenty-five and then conquered twenty-eight kingdoms and at
the age of thirty-nine was dead. But Lancelot held him back from these ambi-
tions, as was clear when Galehaut turned his great honor into his great shame
by begging King Arthur's mercy at the very time he had the upper hand,[18] and

---

[18]See Chapter 7.

again, after that great moment, when the two men of his clan closest to him, once he had crowned them kings, rebuked him in private for the shameful peace he had made for the sake of a single man.

Then Galehaut answered, saying that that had brought him greater gain and greater honor than ever, "for riches," he said, "lie not in land or goods but in worthy men, and land does not produce good men, but good men make land productive; and a truly rich man must always strive to have what no one else has." In this way, Galehaut saw wisdom and gain where others saw loss and folly, and no one would have dared make bold to love good knights so much as he.

[*Galehaut had disturbing dreams, one of them involving a serpent, the other a leopard. He and Lancelot returned to Sorelois, where all the castles were crumbling; Galehaut sent a messenger to ask Arthur to send him the wisest men in his land.*]

14. Guenevere Is Accused of Imposture.

Now the story says that King Arthur was at that time staying at Camelot. When Galehaut's messenger brought the letter, the king was very glad to receive it, and the queen and the lady of Malehaut were more pleased than anyone else. But it did not take long for their delight to give way to great alarm, for once the man had given all his news to the king, a young lady arrived at court and walked boldly up to the king as he was sitting with his knights; and there was a great escort behind her, more than thirty knights and men-at-arms making up her party. The damsel was very beautiful; she came before the king smartly dressed in tunic and cloak of rich silk cloth and wearing her hair in one long, thick braid, lustrous and light. Seeing her come along, the knights made way, and no baron, however noble, failed to leap to his feet; everyone who saw her was sure that she was the most noble lady in the world.

When she came before the king, she pulled off the wimple still covering her head and threw it to the ground, and there was no dearth of men to pick it up, since she was surrounded by the people in her large retinue and others as well. The wimple removed, they were all amazed by her great beauty, and she spoke loudly enough for them all to hear as she said boldly, "God save King Arthur and his knights (saving the honor and the rights of my lady)—King Arthur, worthiest man in the world if not for just one thing!"

"My lady," said the king, "whatever I am, God grant you good fortune! As for the honor and the rights of your lady, I want them to be safe, wherever she may be. Now, though, I would be grateful to you for telling me what failing I have that keeps me from being the worthiest man in the world. After that, you can tell me who your lady is and how I may have wronged her, though I don't think I have ever misbehaved toward any lady young or old, nor would I ever want to."

"King," she said, "if I were not able to make you see both my lady's rights and the failing that keeps you from perfection, I would have had no reason to come to your court. But I have not come without a reason. Indeed, I am here because of the strangest and most extraordinary thing ever to have happened in your household. Like you, your people will be more shocked by it, once they've learned the truth, than by anything else they have ever heard. First, let me tell you that the name of the lady who has sent me to you is Queen Guenevere, daughter of King Leodagan. But before I disclose what rights she claims, I must give you a letter I have here, sealed with her seal; it is meant to be read aloud in front of all your barons."

The young lady looked around, and an old, white-haired knight sprang forward. He handed her a very handsome box sparkling with gold and precious stones. She took the box and opened it, then took out a letter hung with a gold seal and said, "My lord, have this letter read aloud as I have stated, but with the understanding that it will be heard by every lady and maiden at this court; I have a right to ask that. A letter as important as this must not be read in private. You see, even if the largest court that you have ever held were brought together here, there would be no person too insensitive to be shocked by it. You would do well, then, to take up this extraordinary matter with a large group of worthy men."

The king stared dumbfounded at the young woman speaking so boldly, and all those with him were just as stunned.

He sent right away for the queen and all the ladies and maidens scattered through the rooms, and sent a crier through all quarters to make sure that every knight and man-at-arms came to court forthwith to hear the strange news. Once they were all gathered, the young lady spoke and asked the king to have her letter read. He handed it to the clerk whom he knew to be the best spoken and the most learnèd of all. The man unfolded the parchment and, scanning the letter from top to bottom, was so alarmed that the tears of his eyes ran down his face and fell onto his chest. The king stared at him with greater wonder than he had felt before, and everyone there was frightened by the sight.

"Speak!" said the king. "I am more eager to hear this letter than I've ever been."

The clerk looked at the queen, who was leaning against the shoulder of Sir Gawain, and when he saw her, his whole heart turned cold with anguish and locked so tight inside his chest that even to save his life he could not have uttered a word; and he began to totter.

Sir Yvain, who was very kind and gracious, saw what was happening and thought he had detected some threat to the king in the letter; he jumped forward to catch him, and the man fainted in his arms. That astonished the king and made him wonder what the news could possibly be. He sent at once for another reader and handed him the letter. This one scanned it too and broke into sighs and bitter tears; he dropped the letter onto the king's lap and turned away in utter grief. Walking past the queen, he said, "Ah, my lady! my lady! It's such woeful news!"

Thereupon he flung himself into another room and grieved more bitterly than he had ever done. The queen was dumbfounded.

The king could hardly take the matter lightly. He sent for his chaplain and, as soon as he appeared, said to him, "Sir chaplain, read me this letter. I urge you, by the faith you owe me and by the Mass that you have sung today, to tell me whatever you find in it and not hide a thing."

The chaplain took the letter and, when he had scanned it all, sighed deeply and said to the king, "My lord, am I to read this letter aloud?"

"Yes," said the king, "you are."

"The truth is," said the chaplain, "I am very sorry, because what I have to say will grieve and anger all the members of your court. If it were possible, I would ask you to please have someone else read the letter, but you have called on me to do it and I mustn't stand back."

"My lord," said the king, "you have no choice."

The chaplain, speaking loudly enough for the whole court to hear him, began. "My lord," he said, "Queen Guenevere, daughter of King Leodagan, greets King Arthur, as is proper for her to do, together with his whole company of barons and knights. King Arthur, I am hereby lodging a complaint first against you and then against all your barons. I want everyone to know that you have behaved disloyally toward me, while I have behaved loyally toward you. Indeed, you do not deserve to be king, for it is not proper that a king should live with a concubine, as you do. The truth is plain: I was joined to you as wife in true wedlock, anointed and crowned as queen and consort of the kingdom of Logres in the church of Saint Stephen the Martyr in the city of Logres, the head city of your realm.

"But that high honor lasted only a short while, for I was queen but a day and a night and was then taken away and cast out, either by your doing or someone else's. Then in my place was put the woman who was my maid and servant, the very Guenevere you hold to be your wife and queen. She sought my death and destitution, whereas she should have been ready to sacrifice her own self in order to save me. But God, who never once forgets those who wait upon His mercy, sent me a deliverer to whom I owe greater love than anyone else in the world. And though once banished and disinherited, I am now, by God's mercy, restored to my position and my inheritance. So I ask you, out of loyalty and for the sake of right, that, by the judgment and finding of your court, this act of disloyalty be avenged and the woman who has kept you so long in mortal sin be made to suffer torment and die, just as she wanted to make me die.

"That is what I want my letter to make known to you. But inasmuch as in the writing I could not recall every single thing that might have some bearing, I am sending you my first cousin, Clice, the bearer of the letter, to be my heart and my tongue. I urge you to trust whatever she tells you in my behalf, since she knows as much about my troubles as I do, and what she knows she knows properly. Together with her is a man who is even more to be trusted than she is or I: Bertelay the Old, the staunchest knight of his age in all the British Isles."

With that, the chaplain stopped speaking; he handed the letter to the king and walked away downcast and dismayed. The king was dumbfounded by the news; all the others present were stunned and mute. Then the king looked at the young lady who stood before him, and said, "My lady, I have now heard your mistress's message, and if the letter was not read well, you can now make clear whatever is not so, for it seems you bear the heart and tongue of your lady. As for the knight, I would gladly meet the knight who is the staunchest and the most renowned in the world."

At that, the damsel stepped back, took the hand of the knight who had given her the letter, and led him up to the king, saying, "My lord, here is the knight whom my lady sends you to bear witness and to defend her cause."

The king looked at the knight, who struck him as quite old, for his hair was grey and white, and his face pale and lined and covered with scars, and his beard hung down onto his chest. Yet he had long arms and well-shaped shoulders; all his limbs were in fact so well made that you could not have imagined better. He was remarkably tall and robust and stood bolt upright and was more impressive than you could have expected such an old man to be.

"I must say, my lady," said the king, "this man is so remarkably advanced in age that he could surely never be involved in anything disloyal or treacherous."

"My lord," said the young lady, "you would say that even if you knew him well. But there is no need here for any proof of his worthiness, for God can tell easily enough who is a good man. But let me tell you what the letter doesn't speak of: the message that my lady sends through me. I believe you have understood that my lady's complaint is that you should be a loyal husband but are not. It is well known that, when you were crowned king of Britain, news came to you of King Leodagan of Carmelide, who was at that time the most valorous man in the world; he was at home on all the islands of the West and best maintained his knights in high esteem and in great honor.

"My lord the king's renown was great, but it was surpassed by what you heard of the great beauty and virtue of my lady his daughter, who was rightly the most esteemed of all young women. You said that you would not rest until you had seen why the king and his daughter were so admired in all lands. You left your land in the care of others and traveled to the kingdom of Carmelide disguised as a squire, as were the knights traveling with you. There you served my lord the king from Christmas to Pentecost, and that day you carved the peacock at the Round Table and earned the praise of the hundred fifty knights who sat there. Each was served his fill, and you thereby gained the most worthy lady alive, my lady the queen. And my lord the king gave you the noblest wedding gift ever given, the Round Table, which is honored by so many men of valor.

"After that, you took my lady to Logres, your city, and there she was wed, as the letter recounts, and that night you went to bed with her. But when you rose to go to the privy, my lady was betrayed and tricked and thrown out by the very people she trusted the most, and from then on you were coupled with that lady I see there for whom I have such dislike, that Guenevere who betrayed her mistress and threw her into prison and thinks she was killed there! But inasmuch as God was unwilling that the betrayal remain hidden, it has now come out in front of her. My lady, you see, escaped from prison by the will of God and with the help of this knight here; he became a robber for her sake and risked death to carry her out of the tower on his shoulders, which was very dangerous.

"Thus my lady was a long while in captivity, together with her attendants, until, thank God, her barons freed her and gave her back her land and her inheritance. If my lady wished, she could be married very handsomely, as no man under heaven, however highborn, would be stopped by birth or office from accepting her. But her feeling is that, if she loses you who are meant to be her true husband, she will give up wedlock altogether, for it seems to her that she would make no man a good wife but you, and you no woman a good husband but her; and if you were together, you would be a couple without peer, you the most worthy king and she the most worthy queen. That is why my lady urges you to acknowledge the faithful bond that you promised when you wed her, and to satisfy her claim against the woman who sought her doom and whom you have kept against God's will.

"If you do not agree, my lady forbids you, in God's name as in her own and her clan's, to keep from this time forward the noble gift that you received with her hand, that is, the Round Table. Send it back to her as well endowed with knights as when you received it, and take care that no Round Table ever again stand in your house, because it is such a lofty thing that there must not be more than one in all the world.

"To you, my lords called Knights of the Round Table, I say that you must give up that name until it is rightfully conferred on those who deserve the honor, for you might well come to such a pass that the proudest among you would be hard pressed to merit it.

"And you, my lord," she said to the king, "if you or any other person in your house should claim that my lady was not betrayed as you have just heard, I am ready to prove it either in your court or in another, right now or at some fixed time. The evidence will not be a bundle of lies or furnished without a trustworthy witness, but presented by a knight who heard and saw the whole affair. And whoever wants to gainsay him will have to know equally well the cause he tries to defend, for in so important a matter as this, that is how evidence and challenge must be treated."

When the young lady finished speaking, no one uttered a word, and the king was dumbfounded. He gazed upward and crossed himself again and again, astonished at what he had just heard. He was so distressed and so shamed by the damsel's charge that he almost took leave of his senses, and the look on his face made it plain that his heart was in turmoil.

"My lady," he said to the queen, "come forward. It is only right that we should hear you speak. Clear yourself! So help me God, if this young woman's accusation is true, you are more deserving of death than all other women who have ever sinned, and you have gulled us all into thinking you the most valiant lady in the world. You would be the falsest and the most disloyal, if it turned out true!"

At that, the queen stood up, showing no hint of fear, and the king and counts and other lords started toward her. But Sir Gawain stepped in front of her, his switch in hand and so overwrought with anger that it seemed red blood was about to gush from his face.

As the queen remained standing before the king, Sir Gawain took it upon himself to speak, saying to the young woman who had brought the news, "My lady, we want to know if your charge is made against my lady the queen, here present."

She answered, "Not against the queen, as I see no queen here, but against that lady over there, who betrayed her mistress and mine!"

"My lady is innocent, so help me God, of any betrayal," said Sir Gawain, "and she will be proven so! And I want you to know that you have almost driven me to behave as no other woman has ever made me do! If not for the shame it would bring to my lord even more than to me, I would make you realize that you have committed the greatest folly that you could have ever undertaken, for even if your story were sworn to by all the people in your country, it would still not be true!"

Sir Gawain went on, "My lord, here I am, ready to be my lady's champion against one knight or more, as you decide, and I am prepared to prove that she is not guilty of the betrayal she has been charged with, and that she is your wife and consort, rightly anointed and crowned as queen."

"That indeed sounds like a challenge, sir knight," said the young woman, "so it is only right that we should now be told your name."

He answered that his name was never hidden from any knight and certainly not from any maiden, and he said he was named Gawain.

That made the lady smile and say God keep him. "Now I feel better than before, knowing your name, because I know you to be such a noble knight and so loyal that you would not take the oath for the whole kingdom of Logres; and I know too that you would not for the whole world do battle after the oath. Still, many men receive more praise than they deserve, which is what I will soon see in whoever takes up the defense. Let anyone who does it beware! And even if you had more skill in battle than you have, you will soon be in hand-to-hand combat, if you dare take up the defense!"

Then the young lady took the hand of the knight named Bertelay the Old and led him up to the king, saying, "Bertelay, for your sake and your lady's, settle this matter in combat with Sir Gawain or another knight, if any there be bold enough to champion the accused against you!"

He fell to his knees in front of the king and offered to do battle, just as the young lady had said.

[*Neither Gawain nor others wanted to do battle with such an aged knight. Arthur then announced that he would convene court at Candlemas (February 2) and that the matter would be settled at that time.*]

15. Galehaut's Plans and the Interpretation of His Dreams: Lovesickness and Destiny.

Now the story says that Galehaut had been staying with his companion in the kingdom of Sorelois when the messenger came back from court and told him the news of the accusation that had been made against the queen. Hearing it, he felt both sorrow and joy: sorrow because he knew that Lancelot would feel sorrow and anger as soon as he heard the news, but joy because he could surely keep Lancelot with him for a longer time if the queen were separated from the king. Nevertheless, he forbade all his people to disclose the news to Lancelot, since he was very fearful of upsetting him. But it could not be kept from him for long, and indeed he heard it and was more deeply pained than he had ever in his life been.

He ran to Galehaut and, taking him by the hand, pulled him into a private room. It was plain, to look at his face, that he was sorely troubled, and Galehaut, seeing it in his expression, said, "My good, dear friend, what has upset you?"

"My lord," he said, "I've heard news that I think is going to kill me."

That was enough for Galehaut to know that he had heard the news of the queen, and he was deeply distressed, for he would gladly have kept it from him if at all possible. Nevertheless, he asked him what news he had heard, as if he did not know a thing. Lancelot repeated it to him from beginning to end, just as the event had occurred.

"Yes, my dear friend," said Galehaut, "I had known about it for a while but hadn't dared say anything to you; knowing your heart as I do, I was sure it would pain you deeply. Still, if there is anything you should welcome, it is the separation of the king and queen, for in that way you and she could be happy together for the rest of your lives."

"Oh, my lord," said Lancelot, "how could I rejoice over something that brings distress to my lady?"

"No," said Galehaut, "I don't mean that you could be happy if she were not; but she is as truthful in her heart as she is in appearance, and I know she would rather reign over a little kingdom with you than be queen of the whole world without you. And if you and she are willing, I will give the best advice that I can ever give. I can tell you this: that what has happened to you is better than what has ever befallen two lovers, and if you care to follow my advice and trust my plan, I will pull you through."

"There is no doubt," said Lancelot, "that I need help desperately; and whatever harm my lady suffers, I won't ever feel at ease unless she is at ease first."

"Listen then," said Galehaut, "how she can be helped if the king divorces her, which God forbid (though you should welcome it)! I will give her the finest and most prosperous kingdom in the whole land of Britain or in my holding—I mean this kingdom where we are; and I will assure her of it by taking an oath on holy relics the first time we see her. Then, if things happen as we've said, let her come here and be lady not only of Sorelois but of all the land of which I am lord. Then you could often be together and openly enjoy the contact that must now come late and in secret. And if you wanted to go on enjoying your happiness without blame or sin, you might marry; no one, in fact, could find you a better wife, nor could she wed a better knight. Well, that is my plan to make your love last forever."

"My lord," said Lancelot, "that is the plan I'd like best in the world, as long as it were as agreeable to my lady as to me. But there is a great danger that worries me very much: the king has sworn on holy relics to put her to death as soon as she has been found guilty. I am all ready, though, to see she doesn't die alone, please God in whose care I've put myself! And you, please help me, for His sake first and then for the sake of my lady, who has loved you so much, and in the name of the great love that you have devoted to me, that love so great that you let it cost you in one day the mastery of thirty kingdoms that you had as much as conquered."

With these words, he broke into tears and could say no more; he clasped his hands and fell to his knees in front of Galehaut. Galehaut, who could not bear what he was seeing, put his arms around him and raised him as his own tears flowed; and the two were so wracked by their common pain that they fell onto a couch and lay there in a faint for a long while.

When they came to, they went on with their grieving; but Galehaut, who was more mature and better able to control himself, tried to comfort Lancelot, saying, "My good, dear friend, be calm now and don't worry about anything we've spoken of. I will act as carefully as any mortal can; and anything you want will be done, whether it takes cunning or force, even if I have to lose all my lands, then all my kinsmen and even my own life.

"Now, you know for a truth that nothing matters to me more than you. You must reassure me, then, and make every effort you can to save my life; and if you're willing to do it, you will. Let me tell you how. It is true, and you know it, that I have done many things for you that people have deemed more shameful than honorable and more foolish than wise. But there is nothing that I would undo, for, as God is my witness, I have never done anything for you that I don't consider an honor and a gain, and I would give up all the lands under heaven rather than lose your companionship and your love. Indeed, if I can count on your commitment, I can easily overcome any woes; but if I lose you, I can only die.

"That is why, by God, I beg you to make every effort to preserve our love; and when you're with my lady the queen, urge her, as I've said, to let us stay together, and I will urge her, too. Besides, if you love each other at all, you should want to have her with you forever; and then we would all be together, never to part. Let me tell you, at the risk of upsetting you, I had thought of something I might do soon, though I have never in my life been guilty of villainy or treachery; but this I would have done, because fear of death and the strength of my love would have made me do it. I'll tell you what it would have been.

"I had planned that the first time King Arthur traveled toward this part of the country, I would ride as fast as possible, stopping neither by night nor day, to catch him unawares, before he could have any news of me. I would go into his household with a hundred of my best knights, while leaving the rest close by in the woods just in case I needed them; and the men with me would have their weapons hidden under their cloaks. Then I would carry off the queen without being recognized and bring her to this land. In that way I would have both you and your heart right here with me forever.

"But then I realized that such a breach of faith would be too vile and that, if it happened to make my lady angry, you would go out of your mind and surely die, for I know your heart well enough to know that nothing could kill you so easily as her anger."

Then Lancelot answered, "Good God, my lord! You would have killed me, if you had done that! A plan like that can't be carried out without her leave, because if it troubled her, I could never be happy."

"So help me God," said Galehaut, "I can't ever blame you for that. If I hadn't seen the harm it would do to you, I would have found it hard not to go ahead; in fact, no thought for anyone would have stopped me. And all the good I've ever done would have been wiped away by this one misdeed. But a heart that's sorely troubled often risks a great wrong to find some rest."

The two companions spoke at length of their woes, each comforting and reassuring the other as much as he could.

[*Galehaut convened the wise men sent by Arthur. They offered their interpretation of Galehaut's dreams; then one of them, Master Elias, asked to speak to Galehaut alone. Lancelot left the room.*]

Master Elias said to Galehaut in the chapel, "My lord, I believe you are one of the wisest princes of our time in the whole world and I am sure that, if you have behaved foolishly, it was more out of goodness of heart than lack of intelligence, so I'll give you a very useful little lesson: take care, as far as you can, never to say in front of any man or woman with whom you are in love anything that would trouble his or her heart, for everyone should do his utmost to keep anger and distress away from the one he loves. I say this because of the knight who has just left us. I know that you love him with all the love that can exist between two true companions, and would have wanted him to share in this discussion. But it would have been wrong, as he would have risked hearing words that would have burdened his heart with shame and sorrow, and he would perhaps have been more pained than you will be. Of course, you could never care less for his happiness or his welfare than he could, but you are more sensible and reasonable than he."

"Master," said Galehaut, "it seems you know him well, to judge by what you say."

"I do," he answered; "I think I know him, though not through any personal report save that I have heard the man who made peace between you and King Arthur is the finest knight alive. He is the leopard that appeared in your dream and in our findings."

"Master," said Galehaut, "is a lion not a prouder animal than a leopard, and more powerful?"

"Yes," he answered, "of course."

"Then I think," said Galehaut, "that the man who is the finest knight of all should look like a lion, not a leopard."

"By God," said Master Elias, "you are sharper than many another, and I will give you a reasonable answer that you can readily understand. I know quite well that he is truly the finest knight among those living now. But there will come one better than he, just as foretold by Merlin, who never makes a mistake."[19]

"Master," said Galehaut, "do you know his name?"

"I know nothing about his name," he answered; "I have not tried to learn it."

"Then how can you know," said Galehaut, "that there will be a finer knight?"

"It is clear to me," said Master Elias, "that the one who completes the

---

[19]The reference is to Lancelot's son, Galahad.

Adventures of Britain will be the finest knight in the world and will take the last seat at the Round Table; and his emblem will be the lion."

"But this fine knight that you speak of," said Galehaut, "do you know what his name will be?"

The other answered that he did not.

"Then I don't see," said Galehaut, "how you can know that my companion will not be the one to complete the Adventures of Britain."

"I know for a truth that that cannot happen," said Master Elias; "he is not fit to try the Adventure of the Grail or to complete the Adventures or to take the seat at the Round Table where no knight has ever sat without risking life and limb."

"But, master," said Galehaut, "what are you saying? There is no great knightly virtue that he doesn't have! And why do you say that he is not fit to try the Adventure of the Grail? Why, he has the daring to complete more than any other knight even dares to think about!"

"That is all to no avail," he answered, "and I'll tell you why. He cannot regain the qualities needed by the one who will complete the Adventure of the Grail. Above all, that man must be, from birth to death, so utterly virginal and chaste as never to feel love for a woman, married or not. For your companion it is too late, for I know more about what goes on his mind than you think."

Hearing that, Galehaut turned red with embarrassment and said, "By God, master, do you believe that the man who wins the seat at the Round Table will be a better knight than my companion in skill at arms?"

"I'll give you an answer to that," said Master Elias. "I well know that your knight is the finest of those now living and even of all who have ever lived in Great Britain; and I daresay no one could overcome him in hand-to-hand combat. But Merlin, who has never yet lied, tells us that out of the chamber of the Maimed King of the adventure-filled Waste Forest, on the edge of the kingdom of Lists, will come the wondrous beast that will astound the fields of the Great Mountain. This beast will be different from all other animals, for it will have the head and face of a lion, and the body and legs of an elephant; it will have the kidneys[20] and navel of an untouched maiden, and a heart of hard, dense steel that will be proof against swaying or softening; and it will have the speech of a serious woman and the will to make right judgments.

"That is what the beast will look like, and all others will make way for it and welcome it gladly. Then the Adventures of Great Britain and the perilous wonders will come to an end. In all of this you can glimpse the knight who will complete the Adventures. Through this beast you can understand that no man will be his equal in pride, since no animal has so proud a look as the lion.

---

[20]"kidneys": that is, the sensuality.

The body lets you know that no other man could bear the burden of arms that he will bear, since no other animal has the strength of the elephant. The kidneys and the navel let you know that he will be a virgin and chaste, just like an untouched maiden. The heart tells you that more than any other man he will be bold and venturous, free of cowardice and fear; and like the serious woman, he will be spare of speech. You may well understand that his exploits will hardly resemble those of other valorous knights."

"Yes," said Galehaut, "he will be of truly great prowess if his exploits are greater than my companion's; and I never thought that anyone could be better than my companion! But tell me now if you know any prophecy about that good knight."

"Yes," he said. "Merlin said that from the king who would die of grief and his sorrowful queen would come forth an extraordinary leopard who would be fierce and bold and brave, spirited and gay, and he would show greater pride than all animals in Britain who had shown pride before him, and he would be more warmhearted and sought-after than any others. If you know who fathered the knight who has just left this room, then you can easily understand that the prophecy is about him, as he has made it clear that he is better than all the men of Britain who have borne arms before him."

"I know for a fact," said Galehaut, "that his father was king of Benoic and died of grief and that his mother had all the sorrow of a woman who in one day lost her land, the king her husband, and her son still in his cradle. What I also know is that this knight is the most charming and warmhearted and sought-after of men, and that his deeds of arms are such that he deserves to be called the leopard of knights. You know much more about him than I thought, and I see that you are the flower of all learnèd men, just as gold is the flower of all metals."

"Furthermore," Master Elias went on, "I find something in the prophecies of Master Marabon,[21] who lived before there were Christians in Great Britain and who said, 'If the leopard does not have weak kidneys,[22] he will surpass all other earthly beasts, lions as well as the rest.' I know that this prophecy concerned your companion and that if he had kept himself pure, the whole world would have marveled at his feats."

Galehaut was downcast and lost in thought. Master Elias went on, "Do you know," he said, "what Merlin said before the Lady of the Lake had come to know him? He said that from the prideful leopard and the line of Jerusalem would come forth the lion feared above all other animals, and the lion would sprout wings that would cover the world. That's what Merlin said, and I certainly do not see who that leopard could be, except your knight."

---

[21]The prophecies of Master Marabon are apparently an invention of the writer.
[22]That is, if he does not succumb to sensuality.

"By God, master," said Galehaut, "he could well be the one! But tell me something else from the prophecies of Merlin—I am listening very gladly; tell me if there is any prophecy that touches on me."

"Yes," he answered. "Merlin tells us that from the Islands of Jedares, from the home of the Fair Lady,[23] a wondrous dragon will break forth and go flying left and right over all countries, and wherever he appears everyone will tremble before him. The dragon will fly on to the Adventurous Kingdom, and there he will have grown large and massive and have thirty heads of gold, each finer and more splendid than his original head. Merlin said that there he would be so large that the whole land would darken under the shadow of his body and his wings. He would reach the Adventurous Kingdom after having conquered almost everything, but the wondrous leopard would stop him and push him back and put him at the mercy of those he had just been so close to defeating. Afterwards, the two would love each other to the point of considering themselves a single thing, each unable to live without the other; but the golden-headed serpent would come draw the leopard away and take him from his companion and besot his mind. Merlin says that this is how the great dragon will die. I know for a truth that you are the dragon, and the serpent who will take the knight away from you is my lady the queen, who loves or will love him as much as a lady can love a knight. But you know, don't you, that you love the knight with such love that your heart cannot long endure that change."

"No, master," said Galehaut, "I can endure it for a while, but I couldn't go on that way forever. I have given him the deepest love; no other stranger have I ever so loved with all my heart. But I don't see how he could bring about my death, unless he were to die himself. After his death I don't think that I could live, because I would have nothing left in this world that could bring me any pleasure. No, I am sure I couldn't live on after him.

"But there is something that surprises me: it is what you said about the queen. As far as I can tell, he doesn't think about any woman at all; if he did, I would know about it right away."

"I know for a truth," said Master Elias, "that everything is bound to happen as I have said, once she puts her mind to it. In fact, I think she has already started, and she will certainly do her utmost. But let me add that you will also see one of the most astounding things ever to happen in your day: the queen stands accused of the basest wrongdoing that a woman can be charged with. And I believe it stems more from her sin than from any other wrong, for she was so untrue as to dishonor the most honorable man in the world. It was to

---

[23]*La Bele,* the Fair Lady, is no doubt to be understood as *la Bele Jaiande,* the Fair Gi-antess, identified elsewhere as the mother of Galehaut. In other sources, various names are given to these islands.

tell you that I sent out the knight whom you love so much, for I would rather have you hate me for speaking ill of him than let him hear it himself, and I know you to be so honorable and wise that I am sure my words will not be repeated. Indeed, I beg you, in the name of your honor and your rank, not to disclose to my lady anything I have told you that might be to her shame, just as you would want me to keep any secret you might tell me. I have told you many things, you see, for which I could be charged with hate and treachery if they were known. I beg you, then, to safeguard my honor and my welfare, just as you would want me to safeguard yours."

"My dear teacher," said Galehaut, "there is no need to point that out. Whatever you have shared with me that should remain between us will never be repeated. Moreover, I will always remember the lesson I heard you teach; I won't ever say anything to anyone, man or woman, that I know would be upsetting, unless I should want not to hide their shame or harm. No, you have taught me to keep these things from the queen and from the companion I love, to spare him. I know his heart very well; if he knew that there were talk of him and the queen, he would never again be seen in the king's house, because he is free of any shameful thought, and no man is as fearful of shame as he or so open to slights."

"Let's leave all this now," said Master Elias, "and let events show what they will. But you are right to say what you say, and I know a good part of what is happening. I am sorry that I know so much and that what will be cannot be changed. But just as you would rely on me in an important matter rather than on someone else, so I have told you what I would never want to tell the king or queen or your companion himself."

"My dear teacher," said Galehaut, "you have shown me the reason behind all the things you have spoken of, but, by God and by your soul, advise me about the thing I want to know more than any other—I mean the forty-five-plank bridge that I will have to cross, as foretold by the last speaker before you. He told me that he knew each plank stood for a year, a month, a week, or a day, but did not know which of the four lengths of time was meant. And so I ask you, my good teacher, to please tell me the truth, if you will."

"That," said Master Elias, "is a matter that you should not dwell on. No man born into our world down here would ever have an hour of happiness or peace if he knew the time fixed for his death. Nothing, you see, is so frightening as death; and since the death of the body is so dreaded, one should all the more fear the death of the soul."

"Master," said Galehaut, "in the name of everything I owe you, that is why I am asking you when my body will die: because I want to do whatever I can to avoid the death of my soul! I want to watch out for the death of the body in order to avoid the death which is truly frightening, the death of the soul. And be assured that, whatever torment my body may undergo, my soul, please God, will accept it gladly. I would strive more to behave the right way, and more urgently, than if I were just to live out a usual life. It would help me, since I have committed many wrongs in my life, destroying cities, killing people, dispossessing and banishing people . . ."

"Yes, I know," said Master Elias, "that it would help you to change your life, for any man who has conquered as much as you have must have a heavy burden of sins, and it's no wonder. Furthermore, if you knew the day of your death and tried to save your soul, it would be all to the good. But there is a great danger that could arise from this, as has already happened elsewhere. Indeed, we read that in Scotland there was once a lady of great wealth who had for a long time led a very wanton life. In the same land, not far from her, there was a very holy hermit; he lived his very religious life in the depths of a forest. The lady became acquainted with him and would often go to see him, and the hermit spoke such uplifting words to her that she reformed her life. At length, it came to the hermit in a vision that the lady had only thirty days more to live. He warned her to pay greater heed than ever to living the right way and told her the day when her life would end.

"Hearing the day she would die, she felt such fright and trembling in her flesh and was so overcome with fear that her body yielded and she forgot her soul's salvation. She went astray out of hopelessness; the Devil took hold of her as soon as fear for the flesh made her forget the saving of her soul. When the good hermit found out, he began to weep and cry out to Our Lord for mercy as he held Him in his hands, and he prayed that God not suffer the Devil to have power over the sinful woman whom He had called to His service. God, who is always ready to succor those who call on Him sincerely, heard the good man, and a voice came down to the chapel saying that God was granting him the favor that he sought, and he had only to touch the woman and she would be healed.

"The good hermit came to where she lay bound, and she began to scream when she saw him. That was the work of the Devil, who was tormenting her because of the good man's arrival. But as soon as the hermit had made the sign of the cross over her and touched her flesh, the Enemy rushed out of her, bellowing and howling so madly that the whole land shook. No sooner had the lady regained her senses and recalled what her lack of belief had brought about than she renounced this world at once; she had her beautiful locks shorn off, put on a nun's habit, and went off with a single woman companion to a high place between two cliffs, where she remained in her garb of poverty until she died.

"Now you can understand that there is great value in uncertainty and none in hopelessness, for as soon as she lost hope, she was emptied of the Holy Spirit and filled with the Devil. Likewise, Saint Peter sank in the sea as soon as he felt fear, and that is the danger that can come of knowing the day of your death. And so one must not be eager to learn it, because the flesh is so impure and weak that that knowledge makes it fall into fear, and from fear the body falls into hopelessness. So my advice is that you give up such a rash pursuit; and as God wills, so let it be with you. And strive to live the right way as if you were sure that your life would last another thirty years."

"Master," said Galehaut, "I am not afraid, please God, of falling into hopelessness if you tell me the time of my death. I am not so lacking in belief; indeed, I could only welcome the chance to make my life better. God has allowed me till now to have more power and wealth than anyone of my age has ever had, even born into a greater line. And so it seems to me that God will be showing me much love if He allows me to enjoy the pleasure of this world and then look forward to the joy that has no end. And the closer I am to my death, the more I will strive to deserve the everlasting life. So I ask that you counsel me in accordance with what you know of me, for you would not be a loyal counselor if you didn't tell me everything that touches the salvation of my soul.

"If you hide the truth from me, I will call on the Savior of the world to be my guarantor and put your soul in the place of mine if I sin as a result of your failing or the failing of what you teach—because I am relying on your guidance in all matters, and God is a righteous judge who judges every man according to his works. Now take care, then, with your soul at risk, to enlighten me honestly and not foretell a longer time for my life in order to make me feel better. Remember that I would be less bent on living the right way if I thought I had long to live."

Then Master Elias began to weep and said, "My lord, now that you have put my soul at risk, there can be no hindrance to my telling you the truth. In a way I am pleased and in another way I am sorry: pleased because I know you to be so wise that you could only become a better man thereby, and sorry because a man as worthy as you are or might be should never have to die before reaching true old age. Nevertheless, I will not tell you the day or hour of your death, because I find no particular moment that you might not well live past. If you went beyond the day I had foretold, you would hold me to be a liar, which is why I won't tell you. I will, however, go far enough for you to know the day beyond which you could survive in only one way—but you could hasten the day as well."

With that, he rose and went over to the door of the chapel, which was freshly whitewashed. With a piece of coal, he drew forty-five small black circles, each the size of a penny, and wrote over them, "These represent years." After that, he drew forty-five smaller circles below the others and wrote, "These represent months," and below those he drew even smaller circles and wrote in smaller letters, "These represent weeks," and at the bottom he put even tinier circles, with letters saying, "These represent days."

Having done that, he said to Galehaut, "My lord, what you see here represents the forty-five planks standing for the rest of your life. This will show you whether they stand for years, months, weeks, or days."

Then he pointed to the four groups that he had drawn on the wall, explained what each meant, and then said, "My lord, take care not to be startled by anything you may see, as I am going to show you one of the most remarkable things you have ever witnessed. Well, then, if these circles remain as untouched as they are now, you will live exactly forty-five years; but if any are erased, that many years will be cut from your life, and you will see them erased before your very eyes. The same is true of the months and weeks, but when it comes to the days, you will surely have as many of them as there are planks."

Thereupon he reached into his robe and pulled out a little book; opening it, he said to Galehaut, "My lord, here is a little book which treats the meaning and the mystery of all the great spells that can be cast with words. With the explanations given in it, I would know the truth about all the things I am now uncertain of, if I made a point of studying it; I could even pull trees out of the ground and make the earth quake and make water flow uphill. But the truth is, whoever attempts such things puts himself at great risk. When my lord King Arthur could not find any help in understanding his dreams, all his learnèd clerks rushed toward this little book. They opened the cupboard where it was kept, since I was at that time in Rome, and the man who took it from the cupboard to interpret the king's dream did not know what care to take with it and was unaware of the meaning and the power of what had to be done. In the very act of reading, then, he lost his sight and his mind and control over his limbs. That happened just as he was trying to figure out the meaning of the water lion, the drugless doctor, and the prompting of the flower.[24] For that reason, I warn you not to be startled by what I am going to show you, which will be a more extraordinary thing than you have ever seen. You may be sure, at least, that you will not leave here unshaken."

With that, he went up to the altar and took a splendid cross made of gold and gems and the box holding the body of Our Lord. Keeping the cross, he handed the box to Galehaut and said, "My lord, take this box, which encloses the holiest thing in the whole world, and I'll hold the cross, which is the next most noble. As long as we hold them, we need not fear any untoward event."

Then Master Elias sat down on a stone bench, opened his book, and began to read. He went on at length, until his heart grew very warm and his face became flushed; from his forehead sweat trickled down his cheeks, and he began to weep and could not stop.

Galehaut looked on and felt uneasy with what he saw. Master Elias read till he was tired and worn out, and he sighed deeply out of great sorrow. When he had regained his calm, he took up his reading once again and trembled with fear. Then, in almost no time at all, such thick darkness settled over the

---

[24]References to a prophetic dream not included in this volume.

chapel that you could no more see anything there than if it were an abyss. A voice called out, so hideous and shrill that in the whole city of Sorhaut there was no man or woman who did not hear it. Galehaut, stunned by the voice, put the box down in front of him and flattened himself face down on the ground. After a moment, he picked it up again with both hands and held it tightly right before his eyes, as the darkness made him unsure of himself and the piercing voice so stunned him that he could not hear or see a thing. Not far from him, near the altar, lay Master Elias in a faint, with the cross lying on his breast.

Then the darkness faded away and the light of day came back. Master Elias came out of his faint, heaving sad sighs and looking all around. He asked Galehaut how he was, and he answered that all was well now, thank God. But only a moment later the ground began to quake.

"My lord," said Master Elias, "lean against that seat over there! Your body can't support you by itself through the wonders that you're about to see."

Galehaut leaned against the seat, and his master against a stone pillar; and all along Galehaut held on to the box. Soon it seemed to the two men that the whole chapel was spinning. When it stopped, Galehaut looked up and saw nearby, coming through the tightly shut door, a hand and arm that went back as far as the shoulder. It was wearing a wide sleeve of purple satin that trailed down to the floor; the sleeve came down a little below the elbow, and from that point forward to the wrist the arm was covered with a kind of white silk. The arm was extraordinarily long, and the hand was as red as live coals and held a sword just as red, which was dripping red blood from the hilt to the point.

The sword came right up to Master Elias and looked as if it were about to run him through and kill him. In his terror, he held the cross out in front of him, and the sword began to circle him, still threatening to kill him; he kept moving the cross around to face it down. In a while, he became aware that it was moving away from him and straight toward Galehaut. Galehaut held the box out in front of him, just as he had seen Master Elias do, and went on like that until the sword moved away from him as well. With the arm and hand that gripped it, it went up to the wall where the black circles were drawn and struck so sharply into the stone that half a foot of it came away, removing three of the circles and part of a fourth. Having done this, it turned back to the door it had come through and disappeared.

Galehaut was more astonished than he had ever been in his life. When he could speak, he said, "You have really kept your promise to me, master. You have shown me, as far as I can tell, the greatest wonders that have ever been witnessed, and you have let it be clear to me that I still have three years and more to live. I feel more at ease now, and would like you to know that my life will be all the better for it, for no man of my age has ever done as much good as I am going to do in the next three years. I assure you, besides, that I will never let any sadness show that might betray what I know, but will rather do my best to display more cheer than I have done till now."

"Now I'll tell you," said Master Elias, "that I was very worried about your death when I showed you those symbols of it. You might yet live beyond the end indicated, but that depends upon my lady the queen. And if you could somehow have your companion remain with you, you would indeed live beyond it, because your death will only come from his absence. So all you can do is keep up a good appearance until you see how things are going. And remember not to disclose your secret to him or to any other, for one mustn't expose one's inner truth to anyone."

[*Galehaut proposed that he and Lancelot be crowned kings and avenge Lancelot's father's death. Leaving King Bademagu of Gorre in charge, Galehaut left for Arthur's court. Arthur succumbed to the wiles of the False Guenevere; returning to his court, he proclaimed her queen. Guenevere was rejected, and it was decided that her fate would be determined at Pentecost; until then, she would be in Gawain's care. At Pentecost, Lancelot defended Guenevere by defeating three of the best knights of Carmelide.*]

16. The Imposture Is Revealed; the False Guenevere Dies; Arthur Repents and Is Reconciled First with Guenevere, Then with Lancelot.

Thus Galehaut rode off toward his country, taking the queen with him, and after a number of days they arrived. There Galehaut saw to it that Sorelois received the queen with all due homage; and once the land was hers and all oaths of fealty sworn, Sir Gawain left, happy to know that she was properly settled.

Then Lancelot went to speak with the queen, not in public but with Galehaut present, in whom she had great trust. She said, "My dear friend, this is where things stand, as you see: I am separated from my husband the king as a result of my misdeed—yes, I acknowledge it—not that I am not his lawful wife and just as crowned and anointed as he, and daughter of King Leodagan of Carmelide as well, but I have been hurt by the sin of going to bed with a man other than my husband.

"Still, there is no upstanding lady in the world who would not feel impelled to sacrifice something to make an upstanding knight like you happy. Too bad Our Lord pays no heed to our courtly ways, and a person whom the world sees as good is wicked to God. But now I have to beg a favor of you, because I have reached a point where I have to watch myself more closely than ever before. I ask you, then, in the name of your great love for me, to seek no more of me from now on than a kiss or an embrace, if you like, unless at my invitation. This much of me, though, you will have as long as I stay here; and when I find the time and place are right and you are willing, I will gladly let you have the rest.

"But my will right now is that you be patient for a while. You must not doubt that I am yours forever; you have deserved it, and my heart, besides, would never let me give you up. Remember, when my lord the king asked that I urge you to remain in his household, I said more to him than I have said just now, for I told him I preferred being with you to being with him."

"My lady," said Lancelot, "nothing you wish can be a burden to me. I am wholly subject to your will, even if it means pain no less than happiness; and I'll endure whatever you like, because my fulfilment can only come through you."

In this way the queen remained in Sorelois, where she usually had the company of Galehaut and his friend and where the lady of Malehaut stayed with her, too; and if not for the company of these three, she could not have gone on, after all the people and pleasures that she had known. So the queen lived in Sorelois for two years, while King Arthur stayed in his country; and if beforehand he had loved his wife dearly, he now loved the new woman even twice as much. Things reached the point where the pope who was then on the throne in Rome learned about it. He held it a grave offense that so important a man as the king of Britain should have cast aside his wife in disregard of the Holy Church. He ordered then that the vengeance of Our Lord make itself felt throughout the land where he had taken his first wife, until such time as they should be brought back together by the Church. In this way King Arthur's land was placed under interdiction for twenty-one months.

During that time, it happened that the king was at one of his castles in Britain together with a great number of knights as well as the queen and Bertelay the Old, who held considerable sway over the royal pair. The queen had so worked on the king with drugs that he could not oppose any wish of hers, and things had already gone so far that all the barons hated her. At the beginning of Advent, the king had held court at Caerleon, and the queen was there, since he took her along wherever he went, whether military marches, sieges, or tournaments, but he never slept with her except when he was staying in his own room. One time, after a quarrel with the barons, the queen withdrew to her quarters, and that night she lost all the strength in her limbs, so that she became paralyzed, except for her eyes, and her flesh began to rot from the feet up.

The sickness lasted a long time, and eventually she was so badly stricken and, with the onset of the rot, gave off such a stench that no one could come near her. The very night she was at her worst, Bertelay the Old was struck down in the same way. The king was overcome with sorrow and, once this had happened, remained a long while at Bredigan; in the end, though, Sir Gawain took him off to spend some time at Camelot; not wanting to be rebuked by his barons, the king said that he would have no lack of news of the queen if he were there.

[*Arthur fell very ill, and a hermit informed him that it was punishment for Arthur's having rejected the queen and having lived in sin. Arthur confessed*

his sins, took communion, and soon felt healed. When he returned to court,
the queen sent for him, and he advised her to make her confession.]

Just then, one of the queen's knights came in and said to the king, "My lord,
Bertelay the Old is dying downstairs. He asks you please to come see him one
time before he dies."

The king went and, seeing him come in, Bertelay said, "My lord, I have
had you come because I have the greatest need to see you, but I would like all
your knights to come hear what I want to tell you, since it is one of the greatest wonders ever uttered or imagined. Please have them come in."

The king had all his knights come in. Meanwhile, the hermit was speaking to Guenevere. "My lady," he said, "you are likely to die, for no mortal
man can heal you; and whoever loses his body and then his soul as well, loses
too much. You are losing your body; think about saving your soul! Take care
that you not hide something that might harm your soul; remember, there is no
true confession unless you admit all the things by which you feel stained, and
no one can be safe without true confession."

"My lord," said the lady, "you are urging me to save my soul if possible,
but I fail to see how it can be saved, because I am the most disloyal, the most
sinful, the most traitorous of women. I have tricked and betrayed the worthiest man in the world, King Arthur; I made him abandon his loyal wife, who is
the flower of all women in the world. And God is taking vengeance as He sees
fit, for all my limbs are paralyzed; and His vengeance isn't even as great as it
should be!"

Then she told him from beginning to end just how she had betrayed the
king, hiding nothing, telling the whole truth about this sin and others that she
could recall as well; then she said, "Good sir, give me your advice! I am in
great need of it, and my lord the king told me that you would advise me better
than anyone else."

"My lady, I cannot easily advise you on this matter; you might well not
abide by what I have to say."

But she promised that she would.

"In that case," he said, "I recommend that, just as you committed your
sin against the king and his people, you now acknowledge your guilt to the
king in front of his people. Your soul will be much relieved, and you can
thereby reach salvation sooner. If you don't do this, you will lose both body
and soul."

The lady promised that she would do as he said.

Meanwhile, the knights came along whom the king had sent for to hear
what Bertelay had to say. Once they were gathered, Bertelay acknowledged
his part in the betrayal and admitted how he had ensnared the king; he admitted everything else the story has recounted, then said to the king, "My lord, I
am faithless and traitorous, as you have heard, and I want you to know that
the wretched woman who is dying upstairs would never have done anything

wrong if not for me. I beg you, therefore, to take such vengeance on this wretched body of mine, traitorous and disloyal as it has been, that no one hearing of it will ever dare risk a similar betrayal. I believe my soul will thus be relieved, because the more torment the body suffers in this world, the less hardship the soul will meet in the world beyond."

Hearing this extraordinary statement, the king crossed himself vigorously, and all the knights gathered there were very pleased. But Sir Gawain was happier than anyone else, and he said to the king, "My lord, didn't I tell you . . . ? Not that it was thanks to us my lady was not destroyed, but thanks to God, of course, and to Lancelot! It's true, no betrayal can be hidden forever."

As the king was listening to Bertelay's revelations and the words of Sir Gawain, someone suddenly came to call him back to the hermit who was at the queen's bedside. He left, and his knights all followed.

When the queen saw he him come in, she burst into tears and begged his mercy in God's name. "My lord," she said, "I beg your mercy as the most sinful creature alive."

Then she recounted the betrayal from beginning to end, just as she had done it, under the guidance of Bertelay. Then the knights were happier than they had ever been, since now they were sure that it was all true. But the king was as overwhelmed as any man could be, never having imagined that a woman's heart would dare undertake such treason. He turned to the hermit and his barons to help him decide what to do.

"My lord," said the hermit, "wait for the barons whom you have summoned to this city, and then you will do as they advise. It will be much better if they hear the true story from the very two people who have confessed it to you."

The king took this advice and waited for his barons, while Sir Gawain picked a messenger and sent him to the queen with the news of what had happened and word that she could be sure she would enjoy more honor than ever in the past.

[*Everyone asked Guenevere's forgiveness. On the advice of Galehaut and Lancelot, the queen decided to return to Arthur.*]

Thus the queen had stayed in Sorelois two full years plus the time from Pentecost to the last week of February. When she left, she was escorted by Galehaut, his companion, and a great number of his men. Two days away from Carduel, King Arthur rode out to meet them.

Galehaut had asked the queen to forbid Lancelot to rejoin the king's household, so she turned to him and she said, "Lancelot, be sure not to remain with the king, whatever urging you may hear, unless I plead with you myself. And you may be sure that I will not make that plea as long as I can honorably avoid it."

When the king met them, his greeting to Galehaut and to the queen herself was full of joy, even though he had not forgot his longing for the other woman; but, because of his people, he made an effort to put on a good face. For her part, the queen was very humble toward him, and all those who saw her loved her and admired her all the more. But well beyond the joy shown by the king and all the others was the happiness that Sir Gawain showed. As soon as he could see the queen and Galehaut, he ran up to them with his arms out, and he was so obviously overjoyed that no man of feeling could have been more so. He kissed them each in turn.

That night, they stayed in the kingdom of Escalone. As soon as they had dismounted, Galehaut, in his usual way, led the queen to the king's lodging, and Galehaut said to the king, "My lord, here is my lady, whom you charged me to look after and whom I am returning to you. I assure you that I looked after her just as I had promised, so that, so help me God and"—here he pointed toward the chapel—"the saints in that church, she could not have been better guarded, and with all honor to you, had she been my very own sister."

The king thanked him and, with a laugh, said, "My dear friend, I can never pay you back for what you have done for me, because though the will is there, the means are not. There is even something else you have to do, which will cost you very little but will be very important to me; but you won't know what it is until the time is ripe."

He was speaking about Lancelot, whom he wanted to ask back. Indeed, Lancelot was not present at the reconciliation of the king and queen, but was at his quarters, locked up in a room, sad and downcast, seeing nothing that might comfort him, since he was sure that he had lost his lady; but he kept it all to himself, even from Galehaut.

That evening, the king and queen were reunited by bishops and archbishops, and there was great rejoicing. Afterwards, Galehaut stayed on with them for a good week, but Lancelot, with his leave and the queen's, went back to Sorelois before that. Galehaut stayed with the queen for three days after Lancelot's departure, then came to the king to take his leave. The king drew him and the queen aside and said that, in the name of their fealty and their love for him, they should do what they could to make Lancelot forgive him and grant him, as in the past, his love and companionship. Galehaut answered that he would gladly speak to him about the matter, "since I will soon see him," he said, "but my lady will not be seeing him for some time, as he left for my country three days ago."

At these words, the king was sorely irked and said that that was a nasty disappointment. "I was planning," he said, "to make peace with him before he left; in fact, that's the favor I asked of you when you returned the queen to me."

"My lord," said the queen, "at that point it did not seem that Lancelot would do for me what you asked when I went off to Sorelois. Now he has left without saying goodbye to me, and yet I would rather have him go without my leave than see him deny my request."

"Ah, my lady," said Galehaut, "we need to bear with him; he is well worth it. A man who is all upset is not in control of himself, and Lancelot has a heart that forgets nothing. Whatever favor or wrong anyone does him, no matter how small, he never puts behind him; and I have chided him for it many a time, both in front of you and in private. But he sees it as such a great rebuff that my lord the king didn't free you as soon as he spoke up that he cannot change his feelings back into love for him. He has often said to me, 'My lord, how could I ever serve him again, now that he has shown me he has no regard for me or all the service I have ever done him? And I have done him such great service that I'll never be able to match it! No, he is not like you, who in one day gave up your honor for shame!' My lord, that's what Lancelot has often said to me when I would chide him."

When the king heard that Lancelot was so deeply upset, he burst into tears with pain and felt great distress in his heart, for he still loved Lancelot with greater love than anyone else but Galehaut. And later on he showed it clearly a number of times, when the slanderers in his house would say vile things to him and he would answer that it was pointless for anyone to try to turn him against Lancelot, "for there is no wrong that he could do me in this world," he would say, "that would make me hate him. If he did anything base, I could only be grieved."[25]

The king was greatly saddened by Lancelot's enmity. He begged this favor of Galehaut, that he, as he cared for him deeply, please do his very utmost to bring Lancelot back to him. "And to you, my lady," he said to the queen, "I make the same plea, by the allegiance you owe me and in the name of the creature you love most in this world, if you want me ever again to be at peace. Swear to me, you and Galehaut, that you will both do as I ask; then it will be up to Lancelot to respond to me as he likes, and in his own time."

Having said this, he fell at their feet and offered his support in return as urgently as if they were now about to snatch him from death.

At last they granted his plea, and Galehaut promised that, barring some bodily impediment, they would both be with him at Easter. Then Galehaut took his leave of the king and queen, and the queen urged him, as he cared for her deeply, to be sure to bring Lancelot back with him at Easter. "And never fear, my good friend," she said, "what may happen in all this coming and going. I swear to you, by the great faith I have in him, that nothing will ever happen to make you lose his companionship. On the contrary, I will make sure he is with you as often as he has been all along."

With that, Galehaut went back to his country and gave his companion the queen's message. They stayed together in Sorelois until the middle of Lent and then, traveling in short stages, they reached King Arthur on Palm Sunday

---

[25]For the realization of this forecast, see *The Death of Arthur.*

at Disnadaron, for he would not ride on any day of Holy Week, a custom which at that time was observed by many people. When the king learned that Lancelot had come, he was overjoyed and the queen was no less happy, both for her own sake and for the sake of the king, who had been yearning for that return and had often urged her cooperation whenever he thought her most favorably disposed.

All that week they were at prayer, and when it was time for High Mass on Easter Sunday, the king reminded the queen and Galehaut of what he had asked them, urging them to make their effort clear to Lancelot. "And count on me for anything I can do or give," he said to the two of them; "don't hesitate to promise him whatever he may ask that is in my power or yours."

Thereupon Galehaut and the queen sent for Lancelot to join them in the queen's rooms. When he came in, he took the queen in his arms in front of the others who were there (for the lady of Malehaut had been called to this meeting).

Then all four sat down on a couch, and the queen said to Lancelot, "My dear friend, we have reached the point where you and my lord the king must be reconciled; I want it, and so does Galehaut, who loves you very much, as you know. And you ought to be grateful to the king for being so eager for your presence, for he has charged me to promise you whatever you wish of his or of mine; and I know that what you already have of it you like better than all the rest. Nevertheless, I don't insist you do his bidding as soon as he asks you: leave time for me to entreat you, and Galehaut and then all the barons. I want you to be unbending at first! Don't yield till Galehaut and I have fallen at your feet, and then all the knights and ladies and damsels. At that point, go up to my lord, kneel before him, and agree to do as he wishes."

"No, my lady," said Lancelot, "I couldn't possibly allow you to fall to your knees in front of me!"

"Yes, you will," she said; "that's what I want you to do! In the name of all the great love you have for me, I beg you to agree."

So Lancelot agreed, not daring to oppose his lady's will. Then the queen and Galehaut went into the hall where the king and his barons were waiting, while Lancelot and the lady of Malehaut stayed behind. The queen and Galehaut both reported to the king that they were unable to find any readiness for peace in Lancelot. "But we will send for him," said Galehaut, "and if we cannot reach an understanding ourselves, then have your barons do as we do."

With that, they sent for Lancelot, and all the ladies and maidens who were in their rooms came out. Once everyone was there, the queen and Galehaut made the same request to Lancelot that they had made earlier. He was unbending in his refusal, saying that he had no wish at this point to belong to any household or have any companions other than the one he had. Then the queen promised, just as the king had told her to, to give him whatever he would want, and he went on refusing. He said, loudly enough for everyone to hear, "My lady, please don't ask anymore, as it would be in vain. You must not think, though, you or anyone else, that I harbor any hatred for the king. The truth is that I could not be anywhere so far away that I would not come back to stand by him if I found out he needed help."

Lancelot thus rejected her plea, at which point Galehaut and the queen dropped to their knees before him, and all the barons, ladies, and damsels did likewise. Seeing the queen at his feet, Lancelot pretended to be incensed; he bounded forward and raised her by the hand, then did the same with Galehaut. He went up to the king, fell to his knees, simply and humbly begged his pardon, and agreed to abide by his will. Then the king raised him by the hand and, happily kissing him on the mouth, said, "Many thanks, my dear friend! One thing I promise you in front of all your friends and mine, and swear to you in the name of today's holy feast: that I will never again give you any grounds for anger if I can possibly help it."

That is how good terms were restored between King Arthur and Lancelot, and Lancelot remained attached to the Round Table and the household of the king as he had been earlier. There was great joy throughout King Arthur's court both because the king was happy and because so valorous a knight was not lost. Thereupon they all went to hear Mass, which had been delayed by the matter at hand.

That day there was great joy in King Arthur's court. During the king's stay at Disnadaron, he decided that the next court he would hold, at Pentecost, would be the most splendid ever held. At the court's close, as all the barons were about to leave, he commanded them all, if they cherished his love, to join him at Pentecost in London and to come in greater numbers than ever before and with as much pomp as they could afford.

[*Gawain was abducted, and other knights sought him. They found adventures and undertook battles, and some were imprisoned. The duke of Clarence wandered into the Valley of No Return (also called the Valley of False Lovers). Morgan had cast a spell on the valley, and no knight who had been unfaithful to his lady could leave there until one came there who had always been faithful.*]

17. Lancelot Liberates the Valley's Prisoners, but Is Abducted by Morgan the Fay.

Now, according to the story, Lancelot was greeted with much joy and honor at Escalon the Dark when through his great knightliness he mastered the darkness, driving it out, and brought light back to the church and the castle. The next morning, the story says, when he, Sir Yvain, and the damsel had heard Mass, they left and rode, as she led them, straight to the Valley of False Lovers. It happened that they came upon the vavasor who had given lodging to the duke, and he gave them whatever news of the duke he had.

When they left him, they quickened their pace, as they were impatient to catch up with their companion. At the hour of nones they reached the chapel where the road forked, and found the squire who was waiting for the duke. He told them how he had ridden off and when. They were surprised to hear this and troubled not to have caught up with him.

Then Lancelot asked how long the squire had been there with the duke.

"Two long days, my lord," he answered. Then, seeing the young lady, he recognized her easily, as she did him, and the two greeted each other very warmly. "My dear lord," the squire went on, "what are you going to do about the duke? Will you just ride through the valley without waiting for any news of him? He would never leave you there, even at the risk of dying!"

"So help me God," said Lancelot, "he's not going to stay there! We're going in after him, and we'll see why no knight can ever come out!"

With that, Lancelot turned down the road to the left, together with Sir Yvain and the young lady, who was eager to do her utmost to advance Lancelot's renown. When they reached the entry in the smoke-like wall, she said to Lancelot, "There are adventures in which you risk no shame, because one or another of your companions has failed in them; strive for something greater! Here you face one of the most trying adventures in all of King Arthur's realm, for no knight, once entered here, has ever come back out. If you like," she said to Sir Yvain, "you try this adventure first; otherwise, Lancelot will. If you choose the next one, Lancelot will have this one."

[Yvain failed at his adventure.]

Thereupon she came back to Lancelot and said as soon as she saw him, "Now then, noble knight! You are going to see what great honor awaits you! For, as God is my true witness, my heart tells me that today you will set free all the men who are prisoners in this valley because of the evil customs that are in force here. Yet it will not just be a feat you owe to your skill as a knight; you could never carry it through were it not for another virtue you have."

"My lady," he said, "what virtue do you mean? I have far fewer than I'd like of all the many virtues that go into knighthood."

"I'll tell you," she answered. "You will never in your life leave this place if you have been false or unfaithful to your lover, in either deed or thought."

At these words, he began to laugh and then said, "My lady, and what if a knight came along who had never been unfaithful?"

"You can be sure," she said, "that he would soon set free all the people in this place; and it would be no small honor, since there are over two hundred knights here who expect never to leave. However, you are such an upstanding knight that it would be a terrible loss if you were to fall into such a dreadful prison, so my advice is that you would do better to go find Sir Gawain. I don't believe there is any knight alive who has been in love and has not in some way been unfaithful to his lady."

"I'll soon see," he said, "but now come follow me."

Then he boldly strode in, followed by the young lady, who was uneasy and afraid for him. Having left his horse outside, he walked ahead until he came to the two dragons. They made straight for him, but he was already taking aim at the first; he struck him between the eyes, and his sword bounced right back. He was so stung with disappointment that he almost flung it as far away as he could. However, he thought that it might still be of some use to him, so he thrust it back into its scabbard and pulled his shield away from his neck, holding it up in front of his face to protect himself from the flames.

Then he threw himself upon the dragon that was closer to him, aiming his fist at him, but the dragon jumped up and clawed at his shield and spewed hot flames from its gullet. But Lancelot thrust out his hand and dashed the dragon against the nearby wall; then, seizing it with both hands, he gripped it so tightly, with so much tension in his arms, that he snapped its neck. With that one slain, he hurled himself against the other, undaunted by any dreadful harm that might come to him. When the dragon saw him coming, it jumped toward his eyes, but he covered himself with his shield to keep away the hot, thick flames darting at him.

Why should I prolong the telling? Just as he had killed the first, he killed the second; and the young lady, seeing this, was very pleased. Then he went back to where he had left his lance, picked it up, and went ahead as the path led him, until he came to the deep stream where the young lady had seen Sir Yvain fall in; at that point, she was greatly frightened, more so than she had ever been.

When Lancelot reached the stream and saw the long, narrow plank and the three knights on the other bank, he stopped and asked the three whether the crossing was barred to him, but they gave him no answer. When he saw that they were not saying a word, he said that, if ever any true lover were allowed across, he would never let them stop him from crossing. Then, having unfastened his shield from around his neck, he stepped forward with his right foot and went steadily along the plank, just as if it had been an earthen path trodden by the most agile and self-assured of knights.

When he reached the middle and saw the knight who was holding a lance poised to run him through, he stood stock-still; then he held his shield out in front of him as far as his arm could stretch, and couched his lance under his arm. When he saw the other man's lance touch his shield, he strengthened his stance on the plank as well as he could and pushed his shield upward against the lance so mightily that the shaft was shattered. Then he flung his shield to the side, lest it get in his way, and dropped it into the water.

With that, he quickly planned his attack, then ran as fast as his legs could carry him toward the three men who were awaiting him. He struck the lance-holder with his lance just below the throat and tossed him to the ground so dazed that he was powerless to stand back up. Then he hit the other two with such fury that he knocked them both down to the ground and he himself went sprawling down on top of one of them; but it did not take him long to stand up again, as he was very nimble and strong. So he jumped right back up and, grasping the man who had been under him and was all stretched out in a daze, pulled him up to the bridge and threw him into the water. Then, with sword in hand, he turned back to attend to the two whom he had left on the ground, but they were not to be found. Lancelot was extremely puzzled.

He looked toward the young lady, who he could see was delighted. "Good Lord, where have they gone? By whatever you hold dearest, my lady, tell me, if you know!"

She said that she didn't know, so help her God.

Lancelot was very upset, afraid that their escape meant he had lost everything; he stood there awhile, rapt in thought. She asked him what he was waiting for.

"I am waiting," he said, "for those two weak cowards who ran away. I'm afraid they may come back once I am gone and claim that *I* ran away from *them*."

"A foolish fear!" she said. "Aren't you better off if the adventures back away from you than if you run away from the adventures? Go ahead and face the next ones, since you have failed at them so far! I wish you would fail at the rest in the same way."

"So help me God, my lady," he said, "that's not what *I* want! You would be robbing me of the great honor that you have promised me here."

With that, he pulled off the left gauntlet of his hauberk and looked at his ring.[26] Not seeing any trace left of the broad stream and the plank bridge that he had seen and crossed, he realized right away that it had all been a magic spell. Then he put his gauntlet back on, picked up his shield from the ground, and went on till he came to a fire blazing across his path. The fire was so intense that it seemed nothing could enter it without being burned up; and it stretched all the way from the wall on the right to the one on the left. Rising above the fire was a stone staircase that led up to a splendid palace.

The staircase spiraled as it rose; it was very high and was over a foot wide. At the door to the great hall stood two knights fully armed and each holding a large, extraordinary axe; one stood below the other, a little higher than the first step. When Lancelot saw the fire, he wondered what it could mean; but when he saw that his path was taking him up the stairs, he was very glad, as he scorned the obvious attempt to bar his way. He reached the stairs, went up, and at the top faced the first knight.

---

[26]This is the ring given to Lancelot by the Lady of the Lake, which allows him to detect and undo magic spells; see Chapter 3.

[Lancelot defeated several more adversaries. He cut off the head of the last one and brought it to the tent where Morgan was lying.]

He encountered a crowd of knights and young ladies gazing at him in wonderment as he strode in with the head in his right hand.

Now, Morgan had been moaning loudly about being hurt by the bed. When Lancelot heard her moans, he had no doubt that she was the person on whom he had turned over the bed. He was so ashamed that he barely dared to look at her, for of all the knights in the world he was the one most unwilling to wrong any lady or maiden. He fell to his knees in front of her and, showing her the head, said, "My lady, I have come to repair the great wrong that this knight made me commit when he flung himself under your bed."

But seeing him, Morgan was badly frightened and cried out loud. A young lady who was the lover of the slain knight came in, crying aloud like a madwoman and brandishing a spear in her two hands. With all her strength she struck Lancelot between the shoulders, tearing his hauberk and sinking the spear so far into his flesh that red blood spurted out and ran all the way down his back.

When Lancelot felt the blow, he leapt way up and grasped his sword; but when he saw that it was a woman, he was shocked and put the sword back into its scabbard. Meanwhile, she was swearing by everything she could swear by that no one could stop her from killing him, or else he would kill her, "because I don't want to live on after the creature I loved most in life, whom you killed like the faithless scoundrel you are!"

"So help me God, my lady," he said, "no worthy young lady should have loved him, for he was the most cowardly and craven knight that I have ever yet seen, however tall and handsome he was!"

At those words, she was so stung that she almost went out of her mind. She sprang toward him, but he jumped aside, then caught her in his arms and pulled the spear from her hands.

A moment later, a young man came in and, going up to Morgan, said, "My lady, I have very strange news for you."

"What is it?" she said. "Speak!"

"My lady," he said, "the spell over the valley is broken, and the walls are gone. You can already find more than a hundred knights at the gate who have been prisoners here for a long time."

"How did this happen?" said Morgan. "Who did it?"

"My lady," he said, "it was done by this knight here, who has performed greater feats of arms today than any other knight has ever done!"

After the young man had spoken, the knight came in who was Morgan's lover and because of whom the bewitching had taken place.

When he saw Lancelot, he greeted him, saying, "My lord, you are welcome here as the flower of all knighthood," and he fell to his knees before him.

"In God's name, *un*welcome," said Morgan, "as the greatest wrongdoer of all knighthood!"

"My lady," said the young woman who had come with Lancelot, "what have you said? He is the finest knight, the most trustworthy knight ever born of woman, and the most faithful in love as well. It is clear, and you can see it perfectly well."

"Young lady," said Morgan, "if he is faithful in love, that is a great honor and a great joy to his lover, but he has brought more harm to us than joy or well-being to her. There are beautiful and loving young ladies in this place who have been fully satisfied by their lovers, because these knights could go nowhere else. Once they are out, things will change and they won't ever again spend so much time with their ladies. Still, the knight deserves to be honored and admired in every land for the great loyalty he has; and his lover, whoever she is, may well boast that she is the best loved woman of all. And I never thought I would ever see a knight who had not done *something* wrong in love! May God keep him forever just as he is now!"

Then she rose and went up to Lancelot and offered him a very warm and cheerful welcome. In a moment, Sir Yvain came in, together with the other knights of the king's household and a crowd of knights who had been held prisoner for a long time. When those who knew Lancelot saw him, they ran up to him with arms outstretched to welcome the man who was their companion and who had just delivered them from a woeful prison. Morgan had him disarmed in great honor. When she learned that he was Lancelot, she guessed right away that he was in love with the queen, and resolved to cause her some distress. Indeed, she thought that, if the queen loved him as much as he did her, she would deprive her of happiness forevermore, for she hated the queen more than any other woman.

This hatred had arisen between the two as you will now hear. The fact is that Morgan was the daughter of the duke of Tintagel and his wife Ygraine, who later became queen of Britain, the wife of Uther Pendragon and mother of King Arthur, whom she had conceived during the duke's lifetime through Merlin's treachery.[27] When Ygraine came to Uther Pendragon and married him, she had her daughter Morgan with her; she left behind in the dukedom of Tintagel a boy who was the duke's son by a wife the duke had had before Ygraine. The duke was an ugly man, and Morgan, who took after him, was also ugly; and when she came of age, she was so lustful and wanton that a looser woman could not have been found.

Now, when King Arthur was newly married, there was in his household a knight who was a nephew of the queen; this was Guyamor of Carmelide, a very brave and handsome knight. At that time, Morgan was lady-in-waiting to the queen and fell so deeply in love with Guyamor of Carmelide that she

---

[27]For the story of Arthur's conception, see *Merlin,* Chapter 3.

could never have enough of his company. One day, it happened that the two of them were in bed together. The queen had already been warned and had been keeping close watch on them, as she would gladly have kept Morgan chaste lest the king be shamed, and Guyamor as well lest the king punish him, for he would have hated him for such behavior, had he learned of it. That day, then, the queen caught them together in the act; there was no hiding it.

She came to Guyamor and said that he was as good as dead if the king learned of the affair, and with pleas and threats she succeeded in making him give up the young woman. In fact, he did so easily, since he was hardly so in love with her that he could not get by without her. When Morgan saw that he had given her up because of the queen, she was sorely distressed, and all the more as she was pregnant. Seeing that she had failed utterly with him, she decided to run away to Merlin; she would search everywhere till she found him, for she believed she could find no help in her plight from any other man.

She sought him and at last found him, bringing great wealth and many horses with her. She came to know Merlin well, and he loved her more than anything else. He taught her all the spells and bewitchments that she knew later on, and she stayed with him for a long time. The child she had by Guyamor became a knight of great prowess.

That explains the hatred that she felt for Queen Guenevere throughout the days of her life.

She decided, when she saw Lancelot, that through him she could cause her greater distress than by any other means, for she was quite sure that the queen loved him, because he had performed greater feats of arms for her than any other knight had ever done for any other lady.

But so that he would not suspect what she was planning, she was as charming to him as she could be. When he heard her order that he be disarmed, he said that he had to be on his way; but she swore that he had to stay the night, as she was eager to show him great honor and hospitality. "And when you do leave this valley," she said, "it will remain so emptied of knights that not a single person could find lodging here; all these fine houses will fall to the ground and turn to dust, and the valley will be as empty and barren as it used to be. Without you tonight, the knights who are here would be at a loss to find a place to sleep."

Her words at last convinced him to stay. Everyone rejoiced to have him there, and the more Morgan watched him, the more she prized him. At the beginning, though, he did not want to stay, until she promised him that all the knights were free to leave whenever they wished; she promised him, besides, that each of them could leave the valley with the horse and the arms that he had brought in. The night was filled with the rejoicing of the knights as they awaited the new day; and there is no point in describing the splendid feast they had, for they might as well have been in the richest city in the world.

When it was time to go to sleep, the beds were made ready, and they gave Lancelot an especially comfortable one, with Sir Yvain and the duke beside him, as well as the three other knights of the king's household. Then Morgan asked Lancelot and his two companions where they were going; and when she heard the news of Sir Gawain, she was very sorry and said to Lancelot, "If the knight who is holding Sir Gawain in prison were holding you and knew you as well as I do, you would have a bad time of it there, deservedly so."

He answered that the knight might well hold him, if he could live long enough to reach his castle. "But how," he went on, "have I deserved to be killed, if he held me?"

"You killed his nephew today," she said; "it was the man whose head you brought me."

"God!" he cried, "now I am even more pleased than before, because that means Sir Gawain is avenged somewhat! If only I could face him now, without interference from anyone else!"

And she began to laugh. With that, she left and pretended to go to bed; but first she carried out what she had undertaken to do, and only then did she go to bed. Once she was sure that Lancelot was asleep, she came up to him and slipped a ring onto one of the fingers of his right hand. This ring was such that, if it was put onto the finger of a sleeping man, he would remain asleep as long as it stayed in place. When she was done, she went to bed for a while. After sleeping a little, she rose and went back to Lancelot's bedside. She then had four of her men-at-arms move him onto a quilted mattress and carry him out into the meadow, where they put him onto a stretcher attached to two strong, swift horses and hurried away with him. Morgan went along, as did her lover.

They took him far away, to a forest where Morgan had a splendid property and a very beautiful house. In the morning, they lowered him into an underground cell and left him there.

But now the story stops speaking here about Lancelot and Morgan, and turns back to Sir Yvain and the other knights who were still in the Valley.

[*After several adventures, Lancelot liberated Gawain and the others but was imprisoned anew by Morgan, who then sent a messenger to the royal court to denounce the love of Lancelot and Guenevere. Galehaut, Lionel, and Gawain set out in search of Lancelot.*]

18. Galehaut Discovers Lancelot's Shield and Battles Successfully, Though Not Without Being Wounded, to Gain Possession of It.

The story says that, when Galehaut and his companions woke up the next morning and did not find Morgan's messenger with them in the vavasor's house where she had lodged them, they were shocked and disappointed. They left the place in great sorrow and worry, for the vavasor could not show them the right road; in their distress they rode on without stopping till well into mid-morning. At that point, on Galehaut's advice, they separated, the better to scour the countryside. Their search, however, could not succeed; even if there had been a thousand of them, they would never have found Lancelot as long as he remained in Morgan's prison, because the witchcraft that she knew only too well did not let him be discovered. The story nevertheless speaks of the adventures of the four knights, and first of all those of Galehaut, who was more uneasy than his companions.

Galehaut now went off with his four squires. He met no man or woman whom he did not question for some trace of what he was seeking, but none had any facts to tell him; he rode around like that for two whole days without anything happening that the story need speak of. On the third day both face and body showed that he was in a very sad state, his worry over Lancelot having taken away much of his appetite for food and drink. He rode until the hour of tierce, then came into a large, old forest full of tall trees. By midday the sun was hot, as it is in June, and he was overcome by such an urgent desire to sleep that he could not travel any farther, so he dismounted, lay down in the deepest shade he saw, and slept soundly for a long while.

[Galehaut learned that Lancelot was in prison.]

Galehaut saw straight ahead a beautiful battlemented house, moated in the Welsh way and protected by tree-stump hurdles. When he came up to the gate, he saw in the courtyard a great crowd of ladies and maidens and knights, singing and dancing in rounds and enjoying themselves.

In the middle of the courtyard stood a pole with a hook on it, from which hung a shield that seemed very much to be that of a worthy knight, as it had very large lance-holes both above and below the raised center and showed the slashes and slices of swords on top and bottom and was splintered and broken. But enough of its colors remained to make it recognizable: it had a silver field crossed by a diagonal band of red.[28] The shield was displayed right in front of the round-dancers, and every time the knights or ladies came to face it, they would bow before it as before a holy relic.

For a long while Galehaut watched how they were honoring the shield. He recognized it and was sure that it was the shield that Lancelot carried from London when he rushed after Sir Gawain; and he was very glad to see it, because it gave him to understand that he would now have news of Lancelot. Thereupon, fully armed as he was, he rode through the doorway toward the

---

[28]This shield first appears in Chapter 4, where it is the first of the three magic shields sent to Lancelot by the Lady of the Lake.

shield. An elderly knight came up to him, and Galehaut asked him whose shield it was and why all those men and women were bowing before it.

"My lord," said the good man, "it belonged to the finest knight in the world, and that's why we are treating it with such rejoicing and honor."

Galehaut then asked him please to give him whatever news of the knight he might have; and the man answered that it was nothing he could vouch for, "but news did reach us that he is dead, and this castle was for three days plunged into such grief that no one would have dared show a sign of joy. But yesterday evening his shield was brought here to comfort us, and we are rejoicing over it, as you see."

Galehaut thought to himself that, if he could not have the knight, he would have his shield. He took it then and, carrying it out of the courtyard, handed it to one of his squires.

"What are you doing?" said the old knight. "Do you mean to take it away?"

"Yes," said Galehaut; "or else I'll die."

"Well," he answered, "you'll do just that very soon, because there are many brave knights here who will fight you for the shield!"

Galehaut did not go on talking, but galloped back to his squire and ordered him to rush ahead to the nearby woods as fast as his mount could go.

The squire did as ordered, while Galehaut rode more calmly behind him. He had not gone far when he became aware of an armed knight galloping up after him. When he drew near, he bellowed out that Galehaut would be sorry to have taken the shield. Then Galehaut asked for his helmet, laced it on, put on his shield, then took a lance of the sort he used, with a thick shaft and sharp iron head. Then, furiously, like a man more eager for death than for life, he attacked the knight. He delivered a blow above his shield and, the tip being sharp and the attacker strong and furious, he pierced him right through the heart and threw him down dead to the ground.

[*Then Galehaut fought a number of other knights, defeating most but being wounded in the process. His enemy, recognizing his nobility, ordered that the battle cease.*]

"As God is my witness," said the good man, "you are of such noble heart that I would not take a kingdom to let you die on my land for so slight a wrong."

Then he ordered the remaining knights to withdraw, granting him safety. After that, he himself attended to his wound, dressing it as needed. Meanwhile, Galehaut asked him for God's sake to say whether he knew Lancelot was really dead and where his body lay; but the man answered that he could not tell him any more than he had already said.

They parted on friendly terms. The old knight asked Galehaut to tell him his name, which he did, and then the two took leave of each other; the good man would gladly have had him stay on if possible, but he could not persuade him. Galehaut went away anguished and grieving over the death of Lancelot. Rapt in the deepest mourning, he realized that he could not live on after him and resolved to lay his body open to all the risks it could bear, barring, however, anything that would damn his soul.

With such mournful thoughts he rode till evening, when chance brought him to a religious house; the monks received him very honorably, and he spent the night there. It happened that one of them, who used to be a knight, could attend to his wound, since he knew about such things; and so Galehaut stayed at the house until the wound had almost healed, but his general state grew steadily worse. Afraid of not dying the right way, he decided to go back to his land and found churches and hospitals; he would give alms generously for the soul of his friend and for his own as well. Thus he left the monastery that had tended him in his pain and that later, with his gifts, grew into a large, rich abbey.

But now the story turns back to Lancelot.

[*Morgan released Lancelot, on condition that he not see Guenevere before Christmas. Gawain and Yvain later met Lancelot at a tournament, but he refused to return to court with them.*]

19. Lancelot Goes to Sorelois, Only to Find that Galehaut Has Departed; He, Too, Leaves, but in Circumstances that Suggest Suicide.

When Lancelot parted from Sir Gawain and Sir Yvain, he pondered and wondered where he might go; in the end, he made up his mind to go to Galehaut, who had always been so good to him, and he started on his way to Sorelois. If he had known that Galehaut was away looking for him, he would not have gone there; but Sir Gawain had forgotten to tell him, and he would soon be extremely disappointed. When he reached Sorelois, he was welcomed very warmly, but of Galehaut he found no trace, since he and Lionel had gone off to search for him. Lancelot was so deeply disturbed by that that he almost took leave of his senses, since he did not know whom to turn to for comfort, and all the joyous warmth of his welcome only galled him.

One night, he stole away from Galehaut's people at midnight, taking only his tunic, shirt, and underclothes. His great anguish had made his nose bleed while he was still in bed, and he had lost a whole bowlful of blood. Then he went away. When the blood was found the next morning, he was thought to have been killed, and the mourning for him was endless.

But now the story has no more to say about him for the moment and turns back instead to Galehaut, who was searching for him.

20. Galehaut, at Court, Hears that Lancelot Is Back in Sorelois; He Returns, Only to Hear the News of Lancelot's Apparent Suicide, and Dies Heartbroken.

When Galehaut and Lionel left Sorelois, they went first to court and there found Sir Gawain, who gave them news of Lancelot, saying that he was quite sure he had gone to Sorelois, "since I forgot to tell him that you were looking for him."

Then Galehaut went back to Sorelois, but when he heard how Lancelot had disappeared and heard about the blood in his bed, he was sure that he was dead and had even killed himself. From that time on, there was no comfort for Galehaut, who could surely have found some comfort had he not been convinced that Lancelot was dead; but this thought made him lose all hope, so that he spurned all food and drink. Whatever comfort he had came from Lancelot's shield, which he kept at all times before his eyes.

Lancelot's death, says the story, made him go without eating or drinking for eleven days and nights, to the point where the men of religion who often came to see him claimed that, if he died as a result, his soul would be damned. So they forced him to eat, but it was to no avail, for too much harm had been done by the long fast. Besides, another problem arose, in that the wound that he had received when fighting for the shield, having been poorly treated, festered and made his flesh rot. And then he fell into an illness that made his body and all his limbs turn dry.

Galehaut languished in that way from the Feast of Mary Magdalene to the last week of September. Then he took leave of this world, according to all reports, as the worthiest man of his age during those times. It would not be easy to recount all his deeds of charity. He invested his nephew with his lands and secured for him the homage of his vassals, and he did many other good works.

Here the story finishes telling of him and turns back to Lancelot.

Part IV

TRANSLATED BY ROBERTA L. KRUEGER

21. Meleagant Abducts Guenevere; Lancelot, in Quest of the Queen, Rides in a Cart.

Now the story says that after Lancelot had departed secretly from Sorelois and had left the region, he grieved every day and ate and slept little. His head became so empty that he went mad, and he remained that way all summer and all winter until Christmas. He wandered throughout many lands, persisting in his madness. After Christmas, it so happened that the Lady of the Lake, who had raised him, went everywhere in search of him; she traveled for a long time asking for news and looking for signs until she finally found him on the eve of Candlemas lying in a hedge in the forest of Tintagel in Cornwall. So she took him off and healed him and kept him with her all winter long and throughout Lent. Afterwards, he was more handsome and stronger than he had ever been, because she promised him that she would bestow on him again joy as great as the greatest he had ever known. He never learned a thing about the death of Galehaut as long as he stayed with his lady, because she concealed it from him and kept it hidden as best she could.

So he remained with his lady until two weeks before Ascension. Then he set off for King Arthur's court. His lady prepared for him a horse and arms, and said, "Lancelot, now the time has come for you to recover all that you have lost, if you wish. Understand that you must be at Camelot on Ascension Day before the hour of nones. If you are not there at that time, you'll love your death more than life."

"Ah, my lady," he said, "do tell me why."

"Because," she answered, "the queen will be abducted. If you are present, you'll rescue her from the place from which no one has ever been rescued."

"Then I swear I'll be there," he responded, "be it on horse or on foot."

And so she made him set off two weeks before Ascension, so that he arrived precisely at noon in Camelot at the spot where Kay lay beaten and wounded because of the queen whom he had been accompanying, just as the story of the *Charrette* tells it.[29]

On that day, King Arthur held his court at Camelot, which was the city most full of adventures that ever was and one of the most delightful. But this was not one of the great, marvelous courts that Arthur had held during the lifetime of the noble Galehaut and in the presence of Lancelot of the Lake, who everyone thought was dead. Instead, the court was sad and mournful, and many tears were shed before it dispersed.

For when the king had returned from Mass, Lancelot's cousin Lionel entered; he had been seeking his cousin throughout many lands. The king rushed up to greet him, as did the queen, who greeted him more joyfully than anyone, and the lady of Malehaut, whom nothing could make happy, since she had lost the chance to be lady of thirty kingdoms when Galehaut died, and was supposed to have married him within the year.

Great joy greeted Lionel's arrival, but it soon changed into anguish when he told them that his cousin was lost and that he really believed he was dead. The king began to weep, saying that it was out of grief for Galehaut, who had died.

"Indeed," said Sir Gawain, "he is right, because after the death of such a man as Galehaut, no man should deign to live."

This idea made the queen very angry, for she could not accept the idea of Lancelot's death. She faced Sir Gawain and said, "What do you mean, Gawain? Are you saying that there is no nobleman left on earth who is the equal of Galehaut?"

And he replied, "In truth, my lady, I do not know him."

"There is your uncle, at least," she answered.

At that Sir Gawain rose, and his heart grew heavy, and tears came to his eyes. He turned and said as he departed, "Certainly, lady, he should well be."

So the matter was left between them.

Then Kay the Seneschal arrived, holding a staff in his hand. He had removed his coat, and he said to the king that dinner was ready and that "you can eat right now, because the meal will not wait for any adventure."[30] The

---

[29]Refers to *Le Chevalier de la Charrette,* or *The Knight of the Cart,* a verse romance written ca. 1180 by Chrétien de Troyes for Marie, Countess of Champagne. The allusion to Kay's defeat by Meleagant anticipates events that are about to occur. This section of the prose *Lancelot* follows Chrétien's story, with important modifications, up through the death of Meleagant at the end of Chapter 27.

[30]Kay alludes to Arthur's frequent habit of waiting until an adventure has occurred before eating.

king sat down to eat not because he desired to, but to gladden his court. Yet
few of those who were there ate.

Lionel was with the queen in her room, where they consoled each other
in their deep sadness. After the king had eaten, he reclined on a large couch;
he was so sad that he had no desire for the festivities he usually enjoyed.
Instead, he was pensive, and all around him his assembly of barons was
stunned.

While the King was reflecting there, in came a knight armed in a hauberk
and leg armor; his sword was girded, and he wore no helmet. He was tall and
well proportioned in every respect; he strode across the room with long steps.
He clasped the hilt of his sword with his right hand in a show of confidence.
As he approached the king, he spoke very arrogantly and said, "King Arthur, I
have come to make it known that I am Meleagant, son of King Bademagu of
Gorre. I have come to your court to prove my honor and to defend myself
against Lancelot of the Lake because of the wound I gave him last year in a
joust, for I have heard that he complains that I wounded him in treason. If he
says that, then let him come forward, because I am completely prepared to
defend myself."

"Sir knight," said the king, "Lancelot is not here, and we have not known
where he is for a long time, which is a great pity. If he were here, he would
certainly dare to defend his right, either here or in your land, as we well know,
or in any other place."

News of this knight traveled so swiftly that it was known in the queen's
chambers. Lionel, who was there, rushed before the king and hastened to
challenge the knight who had wickedly wounded Lancelot. But the king did
not want to permit the fight to take place, nor did the queen, who did all she
could to prevent it.

Then Meleagant rode away. When he reached the entrance to the hall, he
turned back, and went before the king, saying, "King, I'm leaving your court
without a fight, but I'll do such a thing that, if any nobleman be present, I'll
have one. You know very well that in my land and in the land of my father,
Bademagu, many knights from your land are held imprisoned and enslaved
along with ladies and maidens and young men. It doesn't seem that there are
as many good knights here in your court as they say, since they haven't come
to rescue and free the prisoners! It's neither too far nor too arduous for such
knights as there must be here to cross one bridge and to fight a single knight.
But now they can easily win honor, if they dare. If you're bold enough to entrust the queen—whom I see there—to one of your knights who would escort
her to the forest, and if he can defend her against me, then I will free all the
miserable men and women in Gorre, and I'll become your man, and so will
my father. And then, when your knight has defeated me, you'll keep me imprisoned until you have all your promises fulfilled. But if I conquer the
knight, this won't stop you from doing all that is within your powers, nor me
from doing what I can."

"Noble lord," said the king, "since you hold my people imprisoned, I must endure the situation until I can improve it. But they will not be freed by the queen, any more than they are imprisoned because of her."

Then Meleagant left and mounted his horse, riding all the way to the edge of the forest, glancing back and waiting to see if anyone would follow after him.

Less than two bowshots away, there were a good hundred armed knights waiting for him. There Meleagant waited, and word of the knight's pride and arrogance spread so quickly throughout the king's castle that Kay the Seneschal, who was below eating in the hall, heard it. He rose from the table and went to his room, armed himself, and came before the king, saying, "My lord, I have served you for a long time, but it no longer pleases me to serve you. So I now take leave of you, for I am going away."

The king was completely shocked by this. "What do you mean?" he said. "Seneschal, are you speaking the truth?"

"Yes, my lord," he said, "without a doubt."

"Why is this?" asked the king.

"My lord," he said, "such is my will now."

"You won't do this," said the King, "but if you have a foolish desire, abandon it: I entreat you, for the sake of the love and faith you have for me, please remain."

"Lord," he said, "don't beg me about that now, because there is nothing in the world that would make me remain, save one thing, and you won't find out what that is from me now."

The king cherished Kay and thus tried as hard as he could to detain him, but Kay did not want to tell the one thing that would make him stay. When the king saw that he would not find out by himself, he asked the queen to entreat him. And so she did, very sweetly. "You know very well," she said, "that whatever it is that you want, I'll make sure that you have it."

"Lady," Kay replied, "if I were sure of that, I would tell it."

And the king, who was delighted, promised him what he wanted and he thereby gave him the queen as a guarantee.

"Lord," said Kay, "you have granted that the queen be entrusted to me so that I can lead her to the knight who was just here. For your court would be disgraced if no one were found here who dared to accompany her."

The king could not have been more upset about this matter. And so he gave the queen to Kay, although there was not a knight present who was not crying. The queen wept so bitterly that no one could force a word out of her. Then her palfrey was led forth.

When Dodinel the Wildman heard that Kay was leading the queen away, he was very disturbed, and he confronted the king: "My lord, are you going to permit that my lady be carried off in such a manner?"

"I can't do anything else," said the King.

"No?" asked Dodinel. "May God never help me if he manages to take her very far. It would be better for me to capture her than that a stranger do so."

"You'll do nothing of the sort," Arthur replied, "nor, so help me God, will betrayal ever be found in anything that I promise. Kay will have her, because I have granted her to him. Meleagant will have nothing to fear from me until he returns to his own land, because whatever promise a king has made must not be broken."

"No?" replied Dodinel. "Then I declare that no one is disgraced unless he is a king, and shame on whoever wants to be one!"

Then he departed as distressed as he could be, and the queen mounted her horse as she wept bitterly. And Kay said, "My lady, do not worry."

She looked at Sir Gawain who was dying of grief, and she could not refrain from saying, "Ah, Sir Gawain, today I shall see for myself that after Galehaut all prowess is dead."

Then Kay led her off, and they rode straight toward the forest. Meleagant saw her coming and went to the hundred knights who were waiting for him, and told them about the adventure, and they were overjoyed.

Meleagant returned to where he had been waiting, and when Kay reached him, he asked if it was the queen he had with him.

"Yes," said Kay.

"And who are you?" asked Meleagant.

Kay told his name.

"My lady," said Meleagant to the queen, "uncover your face."

She was so distressed that she wanted to die, and she spoke not a word.

Meleagant lifted her veil and recognized her. "Kay," he said, "we'll go into the best clearing there is, which I'll show you; we'll be able to joust more easily there than we could in these dense woods."

And Kay agreed.

So they went their way, and they came upon a knight in armor. It was Lancelot, who was guarding the path, just as his Lady of the Lake had ordered. He asked who the lady was.

"It is the queen," said Kay.

"Which queen?" asked Lancelot.

"The wife of King Arthur."

"You shall take her no farther," ordered Lancelot.

"Against whom are you willing to defend her?" asked Kay.

"Against all those who would lead her any farther."

"Who are you?" asked Kay.

"I am a knight errant. And who are you?"

"I am Kay."

"Are you abducting my lady in this way?"

Kay did not recognize Lancelot, and told him, "Noble lord, I must defend her against this knight," and he explained how that had come to pass.

Lancelot decided to see how Kay would fare. So he rode off, and the queen, who believed he had recognized her, was amazed. "I dare not think he is Lancelot."

Lancelot followed them throughout the woods until they reached the clearing. Then Meleagant took the queen by her horse's reins and said, "Come along, lady."

"You haven't won her yet," said Kay. "Remove your hand, because you'll soon pay for that."

Then the two backed apart and placed their lances beneath their arms; they knocked the sides of their shields and spurred on their horses; they exchanged heavy blows on their shields. Kay shattered his lance, and Meleagant struck him so hard that he bent him back over the saddle, so that the leather and planks of his shield split, and his hauberk could not endure the great blow: the chains of the mail broke, and the tip of the lance pierced Kay's side and broke one of his ribs; it was driven so hard that the blade passed beside the spine through the fold in the hauberk. Meleagant brought Kay and his horse down in a heap, and he fell so hard to the ground that the whole saddle splintered. Then Kay fainted, and Meleagant, who was very cruel, rode over his body until he was completely crushed and unable to defend himself. Meleagant's knights, who had been waiting, ran up to Kay and raised him in his wounded condition into a litter, and carried him away.

That is how they abducted the queen. When Lancelot, who had been watching to see what the outcome would be, saw that they were carrying his lady away, he was not pleased. He dug his spurs into his horse and shouted after them. And Meleagant saw him coming, and turned to face him, for he would have been quite valiant if he had not been so lacking in honor. The field was flat, the horses were spirited, and the knights were strong and angry. They dashed in from afar and exchanged heavy blows on their shields. Meleagant broke his lance, and Lancelot struck him in the middle of his shield. The knight was strong and resilient, the blow was heavy. Lancelot hit the knight so violently that he sent him flying to the ground, where he fell so hard that he was completed stunned.

The horse fled, and Lancelot pursued the others; he had taken hold of his own lance,[31] and he hit the first knight he reached so hard that he struck him dead. Then he rushed into the field once more and charged against all the knights. He performed so well with his lance that he killed four men, and then he put his hand to his sword and attacked them, like a man who does not fear death. He shattered their shields and smashed their helmets and destroyed

---

[31] *glaive;* the Old French terms *lance* and *glaive* are both used to describe the weapon with long wooden shaft and a sharp metal tip that is used for combat on horseback; the *espee,* "sword," is often reserved for combat on foot.

their hauberks wherever he overtook them. Meleagant, having remounted, saw the marvelous deeds that the knight was performing, and his heart told him that it must be Lancelot. He spurred his horse on, faced Lancelot, took a lance, struck Lancelot's horse right through the middle and killed it. His knights rushed up, but Meleagant was afraid that other knights would follow,[32] and so he told them: "Go away, all of you: leave him alone, for this matter is not yet settled."

So then they all rode away, and Meleagant remained behind. But he did not try to kill or capture Lancelot, for he feared an ambush, and yet he dearly wanted to undertake an important fight. Lancelot's horse was dead and could not be moved, so Lancelot remained behind; he was so distressed he nearly killed himself.

As Lancelot looked about, he saw Sir Gawain ride up in full armor; Sir Gawain had seen Kay's horse fleeing towards the town. The king's men all believed that Kay was dead, and so Sir Gawain had armed himself to rescue the queen and to pursue her all the way to Gorre. He had two horses led along beside him.

When Lancelot saw Sir Gawain, he recognized him readily, but Sir Gawain did not recognize Lancelot. When he had reached him, Lancelot said to Sir Gawain, "My lord, you see that my horse is dead; for the sake of God and for a reward, lend me or give me one of yours until I can return it to you."

Sir Gawain said that he would do so very willingly, "and take the one you prefer."

Lancelot leapt up on one of the horses, but it did not matter to him which one. Sir Gawain asked him who he was.

"Don't worry about who I may be," said Lancelot, "for your horse will soon be returned to you."

At this, Sir Gawain was quite ashamed; he was sorry that he had ever asked the knight who he was.

[*Lancelot pursued the knights and distinguished himself in battle, but his horse was killed. He continued to pursue them on foot.*]

When he had pursued the knights to the point of exhaustion, he looked to his right and saw a cart in the middle of a broad, grassy path.

He headed toward the cart, where he found a hunchbacked dwarf who was a very fine cart driver. "Oh, dwarf," said Lancelot, "if you have any news about the knights who have come through here leading a lady, then tell me, and I promise to be your knight forever."

---

[32]Meleagant presumably fears that other knights will arrive to assist Lancelot.

"Ah," said the dwarf, "you are asking about those who are leading away the queen?"

"Yes."

"Do you greatly desire to know where they are going?"

"Yes," said Lancelot, "more than anything."

"Then," said the dwarf, "climb up on this cart, and I'll take you to a place where you'll learn the truth about them."

"Do you promise me that?" said Lancelot.

"Yes," replied the dwarf.

And so Lancelot leapt immediately into the cart. At that time, there was a custom that whoever wanted to destroy or disgrace a man in all countries would first make him ride upon a cart. From then on he would never be received in a court, but would rather have lost all knightly privileges.

That is how Lancelot rode in the cart. After they had gone some distance, Sir Gawain caught up with them. He had been everywhere Lancelot had performed his brave deeds and had seen all the men he killed; he was amazed by what Lancelot had done. When he saw the knight on the cart, it greatly disturbed him, and he said to the dwarf, "Dwarf, tell me news about the men leading the queen away, if you know any."

"If you were willing to ride on the cart just as this knight is, I would lead you to a place where you would hear news."

"I will never ride in a cart, so help me God," replied Sir Gawain.

"Then you don't have as great a desire to be shamed as this wretched knight," said the dwarf.

Sir Gawain rode behind the cart until dusk began to fall.

Then they came to a castle, and as soon as they had entered, all the people began to shout at Lancelot and to insult him and stone him; they asked the dwarf what he had done wrong. And the dwarf passed through the castle grounds, and when he had reached on the other side, Sir Gawain said to Lancelot, "Lord knight, would you not be seated more honorably on a horse than on a cart? I have two horses here: take whichever one you please; it would be an honor for both you and me."

"In God's name," said the dwarf, "he'll not mount one now, because he must ride on the cart until we reach the place where I will rest tonight."

And Lancelot said that he would do that.

So they rode on, and when they had traveled about two leagues, they arrived at another castle and rode in. If people had said much to shame Lancelot at the first castle, here they insulted him even more. There was no one, young or old, who did not chase after him. And so they escorted him right up to a large enclosure surrounded by a high ramparts; there, the cart passed inside.

"Get down," said the dwarf to Lancelot.

"First tell me news about my lady."

"You'll find out about it here." said the dwarf.

"No, I will learn it some other way," Lancelot replied.

"Then you don't want to sleep here tonight?" asked the dwarf.

"No," he said, "I would rather go on."

"If you want to learn what you're asking about," said the dwarf, "you will sleep here. But unless you're brave and strong, don't stay here, for no one but a valiant man can escape from this place."

Lancelot was most dismayed by this news, for if he remained there, he knew that Sir Gawain would recognize him. But if he left, he knew that the dwarf would think him a coward. He stepped down and saw two young ladies approach who were emerging from a high tower; they welcomed Sir Gawain joyously. Lancelot greeted them, and one of them said, "God help me, my lord, you should have refrained from greeting us."

"Why so, my lady?"

"Because you're disgraced in all lands for having ridden in a cart," she said.

When Lancelot heard this, he was so dismayed that he nearly killed himself with his own sword. But when he reminded himself that he had ridden in the cart for his lady, he returned the sword to its sheath and stopped grieving.

[A maiden showed Lancelot three beds but told him that he would be risking his life if he slept in the splendid one in the middle. He declared his intention to sleep in that very one.]

Then they withdrew and led Sir Gawain away. Lancelot had many servants who disrobed him, and as soon as he was undressed, he climbed into the most splendid bed. Soon afterward Sir Gawain and the two ladies returned; they told him that he slept there at his peril. This did not bother Lancelot, and the young women retired. Then Sir Gawain lay down, even more convinced than before that it was Lancelot who lay in the luxurious bed. Lancelot, worn out by combat and by sorrow about his lady, slept very soundly.

At midnight, the whole house began to shake, and a great crash resounded so loudly that it seemed that everything was crumbling. Then a lance with a white shaft and a red tip descended from above, and a bright red flame burst forth from it. The lance descended as loudly as lightning on Lancelot's bed; it pierced the bedspread and the sheets and struck Lancelot on his left side; then it shot through the foot of the bed to the ground. Lancelot leapt up, saw it transfixed straight through the bed, pulled it out, threw it as far as he could, and said that whoever threw it should be as cursed as a coward, since he did not strike immediately.[33] Lancelot then put out the fire on the bed and placed the sword at his side.

---

[33]Lancelot is angered by the absence of a human agent who would have thrown the lance and who would turn up for a fight.

Sir Gawain had leapt up again, terrified that Lancelot was mortally wounded, and he asked him how he was. "Fine, my lord; now go back to sleep," said Lancelot.

So Sir Gawain returned to bed and stayed there until dawn. The room was dark, and they could not see the daylight. The dwarf who had led Lancelot on the cart came in and called out from the doorway, "Knight who rode the cart, come see those who are leading off the queen."

And Lancelot, who was sleeping in his shift[34] and breeches, leapt up and threw only his tunic on his back and went swiftly to the tower. He saw many young women at the windows overlooking the fields, and he went there; he saw that the knights whom he had seen the previous day were leading the queen away. Alongside them, in a litter, he saw Kay the Seneschal.

When he saw the queen, he was so stunned that he was speechless. The farther she retreated from his sight, the farther he leaned out the window to see her. Sir Gawain had approached, and saw that the knight was there and that he was hanging out the window as far as his thighs. Sir Gawain took him between his arms and pulled him back. When Sir Gawain saw the knight's face, he recognized that he was indeed Lancelot, and he began to kiss him, saying "Ah, dear friend, why do you hate your life? You very nearly died there."

"Indeed, he is right to," said the young women, "for he will never have honor."

"Alas," said Sir Gawain, "then there will be no honor on earth, if this knight doesn't have any. You know very little now about him."

Then they called for their armor and had themselves armed. The maidens asked Sir Gawain who this knight was, and he said that he would tell them under no circumstances without the knight's permission. "But I will tell you this much. He is the very best of noble knights. Don't ask me any more questions, because you would be wasting your effort."

When the men were armed, the maidens had their horses and lances brought forth. But Sir Gawain said that he would not mount before his companion "takes the one of my two horses that pleases him more."

Lancelot took the lance and climbed on one of the horses, and both knights rode away. And the elder maiden asked Lancelot his name.

"My lady," he said, "why do you want to know? I am a knight who has ridden a cart."

"That is truly a great shame," she said. Then she called one of her maidservants and confided to her what she wanted. Then she[35] mounted her horse

---

[34]The Old French word is *chemise,* which refers to male or female underclothing. "Shift" has been chosen here as a translation for Lancelot's garment because the word chemise in modern English refers specifically to female underclothing.
[35]This is presumably the servant.

and accompanied the two knights some distance to show them the path that led to the queen, and then she headed back.

Then the two companions rode on until noon, when they met a young woman riding on a mule that was sweating with exhaustion. They greeted one another, and the knights asked for news of the queen.

"I could certainly tell you news if I wanted to."

They both begged her to do so.

"What will you give me?"

"Lady," said Sir Gawain, "I'll be your knight forever."

"By God's name," Lancelot told her, "ask for whatever you want and you will have it, if I'm able to find it anywhere in the world."

"I'll tell you," she said.

And she told them who had abducted the queen and how arrogantly he had done it.

"All this I know well," said Sir Gawain. "But tell us how to enter his country."

"The entrance is surely not easy," she replied, "because there are two very treacherous passages. Here, on the right, is the path of the Sword Bridge; to the left, there is the Underwater Bridge, which the people of the area call the Lost Bridge."

"My lord," said Lancelot to Sir Gawain, "choose one of these two ways, since you have undertaken the quest."

Sir Gawain chose the Lost Bridge.

"And I'll take the Sword Bridge," said Lancelot.

"My lords," said the young woman, "each of you owes me whatever gift I request."

They agreed, and she left them. The two companions spoke together at length. But Sir Gawain told Lancelot neither about Galehaut's death nor about the queen's chagrin, nor about where he had been, because he saw that Lancelot was too pensive and disturbed. Then they took leave of each other, and Sir Gawain set forth in the direction of the Lost Bridge. But here the story falls silent about Sir Gawain and talks about Lancelot.

22. Lancelot at the Holy Cemetery.

[*A young woman who had subjected Lancelot to a test and had been rescued by him accompanied him toward Bademagu's land.*]

They rode until the hour of tierce and found a deep, wide river. They followed along the riverbank until they arrived at a castle at the edge of Bademagu's land; it was called Wandehenches, and it was very well fortified. You should understand that Bademagu's land was enclosed on the British side by two great rivers which the two perilous bridges spanned. If a wandering knight crossed over one of them, he could ride through without a challenge and travel freely throughout the land that was between the two waters.

Bademagu had conquered that land since he had become king. When he saw that the captives from Britain were increasing, he placed them in that land, which he called the Land Beyond. The region possessed four points of exit, which were at four castles. They had been built only so that the exiles would not escape, although they paid them no heed.

The Knight of the Cart entered the castle along with the maiden who was accompanying him. And the news had already spread far and wide that a knight who had ridden a cart was coming to free the queen; it was soon known everywhere what kind of armor he wore.

The knight entered the castle along with the young lady. Then all the maidens and the ladies of the castle began to cry out, "Flee, flee on account of the disgraceful knight who is coming, for he was carried in a cart!"

And they fixed their eyes upon him and cursed the hour he was born.

All the little children of the town ran about, crying, "Look at the defeated knight! Look at the defeated knight!"

In that manner, the knight rode beyond the castle. The young lady wept softly and cursed the day that a cart was ever made. By the time they passed beyond the castle, it was high noon. They came to a large stone causeway between two rivers and found a tall, armed knight at the entrance.

As Lancelot and the girl approached the bridge, the knight of the causeway jumped forward and, as he recognized the Knight of the Cart, cried out, "Away! You who have ridden in the cart, go away! You won't cross here, for your stench would kill me."

"I certainly will," said the knight, "for this is the way I'm heading."

"You will be doing a foolish thing," said the other.

"Why?"

"By my faith," said the other, "you'll have to give up what I like best of all that you possess or else fight with me."

"What do you mean? Do you ask the same thing of everyone who passes here?"

"Yes, indeed I would, even if Arthur of Britain came by. From his wife herself today I had a very lovely payment for passage."

"What was that?" asked the Knight of the Cart.

He pointed to a stone slab at the end of the causeway. "You could see on that stone over there the most splendid comb you've ever seen; its teeth are full of the queen's hair, which is very beautiful. But her hair must not be seen by a man who has ridden on a cart as you have."

"Whatever kind of man I am, I'll see it anyway," retorted Lancelot.

"Then you will first give me the horse that you are riding," said the other.

"You won't get this horse easily; I will fight first," declared Lancelot.

"No, what a disgrace! I'll never fight with you, God willing, for a good knight shouldn't fight with a defeated man."

"Then I will pass by all the more easily," answered Lancelot.

As Lancelot was about to ride onto the causeway, the knight came forward and told him that if he advanced even a single step, he would lose no less than his head. Lancelot gave no indication that he was alarmed, but rather rode ahead anyway. The knight took his horse by the reins. "Knight," he said, "now you will proceed no farther, for you must fight with me. And understand that if I win, I will cut off your head."

So the Knight of the Cart stopped. And the other knight charged up and down the road, as fast as he could ride. Lancelot did the same, and they exchanged blows on their shields. The knight of the causeway shattered his lance, and Lancelot struck him so hard that he brought him off his horse to the ground. Then Lancelot dismounted, removed his shield from his neck, threw it over his head for protection, drew his sword, and charged against the knight of the causeway, who had jumped up. They exchanged fierce blows on their helmets, shields, and hauberks.

But, at last, the knight of the causeway was so mistreated that he had to abandon his place and could no longer endure the assault; he surrendered the crossing to Lancelot. And Lancelot told him that he would not escape in that manner, unless he declared himself defeated.

"Tell me first," he said, "if it was true that you rode in the cart."

And Lancelot replied that it was true.

"Then surely," said the knight of the causeway, "I'll not be defeated by a man who has been in a cart."

"Then you will die," said the other.

"I would rather have an honorable death than a disgraceful defeat."

"Alas, unlucky one," said the girl, "he was not disgraced by the cart, for he mounted of his own good will for the sake of his great honor."

"Indeed, I believe that he did it with a noble heart, for he is an excellent knight. Take my sword, my lord, because I finally declare myself defeated by your hand."

"First you'll give me the queen's comb, and then you'll go to be imprisoned where I order you," replied Lancelot. "And if you don't want to do this, you'll lose your head, just as you threatened earlier today to cut mine off."

The knight was reluctant to agree to this, but he was finally forced to consent. He led Lancelot to the stone, and he gave him the comb. Lancelot gazed at it so tenderly that he forgot everything else. He lifted the bottom of his hauberk and pressed the comb with the queen's hair against his chest and told the knight that he could leave cleared of any obligations, since he had been so richly rewarded. The knight was very glad for that, and so he departed.

The knight and the young lady traveled on until they entered a forest. When they had ridden until early afternoon, they came to a path so narrow that there was scarcely room for one horse to turn around, because it formed a deep hollow and was bordered on both sides by thick woods.

[*Lancelot did battle to protect the young woman, but the fight was interrupted, and the two proceeded to a monastery, where they could spend the night.*]

Afterwards, they came to a great enclosure surrounded on all sides by high walls; it was a cemetery.[36] In this cemetery lay the body of Galahad, the younger son of Joseph of Arimathea. Galahad was conceived in Hoselice, which was later named Wales for him,[37] because he established there the religion of Our Lord Jesus Christ. With him lay twenty-four of his companions.

Inside there were two tombstones on two tombs which were very marvelous, since no one knew of what they were made. One was located high up in the midst of a beautiful meadow and the other was underground, in a deep cave. The tomb in the meadow had an inscription that said that whoever would raise it would free all the prisoners in the Kingdom of No Return. The tomb in the cave had an inscription declaring that whoever raised it would dispel the enchantments in the Kingdom of Adventures, bring an end to the adventures, and attain the seat at the Round Table. Within the tomb in the meadow lay the body of Galahad; within the tomb in the cave lay the body of Simeon, father of Moses, the one whose body lay in the Dolorous Tomb of the Hall of Great Fears, about which the Great History of the Grail speaks.[38]

The two tombs of the church where the Knight of the Cart was lodged were just as you have heard; those who would raise them had to be issued from this same lineage. The church was named the Holy Cemetery in honor of the sacred bodies that lay within. Merlin had prophesied that as soon as the tombstone of Galahad was raised his body would be carried off to Wales and that as soon as his body passed out of the country, the prisoners in Gorre would be liberated.

---

[36]In Chrétien's *Charrette,* the father and son also follow Lancelot to a cemetery; see lines 1829–2010. There Lancelot discovers and raises his own tombstone, that of the knight destined to free the prisoners of Logres trapped inside Gorre. By contrast, the historical and eschatological allusions have been multiplied and intensified in this scene, which refers to events in the *History of the Holy Grail,* to the Dolorous Guard earlier in the *Lancelot,* to the coming of Galahad, and to the *Quest for the Holy Grail.*

[37]According to this etymology, the Old French *Galles* ("Wales") would derive from Galahad. Galahad is crowned King of Hoselice by his older brother Jospheus, and his subjects name their country after their worthy ruler following his death.

[38]For the story of Moses, son of Simeon, see *The History of the Holy Grail,* Chapter 7. Moses attempts to sit at the table of the Holy Grail, but he is carried off by flaming hands on account of his sins.

Lancelot was greatly honored at the church. Almost immediately, the vavasor who would not let his son fight appeared and took accommodations inside. The monks loved him dearly, for he had been lord of the land for a long time. He entered there, but he did not let Lancelot see him. The next morning, Lancelot attended Mass before he armed himself. When he had put on his armor, the abbot said to him, "My lord, we know that you have set out on this route to rescue the queen. The first test for those who want to undertake such a thing must be attempted here."

"What is the test?"

And he told him, just as the story has explained before.

"Then I will try it," said Lancelot.

So they led him to the cemetery, and when he saw the tombs, he remembered the Dolorous Guard.[39] He came to a huge tombstone, and gazed at it in wonder, because he could not imagine of what it was made; the tomb was erected on four pillars. He seized the tombstone and raised it up without effort until he saw inside the body of a knight in full armor. The dead knight's hauberk was white as the day he was first dubbed, his helmet and shield were as bright and shining as the day they were made, the sword lay bare along his side, and it appeared to be bleeding with fresh blood in several places. The golden shield had a red cross. Lancelot began to read the inscription on the tomb, which said, HERE LIES GALAHAD, CONQUEROR OF HOSELICE, FIRST CHRISTIAN KING OF WALES.

Lancelot held the stone up for a long time. An odor emanated forth that was so pleasing and sweet that he could not satisfy his desire to smell and to gaze at the marvel; instead he forgot all else as he stood there. At that time no knight was buried without his armor, as long as he died in a place where his arms could be had. When the knight let go of the tombstone, a marvelous thing occurred; it stayed right where he had held it, as firmly as if he were still holding it. And then there entered a great crowd of monks who had come from Wales to seek the body of the king who lay in the tomb that Lancelot had opened. The abbot asked how they knew that the tomb had been opened, and they said that they had learned of it in a vision eight days earlier. And everyone marveled at this.

Then, from that holy place, the body of the high king was removed from the sarcophagus and was carried into the land of Wales.

As the Knight of the Cart came forth, he heard a great din arising from the cave of Simeon's tomb. Smoke poured forth that was so thick and so irritating that anyone standing nearby could barely endure it. Lancelot asked where the smoke and noise came from. The abbot replied that it came from

---

[39]At the Dolorous Guard, Lancelot raised the slab of the tomb destined for him and learned his identity as Lancelot, son of King Ban; see Chapter 4.

the most treacherous and hideous place that he had ever seen, and he told him about the adventure from beginning to end.

"I want to see this adventure," Lancelot announced.

The abbot led him through a dark, black vault until they came to a staircase. Then everyone left him, since they dared go no farther. Lancelot descended all the steps until he reached the source of the noise. He stopped and saw a very bright light within, but he could not tell where it was coming from, because he was still dazzled by the light, as would be someone coming in from outside. His vision soon cleared, and he found that he was in a great chamber; he saw in the middle of the room a tomb as great as, or greater than, the one he just raised. It was ablaze on all sides with a flame that leapt higher than the length of a lance and emitted an extraordinary stench.

As the knight observed the tomb in wonder, he was stunned by a voice that he heard within, a voice more horrible than he had ever heard. It brayed and cried and lamented so loudly and so frightfully that no one could hear it without being terrified. Just so did Lancelot hear it, for he drew back, unable to do anything else.

When he reached the steps, he stopped and began to think a little. When he had reflected, he sighed and began to weep bitterly, cursing the day he was born, and moaning, "Oh, God, what a great shame!"

Then he turned to the tomb and covered his face with his shield because of the flame.

As he approached, the voice emanating from the tomb cried out to him, and he listened and heard what it said: "Go away, go back, for you have neither the power nor the right to accomplish this adventure."

"Why?" asked Lancelot.

"I will tell you," said the voice, "but first tell me why you just said, 'Dear Lord God, what a great shame!'"

Then Lancelot, overcome by sorrow and shame, began to weep.

"Tell me truly," said the voice, "and do not lie to me."

"In truth," explained the knight, "I said it because I have basely betrayed and disappointed everyone in the world, for they consider me the best of the noble knights. But now I know well that I am not, because no good knight is ever afraid."

"Now," said the voice, "you do not speak nobly; you are right when you say that a good knight is not afraid, but you are wrong to say 'what a great shame' just because you are not the best of the noble ones. But with the body and the strength that you have, undertake to accomplish this task. For he who will be the Good Knight has not yet come, although his coming is very near. He will be so good and fair and so virtuous that as soon as he steps into this room he will extinguish the painful flame that burns here, ravaging my soul and my body.

"I know you and all those of your lineage very well. You should know that you were baptized in the name of the holy man you freed from the tomb up in the meadow,[40] and that I am his first cousin. But your father called you Lancelot in remembrance of his ancestor who had that name.[41] And from your lineage will come the one who will deliver me and will fulfill the adventure of the Perilous Seat and who will bring the adventures of Britain to an end."

Lancelot asked the knight his name.

"I am Simeon, nephew of Joseph of Arimathea, who brought the Grail to Great Britain from the Promised Land. But on account of a sin I committed against my Creator I am tormented in body and soul in this tomb, since God does not want me to be tortured in the other world. So I will endure this pain until the day God sends the one who will deliver us.[42]

"Now go away, fair cousin, and don't be ashamed. You have all the prowess and valor that a corrupt man can have. You should have realized that if you weren't a sinner you would have accomplished all the marvelous deeds that your kinsman will accomplish and that you have lost all this because of your father's sin, for he sinned one single time against my cousin, your mother.[43] He was a chaste virgin when he lay with her, and he was fifty or more years old. You have lost what I described to you because of this sin. Nevertheless, the good qualities you possess you have inherited from the great virtues that were in your mother, and that still are there."

When Lancelot heard that his mother was still alive, he was overjoyed. But he did not want to leave the cave without trying to raise the tombstone. When Simeon realized that he could not dissuade him, he said, "Good cousin, since it must be so, do what I tell you, or else you will die. Take from the marble stone on my right the water you find there, for it is the water with which the priest washed his hands after he blessed the body of Jesus Christ. Take this water and wet your body with it, or otherwise you will perish. But remove your shield, which would only encumber you."

Lancelot did as he was told and then went to the tomb. But no matter how hard he tried, he could not raise the tomb at all. The fire so tormented him that his hauberk disintegrated before he could climb the steps.

Then, carrying his shield in his arms, he returned to the high cemetery,

---

[40]Lancelot's baptismal name is Galahad, as was explained in the opening lines of *Lancelot*.

[41]Lancelot's grandfather is named Lancelot.

[42]Lancelot's son Galahad will extinguish the flames of Simeon's tomb in the *Quest for the Holy Grail*.

[43]The reference is to the adulterous liaison of King Ban, Lancelot's father, with the daughter or niece of the lord of Mares; Hector des Mares, Hector of the Fens, Lancelot's half-brother, was born of this union.

where all the people were waiting for him. When they saw he was alive, they were delighted.

[*Refusing to identify himself, Lancelot separated from the young woman and rode away.*]

23. The Sword Bridge.

[*A vavasor told Lancelot of the customs of the land of Gorre and predicted that his quest to rescue the queen would be successful. Lancelot and the vavasor's son entered a battle to help the exiles from Logres rout Meleagant's men.*]

Then they rode on until they came to a very large and splendid castle; they entered through the gate and rode to the other side. Everyone came out to see the knight because of the marvelous things that had been said about him. When they had passed beyond the castle, they entered a lovely town, where the exiles lived by themselves; the people of the country lived in the castle they had just ridden past. Lancelot was honored there: all the people came to greet him, singing and celebrating, and the streets were decked with all their dearest possessions. They dismounted at the most beautiful house in the town; the inhabitants greatly honored Lancelot's companions out of love for him.

The meal was prepared and served early. The knights dined, and after they had been seated a long time at table, a knight outfitted in all his armor rode in on horseback (since the house was at ground level), and he asked the lord of the manor to point out the good knight who came to rescue the queen.

"Why do you ask?" said the host.

"Because I very much want to see him."

"You would not be able to recognize him here."

The knight said, "Why is he hiding? A knight as good as he is ought not to hide himself, but should make himself known to everyone. And if he is such a knight that he dares to cross the Sword Bridge, let him say so."

And Lancelot answered, "Sir knight, I am the one who intends to cross it."

"You?" exclaimed the knight. "How dare you undertake a trial so difficult that none of the knights of the Kingdom of Logres could ever accomplish it? You should at least have abandoned it out of shame for having ridden in the cart, since there you lost all your honor and all your joy. You should realize that the miserable prisoners in this country will never be freed by a disgraced man. On the contrary, the liberator must be valiant and loyal and bold above all others, and courageous. That is the sort of man who should undertake this risk, not one with a heart as shameful and cowardly as yours is. Nonetheless, you'll cross the Dolorous River more easily, if you want to, than you'll cross the Perilous Bridge. But when you reach the other side, I'll take from you whichever of your possessions I like best."

Lancelot replied that he would never pay a toll there.

"No? Then make sure you never try to cross by the bridge, because I forbid you to. And if you want to try it despite my interdiction, then come straightway to fight with me. If you can't beat me, how will you vanquish Meleagant, who is one of the best knights in the world, after the agony of crossing the bridge?"

When the lord of the manor heard this, he declared that Lancelot would not fight at that moment, since he had other things to do. But Lancelot leapt up from the table, demanded his arms, and said that since the intruder had provoked a fight, he would have one. Although this greatly upset his hosts and companions, they could not dissuade him.

When Lancelot was armed, they led him outside the town to a field. All the exiles armed themselves as well, for they feared treachery. The whole population, from both castle and town, assembled there, and the men who had led the Good Knight there were very fearful. Lancelot told them all to take comfort and not to worry. Then he spurred himself forward, seized the strap handles of his shield, and lowered his lance under his arm. The two knights charged into each other. The ground was fine and the horses ran swift and fast.

Both knights were very brave. They exchanged such heavy blows that both of their shields split open. Their lance blades came to rest on their strong hauberks. Both lances shattered, and their horses clashed head on, body to body, and then fell dead to the ground. And the men, scarcely wounded, leapt up, although they were staggering with dizziness. When they had recovered, they placed their hands on their swords and exchanged the fiercest blows they could. The Knight of the Cart found himself in fierce battle with the knight, whom he esteemed greatly; he was very valiant, but treacherous and dishonorable.

The combat lasted a long time. They wounded and maimed each other, but, in the end, the Knight of the Cart treated his opponent so badly that he could no longer hold out; Lancelot had seriously injured him. He increasingly lost ground without any other means to defend himself.

When Lancelot saw that his enemy was so overcome, he pursued him and burdened him with blows until he brought him to his knees. As the other knight was about to rise, Lancelot grabbed him by the helmet, ripped it off his head, and hurled it to the middle of the field. And the knight thrust his shield over his head and turned away, which he need not have done, because he finally cried for mercy and held his sword out to the Knight of the Cart. But Lancelot refused to take it and declared that he would never grant his victim mercy unless he first rode in a cart. The other replied that he would by no means ride a cart.

"Then I'll cut off your head," said Lancelot.

"You may indeed do that," replied the knight.

At these words, a young woman arrived at great speed on a black palfrey and greeted the Knight of the Cart, as he did her. She leapt from her palfrey to the ground, and said, "Noble knight, I have come to you with the greatest need I have ever had of you. I beg you and entreat you by the one whom you love best in the world that you give one gift that I will ask of you, by which you will receive greater honor and profit than you have ever had for a service rendered."

Lancelot granted the gift, since he would earn honor and profit, and the girl fell at his feet in joy. "Noble knight," she said, "you have given me the head of this knight, just as you wanted to cut it off."

Lancelot thought that she was asking for protection for the knight's life, and said to her, "My lady, I will spare his head for you; for because of your prayer, I promise never to kill him, if God is willing, although he has done me a great wrong. But I shall not refuse a maiden or a lady any request, provided that it does not redound to my shame."

"Aha, my lord," replied the girl, "you have granted me his head. So give it to me in my hands, because he is the most treacherous knight who ever lived."

The Knight of the Cart was amazed to hear this. And the other knight fell at his feet and begged for mercy. "Don't believe her. She hates me, and I thought she loved me."

By that point, Lancelot did not know what to do, since the young woman had remained on her knees before him, asking for the promise he had made for the sake of the person he loved above all else. Meanwhile, the knight cried for mercy, for pity's sake and for God's. Lancelot had the custom of never killing a knight who begged for mercy, unless he had sworn beforehand to do so, or unless he could not avoid it. But he hoped to fulfill the desires of each, and so turned to the knight.

"Sir knight, if I gave back your helmet and shield, would you fight me? If I conquer you, I will do what I want with you. If you have the upper hand, I will again be at your mercy."

"Then, my lord," replied his opponent, "I would say that you are the flower of all knights."

"I will do this on the condition that if I conquer you, you won't escape with your head."

"Nor will I seek to," said the other.

Then the knight ordered that a fine, whole shield be brought, since his own was in pieces, and he returned his helmet to Lancelot. After that, Lancelot returned to the fray and conquered his opponent more fiercely and more swiftly than he had done earlier. He tore his enemy's helmet from his head and he knocked the ventail down over his shoulders. The knight cried out for mercy.

On the other side, the young woman asked once again for the knight's head on behalf of the person whom Lancelot loved the most. "Noble knight, you should realize that this will be a well-rewarded service, one that will also bring you honor, since this is the most treacherous Christian alive," she said.

So Lancelot raised his sword, struck, and cut off his opponent's head. Then he handed it to the young woman. She mounted her horse and dashed off with the head, riding swiftly until she came to a very deep and ancient well. She threw the knight's head down inside it.

This young lady was Meleagant's sister, the daughter of King Bademagu of Gorre by his last wife. The one whose head she carried was a knight whom Meleagant held dear. That knight had greatly loved the lady and had often besought her love. But the young woman wanted to hear nothing of it, since she was in love with one of the most handsome knights in the world, who was a mere youth. When the knight saw that she refused to return his love, he told Bademagu that he had seen her preparing poison to kill him and his son, so that she could install her lover as king. The king and his son detested her for that reason. Then, the treacherous knight told the king that he had seen his daughter sleeping with her lover. So Bademagu granted to the knight that if he ever found the lover again in a room with the maiden, he should kill him.

This is what the knight did, but it was through treachery, because the knight himself had led the lover there; the lover foresaw no harm in it. And so the young knight was killed without having done anything wrong. Afterwards, the girl wondered how she could avenge his death. When she learned that the Good Knight was coming to deliver the queen, she went to the one who had killed her friend and told him that if he went to fight the knight who was coming to their country, she would be his, "for I hate him more than any man," she said.

He went willingly, since he loved the girl very much. She followed him so that she could deceive him. When she saw him losing so badly against Lancelot, she then entreated the Knight of the Cart on behalf of the one he loved best, since she suspected very well that he was in love. And that is how she came to take revenge on her enemy.

The Knight of the Cart and his retinue returned to the vavasor's house; everyone looked on in amazement. Many came forward to remove Lancelot's armor and look at his wounds. His host made sure that no part of his equipment was lacking: neither ropes nor lashes, neither straps nor handles; there was nothing left for Lancelot to worry about. That night he was provided with all that he could desire. In the morning, when he rose, he heard Mass and armed himself, as did a great number of the exiles. They rode without finding any adventure to speak of until the hour of nones.

Finally, they arrived at the Sword Bridge. By then, there was no one so bold that he was not weeping out of fear for Lancelot. He comforted them all, saying, "Do not fear for me for, God willing, I'll free you; and if He is not willing, then it cannot be. You should take comfort from the adventures that have previously befallen me, for the wise men said that after the body of Galahad was delivered, you would all be freed from prison, and his body has been removed. Now rest assured that if you are ever supposed to be freed, you will now be freed."

He spoke like this at such length that they were comforted. He returned his horse to the host who owned it, and walked to the bridge, and saw that it was fearsome and perilous. He was relieved to discover that the river was hardly very wide, although it was very deep. Then he looked beyond to the other side, where he saw a very beautiful, magnificent city. This was Gorrun, the most important city of the land, after which the entire country was named Gorre.

Queen Guenevere was within that city, inside the king's palace. At that moment, she appeared at the windows, along with the king and Meleagant and knights, ladies, and maidens. From there, they had a fine view of the knights at the bridge, who could see the townspeople just as well. Many had informed the Knight of the Cart that the queen was imprisoned within the city, and so Lancelot gazed tenderly at the tower and then prepared himself. His companions removed the panels of his hauberk from the inside of his thighs, and bound them with strong ropes of deer hide and also with thick iron wires. They sewed his gauntlets, which they coated with hot tar, so that he could hold on more firmly to the bridge.

When he was completely equipped, he commended all his companions to God and stepped up to the bridge. Gazing in the direction of the tower, he crossed himself, bowed down, and climbed astraddle the steel blade and dragged himself over it in great pain, for he was very encumbered by his armor, since he was missing nothing but his shield. In great anguish, he dragged himself across, first leaning lengthwise, then crosswise, now flat, now astraddle, until he at last reached the other side. His feet and hands were bleeding. He wiped the blood off on the green grass and on the tails of his tunic.

And as he looked about, he saw that his companions went down the river to cross over in boats, because they crossed that way whenever they wanted to.

On the other side, King Bademagu went to the queen and said "My lady, for the sake of your welfare and for all the services I have rendered to you and that I will render, I beg you to tell me the name of the knight who has crossed the bridge, because I know very well that he did it for you."

Guenevere said that she would conceal nothing from him where her welfare was concerned. "Indeed, my lord, I don't know for certain, but I think it is Lancelot of the Lake."

King Bademagu replied, "Lady, if I had known that he was alive, I wouldn't have asked you, because I know very well that no one would dare to cross before him. Now I believe that he is indeed alive and that he's the one I see there. You should realize that he is the knight of your lord's kingdom whom I love the most, and I love you even more for his sake than for King Arthur's, since the king's ancestors did great harm to mine."

"My lord," said the queen, "thank you kindly for all the honors you have done me, for I am indeed greatly honored. I will thank him, if it is indeed Lancelot, and I will love him all the more for it, since you have treated me well on his account. Whoever it might be, Lancelot or another, be sure, if it is within your power, that you do nothing you might be blamed for, for you are considered one of the wisest barons in the world."

"My lady, don't worry," replied the king, "I will protect him for the sake of my honor."

24. Lancelot in Gorre; Guenevere's Rejection and Pardon of Lancelot; Lancelot Captured by Meleagant's Seneschal.

Then Bademagu descended from the tower, mounted his horse, and commanded his retinue to ride with him. He had a fine horse led out by hand, and he rode to where Lancelot was wiping the blood from his wounds. Lancelot leapt up when he saw the king, and the king dismounted, embraced him, and greeted him joyfully, before he saw Lancelot's face uncovered.

"My lord," he said, "you have undertaken a great adventure in the hopes of a great honor. May God grant you that honor without my suffering, for that is what I would like. Although I can't see who you are, I think I know, because my lady, the queen of Britain, told me. You should know that you have only my son to fear, for I promise you protection against everyone else."

"Thank you very much, my lord," said Lancelot, "but I have come in search of your son. Let him step forward. Since he must fight with me, there is no need to delay; this imprisonment has lasted too long."

"Now don't be in a hurry to fight, my dear friend," replied the king. "You need to rest. I will see that your wounds and injuries will be healed."

"My lord, I have no wounds or injuries that would make me need to rest, thank the Lord. Hurry up with the battle, because I have many other things to do!"

"It cannot take place tonight," replied King Bademagu, "since I want both my people and yours to be there. You will have to wait at least until tomorrow, since you cannot wait any longer than that."

And Lancelot agreed very reluctantly, since he was extremely impatient. The king had him mount the horse he had brought forth and led him to the house where he himself slept, and he had his armor taken off. When the king saw Lancelot without his helmet, he recognized him at once.

Then the king received Lancelot as warmly as he could, and after some time spent welcoming him, he went to his son and said, "Good son, now an adventure has arisen, for I have heard you wonder before why Lancelot doesn't come to free the prisoners in our country. You said he would never do it as long as you were alive. He has gone so far as to cross the bridge that no knight has ever crossed. For the great boldness he has shown, you ought to surrender to him a good part of your rights, since you know very well that he has come to free the queen, to whom you have no rights. If you give her back to him graciously, you will have earned more honor and esteem from this than he will have for all that he has done, and he has surmounted all the great perils. For everyone will say that you have returned out of generosity what you conquered by force. But if Lancelot conquers her by his prowess, you will have lost all the honor that I've just described to you. Therefore, I advise you to give back the queen, and he will consider your act a great goodness. You will not be doing him any favor, for he would easily conquer her from a better knight than yourself. He would rather have her by a battle than by your generosity, for you know very well that there is no better knight than Lancelot."

[*Meleagant refused to surrender the queen and to forgo battle. With the queen watching, and with Kay's bed nearby, a vicious battle began. After some time, Lancelot clearly had the upper hand.*]

Then Bademagu went to the queen and said to her, "My lady, I have honored you greatly, for I have never done anything against your will. Therefore, I should be rewarded in a matter where you have some power."

And she said that he surely would be. "But why do you ask this?" she queried.

"Lady, I say it for my son who is in the worst situation, which neither he nor I needs. This would be fine with me, so help me God, so long as he is neither dead nor wounded. So I beg you to impose your will that things remain as they are at this point."

"That certainly seems acceptable to me. I was not pleased that a fight ever took place. Now go and separate them, since I greatly desire it."

During this conversation, Lancelot had steered Meleagant so that they were both under the windows, where they heard the words of the king and the queen. From that moment on, Lancelot did not touch Meleagant, but instead slipped his sword back into the scabbard. Then Meleagant struck the hardest blows he could, so that he injured Lancelot; yet despite all this, Lancelot did not retreat. The king came running up and pulled Meleagant back, but his son said, "Leave me to my battle; you will never interfere!"

"I will, too," said the king, "because I see that he would kill you if you let him."

"I have the upper hand again and he's losing," replied Meleagant.

"Nothing that you say is worthy of you," said the king, "because we all see what's happening. Now you have to give up."

"You can take my battle away from me, but I'll pursue it as best I can wherever I think I have the right to do so."

Meleagant then declared to Lancelot that if they separated in such a manner, Lancelot would be defeated. Then the king pulled him aside, speaking so forcefully that he agreed to give up the fight on the condition that whenever he wanted, he could go to Arthur's court and would summon Lancelot to battle and fight with him. The queen swore on relics that she would go away with Meleagant if he could win her in combat.

So the matter was settled between the queen and the king. The queen swore to it first, and Lancelot afterwards. And then they led Lancelot away to take off his armor in the queen's chambers. But Kay the Seneschal was upset about the peace they concluded; he would rather have seen Lancelot fight to the bitter end than have him quit in such a manner. Although this arrangement greatly vexed the queen, she agreed to it before she realized what she was doing. Then she returned to her chambers, for she had spent the whole day in the public rooms.

When Lancelot had removed his armor and washed his face and neck, the king escorted him to see the queen. When Guenevere saw the king, she rose to greet him, and Lancelot knelt from a distance as soon as he could see her, and he bowed to her.

The king said, "Lady, you see here Lancelot, who has paid very dearly to see you, for he has reached you by way of many a treacherous pass."

Guenevere turned to face the king and said, "Surely, my lord, if he has done all this for me, he has been wasting his effort, because I am not at all grateful to him."

"But my lady," protested the king, "he has rendered you so many difficult services."

"He has done so many other things to me," she said, "that I will never love him."

"Alas, my lady," said Lancelot, "how have I done you wrong?"

And she, to destroy him even more, retired to her rooms. Lancelot stared after her as long as he could see her.

The king said to the queen, "My lady, my lady, this last service has surely redeemed all the wrongs."

[*Kay told Lancelot that Meleagant had wanted to sleep with the queen and to marry her, but she had refused.*]

Lancelot rose and said that he would leave in the morning to seek Sir Gawain at the Underwater Bridge. Then Lancelot departed and went upstairs, accompanied by many of those from Gorre and by many of the exiles, all of whom honored him greatly.

In the morning, Lancelot set out for the Underwater Bridge; only seven of the exiles went with him. He instructed the others to remain with his lady until Sir Gawain arrived, and he rode until he reached the bridge. There he was captured by the people of Gorre, who thought that the king wanted him as a prisoner. Lancelot could not defend himself, since he was without armor, thinking he had nothing to fear. After he was captured, he was led away to the king.

The rumor that Lancelot had been killed quickly traveled to Bademagu's court. When the queen learned of it, she was so distressed that she nearly killed herself, but she waited until she could discover the whole truth. At that point, Guenevere decided that she would never eat. She was all the more distressed because she thought that she had killed Lancelot by refusing to speak to him. So she criticized and blamed herself, thinking that "since such a knight has died for me, it would no longer be right for me to live."

Such was her lament; as long as she lay on the bed, she wanted no one to see her great anguish. The king felt very sorry for her and comforted her as best he could, but it was no use, for the story says that she went two days without drinking or eating. And so her great beauty faded, as Lancelot's captors drew nearer to the court.

That night, while they were resting from their journey, news reached them that the queen was definitely dead. The first one who heard it was the vavasor with whom Lancelot had stayed when he fought the treacherous knight. He dared not convey this to Lancelot, but he could not at all refrain from crying, and so he rose from the table where he was seated. When Lancelot saw him get up, he knew that it was for some good cause. So as soon as the table had been cleared, he called him over to consult him and entreated the vavasor as earnestly as he could to explain why he was crying.

The vavasor dared not conceal the matter, and so he told Lancelot what he had heard. The word spread so fast within that everywhere the exiles wept and said that no finer lady had ever died. Everyone lamented her, one and all, except for Lancelot, who was unable to utter a word, but who was extremely anxious to retire. When he was finally in bed, he reflected about how he could kill himself without being noticed, for he had no desire to live a single day longer than the had one who gave him life. Instead, he would follow her, wherever she might be.

Lancelot remained absorbed in this thought for a long time. There were ten armed men stationed continually in front of the bed, so that they would not lose him, and, besides this, the doors of the room where he slept were closed tightly. But when it was around midnight and he thought that everyone was sleeping, there were two candles burning in the room, and you could see as clearly as in daylight. Lancelot was about to extinguish the candles, because he wanted to hang himself. But then he reflected that he would be dying a vile death and that he would never die in such a base manner, God willing.

So Lancelot stole over to one of the guards and thought that he would neatly draw the sword out of his sheath, but the guard grabbed it and seized it with his hands; still he could not prevent Lancelot from striking himself with the sword on his left side so that the sword broke against his side. If his blow had gone a little farther, Lancelot would certainly have been dead. A cry was raised; the men jumped up and tied him; Lancelot was powerless for the rest of the night. When morning came they watched him more carefully than they had before.

When they were fifteen English leagues from Gorrun, the news arrived that Lancelot was alive and well. The queen was as happy as could be when she learned this. She recovered completely and resumed eating and drinking, because she had fasted long enough. When the king learned that Lancelot was near, he mounted his horse and rode out to meet him. He greeted him warmly and privately told him about the great anguish that the queen had suffered on his account.

"You should know," confided King Bademagu, "that I don't think that she will refuse to speak with you when you see her."

Lancelot was overjoyed to learn that Guenevere had not died. Then they arrived in the city, and the queen heard about how Lancelot had tried to kill himself. The king imprisoned all those who had captured Lancelot and said that he would have them all killed. When Lancelot saw the king so angry, he fell at his feet and begged him in God's name to forgive his captors' misdeed, and the king did so. Then Bademagu led him to see the queen; she rose to greet him and took Lancelot in her arms, inquiring how he was, and he replied, "My lady, very well."

Then the three of them sat down together on a couch. But the king, who was very courteous, stayed only for a brief time; he said that he wanted to see how Kay was faring.

Both the queen and Lancelot remained together in conversation, and Guenevere asked Lancelot if he had wounded himself in any way. He replied, "My lady, I have no injury."

And then he entreated her, in God's name, to tell him why she had not wished to speak with him the other day. She responded that he had left London without asking leave of her, and he agreed that he had done something very wrong.

"You have done an even greater wrong," she said.

And then she asked for her ring, and he said, "My lady, here it is," showing her the one on his finger.

"In God's name," she said, "you've lied to me. That's not my ring."

Lancelot swore as solemnly as he could that it was; he really believed he was telling the truth.

At that, she showed him the ring she wore on her finger, so that he recognized indeed that it was the real one. Lancelot was very dismayed to be wearing another ring; he pulled it off his finger and threw it out the window as far as he could. Afterward, the queen told him how the young woman had brought her ring back and the incredible accusation she made. Lancelot remembered everything and realized that the treacherous Morgan had done it. He told her the entire truth about both the dream and the ransom, which astonished her.[44]

After listening to his dream, she said, "Dear friend, let me die if anyone but you shares my body, for I would have chosen very poorly. And I don't think that there could be anyone who would have the right to lie next to me in your place."

Lancelot asked, "My lady, will you forgive me for my grave misdeeds?"

"Dear friend, I forgive you for all of them."

And he begged her in God's name, if it was possible, to come to him that night: it had been a long time since he had spoken with her. And she replied that she desired this even more than he did.

"Let's go see Kay," she said. "You'll see that to the left of my bed there is a window with iron bars where you can speak with me tonight, since you won't be able to get into the room. You'll reach the window through the garden behind it; I'll show you where you can most easily enter the garden."

Next, she led him to a window in the room, where she pointed toward the old, crumbling wall and instructed him to enter that way. After that, they went to see Kay, but the king was still talking to him. And there the queen showed Lancelot where he could enter without being seen. After they had been there for some time, the king led them away, and Lancelot grew very eager for night to fall. When night finally arrived, he retired to bed earlier than usual, claiming that he was ill. And when he saw the right moment, he rose and crawled through the window of the room where he was sleeping. Then he rushed to the garden and ran to the window.

The queen was not sleeping; she went to the window. They threw their arms around each other and exchanged caresses where they could.

"My lady," asked Lancelot, "if I were able to come into your room, would it please you?"

"How could that happen, fair friend?" she asked.

"My lady, if it pleased you, it could be easily arranged."

"Indeed, I would desire it more than anything."

"In God's name, then it will be so: iron bars will never hold me back."

"Now wait until I get into bed," said the queen, "and take care not to make any noise."

She lay down, and he pulled the iron bars out of the window frame so softly that he did not make any noise or break any of the bars; then he thrust

---

[44]Earlier, Morgan had caused Lancelot to dream that Guenevere was sleeping with another knight.

himself through the window. There was no candle or light in the room, because Kay had complained about the brightness.

As Lancelot climbed into her bed, the queen felt the blood that was dripping from him; it fell from his hands, where the skin had been broken by the sharp edge of the iron bars. But she thought that it was Lancelot's perspiration, and neither of them paid any attention to it. And then she told him about the death of Galehaut, of which he knew nothing. Lancelot would have grieved bitterly, except that it was not the place to mourn, and so they gave each other great pleasure. As day neared, they separated and Lancelot went back through the window, returning the iron bars to the places from which he had removed them. Then he took leave of his lady and went to sleep so quietly that no one knew anything about their encounter.

The next morning Meleagant went to visit the queen, as was his custom. She was still sleeping. He saw the sheets spotted with Lancelot's blood and crossed the room to Kay's bed. Kay's wounds had opened and he had bled a great deal; it happened that he bled more heavily at night. Then Meleagant went to the queen and said, "My lady, my lady, now here is a bad affair."

"What are you talking about?" she asked.

And he showed her the blood in one bed and then in the other and declared, "Lady, my father protected you very well from me, but he protected you badly from Kay. This is a great disloyalty from such a woman as they claim you to be; you have disgraced the most valiant man in the world with the most wicked one. You've behaved with great contempt toward me, for you have refused me for him. At the very least I am more worthy than he, since I won you from him in a show of arms. And in fact Lancelot, who has suffered such misfortune for you, is even more worthy. But he has struggled in vain, because anyone who serves woman and the devil is rewarded with shame."

"Good sir," responded the queen, "you may say what you like; God is my witness that Kay never brought this blood into my bed, but rather that my nose often bleeds."

"God help me!" Meleagant exclaimed. "Nothing you say will do you any good; you're guilty. You will never escape from my keep, and you will always be considered disloyal."

At this, Kay became so upset that he nearly flew into a rage. He announced that he was ready to defend himself, either in a judgment in court or in a battle. Meleagant sent for his father, who was still sleeping, and when Bademagu heard the news, he sprang up angrily and had Lancelot awakened to accompany him. And then Lancelot realized for the first time that he had cut his hands at the window; he followed the king.

When they reached the bedroom, Meleagant said to his father, "My lord, look at the blood in these two beds." He continued, "My lord, now give me the rights to this woman for whom I have risked my life. She refused me, and

I have discovered her affair with the worthless man who wasn't able to defend her against me."

"Alas, lady," exclaimed the king, "what kind of behavior is this? How badly you have gone astray!"

"Lord," she replied, "don't believe him. May God never help me if Kay ever had anything to do with me! Lancelot, now you can see if those who know me consider me that kind of woman."

"My lady," Lancelot replied, "God forbid! Certainly Kay never did that, nor would you even have thought of such a thing. There's no knight in the world against whom I wouldn't defend you."

"She'll certainly need your protection," said Meleagant, "because if you dare to defend her against the accusation, I am ready to prove it."

"How so?" asked Lancelot. "Has your wound healed yet?"

"In God's name," Meleagant retorted, "I've no injury that can prevent me from defending my privileges."

"You certainly talk like a valiant knight," replied Lancelot, "but you must have had enough of fighting. If you want more, go get yourself armed."

[*Lancelot and Meleagant did battle again, and again the battle was interrupted by Bademagu, with Guenevere's approval. Lancelot left to seek Gawain, but a dwarf tricked Lancelot and caused him to be imprisoned.*]

25. Gawain, Arthur, and Guenevere Ride in the Cart.

[*Meleagant forged a letter telling the queen that Lancelot was at Arthur's court. She and Gawain returned to court and found that he was not there. Arthur refused to hold a tournament until Lancelot was found.*]

This is how the court lived from Pentecost until the middle of August;[45] then the king had to hold court and wear his crown, as it was customary for a great holiday, and he held the court at Roevent. He would have held it in an even more humble place, had he dared incur his barons' blame, for he had no heart for the great merrymaking and festivities that he used to arrange. When the feast day arrived, after Mass, the king leaned out a window and turned his head towards the fields. He did not want to eat yet, because he had not seen any adventure.[46]

While he was gazing below, he watched the approach of a cart drawn by a horse whose tail and two ears had been cut off. Riding on the horse was a

---

[45]The time of the feast of Assumption, August 15, which celebrates the bodily ascent of the Virgin Mary to heaven.

[46]As has happened before in the *Lancelot,* Arthurian custom dictates that the king refuse to eat until an adventure has occurred.

stout, well-built dwarf, who had a long beard and a broad head covered with gray hair. Inside the cart there was a knight whose hands were tied behind his back and who wore a torn and filthy shift. His two legs were bound to the two shafts of the cart, and in front hung his shield, which was all white with a strap of white silk; beside him were his helmet and hauberk. His horse was hitched to the back of the cart; it had the bit in its mouth and the saddle on its back; it was white as snow and amazingly beautiful.

When the knight saw the king and his knights, he said "Alas, God, who will free me?"

All the knights ran out to see him. The king said to the dwarf who was leading the cart, "Dwarf, what has this knight done wrong?"

"Just as much as the other knight," said the dwarf.

The king did not know what he meant; he asked again, and the dwarf answered the same way. Then the king and all the knights fell silent for a long time. Afterwards, the king asked the knight, "How will you be freed?"

"If only a knight would ride here in my place for me, my lord."

"You won't find anyone to do that today," said the king.

"God forbid," said the dwarf.

With that, the dwarf drove the cart through all the city's streets, and the knight was insulted and assailed by clods of mud and shoes. The king declared that he could certainly eat now, for he had seen a very marvelous adventure. Sir Gawain emerged from the chambers of the queen where he had been sleeping, since he had kept a vigil in the chapel all night. Many people recounted the adventure to him. And Sir Gawain began to weep and cursed whoever had first put a cart to such use; he remembered that Lancelot had ridden in one.

Then the king and all the others sat down to dine. As they looked about them, they saw the cart arrive in the middle of the court. The knight stepped down off the cart and walked over to where the other knights were eating. Each knight exclaimed, "Look at the Knight of the Cart."

He went over to be seated with the knights, but each one shoved him away and said he should not be seated with the knights. He went among them throughout their ranks, but no one would let him sit next to him, and instead each knight pushed him away. After he had tried everywhere, he took a table napkin and went to sit in the ranks of the squires.

But when Sir Gawain saw the knight being pushed and shoved away, he stopped serving the meal and went over to him. Sir Gawain sat down beside him and announced that he would keep him company, since he was a knight. Word spread until the king heard about it; he chastised Sir Gawain and declared that he considered his behavior a disgrace and that he had lost his seat at the Round Table. Sir Gawain retorted that if he were disgraced because of the cart, then Lancelot was also disgraced and that after his disgrace he sought no honor. The knight pretended not to hear these words, and the king was amazed at what Sir Gawain has told him. When the knight finished eating, he rose and said to Sir Gawain, "Many thanks. I now see that what everyone says is true."

[*The knight took away one of Arthur's horses, and several knights pursued him, doing battle with him but losing their horses to him.*]

While they were conversing there, up came the cart, along with the dwarf who was driving it; a young lady sat inside. The dwarf led her straight to the court, and the young woman looked up to the king at the window and called out, "King Arthur, they used to say that no man or woman who had been wronged would come into your court and not find support. But now that seems to be a lie, because the Good Knight has left without finding anyone who would ride the cart for his sake. Now you have earned more shame than honor, since he has led six of your horses away against your will. Now I wonder if I will find someone to deliver me from this cart."

Then Sir Gawain stepped down and asked her, "My lady, how would you be freed?"

"If someone would ride up here, I could step down," she said.

"In God's name," said Gawain, "I'll get in the cart for the sake of the Good Knight who rode there."

Then he rushed to step into the cart, and the lady descended. Ten knights fully armed soon appeared, and they dismounted so that they could place the woman upon one of the most beautiful palfreys imaginable, which they were leading along with them.

Then the queen appeared, and the lady announced to the king, "King Arthur, I am leaving. But before I go, I want you to know that your court's deliverance is near and that the adventures will come to an end; and you should not have failed the knight, but you should have jumped into the cart instead. Because the knight rode the cart only out of love for Lancelot, who rode for this lady's sake; he did what you didn't dare undertake for the sake of the woman who is your wife. In honor of Lancelot, all cart riders should be praised forever more. Do you know who the knight is who defeated your companions? He's a very young knight, twenty-one years old, who was made a new knight on Pentecost. He's Lancelot's first cousin and Lionel's brother. He has gone in quest of Lancelot, although in that respect he is behaving foolishly, because he won't find him."

At these words, the knight she had been talking about rode up, followed by his squire, who led at his side all the horses that his lord had won. The knight removed his helmet and approached the king; he knelt down and said, "My lord, take back your horses. I would never steal them in such a manner."

And then the queen leapt up and raised the knight to his feet, and the king greeted him joyfully for the sake of Lancelot, his cousin. The lady remounted and rode away without saying another word. And the king engaged the knight as a companion of the Round Table. He asked his name and the knight replied that he was called Bors the Dispossessed.

The queen asked him who the departing lady was, and he said that it was the Lady of the Lake, who had raised Lancelot and himself and Lionel. When the queen heard that, she could not have been more upset, and nothing could comfort her. Then the queen mounted her horse and said she would ride until she found the Lady of the Lake. The king accompanied her, and they found Sir Gawain in the center of the city where the dwarf had led him, still in the cart. The queen jumped into the cart, and Gawain got down; the king stepped in next to her, and finally not a single knight of the king's retinue remained who did not ride in the cart. And from that moment on, as long as the king was alive, no condemned man was ordered to ride in a cart; instead, each city kept an old nag without a tail or ears, and the one who was to be disgraced would be paraded through the streets on this old nag.

But the queen rode after the Lady of the Lake, with Sir Gawain beside her, and they rode until they caught up with her. Guenevere called out her thanks and said that she was mortified that she had not recognized her and begged her to turn back with them. And Sir Gawain, whom she had greeted so warmly, entreated her, too, but she said that it could not be. Then the queen drew her aside secretly and urged her, if she had any news of Lancelot, to tell her. The lady replied that Lancelot was alive and in prison, but that he was being kept comfortably and honorably. The moment for his escape had been firmly decided, because if he had escaped any sooner, he would have lost the great honor that he was expecting. "But you should know that you will be able to see him at the next tournament in the kingdom of Logres, if you are present."

The queen was delighted with this news. When she saw that she could not detain the lady, she took her leave and rode back. Then she went to tell the king the news about Lancelot, except that she did not tell him that Lancelot would be at the next tournament. The king was very happy because he had been afraid that Lancelot was dead, but he was troubled by the knight's absence.

So the queen suggested, "My lord, have a tournament announced at the border of Gorre and Logres, for you might by chance hear news of Lancelot. In any case, it will be time for the tournament; the people who have been freed from exile have been asking for one."

So the king agreed and had it decreed everywhere that the great tournament would take place in two weeks' time at Pomeglai; he decreed it so by letter and by messengers. But now the story speaks no more of Arthur or his knights; it returns instead to Lancelot.

26. Lancelot at the Tournament of Pomeglai.

[*Lancelot, imprisoned, heard news of the tournament. The seneschal's wife allowed him to leave long enough to participate in the tournament. Once there, he fought so well that those watching him thought he could be no one except Lancelot.*]

Then the queen called one of her maidservants, since she dared not trust anyone or divulge her thoughts. For the Lady of Malehaut, who was stricken with a fatal illness in her country, was the only person in whom the queen could confide. So she told the girl, "Go to that knight over there and tell him that now he should do his worst, just as he was doing his best, and say that by the signs I give him he should have great grief in the place of great joy."

The young lady went to Lancelot and told him. He took a lance from his squire, moved toward a knight to joust, and faltered. The knight struck him and knocked him flat over the rump of his horse so hard that he could barely rise.

Then Lancelot returned to the fray, and when he had to strike heavy blows, he held on to the mane of his horse and pretended that he was about to fall. From that point on, he stood up to no knights. Instead, he lowered his head and retreated whenever he saw knights coming to attack him. He performed so badly that everyone shouted and cursed at him. The squire who accompanied him was more amazed than anyone. Lancelot continued to fight this way for the rest of the day, until the knights dispersed, and everyone who had considered him to be a valiant knight was ashamed. He returned to his lodgings without anyone daring to speak to him because of his cowardly performance.

The next morning, Lancelot rose and set off for the tournament without his helmet. A young woman rode up to him and recognized him. It was the same person who had led him to the church where he raised Galahad's tombstone; she had been following him. Then, after he had put on his helmet, she pursued him, crying out throughout the ranks: "Now the marvel has arrived!"

When the rogues and the braggarts saw him, they began to shout loudly. At that point, Lancelot began to strike down the knights so fiercely that everyone who watched was amazed.

His good performance continued for some time, until the queen, sending her command by way of her maidservant, asked him once again to do his worst. At that point, Lancelot began to fight as poorly as he could, and the girl who had announced him to the crowd was stunned speechless. Lancelot fought that badly until noon, at which point the queen asked him once more to fight his best, so that he would vanquish all.

From that moment on, people spoke of no one but him. When night fell, Lancelot threw down his shield into the melee and returned to his lodgings.

That evening all those at the tournament knew that the knight had been Lancelot, and they realized that he had performed badly to mock them.

[Lancelot returned to his prison. Meleagant went to Arthur's court to inform the king of Lancelot's agreement to fight him again. Arthur announced that forty days must pass before such a battle.]

27. Meleagant's Sister Frees Lancelot; Lancelot Kills Meleagant at Arthur's court.

Meleagant had a sister about whom the story has spoken earlier; she was the one to whom Lancelot gave the head of the knight he had killed. She was very upset about Lancelot's imprisonment. When the tower in the marsh was constructed, she realized that Meleagant had made it for no other reason than to wall in Lancelot. The wife of the serf who guarded the tower had raised Meleagant's sister, and the girl often performed kind acts for her. At this point, she began to bestow more favors than ever before.

One night, she sought lodging at the house of the serf, who lived at the far end of the swamp on the road; she took great care that no one should see her. She observed how meals were prepared for Lancelot, and then she knew for certain that he was in the tower; she left him there for the moment. She returned one night, determined to do whatever was necessary to free Lancelot from the tower. And that night, after everyone had retired, she made her preparations in a room where she slept with her servant girls. After everyone was asleep, she sneaked out to the little boat, where she put a pick and a thick rope, and she stepped inside. She floated to the tower and found a little basket hanging from the window. Then she tugged the cord of the basket.

Lancelot, lost in thought about himself, was not sleeping. He rose and went to the window and leaned out. The girl called to him softly, and he asked, "Who are you?"

"I'm a friend and I've come to free you," she answered.

Lancelot was delighted to hear this. After the girl had tied the thick rope and the pick to the small rope, which hung from the window, Lancelot pulled the tools up. He cracked the window frame until he was able to crawl out, attached the cord inside the tower, and then climbed down the wall and crept out of the swamp as discreetly as he could. Then the girl lay down in a bedroom with Lancelot at her side.

Lancelot rose in the morning and dressed himself in the girl's best cloak. She placed him on a palfrey and led him away in that manner in front of everyone in the house, and she accompanied him all the way to the land that she held from her mother's side. When she arrived, Lancelot procured the necessary provisions; he was in great need of rest, since his imprisonment had been very harsh. Then the young lady sent a messenger off to Arthur's court for news of Meleagant.

When the lady's messenger arrived in court, he asked why Meleagant had been visiting for such a long time. He found out that Meleagant had been waiting for forty days for a combat with Lancelot, and he learned when the fortieth day would be. Then he returned to his lady and told her what he had discovered at court. She in turn recounted all this to Lancelot, who was by now quite recovered and restored to his former strength and beauty.

Lancelot requested permission to leave, since he was extremely eager to avenge himself against the man he hated most in the world.

"Fair friend," she said, "I will first prepare arms and a horse for you, and then you may leave. Never fear, because there are still eleven days until the time that you must be there. May God help you avenge me against him as well as you did against the knight whose head you cut off. He's the man I hate most on earth; he was never my brother, for he has disinherited me and has done me more harm than anyone in the world."

So Lancelot remained there a week, while the young woman provided him with a horse and arms. Then he set out and rode until he arrived exactly on the date of the battle at Escavalon, where the king was holding court. Meleagant, who was already armed, announced that he would leave, since there was no one who could guarantee the battle for Lancelot. At that, Bors the Dispossessed leapt up and said that he would fight straightway, if they would permit him. But Meleagant said that he would prefer Lancelot, and Sir Gawain declared that he would fight immediately and that no one but he would do it.

"God bless me, my lord," exclaimed Meleagant, "I don't know a knight with whom I'd fight more willingly."

So Sir Gawain ran off to arm himself, and Bors the Dispossessed did the same.

Meanwhile, Lancelot was riding along and had just entered the city when he met Sir Gawain, as he was returning to his lodgings to don his armor. They greeted each other with delight. When news of Lancelot reached the court, there was great joy. First, the king ran to kiss him, and then the queen did so as well, and all the others afterwards. Meleagant was shocked to hear the news; he had not yet heard about the latest adventure, since his serf had fled when he realized that Lancelot was gone.

Lancelot rode up to the lists and announced, "Meleagant, you have raised such a cry that now you have me before you. So now you'll have the battle you've so desired, because I've been delivered from the swamps, thanks to God and the young lady who freed me."

Then they rode to the battlefield, and the lists were set up. The knights then charged on their horses and exchanged great blows. Meleagant shattered his lance, and Lancelot struck him so hard that he crushed his shield against his arm and pressed the arm against the body, which knocked his spine against the saddle, and so brought him down to the ground. Lancelot dismounted with him; they drew their swords and slashed each other's helmets and hauberks as often as they could. The cruel, violent battle continued this way until vespers, when Meleagant faltered. His mortal enemy pressed him hard, and treated him so badly that blood spurted from more than thirty wounds, and he stumbled several times to his knees.

Then they seized each other by the arms and wrestled; Lancelot brought Meleagant down, tore off his helmet and threw it in the field, and knocked off his ventail. The king shouted not to kill him, while the queen made a sign to cut off his head. And Lancelot said to the king, "For your sake, I'll allow him to stand up, but don't ask for anything more."

Meleagant raised himself up, and Lancelot struck and sent his head flying off into the field, while his body fell flat to the ground. Lancelot replaced his sword into its sheath.

Then Kay the Seneschal jumped up, removed Lancelot's shield from his neck, and declared, "Ah, my lord, we welcome you above all the other knights in the world as the flower of earthly chivalry! You have proved your valor here and elsewhere."

After Kay the Seneschal came King Arthur, who embraced Lancelot in all his armor; he removed Lancelot's helmet and handed it to Sir Yvain, and then kissed him on the mouth and said, "Dear friend, you are most welcome here!"

Afterward, Sir Gawain approached and leapt to greet Lancelot with outstretched arms. Finally, the queen arrived, as joyful as could be, and all the other barons followed her, celebrating so merrily that I could not describe a finer welcome. And thus they led him into the midst of such joyous festivities to the great hall. The king ordered the tables to be set up, and they were. The knights all sat down there, although it was only between the hours of nones and vespers.[47]

Then the king did something that greatly redounded to Lancelot's honor, something he had never done for any man before. He bade him sit at the high table where he ate, right in front of him, where no knight had ever sat except at dinner during the important feasts. Whenever some foreign knight won at tilting or the quintain, he would sit there—not right next to the king, but close by. The king would make him sit there so that everyone present would see him and recognize him from that moment on. No other knight had ever had the honor of sitting there, no matter how noble he was. But on this day, Lancelot took his place in that seat at the behest of the king and the commandment of his lady the queen. He was very disturbed and embarrassed by this, but he agreed to it out of obedience for the king and the queen.

---

[47]In other words. it was earlier than the usual dinner hour.

28. Lancelot Agrees to Fight at Bademagu's Court, Defends Guenevere, and Rediscovers Lionel and Hector at the Castle of Maidens.

Great were the joyous festivities that the king held for Lancelot, since he had not seen him for so long. He began to speak with him and inquire about all that he had done. And Lancelot replied that he had fared well, thanks to God; he was completely safe and sound. But the king dared not tell him the news of Galehaut's death, since he did not believe that Lancelot knew anything about it.

In the midst of their conversation, a knight in full armor entered the hall; he had left his charger down in the courtyard. The knight was tall and well built and wore red armor; he strode right up to the tables without so much as a greeting for anyone. After observing for some time those who were eating, he spoke loudly enough for all to hear and said, "Alas, where's the disloyal, the treacherous, the most disgraceful of all knights, who killed Meleagant, the son of King Bademagu? Where is Lancelot? Where is the one on whom we bestowed all the honors of the kingdom of Gorre and who has now betrayed us by killing the best knight in the world?"

At that, Lancelot looked up, and the knight, recognizing him, said to the king, "What have you done, my lord? You're considered one of the most valiant men in the world, and yet you have the most treacherous knight alive seated at your table. This truly astounds me."

At that, Lancelot leapt up from the table, very ashamed because of the grave insult the knight had uttered. "Lord knight," he said, "you are hardly courteous to speak of my dishonor with no cause."

"It is true," the knight replied, "that one should not speak about dishonor to you; rather, one should *act* to dishonor you as much as possible, because you have murdered my cousin Meleagant."

"I did not murder him," retorted Lancelot. "There were more than two hundred people who witnessed the battle."

"But surely from the moment he begged you for mercy and you subsequently killed him, you acted unlawfully and wickedly. I am ready to prove that you're wicked and a traitor in another court than this one, if you dare to defend yourself."

"There's no court in the world where I wouldn't stand up confidently against you to prove that my deed was neither treason nor a crime," replied Lancelot.

"In God's name," said the other knight, "if you dare to defend yourself in King Bademagu's court, I will convict you of just what I said."

Lancelot declared that he would vindicate himself.

"Then be there on Monday in one month, on the day of St. Mary Magdalene. I swear to you on my honor that you will find me there."

"And I swear that I will be there on that day, unless death or prison detains me."

Thereupon the knight, who wanted to delay no longer, departed, and Lancelot took his seat again at the king's command. Then everyone throughout the room began to talk about the red knight, agreeing that he was very wicked and that he spoke out very foolishly against Lancelot.

It was not long before a squire entered, who announced to the king, "My lord, the red knight has had Meleagant carried off in the most luxurious litter that I've ever seen. He has more than twenty armed knights in the escort. I have never seen anyone grieve as bitterly as they are mourning together."

"I certainly wish that this matter had been settled in some other way than it has been," sighed the king. "For the sake of my love for Bademagu, I would prefer that Meleagant had not been killed in my court. I wish that he had died in some other court than mine. But since it happened this way, I must accept it."

After the knights had eaten, the tables were cleared away, and people returned to their lodgings. But the king detained Lancelot with him, and led him over to the windows of the great hall. The queen was with him, along with Sir Gawain and Bors the Dispossessed, who joyously received Lancelot. They sat down on a couch. The king took great pains to treat Lancelot courteously. He asked him on his oath to tell him, in front of all the companions gathered about, all the adventures that had befallen him since he had left the court. Lancelot recounted some of them, and some of them he concealed. The king and the queen listened to them very willingly as well, and the king had them promptly put into writing, so that they would be remembered after their death.

Afterward, Lancelot asked for news of Lionel. "In fact," said the king, "he's been looking for you continually for a good six months, because everyone said that you were dead, and we haven't seen him since."

"Oh, my God," exclaimed Lancelot, "wherever he may be, watch after him!"

Then the king told how Bors had come to court, about the feats of prowess that he had accomplished against his own men, and about how all the knights rode in the cart. At that news, Lancelot smiled to himself. He greeted Bors very joyfully, kissed him affectionately, because he had not seen him for some time, and said, "Dear cousin, now make sure that you behave so that everyone will talk about you from now on as they do today; you have not begun your chivalry only to abandon it so soon, but to improve it and to strive farther and farther ahead. Make sure for the love of me that no lady or maiden who seeks your help will ever be refused by you; rather, help and serve all of those who you believe will need your service."

With such joy and festivity, Arthur kept Lancelot with him the whole week. There was no earthly delight of which Lancelot did not partake, since he had all the pleasure he desired from his lady, from whom all his joy derived.

At the end of the week, when Lancelot had to leave, there was no one among them who was not distraught about his departure. The queen wept bitter tears, but so discreetly that no one but the two of them knew it. After Lancelot heard Mass on Monday morning, he armed himself and mounted his horse, and he left court without anyone but the queen knowing about it. He rode all day without finding any adventure to speak of, and he stayed that night with a forester who provided fine accommodations.

The next day, as soon as he saw light, he began his journey and entered a forest called the Sapinoie. Then he discovered on his right a narrow path that he thought was scarcely inhabited, which is why he headed in that direction and traveled along that road until the hour of tierce. At that point, he came upon a knight in full armor who was riding all alone. Lancelot exchanged greetings with the knight as soon as he reached him. The knight asked Lancelot where he was from, and Lancelot replied that he was from the land of Gaul.

"My lord," asked the knight, "were you ever in Arthur's court?"

"Yes," Lancelot answered," I have been there a few times."

"And did you ever see the queen?"

"Yes, of course I saw her."

"Then you can say that you saw the most unfaithful woman there ever was, when you saw the queen."

"How do you know?"

"I know it for a fact, and I'll tell you how. It happened this year that I had gone to Arthur's court, when a young lady arrived who announced that Lancelot was dead and that he had begged pardon from King Arthur for having slept with his wife. The girl carried such proof that it had to be believed."

"What proof?" said Lancelot.

"The ring that the queen had given Lancelot as a love token, which the girl had held out to her as a sign that she should be believed. The queen was never the kind of woman who would deny the truth; instead she admitted before everyone that she had truly loved Lancelot and that she had given him the ring. It's obvious, therefore, that she is just the way I've described her to you, in my opinion."

Lancelot became very angry at this and replied, "This is a foolish thing to say, my lord, unless you can come forth and prove it."

"There's no knight in the world I wouldn't prove it to except for one."

"Who's that?"

"Lancelot of the Lake, the son of King Ban of Benoic. I would dare to prove it against all other knights but him."

"But everyone knows everywhere that Lancelot has been dead for over a year," replied Lancelot.

"Is that the truth?" he asked.

"I didn't see him die, but that's what everyone says is true."

"Then there's no one in the world against whom I wouldn't dare to prove and to show that Guenevere is the most unfaithful of all women, since she allowed another knight to sleep in the place of King Arthur, who is the most faithful of all knights."

"In God's name," said Lancelot, "there are many knights in this country who would defend her willingly against the blame you're casting on her, if they heard you talk like this."

"You are not one of them," observed the other knight.

"You don't know that," said Lancelot.

"Prove it if you are. I am ready to prove that she is the way I've said, and even more unfaithful."

"And I am ready to defend her," said Lancelot.

"Then be on your guard against me from now on!"

"And you, against me," said Lancelot.

[*Lancelot defeated the knight and forced him to go to court and ask the queen's pardon. He then did battle with many knights who hated both the queen and those who served her. He sent one of his victims to court to seek her pardon. He then rode on and came to a tournament between the knights of the Castle of Ladies and those of the Castle of Maidens. He joined in the tournament and distinguished himself, though he wounded Hector and his own cousin Lionel. Lionel was reunited with Bors and told him on Lancelot's behalf that he, Bors, must leave to seek adventure. Bors distinguished himself in tournaments, battles, and service to those in need.*]

29. Lancelot Discovers Galehaut's Casket and Defends It; Lancelot Rescues Meleagant's Sister.

[*Lancelot learned that Meleagant's sister had been accused of murder (for freeing him to kill Meleagant) and that she would be burned at the stake the next day. He set out to rescue her.*]

Lancelot rode until he came out of the forest, and he saw a monastery before him. He headed toward it to seek lodging. [. . .] He went into the church to pray, and as he was kneeling, he turned to his right and saw a silver choir screen richly adorned with little golden flowers and birds and animals. Within the choir were five armed knights, helmets on their heads, swords in hand, ready to defend themselves as if someone were about to attack them. This amazed Lancelot; he stood up quickly and went over there; he greeted the knights and they welcomed him.

Lancelot entered the choir by a little gate and gazed at the screen, which was so richly decorated that he did not think even a king could afford it. Then, beside the knights, he saw a tomb, the most splendid that man had ever crafted, for it was composed entirely of pure gold with beautiful precious stones worth far more than a vast kingdom. If the tomb was extremely beautiful, its beauty was surpassed by the value of its materials, and, furthermore, it was the largest tomb Lancelot had ever seen. He wondered who the prince buried inside could be. He inquired of the knights stationed there.

"My lord," they answered, "we are protecting the body that lies in this tomb so that it will not be carried off from here. We five stand guard during the day, and at night there are another five who provide the same service we do during the day."

"And why are you afraid that the body will be carried away?"

"Because, my lord, one of the monks here who is very noble and holy has told us that a knight will soon appear who will remove it by force and have it carried out of the country. And we, the people of this land, would rather die than have him taken from our presence. That is why we stand guard here as you see: the good monk told us that the knight would soon arrive."

"Now tell me," queried Lancelot, "wasn't he a very noble prince to have such a splendid tomb made for him?"

"Lord, he was a rich and noble man; besides being noble, he was the most worthy who ever lived in his time."

"Pray God, who was he?"

"If you know how to read, sir, you can see for yourself, for his name is written at the head of this tombstone."

So Lancelot turned there and stared at the letters which said, HERE LIES GALEHAUT THE SON OF THE GIANTESS, THE LORD OF THE DISTANT ISLES, WHO DIED FOR THE LOVE OF LANCELOT.

When Lancelot saw this, he fell down in a swoon and lay speechless for a long time on the ground. The knights ran over to help him up and wondered very much who he could be. After recovering from his swoon, Lancelot cried to himself, "Alas! What sorrow and what shame!"

And then he beat his fists together and scratched his face until the blood streamed from all over; he pulled his hair and beat his brow and chest with great blows and cried so loudly that not a soul did not feel compassion for him. He cursed himself and the hour he was born, crying, "Oh, God! What shame, what loss of the most valiant knight in the world, who died of love for the basest and most wicked knight there ever was!"

Lancelot lamented so bitterly that all the people there came to watch him in amazement. They asked him who he was, but he was unable to utter a word. Instead, he cried all the while and beat himself and tore his clothing. After he had mourned for a long time, he gazed at the inscription explaining that Galehaut had died for him. And so he told himself that now he would be

too wicked if he did not in turn die for Galehaut. With that, he leapt beyond
the screen and decided to seek his sword and kill himself with it, for his
sword had also been Galehaut's.

But just as he emerged from the church, he met one of the young ladies
of the Lake, the one to whom Bors had spoken in front of Hungerford Castle.[48] She recognized him easily and took him by the sleeve of his tunic and
stopped him.

"What is the matter? Where are you going like this?" she asked.

"Ah, lady, allow me to bring my misery to an end, for I will never again
have joy or rest in this world."

"Tell me about it," she said.

Lancelot said not a word, but instead dashed away to escape from her
hands. When she saw him run off, she cried after him, "I forbid you by the
one you love most in the world to go any farther without speaking to me."

And Lancelot stopped and looked at her, and when he recognized her, he
told her that she was welcome there.

"In God's name, you ought to greet me more warmly than that, at the
very least because I am the messenger of your Lady of the Lake."

"Alas, my lady, pray do not be disturbed. I surely have known so much
sorrow that no one but God could comfort me. Don't think that I could ever be
happy about any adventure that might befall me."

"In God's name," replied the young lady, "you will indeed be happy. Listen to what my lady commands you to do."

"Go ahead and tell me," said Lancelot.

"She wants you to remove Galehaut's body from the church and have it
carried in a litter to the Dolorous Guard, where he will lie in the very tomb
where you found your name inscribed. She desires that it be so because she
knows that your body will be buried in the same place."

When Lancelot heard this, he was very glad and said that the news was
very pleasing and that he would do everything just as she had said. Then he
asked how his lady arranged this.

"She has been very distressed for a week because she learned from her
oracle, as she herself told me later, that as soon as you discovered Galehaut's
tomb, you would kill yourself in grief, if you weren't prevented. She sent me
here to you in great urgency so that I would order you to stop mourning—
since it could only harm you—and beg you by the one you love the most to
console yourself as best you can. I was to tell you that if you did not follow
her instructions, you should know that the next time you needed her, she
would fail you."

Lancelot said that since his lady desired it, he would console himself.

---

[48] An earlier event not included in this volume.

[*Lancelot defeated the five guards and sent one to take Galehaut's body to Dolorous Guard. He sent Galehaut's sword to Bors, then rode on to Floego Castle to save Meleagant's sister.*]

He stared at the field outside the city and caught sight of a huge crowd of people surrounding the fire where Meleagant's sister was to be burned. When he saw the fire, he feared for her life. Then he spurred his horse on in that direction and rode as fast as his horse would carry him. When he reached the spot, he looked and saw the young woman who had already been led to the fire to be killed. She was wearing only her chemise. Six ruffians held her, three on one side and three on the other. They were waiting only for the judges' order to throw her into the fire. She wept very bitterly and lamented Lancelot's absence.

"Oh, noble knight Lancelot, may it please God that you hear news of this and that you be half a league away! Surely with God's help and yours I would be rescued yet today in spite of all my enemies. But you don't know this, so I will have to die now for the life that, after God, I saved for you. Yet, truly, this doesn't disturb me so much for myself as it does for the chagrin that you'll have when you learn what has happened. I console myself with the knowledge that maidens will gain so much by my death: you will never fail any young lady who requests your help as long as you remember me. For your heart is so noble that it could not exist unless it gives great service to all women who invoke my name. So it seems to me that it's better for me and for my soul that I die out of loyalty to you, and for having freed a man as valiant as you from prison, than that you should die by the disloyalty of Meleagant who threw you into prison treacherously."

The young woman was speaking in just this way, weeping softly, when Lancelot came riding fast to the place where he saw her. He said to those who were holding her, "Let the young lady go!"

"Why should we let her go?" demanded one of the armed knights who sprang forward.

"Because you have no right to hurt her," replied Lancelot.

"Yes, we do. We have every right, because we have convicted her of the murder of which I accused her and she proposed to defend herself. But she found no one to take up the sword for her, which is no wonder, since everyone knows that she has behaved dishonorably."

"In what way?"

"Because she freed Lancelot so that he could kill her brother, Meleagant."

"If you dare to claim that she has committed treason or murder, I will be ready to defend her," announced Lancelot.

"Who are you?" asked the other.

"I am a knight who has come here to defend this lady."

"In faith," said the knight, "if I wanted to, I wouldn't have to fight, because she has been condemned since yesterday, since she couldn't find a champion to defend her. But I feel that my case is so legitimate and just that there's no knight in the world against whom I wouldn't dare put the strength of my claim to the test."

"We'll see about that, by God, for I am ready to defend her against you," Lancelot replied.

"Then, by heaven, you will assuredly die like a traitor and infidel," retorted the other.

So they dragged the young woman away from the fire, and the knights backed apart and then charged each other as fast as their horses would carry them. They struck each other so hard with their lances that they sent them flying into bits. They clashed bodies and heads together so violently that both were completely stunned and confused. Lancelot's opponent was so dazed that he could not hold his saddle; instead he flew down from the horse and in the fall the point of his helmet stuck into the ground, so that he nearly broke his neck.

When Lancelot had turned around, he dismounted, for it would have been disgraceful to pursue on horseback a knight who was on foot. He drew out his sword and ran over to the knight, who was now rising. And he gave him such a blow on the helmet that he sent him down on his hands and knees to the ground. Then he dealt another blow, sending him flat on the ground. Lancelot seized the knight by his helmet, dragged him to the fire, and threw him in. The knight was so stunned and had lost so much strength that he could not stand up; he had to remain in the fire and die in that way.

[*He then took the woman back to her castle and continued on his way to Bademagu's court.*]

30. Lancelot Buries Galehaut at the Dolorous Guard.

[*Lancelot arrived at Bademagu's court and defended himself against accusations made against him. He refused to stay afterward, telling Bademagu that the latter had offended him. He rode on to Dolorous Guard.*]

Although the people within the country called it the Joyous Guard, for foreigners it never changed its name.[49]

When Lancelot entered and saw Galehaut's body there, one need not ask if he wept: all who witnessed his grief thought he would die on the spot.

---

[49]The changing of the castle's name, from Dolorous Guard to Joyous Guard, was recounted in Chapter 5.

When the people of the castle recognized him, they comforted him as best they could because they were very upset by his distress. Then he ordered that the most beautiful tomb one could imagine should be built.

"Why, my lord?" asked the people.

"Because I want his body to lie there."

An old woman spoke up: "In God's name, my lord, within the castle there is the most splendid tomb in the world, but we do not know for certain where it is. If you wish to find it, call forth all the old men from within, and then you will hear the truth, I think."

Lancelot did just as the old lady advised. He summoned the oldest men from within the castle and had them assemble in private. After they had deliberated, they came before him and told him that it was in the main chapel, beneath an altar: "You should realize that it's the most splendid tomb in the world and was made for King Narbaduc, who was the author of the law upheld by the Saracens after Mohammed. This castle was the pagan's mosque before Joseph of Arimathea arrived in this country; they buried the king inside and placed him in the tomb, which they considered holy. But with the advent of Christianity, the body was removed and thrown into the moats beyond the city. They left the tomb in its place; it has not been touched by human hands ever since then."

Lancelot was delighted to hear this news. He had the tomb dug up from where it had been placed. When he saw it, he esteemed it more than anything that he had ever seen, which was no wonder, since it contained neither gold nor silver, but rather was crafted entirely of precious stones joined together so subtly that it did not seem as if a mortal man could have made such a work. When the tomb was carried to the place where Lancelot had found his name, they placed it before a marble armory, and they lay Galehaut's body within. He was armed in full armor, as was customary in those times. And Lancelot himself lay his companion to rest inside the tomb. After he had laid Galehaut down, he kissed him three times on the mouth in such agony that his heart nearly leapt out of his chest. He then covered him with a rich silken cloth decorated with gold and precious stones and placed the tombstone on top. Afterwards, he left the castle and commended the people of the castle to God. He left behind the young woman whom he had escorted there.

Then Lancelot resumed his journey and rode on until he came to the court of King Arthur, who was staying at Camelot. When the king learned that Lancelot was arriving, he went down from the hall, along with all his barons and the queen and her maidservants. They received him as joyously as if he were God himself. After that, Lionel, Hector, and Meliaduc the Black came forward. They greeted him as joyously as they should have. After he had removed his armor and had eaten, the King called forth his clerks, who set the adventures contained within this book into writing. They wrote down Lancelot's adventures just as he had told them.

When the king heard him talk about the knight who vowed that he would take the queen from the escort of four knights, he announced that for the next year he would never venture into the forest without the queen, and that four armed knights would always escort her. "And I beg you, Lancelot, to be one of them," said Arthur.

Lancelot agreed, and the king appointed Sagremor the Unruly, Kay the Seneschal, and Dodinel the Wildman along with him. The King assigned the escort of the Queen to those four knights whenever he ventured into the forest during the next year. And so the moment arrived when the three knights would not have been able to prevent Guenevere's abduction if Lancelot had not been there, as the story will describe further on.

[*Amid adventures of Bors, Sagremor, and others, Guenevere mistakenly thought Lancelot dead and announced his loss at court. Gawain, leaving court in quest of Lancelot, found a knight with two swords and asked about them. One was broken, and Gawain and his companions were unable to join the two parts, whereupon they were told that it was the sword that injured Joseph of Arimathea and that it could be repaired only by the chosen knight who would achieve the adventures of the Holy Grail.*]

31. Sir Gawain Fails at the Grail Castle and Learns the Significance of His Adventure from a Hermit.

[*Gawain came to a castle and was welcomed by its king.*]

As they were speaking in this way, Sir Gawain looked about and saw through a glass a white dove that carried in its mouth a censer of magnificent gold. As soon as the bird had entered, the hall was filled with all the sweet odors that a mortal heart could imagine or a mortal tongue describe. At that moment, everyone was so dumbstruck that not a soul uttered a word. Instead, they all knelt down as soon as they saw the dove, which flew straight into a room. Then those from the palace leapt up and placed the dinner cloth on the tables. They sat down next to one another without anyone saying a word, nor was anyone called. Sir Gawain marveled greatly at this adventure. He sat down with the others and observed that everyone was praying and worshiping.

They had scarcely been seated when Sir Gawain saw the most beautiful young woman he had seen in his life emerge from the room where the dove had flown. She was without a doubt the loveliest maiden who had ever been born or has ever been born since. The young lady was bareheaded and her hair was braided; she had the most beautiful face a woman could possess, and she was so splendidly imbued with the fine attributes that belong to woman that a more beautiful woman has never been seen, save for the Virgin Mother who carried Jesus Christ in her womb. And she emerged from the chamber, carrying in her two hands the most splendid vessel that had ever been seen by earthly man, which was made in the semblance of a chalice; she held it above her head so that she was constantly bowing before it.

Sir Gawain looked at the vessel and admired it more than anything he had ever seen, but he was unable to learn what it was made of, for it was composed neither of wood nor of any kind of metal, nor of stone, nor was it of horn or bone, which amazed him. Then he gazed at the maiden, marveling more at her beauty than at the vessel's, for he had never seen a woman whose beauty compared to hers; he gazed at her so intently that he thought of nothing else. As the maiden passed in front of the dining table, each knight bowed down before the holy vessel. The tables were at once replenished with all the delightful nourishment that one could describe. The hall was filled with delicious odors as if all the spices in the world had been scattered there.

After the maiden had passed once in front of the table, she returned to the chamber from which she had come. Sir Gawain followed her with his eyes as far as he could. When she was out of sight, he looked before him at the table where he was seated, but he saw nothing for him to eat. Rather, the table lay empty in front of him, although there was no one else who did not have a great abundance of food as though it grew there. When Gawain saw this, he was too shocked to know what he should say or do. He realized that he had done something wrong, since he had nothing to eat as the others did. He restrained himself from asking until the dinner was over.

After dinner, when they had risen from the tables, the people left the hall and went off in separate directions, so that Sir Gawain did not know what had become of them. As he was about to go down into the courtyard, Sir Gawain discovered that he could not leave the room, because the doors were tightly locked. When he realized this, he went to lean out of one of the windows and began to reflect very intently.

Just then he saw a dwarf with a stick in his hand emerge from a room. When he saw Sir Gawain, he said, "What is this, sir worthless knight? By what misfortune are you leaning out our windows? Get out of here, you shouldn't be here, for you are too full of evil. Go hide yourself in one of these rooms so that no one will see you!"

Then he raised his stick to hit Sir Gawain, but the knight thrust his arm against it and took it from him. When the dwarf saw this, he said, "Ah, knight, that won't do you any good. You certainly won't be able to leave this place without incurring shame."

Then he retreated into a room. Sir Gawain looked at one end of the room, where he saw the most splendid bed in the world. He walked over to it, for he was very eager to sleep. Just as he was about to sit on the bed, he heard a young lady crying out to him, "Alas, knight, you'll die now if you sleep there without your armor, for this is the Adventurous Bed.[50] But here is a suit of armor. Take it and then be seated there, if you wish."

Sir Gawain ran to where he saw the armor, took it, and outfitted himself as best he could. When he was all armed in hauberk, helmet, shield, and sword, he went back to sit on the bed. But as soon as he was seated, he heard the ugliest and most hideous cry he had ever heard: he really believed that it was the devil.

Then he saw emerge from a room a lance whose tip was ablaze; it struck Sir Gawain so hard that neither the shield nor the hauberk prevented the blade from penetrating all the way through his shoulder. Sir Gawain fainted. The lance was extracted from his shoulder, although he did not know who removed it. He bled an astonishing amount, but he did not move from the bed. Instead he said that he would drop dead or he would see more than he had yet seen. Yet he felt that he was very badly wounded.

Sir Gawain remained there for a long time, until the night grew so dark that one could have seen only dimly within the room had it not been for the moonlight that streamed in through more than forty open windows. So Sir Gawain peered into a room—into the one that was closest to him—and he saw the hugest and most wondrous serpent that he had ever seen. Any man in the world would have been completely terrified at the sight of it. Nor was there any color in the world that one could not find in it: it was red and indigo and yellow and black and green and white. The serpent had huge, red, swollen eyes, broad jaws, and a thick belly. It began to slither up and down across the room, playing with its tail and striking the ground. After it had played for a long time, it turned itself upside down and began to moan and bray and flail about violently.

After it had thrashed about for some time in this way, it stretched itself out as if it were dead. Sir Gawain watched in amazement as a hundred little serpents swarmed out of its jaws. After this, it slithered out of the room and went to the great hall, where it found the fiercest leopard in the world, and they rushed to attack each other. Then the two of them began to wage the most savage battle on earth, for the serpent believed the whole time that it could vanquish the leopard, although it could not. As they were fighting there, such an adventure befell Sir Gawain that he could no longer see a thing, although the moon was shining brightly. But after a time his eyesight returned, so that he could see the serpent and the leopard, which were still fighting.

The battle between the two beasts lasted for a long time, so long that Sir Gawain could not tell which one was winning. When the serpent realized that it could not get the better of the leopard, it returned to the chamber from

---

[50]This scene contrasts strikingly with an earlier one—summarized in Chapter 21— where Lancelot emerges unscathed from an encounter with a lance in a perilous bed, as Gawain observes him.

which it had come. Just as soon as it entered, the little serpents rushed up to attack it, and the big serpent fought back. The little serpents defended themselves vigorously and helped one another as best they could. Their melee went on through much of the night until, finally, in the end the big serpent killed the smaller serpents, and the smaller ones killed the big serpent. [. . .]

Then the whole hall began to shake and tremble, and the windows began to rattle and knock, and it began to thunder and spark lightning violently. It was the most inclement weather in the world, except that it did not rain. Sir Gawain was terrified by this adventure, but he was too tired and exhausted to raise his head. Besides this, his brain was so addled by the sound of thunder that he did not know if he was alive or dead; he lay there like a dead man. Next, there arose such a sweet and soft wind that it was a marvel. Finally, a chorus of voices—perhaps as many as two hundred—came down into the great hall singing so sweetly that nothing in the world could compare to the sound.

Sir Gawain could scarcely understand what the voices said except that he heard them all at once singing glory, praise, and honor be to the King of Heaven. A little before the voices were heard, all the good odors of earth were spread about. Sir Gawain listened carefully to the chorus; he heard voices so sweet and melodious that he felt they were celestial rather than earthly sounds, as indeed they were. He opened his eyes, but he saw nothing around him, and then he believed that these were not earthly sounds that he had heard, for he could not see their source. He would gladly have risen, if he had been able to, but he could not, for he had lost the power of all his limbs and the strength of his body.

Then he saw the beautiful maiden who had carried the splendid vessel before the tables emerge from the room. Preceding her were two candles and two incense burners. When she reached the middle of the hall, she placed the vessel on a silver table, and Sir Gawain saw ten censers around it that continuously burned incense. Then all the voices began to sing together more sweetly than a mortal heart could imagine or than an earthly tongue could describe, and everyone chanted in unison, "Blessed be the Father of Heaven."

After the song had continued for some time, the maiden took the vessel and carried it back to the room she had left, and, at that moment, all the voices departed and went back where they had come from. Then all the hall windows closed, and the room became so dark that Sir Gawain saw nothing. But it was all the more fortunate for Sir Gawain that he felt as strong and healthy as if he had never had any pain or injury; nor did he care about the shoulder wound, for he had completely healed. He stood up glad and joyful and went off to find the knight who had fought against him, but he could not find him.

Then he listened and heard a great crowd of people approach. He felt someone take him by the shoulders, feet, and head, and carry him out of the room, and they tied him firmly to a cart that was in the middle of the courtyard. The next morning at daybreak, Sir Gawain woke up to find himself in the ugliest cart in the world, and he saw his shield tied to the shafts of the cart and his horse hitched to the back.[51] Supporting the shafts in front was such a haggard, miserable nag that it seemed scarcely worth three pence. When he realized that he was in such a terrible situation, he was so upset that he would rather have been dead.

Then an old woman with a whip came toward the cart, and she began to beat the nag and drive it swiftly through the city streets. When the workers and craftsmen of the town caught sight of the knight of the cart, they ran after him hooting and shouting. They escorted him in this manner out of the town. They threw manure, mud, shoes, and all the refuse they could find. When he had crossed over the wooden bridge, the old lady stopped and untied him, and then she ordered him to jump out of the cart, for he had sat there long enough. He jumped down, mounted his horse, and asked the old lady what the castle was called, and she replied, "Corbenic." Then Sir Gawain rode off, lamenting as bitterly as he could and cursing the hour he was born and that he had been invested as a knight, for now he had become the basest and the most shameful of all men.

Then Sir Gawain left, weeping, lamenting, and mourning, and he wandered all day without drinking or eating. In the evening, he arrived at the abode of a hermit who was called Hermit Segre. Sir Gawain arrived before the good man had sung vespers, and he listened to the service with pleasure. Afterwards, the noble man entered into his abode. Then he inquired who his guest was and what country he came from. Sir Gawain told him the entire truth.

"Ah, sir," said the hermit, "you are most welcome here! Indeed, you're the man in the world I most desire to see. But, for God's sake, where did you sleep last night?"

At that, Sir Gawain was so upset that he was unable to reply; his eyes welled with tears. Then the good man realized that Sir Gawain was upset about something, and so he stopped speaking, except to tell him, "My lord, for heaven's sake, don't be sad about something that happened to you, for there is no valiant man who does not meet with some misfortune."

"That is so, my lord," replied Sir Gawain, "I realize that many good men have bad luck, but never has so much misfortune happened to a single man as has befallen me in the past two weeks."

And then Sir Gawain recounted all the adventures that had occurred that fateful evening. The good man observed him and was so stunned that he said nothing for a long time. When he was able to speak again, he said, "Ah, my lord, you were indeed unfortunate, because you saw it but did not recognize it."

---

[51]This scene recalls Gawain's refusal to ride the cart on the occasion when Lancelot does so in Chapter 21.

"Oh, my dear sir," said Sir Gawain, "for God's sake, if you know what it was, then tell me."

"Indeed," explained the hermit, "it was the Holy Grail, where the blood of Our Lord was shed and gathered. Because you were not humble and simple, it is right that His bread should be refused to you, as it was; this you saw clearly, when everyone was served and you were forgotten."

"Tell me the truth and the whole truth about the adventures I saw, if you know."

"You will never hear anything from me, and yet it will not be long before you find out."

"Kind sir, at least tell me what the serpent signifies, if you know."

"I'll tell you that much," replied the good man. "But don't ask me anything more afterwards, for I won't tell you any more.[52]

"It was true that you saw in the room the serpent that played and spat out the little snakes that he left in the room. Then he left to go to the great hall, and once there he found the leopard with which he fought but which he was unable to vanquish. When he realized that he wouldn't be able to defeat the leopard, he returned to the room where the snakes rushed to attack him, and they killed him as he killed them. Did you see all this?"

"I truly did," said Gawain.

"Now I'll tell you what it means," continued the good man. "The serpent, which was so big and strong, signifies your uncle, King Arthur, who departed from his land just as the serpent left his room, leaving his men and his kin in his country, just as the serpent left the little snakes. And just as the serpent attacked the leopard and fought with him but was unable to defeat him, so will the king attack a knight, but will be unable to wound him, try as he might. And just as the serpent returned to his room when he realized that he couldn't defeat the leopard, so the king will return to his country when he sees that he won't be able to wound the knight. And then a marvelous adventure will happen to you, because just as you were deprived of your eyesight as long as the battle of the leopard and the serpent lasted, so at this point will the light of your prowess be dimmed.[53] Afterwards, when the King will have returned to his country just as the serpent returned to the room, his men will attack him in the same way the little serpents attacked the serpent. The battle will last until he slays them and they him. Now you've heard what the serpent means. So I've done what you want, and by the same token I want you to do what I request."

---

[52]The hermit's explanation prefigures the battle between Arthur and Mordred in *The Death of King Arthur*, Chapter 7.

[53]This is presumably a reference to Gawain's failing health and eventual death after he is wounded in a battle against Lancelot in *The Death of King Arthur*. As a result, Gawain is weak and ineffective in Arthur's Roman War, and he dies in Chapter 6.

Sir Gawain promised that he would do it.

"You must swear on relics that you'll never speak about what I've told you ever in your life and that you won't reveal it to any man or woman alive."

Sir Gawain swore it on the relics, although he was frightened by the hermit's words. Still, he let the matter rest and put on a cheerier face than he felt in his heart of hearts. He remained at the hermitage that night and was provided with whatever the good man could offer. In the morning, as soon as he heard Mass sung by the hermit himself, Sir Gawain took up his arms and mounted his horse, just as he had done the preceding day. But now the story stops talking about him and returns to Hector who had set off on his quest.

[Hector defeated Marigart the Red in battle, and Yvain continued to search for Lancelot.]

32. Sir Gawain and His Brothers Described.

Now the story says that the day Mordred left his companions, he wandered all alone and rode all day long without drinking or eating; he suffered greatly, for it was very hot and he had not yet learned to endure hard work, since he was a mere youth of twenty. Nevertheless, he was a large, tall knight; he had curly, blond hair and would have had a very handsome face, if his demeanor had not been not so wicked. In this he did not resemble Sir Gawain at all, since Sir Gawain had a simple, pleasant countenance and a compassionate expression. The truth was that Sir Gawain had the most handsome body of all his brothers, although his stature was small. Since I have never described his brothers to you, I shall describe them to you right now, just as the story describes them.

The truth is that Sir Gawain was the eldest of his brothers and had a very handsome physique; all his limbs were well formed, and he was neither too tall, nor too short, but of fine proportions. He was more chivalrous for his age than any of his brothers. Nevertheless the story says that Gaheriet his brother had accomplished feats of arms almost as great as Sir Gawain had, but he never put as much effort into it as Sir Gawain always did, which is why Gaheriet was not as renowned.

However, what made Sir Gawain most memorable was that he loved poor people and was kind and compassionate towards them; he gladly did more good for lepers than for others. And another trait assured that his reputation would remain forever great (for there were many who, as long as their stamina lasted, would have been better knights at King Arthur's court if it were not for this particular feature of Sir Gawain): around noon he doubled his strength, which is why no one was able to conquer him in a sword fight, although there were many more skilled with lances.

But no one was so gracious toward the poor. And his custom was such that, if he were fighting any knight in the field, he would rather have died on the spot than not get the better of him. Sir Gawain was a very fine knight of great bearing and was very loyal toward his lord all the days of his life. He was neither spiteful nor jealous; on the contrary, he was more courteous than any knight at the court. This courtesy inspired many ladies to love him, less for his chivalry than for his courtesy. He never boasted among knights about anything he had done. He was wise and moderate always, without calumny and without baseness, and he never bragged about his prowess.

The next eldest after him was Agravain. He was taller than Gawain, and his body was somewhat misshapen; he was quite a fine knight. But he was too arrogant and full of evil words, and was jealous of all other men, which caused his death at the hand of Lancelot himself, as the story will tell you later on.[54] Agravain was without pity or love and had no good qualities, save for his beauty, his chivalry, and his quick tongue.

The next after him was called Gaheriet. He was the most charming of all the brothers; he was valiant in chivalry, brave, swift, handsome, and noble. His right arm was longer than his left. He performed numerous acts of prowess without speaking of any, unless he was forced to. He was the most restrained of all his brothers but, when overcome by anger, he was the most unruly. He was the least well spoken of all his peers.

The next after him was Guerrehet. He was a fine knight, valiant and diligent, who never ceased seeking adventures during his whole life. He was strong and had a marvelously handsome face; he always comported himself more elegantly than any of his brothers. He had such great endurance that he could suffer great pain; even so, he did not have Gawain's prowess. He was a lover of ladies, and they loved him greatly; he was very generous, and he did many good deeds as long as he lived. He was the brother whom Sir Gawain loved the most, and he loved Sir Gawain more than all the others.[55]

The youngest brother was named Mordred. He was greater in stature than any of the others and the worst knight; although he had great strength and was more inclined to do evil than good, he nevertheless delivered many fine blows. Envious and deceitful, he never loved a good knight since he first bore arms. He killed many people and did more evil in his life than his whole family did good, because on his account more than a thousand men died in one day. He himself died in the debacle, as did the king his uncle, which was a great sorrow, as the story will tell you clearly.[56] This man was truly the

---

[54] Agravain's death occurs in *The Death of King Arthur* in a battle that takes places when Lancelot rescues Guenevere from the pyre (Chapter 4).

[55] This relationship is described differently elsewhere; *The Death of King Arthur* (Chapter 6) tells us that Gaheriet was Gawain's favorite.

[56] This announces the final battle on Salisbury Plain near the end of *The Death of King Arthur;* see Chapter 7.

devil; he never did any good except during the first two years he bore arms. Nonetheless, his body and all his limbs were very well formed.

Sir Gawain and his brothers were just as I have told you. Now I will be silent about them and I will return to my material, for it is certainly the moment and the time. [. . .]

Part V

TRANSLATED BY WILLIAM W. KIBLER

33. Lancelot Is Captured by Three Sorceresses; At a Tournament He Fights for King Bademagu; At the Castle of Corbenic He Witnesses the Grail Procession and Fathers Galahad at Case Castle.

[*Lancelot was captured by Morgan and two other sorceresses; they took him to Cart Castle and informed him that he could leave only if he chose one of them as his lady. He refused and stayed in prison until a maiden who was serving him agreed to free him. He went to help Bademagu in a tournament against the king of North Wales. Later he met a lady who praised his prowess and promised to accompany him to Corbenic.*]

That night he had a comfortable bed and rested, because he was very tired and exhausted, and slept until nearly the hour of prime. When he awoke, it was long past sunrise; the lady had prepared him a new and comfortable linen robe, which he took and put on. After he was dressed and ready and had heard Mass, breakfast was prepared. Once they had eaten and the tables were removed, Lancelot requested his weapons and the lord begged him to stay for the day, but he said that there was no way he could do so. When he was fully armed and mounted on his horse, he took his shield and called for a spear, which was brought him. Then he said to the lady, "My lady, do you remember your promise to me?"

"Yes, my lord, very well," she replied.

"Then I pray you," he said, "to keep it as you should."

And she said she would gladly do so.

Then she had a palfrey saddled and told a squire to follow her.

"My lady," her husband inquired, "where do you have to go?"

"My lord, I'll escort this knight to Corbenic, for I've promised to show him the most beautiful creature in the world."

"Go then," said her husband, "and take care to return."

At that she left the castle and rode on with Lancelot; she was well wrapped to protect herself from the sun. They rode along in this manner until just after the hour of nones, when they came into a valley and saw in front of them in the distance a small and very well-situated castle, surrounded entirely by deep water and well fortified walls. As they approached they met a maiden who said to the lady, "My lady, where are you taking this knight?"

And she replied, "To Corbenic."

"Then truly, my lady, you have no love for him, for in God's name you're taking him to a place he cannot leave without shame and injury."

They rode on until they came to the castle and found the bridge to cross. They entered the castle, and as they rode up the main street people began to say, "Sir knight, the cart is waiting for you!" And he said under his breath that if he had to climb into it, it would not be the first time.[57] They rode on until they neared the main tower; he admired it greatly, for he thought it was the most beautiful and strongest he had ever seen. He looked to the right and heard a woman's voice that sounded very close. He went in that direction and saw that she was the maiden Sir Gawain had tried in vain to free from the basin.[58] And she was shouting, "Holy Mary, who'll get me out of here?" As soon as she saw Lancelot approaching, she said, "Ah, my lord, get me out of this burning water!" He came to the basin, took her by the arms, and pulled her out. As soon as she saw she was free, she fell at his feet, kissed his leg and shoe, and said, "Oh, my lord, blessed be the hour you were born, for you've saved me from the greatest pain a woman ever endured."

The room immediately began to fill with ladies and knights: everyone in the town gathered to see the maiden and led her into a chapel to thank Our Lord. Then they took Lancelot to a cemetery below the tower and showed him a splendid tombstone upon which carved letters proclaimed, THIS TOMB-STONE WILL NOT BE LIFTED UNTIL THE LEOPARD, FROM WHOM IS TO DESCEND THE GREAT LION, PUTS A HAND TO IT, AND HE WILL LIFT IT EASILY, AND AFTERWARDS THE GREAT LION WILL BE BEGOTTEN IN THE BEAUTIFUL DAUGHTER OF THE KING OF THE LAND BEYOND. After he had read the writing, he did not understand what it meant, and the people around him said, "My lord, we are certain that this writing speaks of you, because we know by your freeing the maiden that you're the best knight of all those now living."

"What do you want me to do? I'm ready to do whatever you wish."

"We want you to lift up this tombstone and see what's beneath it."

He put his hand on the thickest end and lifted it easily; inside he saw a more horrible and fiendish dragon than any he had ever heard of. As soon as it saw Lancelot, it spat fire so hot that Lancelot's hauberk and weapons were all

---

[57]The first time Lancelot entered the cart was recounted in Chapter 21.
[58]See Chapter 21.

burned; then it flew from the tomb to the middle of the cemetery, and all the bushes there began to burn from the heat of the fire. The townspeople all turned and fled to the upper windows to see what would happen. Lancelot lifted his shield in front of his face and, unafraid of any adventure that might befall him, headed toward where he saw the dragon. The dragon spat poison fire that burned the outside of his shield, but Lancelot struck it through the chest with his spear, leaving point and shaft embedded in its body. It began to beat the earth with its wings like a dying creature; Lancelot gripped his sword and whacked at it wherever he could until he managed to send its head flying. At that moment, the other knights came forward fully armed to help Lancelot; but when they saw he had already killed the dragon, they welcomed him joyfully and began to ring all the bells. Knights, ladies, and maidens all gathered at once, a marvel to behold, and welcomed him above all other knights in the world; then they led him to the main palace and removed his armor.

As they were disarming him, a tall knight came forth with a great company. He was one of the most handsome knights Lancelot had seen since leaving Camelot and gave every appearance of being a noble gentleman. When the people saw him coming, they rose to greet him and said to Lancelot, "Sir, here's the king coming." Then Lancelot rose and welcomed him, and the king returned his greeting and threw his arms around his neck, saying, "Sir, for so long now we've wished to see you and have you among us! Thank God, you've come at last. Mark me well: we're in great need of you, for our land has been so long destroyed and laid waste, and the poor people have lost their meager holdings, that it's only right, if it please Our Lord, that their losses be redeemed and their possessions restored, which they've done without for so long."

Then they sat down beside each other, and the king asked him his name and where he was from.

"Lancelot of the Lake," he replied.

"Now tell me," said the king, "was not King Ban, the gentleman who died of grief, your father?"

"Yes, sir, he was," said Lancelot.

"Upon my word," said the king, "then I'm convinced that either you or someone begotten by you will deliver this land from the strange adventures that occur here day and night."

Then a very ancient lady, who could easily have been a hundred years old, came forward. She called to the king, saying, "Sir, I wish to speak with you."

The king left Lancelot, after giving orders to his knights to keep him company, and they said they would. Then he followed the woman into a room, and when he was seated she said, "Sir, what can be done with this knight God has sent us?"

"I don't know what we should do, except that he'll have my daughter to do with as he will."

"In the name of God," said the woman, "I know for certain he won't want to take her when she's offered to him, because he loves the queen, King Arthur's wife, so dearly that he'll refuse to have anyone else. Therefore, we'll have to do it so subtly he won't notice."

"Then see to it as you will," said the king, "because it must be done."

"Don't you worry about it anymore," the woman reassured him, "for I'll see that it's accomplished."

At that the king returned to the hall and came to keep Lancelot company; they conversed and came to know each other as best they could. Lancelot asked him his name, and he replied that he was called Pelles of the Land Beyond. While they were talking in this way, Lancelot looked and saw a dove enter the window; it was the same dove that Gawain had seen before,[59] and in its beak it was carrying a very precious golden censer. And as soon as it had entered, the palace was filled with all the sweet scents a man's heart could imagine. Everyone there grew silent, no one said a word, and they all knelt down when they saw the dove enter. Then it flew immediately from the hall into a room.

The servants quickly sprang forth and placed cloths over the dais; then one and all sat down without anyone saying a word or summoning them. Lancelot marveled at this, but did like the others and sat beside the king; he noticed that they were all praying, so he did likewise. Not long after they sat down he saw coming forth from a room the maiden that Gawain had stared at for so long, and she was so beautiful and attractive in every respect that Lancelot himself acknowledged he had never before seen such beauty in a woman, unless it was in his lady the queen, and that the lady who had brought him there had spoken the truth. He looked at the vessel the maiden was holding in her hands, which was to his mind the most precious that mortal man had ever seen, and was in the shape of a chalice; he thought, and truly believed, that it was a holy and worthy thing. He folded his hands and extended them toward it and began to bow humbly before it. And at the moment the maiden passed across the dais, everyone knelt in front of the holy vessel, and so did Lancelot. The tables were immediately covered with every fine food one could imagine, and the palace was filled with every pleasant scent, as if all the good spices in the world had been poured out there.

After the maiden had crossed the dais one time, she returned right to the room from which she had come. After she had gone, King Pelles said to Lancelot, "Indeed, sir, I was very fearful that Our Lord's grace might fail this time as it did the other day, when Sir Gawain was here."

---

[59]See Chapter 31.

"Good sir," said Lancelot, "Our Lord, who is so gentle, could not remain forever angry with sinners."

After the king had eaten at his leisure, they removed the cloths, and the king asked Lancelot what he thought of the precious vessel the maiden had carried. "It seems to me," answered Lancelot, "that it was costly and splendid. And I've never seen such a beautiful maiden: I speak only of maidens, not ladies."

When the king heard this, he immediately remembered what he had heard about Queen Guenevere and was convinced that he had been told the truth. He went to Brisane, his daughter's tutor, the one who had spoken to him earlier, and told her what Lancelot had answered about this daughter.

"Sir," she said, "I told you so. Now wait a bit for me and I'll go speak with him."

She went to Lancelot and began to ask him news of the king, and he told her what he knew of the queen.

"My lord," she said, "I didn't ask you about her, because I saw her healthy and happy just a few days ago."

And he trembled with happiness at her words and asked her where she had seen the queen.

"My lord," she replied, "just two leagues from here, where she'll be sleeping tonight."

"My lady," he said, "you're lying to me!"

"So help me God, I'm not. But if you refuse to believe me, come along and I'll show her to you."

"Most willingly, my lady."

Then he sent for his weapons, and she hurried meanwhile to the king who was waiting in his room. He asked her how she had managed.

"Have your daughter mount at once," she said, "and send her to Case Castle as fast as you can, and Lancelot and I will come along afterwards. When we arrive there I'll convince him that she's the queen. I've mixed a potion I'll give him, and after he's drunk it and it's gone to his brain, I've no doubt that he'll do everything I want, and so what we're all seeking will come about."

The king had his daughter prepared and gave her twenty knights to escort her to Case Castle. As soon as they arrived and had dismounted, they set up the most splendid bed possible in a hall, and the maiden lay down in it, according to the wishes of those who had brought her.

Meanwhile, Lancelot had donned his armor, mounted his horse, and departed, leaving the one who had brought him. Then he and Brisane rode until they reached Case Castle. When they arrived it was after dark and the moon had not yet risen. They dismounted, and Brisane took him into a room where the knights were; as soon as they saw him coming, they stood up and welcomed him and removed his armor. The room there was brightly lit by some twenty burning candles. Brisane, who had acquainted one of her maidens with what she intended to do, had given her the potion and said, "When you hear me calling for drinks, bring a full cup of this and give it to Lancelot, and don't bring him anything else until he's drunk it." And she agreed to do so.

Once Lancelot was out of his armor, he was eager for drink, because he had become hot on the way there; and he asked where his lady the queen was. "My lord," she said, "she's in this room, and I think she's already sleeping." He called for wine, and the maiden who had received Brisane's instructions brought him the potion, which was the color of wine and more sparkling than spring water. The cup was not large, but was filled to the top. He was thirsty, and the lady said to him, "My lord, drink it all; it will do you good, for I don't think you've ever drunk anything like it." He took the cup and emptied it and found the potion sweet and good; he asked for more, which she brought him, and he drank it down.

Then he became more animated and talkative than usual; he asked Brisane how he could see his lady the queen. She looked at him and saw that he was completely transformed: he did not know where he was or how he had come there; he really thought he was in the city of Camelot and was talking to a lady who had been the queen's principal lady-in-waiting ever since the lady of Malehaut had died. Once she saw how confused he was and was sure he could easily be tricked, she said, "Sir, my lady might already be asleep. Why have you waited so long to go to her?"

"Since she hasn't yet sent for me," he said, "I don't wish to go to her; but if she were to send for me, I'd go."

"By God," she said, "you'll hear from her soon."

She entered the room and pretended to talk to the queen; then she returned to Lancelot and said, "Sir, my lady is awaiting you and has sent word for you to come speak with her."

He immediately had his boots removed and went into the room in undershorts and shirt; he came to the bed and lay down in it with the maiden, thinking she was the queen. And she, who wanted nothing so much as to possess the man who was the light of earthly chivalry, welcomed him happily and joyfully, and he entertained and delighted her as he would have his lady the queen.

And so the best and most handsome knight who ever lived and the most beautiful and highest-born maiden of that day were joined together. Their desires stemmed from different motives: she did it not so much for his beauty or from lust or bodily desire, but so as to receive the fruit that would restore that entire land to its original beauty, that land which had been laid waste and destitute by the dolorous blow from the Sword with the Strange Straps, as is clearly recounted in the *History of the Grail*.[60] But he desired her in a very

---

[60]See *History of the Holy Grail*, Chapter 8.

different way, because he did not covet her for her beauty, but believed she was his lady the queen; and this inflamed him to know her as Adam knew his wife, but not in precisely the same manner, because Adam knew his wife faithfully and by the command of Our Lord, whereas Lancelot knew her in sin and adultery and in opposition to God and Holy Church. Yet nonetheless the Lord, who is the font of every mercy and who does not judge sinners by their deeds, looked on this coupling in light of its value to the land, for He did not wish it to remain a wasteland forever: so He permitted them to engender and conceive a fruit, by virtue of which the flower of virginity that was corrupted and violated there blossomed forth in another flower whose goodness and tenderness would replenish and console many a land. For just as the *Story of the Holy Grail* informs us, from this lost flower blossomed forth Galahad, the virginal, the most excellent knight, who achieved the adventures of the Holy Grail and sat in the Perilous Seat of the Round Table, where no knight had ever sat and lived to tell of it. And just as the name Galahad had been lost to Lancelot by the flame of desire, so too was it restored in this offspring by mortification of the flesh, for he remained a virgin in thought and fact until he died, as the story tells us.

And so flower blossomed forth from flower, because as Galahad was conceived the flower of maidenhood was destroyed and crushed; he who was to become the flower and mirror of chivalry blossomed forth from this mutual coupling; and if virginity was harmed as he was conceived, the wrong was made right in his life through his own virginity, which he returned whole and entire to his Savior when he left this world, and through the great deeds he did during his lifetime.

Now the story leaves him and returns to Lancelot, who lay all night with the maiden; he took from her the name she could never truly recover, for although they had been able to call her a maid that evening, her name had changed to woman by morning.

34. After Further Adventures Lancelot Is Entrapped in a Magic Dance.

When morning came, Lancelot awoke and looked about himself, but saw no light because all the windows were so blocked that no sunshine at all could enter. He began to wonder where he was and to grope about himself. He found the young woman and asked her who she was, but already it was coming back to him, for the strength of the potion began to weaken as soon as he knew the maiden carnally. She said, "My lord, I'm the daughter of King Pelles of the Foreign Country."

As soon as she said this, Lancelot realized how he had been tricked; he leapt out of the bed, more grieved than words can express, took his undershirt and pants, dressed and put on his shoes, and took his armor. After he was fully armed, he returned to the room where he had slept and opened the windows; when he saw the young woman by whom he had been tricked, he was so grieved he thought he would go out of his head; he intended to avenge himself without delay. He drew his sword, moved toward her, and said angrily, "My lady, you'll be the death of me! So you too must die, for I don't want you ever to trick another man as you've tricked me." He raised his sword above his head, and the woman, afraid she would be killed, pleaded for mercy with joined hands, saying, "Oh, noble knight, don't kill me! Have pity on me as God did on Mary Magdalene!" Troubled, Lancelot stopped and saw she was the most beautiful creature he had ever laid eyes on, but he was shaking so with anger and wrath than he could barely check his sword. He said nothing and pondered what to do: whether he should kill her or let her live. She kept pleading with him for mercy and was on her knees in front of him in nothing but her shift; and he looked at her eyes, her face, and her mouth, and saw there such beauty that he was amazed. Then, more grieved than words can express, he said: "My lady, I leave you as a man overwhelmed and defeated, a man who doesn't dare take vengeance on you, for I would be far too cruel and false were I to destroy such great beauty as you possess. I beg you to forgive me for having drawn my sword against you, for anger and wrath made me do it."

"My lord," she said, "I forgive you on condition that you no longer be angry with me."

He agreed, since he saw he had no choice; he put his sword back in its scabbard and bade her farewell.

When he came down into the courtyard, he found his horse saddled. Brisane had had it made ready so Lancelot would find it when he came down, for she well knew that he would not remain there after he discovered the deceit. Once he had mounted and taken his shield and a spear he found leaning against a tree, he set off sad and angry along his way, so downcast he did not know what he was doing.

King Pelles came early in the morning to Case Castle to see his daughter, for they had already brought him word of Lancelot's departure. As soon as Pelles arrived, he found her languishing and dispirited because of the fright Lancelot had given her when he almost killed her; she told her father everything just as it had happened. When he knew the whole truth about her and Lancelot, he cherished her and watched over her with more honor than before. Less than three months later he learned she was pregnant, from the physicians who told him and from his daughter who assured him it was true; they were both happier than words can express, and the people of that land rejoiced.

[*Lancelot, meeting a maiden who had earlier saved him, defended her against a knight who wanted to rape her. Then he went on to the castle where King Ban had engendered Hector; told of this event, he learned that Hector was his half-brother. The following day he left that castle to look for Hector and for his cousin Lionel.*]

The heat had grown most oppressive and it was uncomfortable to ride, so he removed his helmet, which seemed to hurt him the most, and gave it to a squire he encountered along the way. Then he rode along in this manner until the hour of nones, when he came to the entrance of an ancient and venerable forest. There he saw the chapel of a very worthy hermit, and all around the chapel was a cemetery, at the entry to which was a cross and a large marble slab. Upon the slab he saw a red inscription that read, BEWARE, KNIGHT ERRANT WHO COMES THIS WAY SEEKING ADVENTURE: UNLESS YOU WISH TO DIE, DO NOT ENTER THIS FOREST, FOR YOU WILL NEVER ESCAPE WITHOUT SHAME OR DEATH. The squire read this sign and said to Lancelot, "My lord, do you understand clearly what this message means?"

"Yes," he answered.

"Then I'm sure you won't go on," said he, "since this sign forbids it."

"And where are you going?" asked Lancelot.

"My lord, to a castle on the other side of this forest."

"Then you'll have to take this road, for there's no other."

"That's true," he said; "I have no choice."

"Then proceed with confidence," said Lancelot, "for I'll follow you."

"Oh, my lord, for the love of God," said the squire, "don't come along, for it would be too great a folly! Don't you see what this sign says?"

"That sign won't keep me out," said Lancelot, "for nothing will stop me from going there."

Then he looked off to the right and saw the hermit who had opened the door to his chapel and was about to sing vespers service. He went there, greeted him, and the worthy man returned his salutation and asked him who he was, and Lancelot replied that he was a knight errant.

"What are you seeking?" he asked.

He said he was seeking a cousin of his named Lionel.

"And what is your name?" asked the hermit.

"Sir, I'm called Lancelot of the Lake."

"In the name of God," he said, "I've heard of you before. Many people say you're the best knight in the world, so it would be a real pity if you were to go somewhere you couldn't leave, for many people have been lost there. So I urge you to return along the path that brought you here, for I don't see any way you could get through this forest along this path. In the past two years some two hundred knights have entered here, all of whom promised me as they left that if God gave them strength to escape death they'd return here to tell me what they'd found, but none has returned, so I know they're all dead. I tell you this, sir, for in these days you are the pillar of chivalry; I tell you not to enter this forest, for I know you won't come out."

"Tell me now," said Lancelot, "about that sign; you must know who wrote it."

"Indeed I don't," replied the hermit.

"Has it been there a long time?"

"Yes," he answered, "more than six years."

"Now I bid you farewell," said Lancelot, "for I've tarried too long."

"Will you not do as I told you," said the hermit, "and abandon this path through the forest?"

"No indeed," said Lancelot. "Nothing I see will stop me from taking it, for it would be most cowardly on my part if I were to show fear before I knew why."

"Then I'll tell you what you must do," said the hermit, "since you refuse to turn back. Stay here today, for it's almost night, and it's the best thing I see for you. If you were to go into this deep and dense forest now, night would probably fall before you've gone two leagues, and you'd have to sleep under a tree or on the bare earth, and neither you nor your horse would have any food. But here you can sleep comfortably and eat, and your horse will have hay and oats, and the squire can rest, which he couldn't today otherwise."

"Since it pleases you for me to stay, I will," said Lancelot, "though it's still a bit early."

Then he dismounted; the hermit steadied his stirrup and asked him to stay the day with him, "and I tell you loyally that I'll accompany you tomorrow through the forest." Lancelot stayed with him, seeing he could do no better. That night Lancelot was well served and put at ease in every way the hermit could, for he sent his clerk to a nearby castle to buy fish as on Friday, and they ate it in large portions. After supper Lancelot asked the worthy man the name of the forest. "My lord," he said, "the people of this land call it Lost Forest, because there's no one who knows anything about what's there, since everyone who enters is lost and no one ever hears another word about them."

"Upon my word," said Lancelot, "it's a marvel that no one returns. I think this must be the Path of No Return. May God never help me again if anything keeps me from going there and learning where they've all disappeared."

"May God be with you," said the hermit, "because, so help me God, I've never been so afraid for anyone who's gone there as I am for you."

That night Lancelot was as comfortable as the worthy man could make him, and in the morning after he arose, the hermit sang the Mass of the Holy Spirit for him; then he donned his armor, and when he was armed he bade farewell to the worthy hermit. As he saw him leaving, the hermit prayed to Our Lord that He bring him safely through. Then Lancelot and the squire plunged into the forest. Lancelot asked him whose man he was.

"A squire of King Pelles of the Land Beyond, who has sent me with a message to the duke of Oc."

So on they rode in the shade of the wood until after the hour of prime, when they met a young woman carrying a dog in her arms. Lancelot had removed his helmet as it grew hotter and his face was exposed; he greeted the young woman as he approached her, but instead of responding she only stared at him, for he seemed so handsome that she was quite amazed and stopped to see him better, and he wondered why she was staring at him so, and said, "My lady, what are you thinking?"

"Indeed, sir, I'm thinking it's a great pity when such a handsome man rides to his death and dishonor. I think God Himself is very much to blame for leading you this way, for you couldn't go to any more perilous place."

"Don't be worried, my lady," said Lancelot; "all the evils you're imagining won't happen to us, God willing."

"May God grant it," she said, "because, so help me God, I hope you're right."

Then they proceeded their separate ways. After they had gone a short distance, the squire said to Lancelot, "My lord, in God's name take some advice: have pity on yourself and turn back. Didn't you hear how this young woman, who's never seen you before, is sorrowful on your account and has said you're going to your death? Imagine how sad it will be for those who know you, when those who've never seen you before are grieved. For God's sake, turn back while you still have time, and for love of you I'll turn back also to accompany you until you're out of the forest."

But Lancelot said that nothing could force him to turn back, so he should speak no more of it; and the squire said he would say no more about it, since Lancelot's heart was set upon it.

So they rode on until they reached a very beautiful meadow below a tower, and in the meadow were set up some thirty of the most beautiful and finest tents Lancelot could ever remember having. In the middle of the tents were three tall, fully mature pine trees, standing touching one another in a circle, and in the middle of them was an ivory throne covered with a cloth of red samite, and on the samite was placed a large and heavy gold crown. All around the pines were knights and ladies; some of the knights were in armor, and others not. Some were dancing with helmets laced on, as if this had been agreed upon, and others were dancing in cloaks and mantles and holding maidens by the hand, and still others were holding neither maidens nor ladies, but knights by the hand, since there were many more knights than women.

As Lancelot approached the place and saw them dancing around the pines, he was quite surprised and said to the squire, "What a joyful and noble gathering! You can't tell by looking at them that it's dangerous to travel through this forest, so may I be damned if I don't go see why they're so happy."

Then he struck among the tents and no sooner had he reached the first than he grew pale and his whole heart changed: if before he had only a mind for chivalry, leading assaults, and starting battles, now his desire had shifted and he wanted only to dance. He totally forgot his lady, his companions, and himself; he dropped down from his horse and gave it to the squire to watch, threw his shield and lance to the ground, and entered the dance in full armor, his helmet laced on, taking the hand of the first maiden he met. Then he began singing and stamping his feet like the others, making merry and skipping much more than he had ever done before, so much so that the squire looked at him and thought him a fool. They were singing a song written about Queen Guenevere, but they were singing in Scottish, so the squire could not understand well what they were saying, but nevertheless he knew enough to understand that the words meant, "Truly we have the most beautiful queen of all."

After the squire had waited there a long while, he grew tired of delaying, because it seemed to him he was wasting his day. He came to Lancelot, took him by the edge of his hauberk, and said, "My lord, come on, you've tarried too long."

But Lancelot replied angrily to his words, "Get away from here! Leave me alone! I won't leave here for you or anyone else."

When the squire heard him refuse to leave, he thought perhaps he was angry because he had called him too soon. So he withdrew and waited a little longer to see whether he would leave, but Lancelot gave no sign of it. The squire waited until the hour of nones, and when he saw that the sun had already started down, he thought himself a fool for having waited so long. He went back to Lancelot and called him again, telling him to come along. But Lancelot, who had no mind except to dance and make merry, answered, "It's truly good to be in love," which was the song they were singing. Then the squire realized that Lancelot had been deceived and taken in by the dance; he began to lament bitterly and curse the hour they had come there, since the best knight of all was overcome by folly and enchantment. He wept and lamented bitterly. When he saw that he could do nothing more, he set off once more along his path and rode rapidly away, leaving Lancelot in the dance. But now the story leaves both of them and returns to Yvain, for it has long been silent about him.

[*Yvain was wounded in battle with Bors; both of them had further adventures. Gawain met a maiden who told him that Lancelot had been at Corbenic; he decided to go there in hope of finding Lancelot.*]

35. Lancelot Escapes from the Magic Dance; His Adventures with the Maiden Who Rescues Him from a Well Filled with Poisonous Snakes.

Now the story says that after the squire had left Lancelot in the dance, he set off and rode swiftly, for he was of the opinion that he had tarried too long; he was lamenting bitterly, because he thought that Lancelot would stay there forever. Lancelot made merry and sang just like the others, staying there until the hour of vespers. When it was time for supper, a maiden came to him and said, "Sir knight, you must go sit on that throne; we'll put this gold crown upon your head."

He said he did not care for crowns or gold thrones; all he wanted to do was rejoice and make merry.

"You must go there," she insisted, "because that is how we'll know whether or not you'll be the one to free us. If you don't release us, then you too must stay here with us and wait until God sends us the one who is to free us from this madness we live with."

He said he would gladly go, since she wished it; so he went to sit upon the throne, and she put the crown on his head, saying, "Good sir, now you can claim to have your father's crown upon your head."

He looked about and saw a magnificently carved statue resembling a king fall from the top of a tower and shatter on the ground into many pieces. Then the enchantment was lifted immediately and all those who had long lost their minds and memories had them restored.

When Lancelot saw that he had a gold crown on his head, he seized it and threw it down and sprang from the throne where he felt he had no right to sit, since it was the sign of royalty. The knights, ladies, and maidens all ran to embrace him and rejoiced more over him and fêted him more than ever anyone had a man, saying, "My lord, blest be the hour of your birth, for you've cast us out of the greatest madness we've ever endured, from which only death would have brought us release, had God not led you here."

Then they led him up into the tower and helped him remove his armor. An old knight came into the room and said to Lancelot, "Lancelot, dear son, truly I said that the enchantments of this place would not end until you came here. Now it is clearly proven that you are the best knight in the world and the fairest: everyone should love and cherish you dearly from this day forth, for they would not have escaped except for you."

"Good sir," said Lancelot, "tell us the origin of this wonder, why everyone who joined in this dance lost their minds and memories and couldn't leave."

"This I'll gladly tell you," he said. "It happened in the days after King Arthur had promised to wed my lady Queen Guenevere and the wedding was about to occur, that all the noble men who were vassals of the king came into this land to receive their fiefs and do him homage. And it happened, a good two weeks after the wedding ceremony, that your father King Ban was riding through this forest with his knights. When he reached this tower, beneath these trees you still see here today, he found six maidens dancing and singing a new song just composed about Queen Guenevere. In the middle of the circle of dancers was a throne on which was seated one of the loveliest maidens in the world, the daughter of royalty. Though King Ban was very elderly, there was no knight in his company as spry as he. He stopped to watch the dancing, and beside him was a cousin of his, a learned clerk who was handsome of body, gay, lively, and a good singer, though he had never fallen in love; but he knew more than anyone in the world about enchantments and necromancy. The king watched the maidens singing while the young clerk watched the one on the throne and found her so beautiful and attractive that he was of the opinion that whoever could possess her could consider himself fortunate. He loved her so deeply that he felt he'd never be happy if he couldn't have her, but he didn't see how this was possible.

"After the king had observed the dancing for a long while, he said that it would be more appropriate if each maiden had a knight. He immediately had six knights who were with him dismount and join the dance, so that each maiden had her knight. When the young woman on the throne saw this company, she said that she would consider herself most fortunate if she could have such dancing and such company every day. After the clerk heard the young woman speak, he replied, 'Indeed, my lady, if you wish, you can have even better dancing and company than this, such as will continue as long as there's fair weather, both winter and summer.'

" 'By God,' said she, 'I'd like this very much, and there isn't anything I wouldn't do if you promise it will be as you've said, for I could think of no finer and more agreeable pleasure than what you've described.'

" 'If you'll grant me your love and swear before my lord here present that you'll love no other as long as I'm alive, I'll do even better than I've described, and I'll tell you how: I'll enchant everyone here in such a manner that for all their lives they won't become wearied or exhausted from dancing, but will dance both winter and summer whenever it's good weather, and it will never bother them as it does now. And since there are but few dancers, I'll arrange it that all others who enter this meadow, if they're in love or have ever fallen in love, will remain with them to dance and will never recall anything except the dance. And they will dance just as they come: if they come in armor, they'll dance in their armor; if they come without arms, they'll dance without them; and they'll dance each day until the hour of vespers, when every night they'll enter this tower to eat and sleep. But no one can join in the dance unless he has loved or is in love, for anyone who does not love happiness cannot stay among happy people, and no one can attain true happiness if he isn't in love or hasn't loved. This dance will last as long as we live and will continue after our deaths until the most loyal, the best, and the most handsome knight comes; and on the day he comes, the dance will end in the same way that it began, for it will begin with you, my lady, who to my mind are the most beautiful woman in the world, and it will not end until the most handsome knight in the world arrives. And so it will begin with beauty and end with beauty.'

"When the young woman heard this, she thought it was all a lie and believed there was no way he could do this, so she promised faithfully to do whatever he wished, and he said he asked for nothing more. He cast his spell at once and so bound the knights King Ban had sent to join the dance that not one of them could leave it, and he did likewise to the young woman's companions. When the king realized that the enchantment was a fact, he said that his crown could find no better use than to be given to the best and most handsome knight in the world, and so he left it upon the throne in order that the one who was destined to end the spell would have it. When the king left, the clerk remained with the young woman, and all his desires were satisfied, as she had promised.

"When the people of the land heard tell of this, they began to come and behold the wonder, and many among them were powerless to return, for so many were bound by the strength of the spell that I saw in one day a hundred and fifty who stayed on to join the dance. So the dancing continued in this fashion for over fourteen years, grand and wonderful, until the young woman became bored and asked her lover to remove the spell, but he said that it could not be removed before the time he had set. 'Then I pray you,' she said, 'on your love for me, to create another game that we can play, a game so clever that all who see it will marvel at it.' And he said that it would be done since it was her wish.

"Then he created a chess set with gold and silver pieces, the most precious and beautiful that any man had ever made or seen, and even formed a chessboard from a precious stone worth over a thousand pounds. After he'd made the chessmen and board, he brought them one day after dinner to the young woman and said, 'This is a chess game unlike any you've ever seen.'

"'Why?' she asked.

"'By heavens,' he said, 'I'll show you.' Then he arranged the pieces as if to begin a game and asked the young woman to choose hers, for she was obligated to play.

"'Whom shall I play against?' she asked. 'It can't be you, because you're not clever enough to play me.'

"'Go ahead and play your best,' he said, 'because you can't play well enough to keep from being checkmated.'

"When she heard this, she moved a pawn ahead to see what would happen, and immediately an opposing pawn advanced without anyone having touched it. When she realized that the chessmen themselves were playing against her without anyone's help, she strove to play her cleverest game to see what the result would be, and she knew more about chess than any woman there was in those times. But no matter how cleverly she played, she was always checkmated. After she had tried the game, she said that it was masterfully made and adroitly created, and asked whether everyone who played would be checkmated. 'No,' he replied, 'a knight will come, gracious and desired and beloved over all others, and he will be so skilled in chess and other games that he'll not find his equal in this world. That knight will checkmate this game, but everyone else who plays it will be checkmated except him, and the power of this game will last all his life, but at his death it will end and the chessmen will never play themselves again.'

"And so the clerk established the dance just as you've witnessed it in the way I've told you, and destined it to end, I believe, with your arrival. After she had enjoyed the dancing for many years, and the chess game too, the clerk died, as did the young woman for whom he had cast his spells. Those who were caught up in the enchantment remained a part of the adventure and would never have escaped had you not come. But God in his mercy has led you here to overcome their madness and restore their memories; and even had you done nothing else in all your life, still everyone should laud and admire you, for you have garnered much glory here."

"Now, since this adventure is ended," said Lancelot, "I must see the chess game, because otherwise I could never leave this place without dishonor."

Lancelot commanded that the chessmen be brought to him at once; they were brought and placed on a quilted cover along with the chessboard. Lancelot stared for a long while at the men, for they were skillfully carved and beautiful. He took the silver ones and arranged them, and also the gold. After he had set them all out in their proper positions, he began by moving the pawn in front of the queen, and the other side did likewise. After he had made several pawn moves, he changed his attack subtly, moving his rooks and other pieces so that they were all well protected; then he doubled his rooks, played his knights to the right, and played so cleverly for all to see that he cornered the gold king and said, "Checkmate!"

When the people there saw this, they were astonished and said to Lancelot, "My lord, the game is yours! You've won! Mark well: since you've not been checkmated, it was created to reflect your intelligence and skill: just as you weren't checkmated or vanquished by these pieces, you won't be checkmated or vanquished in battle as long as you live. This should be most reassuring to you." He said that he was very happy for this and had never heard anything more reassuring.

Everyone there began to rejoice and make merry, for they were overjoyed that God had freed them through Lancelot; they prepared the meal, for it was certainly time. That night Lancelot was served to his heart's content, for everyone sought to honor him, both for love of him and in thankfulness for their deliverance through him. After eating, they prepared his bed in a lovely room a little removed from the others, so he would not be disturbed by the noise, for they were intent upon offering him every service they could that he might appreciate.

[*The following day, Lancelot left. He was attacked by thirty knights who threw him into a well full of poisonous snakes. A maiden rescued him, and they left.*]

With that Lancelot and the maiden departed and rode until they arrived on the day specified at Cart Castle, where Lancelot had been imprisoned by the three ladies, and that was the day for the wedding of the brother of the queen of Sorestan and the daughter of the duke of Rocedon. When they arrived at the entrance to the castle, a child came up to them and said to Lancelot, "Sir knight, for love and courtesy, tell me your name."

"Why do you ask, young man?" inquired Lancelot.

"Sir, I ask it only for good reason, so tell me if you please."

And he said that he was called Lancelot.

"Truly you are welcome," the youth exclaimed. "By God, I've been waiting a long time for you!"

"Why?" asked Lancelot.

"Because I intend to take you to the church when it is time to deliver my cousin, the maiden who released you from prison. You remember why you came here? Well, now you have even greater reason to accuse him of treason than before. Since you left here we've learned that this past Christmas he killed his own nephew, the son of the lady of this castle, as he was going to Carlion.[61] If you accuse him of treason, everyone here will be delighted, because they hate him so and because he's such a coward he'd never dare fight against you."

"Have no fear, good friend," Lancelot replied, "because before nightfall I intend to see to it that the maiden is released according to her wishes."

Then they listened and heard the bells ringing loudly throughout the castle. "My lord," said the youth, "now she's being taken to the church."

"Then let's go," said Lancelot.

He told the maiden with him to wait until he returned, which she most willingly agreed to do. Then he said to the child, "Young man, take me to the church where your cousin is to be married."

And he said, "My lord, follow me."

"Go quickly, I'm following," replied Lancelot.

They hurried on until they reached the church, where many great barons and noble ladies were gathered. The priest was already vested and at the door of the church to perform the wedding ceremony. Lancelot, who had ridden right up to them fully armed, did not dismount but said to the knight who intended to marry the maiden, whom he easily recognized by his armor which had been described to him, "Sir knight, you may intend to marry this maiden, but I forbid you from this moment on to do anything more than you've done, for you are so wicked and disloyal that you're unworthy of such a noble wife."

"In the name of God," he said, "you can't prove that!"

---

[61]This knight was the fiancé of the girl who released Lancelot from prison and who is now about to have to marry his killer.

"But I will," said Lancelot, "and more than that, for I'll prove that you unlawfully killed your nephew, if you'll dare to counter my challenge."

"Upon our solemn oaths," said the others to him, "you'll be granted no delay. Since he accuses you of treason, you must defend yourself; and if you don't, your treachery will be known, and we'll hold you guilty of the charge he's made against you."

When he realized that he could not escape except through single combat, he did not know what to do, for he was well aware that the man who brought this challenge against him was a dreaded adversary; and moreover, he was even more frightened because he knew he was guilty of the charges of wrongdoing and treason. So he decided that he would offer his pledge for all to see, but when he was supposed to put on his armor, he would mount his horse and leave the country. And so he could avoid this combat, which he would never undertake in any event, for he was the most cowardly of all men.

Then he said to Lancelot, "Good sir, I am ready to defend myself against the charges you made against me, if you dare repeat them." He placed his pledge in the hand of the queen his sister, and she accepted it. Lancelot came forward and said that truly he challenged him on all counts, then offered to prove it and gave his pledge to the queen, who took it.

Then the knight pretended to go fetch his armor, but went to his sister's courtyard, took and mounted the best horse there, and went sneaking down the side roads of the town until he came to the castle gate. Once he was out, he rode as fast as he could to put as much distance as possible between himself and the town, for he had no desire to return. A youth came to Lancelot, who was still waiting with the others for the knight to return, and told him, "My lord, you're wasting your time waiting for the knight who's supposed to fight you, for he left some time ago and must be two leagues and more away by now."

When the queen heard this, she said that so help her God she was glad, and all the others agreed. Then Lancelot said to the queen, "My lady, since we are thus rid of the knight who offered in your presence to do combat, I pray you to return her lands unconditionally to this maiden, who is the daughter of the duke of Rocedon, so that she may do with them as she pleases and rule them as she should."

The queen invested her with them at once, and the maiden was happy and delighted at the outcome of this adventure. And Lancelot asked her if she wished him to do anything further. "Not now, my lord," she replied, "for you have done everything I wished, thanks be to God and yourself."

He said that he was satisfied and immediately asked leave of all those there, for he wished to depart. But Morgan, who was standing right beside him, was very eager to have a look at him to see if she recognized him, because she was certain he was from the house of her brother Arthur. So she said to him, "Sir, as God is your protection, tell me who you are."

But he looked at her, knew who she was, and was very fearful that she would recognize him, for she was the woman he most feared in all the world, since he knew that she had often made trouble for him and many another worthy man. So he did not dare uncover his face, fearing that some evil would come to him from it, but responded nevertheless, "My lady, I am a knight errant from the house of King Arthur, a member of the Round Table and knight of my lady Queen Guenevere."

"Tell me your name," she insisted.

But he told her she would learn no more at this time.

"No?" she said.

Immediately she thought it must be Lancelot, the man she most hated in the world. He was about to leave when she called him back, but he barely turned around, as he cared very little for her. She said, "Sir knight, you won't tell me your name?"

"Truly I won't, my lady," was his reply.

"Now I pray you," she said, "in the name of whomever you love most in this world, to remove your helmet so I can see your face plainly."

When he heard these words, he was sadder than words can express, but removed his helmet. As soon as she saw him, she recognized him. "Aha!" she exclaimed. "Lancelot! If only I'd recognized you the other day as well as I do now![62] But I didn't recognize you because you'd had your hair cut; we were wickedly deceived!"

"My lady," he said, "I escaped, though many of you may not like it. So help me God, I swear that if you weren't a woman, I'd see to it that you'd never harm another knight errant or worthy man, for your body harbors nothing but disloyalty and treason."

"Truly, Lancelot, you've had your say. But I swear to you upon my word that you won't see this year pass without regretting these words more than you've ever regretted anything you've done before."

"Indeed, my lady," said he, "if you live long, I know you'll do much more evil than good. But if it please God, some worthy man will yet come who'll take you in hand and free this world from you, which will be a great joy, for you are intent only on doing evil."

"God be praised for these fine words," she replied. "Be on your way now and rest assured I'll take the first opportunity that comes my way to do you ill."

Lancelot immediately laced back his helmet back on, for he wished to be off, fearful as he was of Morgan's deceitfulness and charms. He rode on to where he had left the maiden. As soon as she saw him coming, she greeted him and asked him how he had done, and he told her the whole adventure,

---

[62]A reference to material summarized in Chapter 33.

how the knight he was supposed to fight had fled, and how King Arthur's sister Morgan had made him known to everyone there, and how she had threatened him. "So we must leave here as quickly as possible," he continued, "because if she happened to follow us, I fear she might detain us through some charm, for she's the most deceitful of all creatures." Then they left Cart Castle and rode straight toward Camelot, where Lancelot hoped to attend the tournament, since his lady the queen had summoned him, as the story has already told.

Meanwhile, the knight who was carrying the woman's body, the one he had killed to spite Lancelot, had ridden until he had reached Camelot at the hour of prime on a Wednesday. That day there were many people there, because all the knights from foreign lands had gathered for the tournament, which was to begin the following Monday; so the palace was filled with kings, counts, and other barons.

After the knight dismounted in the courtyard, he took in his arms the still naked body of the woman, just as Lancelot had found her. He climbed up to the palace, and when the people there saw him coming, they opened a path to the king and followed him to hear what he was about to say. He greeted the king, laid down the woman's body, and said, "My lord, if my lady the queen is here, have her come forward, for I must address her and the ladies here. They will hear of an adventure that recently befell me." The king immediately summoned the queen, telling her to bring with her the ladies and maidens who were there.

Once the queen had heard King Arthur's summons, she did not delay long, but came as quickly as possible, bringing with her a great company of ladies and maidens. As she entered the room, everyone stood to greet her, and the knight came before her and knelt down, and he still had the woman's head hanging around his neck just as Lancelot had placed it. He unlaced his helmet, which was still on his head, and set it on the ground; then he removed the woman's head from around his neck, greeted the queen, and said, "My lady, a knight who defeated me by his skill in arms has sent me to you because I took vengeance on this woman to spite him. Let me tell you about it: the truth is that I loved this dead woman so much that I married her for love, though I was a man wealthy in land and friends and she was a poor maiden. I lived with her a long while, holding her in great honor and esteem as if she were a queen. For love of her and to win honor I left my castle and went seeking wondrous adventures like other knights here, and there was nothing I wouldn't have done for her had I the power to do it.

"The other day I chanced to pitch my tent at the edge of a forest and left her to sleep all alone one night; I had gone into the forest to discover the true source of a voice I'd heard. After I'd found what I was seeking and stayed a while there, I returned to my tent and found a knight sleeping in my bed naked with this woman. When I saw that, I was terribly angry, drew my sword, and killed the knight (for which I have no regrets), and then I seized this woman, dragged her from the tent, and was pulling her along beside my horse by her braids and beating her, when a knight came charging at me to rescue her, saying he'd kill me if I didn't let her go that minute. When I heard that, I was enraged the more, pulled out my sword, cut off the woman's head, and threw it at the knight, saying I'd done it to spite him. He charged me straightway to kill me, but when I saw he'd drawn his sword, I didn't dare wait for him, because he clearly had the look of a man to be feared, so I fled as fast as I could, but he gave chase and overtook me and would have killed me if I hadn't begged for mercy. But he let me go and told me that I must carry into your presence this woman I'd killed so wrongfully and obtain the pardon of ladies and maidens, and if you judge that I deserve to die, I am to hand you my sword and permit you or another to kill me, since that would be a lawful judgment."

Then he drew his sword from its scabbard and handed it to the queen, saying, "My lady, now you may do with me as you will." The queen took his sword and asked the king what should be done—whether the knight should be slain or allowed to live.

"Indeed," answered the king, "he's wronged all the ladies in the world so much that he shouldn't be spared, yet it's possible that some knight sent him to you for whose merits you should pardon him an even greater offense: therefore I advise you to ask who sent him."

So she asked him, "Good sir, who was the knight who defeated you and sent you to me?"

"My lady, the same knight who sent you the golden chess set."

The king and everyone else who heard these words were immediately overcome with delight. And the queen said to the king, "My lord, you have no doubt now who the knight is who sent him here to you. We will do whatever you wish."

"Upon my word," said the king, "I could never consent to see him come to bodily harm; nor could you consent to it, out of love for Lancelot who sent him to you, for no man alive has better served both you and me. And even had he not served you well, still he is such a worthy knight that out of love for him one should be prepared to pardon a great offense. Therefore, I desire that you should grant the knight pardon for all his wrongs."

And the queen handed him back his sword and pardoned him in the presence of everyone there. Then the knight was overjoyed and said to the king, "My lord, for God's sake, advise me now what to do."

"In what way, dear friend?" asked the king.

And he told him how he was still obliged to carry the woman's body to the courts of King Bademagu and the king of North Wales and offer himself in each place to the ladies and maidens to obtain forgiveness "just as I did here."

[*Lancelot distinguished himself in a tournament and afterward spent two nights with Guenevere. When the tournament resumed, Lancelot again prevailed. Arthur asked his identity, and Lancelot identified himself. A great feast followed, and only Lancelot could defeat the magic chessboard. Arthur had Lancelot's adventures written down; he then calculated that Lancelot had defeated sixty-four knights of the Round Table.*]

36. Bors Frees Yvain; Lancelot Kills Tericam, Freeing Hector, Lionel, and Many Others.

After the companions of the quest had related their adventures, the king said, "Only four of you have returned, and there should have been fifteen, for that's how many I was told undertook the quest. Therefore, if you truly wish to be considered companions, you must seek until you find those who set out with you."

"My lord," said Lancelot, "what you say is true, and I am prepared to set out questing for them tomorrow or the day after, and it is right that I do so, for they set out to seek me."

And Sir Gawain said that as soon as he was recovered he would leave court to seek his brothers, three of whom were still out questing. Bors stated that he would accompany him to seek his own brother. Gaheriet said that he would accompany them and not let them leave without him. And so they all four promised to keep one another company, and so began anew the quest that would not end for a long while.

That day there was much joy and great merrymaking in Camelot; they spoke of many things, until it happened that the queen was at the palace windows with Lancelot, and they were all alone and so far from the others that no one but they could hear what they said. Then the queen said to him, "Ah, Lancelot, did you hear what Sir Gawain said when he told of the adventure in the Waste Chapel, when he said that no man would complete this adventure until the unhappy knight came there who because of his miserable lust had failed to complete the adventures of the Holy Grail? And elsewhere they called the knight the Son of the Sorrowful Queen. Tell me if you know who this knight is."

"My lady," he answered, "I don't."

"Good heavens!" said she, "it was *you* the letters spoke of, for you are the Son of the Sorrowful Queen. I am very distressed that the flames of passion have caused you to fail to achieve the adventure for which all earthly knighthood must strive: you can rightly say that you have paid dearly for my love, since on my account you have lost something you can never recover. Understand that I am no less sad about this than you, and perhaps even sadder, for it is a great sin, in that God had made you the best and most handsome and most gracious of all knights and moreover had granted you the happiness of witnessing with your own eyes the wonders of the Holy Grail: yet now you have lost all this because of our love. It seems it would have been better for me never to have been born than to have so much good go undone as will be left undone because of me."

"My lady," said Lancelot, "what you say is wrong. You must understand that without you I would never have achieved as much glory as I have, because at the beginning of my knighthood I would never have had courage enough to undertake those deeds that others abandoned for lack of strength. But because I aspired to you and your great beauty, my heart was made so proud that every adventure I undertook I was able to complete. For I was well aware that if my valor did not bring me through the adventures, then I would never be able to win you, and I had to win you or die. Therefore, I tell you in all sincerity that this more than anything else increased my strength."

"Then I don't regret that you loved me, since you were inspired to such valor; but I do still regret that you failed to complete the high adventures of the Holy Grail for which the Round Table was founded."

"What you say astounds me," said Lancelot, "and I'll explain to you why. I don't believe that I would have attained the great valor I did without you, for I was a young and silly youth, far from my homeland, and without valor I could never have accomplished this quest you speak of, and would have achieved nothing if I had not been as favored by you as I am."

Then Guenevere asked him about Morgan, King Arthur's sister who had threatened him, and he told her everything. She was very perturbed, because she felt that Morgan hated him only because of her, and said, "If Morgan hates you, I advise you to beware of her. She is much to be feared, for she knows so many spells that she can cast them over the most worthy man in the world. The only advice I can give you is to wear on your finger a ring that your Lady of the Lake gave me just after you were knighted, because it exposes spells and makes them known, and that is something you'll need against her." Then Lancelot took the ring and placed it upon his finger.

That night King Arthur had Lancelot's bed set up in the master room and moved his own, which caused the people who saw this to say that the king paid more honor to Lancelot than to anyone else in his court.

The next day at the hour of prime, news reached there that a knight of the Round Table had died of wounds inflicted by Lancelot at the tournament. The knight was named Ganor of Scotland and had been a good and brave knight of high lineage. Then King Bademagu came to Lancelot and said to him, "My lord, if my valor or chivalry—not just my wealth—makes me worthy to become a companion of the Round Table, I pray you to ask King Arthur to accept me in lieu of the dead knight."

"Indeed," said Lancelot, "I know you to be so worthy and wise that your intelligence could give you more rights than another's chivalry. I will gladly beseech him, and I truly feel he'll do something of what I wish."

Then Lancelot went into the king's room and found him already up and about to go to church. Lancelot greeted him, saying he hoped that God would grant him a good day.

"In God's name," replied the king, "welcome to you! But why have you come so early?"

"Because I couldn't sleep," answered Lancelot. Then he continued, "Sir, one of our companions of the Round Table died today, and King Bademagu has asked me to beseech you to accept him as a companion in lieu of the dead knight, if you feel that his chivalry, not just his noble birth, makes him worthy to become a knight of the Round Table."

"Indeed," said the king, "it will be as you wish, for he is very worthy in wisdom and chivalry to be seated alongside the others. You are a companion and master as much as I, and are sworn just as I am not to elevate anyone purely out of love for him, if to your mind he's not worthy, any more so than you should refuse him a place out of enmity toward him."

"So help me God," said Lancelot, "he is more chivalrous than any seven others; and were he not as good a knight as I say, still he would be so worthy a man that we'll be more honored by his company than by that of any ten others. Therefore, I say that truly and rightfully he should be a companion, for he is still in his prime and at the peak of his powers, being no more than forty-six years old."

"Upon my word," said the king, "then he *will* be a companion, since you wish it." [. . .]

That day King Bademagu was seated at the Round Table by common accord of all those there and swore the same oath as all the others always to come to the aid of widows, maidens, and impoverished and disinherited noblemen, if ever he was summoned to do so or there was need. Then the queen came and sat Lancelot down beside her and said, "My lord King Bademagu, I love you dearly and for that reason I give you this man to be your companion; I pray him to offer you his company from this day forth and to consider you his closer friend and companion than anyone else."

"My lady," said Lancelot, "I grant that, since it is pleasing to you."

Then King Bademagu profoundly thanked them both.

Great were the festivities that King Arthur held to honor King Bademagu, and all who heard of them were delighted; the feasting and rejoicing continued for two full days. And the fourth day following, Lancelot said to the queen, "My lady, if it were your pleasure, I would set off tomorrow in quest of my brother Hector and my cousin Lionel. I am very distressed not to know where they are."

"My lord," she said, "were the need not so great, I would never have you leave here, for I am never much at ease the day I don't see you. Therefore I pray you to hurry back as soon as you can, if ever you want me to do anything to please you." And he replied that he would return as quickly as he could.

[*Lancelot, Bors, Gaheriet, and Bademagu set out and rode to White Thorn Castle, where the found people insulting and mistreating Mordred. Learning that all knights of Arthur's court were treated that way, they did battle with sixty knights and burned the city. The companions separated, and Lancelot learned that Tericam had imprisoned Lionel and some sixty others. He defeated Tericam, liberated the prisoners, and rode on.*]

Then Hector of the Fens and Lionel and the other companions of the quest hastened forward, and when Gaheriet saw them, he took his helmet from his head and showed them who he was, and they all rushed to embrace and welcome him joyfully. And he said to them, "Gentlemen, my lord Lancelot of the Lake sends greetings, both to those he knows and those he doesn't, and informs you that you may leave this prison whenever you like, for you've all been freed because he vanquished in arms the one who held you prisoner. Now he's ridden off after a maiden, but he sent me here to free you: you can leave whenever you please, since there's no one left here who'll hold you against your will, for the huge knight lies dead in front of the spring, slain by Lancelot's sword."

When the companions heard this news, they were more joyful than I could tell you in words; they came forth from the prison happy and joyful for this good fortune that had befallen them, and came out of the hall. Once they had come out, Gaheriet counted them to see how many there were and found that they numbered some sixty-four knights, from both King Arthur's court and elsewhere, since knights go seeking adventures through strange lands. And after they had all been set free, the seneschal Kay spoke up so that all there could hear, "I was right," he stated, "when I said that we wouldn't be delivered until Lancelot freed us, but that we *would* be delivered as soon as he passed this way."

And the others said, "He's clearly shown himself to be an exemplary knight wherever he goes." [. . .]

And so the companions remained there. In the evening, after they had eaten, they asked Gaheriet if he knew any news of the court, and he told them that he had left it only a short time ago. So he told them about the most splendid tournament that had been held in the kingdom of Logres since King Arthur was crowned, and then he told them about the great crowds and marvelous deeds of chivalry there, and how the knights of the Round Table had been defeated by Lancelot, who had gone over to King Bademagu's side. After hearing this report, they said that truly Lancelot was the most wonderful man in the world. "So help me God," said Kay, "in this fashion he has clearly proven that the Round Table is given more glory by him alone than by half of those who belong to it combined."

37. Imprisoned by Morgan, Lancelot Paints the Walls of His Room with Scenes of His Love for Guenevere.

[*Lancelot killed two giants who were guarding a castle. He was welcomed as the new lord of the castle, but he left as soon as possible.*]

With that, Lancelot entered the forest and rode all day until in the evening he came into a deep valley. There he met a maiden who greeted him and asked him his name, and he replied that he was named Lancelot of the Lake, son of King Ban of Benoic.

"By God," she said, "it is you I've been seeking. You are a most welcome sight, for you released me from the greatest suffering any woman ever endured: I had set off to find you and would never have stopped my wanderings until I did."

"And why were you seeking me?" he said.

"Because there is an adventure in this forest," she replied, "the most marvelous in all the world, and it can be accomplished only by you. That is why I was seeking you: so you would attempt it."

He said he would gladly go see what it was. And so Lancelot followed the maiden, thinking to do well, but it was to cause him harm and trouble, for the maiden had betrayed him and was taking him to Morgan's prison. Morgan was living in that forest, where she had built the most beautiful manor house in the world, planning to hold Lancelot there forever. She had sent twelve maidens out through distant lands in quest of Lancelot, telling them when they found him to bring him back with them on the pretense of accomplishing adventures. She who was bringing Lancelot was one of the twelve.

And so they rode together until they came to a splendidly fortified house surrounded by walls and moats; they entered it and the maiden spoke to Lancelot, "My lord, we'll take our lodging here tonight, for it is quite late and we could ride no farther today without night overtaking us. Tomorrow as soon as it is day I'll take you to the place I mentioned." He agreed and dismounted.

"Wait for me here until I return," she said.

"Go on," he said, "and don't tarry."

She went in, came to Morgan in a room where she was resting, and said, "My lady, I've brought you Lancelot. What do you want me to do with him?"

"By God," replied Morgan, "I am glad to see you! You have served me according to my wishes. Now I'll tell you what you'll do: have him remove his armor, and when it is time for dinner, have the table set and give him plenty to eat. When he is nearly finished, here is a potion I've concocted you'll give him to drink. He'll find it sweet and drink it gladly, and once he has drunk it we can do with him as we like."

She agreed to this plan, thinking this was just the way to trick him. Then she returned to Lancelot with three servants, one of whom took his horse and led it to the stable, while the two others led off Lancelot, removed his armor in the shade of an elm in the courtyard, then escorted him into the main hall and brought him a bright silk robe to wear. Next they set up the tables and took their places, but Lancelot did not make any inquiries about the place, for he did not wish them to find him churlish. When he had nearly finished eating, he drank the potion the maiden had prepared for him in a silver goblet. He found it sweet and good and drank it gladly, for he had no idea he had been so cruelly deceived. After he had eaten and drunk, he was so eager to sleep that he wondered why; he asked the maiden to have his bed prepared, for he wanted to lie down.

"My lord," she said, "it's all ready. You can lie down whenever you wish."

He rose from table at once, for he had lost all strength in his body from drinking the potion; he lay down and went to sleep immediately. Then the maiden went to Morgan and said to her, "My lady, Lancelot is already in bed asleep."

"By God," she replied, "I am glad for that."

Then she left her room, taking a box full of powder she had prepared for Lancelot, and came to where he was lying so soundly asleep he could not be roused. She filled a silver straw with the powder, placed it in Lancelot's nostril, and whiffed it into his brain. He stiffened from the pain he felt, but was so overcome by the brew he had drunk that nothing could awaken him. After Morgan had done this, she said to the maiden with her that now she had avenged herself well, "for I truly believe he'll never return to his good senses as long as this powder is working in his brain." Then she took the container and powder, thinking she might have need of it again. And the maiden asked her why.

"I'll be glad to tell you," said Morgan. "The truth is that when the knights of the Round Table fail to hear any news of Lancelot, they'll quest for him in every land. And he has two cousins, one named Lionel and the other Bors, who are excellent knights; I hate them so much for love of Lancelot that if by chance they come here I will take my vengeance on them gladly. So that's why I'm saving this powder: to give it to them if they come."

Then she had Lancelot taken and carried into a wide, high, and well fortified room, which was a good sixty feet wide by a hundred twenty long, with iron-barred windows that opened on a garden. She had a bed set up as if it were for King Arthur himself. "Lancelot will sleep here for as long as he lives," said Morgan. She was convinced he would never escape.

Then Morgan left the room, leaving Lancelot to sleep all night with no possibility of awakening. In the morning when he did awaken and discovered where he was, he was very surprised. He was positive he had not gone to bed there the evening before, so he was quite confused as to how he had come there. And he felt sick and uncomfortable, and thought that the house was spinning around him. He did not know what to do, for he was certain he could not ride on, since he was feeling so miserable; and he was especially surprised not to see anyone around to comfort him.

And so Lancelot waited until about midday; he did not have the strength to get out of bed, so he just lay there. Then Morgan came to a barred window to see if he was still asleep; and when she saw he was ill, she said to the maiden who accompanied her, "By my head, our potion is doing the trick: I don't think Lancelot has strength enough to rise. Go to him and ask how he feels, but be careful not to tell him he's in prison, because if he realized it, I think he would die of sorrow." She promised she would not utter a word about it. She opened the door of the room in which Lancelot was lying and found him pale and weak; she asked him how he was feeling, and he replied that he was very sick and so miserable that there was no way he could ride on.

"Then you can stay here," she replied, "because you cannot leave today in the terrible condition you're in."

"Certainly not," said Lancelot. "Even if I wanted to, I couldn't ride."

So Lancelot stayed there a full month until he was completely healed, before he realized he was in prison. And when Morgan learned that he knew, she wondered how it was possible. He had asked the maiden when she would take him to where she had promised, and then she had told him there was no way out, for he must remain a prisoner there. When he heard this, he was very distressed and said, "My lady, why have you betrayed me?"

"Upon my word," she said, "I had to do it or be killed."

"And why are you keeping me in prison?"

"That I cannot tell you," she said. So he asked no more and stayed there from September until Christmas.

After the cold of the Christmas season was passed, it happened that one day Lancelot went to rest against one of the iron windows, from which one could easily see into the palace. He opened the window and saw a man there painting a mural depicting an ancient legend, and over each picture was writing, and he recognized the story of Aeneas and how he had fled from Troy. Then he thought that if the room he was in were decorated with his own feats and words, he would be most pleased to behold the fair deeds of his lady, and this would be a great comfort in his sufferings.

So Lancelot asked the man who was painting to give him some of his paint to make a picture in the room where he slept, and he said he would be glad to. He offered him some paint and the necessary implements of the trade. Lancelot took what the man gave him and closed the door so that no one could see what he was doing. Then he began to paint first how his Lady of the Lake sent him to court to become a knight, and how he came to Camelot and was overwhelmed by the great beauty of his lady, when first he saw her, and how he went to rescue the lady of Nohaut. This took all of Lancelot's day; and the paintings were as skillfully and well done as if he had practiced this trade all the days of his life.

Morgan came there at midnight, as she did each night as soon as he was asleep, for she loved him as much as a woman could love a man for his great beauty; and she was very sad that he refused to love her, because she did not hold him in prison out of hatred, but hoped to vanquish him through persistence. She had often pleaded with him, but he refused to listen. And as soon as she saw the paintings, she knew exactly what they meant, for she had often heard how he had come to court and in what clothing.

Then Morgan said to the maiden who accompanied her, "Upon my word, you are witness to a miracle in this knight, who is so skilled in chivalry and all things. Truly love can make the dullest of knights artful and clever: I say so because of this knight, who never in his life would have been able to paint so well had he not been overwhelmed by love, which brought him to this. But now that he's put his mind to it, there is no one in the world to compare to him."

Then she showed the maiden the images he had painted and explained the meaning of each one to her, saying, "Here you see the queen, and here you see Lancelot, and here King Arthur," until she knew what each one meant. "There is no way now," she continued, "that I would free the painter before he has covered this whole room, because I know for certain that he'll depict all his deeds and words and all the doings between himself and the queen. And when he has painted it all, I'll see to it that my brother King Arthur comes here, and I'll show him the facts and truth about Lancelot and the queen."[63] Then they left, closing the door behind them.

In the morning after Lancelot had risen and opened the windows onto the garden, he came into the painted room. When he saw the image of his lady, he bowed in front of it, saluted it, came over and kissed it on the mouth, and took much more pleasure in that image than in any woman except his lady. Then he began to paint how he came to Dolorous Guard and won the castle by his prowess. The following day he painted all he had done up to the tournament in which he wore the red armor, that day when the king of the Hundred Knights wounded him. Next he painted his story day by day, not only his own, but that of the others as well, as the tale has related. He kept at it all season until after Easter. Now the story ceases to speak of him and returns to Sir Gawain.

[*Gawain and other knights continued to look for Lancelot.*]

---

[63]Morgan's intention will be realized in *The Death of Arthur,* Chapter 2, when she lodges Arthur in the same room and gives him the opportunity to see the murals.

Part VI

TRANSLATED BY CARLETON W. CARROLL

38. Lancelot Escapes from Morgan's Prison.

Now the story tells that Lancelot remained in Morgan's prison through two winters and one summer, until it happened that after Easter he saw the garden outside his room turning green anew. The trees were in leaf and loaded with flowers, and the rose bloomed each day before his window, for Morgan had had a fine garden planted so that Lancelot would be at ease through the summer. In the winter he had suffered greatly, for the prison where he had been so long distressed him much and would have distressed him more had it not been for the pictures he had painted in his room. There was no valorous deed he had ever performed, small or large, that was not portrayed there, each according to its manner, so that it was a wonder to behold. Each morning after rising, he went to each figure representing the queen and kissed the eyes and mouths just as if it were his lady the queen, and he wept and lamented most bitterly. And when he had at length lamented and bewailed his ill fortune, he returned to the pictures and kissed them and showed them the greatest honor he could and so consoled himself, and that was the thing that most pleased him.

After Easter, at the beginning of May, when Lancelot saw the trees full of leaves and flowers and the foliage that made his heart rejoice and the rose that bloomed each day fresh and red, he remembered his lady the queen and her bright complexion of which the rose reminded him every day—for when he looked at the rose it seemed it was the color of his lady, and he did not know which was the brighter hue, the rose or his lady, and that was the thing that was most responsible for his torments.

One Sunday morning, Lancelot had risen as soon as he heard the little birds singing; he went to a barred window and sat to look at the foliage, and stayed there until the sun had spread through the garden. Then he looked at the rosebush and saw a newly opened rose that was fully twice as beautiful as the others. "In this way I saw my lady more beautiful than the others at the tournament at Camelot, and because I cannot have her I must have this rose that reminds me of her."

Then he thrust his hand out the window and stretched it out to take the rose, but in no way could he reach it, for it was too distant. Then he drew in his hand and looked at the iron bars and saw that they were wondrously strong. "What is this?" said Lancelot. "Will this fortress hold me so that I cannot do as I wish? Indeed not!" Then he seized one of the bars with each hand, pulled so hard that he broke them, and threw them into the middle of the room. This so tore the flesh from his fingers that the blood spurted from them to the ground, but he felt it but little. Lancelot slipped out of the room, went to where he had seen the rose, and kissed it for the love of his lady, whom it resembled; he touched it to his eyes and mouth and placed it in his bosom next to his flesh.

Then he headed toward the keep, found the door open, went in, found helmets, hauberks, and arms in abundance, and immediately armed himself as best he could and took a sword he found atop a chest. He came down from the keep so well armed that he feared no man who might attack him; he went from room to room until he found two strong, swift chargers. He saddled and bridled the one he judged the better, then mounted it.

It was still so early that no one was up except for the man who guarded the gate. He was much astonished to see Lancelot coming, for he believed there was not a single knight within. Lancelot asked him who was the lord of that castle.

"My lord," he replied, "there is no lord, but a lady to whom this manor belongs."

"And what is her name?" asked Lancelot.

"My lord, she is called Morgan the Fay, and she is the sister of King Arthur."

When Lancelot heard this, he thought he should go back to kill her, but he refrained out of love for King Arthur and because she was a woman. He said to the youth, "Good friend, you will tell your lady that Lancelot of the Lake, who is leaving, greets her as he should, as the most disloyal woman in the world. And be assured that had it not been for my love for King Arthur, I would have done to her what one ought to do to a disloyal and traitorous woman. Tell her I send her this message."

The man replied that he would certainly deliver that message. He went to his lady, who was still asleep, woke her, and gave her Lancelot's message. When she heard it, she was greatly distressed; she put on her shift and went to the room where Lancelot usually slept. When she did not find him, she was extremely sorrowful and said, "Alas, we've done a poor job of guarding what we were to guard!" Then she began the bitterest grieving ever seen and began to look at the bars that Lancelot had twisted and broken; she showed them to those who were with her, saying, "Have you ever seen such marvels as that devil performed, breaking such strong iron bars with the force of his bare hands? Upon my word, no man ever wrought such deviltry!"

[Lancelot found Lionel and freed him; then he liberated other imprisoned companions. In the Perilous Forest, he learned of Galahad's birth. Claudas rejected a request from Guenevere and sent her an insulting message. An old man prophesied that Mordred would cause the downfall of Arthur's kingdom.]

39. Bors, in the Palace of Adventures at Corbenic, Sees Galahad, the Grail, and the Lance.

[. . .] Bors left at once, thinking to go to Camelot, for there was, he told himself, no time to lose if he wanted to be there for Pentecost.

So Bors rode on for many days without finding any adventure worth recounting, until one Tuesday evening he reached the town of Corbenic. [. . .]

Squires came forth, saying, "Welcome, my lord!" He returned their greeting, and one took his horse and another escorted him into the palace, where they removed his armor. Then knights, ladies, and maidens came to him and asked him who he was, and he replied that he was of King Arthur's household and was named Bors of Gaunes.

When they heard that, they said, "Oh, welcome, my lord!" They rejoiced over him and went through the halls bearing news of him, each one repeating, "The cousin of Sir Lancelot of the Lake has come here!"

Very shortly thereafter, King Pelles came forth from a room, sumptuously dressed in a samite tunic and cloak; he brought with him a great company of knights. Bors recognized him as soon as he saw him, for he had seem him many times before. As soon as the king saw him, he said, "Bors, welcome!"

"My lord, God bless you!" he replied.

Then they sat down upon a silken quilt in the middle of the hall. They began speaking to each other, and the king asked him about Lancelot's situation and how he had been, "for it has been so long since I last saw him or he was at King Arthur's court that I very much wonder what can have become of him. More than seven times in the last year, I sent to King Arthur's court for news of him, but word came back that he hadn't been at court for over a year."

"Indeed, sir," said Bors, "my lord is in the best of health, I believe, for not a week ago I saw him carry the day in a tournament at Penning Castle, where there were some of the best knights in the world."

"And where has he been so long," asked the king, "that he hasn't gone back to court or come to see us for more than a year and a half?"

"Indeed, my lord, for a year and a half he was in a lady's prison, as he told me; he left me a few days ago and is headed for court, where he will be for Pentecost, if God grants him health."

"Since he's in good health," said the king, "I'm not concerned about the delay, and God be praised that he is out of prison! Indeed, everyone must rejoice, for to my knowledge he's the world's best knight, and may it please God he is as well as you are. God help me, that would give me more pleasure than the gift of a hundred marks of gold."

While they were speaking thus, King Pelles's daughter came forth from a room, so beautifully and splendidly adorned that her clothes were a wonder— but her great beauty surpassed all else, for she was without doubt the most beautiful young lady of that time. When she came into the hall, she brought with her a great lot of people. All those present rose at once to greet her; she was not the least dismayed, being courtly and wise, but rather went toward Bors, greeted him, and told him he was welcome. He returned her greeting as politely as he could. She sat down beside him and asked him for news of the man she was very eager to see,[64] and he told her what he knew.

While they were speaking about this, an aged knight came among them carrying in his arms a very young child who could not yet be a year old— rather, he lacked two months of that age. The child was as fair as a child can be and was wrapped in silken cloth. The knight showed him to Bors and said, "My lord, you don't know who this child is: he's your young relative, whom you've never seen before. I tell you that he descends from the highest Christian lineage of any man, and he is your cousin, you may know this for a fact."

When Bors saw the child, it immediately seemed to him that this was Lancelot, and without doubt he resembled him as much as any man's face can resemble another's. So he asked who he was.

"My lord," said the knight, "do you know anyone he resembles among your kin? Now take a good look, and I'll be very surprised if you don't easily recognize him."

Bors dared not say what he thought, for it seemed to him that this must be Lancelot's child, but because he knew the truth about him and the queen, he dared not admit what he thought. Nevertheless, because he had to respond to what the knight asked, he said, "Indeed, my lord, I think he resembles Sir Lancelot more closely than anyone else."

"God help me," said the knight, "he ought to resemble him, for he descended from him as surely as you descended from your father."

When Bors heard these words, he was happier than about anything else he had ever heard; he asked his name, and the knight told him he was called Galahad. He took the child in his arms and kissed him more gladly than he

---

[64]Lancelot; see Chapter 33.

would have done with any other creature then alive, and weeping with tenderness he said to him, "My lord, your birth was most fortunate, for I believe you'll be the head and standard of your line. God be praised for bringing me this way, for, God help me, I wouldn't be so glad if someone gave me the best castle in the world, as I am at this news."

As they were speaking together, a dove entered, carrying a golden censer in its beak, and flew into a nearby room. The palace was immediately filled with all the good smells in the world. Then the servants spread the tablecloths, and all sat down to eat without anyone being called, for no one present said a word, but rather all were at prayer, old and young alike.

Shortly after they were all seated, a maiden emerged from the room[65] carrying the Holy Grail. As soon as she entered the hall, all those present knelt down before her and said in a low voice, "Blessed be the Son of God, amen, who fills us with His grace."

As the young lady passed among the tables, they were immediately covered with all the finest foods. And when she had passed before all the tables, she went back into the room from which she had emerged. Then those in the hall who had been silent began to speak. After they had finished eating, the tablecloths were removed.

The king went to relax at one of the windows of the palace, taking Bors with him. They began to speak of him who meant so much to them, that is of Lancelot, until at length Bors asked the king the truth about the child. The king immediately told him about Lancelot and his daughter, and how he was so cleverly ensnared that he knew her in the way that a man knows a woman.

"Blessed be God," said Bors, "for devoting His attention to such a ruse! Never did such great good come from any ruse as will result from this, for without doubt the True Knight by whom the adventures of the Holy Grail are to be accomplished, and who will sit in the Perilous Seat of the Round Table—in which none has ever sat who did not die—is to descend from your lineage. And if he's not that child, I don't know who he can be, for my lord is the best of all knights in the world, and yet I'm certain this child will be an even greater knight, and the hermits assure us this is the truth.

"Now tell me, my lord," continued Bors, "is this palace called the Palace of Adventures?"

"Yes, my lord, and you've heard of some fine ones, since you came, for it is a marvelous adventure when each day the Holy Grail gives us whatever food we request."

"Indeed," replied Bors, "that is truly a fine one! God help me, since I'm here, I'll never leave until I've stayed the night and seen the wonders Sir Gawain described, when he was here."[66]

---

[65]That is, the room into which the dove had flown.
[66]Gawain's experiences at Corbenic are related in Chapter 31.

"Oh, my lord," exclaimed the king, "for God's sake, don't say that! By my faith in Our Lord, you will not stay tonight, for I am certain you would never leave without shame and loss; I wouldn't want shame to come to you, if I could keep you from it, not for half my lands, for I would be blamed by many people."

"My lord," said Bors, "when I came here before, I learned nothing, and was mocked and derided wherever I went thereafter. For that reason I tell you I'll never leave here unless I'm dead, until I've learned more than I have so far."

"Upon my word," said the king, "I would not try to make you break this oath: tonight you will not stay here, but tomorrow evening, since your mind is made up, I will permit you to stay, in the hope that Our Lord may let you leave here without shame or loss."

"And why won't you allow me to stay?"

"I'll tell you," said the king, "before you leave here."

That night Bors slept in a room beneath the tower, and the king showed him all the honor he could. In the morning, when they were to hear Mass, the king said, "Bors, you are to sleep in the Palace of Adventures tonight."

"That is true, my lord."

"Then I tell you," said the king, "to go speak to one of our chaplains and make a full confession of your sins, before you go before the Holy Grail, for since you will be clean and purified, I believe it will not go so badly for you, as it would if you came before it vile and filthy."

Bors considered this to be good and loyal counsel. As soon as he had heard Mass, he left there, called one of the chaplains, and confessed all the sins of which he felt himself guilty in the eyes of God. The chaplain asked him about his situation, and he told him the story of his whole life, concealing nothing; he found Bors so moral and so religious that he was quite amazed, when he learned he had never sinned except with one woman, and that was with Brandegorre's daughter, who had given birth to Helain.

When Bors had made his confession, with his heart as well as with his lips, he received the body of the Lord, for he was not at all confident about the adventures of the palace and did not know whether he would escape them or die there. He left the church happy and joyful, and the rest of the day refused to eat anything.

In the evening he put on his armor and went up all alone into the great hall; the others all withdrew and, filled with fear, left him. He waited until it was night, staying by the windows as long as he could see any daylight. When day had been darkened by the arrival of night, he went to sit on the Bed of Wonder, which stood at the head of the hall. As soon as he was seated, the loudest din in the world began, and a great wind arose, so wondrous that it began to make all the windows shake at once, and there were more than a hundred of them. It seemed to him who heard them that the palace was about to crumble from the great noise the windows were making.

When all this had ceased, from a room there came forth a large, long lance, its iron tip flaming like a lighted candle; it came straight at Bors as swiftly as lightning and struck him so violently that through his shield and hauberk it penetrated half a foot into his left shoulder. When he felt himself wounded in this way, he was totally dismayed, for he could not see who was holding the lance—and yet he felt it being pulled out of him, but he did not know who was doing it. And after the lance had been withdrawn from him, it went back to the room from which it had come. Bors remained on the bed, so ill and wounded that any other would have felt he was surely dying, but he did not stir, determined to stay there all night, come what may.

[*An armed knight entered the room, and Bors defeated him in battle, after which he witnessed a symbolic battle between a dragon and a leopard.*]

Bors went to sit on the bed, but as soon as he had sat down, quarrels and arrows began to rain down from every window, striking him on shield and hauberk in more than a hundred places and wounding him severely. Nevertheless, he did not stir, but sat as firm and confident as if he felt no pain, waiting for the adventures of that place, for he was sure he would see plenty more. When the quarrels had stopped coming, the windows all closed again, making a great din, as if the palace were about to crumble. Then it was quite dark, for the moonlight could no longer pass except through a few glass windows that were open.

When the palace was quiet again, a huge and wondrous lion emerged from one of the rooms and came bounding toward Bors, its mouth wide open. When he saw it coming, Bors sprang up, threw up his shield, and raised his sword to strike it upon the head. The lion came at Bors with tooth and claw, to catch him by the hauberk; it seized his shield, tore off the top as if it had been cloth, and nearly knocked him down. But Bors was strong enough to stand firm, and he struck the lion between the ears so violently that he cut through its neck and it fell dead upon the floor.

Bors sat down again to rest, but very soon he saw the dragon come forth, the one Sir Gawain had seen.[67] It was so huge and terrible that anyone who saw it would have been afraid; every color could be seen upon it, and its eyes were red and glowing like two burning coals. After it came forth from the room, it advanced slowly through the hall, spewing fire and flame, but not very much, and playing with its tail like a child with a toy. It had letters written on its forehead, and Bors could see them clearly by the light from its eyes; the inscription said, THIS IS THE SYMBOL OF KING ARTHUR.

When the dragon had advanced to the middle of the hall, Bors saw a

---

[67]In Chapter 31.

proud, fierce leopard come forth against it, but he did not know where it could have come from. At once the dragon charged the leopard, spewing fire and flame and doing its worst. But the leopard defended itself so well that it was a wonder to behold, for it seized the dragon with its teeth and claws and never retreated, but pressed constantly forward, gaining ground on the dragon. If the leopard had been as strong as the dragon, the latter could not have held out against it, despite its great strength and burning fire. Bors observed this battle for a long time, deeply puzzled as to what it might mean, for he had never seen such cruelty in two mute beasts, and he was sure this must signify something.

When the battle had gone on so long that neither creature could take any more, the dragon departed, and the leopard disappeared so that Bors never knew what had become of it. As soon as the dragon reached the entrance to the room, it began to roll about and contort itself, just like an animal in great pain when it is about to give birth: so the dragon thrashed about for a long time. And when it was calm again, it began to spout little dragons from its mouth, as many as a hundred of them; then began the battle of the little dragons, which were intent on killing the dragon from which they had sprung, but it was so strong that they could do it little harm.

Yet, the fighting went on until the little dragons and the big one were all dead. Bors was more mystified by this than by anything else he had ever seen, for he was certain this must signify something, but he could not see what.

[An old man told Bors that he could leave because he would see nothing more, explaining that the adventures of that place would not be finished until the Good Knight came who was to end the adventures of the Holy Grail.]

Then the man left without another word. Bors wanted to ask him many things, but the man could stay no longer and went back to the room from which he had come. Shortly thereafter, the dove came in through the window, carrying a golden censer in its beak, and flew into the room from which the Grail had emerged the previous day. Then the palace was quiet and serene and filled with all the good smells in the world.

Next four very young children came out of the room, so beautiful that Bors, as he observed them, thought they could not be earthly beings, but rather spiritual ones. They carried four lighted candles in four candlesticks; a censer went before them, and after them came an ancient white-haired man dressed like a priest but without any chasuble, carrying a lance before him. The more Bors watched, the more he was amazed, for he saw that drops of blood issued from the iron lance head, running down the wooden shaft one after the other, but he did not know what became of them. Then Bors, thinking this must be a holy and worthy thing, rose and bowed before it.

The man carrying it went straight to the chair, sat down, and said to Bors,

"Sir knight, you are the purest and worthiest man who ever came here from the household of King Arthur. Now when you go back to your own land, you can say you have seen the avenging lance; yet you do not know what this is, and you will not, until the Perilous Seat of the Round Table has found its master: through him who is to sit there, you will know the truth of this lance and who brought it to this land and where it came from. And yet, if your cousin Lancelot had kept himself, as you intended to keep yourself, at the beginning of his knighthood, he would have brought to an end everything from which you now suffer, for he is so illustrious in knighthood that he's unequaled in all the world. But on the other hand he is so debased that all the virtues that should be in him have declined and died through the frailty of his loins."

Then he withdrew into the Grail room, along with the lance that he had brought. [. . .]

Shortly before midnight, Bors went before the Grail room and saw a great brightness, as if the sun had made its home therein, and the brightness was constantly increasing. He at once went to the door to the room, but when he tried to go in, he saw a sharp, shining sword ready to strike him if he went any farther. At this adventure he turned back, convinced that this must be caused by God rather than anything else. He nevertheless looked into the room and saw a silver table upon four wooden supports, splendidly decorated with gold and precious stones—but they were still more wondrous, as the divine writing of the Holy Grail will relate, at the proper time and place.[68] Upon the silver table was the Holy Grail, covered with a piece of white samite, and before the table was a kneeling man, dressed like a bishop. After he had stayed there a long time, he stood up, went to the Holy Vessel, and removed the samite that covered it. At once the room was filled with the greatest brightness that I could describe.

At the moment the holy man withdrew the samite from the Holy Grail, such a great brightness spread throughout the place that it seemed to Bors that a beam of sunshine had struck him in the eyes; he was so dazzled that he was blinded for the whole night and could not see a thing. Then he heard a voice that said, "Bors, do not come any closer, for you are unworthy of seeing more than you already have of the secret things in this place. And if you are so bold as to approach in spite of this interdiction, know that you will not escape without losing the power of your limbs, unable to come or go, forever like a piece of wood, and that would be a shame, for you are both worthy and bold."

When Bors heard these words, he was more than a little afraid, for he believed the voice was telling the truth; he turned back and went toward the bed where he had sat, but he could see nothing. Nevertheless, he felt completely recovered from the wound inflicted by the flaming lance. He went up and

---

[68]See *The Quest for the Holy Grail,* Chapter 17.

down in search of the bed, but could not find it. When he saw that he would not find it, he sat down on the floor, worn out from seeking what he could not find. He stayed there until morning, appalled that he had lost his sight forevermore. And if Sir Gawain, on his visit,[69] had heard the splendid melodies of voices singing the praises of Our Lord, that night Bors heard even more joyous sounds, and was very glad that he had come. He was awake all night, neither sleeping nor resting, full of dread that Our Lord had become angry with him. But when day began to break and the light came in through the many windows and he saw it, there is no need to ask whether he was glad: he had not for a long time had such great joy as this.

Then King Pelles entered, with his daughter and many knights. And when they saw Bors safe and sound, they rejoiced over him, and the king said, "God help me, Bors, we were most concerned for you last night, and never thought to see you so strong and well as you now are, for every knight who ever stayed here as you have done either departed shamefully or was found dead. It has gone better for you than it ever did for any other man, and I can tell you I am very pleased."

Bors stayed in the palace that day, for they would not let him leave, no matter what he did: they celebrated him and treated him with great honor, for they were overjoyed at the fine adventure God had granted him. The king asked him, "My lord, for God's sake, did you see my father?"

"In truth, I do not know him."

"My lord, he is the Maimed King, whom people call the Fisher King, the boldest and worthiest knight of our time."

"And how was he wounded?" asked Bors.

"My lord, it was through the misdeed he committed when he drew from its scabbard the sword which was not to be drawn except by him who was to accomplish the adventures of the Holy Grail. But because he drew it despite the interdiction placed upon it, he was struck through the thighs by the sword itself; he was maimed, and will never be healed until the Good Knight comes and anoints his wounds with the blood of the lance."

"My lord, I did not see him, but for God's sake, tell me the truth of the lance of which you speak, which fills me with wonder. I clearly saw that drops of blood issued from it, and it's something I'd very much like to know about, if that may be."

"In truth, Bors," replied the king, "it is not right that the truth of the lance be known or disclosed to you or to any other, but when the last quest of the Grail is undertaken, and all the world's knights make great efforts before they learn the truth of it, then what you ask will be disclosed to you and others, but not before."

---

[69]See Chapter 31.

Bors said that he would accept that, since he had no choice. He stayed there all that day and that night as well. The next morning, fully armed, he set out and rode for many days until he came to Camelot, but the story does not speak of any adventure that befell him after he left Corbenic, and just brings him back to court for Pentecost. And now the story leaves off speaking of him and returns to Lancelot.

[*Lancelot defeated Gawain, Yvain, Hector, and Sagremor without knowing who they were; learning their identity, Lancelot was ashamed of having defeated those he loved. He fled.*]

40. Lancelot Returns to Camelot; Logres and Gaunes Prepare for War.

[*Gawain took Lancelot's shield back to Arthur's court.*]

As soon as the king recognized them, he was overjoyed: he ran to Sir Gawain with open arms and kissed him more than a hundred times, then ran to the others and kissed them one after the other, asking them how they had fared. They replied, "Well, thank God," for they were in good health and believed they had achieved the object of their quest.

When the queen saw that Sir Gawain had returned, and Hector, and the other companions, but that he was not there whose presence would have brought her more joy and happiness than all the others together, she was so distressed that her heart nearly failed her. She left the hall and went to a room, where she began to mourn bitterly, saying, "Oh, God, won't he come, he whose arrival would do more to improve this court than that of half of those who are now here? Surely, if I didn't desire him so, I believe he would already have arrived long since!"

Great was the joy with which the people there welcomed Sir Gawain and the other companions. Sir Gawain ordered that the shield he had brought be hung in the middle of the hall so that all who came in would see it. The king asked him why.

"My lord, because I want to make an example of it for all who come in, for I can tell you that he who bore it against us is to my knowledge the world's best knight, and I believe it was Lancelot." Then he told the king how a single knight had unhorsed all four of them one after another, and how he had thrown his shield upon the ground when he found out who they were. When he had seen the shield of such a worthy knight lying on the ground, he had hastened to pick it up, "and I left my own there and said I'd bring that shield here and the lance as well." Then the king had the lance brought and placed beside the shield, to the knight's glory and honor, after which he asked for news of Lancelot.

"In truth," said Sir Gawain, "I haven't seen him since he was victorious in the tournament at Penning Castle, but there I saw him do more—and those of the quest here present can testify to this—than he ever did at the last tournament at Camelot, when he carried the day against the companions of the Round Table."

While they were speaking in this way, Sir Gawain's four brothers—Agravain, Gaheriet, Guerrehet, and Mordred—dismounted in the courtyard. When they had removed their helmets, they were recognized by the people there, who went to tell the king, and the king rose to go meet them. "Gawain, dear nephew," said the king, "let's go see your brothers."

They entered the hall, and the king kissed them and made them welcome, as did everyone there. Then Mordred asked the king, "My lord, has Sir Lancelot returned yet?"

"No," replied the king, "he hasn't; this grieves me, and I pray God may bring him to us very soon, for now there's nothing else in the world that I wish as much to see."

Then the queen came forth from her room, sad and upset because Lancelot had not come. When she saw Sir Gawain's brothers, she asked them for news, but they said that they had not seen him since the tournament at Penning. "My lord," said the queen, "it's time to go to church."

"Then let's go," he replied. Then he put on his royal robe, placed the golden crown on his head, and held in his hand a scepter on which there was a pommel surmounted by a golden eagle. The king was very handsome and looked the very picture of a worthy man, being no more than fifty years of age. That day he looked at his lords, of whom there was a great number, and said so loudly that all therein could hear, "Oh, God, this great celebration should be postponed, since he is not here whose prowess would illuminate this court! Oh, blessed Lord God who have granted so many of my wishes, please grant me that he may come tonight or before high Mass tomorrow." He wept as he said this, and then they went to the Church of Saint Stephen, which was then the principal church of Camelot, for it was the king's custom, at great feast days, to hear Mass at the main church of the town or city where he held court.

When he had heard Mass, he went back to his palace and found Bors and Lionel, who had come from the quest and had brought with them all the rest of the companions, so that of all those who had been on the quest, only Kay the Seneschal and Lancelot of the Lake were still missing. [. . .]

The tables were set and the companions of the Round Table sat down, and when each had taken his place, they found that of the one hundred fifty companions who were to fill the seats, twelve were missing. This weighed heavily upon the king, for they should all have rightly been there for Pentecost, if they were not ill or imprisoned. [. . .]

Then the joy and the festivity began[. . .], and they were now even more desirous of Lancelot's arrival. The king said that if he did not arrive that night or the next day, he would be more upset than he had ever been by one knight's absence.

"Have no fear of that," said Sir Gawain, "for I'm sure he'll be here tonight or before the hour of tierce tomorrow."

"I only fear," said the king, "that he might be ill or dead, for if he is alive, I know that no prison could hold him at this point."

Thus all at court were eager for Lancelot's arrival and said that if they did not believe he might still be five or six leagues away, they would go to meet him with a great company of knights. But because they did not know whether he was near or far, they would not stir, for they would not know where to find him. So the court was happy in anticipation of Lancelot's coming, and sad because he was taking so long: all the others had arrived safe and sound, but he who should have come sooner was taking longer, and for that reason they were afraid and concerned for him, so much so that their dismay was considerable. But they were somewhat comforted by the fact that the appointed day was not yet over and he might yet come in time. And so things reached the point where they did nothing but speak of Lancelot, and they proposed to have a great celebration if God brought him there before dinner the next day.

In this way they waited until vespers that day. [. . .]

They waited a long time to see whether Lancelot would come; then, when they saw that he would not, they went to their lodgings for the night. The king slept in one of the rooms of the palace and the queen in another; she did not sleep much, but wept all night until dawn, fearful that by some great misfortune Lancelot had been killed. And on the other hand she was most eager to see him, since she had not seen him for a long time, and to find out what insurmountable obstacle had kept him away from the kingdom of Logres for so long—for when he had left her, she had no idea he would stay away so long, unless he were ill or dead. She slept little that night, for she did not know whether to think him alive or dead.

But if she was dismayed and sorrowful, Hector was yet more so, and so distraught he thought he would die. He wept copiously that night, as did Bors and Lionel, but of all those who were not Lancelot's kin, it weighed most upon Sir Gawain, for he was the man who most loved Lancelot in all the world, apart from King Arthur and Lancelot's kinsmen. Without doubt King Arthur loved Lancelot so much that if he had known just how much he loved him, he would have been amazed, and he often said privately that he did not know which one he loved more, Sir Gawain or Lancelot. And that great love would never have ceased, had it not been for Agravain the Proud and Mordred, who, moved by great envy, later told the king that Lancelot had brought him shame and dishonor through his wife, whom he was keeping behind the king's back. They said so much that the king's great line was brought to death and destruction, and he himself along with the two of them, and all the brothers were later killed, and the king who was so valiant died, a great loss and a shame, for at that time no other man was as powerful as King Arthur, nor as gracious with his wealth nor as courtly.

In the morning, as soon as it was light, the king rose and heard Mass along with a great number of lords and knights. When he came into his great hall, he asked whether Lancelot had arrived, and was told that he had not. "Oh, God," exclaimed the king, "bring him to us soon!"

"Surely," said Sir Gawain, "he'll come before the hour of tierce."

Then the king left his barons, went to his great tower, and climbed up the steps to the top; from there he could look out over the whole land to a distance of more than ten leagues, except where the forest blocked his view. He looked for a long while, but near or far he saw no knight coming toward Camelot; he believed he could quickly recognize a knight if he had previously seen him ride. When he was about to come down from the tower, he said to himself, "Oh, God, won't he come, he whom I wish to see above all others?"

Then he looked toward Camelot Forest and saw a knight in red armor ride slowly forth, so proudly that he looked like a man with great powers of resistance, but he saw neither servant nor squire with him. As soon as the king saw him, he was certain this was Lancelot. He came down from the tower as fast as he could, went into the great hall, and said to the waiting lords, "Let's mount and go to meet Lancelot, for I've seen him coming and he's already near." [. . .]

Great was the lords' rejoicing over Lancelot, but some were more joyful than others; it would not be easy to relate Hector's welcome, for he could not keep himself from weeping. Whenever he looked at Lancelot, he called him brother and lord, and showed him so much honor, moved by the great love within him, that all those who heard him were deeply affected. With such rejoicing and festivity was Lancelot received in the city of Camelot on Pentecost Day, and that was four hundred twenty-six years after the incarnation of Our Lord. And when he came to the main street, he found it as richly hung with silken sheets and vair and miniver as if God Himself were to arrive there, but the king did this for love of Lancelot and to honor him.

When they reached court, they dismounted and escorted Lancelot to the main hall. When the queen saw that he had arrived safe and sound, she was overjoyed: she ran to him with open arms, embraced him, rejoiced and exulted over him so that all present could see, and wished him welcome. The king speedily had Lancelot's armor removed and then had a beautiful, rich robe brought to him, one that was appropriate for such a man. And after his armor had been removed, the knights who had participated in the jousting removed theirs and changed their clothes.

Then the king put on his robes and made ready, his golden crown upon his head, and set out at once for Saint Stephen's, the principal church of Camelot. The king led the way, followed by the queen, then other kings and dukes, according to their valor and lineage.

When Lancelot entered the church and saw the dragon of which the wise man had spoken, the one Mordred had killed, he was convinced the old man had been telling the truth; then he grew angry and pensive that such a great lineage as the one he saw before him would be destroyed for the sake of just one man. He would gladly have turned Mordred away from such destruction, if that were possible, but he thought he could not do so without killing him, and if he did that he would incur the hatred of all his kinsmen, something he in no way wished to do, and for that reason he refrained from killing him. In such a way Lancelot long remained lost in thought, looking now at Mordred, then at the king, then at the dragon, and had eyes for nothing but these three things. This went on so long that the queen noticed; she was sure he was not just daydreaming, and resolved to ask him about it as soon as she was alone with him.

After the Mass was over, the kings and counts went back to the great hall and found the tables set; they sat down as soon as they had washed. Something happened there that day that made them glad, for they saw that of the hundred fifty knights of the Round Table, not one was missing, and both intimates and strangers were glad of this. One of the knights conveyed this news to the king: "My lord, you may see something wondrous."

"What's that?"

"All the companions of the Round Table have come at the appointed time, and not one is missing."

"Indeed," said the king, "if Lancelot hadn't come, neither would the twelve who were missing yesterday.[70] This pleases me greatly, for I'm sure I've never before seen them all together."

The lords spoke of this at length. Lancelot, sitting beside the Perilous Seat, saw there a newly written inscription that said, TODAY BRUMAND THE PROUD MUST DIE HERE, AND IF HE DOES NOT, THEN MERLIN LIED IN HIS PROPHECIES. Then Lancelot summoned the clerks and had them read the inscription; they looked at it and explained its significance to him: "My lord, this is a wondrous adventure; but say no more about it now, for I believe you'll see some other adventure before the day is over. And you should know that this inscription was made today by some supernatural power."

"I'll speak no more of this," he said, "since you tell me not to."

When the lords had eaten and the tablecloths were to be removed, they saw a knight come in, dressed in white armor. He had left his horse in the courtyard below. Upon seeing the king, he said to him, "My lord, I have come to live or die, I don't know which, but I must make the attempt."

"Sir knight," replied the king, "I wouldn't want you to have come here for your death, and I would turn you or anyone else away from what you intend to do, unless you were so fully deserving that you could escape without death."

---

[70]The logic of this sentence is puzzling, but this is clearly what the text says.

The knight took off his helmet, his hauberk, and all his armor. When he had removed everything, the others looked at him and saw he was so handsome and well proportioned that he clearly looked like a man of some value, but he was weeping as bitterly as if he saw everyone dead before him.

Filled with pity, the king looked at him and said, "My lord, why are you weeping?"

"Because, my lord, I believe I have come to my death." Then he passed by those who were seated at the Round Table and went to the last seat, called the Perilous Seat. Seeing Lancelot there, he said to him, "Lancelot, I must die in order to perform the act of boldness that you never dared perform, for without further delay I will sit in this seat where you never dared sit." Then he sat in the seat where no man had ever sat without regretting it; he drew from his breast a letter, handed it to Lancelot, and said, "Lancelot, take this letter, and if I die in this seat, read it so that all those present can hear, that they may know who I am and of what people. And if I escape safe and sound, I know you'll willingly give it back to me."

Then he gave Lancelot the letter. All those present began to say that this knight had performed a great act of boldness by sitting in the Perilous Seat, but very soon he began to cry out, "Oh, God, I'm dying! Oh, Lancelot, your prowess is of no use here, for you are not the one who will accomplish the adventures. If you were, you could save me from this death." Then he began to cry out, in such torment that every man present was filled with fear. Suddenly a fire came down from above with such fury that those present never knew where it had come from; it fell upon the knight, and very soon he was burned to a crisp. They were amazed, for they could never see anything left of him, neither flesh nor bone. And while the knight was burning, he cried out, "Oh, King Arthur, pride brings one nothing but shame! I'm well aware of this: because I aspired after something I could not and should not have, I must die so atrociously that such vengeance was never inflicted on any other knight, yet I did not believe I deserved it."

No sooner had the knight uttered these words than they saw that there was nothing left of him but ashes on the seat; it gave off a foul smell, and all those present felt ill. Many were far from glad when they saw the knight burn, fearing that the fire might spread to Lancelot: they told him not to move or he would burn, and he said he would not stir, since the company was seated at the table. He endured in such a way, and it turned out that he was unharmed, for which all were happy and joyful.

When all was finished and there was nothing left of the knight, the king said so that all could hear that he had never seen such a wondrous occurrence, "and I always said we'd see wonders produced by this seat; we've seen some, and we'll see others, I believe."

Then he told Lancelot to look at the letter the knight had given him and see what was in it, and he said he would gladly do so.

*[The letter explained that Brumand had earlier boasted that he was more
bold than Lancelot and that he would attempt to prove it by sitting in the Perilous Seat. Arthur commented that Brumand had been foolish, since the seat
was prepared for the chosen Good Knight.]*

That day the queen was seated beside Lancelot, with so few others that
there was no one from the king's party with them, but only Lancelot's kin.
Then the queen began to ask him where he had stayed so long, and he told her
how he had been in Morgan's prison for two winters and a summer.

"Ah, Lancelot," she said, "your education will never be complete! I had
clearly told you to be on your guard against her: one other time you'd already
been in her prison, and yet you couldn't refrain from going to her! But how
the devil did you fall into her hands this last time?"

And he told her how he was tricked by a maiden who led him off in
search of adventures;[71] she was in Morgan's service, but he did not know that
and so fell into her prison by misfortune.

"And while you were there, what did you do and how were you served?"

"In truth, my lady, there's no good food in all the world that I didn't have
in abundance, and as long as I stayed there, at every feast day I had a new
robe, as splendid as any King Arthur ever had, I'm sure. What can I say? She
took such good care of me that no knight was ever so well served as I was
there, though I don't know why she did it."

"And how did you come to escape?" asked the queen. "Was it by her
will?"

"No, indeed," he replied, and he began to blush from shame, not daring
to tell her.

"I beg you, by the allegiance you owe me, tell me how you escaped."

"My lady, since you entreat me so, I'll tell you. But be aware that I
wouldn't have revealed it if I hadn't been forced to do so." Then he began:
"My lady, the truth is that one day in May I had risen early because I was too
bored in prison, and I went to a barred window that opened onto a garden next
to the room where I was imprisoned.[72] While I was seated there, I saw roses
opening up to greet the sun; I greatly enjoyed looking at them because of one
that stood out among the others, so fresh and red that all the rest paled in com-
parison. I immediately thought of you, for it seemed to me that just as its
beauty surpassed that of all its companions, so you surpassed in beauty and
excellence all the ladies who were with you in the stands, the day of the last
tournament in the field of Camelot. This recollection distressed my heart,
which urged me to see the rose that made me think of you, since I couldn't

---

[71]See Chapter 37.
[72]Lancelot's escape is first related in Chapter 38.

have you; at once I seized the bars of the window and broke them with my hands. In that way I escaped. Now I've told you why I took so long to come back to court. And you may be sure that had it not been for that insurmountable obstacle, there's no way I would have stayed away so long, for I was extremely eager to be here."

[*The queen told Lancelot that she had been insulted by Claudas, who hated Lancelot and, when the latter was a small child, had reduced him to poverty and dispossessed him of his land. Lancelot explained that he would have died had he not been taken away and raised by the Lady of the Lake. He declared his intention of waging war on Claudas, and Guenevere said that Arthur and the knights of the Round Table would surely support him.*]

There the king performed a feat that was much discussed, for when he had caught up with Sir Gawain, he cried out, "Gawain, be on your guard!" He spurred toward him, dressed in nothing more than his cloak, flung his arms around him, lifted him from the saddle, placed him in front of him on the horse's neck, and carried him all the way to his door, in full sight of all those present. Everyone laughed and declared that the king was a most excellent knight.

Then Lancelot said to the queen, "Truly, my lady, for all the world I wouldn't have believed my lord the king could do that."

"Lancelot," she replied, "I can tell you that my lord has been the most wondrous man you ever saw, and would be again, if need be."

The king set Sir Gawain down and said, "Dear nephew, I've seen no one in whom I trust as much as in you, and for that reason I've shown you that one may be worth more in time of need than is generally believed."

Sir Gawain laughed and said he was very glad. Then they dismounted and went up into the great hall; they found the tables set, sat down, and were served with all the splendor appropriate to the feast day.

After the tablecloths were removed, Lancelot summoned his brother Hector into a room, along with Bors and Lionel, and told them of the queen's wishes.

"And what do you say?" asked Bors.

"I say you're to attack with a great force of men, and if you can't accomplish what you wish, I'll go right after you, and so exert myself, with God's help, that he'll repent as a disloyal traitor should repent for dispossessing a little child who is the son of a king."

When they heard this, they raised their hands toward heaven and blessed God for giving him this will, "but we don't want you to come," they said, "for we'll accomplish the task, God willing."

Then Lancelot sent for King Bademagu, in whom he placed much trust, and as many as forty other companions of the Round Table who were renowned for their prowess and in whom he trusted most, and when they had come before him, he had them sit down on the green grass with which the room was strewn. Seeing them before him, he told them the truth of the war he intended to begin and asked them whether they were willing to help him in that task.

Sir Gawain, who did not wish to reply for all the other companions, said to King Bademagu, "My lord, why do you not reply to what Sir Lancelot asks?"

"As for me," he said, "he can dispose of myself and my men as of his own property, for I give him my person and my wealth and am immediately ready to lead my men: they'll come whenever he wishes. Then I'll set out with him at his command and attack King Claudas with my army in such a way that he won't escape alive, unless I can dispossess him. All this I will do for love of him, whom I most love in all the world, even though he killed my son Meleagant, the dearest creature in the world to me.[73] But he's done so much for me since then that I gladly forgive him for that wrong."

"God help me, my lord," said Sir Gawain, "you have pledged much, and if I were as rich as you are, God help me, I'd place all I had in his service, just as you have done, but I offer him what I have for his use, that is my own person for his: that's what a simple knight can give, and I freely make this offer, wishing to place my own person at his service. And so that no one will say I'm going there alone, I give him the help of my four brothers and any other men I can gather by entreaty or reward. I pledge to you here and now that I will not leave Gaul, unless I'm ill or dead, until I see King Claudas dispossessed of all his land."

Sir Yvain swore the same oath, as did all the others who were there.

Then Sir Gawain said, "It would be proper for us to send word to the king and inform him of this matter, to see what he has to say."

They all agreed to that, and sent Bors and Hector to deliver the message. They came before the king and said, "My lord, some of the companions of the Round Table have been meeting privately together; they would not want this generally known before you had heard it, and for that reason they wish you to come and advise them concerning what they will tell you."

The king rose and went to the companions. When they saw him coming, they rose to greet him; he bade them to sit down again and sat among them. King Bademagu, the wisest of them all, told him what they had undertaken and how all had pledged to go in force against King Claudas of the Land Laid Waste and do everything in their power to dispossess him so that he would not have a foot of ground left.

When the king heard this, he was all in favor of the undertaking, saying

---

[73]See Chapter 27.

that it greatly pleased him and that he wanted to do it in that way, "and because I want you to go more confidently," he said, "I'll give you so many of my men that I'm sure King Claudas will never be so bold as to resist you. There will be so many that you can leave Lancelot to keep me company, and if it happens that Claudas is able to hold out against you by strength of numbers, Lancelot and I will follow you with all my forces."

All approved of what he had said and agreed to go against Claudas. When the king saw they were so eager for this thing, he sent at once for the kings and great lords who were in the main hall. When they had gathered before him, he told them of the war that those of the Round Table had undertaken for love of Lancelot, and how they were to go against Claudas, to dispossess him and drive him from the land of Gaul, "and because," he added, "I don't want this thing to be undertaken without you, I ask those present to go with these others." With one voice they cried out that they would gladly do so. [. . .]

In such a way was the war begun, by which King Claudas was later dispossessed and driven from his land, and many good knights died on each side, and the news spread up and down until it was known to all.

[*Claudas learned that war would be waged against him. He prepared for war, but many of his knights left, and he had few men. He then received news that the Romans would send him a great force in winter. Bors spoke to Lancelot about the latter's son, Galahad, but Lancelot asked Bors not to speak to the queen about Lancelot's fathering a child. Preparations for war continued, and ten thousand knights and men-at-arms set out for Gaul. (Lancelot stayed with Arthur and the queen.) Arthur's forces prevailed at first, but many were killed, wounded, or imprisoned on both sides. The Romans approached and prepared to attack the army from Logres, but the Lady of the Lake gave warning of their intent. The battle continued for a week.*]

41. Lancelot and Arthur Go to Gaul; Claudas Abandons Gaunes; King Pelles's Daughter Deceives Lancelot; Guenevere Expels Lancelot.

Now the story tells that when the squire had left Sir Yvain,[74] he rode rapidly for many days until he reached the sea, crossed, then journeyed until he came to a thicket near Camelot where King Arthur was hunting. This was on a Tuesday, and the king had had no news; he was all alone, riding slowly along the road. He had not gone far when he looked about and saw Lancelot's squire coming. The king stopped, thinking this was either a spy or a messenger.

---

[74]As recounted in the previous chapter, not included here.

The squire hastily rode right up to the king, whom he easily recognized, and greeted him, and the king returned his greeting, recognizing the squire because he had the impression that he had often seen him. He asked him where he was coming from, but the squire dared not tell him. Then the king seized him by the arm and swore by God that he would kill him if he did not tell him. When the squire heard this, he feared for his life and cried, "Oh, my lord, for God's sake, mercy!"

"I'll have no mercy," replied the king, "unless you give me your word that you will tell me where you're coming from."

The squire gave the king his word. Then the king released him and ordered him to tell him. The squire said, "My lord, I come from Gaul. I was at the city of Gaunes, where the knights of this land are laying siege to Claudas; there I spoke to Sir Yvain, who sends word to Lancelot to come help him as soon as he can, for Claudas has so many men, thanks to the Roman forces that have come to help him, that our knights can barely hold out against them, and if they weren't such good knights as they are, they could never hold out because the enemy has so many men, and they've captured King Bademagu and many other knights, making our knights most uneasy."

"By God," said King Arthur, "blessed be you for telling me this, for God help me, I'm very glad of it and would consider myself nothing if I didn't march against the disloyal traitor Claudas; I couldn't be happier about anything."

Then the king put his hunting horn to his lips and blew so loudly that the sound carried afar. Very shortly his servants came, and when they had reached him, he asked them where Lancelot was.

"Upon my word," they replied, "we believe he's looking for you, just as we were just now."

Then the king again put the horn to his lips and blew it as if to announce a kill. Very shortly Lancelot came riding along a narrow path, with all the speed he could get from his horse. When he drew near, the king began to cry out, "Lancelot! Lancelot! Sir Yvain greets you and sends word that we're to help them; they need it, for a great force has arrived from Rome to help Claudas."

When Lancelot heard this he was deeply disturbed and replied, "My lord, since he sends for me, I will gladly go, and I must do so."

"By God," said the king, "I will go at once and accompany you, and I'll take so many troops with me that Claudas will be mad to resist me."

"My lord," replied Lancelot, "saving your grace, you won't do this, for this mission can be well accomplished without you, and it is not right for you to make such efforts for me."

The king was more annoyed with Lancelot because of this than about anything else he ever said, for Lancelot had done so much for him, on so many occasions, that the king felt he could never repay Lancelot for even half his service, even if he gave him the kingdom of Logres. For that reason he was deeply upset, and he let it show, for as soon as he had returned to Camelot and had told the queen the news, he sent out letters bearing his seal, commanding all those who held lands from him to come to court prepared to march against Claudas. Delighted at this order, they did their best to make ready, so that before two weeks had passed one could see more than twelve thousand men in his castle, every one of them a good knight or man-at-arms.

Thus King Arthur assembled his forces. When he saw that it was time, he set out, along with Lancelot and his followers, of whom there were a great number. When the queen saw that they were going, she was most upset, for she was greatly distressed at being separated from Lancelot. But seeing that it had to be, she kept silent. She wept most tenderly when they left; she commended them to God, that He might guide them wherever they went, and she beseeched Lancelot to come back as soon as he could.

Then they set out and spent their days traveling until they reached the sea, where they found the fleet that the king had ordered prepared, as beautiful and splendid as befitted such a man. They boarded the ships and set sail; the weather was rough, typical of the season around All Saints' Day. Yet things went well for them, and they crossed safely, with never a man lost or a ship damaged, and amid great rejoicing they arrived on the opposite shore. When they had left the ships and removed their equipment, they put on their armor, because they had entered a land at war.

[*Arthur made Lancelot overlord of Gaul, but a German count named Frollo wanted the kingdom for himself. After a battle between Arthur's forces and Frollo's, the latter sent a messenger to Arthur.*]

The messenger left Frollo and went to King Arthur in his tent, where he had had his armor removed. Lancelot was with him. The messenger said, "King Arthur, Frollo the Valiant sends me to you with this message: it is an evil thing for your people and his to die in such a way, for they have not deserved it. He therefore challenges you to fight alone against him, in single combat. Then if you can defeat him with your sharp sword, he will acquit you completely, and if he defeats you, you will be at his mercy, to do whatever pleases him. In this way only one of you will die."

When King Arthur heard this, he esteemed Frollo more than he had before, and said to the messenger, "Since Frollo wishes to fight, he will have it just as he has set forth, and he has done a very worthy thing by sending this message." [. . .]

With that they mounted and drew apart, then came together with all the speed they could get from their horses; they struck each other, driving the iron tips of their lances through shield and hauberk, into the naked flesh, then smashing into each other, shield and body, with such violence that both were thrown over their horses' rumps to the ground. They broke their lances in their fall and lay a long while on the ground, so stunned that they did not know whether it was night or day.

King Arthur was the first to get up. He drew his sword and ran at Frollo, who was already getting to his feet. Wounded as they were, they went at each other; they exchanged great blows on their helmets, cut up their shields, and ruptured the hauberks on their shoulders and flanks, sending the links of mail flying onto the green grass, so that the field around them was strewn with them. They struck each other repeatedly, so that they made the blood gush from the blows of their swords. Frollo found such great resistance in King Arthur that he was quite amazed, for he thought there could not be such boldness and prowess in any two men. Each held his position so fiercely that neither could gain a foot of ground against the other, and so the battle lasted from the hour of prime until high noon, in such a way that no one could tell which of them was getting the better of it.

But then Frollo began to grow very tired, for he had made great efforts to strike King Arthur. The king often caused him to miss his mark; he had a much better sword than did Frollo, who had already lost a lot of blood, and that was what gave the king the advantage. Then the king, seeing that Frollo was weakening, charged him again and again, striking him upon the helmet so many times that he was too dazed to stand, but fell to his knees. The king raised his sword and struck again, so many blows that he laid him out face down. Then the king jumped onto Frollo, seized him by the helmet, and tugged mightily, but he could not tear it off. Then Frollo, having regained his strength and his wind, and being extremely strong, struggled to his feet and charged the king, thinking to seize him in his arms, for if he held him, he thought Arthur could never hold out against him.

But the king was a man of great prowess: he jumped back, threw his shield to the ground, took his sword in both hands, and ran at Frollo, mad with rage. He dealt him such a blow upon his helmet that he split it more than two fingers' breadth, and if the sword had not turned aside, he would certainly have killed him. The blow was great and heavy, and Frollo was so dazed that he fell full length upon the ground, since he was very weak from the blood he had lost. Then the king seized him by the helmet, cut the laces, and threw it away, after which he turned down his ventail, gave him a great blow on the head with the hilt of his sword, and declared that he would kill him if he did not admit defeat. But Frollo was both more malicious and more arrogant than any other, and declared that knighthood would never be abased by his saying something that might be considered recreancy.

"No?" said the king. "Then by the Holy Cross, you will die here and now!"

Frollo replied that he did not care; the king raised his sword and gave him such a blow that he sent his head flying.

Then he put his sword back into its scabbard. Lancelot came forward, overjoyed, and said, "My lord, God help me, you must truly have this kingdom, since you've won it so well."

Then the king had his armor removed and had his wounds examined by a doctor, who declared that he had no wound that would not soon be healed. After that the king ordered them to make ready to set out the next day to march against King Claudas.

[*Claudas fled to the emperor of Rome and sent word back to say that the people would have to fend for themselves, for he would not be there to help defend his people. His son Claudin received Arthur and Lancelot, giving Arthur the keys to the city of Gaunes. Lancelot refused to become king of Gaul and suggested that Hector and Lionel become the kings of Benoic and Gaul, respectively.*]

King Arthur stayed in Gaul until Easter, when he held a great and wondrous court in the city of Gaunes, at which there were so many people gathered together that it was a wonder to behold. Two weeks after Easter he departed: the lords who were with him advised him to return to Britain, and he agreed. They left Gaunes at once, traveled to the sea, crossed over as quickly as they could, and rode until they came to Camelot, a week before Pentecost.

When the queen, who had stayed there all this time, heard that the king was coming, she was very glad, because of him and because of Lancelot, for she was sure that he would come with the king. She went forth to meet them with a great company of ladies and maidens, and received the king and the other lords with every display of honor.

After the king had returned to Camelot, he sent out word to all his lords in Britain and to all those who held lands and fiefs from him that he would hold court at Pentecost, the greatest and most splendid he had ever held, and instructed them to come with all possible pomp and pageantry. The news traveled quickly and was soon known in Scotland, Ireland, and all the nearby islands; knights, ladies, and maidens made ready to do the king's will and to see the great celebration, which they expected to be very grand.

The news traveled so far that it reached the court of King Pelles. His daughter, the mother of Galahad, and who loved his father Lancelot as much as any woman can love a man, asked her father's permission to go see him at this festive court, and he readily granted it. When she had his leave, she took her governess Brisane and as many as eighty ladies, maidens, knights, and squires, and also Galahad, whom a squire carried before him on his strong, swift, and easy-gaited palfrey. She journeyed in that way until she came to Camelot on the day before Pentecost. She dismounted in the courtyard, and the king came to meet her and led her by the hand up into the palace. And when he knew who she was, Bors welcomed her with great joy as soon as he saw her, but that was nothing compared to his welcome of Galahad.

When those present saw her great beauty, they swore that they had never seen such a beautiful woman as she. The queen showed her every kindness, because she saw that she was beautiful and descended from such a noble line, and she gave her a part of her own room for her use. When Lancelot saw how beautiful she was, he said to himself that he would have acted far too cruelly if he had killed such a beautiful woman as this;[75] he was so sorry for having shown that he wanted to do so that he dared not look at her. But she loved him so much that she could have had such love for no other; she eagerly looked at him and delighted in seeing him, but complained secretly that he did not look at her as eagerly as she looked at him. She did not conceal this from her governess: "My lady, I behaved most foolishly, setting my heart on such a high-born man as Lancelot, who doesn't even deign to look at me."

"Now don't be dismayed, my lady," said Brisane. "God help me, before we leave here, I'll put him in your power so that you'll have whatever you desire from him."

The day before Pentecost, the festivities began with show and merriment, and it was much better because of the maiden; the king was most impressed by her beauty and so were all the others, and rich and poor alike sought to serve her. But the three cousins, Bors, Hector, and Lionel, showed her greater honor than all the rest, and this they did for love of Lancelot: they knew the truth of what had happened between him and the maiden, and nothing else pleased them as much as the sight of their cousin, the little child called Galahad.

But on the Tuesday evening following Pentecost, the queen told Lancelot she would send one of her attendants to fetch him, and he replied that he would come as soon as she sent for him, being totally devoted to his lady the queen. Now Brisane, who was most eager to deceive Lancelot, overheard these words and was overjoyed; she told her mistress that she would bring Lancelot to her that evening, that she could count on it. She replied that that would give her much pleasure and joy, for she loved Lancelot more than any other woman could love a man.

That evening, after all had gone to bed, Brisane, fearful that the queen might get to Lancelot ahead of her, came to his bed and said, "My lord, my lady awaits you; come quickly to us."

Believing her to be the queen's messenger, he replied, "At once, my lady." Then he got up, in breeches and nightshirt, and she took him by the hand, led him straight to the maiden's bed, and laid him down with her. And he lay with her as he did with his lady the queen, for he truly believed that this

---

[75]See Chapter 34.

was she. They both fell asleep in joy and delight, he on one side and she on the other, and each was extremely glad, he because of his lady whom he believed he held, and she because of the man she most loved in all the world.

Now the queen lay in her bed, awaiting Lancelot's arrival, and when she had waited a long time and saw that he was delaying so long, she was puzzled as to what this might mean, for he always did immediately whatever she ordered him to do. Then she called her cousin, she who had been so long in prison in Gaunes: the queen trusted her so completely that she had told her how things stood between her and Lancelot. She told her cousin to go to Lancelot's bed and bring him to her, and she replied that she would gladly do so.

Then the lady went straight to where Lancelot lay and felt all over the bed, but did not find him; she felt high and low, but to no avail, for he was not there. After lingering a long time in that way, she went back to her lady and told her that she could not find him. When the queen heard this, she could only suppose that he had gone to the toilet; she waited a while longer and then sent her cousin to him again, but she could not find him any more than the first time. She went back to tell her lady, filling her with great sorrow.

Now, the room in which she lay was large and broad, so that King Pelles's daughter, along with her attendants, had part of it, and the queen and her cousin were in the other half; the queen had sent away her attendants that night, so that they would not see Lancelot's arrival.

After midnight, Lancelot began to moan in his sleep, as it often happens that people moan. The queen recognized Lancelot as soon as she heard the moan, and knew that he was lying with King Pelles's daughter. She was so sorrowful that she did something she later bitterly regretted, for she was not in the habit of being angered by Lancelot; she was so sorrowful over what had happened that no man could describe it for you. She could not hold herself back, but sat up and began to cough. Lancelot awoke at once and heard the queen at some distance from him; he recognized her, and when he felt the woman next to him, he knew that he had been deceived. He put on his shirt and was about to leave, but the queen, who had approached in order to catch them together, seized him by the hand; she recognized the hand that she had often seen, and felt she would go mad. "Ah, scoundrel," she cried, "you disloyal traitor who have indulged your debauchery in my room and in my presence, get out of here, and take care never to come to any place where I am."

Upon hearing this order, he made no effort to speak, but left just as he was, without his clothes; he went down to the courtyard, headed toward the garden, entered, followed a path until he reached the walls of the city, and went out through a postern. When Lancelot was outside the walls of Camelot, he remembered his lady and the great joy he had had with her on many occasions, but now he would have to endure hardship, trouble, and travail: you would have seen a man deranged, weeping loudly and tearing his beautiful hair and scratching his face so that the blood spurted forth in many places. Then he began to grieve and to curse this misfortune that had been so cruel and wicked to him, who had to that point been the most fortunate man in the world—but now he would have to spend the rest of his life in tears, weeping, and misfortune. This thought filled his heart with such sorrow that he would rather have been dead, by any kind of death.

Thus Lancelot lamented and distressed himself until daybreak. And when he saw that daylight was coming and that he must go away, he was so sorrowful he did not know what to do, and cried, "Oh, Camelot, good and beautiful city, endowed with all knighthood, blessed with all the beauty of ladies, it was in you that my life began!" He said this because of his lady, for it seemed to him that he lived through her. "And now in you my death has begun, and I have without fail come to that grief by which I shall die." With that, Lancelot plunged into the forest, crying "Death, Death, hasten to me, for I have had quite enough of life!"

He wandered through the forest for three days, neither eating nor drinking, in the wildest places he knew, for he had no wish to be recognized by any man who might look for him. Lancelot spent six days in this way, grieving so bitterly that it was a wonder how he could go on living. Thus he continued during this time, since he had no one to comfort him; he neither ate nor drank, and lost his mind so completely that he did not know what he was doing. He attacked everyone he met, man or woman, and harmed many people during this time, for he mistreated every lady or maiden he met; it was a wonder that this did not get him killed one time or another. But now the story leaves off speaking of him and returns to King Arthur and those who were with him.

42. Lancelot Sought by Bors and Later by Perceval; Perceval and Hector Do Battle and Are Healed by the Holy Grail.

Now the story tells that when Lancelot had left the room where he had been caught, King Pelles's daughter, knowing very well that he was going to grief and perdition unless God intervened, said to the queen, "Oh, my lady, you have acted unwisely in driving the world's most valiant man from your court. You will most certainly regret it."

"My lady," said the queen, "it is you who have done all this to me and brought it about; I tell you truly that if I have the chance, I will repay you, for such a wondrous repayment was never made. It was a great misfortune that you were ever so beautiful, for many worthy men will pay for your beauty, and Lancelot himself, which is a great shame. You may say that because of this, grief and sadness will yet come to this court, which has known such joy and gladness at this Pentecost, for as soon as they cannot find him who has gone away, they'll begin a quest for him, the greatest that ever was."

The lady did not know what to say to this, for she felt that the queen was speaking the truth. She sat down upon her bed and dressed and made ready, weeping most bitterly. So did the queen, who deeply regretted what she had done; she thought that she would not see him again for a long time, and this filled her with sorrow and anger, for she loved him above all men.

[*Bors, Hector, Lionel, and thirty-two other knights went in search of Lancelot, but no news was heard of him for two years. The story then turned to one of the questers, Agloval, and to his brother, Perceval.*]

At last, after Agloval had ridden so long, chance brought him to the home of his mother, a good lady of noble lineage, but out of grief for her dead lord and her sons, worthy knights who had been killed, she was so disheartened that she lived very poorly. But do not ask whether her joy was great when she recognized Agloval, for she had not seen him in more than five years and had concluded that he was dead. When she recognized him, she wept for joy.

As soon as Agloval had dismounted, a youth came before him, handsome, young, unaffected, and well proportioned in all his limbs; he was no more than fifteen years old.

"Dear son," said the mother, "do you know this child?"

"No, my lady," he replied.

"This is your brother Perceval, the youngest of all my children."

When Agloval heard this, he ran to embrace him, for Perceval impressed him as a man destined to come to great things, if God had provided him with goodness as He had with beauty; Agloval was as joyful over him as he could possibly be, and said to his mother, "My lady, I will take this lad with me to King Arthur's court, and he'll receive the order of knighthood from King Arthur's hand."

"Dear son," said the mother, "what are you saying? May it never please God that he should be a knight, for through knighthood he could never attain greater honor than my other children did, who died painfully, by the lance! Since the others are dead, I will keep the last one, so that I will never lose him, God willing, no matter what pain may come to me. Oh, dear son, don't you know I used to have a fine family of six sons, whom God has so reduced as to leave me none but you, and until this very morning I believed that you were dead as well?"

"My lady," he said, "what do you intend to do with him?"

"I want him to be with me as long as I live, for I love him so dearly that I would die at once if he left me; he's my only comfort after all my other losses and all my misfortunes."

At that point Agloval said no more of this and spoke of other things.

When it was time to eat, they ate well and richly, but nothing Agloval saw there pleased him as much as his brother's beauty. He said to himself that it would be a great pity if such a handsome lad as his brother spent his youth beside his mother, for if he were a knight at his present age, he could not fail to achieve great things, with God's help, since he was descended from good knights on all sides. But if he passed his youth and reached the age of thirty without being trained in knighthood within that time, he could never thereafter become accomplished in arms, and so it would be a great pity if he delayed in becoming a knight.

He thought about this all through the meal. After the table was cleared, Agloval went for a walk in a garden behind his mother's house, and she sent Perceval to him to keep him company. The youth, who was pleased by this and desired his brother's company more than his mother's, found Agloval lying beneath an apple tree; he gave him a fine greeting and sat down beside him. Agloval gently welcomed him and asked him whether he would come to King Arthur's court to be a knight.

"Indeed," said Perceval, "I never wished anything else as much as to be a knight, if that pleased Our Lord, and if I thought you'd take me to King Arthur's court and have me knighted, I'd go with you when you left."

"Certainly, dear brother, if you're so eager to be a knight, I'm very glad, and I promise you on my honor that I'll take you there as soon as I leave here, and that will be soon, for there's no way I'd stay in this land for long. But I don't want you to speak of this yet, for if our mother knew of it, she'd have you so closely guarded that you'd never be able to leave."

The youth replied that he would speak of it to no man or woman.

Agloval stayed there for four days and was well cared for and shown much affection by his mother and all the members of that household. On the fifth day, Agloval said to his brother Perceval, "What are you going to do? I will stay here no longer, but will set out in the morning. Will you stay here, or will you come with us?"

"My lord," said Perceval, "I promised to go with you, and I'll keep my word so well that I will follow you whenever you wish to leave."

"Then," said Agloval, "we'll have to act in such a way that neither our mother nor anyone else here realizes what we're doing, for if she did, I'm sure she'd guard you so closely that you'd never be able to escape her."

"Don't be concerned," said Perceval; "I'll take care of this, and I'll tell you how: when you're armed and mounted, I'll ask her to give me leave to escort you. She will willingly do this, and I'll set out at once with you and will never come back before I'm a knight."

Agloval said that they could certainly do that and that no one was likely to oppose them.

That night Agloval said to his mother, "My lady, I've stayed here a long time, more out of love and pity for you than for anything else, for my need to travel was greater than my need for rest. I therefore beg you to give me leave so that I may be on my way tomorrow, for I'm very eager to get back to King Arthur's court, where I haven't been for more than two years."

When the mother saw that he wished to leave and that he would stay no longer, she willingly gave him leave, though she wept at this news.

The next morning, as soon as the day dawned bright and clear, Perceval got up, very anxious about this matter. He prepared his brother's armor, and it was brought to him. When he was armed and ready, he commended his mother to God, then mounted and left the house. When he was at the gate, Perceval went to his mother and said, "My lady, give me leave to escort my brother as far as the edge of that little wood over there. It's something I'm eager to do, for I don't know if I'll ever see him again."

"Dear son," said the mother, "go ahead, and I commend you to God. Take care not to tarry, and take a squire with you to keep you company. Be sure to come back right away, not for you, but to cheer me up, for you may be sure that I'll never be happy until I see you again."

Perceval, who had no intention of coming back as soon as she wished, but rather wanted nothing more than to go with his brother to King Arthur's court to become a knight, did not want anyone to go with him, but she said that someone would. At once she had a squire make ready and mount his horse; she ordered him to bring her child back to her, and he replied that he would, God willing.

Then Perceval left his mother, accompanied by the squire; the two of them rode until they caught up with Agloval at the edge of the little wood. Agloval had ridden slowly while waiting for his brother, for he was sure that he would follow him as soon as he could get his mother's leave. When he saw him coming, he was very glad; they rode into the wood and went on speaking together of many things until the day was well advanced.

This troubled the squire, who said to Perceval, "My lord, let's go back. Don't you remember what your mother told you? I'm very much afraid she'll be uneasy, for I can clearly see that we won't get back before the end of the day."

Perceval said to him, "Good friend, I clearly see that, but let me go on a bit longer, and then I'll go back."

Then the squire kept quiet, and the two brothers rode on until the hour of nones and beyond, and it was nearly vespers. Then the squire spoke to Perceval again: "Oh, my lord, I believe you have forgotten yourself: you've ridden so far that you'll never get home by daylight today."

And Perceval replied, laughing, "How's that, dear friend? Do you think I've left my mother so that I may go back so soon? I tell you truly, I won't return until I'm a new-made knight and have stayed at the court of King Arthur, who will knight me, God willing, before I see my mother again. Therefore, I want you to go back home and tell my mother not to be afraid for me, for I'm going to King Arthur's court with my brother. Be sure to tell her why I'm going, and assure her that as soon as I have a chance, I'll come back to see her; I love her dearly, as I should, for she raised me most lovingly."

When the squire heard this, he was as sorrowful as he could be; he began to weep bitterly and said, "Oh, my lord, for God's sake, what's this you say? You will not do this!"

"Yes, I will, I assure you."

"My lord," he replied, "since it is thus, let me go with you, that I may serve you as a knight as I have served you as a youth; it seems to me that you must do this, and so I beg you to let me go with you and serve you as a knight as I have served you as a boy."

"I grant you this," said Perceval, "but first you must go back and tell my mother that I'm going with my brother to King Arthur's court to be made a knight. When you've delivered this message, come to the king's court; if you can't catch up with us between here and there, you'll find us there."

The squire thanked him for this favor and said he would be sure to deliver the message; then he left his lord and, at the hour of vespers, reached his lady's lodgings. But when he had dismounted and had told her the news as he knew it, the mother, who loved Perceval as much as any mother can love her son, began to weep from grief for him; she asked at once for her chaplain, received confession and Holy Communion, and passed away that very evening.

[*Arthur knighted Perceval. A maiden instructed Perceval to sit at the Round Table, next to the Perilous Seat. Eventually, Perceval left to seek Lancelot. He then met Hector, and the two of them engaged in a fierce battle before revealing their identities to each other. Both were seriously wounded.*]

At the point when they were in such danger and anguish that they truly thought they would die, they saw a great brightness coming toward them, as if the sun were descending upon them, and they were mystified as to what this might be. They looked and saw a vessel made like a chalice and covered with white samite; it was preceded by two censers and two others followed it, but they could not see who carried them or who was holding the vessel. Nevertheless, the vessel seemed to be a holy thing, and they hoped for so much virtue from it that they bowed down to it, despite all the pain they were suffering. And immediately such a wondrous thing befell them that they felt hale and hearty, recovered from their wounds. Before long the holy vessel vanished so quickly that they did not know what had become of it.

After a while Perceval spoke and said to Hector, "My lord Hector, did you see what happened to us?"

"Yes, indeed; I saw it, but I don't know what it was. As soon as it was here with us, I was healed of the wounds you'd given me, so that now I'm as healthy as I ever was."

"Upon my word," said Perceval, "I can say the same for myself: I've recovered from every wound you gave me today. God has saved us through His grace and His mercy, for otherwise we'd never have seen tomorrow's light.

Now we can truly say that Our Lord took pity on us, since He healed us by sending us such a beautiful miracle."

They spoke together at length of this matter, each asking the other what it could be that they had seen. "As for me," said Perceval, "I cannot tell what it was."

"Then I'll tell you," said Hector, "since you don't know. Believe me truly, that was the Holy Grail, because of which so many wondrous adventures have happened in the kingdom of Logres. And in many other lands Our Lord has revealed many great miracles for its sake."

"Grail, my lord?" asked Perceval. "What can that be?"

"I'll tell you," said Hector. "The Holy Grail is the vessel in which Our Lord ate the lamb with his disciples, on Easter Day, in the house of Simon the Leper." Then he told him how Joseph of Arimathea had brought it to the kingdom of Logres, "and since then," he continued, "it has been seen to produce such miracles that by its grace his descendants have been fed, and King Pelles and all his household are still fed by it every day, and will continue to be as long as he stays in this land."

"In God's name, my lord Hector," said Perceval, "these are wondrous things you tell me, but I do believe it is the truth. And because of the great power and virtue we have experienced, I declare that I will never rest easy until I've seen it plainly, if it is given to mortal man to see it."

Then they gave thanks to God that they had been shown such beautiful mercy, and waited there until daybreak.

In the morning, when daylight appeared, they stood up, went to embrace each other, and pledged that they would never fail each other as long as they lived, but would henceforth be loyal companions, since they had been saved and healed together. They took up their armor, such as it was, for it was still better to have it than to go without armor; then they hunted about for their horses until they found them. When they had mounted, Perceval said to Hector, "My lord, what shall we do?"

"Whatever you wish," said Hector.

"What were you seeking, when we met?"

"I was going in search of Sir Lancelot, my brother, whom I haven't seen for two years. Since then I have searched so much for him that I'm quite worn out, but I still haven't heard any news to my liking. This fills me with sorrow, for he was the best and handsomest knight in all the world."

"What?" exclaimed Perceval. "And since he disappeared, you've heard nothing of him?"

"Indeed not, but I'm still hopeful he's alive, for if he were dead, it's impossible we would have heard no news."

Perceval agreed that that could well be. "Now let's set out together," he said, "to see whether God will guide us to some place where we may hear news of him."

So they both went on their way and rode together for many days. But now the story leaves off speaking of them and returns to Lancelot.

43. Lancelot's Madness and Subsequent Cure.

Now the story tells that when Lancelot had reached the point where he had completely lost his customary reason and memory, so that he knew neither what he was doing nor where he was going, he wandered about on foot for many a day, clad only in the nightclothes he had when he left Camelot. He went this way and that, as chance took him, and he was soon colored and blackened by the sun, and much the worse off because he suffered much hardship and ate little. He was in such a condition, before the first winter was past, that no one who had seen him before and who saw him then would ever have recognized him as Lancelot, without examining him at great length.

One winter day when it was terribly cold, chance brought Lancelot, in his ragged breeches and shirt, to a pavilion that was set up in a meadow. Inside lay a knight and a maiden; in front on a post hung a white shield, and beside it were a lance and a sword. Lancelot came that way and looked at the shield, then seized the sword and drew it from its scabbard. Then he began to strike great blows upon the shield, making as much noise as if ten knights were fighting together, cutting the shield to bits and ruining it, like a man who did not know what he was doing.

Hearing the noise and racket that Lancelot was making, a dwarf came forth from the pavilion; when he saw a man cutting the shield to bits and ruining it, he was so bold as to try to take the sword from him, for he did not think him as completely out of his mind as he was. He went up to him, seized him by the hand, and pulled with all his strength, but he could not manage to take the sword from his hand. Then the madman flew into a rage, seized the dwarf by the shoulders, and threw himself on top of him so furiously that he nearly broke his neck; he did him no more harm, however, and went back to striking the shield as he had done before.

When the dwarf was thrown to the ground, his fear was so great that he began to cry out, "Help! Help!" and very shortly a knight came out, wearing boots and a richly lined cloth robe. When he saw his dwarf, he asked him what the matter was.

"My lord," said the dwarf, "this devil nearly killed me!"

The knight looked at Lancelot, who was engaged in a terrible battle with the shield; seeing that he was in such poor condition and so poorly clothed, he was certain this man would not have gone about in such a way if he had been in his right mind, for everyone was very cold and yet he was barefoot and wearing only his shirt and breeches, as if it were midsummer. Then the knight had the idea that it would be an act of great charity if one could make him rest and see whether he could be brought back to his senses. At once he went toward Lancelot to take the sword from his hand, but Lancelot cried out to him, "Sir knight, come no closer, but leave me to my battle. God help me, if you interfere, I'll kill you." Then he raised the sword to strike him.

When the knight saw the blow coming, he thought he would be mad to wait for it, since he was unarmed; he drew back, went into his pavilion, and put on his armor, then went back to Lancelot and told him to put down the sword, reaching out his hand to take it from him. But Lancelot, as soon as he saw him approaching, raised the sword and struck him on the helmet with such violence that he broke the sword into two pieces. The knight was so dazed by the blow that he could not remain on his feet; he fell stretched out upon the ground, his brain all in a muddle.

Lancelot left him lying there and went into the pavilion, where he found the maiden awake. As soon as she saw him coming, she knew that he was out of his mind: she cried out, jumped from the bed in her shift, and ran from the pavilion. Lancelot got into the bed; it seemed warm and pleasant, since he was cold, and so he lay down and began to cover himself up. [. . .]

The knight who wanted to keep Lancelot with him was named Bliant, and the other was called Celinant; they were brothers and knights of great prowess.

[*The two tied Lancelot to the bed and took him to Bliant's castle, where Bliant hoped to heal him. He stayed for nearly a year without regaining his memory. Eventually, he broke his chains, but only to defend Bliant. Lancelot then stayed there for two more years. One day he joined a hunt and was seriously wounded by a boar. A holy man cared for him and healed his wounds, but Lancelot remained sickly and mad.*]

But because of the pain he had suffered and the poor fare to which he was not accustomed, he grew much worse during that time; he was pale, weak, and poorly clad, and thus was even less in command of his faculties than he had been before. For that reason he left there without their knowledge, barefoot and poorly clad in the worst cold of winter, so thin and sickly that one would scarcely have known him for Lancelot.

In such a way Lancelot wandered until he came to Corbenic. When he entered the town, the children and serving boys recognized that he was out of his mind and began to beat and strike him and to raise a great hue and cry; they battered him so that he picked up stones and began to throw them at them, wounding many. And when he ran out of stones and found nothing else to throw, he ran at them and threw them to the ground; he wounded many that day, until at last they began to flee before him, because he found none so strong that he did not break him by throwing him down. As they fled they cried out, "Away! Away! Here comes the madman!" In short order the word had spread throughout the town, so that all wanted to see him. He did not stop anywhere, but went from street to street chasing one group and another. He found many who did him harm that day, and in many places received many blows with sticks on his arms and shoulders, until at last he could no longer stand the misery they were causing him. He turned his back on them and fled until he reached the main castle; he went in, finding no one to turn him away, for the servants of the castle were most courteous and gracious.

Lancelot entered when those at court were eating, and when they saw him coming and recognized that he was mad, each one gave him something to eat, and they began to call to him. He ate heartily, being overcome with great hunger. When he had eaten, he went to lie down at the foot of the great hall, on some straw he found there. He was there for a long while without anyone recognizing him, for they would never have suspected it might be he. He had plenty to eat and drink, and the servants gave him their old clothes to wear, and because of the comfort and repose he found there, he soon improved so that he had regained some of his good looks and his strength.

One day after Easter, it came about that King Pelles had knighted one of his cousins, and for honor and out of love for him he had given arms to many. Now this young man, who was the king's cousin, dearly loved Lancelot and constantly kept him with him, never leaving him no matter what he did. As soon as he had been knighted and had removed his fine, rich robe, he called one of his servants and said, "Go get the madman." The servant did so at once, and when he had come to him, the new-made knight gave him his robe and made him put it on in his presence. As soon as Lancelot had donned the robe, since he was extremely handsome, all those who saw him were filled with pity; all lamented, saying that it was a great misfortune, when such a handsome man as he was had lost his mind and his memory. And King Pelles, when he saw how handsome Lancelot was in that robe, declared that he would not believe that he had not been a highborn and worthy man, for that was exactly what he looked like.

That day after dinner, it came about that Lancelot went into a garden below the tower; it was beautiful and full of trees, and in the middle, under a sycamore, there was a delightful spring. When he got there, he drank from the spring and went to sleep beside it fully clothed. And shortly after he had gone to sleep, King Pelles's beautiful daughter, she because of whom Lancelot had been driven from court,[76] came into the garden, along with quite a number of maidens. They began to play, to sing, and to chase one another through the garden, as maidens often do. And while they were intent upon their games, one of them, a noble lady of high birth, chanced upon Lancelot, asleep beside the spring. At first she was very much afraid, but she was reassured when she saw that he was asleep; she drew near, began to look at him, and saw that he

---

[76]See Chapter 41.

was so handsome and so attractive that she thought she had never seen such a fine-looking man.

After looking at him for a long while, she went back to her companions and left him sleeping. When she saw King Pelles's daughter, she said to her, "My lady, if you'd like to see the handsomest man I ever saw, I could show him to you, but I wouldn't want another soul besides you and me to come along, so that he won't wake up."

"What's this?" exclaimed the lady. "Did you find him asleep?"

"Yes, beside that spring."

"Then let's go there together, and no one will accompany us."

Then they left their companions, so cleverly that no one noticed, and went to the spring where Lancelot was sleeping. They looked at him for a long time, exclaiming how handsome he was; they sat down beside him, looking at him and conversing at length together. And King Pelles's daughter studied him attentively until at last she realized that this was Lancelot. Then she was at once extremely joyful and extremely sorrowful, joyful because she had found him and sorrowful because he was out of his mind, for she knew that this was the madman who had stayed so long at her father's court. But she did not want to tell her companion that this was Lancelot, and so concealed the fact. Then she left that place and returned to her companions, who had been going through the garden in search of her. She told them that she wished to leave, because she felt a little unwell; she told them to accompany her, and they did so at once.

When the lady reached the palace, she asked where her father was and she was told. She went to him, drew him to one side far from other people, and said, "Sir, I have wondrous news for you."

"What news?" he asked. "Tell me."

"My lord, Sir Lancelot of the Lake is in this palace, and we knew nothing of it."

"Keep still, fair daughter. I can tell you that Lancelot has long been dead, as those of the Round Table truly say."

"In God's name, sir, he is not, for I saw him just now, quite sound in all his members. Come with me right away, and I'll show you."

"All right," he replied, "let's go."

Then they went into the garden together, without any other company, and went to the spring where Lancelot was sleeping. When the king got there, he recognized that this was the madman who had stayed so long at his court.

"Sir," she said, "what do you think? Is this not Lancelot of the Lake?"

He said nothing in reply, but looked more and more closely and studied him until at last he recognized that it was Lancelot. But then he could keep silent no longer, but sighed deeply, and the tears ran down his face. When he spoke, he said, "Oh, God, what a pity!"

Then he said to his daughter, "This is truly the man you named. Now let's

leave here, lest he wake up, and I'll give this matter my keenest considera-
tion."

Then the king went back to his palace; he told his daughter to tell no one
that this was Lancelot, and she said that she would not, no matter what might
happen.

Then the king took six big, strong squires, led them to the spring, showed
them the madman, and told them to take him by force, without injuring him,
to bind him hand and foot, and that then he would do as he wished with him.
The squires were very much afraid that the king was going to have him killed;
nevertheless, because they dared not refuse his order, they captured him as he
slept. Lancelot tried to get away from them, but he could not, for they were
skillful and strong; they took him by force, bound him up, and carried him to
the room beneath the tower.

In the evening, after people had gone to bed, the king had him taken to
the Palace of Adventures; they left him there all alone, thinking that, as soon
as he came into the palace, Lancelot would be cured by the power of the Holy
Grail and would regain his memory. And it happened just as they thought, for
when the Holy Grail came into the palace, as was its wont, Lancelot was
cured at once, and he stayed there until the next morning.

In the morning, when bright daylight appeared through the many glass
windows and Lancelot lay in the palace where he had been once before, he
was profoundly puzzled as to how he had come there, but he was even more
dismayed when he saw how he was bound. Then he began to break the bonds,
in the bed where they had placed him. And when he had freed himself, he
went to the windows, on the side toward the garden where he had once killed
the serpent; he opened them, began to look at the garden, and saw the king
and his household, who had already risen and were preparing to go to the
palace to find out how things had gone with Lancelot, for they would have
been very glad of his recovery, if God had wished to grant it.

The king said to his lords, "My lords, let's go see how it has gone with
our knight." He had revealed to them that the madman who had been among
them had been the world's best knight, "and if it pleases Our Lord that he
should be cured, I will acquaint you with him."

Then they went to the door of the palace, opened it, went in, and saw
Lancelot leaning on a windowsill and still looking out at the garden. When he
saw the king, whom he knew well, coming toward him, he left the windows
and went to meet him, and they exchanged greetings.

"My lord," said the king, "how is it with you?"

"Well, my lord, thank God," replied Lancelot, "for I have regained my
health." Then Lancelot drew the king aside and said to him, "My lord, for
God's sake, tell me how I came here, for I know neither in what way nor
when."

"My lord," said the king, "I'll tell you, but I fear you may be more upset than before." Then he told him how he had come to Corbenic so mad and out of his mind that no one could stand against him, and so thin and naked that "no one would ever have recognized you for Lancelot. And so you've stayed with us a long time, and I would never have realized who you were, had it not been for my daughter, who found you sleeping beside a spring and came to tell me. And when I heard this news, I went to you at once, very glad that you were with us; I had you captured by my men and placed in this palace, where I was certain you'd be restored to health, as soon as the Holy Grail came. And it happened just as I thought, thank God, for you are cured. Now I've told you what I know of your situation; do not be more upset than you were before, for things have turned out very well for you, thank God, considering the adventures that have befallen you. Now take comfort and be merry and stay here with us, and I promise you on my honor as a king that I will never fail you in anything I can do, but will relinquish to you my land, my wealth, and the authority over my men, so that you will be able to do as you wish with my kingdom, just as I can myself."

[*Lancelot then had Pelles find him lodgings where his identity would not be known. He was lodged on the Isle of Joy, in Bliant's castle.*]

And every day it was Lancelot's custom, before eating or drinking, to go to the end of the island toward the kingdom of Logres and look toward the land to which his heart was completely drawn. And after looking for a long time and regretting the great delights that he had so often had and from which he was now so far away, so that he thought he could never recover them, he began anew such wondrous mourning that none but he could have borne the pain. And he himself could not have borne it, but the pain and anguish he suffered for love afforded him great relief, for it brought such great sweetness to his heart that it seemed to give him great comfort.

After Lancelot had stayed on the island in this way until the beginning of winter, he realized that he had completely lost the habits of arms and knighthood; he thought of a means whereby knights would come to see him but would not recognize him, and he would find out how the men of that land bore arms. One day he went to see the king and said to him, "My lord, I beg you to have a shield made for me, for there are a great many other arms here."

The king asked him about the design of the shield, and he described what he wanted. Three days later a squire brought in the shield, just as he had described it. When the people of the castle saw it, they were amazed, for they had never seen the like, and without doubt it was the most extraordinary shield in the kingdom at that time. It was blacker than a mulberry, and in the middle, where the boss should have been, was painted a silver queen and a knight on his knees before her, as if he were begging for mercy. The people there who saw the shield and the pictures did not know what this meant, except for

Lancelot and King Pelles's daughter. Once the shield was made as I have described it to you, Lancelot hung it on a pine tree in the middle of the island, and from then on he went there every morning to indulge his grief, so great that all who saw it were amazed. [. . .]

44. Hector and Perceval Find Lancelot, and They All Return to Camelot; Galahad's Arrival Is Announced.

[Perceval and Hector eventually came to Bliant's castle and found Lancelot.]

Then as many as seven knights came forth from the castle, aged and venerable knights, and in their company was the beautiful lady, the daughter of King Pelles. When she saw Hector, she welcomed him with great joy, then led them back to the castle and had their armor removed. Then began the joy and the celebration.

After Hector had recognized the beautiful lady, the daughter of King Pelles, he asked her for news of Galahad, who was Lancelot's son and his own nephew, and she told him that Galahad was the handsomest child in the world and already quite grown, being now about ten years old.

"Indeed," said Hector, "I would be very glad to see him."

"My lord," she replied, "he is with my father, King Pelles, where he has been raised since birth; you will soon be able to see him, for I'm sure he will escort his father when he leaves this land."

"And how did he come to this land?" asked Hector.

"My lord, he came here so out of his mind, wearing nothing but tatters, that anyone could scarcely have recognized him as Lancelot. But as soon as he approached the Holy Grail, he was cured. He came to this island because he wanted no one to recognize him, and since then he has concealed himself so well that no one knew it was he, apart from my father and the people of this castle."

They spoke at great length of this matter until the following day, when Hector said to Lancelot, "My lord, my lady the queen summons you, and so you must come to court."

"That cannot be," said Lancelot; "I may never go back, for she has forbidden it."

"I tell you truly," said Hector, "that she has summoned you."

He replied that in that case he would gladly go.

Then he sent word to King Pelles that he would set out two days from then. The king was greatly saddened by this news and said to Galahad, "Dear grandson, your father wishes to leave."

"My lord," said the child, "he will do as he wishes, but wherever he goes, I wish to be so near him that I may see him often."

When the king heard what the child wanted and saw that he could not retain him, he asked what he might do.

"My lord," said a knight, "in Camelot Forest there's an abbey where your sister is abbess. Send the child there, with two knights who will take care of him; when he's there, he'll be able to see his father frequently."

The king agreed with this and did all he could to make the child ready; he gave him four knights to escort him and six squires to serve them, and gave them enough of his wealth that they could live well wherever they might go. Two days later Lancelot came to Corbenic with a great company of knights. Then Hector asked to see Galahad, and the child came, and when he saw him, he esteemed him more highly than he could have esteemed any other child. When the mother learned that Galahad was to go away, she was near to distraction, and would have let nothing keep her from going with him had her father the king not forbidden it, and so she stayed there.

In the morning, when they were ready to mount, the king brought Galahad before Lancelot and said to him, "My lord, wherever you find this child, consider him as your own, for I tell you truly that you fathered him on my beautiful daughter."

He replied that he was quite glad at this news. With that he set out. After the king had escorted him a long way, Lancelot made him turn back and continued on his way with Hector and Perceval. They rode for many a day until at last they reached Carlion, where they found King Arthur, Bors, and Lionel, who had brought Helain the White, the handsomest youth of his station, who was soon due to be knighted, and so without fail he was, by the hand of Bors himself.

When they heard that Lancelot was coming, they all went out to meet him; they welcomed him with great joy and did all they could to serve him. Yet the finest welcome was the queen's, for her joy was as great as may be imagined by the heart of man.

Galahad, having left his grandfather, rode until he reached the abbey of nuns; he stayed there until he was a grown youth of fifteen. Then he was so handsome, worthy, and agile that his equal could not have been found in all the world.

Near the abbey there was a worthy hermit who often came to see Galahad and who, by the will of Our Lord, had some idea of the child's goodness. One day after Easter he said to him, "Dear son, you have now reached the age of knighthood. Will you not be knighted at this Pentecost?"

"Yes, my lord, God willing," said Galahad, "for so my masters tell me."

"Now take care," said the worthy man, "that you enter that order after confession, so that you are pure and cleansed of all filth."

He replied that he would be, God willing.

They spoke together at length that day. The following day, at the hour of prime, King Arthur, who was hunting in the woods, came there to hear Mass, and after it had been sung, the worthy hermit called to him and said, "King Arthur, I tell you in the true spirit of confession that on this coming Pentecost there will be a new-made knight who will put an end to the adventures of the Holy Grail. That day he will come to your court and will without fail sit upon the Perilous Seat. Now be sure to summon your men, so that they will all be at Camelot on the eve of Pentecost, to see the wonders that will occur there."

"Good sir," said the king, "is this true?"

"I tell you this," he replied, "on my word as a priest."

The king, overjoyed at this news, mounted at once, rode off, and remained in the woods until evening. When he was back in Camelot, he sent word throughout the kingdom of Logres telling his lords to be at court for Pentecost, for he would hold the greatest and the merriest court he ever held. And so there were so many assembled on the eve of Pentecost that anyone who saw it would have been filled with wonder. And here Master Walter Map concludes his book and begins the *Grail*.

The Quest for the Holy Grail

TRANSLATED BY E. JANE BURNS

1. Lancelot Dubs Galahad, and the Knights Discuss the Perilous Seat.

Early in the afternoon on the day before Pentecost, when the knights of the
Round Table who had come to Camelot and heard Mass were about to eat, a
beautiful young woman entered the room on horseback. Clearly she had
come in great haste; her horse was still soaked in sweat. Dismounting, she approached and greeted the king, who welcomed her:

"Sir," she said, "can you tell me, in God's name, if Lancelot is here?"

Pointing to Lancelot, the king said, "Yes, you'll find him over there."

She went to him and said, "Lancelot, I ask in the name of King Pelles
that you follow me into the forest."

He asked who her overlord was. She replied, "The man I just named."

"And what do you need from me?" asked Lancelot.

"You'll see soon enough," she said.

"As God is my witness," he replied, "I'll be glad to go."

Lancelot instructed a squire to saddle his horse and bring his armor. The
king and all others in the palace were dismayed to see this command carried
out. But when they realized that Lancelot would not stay, they relented. The
queen said to him, "What is this about, Lancelot? You're leaving us on such a
solemn day?"

"Lady," the damsel replied, "I assure you that he'll be back tomorrow
morning."

"Let him go, then," she said. "But if he were not expected back tomorrow, I wouldn't consent to his leaving today."

Lancelot and the young woman mounted their horses and rode away
without delay, accompanied only by her squire.

Having left Camelot, they rode until they came to the forest. They
traveled along a good road for about half a league until they came to a valley
where an abbey of nuns stood in their path. As the young woman approached
the abbey door, the squire called out, and the door was opened. They dismounted and went inside. When the inhabitants learned that Lancelot had
come, they greeted him enthusiastically and led him to a room where they
took off his armor. There, he was delighted to find his cousins, Bors and Lionel, sleeping on two beds. He woke them, and when they saw Lancelot, they
hugged and kissed him, all the cousins rejoicing in one another's company.

"My lord," said Bors to Lancelot, "what adventure brought you here? We
had expected to see you at Camelot."

Lancelot explained how a young woman had led him there without revealing the reason why.

While they were talking, three nuns entered the room, ushering in Galahad before them. He was a child of unparalleled beauty and grace. Holding
him by the hand and weeping softly, the eldest nun led Galahad to Lancelot
and said, "Sir, I bring you this child whom we have raised to embody all our

joy, our comfort and our hope, so that you can knight him. No finer man, it seems to us, could receive the order of chivalry from you."

Lancelot looked at the child, who was endowed with exceptional beauty. He felt he had never seen anyone so perfectly formed. And the child's innocence made Lancelot believe that he would accomplish such extraordinary things that Lancelot was pleased to make him a knight. He told the ladies he would not deny their request.

"Sir," said the one leading Galahad, "we would like you to perform the ceremony tonight or tomorrow."

"In God's name," he said, "it will be as you wish." Lancelot stayed the night at the abbey and had the young man keep a vigil in the chapel. At the hour of prime Lancelot made him a knight, putting on one of his spurs while Bors attached the other. Then Lancelot girded his sword about him and gave him the traditional accolade, praying God to make him a valiant knight worthy of his extraordinary beauty.

When he had completed the dubbing ritual, Lancelot said, "Good sir, will you accompany me to my lord King Arthur's court?"

"No sir," he said, "I can't go with you."

Then Lancelot said to the abbess, "Lady, won't you permit our new knight to come with us to my lord King Arthur's court? It will benefit him more to be there than to stay here with you."

"Sir," she said, "he will not go now, but as soon as we feel the time is right, we'll send him."

Lancelot left with his companion, and they rode until they reached Camelot at the hour of tierce. The king and a number of powerful lords had gone to hear Mass in the chapel. When the three cousins arrived, they dismounted in the courtyard and went upstairs to the hall, where they talked about the young man whom Lancelot had knighted. Bors remarked that he had never seen anyone who resembled Lancelot so closely. "I'll never believe it could be anyone but Galahad," he said, "the child of the Rich Fisher King's beautiful daughter. His resemblance to that family and our own is too striking.

"Yes," said Lionel, "I too believe it is Galahad, because he looks so much like my lord Lancelot."

They discussed the subject for a long time to see if they could draw Lancelot into the conversation. But no matter how much they spoke of it, Lancelot said nothing. So they let the subject drop and began to examine instead the seats at the Round Table. They discovered an inscription on each one: So-AND-So SHOULD SIT HERE. When they reached the great seat called the Perilous Seat, they found words that seemed to have been written recently. As they read the words before them—FOUR HUNDRED FIFTY-FOUR YEARS HAVE PASSED SINCE THE PASSION OF CHRIST; ON PENTECOST, THIS SEAT WILL FIND ITS MASTER—they said to each other, "This is an extraordinary event."

"By God," said Lancelot, "if we calculate the time elapsed, according to this inscription, from the Resurrection of Our Lord to the present day, we will see that this is the very day that the seat is to be occupied. Today is Pentecost, four hundred fifty-four years after the Resurrection. No one should see this inscription before the arrival of the one destined to try the adventure."

Lancelot's companions assured him that they would hide the inscription, and they had a silk cloth brought in to cover the seat.

When the king came back from the chapel and saw that Lancelot had returned with Bors and Lionel, he welcomed them and greeted them warmly. Delighted by the return of the two brothers, the knights of the Round Table began a lavish celebration. When Sir Gawain asked how they had been since they left court, they answered, "Very well, thank God," since they had been healthy.

"I'm glad to hear it," said Gawain as the courtiers gave Bors and Lionel a hearty welcome. It had been a long time since they had been seen at court.

The king gave the order to set the tables, thinking it was time to eat.

"Lord," said the seneschal, "if you sit down to eat now you will be ignoring an established custom of this court. We have always known you not to come to the table on solemn feast days until an adventure was witnessed by the barons of your household."

"Indeed, Kay," said the king, "you speak the truth."

"I have always observed this custom, and I'll do so as long as I can. But I was so happy that Lancelot and his cousins had arrived safely at court that I forgot about it."

"I hope you'll remember it in the future," replied Kay.

2. Gawain and Lancelot Attempt to Remove the Sword in the Stone.

While they were talking, a young man came in and said to the king, "My lord, I bring extraordinary news."

"What news?" asked the king. "Tell me at once."

"My lord, down below your palace, I saw a large stone slab floating on the water. Come and see it. I know this is a marvelous adventure."

The king went to see the marvel with all the others. When they came to the riverbank, they found the stone slab, made of red marble, on top of the water. A sword, which appeared to be very beautiful and valuable, was stuck into it. The sword handle, made of precious stones, was carefully inscribed with gold letters, which the barons read: NO ONE WILL EVER WITHDRAW ME FROM HERE, EXCEPT THE ONE WHO WILL HANG ME AT HIS SIDE. HE WILL BE THE WORLD'S BEST KNIGHT. When the king saw these words, he said to Lancelot, "Good sir, this sword belongs rightfully to you; I know you are the best knight in the world."

A distraught Lancelot replied, "Indeed not, my lord. The sword is not mine, and I would not have the courage or boldness to lay a hand on it. I'm not worthy or deserving enough to withdraw it. So I won't touch it; that would be madness."

"Try it anyway," said the king, "and see if you can pull it out."

"My lord," said Lancelot, "I won't do it because I'm certain that whoever fails at this will be wounded."

"What makes you so sure?" asked the king.

"I know it's true, my lord," Lancelot replied. "And I'll tell you something else; I want you to know that today the extraordinary adventures and the great wonders of the Holy Grail will begin."

When the king realized that Lancelot would not do as he wished, he said to Sir Gawain, "Good nephew, you try it then."

"With your permission, my lord, I won't do it either, since Lancelot doesn't want to try. My efforts would be in vain since, as you well know, Lancelot is a better knight than I."

"Try it anyway," said the king, "not so much to get the sword as because I ask you to."

Gawain grasped the pommel of the sword and pulled, but he could not withdraw it. The king said to him, "Good nephew, that's enough; you have done as I asked."

"Gawain," said Lancelot, "be forewarned that this sword will touch you so closely one day that you'd give anything, even a castle, not to have touched it today."

"What else could I have done, sir?" asked Gawain. "I would have obeyed our lord's command even if it meant dying."

When the king heard this, he regretted having forced Gawain to act. Then he told Perceval to grasp the sword and Perceval said he would gladly comply to keep Gawain company. Perceval placed his hand on the sword and pulled, but he could not withdraw it. Then everyone in attendance was convinced that Lancelot had been telling the truth and that the inscription on the pommel of the sword was accurate. No one else was daring enough to touch the sword. Sir Kay said to the king, "My lord, my lord, now you can certainly sit down to eat as soon as you wish; there's been no lack of adventure here, to be sure."

"Let's go, then," said the king, "it's time to eat." The knights went off, leaving the stone at the riverbank. The king gave the order to announce that the meal was ready and took his seat on the raised dais. The knights of the Round Table sat in their respective places. That day they served four crowned kings there and a great many powerful lords; it was an extraordinary occasion. Seated on the palace dais, the king ordered the large gathering of important men to be served along with himself. Once everyone was seated, they discovered that all the knights of the Round Table were there and that all the seats were occupied, except the chair called the Perilous Seat.

3. Galahad Arrives at Arthur's Court.

After they had eaten the first course, an extraordinary event took place: all the doors and windows of the palace closed by themselves, without anyone touching them. However, the room was not darkened, which surprised everyone present, wise and foolish alike. King Arthur, who spoke first, said, "In God's name, good lords, today we have seen wondrous things, here and at the riverbank. But I believe we will witness even more marvelous things before nightfall."

While the king was speaking, an old man dressed in a white cloak entered the room. But no knight in attendance there knew how he had come in. The worthy man approached on foot, leading by the hand a knight in red armor, without sword or shield. Once he had fully entered the room, he said, "Peace be with you." And turning to Arthur, he continued, "King Arthur, I bring you the Desired Knight, descended from the noble lineage of King David and the family of Joseph of Arimathea.[1] He will put an end to the wondrous events now taking place in this land as well as in far-off lands. Here he is."

Delighted by this news, the king said to the worthy man, "Sir, if these words are true, a warm welcome to you and to the knight. If he is the one we've been waiting for to undertake the adventures of the Holy Grail, he will receive a heartier welcome than anyone ever has. And whoever he may be, whether the one you specify or another, I hope he will succeed, since he is such a noble man and of such distinguished lineage, as you say."

"I give you my word," said the worthy man, "you will soon see evidence of my claim." Then he had the knight's armor removed so that he stood there in a tunic of red silk. The worthy man then gave him a red brocade cloak, lined with white ermine, which he wore over his shoulders.

4. Galahad Sits in the Perilous Seat.

Once the knight had put on the cloak, the worthy man said, "Follow me, sir knight," and led him directly to the Perilous Seat, next to which Lancelot was

---

[1]Galahad has a complex genealogy in the *Quest*. His parents are Lancelot and the daughter of the Rich Fisher King, who is sometimes identical to King Pelles, guardian of the Grail at Corbenic. At other times, however, Galahad is said to be the grandson of the Fisher King and nephew of King Pelles. But Galahad is always linked, on one side, to the Grail keepers. On the other side, he descends from King David through Lancelot's mother, Elaine (as explained in the *Lancelot,* in a chapter not included in the present volume). Galahad is related more indirectly to Joseph of Arimathea since Lancelot descends from Nascien, who is a friend of Joseph; the fisher kings descend from Bron, Joseph's brother-in-law.

seated. Lifting the silk cloth that Lancelot had put there, the worthy man found the letters which read: THIS IS GALAHAD'S SEAT. As the worthy man looked at the letters, which appeared to be recently inscribed, he deciphered the name and said in a loud voice so that everyone could hear, "Sir knight, sit here, for this place is yours."

The knight sat down without hesitating and said to the worthy man, "You can leave now, sir, for you have accomplished your task. Give my regards to all those who live in the holy site, to my uncle King Pelles and my ancestor the Rich Fisher King. Tell them that I will see them as soon as I can."

The good man departed, bidding King Arthur and the others farewell. When they asked who he was, he cut them off brusquely, saying that he would not tell them at that time. They would know soon enough if they dared to ask. When he came to the main palace door, he opened it and descended into the courtyard where some fifteen of his knights and squires who were waiting for his return. He then mounted his horse and rode away from court, so that no one learned any more about him that day.

When the people in the hall saw the knight sitting in the seat that so many brave men had feared and where so many great adventures had taken place, they were truly amazed. This knight was so young that they did not know how he could merit such a distinction if not by the will of Our Lord. Great rejoicing broke out in the hall. Everyone honored the knight because they felt sure he was the one destined to put an end to the adventures of the Holy Grail. They knew this because of the trial of the Seat, which no one had occupied previously without misfortune befalling him. Thus they paid the knight all due respect, treating him as a master and lord who ranked above the knights of the Round Table. And Lancelot, looking at the knight in wonder, was delighted to realize that this was the young man he had dubbed earlier in the day. He paid the young knight the greatest respect by conversing with him on various subjects and then asked him to say something about himself. The knight, who barely knew Lancelot and did not dare refuse him, answered everything he was asked.

Bors, who was even more delighted than the others to realize that this was Galahad, the son of Lancelot, the one destined to bring the adventures to a close, said to his brother Lionel, "Brother, do you know who the knight sitting on the Perilous Seat is?"

"I don't really know," said Lionel, "except that he was knighted today, dubbed by Lancelot's own hand. He's the knight you and I have been discussing all day, the one Lancelot fathered with the Rich Fisher King's daughter."

"Yes, in truth, that's the one," Bors replied, "and he's a close relative of ours. We should all rejoice at this adventure. For there's no doubt, a more extraordinary thing has never happened to any knight I know. The adventures have begun auspiciously."

As the two brothers and everyone else at court talked about Galahad, the news spread so widely that it reached the queen. She heard about Galahad's arrival from a young man who announced, while she was eating in her quarters, "My lady, wondrous things are happening here."

"What do you mean?" she said. "Tell me."

"I swear, my lady, that a knight has come to court and fulfilled the adventure of the Perilous Seat. He's so young that everyone wonders how he could merit such a distinction."

"Can this be true?"

"Yes," he said, "be assured of it."

"By God," she said, "this has turned out well for him. Every other knight who has wanted to carry out this adventure has either died or been maimed before he could complete it."

"Truly," exclaimed the ladies in waiting, "the knight was born at an auspicious hour. No man, no matter how great his prowess, has been able to succeed at what this one has done. By this feat, one can recognize him as the knight who will bring an end to the adventures of Great Britain and heal the Wounded King."

The queen said to the young man, "Dear friend, with the help of God, tell me what he is like."

"In truth, my lady, he's one of world's most handsome knights. But he's surprisingly young, and he resembles Lancelot and King Ban's family so closely that people are saying he comes from that line."

The queen wanted to see him now more than ever before. What she had heard about the knight's appearance made her think he must be Galahad, son of Lancelot and the Rich Fisher King's daughter. She had heard the story many times of how Lancelot had been tricked into fathering the child. This more than any other event would have provoked her anger toward Lancelot, if he had been at fault.

After they had eaten, the king and the knights of the Round Table rose from their seats, and the king himself went over to the Perilous Seat, lifted the silk cloth, and saw the name of the knight he so wanted to meet: Galahad.

Showing the inscription to Gawain, he said, "Good nephew, now we have among us Galahad, the perfect knight, whom we and the knights of the Round Table have so wanted to see. Let's attempt to honor and serve him as long as he is with us; he won't linger long, I'm certain, because of the great Quest for the Grail, which I believe is soon to begin. Lancelot explained this to us earlier today, if his words were accurate."

Gawain replied, "We should all serve him as the one sent by God to free our land from the great wonders and strange adventures that have been taking place here for so long."

Then the king approached Galahad and bade him welcome. He said, "We had so hoped to see you. Now that we have you among us, we thank God and you as well for deigning to come."

"My lord," the knight replied, "I came because I had to, because all those undertaking the Quest for the Holy Grail will depart from here, and they will be leaving soon."

The king said, "Sir, we are in great need of your help to put an end to the extraordinary wonders of this land and to bring to a close an adventure that no one among us has been able to accomplish. I know you will succeed at it, since you are destined to fulfill adventures that others cannot. This is why God has sent you among us: to do what others could never accomplish."

Galahad answered, "Lord, where is the adventure you speak of? Can you show it to me?

"I will show you," said the king. He took Galahad by the hand, and they left the castle, with all the barons following behind, eager to see how the adventure of the stone would be resolved. Everyone ran after them, leaving no knight behind in the castle.

And now the news came to the queen. As soon as she heard about it, she had the tables cleared and said to four of her noblest ladies, "Ladies, come with me to the riverbank. I cannot miss seeing this adventure for anything in the world, if only I can arrive in time." The queen left the castle in the company of many ladies, young and old.

When they were at the water's edge, the knights who saw them approach exclaimed, "Look, here comes the queen! Stand back!" As the most valiant among them made way for her, the king said to Galahad, "Sir, here's the adventure I spoke of: to pull the sword from the stone. The most highly esteemed knights of my court were unable to do so earlier today."

Galahad replied, "My lord, that's not at all surprising since the adventure is mine, not theirs. It is because I was so sure of obtaining this sword that I didn't bring one to court, as you can see."

He put his hand on the sword and pulled it out of the stone so easily that it seemed not to be stuck at all. Then he took the sheath, placed the sword in it, and belted it around his waist, saying to the king, "My lord, now I'm better equipped than before; I need only a shield."

"Good Knight, God will send you a shield somehow," said the king, "as he has sent you this sword."

5. A Stranger Announces the Arrival of the Grail, and King Arthur Holds a Tournament to Celebrate.

They looked up river and saw a young lady approaching swiftly on a white saddle-horse. When she reached them, she greeted the king and his company and asked for Lancelot. Standing directly in front of her, he answered, "I'm right here, my lady." She looked in his direction, recognized him, and began weeping as she said, "Oh, Lancelot, how your luck has changed since yesterday morning!"

Hearing this, Lancelot replied, "What do you mean, lady? Tell me."

"As God is my witness," she said, "I'll tell you here, publicly. Yesterday morning, you were the world's best knight. Anyone who might have called you 'Lancelot the best knight of all' would have spoken the truth. But to say it now would be a lie, because there's a better knight than you. It has been proved through the adventure of the sword that you didn't dare touch. That's why your name has changed and why, as I have indicated, you can no longer consider yourself to be the world's best knight."

Lancelot answered that he would never make that mistake, because this adventure had convinced him otherwise. The young lady then turned to the king and said, "King Arthur, the hermit Nascien has asked me to announce that later today you will experience the greatest honor ever to befall a knight in Brittany. Yet it will not be for you, but for another. Do you know what I'm referring to? The Holy Grail, which will appear in your court today and feed the knights of the Round Table." After making this announcement, she turned her horse around and left the way she had come. Many of the barons and knights at court wanted to detain her to learn her identity and where she had come from. But she refused to stay, despite their requests.

Then the king said to his barons, "We have now been assured that you'll soon undertake the Quest for the Holy Grail. Knowing that I will never again see you gathered together as you are now, I want to hold a tournament in the fields around Camelot, a tournament so wonderful that it will be remembered by our descendants long after our death."

All agreed and returned to the fortress to take up their arms. Some gathered enough weapons to joust fully protected, while most used only horse coverings and shields because they could rely on their strength. The king had put this plan in motion for no other reason than to verify Galahad's chivalric ability. He felt that after leaving court, Galahad would not return for a long time.

When all the knights, of greater and lesser distinction, had assembled on the fields of Camelot, Galahad donned his hauberk and helmet at the request of the king and queen, but he refused to carry a shield, despite their entreaties. Gawain, who was most pleased by this, offered to carry his lances, as did Yvain and Bors of Gaunes. The queen was stationed on the walls along with a great company of ladies, young and old. Galahad, who had come to the field with the others, began to shatter lances with such force that anyone watching would have been astounded. He accomplished so much in a short time that any man or woman witnessing this display of chivalric prowess would have considered it wondrous, the best ever seen. Those who had never seen him fight agreed that he had launched a stunning chivalric career. It seemed, based on his performance that day, that from then on he would easily surpass all other knights in valor. When the tournament ended, they realized that he had vanquished all the knights of the Round Table who had taken up arms, save two: Lancelot and Perceval.

The tournament continued in this way until after noon, when the king himself had the knights depart, for fear that discord might surface among them. He had Galahad unlace his helmet and hand it to Bors of Gaunes. Then the king led the knight from the jousting field to the fortress at Camelot, where he entered the main street with his face uncovered so that all could see him. When the queen looked at Galahad, she remarked that Lancelot must surely be his father, because no two men had ever resembled each other so closely. For this reason, it was not surprising that he had distinguished himself in chivalry; to do otherwise would be to disgrace his lineage. A lady who heard these words challenged the queen, "By God, my lady, does that necessarily make him as good a knight as you suggest?"

The queen answered, "Without a doubt. He is descended from the world's best knights and from the noblest family known."

The women came down from the walls to hear vespers on this solemn day. After leaving the church, the king entered the upper hall of the castle and ordered that the tables be set. The knights resumed their places in the seats they had occupied that morning. Once they were seated and quiet, they heard a thunderclap so astoundingly loud that they thought the castle would collapse. Then a ray of sunlight shone down, making the castle seven times brighter than before. The people inside seemed to have been illumined by the grace of the Holy Spirit. They looked at one another, wondering where this could have come from. No one could talk or utter a single word. All stood silent for a long time. Unable to speak, they simply looked at one another like mute beasts. Then the Holy Grail entered the room, covered with a white silk cloth, but no one could see who carried it. It entered through the main door of the hall. And as soon as it arrived, the room was filled with a delicious fragrance, as if every earthly spice had been strewn there. The Grail traveled through the room, around the dais. And as it passed the tables, each place setting was filled with the food its occupant most desired. When everyone was served, the Grail left in such a way that no one knew what became of it; nor did they see which way it went. At this point, the castle inhabitants regained their speech. They thanked Our Lord for having granted them the great honor of being nourished by the grace of the Holy Vessel. Happiest of all was King Arthur, because Our Lord had rewarded him more generously than any previous king.

Visitors and court inhabitants alike were encouraged by this event. They felt it indicated that Our Lord had not forgotten them, since he had shown them such good will. They talked about it throughout the meal. Even the king began to discuss the event with those seated closest to him. He said, "To be sure, barons, we should be very happy that our Lord showed us a sign of such great love, that he would nourish us with his grace on such a solemn day as Pentecost."

"My lord," said Gawain, "there's something else that you haven't noticed: every man here has received whatever he wished for. This has never happened except at the Maimed King's court.[2] But the observers there were so deceived that they couldn't see the Grail clearly; its true form remained hidden from them. For that reason, I now make this vow: that tomorrow morning I will undertake the Quest, pursuing it for a year and a day and longer if necessary. I will not return to court, no matter what happens, until I have seen the Grail more clearly than I did today, assuming that I see it at all. If I cannot, I will come back."

[*All the knights swore to undertake the quest. Arthur grieved for them all; the queen, for Lancelot. A wise man predicted that God would reveal great secrets to Galahad. The latter confirmed that he was Lancelot's son.*]

6. The Knights Swear Solemn Devotion to the Quest.

Then, turning to Gawain, the king said, "Gawain, Gawain, how you have betrayed me. All the good you have done for my court does not offset the harm you bring upon it today. Never again will this court be honored by knights as noble and valiant as those whom you have spirited away by your initiative. I feel even greater distress for you and Lancelot than for them. I loved you both with all the love one man can have for another, not only recently but from the very moment I learned of the great virtue you both possessed."

Having said this, the king fell into a deep and thoughtful silence. As he thought, tears began to roll down his face. Those who saw this and were sadder than words can tell did not dare say anything. They realized how distraught the king was. He remained in this state for a long time and finally said, "God, I never thought I would be separated from this company of men whom good fortune has sent to me." Then he said to Lancelot, "Lancelot, I ask you, by the faith and the oath that exist between us, to give me good counsel."

"Lord," said Lancelot, "tell me how I can help."

"I would very much like to prevent this quest, if at all possible."

"My lord," Lancelot replied, "I have heard so many valiant knights swear to carry out the quest; I don't believe they would renounce it for anything. They would all have to perjure themselves. To ask that of them would be unfair."

"Indeed," said the king, "I know you are right. But the great love I feel for you and the others made me suggest it. If it had been appropriate to recon-

---

[2]Allusion to Gawain's visit to Corbenic (*Lancelot*, Chapter 31) or to Lancelot's (*Lancelot*, Chapter 33).

sider the decision, that would have made me happy. It will grieve me so to see everyone depart."

The two men talked until the sun was high and had begun to disperse the dew and the barons of the realm began to gather at court. After the queen rose she went to the king and said, "Lord, the knights await you to hear Mass." The king got up and wiped his eyes so no one would see the sadness he endured.

Gawain and Lancelot asked that their armor be brought in. As soon as they had put it on, except for the shields, they went to the main hall and found their companions ready to go. Suitably armed, they all went to church and heard the service. After returning to the castle keep, those participating in the quest sat next to each other as King Bademagu announced, "Since you cannot be dissuaded in your resolve to undertake this task, I think it wise to bring out the relics. Those knights departing on the quest can then take the appropriate oath."

"I concur with your wishes," added King Arthur, "since it cannot be otherwise." The palace clerics called for the relics upon which oaths were sworn at court, and when they were brought before the high table, the king said to Sir Gawain, "You inaugurated this quest. Come forward and be the first to swear the oath that must be taken by those participating in it."

"If you please, my lord," said King Bademagu, "Gawain should not be the first to take the oath, but Sir Galahad, who will be recognized by all as lord and master of the Round Table. Once he has sworn the oath, we will repeat his words exactly. It must be done this way."

Then Galahad was called. He came forward, knelt before the relics, and swore on his reputation as a loyal knight that he would pursue this quest for one year and one day, or longer if necessary. He swore he would not return to court before learning the truth about the Holy Grail, if he could. Next Lancelot took the oath just as Galahad had done. He was followed by Gawain, Perceval, Bors, Lionel, and Alan the White, then all the knights of the Round Table in turn.

Once all the knights had taken the oath, the scribes recording their names noted that they numbered one hundred fifty, all valiant men without a coward among them. The knights ate a light meal, at the king's request, and then put on their helmets, making it clear that they were about to depart. They bade a tearful farewell to the queen. [. . .]

7. King Bademagu Wrongly Takes the Shield from the Abbey.

Now the story says that when Galahad left his companions he rode for three or four days without finding an adventure worth recording. On the fifth day, after the hour of vespers, it happened that his path led him to a Cistercian abbey.[3] When he knocked at the door, the brothers who came out saw that he was a knight errant and helped him down from his horse. While one man took his steed, another led Galahad to a lower room where they removed his armor. There, Galahad saw two knights of the Round Table: King Bademagu and Yvain the Bastard.[4] As soon as these knights recognized Galahad, they ran to greet him with open arms, for they were delighted to see him. After they had explained who they were, Galahad recognized them and greeted them warmly and with great respect, as one greets brothers and dear friends.

In the evening, after they had eaten, they strolled to a lovely nearby orchard and stretched out beneath a tree. Then Galahad asked what adventure had brought them there. "To tell the truth," they replied, "we came here to witness what we were told would be a wondrous adventure. There is a shield in this abbey that no one can wear or carry off without being killed, wounded, or maimed within a day or two. We have come to find out whether what they say about this shield is true."

"I plan to try taking it away from here in the morning," said King Bademagu. "Then I'll know whether or not the stories about the shield are true."

"This is a truly amazing story," said Galahad, "if the shield has the properties you describe. And if you are unable to carry it off, I'll be the one to use it, since I have no other shield."

"We'll leave it to you then, since we know that you won't fail at the adventure."

"I want you to try it first," Galahad said, "to see if what they told you was true." The two companions agreed to this. That night the knights were welcomed and made to feel comfortable by the most generous hospitality the monks could provide. They extended special respect to Galahad, about whom the two knights had spoken so highly, preparing for him a sumptuous bed in keeping with his stature. King Bademagu and his companion slept next to Galahad.

The following day, after they had heard Mass, King Bademagu asked one of the brothers where they might find the shield that was so widely talked about in the realm. The worthy man asked in turn, "Why do you want to know?"

"Because I plan to take it away and find out whether it has the special qualities attributed to it."

---

[3]The expression in Old French is *blanche abaie* ('White Abbey'), which refers throughout the *Quest,* according to Albert Pauphilet, to the order of the Cistercian monks. See *Études sur la "Queste del Saint Graal" attribueé à Gautier Map* (Paris, Champion, 1921) 55 ff. It was long assumed that the author of the *Quest* was himself a Cistercian, but that assumption has recently been questioned.

[4]Yvain the Bastard (*Yvains Li Avoltres*) is the half-brother of Yvain.

"I wouldn't advise it," said the worthy man. "I'm afraid you'll only incur shame."

"In any case, I want to know where it is and what it's like." The monk led Galahad behind the main altar where he found a white shield marked with a red cross.

"Here is the shield you asked for." They examined it and agreed that it was the most beautiful and lavish shield they had ever seen. It also released the most delicate odor, as if all the spices in the world had been spread over it. When Yvain the Bastard saw it, he said, "So help me God, this is the shield that only the best knight will be able to hang around his neck and shoulders. Certainly I will never wear it because I'm not valiant or worthy enough."

"In God's name," said King Bademagu, "I'll carry it away from here, whatever the consequences." Then he put the shield on and walked out of the church. When he reached his horse he said to Galahad, "If you please, sir, I want you to wait for me here until I can report the results of the adventure. I want you to know if I fail, because I'm certain that you'll succeed readily at this task."

"I'll gladly wait," said Galahad. Bademagu mounted his horse and the monks sent a squire with him to bring back the shield if necessary. Galahad stayed behind with Yvain, who wanted to keep him company until they learned the outcome of the adventure.

King Bademagu, who had set out with the squire, rode for more than two leagues before coming to a hermitage nestled in a valley. As he looked toward the hermitage, Bademagu saw a knight in white armor approaching as fast as his horse would carry him, his lance lowered for combat. Just as Bademagu prepared for the attack, his own lance broke against his opponent and flew into pieces. The white knight, who had taken him by surprise, struck so hard that he broke the chain mail on Bademagu's hauberk and drove the blade of his lance into the king's left shoulder. The blow was struck with such force and impudence that Bademagu fell to the ground. As he fell, the knight pulled the shield from his shoulders and shouted so that both he and the squire could hear, "Sir knight, you were foolish and naive to wear this shield. No one will be allowed to carry it but the world's best knight. Because of your sinful deed, Our Lord sent me here to avenge the wrong you have done."

The knight approached the squire and said, "Here, take this shield to Jesus Christ's soldier, the Good Knight called Galahad whom you left behind at the abbey. Tell him that the Almighty orders him to wear it. It will always be as new and strong as it is now. He should thus value it highly. Give him my greetings when you see him."

The squire replied, "Sir, tell me your name so that I can relay it to Galahad when I see him."

"You can't know my name," he said. "It cannot be known by anyone. You will simply have to accept that, and do as I command."

The squire replied, "Sir, since you won't tell me your name, I ask and implore you, in the name of what you hold dearest in all the world, to tell me the truth about this shield: how it was brought to this land and why so many wondrous adventures accompany it. Truly, no man can use the shield without coming to harm."

"Since you persist in asking, I'll tell you," said the knight. "But I won't speak to you alone. I want you to bring with you the knight destined to receive the shield." The squire agreed.

"Where can we find you when we return?" he asked.

"You'll find me right here." Then the young man approached King Bademagu and asked if he was badly wounded.

"Indeed," said the king, "it's a mortal wound."

"Can you ride?" asked the squire. Bademagu said he would try and stood up, wounded as he was. Then the young man helped him walk to his horse. The king mounted the horse in front with the squire seated behind so that his legs would hold the king steady. He feared, and rightly so, that Bademagu would fall otherwise.

Thus they left the place where the king had been wounded and rode back to the abbey, where the monks ran out to greet them. Helping the king down from his horse, the brothers led him to a room where they could care for his wound, which was large and surprisingly deep. Galahad asked one of the monks who was treating Bademagu, "Do you expect him to recover, sir? I think it would be a terrible shame if he died because of this adventure."

The monk replied, "Sir, he'll survive, if God wills it. But I warn you that he's very seriously hurt. Yet one shouldn't feel too sorry about it, for we told him that misfortune would befall him if he tried to take up the shield. He foolishly ignored our warning."

8. Galahad Wears the Shield, and "The White Knight" Recounts Its History.

After the monks had done everything they could for Bademagu, the squire said to Galahad as the others listened, "Sir, the fair knight in white armor who wounded King Bademagu sends you his greetings along with this shield. He asks on behalf of the Almighty that you carry it from this day forward. He says you're the only one who can carry this shield. That is why he asked me to bring it to you. If you want to know about the shield's many adventures, come with me to meet this knight. He promised me that he would explain the adventures to us."

Upon hearing this news, the monks bowed humbly before Galahad, remarking what good fortune had brought him to their abbey. For they knew that the perilous adventures would soon be brought to an end. Yvain the Bastard said, "Sir Galahad, hang this shield from your shoulders; it was made for no one other than you. Thus will my wish be fulfilled, for I never wanted anything as much as to see the Good Knight worthy of possessing this shield."

Galahad responded that he would take up the shield because it had been sent to him, but first he asked for his armor. After putting it on, he mounted his horse. Then he suspended the shield across his chest and departed, bidding the monks farewell. Yvain the Bastard also donned his armor and mounted his horse, announcing that he would accompany Galahad. But Galahad replied that that could not be; he would go alone, accompanied only by a squire. The two knights then parted company and followed separate paths.

Yvain entered the forest while Galahad and the squire rode until they found the knight in white armor whom the young man had seen earlier. When he saw Galahad coming, he rode out to greet him, and Galahad returned the greeting as graciously as possible. They spoke lightheartedly together until Galahad inquired, "Sir, I have heard that the shield I'm holding has provoked many wondrous adventures in the realm. I beg you in the name of loyal friendship to tell me the truth about it—how and why these adventures occurred—for I think you know the answer."

"Indeed, sir," said the knight, "I'll gladly tell you, for I do know the true story. So listen, Galahad, if you will. Forty-two years after the Passion of Jesus Christ, Joseph of Arimathea, the knight who took Our Lord down from the true Cross, left the city of Jerusalem along with many of his relatives. Following God's commandment, they set out and journeyed until reaching the city of Sarras, held by the Saracen king, Evalach. At the time Joseph came to Sarras, King Evalach was waging war against the rich and powerful King Tholomer, whose land bordered his. As Evalach prepared to fight Tholomer, who was threatening to overtake his land, Josephus, son of Joseph,[5] told him that if he entered the battle so poorly equipped, he would be defeated and dishonored by the enemy.

" 'What do you suggest?' asked Evalach.

" 'I'll tell you,' said Josephus as he began to recount the articles of the new dispensation, 'the truth of the gospel and the crucifixion of Our Lord, and the resurrection.' Then he had a shield brought in on which he marked a red cross and said, 'King Evalach, now I will show you clearly how you can know the force and the power of Him who was crucified. The wayward Tholomer will hold sway over you for three days and three nights, making you fear for your life. But just when you feel the end is near, uncover the cross and say, "Dear God, as I carry the sign of your death, protect me from this danger and lead me safely to receive your faith.' "

---

[5]Josephus is a character invented by the author of the *Quest* to be the son and double of Joseph of Arimathea. However, the son, in addition to being a knight and a priest, is also a virgin and can thus more fully prefigure Galahad.

"With that the king departed to fight Tholomer, and he experienced exactly what Josephus had predicted. As soon as Evalach felt himself to be in mortal danger, he unveiled his shield and saw upon it a crucified man, bleeding. As he uttered the words that Josephus had taught him, he was freed from the hold of his enemy and won an honorable victory over Tholomer and his men.

"As soon as Evalach returned to the city of Sarras, he told everyone about the truth he had discovered from Josephus, and he proclaimed so convincingly the existence of the Crucified one that Nascien consented to receive baptism. During the baptism, a man whose hand had been cut off passed by, holding the severed hand in his opposite palm. Josephus asked him to draw nearer, and as soon as the man touched the cross marked on the shield, the severed hand was healed.

"And yet another wondrous adventure occurred. For the cross that had been on the shield disappeared entirely and adhered instead to the man's arm. Thus did Evalach receive baptism and become a servant of Jesus Christ. He revered him with great love and had the shield carefully preserved.

"Later, when Josephus and his father left Sarras and came to Great Britain, they encountered a cruel and treacherous king who imprisoned them along with a great many other Christians. After Josephus was taken captive, the news spread far and wide, because no one in the world was so well known. Soon King Mordrain heard of the capture and called his vassals together with those of Nascien, his brother-in-law. They traveled to Great Britain and mounted an attack against the king who held Josephus prisoner. They seized his possessions, overcame the country's inhabitants and spread Christianity throughout the land.

"Evalach and Nascien so respected Josephus that they stayed with him and followed him wherever he went. When Josephus was on his deathbed and Evalach realized he was about to leave this world, he wept tenderly at the king's bedside, saying, 'Sir, as you leave me now, I will be all alone in this land, for I left my own realm and sweet homeland for the love of you. In God's name, since you must leave this world, give me a sign to remember you by after your death.'

"'Sir,' said Josephus, 'let me think about it.'

"After thinking for a long time about what he might leave to Evalach, Josephus said, 'King Evalach, bring that shield that I gave you when you fought against Tholomer.' The king agreed readily. The shield was close at hand since he carried it with him everywhere. When the shield was brought before Josephus, his nose began to bleed profusely and could not be stopped. He took the shield and made of his own blood the cross you now see upon it. I assure you that the shield before us is the very one I have been describing. After marking out the cross, just as you see it now, Josephus said to Evalach, 'Here is the shield I leave to you as a way to remember me. You will never look upon it without thinking of me, for you know that this cross is made of my own blood. For the life of the sword, the cross will remain as freshly painted and as bright as you see it today. It will endure a long time because no one will hang this shield from his shoulders without regretting it, not even a knight, until Galahad the Good Knight, the last in Nascien's line, wears it. Thus let no man other than God's chosen one be so impudent as to try it, and for the following reason: just as this shield produced greater wonders than any other, so too the chosen knight will demonstrate more amazing prowess and virtue than any other.'

"'Since you leave me such an apt token of remembrance,' said the king, 'tell me where you want me to keep the shield. I want to assure that it's placed where the Good Knight will find it.'

"'Here's what you should do,' said Josephus. 'After Nascien dies, leave the shield at the place where he's buried. The Good Knight will go to that spot on the fifth day after becoming a knight.'

"And thus did it happen as Josephus foretold. On the fifth day after you were knighted you came to the abbey where Nascien was buried. I have now told you why the wondrous adventures befell those foolishly audacious knights who, despite fair warning, tried to wear the shield destined only for you."

[*Galahad and the others had numerous adventures, and wise men explained their significance. The knights liberated the Castle of Maidens, in which many young women had been held captive for ten years.*]

9. Galahad Battles Lancelot and Perceval; A Knight Is Healed by the Grail.

Here the story says that Galahad, after leaving the Castle of the Maidens, rode for several days until he reached the Waste Forest.[6] One day he met Lancelot and Perceval, who were traveling together, though they did not recognize him for they had never seen his armor. Lancelot attacked first and broke his lance against Galahad's chest. Galahad then struck Lancelot so hard that he knocked him to the ground, along with his horse, but did them no further harm. Having broken his lance, he drew his sword and struck Perceval so hard that he split open his helmet and the chain mail hood beneath. If the sword had not slipped

---

[6]The "Waste Forest" appears in Chrétien de Troyes's *Conte du Graal* as the region inhabited by Perceval's mother. The term "Terre Gaste" (Waste Land) is used in the *Quest* to indicate the region occupied by Perceval's aunt before she secluded herself in the "Forest Gaste" (Waste Forest) to escape King Libran's attack. But the "Terre Gaste" also refers to the entire realm of Logres after King Varlan struck the fateful blow (*coup douloureux*) against King Lambor, father of the Maimed King also called Parlan or Pellehan. Pellehan is cited as Perceval's father in the *Quest*, but in the *Lancelot* he figures as the father of Pelles and grandfather of Galahad.

in his hand, he surely would have killed him. Even so, Perceval did not have the strength to remain in the saddle and flew to the ground. He was so weakened and stunned by the blow he had received that he did not know whether it was day or night. This conflict took place in front of a hermitage where a recluse lived.

When she saw Galahad leaving, she said, "May God protect you! In truth, if these knights knew you as well as I do, they would never have been so audacious as to attack."

Afraid that he might be recognized, Galahad spurred his horse into a gallop and sped away as quickly as possible. When the defeated knights realized that Galahad had departed, they mounted their horses as fast as they could, but soon saw that he was out of reach. They turned back in such dismay and anger that they wanted only to die, so disgusted were they with their fate. The two men then entered the Waste Forest.

Lancelot's dismay and anger at having lost the knight's trail lingered as he crossed the Waste Forest. "What can we do?" he asked Perceval, who had no advice to give. The knight had fled so rapidly that they would never be able to find him.

"You see yourself how nightfall has overtaken us," explained Perceval, "making it impossible for us to leave the forest without some luck. I think we're better off retracing our steps. For if we lose our way in here, it will be difficult to find the right road again. You can do as you wish, but I think we should turn back rather than push ahead."

Lancelot said that he could not readily agree to turn back. He would rather pursue the knight who carried the white shield, for he could never rest until he knew who he was.

"You can at least wait until tomorrow," said Perceval, "and we will pursue him together." Lancelot said he would have no part of it. "Then may God be with you," said Perceval, "because I'll go no farther, but will return instead to the recluse who said she knew him well."

The knights then parted company, as Perceval returned to the recluse and Lancelot pursued Galahad through the forest. Allowing chance to guide his way, Lancelot deserted the established trail and tried to follow a course of his own. But to his dismay, he could see no way to proceed, whether close by or in the distance, because of darkness of night.

He pushed on nonetheless until he reached a stone cross at the parting of two paths in a deserted place. Drawing near, he thought he saw beneath the cross a marble slab that bore an inscription. But it was so dark, he could not make out what the letters said. Beyond the cross, he saw an old chapel and started toward it, thinking he might find people there. Once he was close to the chapel, he dismounted, tethered his horse to an oak tree, removed his shield, and hung it from the tree. Approaching the chapel, he found it to be deserted and in ruins. As he was about to enter, he encountered an iron grate whose prongs were so closely joined that it would be difficult for anyone to enter. But he looked through the bars and saw an altar, richly adorned with silk cloth and other objects. In front of the altar a large silver candelabrum that held six lighted candles cast a bright light. The sight of it made him want to go inside and discover who lived there. He had never imagined that he would find such beautiful things in such a dismal place. But after reexamining the grill he confirmed that he could not open it, and with great sadness he left the chapel, returned to his horse, and led it by the reins to the cross. Removing the saddle and bridle, he allowed the horse to graze. He unlaced his helmet and placed it in front of him. He removed his sword and stretched out on his shield in front of the cross. Being tired, he quickly fell asleep, but did not forget the Good Knight who carried the white shield.

After some time had passed, Lancelot saw two horses approach, pulling a litter on which a sick knight moaned in agony. As the knight drew near, he stopped and looked at Lancelot but said nothing, for he believed him to be asleep. Lancelot, who was in that dreamy state between waking and sleep, said nothing either. The knight on the litter, who had stopped at the cross, began to lament loudly, saying, "My God! Will my pain ever cease? My God! When will the Holy Vessel, which can stem the violence of this pain, arrive? My God! No man has ever suffered such pain for so small a misdeed." The knight carried on this way for a long time, complaining to God about his hardship and suffering. Lancelot, who remained in a trancelike state, did not move or speak. But he saw the other knight clearly and heard what he said.

After a long time, Lancelot, who had been carefully surveying his surroundings, saw emerging from the chapel the silver candelabrum and candles, which he had previously observed inside. He watched the candelabrum move toward the cross, but to his amazement, no one was carrying it. Then he saw the Holy Vessel approach on a silver table, the same vessel he had seen at the Fisher King's palace. It was the one they called the Holy Grail.[7]

When the sickly knight saw the Vessel approach, he fell to the ground, clasped his hands, and said, "Dear God, who have accomplished so many miracles in this land and in others with the help of the Holy Vessel I see drawing near, Father, have mercy on me and alleviate the pain I suffer so that I too can undertake the quest that the other knights have begun." He dragged himself on his arms over to the marble slab which held the Holy Vessel on its silver table. He pulled himself up on two hands, kissed the silver table, and touched it with his eyes. His pain disappeared completely, and he cried out, "My God! I am healed!" And he fell quickly into sleep.

---

[7] The reference is to Lancelot's visit to Corbenic, just prior to the conception of Galahad in the *Lancelot*. See *Lancelot*, Chapter 33.

After a short time, the Vessel and candelabrum returned to the chapel, though Lancelot never understood who had carried them to and fro. Whether because he was so overcome with fatigue or because he was weighed down by the sins he had committed, Lancelot did not move or react at all when the Grail appeared. Later he was shamed for this and suffered for it in many ways during the Quest.

After the Holy Grail had entered the chapel, the knight on the litter stood up hale and hearty and kissed the cross. A squire then arrived bearing a splendid suit of armor. He approached the knight and asked how he was. "Very well, thank God!" the knight said. "I was cured as soon as the Holy Grail came to me. But I'm amazed by the knight who slept through the Grail's visit."

To tell the truth," replied the squire, "that knight is living under the weight of a great sin that he has never confessed. He happens to be so impure that Our Lord didn't want him to see this extraordinary event."

"Whoever he might be, he's an unfortunate soul," said the knight. "I believe he's one of the knights of the Round Table who have taken up the Quest for the Holy Grail."

"Sir, I have brought your armor," said the squire. "Put it on when you're ready." The knight acknowledged that he now had everything he needed. He donned the armor, including the mail leggings and the hauberk. The squire then picked up Lancelot's sword and helmet and gave them to the knight. He saddled and harnessed Lancelot's horse. When he had everything ready, he said, "Mount, my lord, you have a good sword and steed. I'm certain you will put the things I've given you to better use than did the wretched knight lying there."

The moon shone bright and clear; it was already past midnight. The knight asked the squire how he knew about the sword. He said he had presumed it was a good weapon because of its beauty. He had already withdrawn the sword from the sheath and found it to be so beautiful that he wanted to keep it for himself. Once the knight was fully armed and mounted on Lancelot's horse, he raised his hand toward the chapel and swore that, with the help of God and the saints, he would search until he understood how the Holy Grail had appeared on so many occasions in the realm of Logres and who had brought it to England and why. He would continue his quest until he or someone else learned the truth about these events.

"In God's name, that's well said," interrupted the squire. "May God grant that you finish this quest honorably and secure the salvation of your soul; surely you cannot sustain the quest for long without being in mortal danger."

"To die on this quest would be an honor, not a disgrace; no worthy man should refuse to undertake it, whether for fear of death or love of life." The knight left the cross in the company of his squire, carrying Lancelot's arms and heading off where adventure might take him.

[*Lancelot talked with a hermit and confessed his sin with the queen; he vowed never again to commit such sin.*]

10. The Recluse Reveals Her Identity to Perceval.

Now the story says that when Perceval and Lancelot parted ways, Perceval returned to the recluse from whom he hoped to hear news of Galahad, the knight who had escaped them. At first he could not find the path that would lead him there. But he went in what he thought was the right direction and arrived at the chapel. He knocked on the recluse's window and found she was not yet asleep. She leaned out and asked who he was. The recluse was delighted to learn that he was Perceval the Welshman, from King Arthur's court. She loved him dearly, as well she should, since he was her nephew.

The recluse ordered her people to open the door for the knight standing outside, feed him if he was hungry, and help him in every possible way, for she loved him more than any man on earth. Carrying out her orders, the residents unlocked the door, welcomed the knight, removed his armor, and served him a meal. When Perceval asked if he could speak to the recluse that day, they replied, "No, sir, but we think you can talk with her tomorrow after Mass." Without insisting further, Perceval lay down in the bed they had prepared for him and slept soundly through the night, since he was tired and worn out.

At daybreak Perceval got up and heard Mass celebrated by the resident priest. He then put on his armor and went to see the recluse. "Lady," he said, "in God's name give me news of the knight who passed this way yesterday, the one you said you had good reason to recognize. I can wait no longer to learn who he is." The lady asked why he wanted to know.

"Because I won't rest until I do battle with him. He wronged me so that I must pursue him to maintain my honor."

"Perceval!" she exclaimed, "what are you saying? That you want to fight with him? Do you want to die like your brothers, who were killed by their own rage? It would be such a pity for you to die as they did, and such a great loss to your family. Do you know what you would lose if you fought this knight? I'll tell you. You are one of the questers, I believe, on the Great Quest for the Holy Grail, which was begun recently and will soon end, whenever God wills it. You will achieve far greater honor than you can imagine simply by refusing to fight with this knight. For we are certain that in the end only three special knights will have the honor and glory of the quest. Two of them will be virgins and the third chaste. The knight you seek will be one of the virgins and you the other. The third will be Bors of Gaunes. The Quest will be completed by these three alone. Since God has prepared this honor for you, it would be a great pity if you met your death in the meantime. You will certainly hasten its arrival by fighting with the knight you're pursuing.

He is, without question, a better knight than you are, better in fact than any man."

Perceval replied, "My lady, it seems, based on your reference to my brothers, that you know who I am."

"I know you," she said, "and well I should. I am your aunt[8] and you my nephew. Don't let my humble surroundings confuse you; be assured that I was formerly the queen of the Waste Land. You saw me before under very different circumstances; I was one of the richest women in the world. However, my wealth never pleased me or suited me as much as the poverty I now experience."

Perceval began to weep with compassion, and, remembering his past, he recognized his aunt. He sat facing her and asked for news about his mother and his family. "Is it possible, dear nephew, that you've heard nothing about your mother?"

"No, my lady, nothing. I don't know whether she's dead or alive. Many times she has come to me in a dream and said she had more reason to chastise than to praise me, since I had mistreated her."

The lady answered in a sad and mournful voice, "Indeed, you will not see your mother again, except in a dream. She died the day you left for King Arthur's court."

"How did it happen, my lady?"

"As God is my witness," she said, "your mother was so dismayed by your departure that she died the very day you left, just after making confession."

"May God have mercy on her soul," said Perceval. "This truly weighs heavily on me. But since it has happened, I'll have to endure it, for death comes to us all eventually. But I had heard nothing of it before now. But in reference to the knight I'm tracking, do you know, in God's name, who he is or where he's from or whether he's the one who appeared at court in red arms?"

"Yes, I am certain that was he," replied the recluse. "It was fitting for him to go there, and I'll tell you why."

11. Perceval's Aunt Recounts the Story of the Three Tables.

"You know that since the time of Jesus Christ the world has seen three famous tables. The first was the table where Christ ate on several occasions with the apostles. This table sustained body and soul with the food of Heaven, and those who sat around it were brothers in body and soul. In his book the prophet David said a wonderful thing that pertains to these men: 'It is a good thing when brothers live together, united in one will and one work.'[9] Thanks

---

[8]Perceval's aunt, queen of the Wasteland, does not appear in Chrétien de Troyes's *Conte du Graal* or in *Lancelot*.
[9]Psalm CXXXIII. 1.

to the brothers who sat at this table and in whom one could see all good works, there reigned peace, harmony, and patience. The table was established by the Lamb without blemish who was sacrificed for our salvation.

"After this table, another was made that resembled the first and preserved its memory. It was the Table of the Holy Grail, which was responsible for the great miracles that took place at the time of Joseph of Arimathea, when Christianity was first brought to this land. Everyone, believers and nonbelievers alike, will remember these miracles. It happened that Joseph of Arimathea came to this land with a great following of about four thousand people, all of them poor. When they arrived, they were afraid there would not be sufficient food to feed them, since they were so numerous. One day they wandered into a forest where they found nothing to eat and no people at all, which distressed them greatly for they weren't used to it. They suffered through that day, and, after searching high and low the next day, they found an old woman who was taking twelve loaves of bread out of the oven. They bought the loaves. But when they attempted to divide them, anger and ill will broke out. They could not agree on how to proceed. When the event was recounted to Joseph, he became very angry and asked that the bread be brought to him. Those who had purchased the bread also came before him, and he learned from their own mouths that some were unwilling to agree with the others. Then Joseph ordered everyone to sit down as if they were at the Last Supper. He broke the bread, placing pieces here and there, and then put the Holy Grail at the head of the table. It caused the twelve loaves of bread to increase so that everyone, all four thousand people, could be wondrously nourished and fulfilled. They all thanked Our Lord for having helped them so demonstrably.

"At this table a seat was reserved for Joseph of Arimathea's son, Josephus. The seat was destined for their master and pastor alone. No one else was authorized to sit there, for it had been hallowed and blessed by the hand of Our Lord himself, as the story tells it, and had been invested with the authority that Josephus was to exercise over the Christian people. Our Lord had seated him in that chair, and no one else dared to sit there. This seat had been patterned after the seat that Our Lord occupied on the day of the Last Supper, when he appeared among his apostles as their master and pastor. Just as he was lord and master of his apostles, so should Josephus lead those who were sitting at the Table of the Holy Grail, as their lord and master.

"But it so happened that when they arrived in this land, after having wandered for a long time in foreign lands, two brothers, who were Josephus's relatives, were jealous that Our Lord favored Josephus over them and had chosen him as the best among them. They discussed it privately and decided that they could not bear to have him as their leader. Since they were from as distinguished a lineage as he, they would no longer serve as his disciples or call him their master.

"The following day, everyone climbed to the top of a hill where the tables were set up. When they asked Josephus to sit in the place of honor, the two brothers objected and, in front of everyone, one of them sat in the special seat himself. Then a miracle occurred: the earth swallowed up the brother who had taken Josephus's seat. As news of the miracle spread throughout the land, the seat became known as the Feared Seat. From that time on no one dared to sit there except the man Our Lord had chosen.[10]

"After the Table of the Holy Grail there came the Round Table, established according to Merlin's advice and laden with symbolic meaning. The name Round Table signifies the round shape of the earth and the disposition of the planets and other elements in the firmament where one sees stars and other heavenly bodies. One can thus rightly assert that the Round Table represents the world. You can see that to the extent that knights come to the Round Table from any country where chivalry exists, whether Christian or pagan. If God grants them the privilege of becoming a member of the Round Table, they consider themselves more fortunate than if they controlled the whole world. They abandon their fathers, mothers, wives, and children for it. You yourself have seen this happen. Ever since you left your mother and became a member of the Round Table, you have felt no desire to return but have been overcome instead by the tenderness and fraternity that exists among these companions.

12. Perceval's Aunt Recalls Merlin's Prophecies.

"When Merlin established the Round Table, he said that the truth of the Holy Grail, at that time a secret, would eventually be made known through the members of the Round Table. When he was asked how one could recognize the most worthy participants, he answered, 'Three questers will succeed: two of them virgins and the third one chaste. One of the three will surpass his father just as the lion surpasses the leopard in strength and courage. He will become the master and pastor of all the others. Until Our Lord sends this man among them with a suddenness that will take them by surprise, the members of the Round Table will waste their time searching for the Holy Grail.'

"When the people heard this they said, 'Merlin, since by your account this chosen one will be so extraordinarily valiant, you should create a special seat destined for him alone and make it much larger than the others, so it will be easily recognized.'

"'I will do that,' said Merlin. And he fashioned a large and wonderful seat among the others and then kissed it, saying he had done this for the love of the Good Knight who would sit there.

---

[10]The Feared seat at the Table of the Holy Grail is analogous to the Perilous Seat at the Round Table. This seat first appears in Robert de Boron's *Joseph d'Arimathie,* ed. William Nitze (Paris: Champion, 1927), ll. 2527–2530.

"Then the others asked, 'Merlin, what will happen to this seat?'

" 'Indeed,' he replied, 'many amazing things. No one will sit here without being killed or maimed until the True Knight takes his place on this seat.'

" 'So anyone attempting to sit there runs a great risk?' they asked.

" 'A perilous risk,' said Merlin. 'And for that reason the seat will be called the Perilous Seat.' "

Perceval's aunt then said, "Dear nephew, I have now told you why Merlin founded the Round Table and the Perilous Seat, which has killed many knights not worthy of sitting upon it. Now I will tell you how the Good Knight came to court wearing red armor.

"You know that Jesus Christ was master and pastor of his apostles at the Table of the Last Supper. Joseph served the same function at the Table of the Holy Grail, and this knight at the Round Table. Our Lord promised his apostles before the Passion that he would pay them a visit. They waited, sad and dismayed, for the promise to be fulfilled. On Pentecost, when they were gathered together in a house with the doors closed, the Holy Spirit descended among them in the form of fire to comfort them and allay their fears. Then it sent them out into the world to preach and teach the Holy Gospel. Thus did Our Lord visit and comfort the apostles on Pentecost.

"It seems to me that in the same way the Good Knight, whom you should hold as master and pastor, came to comfort you. Just as Our Lord appeared in the form of fire, so did the Good Knight appear in red armor the color of fire. And just as the doors of the house containing the apostles were closed when Our Lord entered, so too were the doors of the palace closed when the Good Knight came in. In fact, he appeared so suddenly that not even the wisest person among you could discern how he had entered. That very day the Quest for the Holy Grail and for the Lance was inaugurated,[11] a quest that will not cease until we learn the truth about the many adventures that have taken place in this land.

"I have told you the truth about this knight so that you will not fight with him. Indeed you must not, since you are his brother through your mutual participation in the Round Table and because you will never stand a chance against him; he's a much more accomplished knight than you are."

"Lady, you have told me enough to make me never want to engage him in battle," said Perceval. "But in God's name tell me what to do and how I might find him. If I could travel in his company I would never leave him."

---

[11]The lance, not mentioned in the initial oaths sworn by the questers, reappears at the end of the *Quest* during the Grail liturgy and the healing of the Maimed King (See below, Chapter 24).

[*Perceval had numerous adventures, and a hermit explained to him the Old and the New Laws. Perceval was tempted by a woman, but he repented his weakness. The story returns to Lancelot, who was berated for his sin and failure and who, after a tounament, was lost in the wilderness. Gawain and Hector traveled together and had visions that were later explained by a hermit. Bors too had strange visions, was tempted by a maiden, and was commanded by God to meet Perceval at the sea.*]

13. After a Tournament, Galahad Rides to the Magic Ship and Meets Bors and Perceval.

Now the story says that when the Good Knight left Perceval, after rescuing him from the twenty knights who had attacked him, he set out on the main road through the Waste Forest and wandered back and worth for many days, guided by chance adventures. He encountered and resolved many adventures, which the story does not recount at all, because it would take too long to tell them. After the Good Knight had ridden across the kingdom of Logres, seeking out every adventure he had heard about, he decided to change course and headed toward the sea. He happened to pass a castle where an extraordinary tournament was taking place. But the attackers had already shown such great prowess that the castle inhabitants were fleeing.

When Galahad saw that those inside were in deep trouble and were being killed at the castle gate, he headed toward them with the intention of helping. He lowered his lance, spurred his horse, and struck the first man he met so hard that he drove him to the ground as his lance flew to pieces. He then expertly took his sword in hand and attacked where the knights were thickest, striking down knights and horses and performing such extraordinary feats of arms that anyone watching would have deemed him a champion. Sir Gawain and Sir Hector had come to the tournament and were helping the attackers. But when they saw the white shield bearing a red cross, they said to each other, "That's the Good Knight! We would be fools to wait here for him; no armor can withstand his sword." As they spoke, as chance would have it, Galahad rode toward Sir Gawain and struck him so hard that he split his helmet and the chain mail coif beneath. Sir Gawain, who felt surely that he was dead from the blow he had received, lunged forward over the saddle horn. And Galahad, who could not restrain his thrust, struck Gawain's horse in front of the saddle horn, cutting so deeply into the animal's shoulders that it fell down dead on top of Sir Gawain.

Seeing Gawain on foot, Hector pulled back, for he knew that it was senseless to take on someone who could deal such blows, and because he was bound to protect and love Galahad as his nephew. Galahad, meanwhile, charged up and down and did so much in such a short time that the once-defeated castle inhabitants were now reinvigorated. They persevered in attacking and striking, until the outsiders were defeated by sheer force and fled to safety. Galahad pursued them for a long way, and once he was sure that none of them would return, he slipped away quietly so that no one knew where he had gone. But he carried off the praise and the prize of both parties in the battle. Sir Gawain, who was in such pain from the blow he had received from Galahad that he thought he would not survive, said to Hector, "On my honor, the words that were spoken to me on the day of Pentecost have now come true: that before the year was out, I would receive such a blow from the sword that I attempted to pull from the stone, that I would give a castle not to have been struck by it. I swear that this knight has struck me with that very sword. Thus can I say that the prediction has come true."[12]

Then Hector asked, "Has the knight really wounded you as severely as you claim?"

"Indeed," Gawain replied, "I won't recover without God's help."

"What are we to do, then?" Hector asked. "It seems that our quest is over, since you're wounded."

"Mine may be over, sir, but not yours. But I will follow you as long as God allows it."

While they were talking, the knights of the castle gathered together. When they recognized Sir Gawain, many were very distressed to see how severely wounded he was. For without a doubt, of all the world's men, he was the best liked by strangers. They took him up and carried him to the castle, removed his armor, and put him to bed in a quiet and peaceful room, far from other people. Then they sent for a physician and asked him to look at the wound to see whether he could heal it. The doctor assured them that he could restore Gawain to health; within a month the knight would be able to ride and bear arms. The knights of the castle promised that if the physician could do this, they would pay him enough to make him rich for the rest of his life. The doctor assured them that he would do as he said. So Sir Gawain stayed there along with Hector, who did not want to leave until Gawain was well.

The Good Knight, after leaving the tournament and riding where adventure might lead him, came that night within two leagues of Corbenic. As the sun set, he happened to be near a hermitage, so he dismounted and knocked at the hermit's door until it was opened for him. The hermit readily welcomed the knight errant, took care of stabling his horse, and removed his armor. He offered the knight what food God had provided him, and the Good Knight accepted it readily, having eaten nothing all that day. Then Galahad fell asleep on a bundle of hay.

When the two men had gone to bed, a young woman knocked at the door and called to Galahad until the good man rose and asked who it was that

---

[12]The prediction was made in Chapter 2 of the *Quest for the Holy Grail*.

wanted to enter the hermitage at such an hour. The young woman replied, "Sir Ulfin, I want to talk to the knight who is inside. I am in great need of his help."

The worthy man woke Galahad and said, "Sir knight, a young woman who seems in great need of your help wants to speak with you. She is outside." Galahad got up, went to the woman, and asked what she wanted.

"Galahad," she said, "I want you to arm yourself, mount your horse, and follow me. I promise to show you the most lofty adventure that a knight has ever seen." When Galahad heard this, he took up his armor and put it on. He saddled his horse, mounted, and bade the hermit farewell, saying to the young woman, "Now you can go where you wish. I'll follow you anywhere." She galloped away as fast as her saddle horse would carry her, with Galahad close behind. They rode until dawn. As the sun shone brightly, they entered a forest called Celibe, which extended to the sea. They followed the main road all day without stopping to eat or drink.

In the evening, after vespers, they came to a castle set in a valley. The castle was well furnished in all respects and surrounded by flowing water, good strong walls, and deep moats. The young woman, still leading the knight, entered the castle with Galahad behind her. Seeing the lady approach, the castle inhabitants welcomed her and received her with great rejoicing, for she was their lady. She told them to make much of the knight, since he was the most valiant knight ever to carry arms. As soon as they had helped him dismount, they hurried to remove his armor. Galahad asked the lady, "Are we going to stay here today?"

"No," she replied. "As soon as we have eaten and slept a little, we'll be off." Then they sat down to eat, and afterward went to sleep. No sooner had the lady fallen into her first slumber than she woke up and called out to Galahad, "Get up, sir!" and he did. The castle inhabitants brought candles and torches so he could see to arm himself, and he mounted his steed. The lady picked up a beautiful and lavish chest, which she set in front of her after she too had mounted her horse.

They left the castle and rode at a fast pace through the night until they came to the sea. There they found Bors and Perceval waiting at the edge of their ship, not asleep, but shouting to Galahad from a distance, "Welcome, sir! We have waited for you so long, and here you are at last, thank God! Come ahead, for nothing remains but to seek the lofty adventure that God has prepared for us."

When Galahad heard them, he asked who they were and why they claimed they had been waiting for him so long. Then he asked the young woman whether she would dismount. "Yes," she replied, "and leave your horse here as I will do, too." Galahad dismounted, removed the saddle and bridle from his horse, and did the same for the young woman's palfrey. He crossed himself on the forehead and commended himself to Our Lord. Then he entered the ship followed by the young woman. The two companions gave them the warmest and most joyous welcome. Then the ship began to sail swiftly out to sea, propelled by a strong wind. When day broke, the knights recognized each other, and all three wept tears of joy at finding themselves thus reunited.

Bors removed his helmet; Galahad took off his helmet and sword, but wished to retain his hauberk. As he looked at the ship, which was so beautiful both inside and out, he asked his two companions if they knew where such an extraordinary ship might have come from. Bors said he had no idea. Perceval explained what he knew of it, recounting what had happened to him on the rock, including how the good man, whom he thought to be a priest, had bade him enter the ship. "Indeed, he said that it would not be long before you two would join me, though he said nothing of this young woman."

"Upon my word," said Galahad, "I don't think I would ever have come here if she hadn't guided me. That means that I came more because of her than on my own. I have never traveled this road before, and I never thought I would hear news of you, my companions, in such a strange place as this." At this they began to laugh.

Then each knight recounted his adventures to the others until Bors said to Galahad, "If only your father, Sir Lancelot, were here, I feel we would want nothing more." But Galahad replied that this was not God's will.

14. Perceval Meets His Sister on a Second Magic Ship.

Conversing this way, they drifted until the hour of nones. They must have been some distance from the kingdom of Logres, because the ship had sped through that night and the following day under full sail. Finally, they arrived at an island wilderness, wonderfully secluded between two cliffs in what must have been a bay.

There they spied another ship, behind one of the cliffs, which could not be reached except on foot. "Good sirs," said the young woman, "in that other ship lies the adventure for which Our Lord brought you together. You'll have to leave this ship and go to that one." They consented willingly and left the ship, helping the young woman out, too. Then they tied fast their ship so the waves would not set it adrift. Once they were on the rock, they went single file in the direction of the other ship. When they reached it, they found it to be even more lavish than the one they had come from. Yet they marveled at finding no one there.

As they drew nearer to see what they could discover, they found on the side of the ship an inscription in Chaldean that would inspire fear and trembling in anyone wishing to board the vessel. The inscription read, YOU WHO WISH TO ENTER ME, WHOEVER YOU MAY BE, BE CERTAIN THAT YOU ARE FULL OF FAITH, FOR I AM NOTHING BUT FAITH. AND FOR THIS REASON, BE SURE BEFORE YOU ENTER THAT YOU ARE WITHOUT BLEMISH. FOR I AM NOTHING BUT

FAITH AND BELIEF. IF YOU DESERT YOUR FAITH, THEN I WILL ABANDON YOU, AND YOU WILL RECEIVE NO SUSTENANCE OR HELP FROM ME. RATHER, EVERY-THING WILL BE LACKING TO YOU WHENEVER YOU FALL INTO DISBELIEF, HOWEVER SLIGHTLY YOU ARE AFFLICTED BY IT.

After reading the inscription, they looked at one another. Then the young woman said to Perceval, "Do you know who I am?"

"Certainly not," he replied, "I don't believe I've ever seen you before."

"Be assured that I am your sister, daughter of King Pellehan. And do you know why I have revealed my identity to you? So that you will more readily believe what I have to tell you. I will say first of all," she said, "to you whom I hold dearest, that unless you believe fully in Jesus Christ, you cannot enter this ship, or you will perish immediately. The ship is such a lofty place that no one marked with evil vice can stay in it without facing danger."

Hearing these words, Perceval looked closely at the young woman until he recognized her to be his sister. He then rejoiced and said to her, "Indeed, dear sister, I will enter the ship, and do you know why? So that if I lack faith, I may die there a faithless man, or if I am filled with faith, as a knight should be, I may be saved."

"Enter then," she said, "with the knowledge that Our Lord will protect and defend you."

15. The Knights Discover the Magic Sword.

Galahad, who was nearest the ship, crossed himself and went aboard. While he was looking around the ship's interior, the young woman crossed herself and stepped on board. Then Bors and Perceval boarded without delay. As they examined the ship's interior, they exclaimed that there could be no vessel on land or sea as beautiful and lavish as this one. After searching the entire ship, they looked toward the center, where they found a rich cloth hung like a curtain around a large and sumptuous bed.

When Galahad approached and lifted the canopy, he discovered the most beautiful bed he had ever seen. It was vast and luxurious. At its head was a crown of fine gold, and at its foot lay a beautiful, shining sword, partially withdrawn from its scabbard.

The sword had various peculiarities: the pommel was made of a stone containing all the colors on earth. And it had another more precious aspect: each color contained a virtue of its own. The story tells further that the hilt was formed from the ribs of two beasts. The first was a kind of serpent called a *papalustes,* found more often in Caledonia than elsewhere. This serpent was such that anyone holding one of its ribs or its bones would be protected from feeling extreme heat. The other rib on the sword hilt was from a medium-sized fish found in the Euphrates river and called the ortenax. As soon as any-one takes hold of one of this fish's ribs, he can remember no joy or pain he has experienced, but only the reason he took hold of the rib. As soon as he puts it down, however, he will regain the thoughts of a normal man. These were the properties of the two ribs that were set in the sword hilt and covered with the most sumptuous red cloth, which in turn was covered with letters that read, I AM A MARVEL TO SEE AND KNOW, FOR NO ONE HAS EVER BEEN ABLE TO SEE OR GRIP ME, AND NEVER WILL, NO MATTER HOW LARGE HIS HAND, EXCEPT ONE MAN ONLY. AND THIS MAN WILL SURPASS IN SKILL ALL THOSE WHO HAVE COME BEFORE HIM AND ALL WHO WILL FOLLOW AFTERWARD.

This is what the inscription on the hilt said. And as soon as those who were able to decipher it had read it, they looked at one another and said, "In truth, there are wonders to be seen here."

"In God's name," said Perceval, "I will try to grasp this sword." And he placed his hand on the sword but was unable to grip the hilt. "On my honor," he said, "I think the inscription speaks the truth." Then Bors tried his hand at it but could do nothing. So the two knights said to Galahad, "You try this sword, sir. We are certain that you will complete this adventure since we have failed at it." But Galahad refused.

"I see something more amazing here than I have ever seen," he said. And, looking at the sword blade, which, as you have heard, was withdrawn slightly from its scabbard, he saw another inscription, as red as blood, which read, LET NO ONE BE SO BOLD AS TO DRAW ME FROM THIS SCABBARD UNLESS HE CAN FIGHT BETTER AND MORE BOLDLY THAN ANYONE ELSE. WHOEVER MIGHT DRAW ME OUT SHOULD KNOW THAT HE WILL BE KILLED OR WOUNDED. THIS HAS ALREADY HAPPENED ONCE.

When Galahad saw this, he said, "Upon my word, I intended to draw this sword, but since the prohibition is so strong, I won't touch it." Perceval and Bors said the same thing. "Dear sirs," said the young woman, "know that drawing the sword is prohibited to all but one man. I will tell you how this came to pass not long ago."

16. Perceval's Sister Recounts the Story of the Sword.

"The truth is," the young woman continued, "that this ship arrived in the kingdom of Logres at a time when a bloody war was raging between King Lambor, father of the man called the Maimed King, and King Varlan, who had been a pagan all his life but had recently converted to Christianity and was then considered one of the finest men alive. One day it happened that King Lambor and King Varlan assembled their armies on the shore where the ship had landed. King Varlan was losing the fight, and when he saw his men being killed and realized his defeat, he began to fear for his life. So he went to the ship, which was beached on the shore, and leapt onto it. He found the sword, withdrew it from the scabbard, and returned to shore, where he met King Lambor. a Christian of intense faith and belief who had the Lord within him.

When King Varlan saw King Lambor, he raised the sword and struck his helmet so hard that he split the knight and his horse in two. This was the first blow struck by that sword in the kingdom of Logres. And there resulted from it such a great pestilence and persecution in both kingdoms that the earth no longer produced when cultivated. From that time on, no wheat or other grain grew there, no tree gave fruit, and very few fish were found in the sea. For this reason, the two kingdoms were called the Waste Land; they had been laid waste by this unfortunate blow.[13]

"When King Varlan saw how effective the sword was, he considered going back to retrieve the scabbard. So he returned to the ship and replaced the sword in its sheath. But then he immediately fell down dead beside the bed. Thus was it proved that no one would draw this sword without being killed or maimed. The king's body remained beside the bed until a young maid removed it, for no man dared to enter the ship because of the prohibition inscribed on its side."

"Upon my word," said Galahad, "this is a remarkable adventure, and I believe it happened as you recount. For I'm convinced that this sword is more amazing than any other." And as Galahad approached to withdraw it, the young woman said, "Wait, Galahad, wait a little while, until we have seen the marvels it contains." Galahad pulled back his hand, and they all began to examine the scabbard, not knowing what it could be made of, unless it was snakeskin. They noticed, however, that it was red as a rose petal and inscribed with letters, some gold and others blue. But when they came to look at the sword belt, their amazement increased. For it was hardly suited to the splendor of the weapon, being of such poor material as hemp cord, and so weak that it seemed it would not support the sword for an hour without breaking.

The inscription on the scabbard read, THE MAN WHO WILL CARRY ME MUST BE MORE VALIANT AND CONFIDENT THAN ANY OTHER IF HE IS TO CARRY ME AS PURELY AS HE SHOULD. I CANNOT BE TAKEN TO ANY VILE OR SINFUL PLACE. HE WHO WOULD PUT ME IN SUCH A PLACE WILL BE THE FIRST TO REGRET IT. BUT IF HE TAKES PROPER CARE OF ME, HE CAN GO EVERYWHERE SAFELY. THE MAN WHO HAS ME AT HIS SIDE CANNOT BE VANQUISHED AS LONG AS HE IS GIRDED WITH THE BELT FROM WHICH I HANG. LET NO ONE BE SO BOLD AS TO REMOVE THIS BELT. NO MAN IS AUTHORIZED TO DO SO NOW OR IN THE FUTURE. IT CAN BE REMOVED ONLY BY THE HAND OF A WOMAN, DAUGHTER OF A KING AND QUEEN. SHE WILL REPLACE IT WITH ANOTHER BELT MADE

---

[13]Although a number of texts attribute the Waste Land to the Dolorous Stroke, the circumstances of the latter vary widely. In many cases, including Malory, the blow was delivered by Balain. Typically the dolorous stroke reduces the kingdom of Logres to a wasteland and causes the maimed king to languish in ill health for many years until he is cured by Galahad. The Dolorous Blow sequence from the Post-Vulgate Cycle is given later in this volume.

FROM THE THING ON HER PERSON THAT SHE VALUES MOST. AND IT IS IMPOR-
TANT THAT THE YOUNG WOMAN BE A VIRGIN FOR LIFE, BOTH IN DESIRE AND
IN DEED. IF SHE LOSES HER VIRGINITY, LET HER BE ASSURED THAT SHE WILL
DIE THE MOST VILE DEATH THAT A WOMAN CAN SUFFER. THIS YOUNG WOMAN
WILL CALL THE SWORD BY ITS RIGHTFUL NAME, AND ME BY MINE, SOMETHING
NO ONE WILL BE ABLE TO DO UNTIL THAT TIME.

Once the companions had read the inscription, they began to laugh, say-
ing that these were extraordinary things to see and hear. Then Perceval said,
"Turn the sword over, sir, and see what is on the other side." And when he
turned it over, he discovered that it was blood red and held an inscription that
said, HE WHO WILL PRAISE ME THE MOST WILL BLAME ME MORE IN TIME OF
NEED THAN HE MIGHT IMAGINE; AND I WILL BE MOST CRUEL TO HIM TO
WHOM I SHOULD BE MOST HELPFUL. THIS WILL HAPPEN ONLY ONCE, FOR
THAT IS AS IT SHOULD BE.

When the companions saw these words inscribed on the reverse side of
the scabbard, they were more baffled than before. "In God's name," Perceval
said to Galahad, "I intended to encourage you to seize this sword. But since
the inscription indicates that it will fail in time of need and be cruel when it
should be kind, I would not now allow you to take it. It could dishonor you
with a single blow, which would be a great pity."

When the young woman heard this, she said to Perceval, "Brother dear,
these things have already happened, and I will tell you when and who experienced them. No one should be afraid to seize this sword, provided he is worthy of it.

"It happened long ago, a good forty years after the Passion of Jesus
Christ, that Nascien, King Mordrain's brother-in-law, was carried by the will
of God in a cloud, on a fourteen-day journey away from his land. He arrived
at an island known as the Turning Isle, out toward the western kingdom, and
found the ship we are standing in at the foot of a cliff. After entering the ship,
he discovered the bed and the sword that you see here. He looked at the sword
for a long while, overcome with an intense desire to have it for himself. But
he lacked the courage to withdraw it. Tormented by his ambition and desire to
possess the sword, he spent a week in the ship without eating or drinking
much of anything.

"At week's end a strange and mighty wind blew him off the Turning Isle
and carried him to a far-distant western island. He sailed right up to a cliff and
then went ashore to meet the largest and most amazing giant in the world,
who was shouting at him that he was a dead man. Nascien feared for his life
when he saw this monster running toward him. Looking around, he saw nothing he could use to defend himself. Hounded by mortal fear and anguish, he
ran for the sword and drew it from the scabbard. When he saw the naked
blade, he valued it more than anything in the world. But when he brandished
it and struck the first blow, the sword snapped in two. Then Nascien began to

reproach the very thing he had most admired in all the world, and rightly so, for it had failed him in his hour of need.

"Nascien placed the broken sword pieces on the bed and left the ship to fight the giant, whom he killed. When he returned to the ship, a chance wind caught the sail and blew him out to sea where he met another ship carrying King Mordrain, who had been assailed by the devil on the cliffs of the Perilous Port. When the two men saw each other, they rejoiced heartily, for they loved each other dearly. They inquired about each other's health and the adventures they had had, until Nascien said at last, 'Sir, I don't know what you'll tell me about your worldly adventures, but since you last saw me, I've had a most extraordinary adventure which, I believe, has been experienced by no one else.' Then he told the story of the magnificent sword, how it broke when he needed it most, just when he hoped to kill the giant.

"'Indeed,' Mordrain said, 'this is an amazing tale. And what did you do with the sword?'

"'I put it back where I found it,' Nascien replied. 'You can see it if you wish; it's inside the ship.' Mordrain stepped from his ship to Nascien's, and drew near the bed. When he saw the pieces of the broken sword, he admired it more than anything he had ever seen. Then he explained that the break was due not to a defect or weakness in the sword, but to some hidden meaning or some sin of Nascien's. Then he put the two parts of the sword together, and as soon as the metal pieces were joined, the sword fused together as easily as it had snapped. Mordrain smiled and said, 'In God's name, how wonderful is the power of Jesus Christ who mends and breaks more easily than we can imagine!'

"Mordrain returned the blade to its scabbard and placed it where you see it now. Then a voice spoke to the men, saying, 'Leave this ship and enter the other one, for if you have sinned and are found on this vessel, you will not escape alive.' As they were departing, Nascien was struck so hard in the shoulder with a flying sword that he fell backward, shouting, 'My God, I'm wounded!'

"Then a voice said to him, 'This is for the wrong you did in drawing the sword. You shouldn't have attempted it, for you were unworthy. Next time, be more careful not to offend your Maker.'

"This is how the prophecy written here came true: 'He who will admire me most will reproach me in time of need,' just as I have described. The man who most admired the sword was Nascien, and it failed him in his hour of need, as I have explained."

"In God's name," said Galahad, "you have given us a thorough account of this incident. Now tell us about the other one."

"Of course," said the young woman.

"The truth is," she began, "that as long as he was able to ride, King Parlan, whom they call the Maimed King, greatly furthered the Christian cause: he honored the poor more than anyone else and lived more piously than any other Christian. But one day he was hunting in one of his woods, which stretched to the sea, and lost sight of his hounds, his huntsmen, and all his knights, except one who was his cousin. Realizing that he had strayed from all his companions, he did not know what to do, for he was too deep in the forest to find his way out. So he and his knight set out and wandered until they reached the sea that faced Ireland. There he found this very ship, came on board, and discovered the inscription that you have read. But King Parlan was not dismayed, for he believed he had served Jesus Christ with all his ability as an earthly knight. So he entered the ship alone, his chivalric companion not being bold enough to go with him. As soon as King Parlan found the sword, he drew it partially from the scabbard as you can see—before that the blade was not visible at all—and fully expected to withdraw it completely. But a lance entered the ship and struck him so hard between the thighs that he was wounded, as he still is today, and was never able to recover from it, and will not recover before you see him. Thus was he maimed for his audacity. And it was to avenge this act, they say, that the sword was cruel to him when it should have been kind, though he was the best and most valiant knight who ever lived."

"In God's name, lady," her listeners responded, "you have shown us clearly that these inscriptions should not prevent us from taking up the sword."

They looked closely at the bed and saw that it was made of wood but had no bedding. On the side of the bed facing them, there was a spindle, sticking straight up from the beam that ran the length of the bed, at its midpoint. On the other side, across from this spindle there was another, also standing straight up. The distance between the two equaled the width of the bed. And on them lay a thin crosspiece, which was squared off and attached to both spindles. The upright on the front side was whiter than new-fallen snow, and the one behind it was as red as drops of blood. The crosspiece was as green as an emerald. Be assured that the colors of the three spindles over the bed were natural, not artificial; they had not been painted by human hand, either male or female. But since many listeners might find this tale hard to believe if they were not told just how this could have happened, the story here veers away from its straight path and its rightful subject to describe the three colored spindles.

17. The Legend of the Tree of Life.

Now the story of the Holy Grail says that when the sinful Eve, the first woman, took advice from her mortal enemy the devil, who from then on deceived the human race, he incited her to commit the sin of covetousness, for which he himself had been thrown out of paradise and had fallen from heavenly glory. He did so by inspiring in her the impious desire to pick the mortal fruit from the tree and the tree branch along with it. For it often happens that the branch remains attached to the fruit when it is picked. And as soon as she brought the fruit to her husband Adam, whom she had advised and encouraged to eat it, he grasped it and broke off the branch, consuming the fruit at his peril and our own. This act resulted in his destruction and ours as well. And when Adam pulled the fruit off the branch, as you have heard, the branch remained in his wife's hand, for it happens sometimes that we hold an object without even realizing it. As soon as they had eaten from the deadly fruit, which should rightly be termed deadly, for it caused the death of these two and all others after them, it completely transformed their nature: they now saw that they had naked bodies. Previously, they were spiritual beings, although in possession of a body. Of course, the story does not affirm that Adam and Eve had been purely spiritual; anything made of so lowly a substance as clay cannot be pure spirit. Yet they had resembled spiritual beings, since they were destined to live forever as long as they did not sin. But when they looked at themselves and saw they were naked, they discovered their shameful members. Looking at each other made them feel the force of their misdeed. So they each covered the basest parts of themselves with their hands. Yet Eve continued to hold the branch that had detached from the fruit, and she never let it go.

When He who knows everyone's thoughts and desires learned that the first couple had sinned, He came to them, speaking first to Adam. It was reasonable that he be held more accountable than his wife, since she was of a weaker disposition, having been made from the man's rib. It made sense that she should be obedient to him rather than him to her. And for this reason God addressed Adam first. And once He had uttered the fateful words, "You will earn your bread by the sweat of your brow,"[14] He did not want the woman to escape unscathed; she too should partake of the punishment since she had participated in the offense. So God said to her, "You will bear children in pain and suffering." Then he threw them both out of paradise, which the Scriptures call the garden of delights. Once expelled from paradise, Eve discovered that she still held the branch in her hand, though she had not realized it until then. And it was still green, for it had just been picked, and it reminded her that the tree from which the branch had been taken was the reason for her exile and her misery. So she vowed to keep the branch as long as she could, in remembrance of the great loss she had suffered through that tree. She would look upon it often as a reminder of her great misfortune.

Then Eve realized that she had no chest or other box to put the branch in; at that time no such object existed. So she stuck it into the ground, straight up,

---

[14]This passage follows in large part Genesis III, 1–23, with one major modification: in the Bible, Adam is forbidden to eat from the Tree of Knowledge, whereas in the *Quest*, Eve picks the forbidden fruit from the Tree of Life.

thinking that this way she would see it often. But the branch that had been thrust into the ground came to life, took root, and grew by the will of our Creator who has dominion over all things.

This branch, which the first sinner brought with her out of paradise, was charged with meaning. The fact that she carried it in her hand signaled a great happiness, as if she were speaking to her heirs who were yet to come, for she was still a virgin. The branch sent them the following message: "Do not dismay that we have been cast out from our inheritance; we have not lost it forever. Take this branch as a sign that we will retrieve it some day." And whoever might question the book about why the woman and not the man carried the branch out of paradise, since the man is a superior being, would learn that it was more fitting for the woman to carry the branch. To have her hold it would signify that the life that was lost by a woman would later be restored by a woman, meaning that the inheritance that had been lost at that time would be restored through the Virgin Mary.

Now the story returns to the branch that stayed in the ground, explaining that it grew and expanded so much that in a short while it became a large tree. When it had developed into an ample shade tree, its trunk, branches, and leaves were white as snow, which signified virginity. Virginity is the virtue that keeps the body clean and the soul pure. The fact that the tree was completely white means that the woman who planted it was still a virgin at the time of planting. Indeed, when Adam and Eve were expelled from paradise, they were still virgins and free from the filthiness of lust.

Be assured that virginity and maidenhood[15] are not identical, but distinctly different. Maidenhood cannot be equated with virginity for the following reason: maidenhood is a virtue shared by all men and women who have not experienced carnal relations. But virginity is a loftier thing and more virtuous. It cannot be found in any man or woman who has even felt a desire for carnal coupling. Yet at the moment of her expulsion from paradise and the great delights it held, Eve possessed this kind of virginity. And when she planted the branch, she had not yet lost her virginity. Only later did God order Adam to know his wife, meaning that he should lie with her carnally, just as nature requires a man to lie with his wife and a woman with her lord. Thus did Eve lose her virginity, and from then on the couple were one flesh.

A long while after Adam knew his wife, as you have heard, it happened that the two were sitting beneath the tree. As Adam looked up at it, he began to lament his suffering and exile. Then they both began to weep bitterly for each other. And Eve said it was not surprising that the place reminded them of their pain and worry, since the tree contained those things within it. Indeed,

---

[15]The Old French words are *virginitez* and *pucelages;* both refer to a virgin state, but the author of the *Quest* draws a moral distinction between them.

no one, no matter how happy, could sit beneath it without feeling sad when he left. It was only right that they were unhappy, for this was the Tree of Death. No sooner had Eve uttered these words than a voice spoke to the couple, "Miserable wretches! Why do you predict and foretell death to each other? Do not prejudge things as hopeless, but comfort each other, for the tree has more life than death in it." Thus did the voice speak to the two unfortunate souls, and they were so comforted by it that from then on they called the tree the Tree of Life. And because of the great joy it gave them, they planted many more trees from this one. As soon as they broke off a twig, they stuck it into the earth, where it came to life and readily took root, retaining the color of the original tree.

The original tree continued to grow and develop, and Adam and Eve sat beneath it more readily and more often than they had before, until one day, when they had been sitting together beneath it for a long while—the true story says it was a Friday—they heard a voice tell them that they should engage in carnal union. Both Adam and Eve were so overcome with shame that their eyes could not bear to watch each other do such a vile deed. The man felt as ashamed as the woman. Yet they did not know how they would defy the order of Our Lord, for they were still suffering the punishment of disobeying his first command. As they looked at each other with great shame, Our Lord saw their embarrassment and took pity on them. But since His command could not be breached, and because He wanted these two to establish the human race and restore the tenth legion of angels who had fallen from heaven because of their pride, He comforted them in their shame. He placed between them a darkness so thick that they could not see each other. The couple were amazed that this darkness had materialized between them so suddenly. They called to each other and touched each other without being able to see. Because everything must be accomplished according to the will of Our Lord, it was necessary that their bodies come together in carnal union, as the true Father had ordered. When they had lain together, they created a new seed in which their great sin was somewhat remedied. Adam had engendered and his wife had conceived Abel the Just, who first served his Creator by loyally rendering Him his tithes.

Thus was Abel the Just engendered beneath the Tree of Life, on a Friday, as you have heard. Then the darkness faded and the couple saw each other as before. They realized that Our Lord had done this to hide their shame, and they were delighted. Then an amazing thing happened. The Tree, which had been completely white, became as green as grass, and all the saplings that derived from it under this union had green trunks and leaves and bark.

Thus did the Tree change from white to green. But the saplings that had descended previously from it retained their original color. By contrast, the Tree of Life, having become thoroughly green, began from that day forward to flower and give fruit, though it had never done so before. The fact that the tree lost its white color and became green signifies that the woman who planted it had lost her virginity. The green color it took on and the flower and fruit represent the seed that had been sown beneath it, which would always be green in Our Lord; that is to say it would always have pious thoughts and feel love toward its Creator. The flower signifies that the creature engendered beneath this Tree would be chaste and clean and pure in body. The fruit signifies that he will work diligently and will exemplify the cause of religion and goodness in all his worldly deeds.

The Tree remained green for a long time, along with the saplings that derived from it after the couple's union. When Abel grew up, he was so devoted to his Creator and loved Him so much that he offered Him the tithes and the first fruits of the finest things he had. But his brother Cain offered the most vile and most despicable things he had. As a result, Our Lord gave a wonderful blessing to the one who had given the finest tithes, so that when Abel climbed the hill where he customarily burned his offerings, as Our Lord had commanded, the smoke rose straight up to heaven. But the smoke from Cain's offerings spread out through the fields, black and stinking, in contrast to the white and sweet-smelling smoke from Abel's sacrifice. When Cain realized that his brother Abel was more blessed for his sacrifice, which the Lord received more willingly than his own, he was very distraught and came to hate his brother beyond measure. Cain began to plot ways to take revenge and even considered murdering his brother, for he did not see how else he might be fully avenged.

[*It is explained that, after the death of Abel at Cain's hand, prefiguring the death of Christ, the Tree of Life turned completely red, and all the shoots taken from it always died.*]

18. The Tree of Life Throughout Time.

For a long while the Tree retained the color and beauty that you have heard me describe. It never grew old, or withered, or deteriorated at all, except that it bore no flower or fruit after the hour of Abel's death. But the saplings that grew from it flourished and bore fruit, as trees naturally do. The original Tree remained as it was until the people of the earth had increased and multiplied. The descendants of Adam and Eve had great reverence for it; all of them honored it. One generation told the next how the first mother had planted it, and young and old found solace there. They came to be comforted when they were in distress, and because it was called the Tree of Life, it held happy memories for them. And as this Tree grew and flourished, so did all its offshoots, the white ones and the green ones. No one dared remove a twig or leaf from it.

Then another extraordinary thing happened to this Tree. When Our Lord sent the great flood to earth, by which the world perished in its wickedness, the fruits of the earth and the forests and ploughlands suffered such ravages that they lost their original sweetness; everything took on a bitter taste. But the trees that had grown from the Tree of Life bore no sign of harm, whether in flavor or fruit or change of color.

These trees survived until the time when Solomon, son of King David, ruled over his father's land.[16] Solomon was so wise that he possessed all the knowledge a mortal man can have. He knew the properties of precious stones and herbs, and he knew the course of the heavens and the stars nearly as well as God himself. Yet all this wisdom could not withstand the scheming of his wife. She deceived him often, whenever she wanted. And this should surprise no one. For it is well known that as soon as a woman turns her thoughts to deceit, no man's good sense can stop her. This is not new to our time, but dates back to the first mother.

19. Solomon's Wife Suggests How to Signal that Galahad Is Anticipated.

When Solomon saw that he could not protect himself from his wife's wiles, he marveled at how this could happen and was angered by it. But he did not dare to address the matter. He states in his book, called the Parables,[17] "I have circled the globe and searched it as thoroughly as any man can, but in all my wandering I have not found one good woman." Solomon made this statement out of anger toward his own wife, whom he could not resist. Though he tried in varied ways to change her disposition, nothing worked. Realizing this, he began to ask himself why women were so willing to anger men. And as he was thinking it over, a voice answered his question, saying, "Solomon, Solomon, if woman was and continues to be the source of man's sadness, do not let it bother you. For a woman will also bring to man a joy that is one hundred times greater than his sadness, and this woman will issue from your family line."

When Solomon heard this, he realized he had been a fool to blame his wife. He began to ponder the visions he had while sleeping and awake to see if he could learn the truth about the end of his line. He searched and thought for so long that the Holy Spirit finally showed him the coming of the glorious Virgin, and a voice revealed to him part of what was to come. Then Solomon

---

[16]*The History of the Holy Grail* also recounts—though not in the excerpts we include—the story of Solomon and the ship, although with significantly greater emphasis on the perfidy of his wife and of women in general.

[17]The term *parable* is used in the Lancelot-Grail Cycle to identify the book of Proverbs.

asked if that would be the end of his line. "No," the voice replied, "a virgin man will be the last in your line. He will be as superior in knighthood to your brother-in-law Joshua[18] as the Virgin will be superior to your wife. Now I have verified what has been troubling you for so long."

Solomon was very pleased to hear that the last descendant of his line would be rooted in such virtue and high valor. He thought about how he might communicate to the last man in his line that he, Solomon, who had lived so long before him, had known that he was coming. He pondered this for a long time but did not see how he could possibly announce to a man who was to come so long after him that he had known anything at all about him. Solomon's wife saw that he was attempting the impossible. She loved him dearly (though many wives love their husbands more), and she was very shrewd. She did not want to ask him immediately, but waited for the right occasion, until one evening when she saw he was happy and joyful and in a good mood. Then she asked if he would tell her what she wanted to know. He said he would indeed, without suspecting what she had in mind. So she said to him, "Sir, you've been thinking all this week and last, and for a long time before, without giving your mind a rest. So I know that you've been pondering a problem that you can't solve, and I would like to learn what it is. For there's nothing in the world that I cannot solve with your great wisdom and my great shrewdness."

Solomon considered the offer, thinking that if any human mind could help him solve this matter, it would certainly be his wife. He had found her to be more shrewd than anyone he could think of. So he confided in her. And once he had told her the truth of the matter, she thought for a moment and then replied, "What? You can't figure out how to convey to this knight that you know about his coming?"

"Indeed," Solomon replied, "I can't imagine how it could be done. It's the length of time from now to then that puzzles me."

"Upon my word," she said, "I'll tell you the answer, since you can't figure it out. But first tell me how long you think it will be before he arrives."

Solomon said he thought it would be more than two thousand years. "I'll tell you what to do," she continued. "Have a ship built of the best and most durable wood that will not rot from water or other substances." Solomon agreed.

The following day, Solomon called together all the carpenters in his land and ordered them to make the finest ship they had ever seen out of wood that would not rot. They agreed to follow his instructions, began searching for wood and timbers, and soon started to build. Then Solomon's wife said to

---

[18]Solomon's brother-in-law is an imaginary figure. Here reference seems to be to Joshua. the valiant warrior who succeeded Moses.

him, "Because the knight you have described is destined to surpass in valor all those who have preceded him and those who will follow afterward, it would be a great honor to him if you fashioned some armor for him that would surpass all other armor, in the same way that he will surpass all other knights."

Solomon replied that he did not know where to obtain the kind of armor she described. And his wife answered, "I will tell you where: in the temple that you built to honor your God lies the sword of your father King David. It is the keenest and most amazing sword that has ever been handled by a knight. Take it and remove the pommel and the hilt, so that we'll have the naked blade alone. Then you, who know the properties of precious stones and herbs and the way of all terrestrial things, should make a handle of precious stones so finely joined together that no one who looks at it in the future will be able to discern one from another. Rather, anyone who sees it will think it is a single piece. Then make a hilt of such extraordinary virtue that it will have no equal in the world, and fashion a scabbard as remarkable as the sword itself. Once you have done all this, I will fashion the belt to my liking."

20. Solomon Constructs the Ship and Dreams of Its Consecration.

Solomon did as his wife had instructed except for the sword's pommel, in which he set only one stone, but it contained all the colors one could imagine. And he added a wonderful hilt described elsewhere.

Once the ship had been built and launched, Solomon's wife had a huge and magnificent bed put in it, along with several decorative coverlets. The king placed his crown at the head of the bed and covered it with a white silk cloth. He now asked his wife for the sword he had given her so that she could attach its belt, saying, "Bring the sword so I can place it across the foot of the bed."

When she carried it in, Solomon saw that she had fixed to the sword a belt of hemp. And he was about to express his anger when his wife interrupted him, saying, "Be assured that I have no material of high enough quality that it would rightfully support such an important sword."

"Then what can we do?" Solomon asked.

"Leave it as is," she replied. "It's not up to us to attach the proper belt to this sword. A virgin will do that, though I don't know when." So the king left the sword as it was and had the ship covered with a white silk cloth that was not susceptible to damage from water or anything else. But even after these preparations, the woman felt that the bed lacked something.

She set out with two carpenters to the Tree where Abel had been killed, and instructed them, "Cut me enough of this wood so that I can have a spindle made."

"We wouldn't dare, lady," they said. "Don't you know that this Tree was planted by the first mother?"

"I suggest you do it," she continued, "because if not, I'll have you killed." The carpenters agreed to do as she asked under the circumstances; they preferred to do wrong rather than lose their lives. So they began to strike the Tree, but had barely cut into it when, much to their astonishment, they saw quite plainly that drops of rosy red blood were spilling out. Though they wanted to stop cutting, Solomon's wife made them try again, against their better judgment. So finally they chopped off enough wood to make a spindle. Then Solomon's wife had them take a sample from one of the green trees that had grown from the original one, and another from one of the white trees.

Once the carpenters had gathered the three woods of different color, they returned to the ship. The lady entered first and had them follow her, saying to them, "I want you to fashion from this wood three spindles, fixing one on this side of the bed, the other on the far side, with the third one above them, as a crosspiece bolted to the uprights. The carpenters did as she asked and attached the spindles to the bed. Not one of them changed color during the life of the ship.

When this task was complete, Solomon looked at the ship and said to his wife, "You have accomplished something wondrous. If all the world were here, they would not know how to interpret the meaning of this ship unless Our Lord instructed them; even you who had it built don't know what it means. And despite what you've done, the knight will not know that I had heard of him, unless Our Lord explains it."

"Leave the ship as is," Solomon's wife advised. "In time you will discover more about it, things that you cannot now imagine."

That night, Solomon slept in his tent next to the ship, along with a few men. As he slept, he saw the image of a man coming down from the sky in the company of many angels. After setting foot on the ship, the man took water from a silver pail carried by one of the angels and sprinkled the ship with it. When he drew near the sword, he wrote inscriptions on the pommel and the hilt. Then he approached the side of the ship and placed an inscription there. After that, the man lay down on the bed. But from that point on, Solomon did not know what happened to him; he and his entourage simply vanished.

The following day, as soon as Solomon awoke, he went to the ship and found on its side an inscription that read, YOU WHO WISH TO ENTER HERE, BE CERTAIN THAT YOU ARE FULL OF FAITH, FOR I AM NOTHING BUT FAITH AND BELIEF. IF YOU DESERT YOUR FAITH, THEN I WILL ABANDON YOU, AND YOU WILL RECEIVE NO SUSTENANCE OR HELP FROM ME. RATHER, I WILL LET YOU FALL AS SOON AS YOU ARE TOUCHED BY DISBELIEF.

Solomon was so astonished to see these letters that he did not dare to step on board the ship, but pulled back from it. And the ship slid down into the sea and sped away so quickly that he soon lost sight of it. Sitting down on the shore, Solomon began to think about what had happened, and a voice said to him from above, "Solomon, the last knight in your family line will rest in the bed you have made and will receive news of you."

Solomon was so delighted to hear this that he woke his wife and the members of his company and told them of the adventure, explaining to friends and strangers alike how his wife had solved a problem that had baffled him. And so the story relates to you, for reasons already explained in this book, why the ship was built and how the spindles bore the natural colors of white, green, and red without being painted. But now the story falls silent about this event and speaks of something else.

21. A Belt Is Fashioned from the Hair of Perceval's Sister.

The story now says that the three companions stared at the bed for so long that they understood its spindles to be naturally colored rather than painted. This amazed them, and they did not know how it was possible. But after a long while, they lifted the cloth and saw the gold crown beneath it, and under the crown a luxurious alms purse. Perceval opened it and found a letter inside, which the others hoped, God willing, would tell them about the ship, where it had come from and who had made it. Perceval began to read the letter, which described the nature of the ship and its spindles, just as the story has narrated. Everyone who was listening began to weep as they heard this account, which called their attention to solemn deeds and men of lofty heritage.

When Perceval had described for them the nature of the ship and its spindles, Galahad said, "My lord, now we must search for the young woman who will exchange this belt for another. No one should remove the sword from here without that belt."

But the others confessed they did not know where to look for her. "Nonetheless," they said, "we will gladly begin the search, since we must."

When Perceval's sister overheard this discussion, she interjected, "My lord, don't despair, because with God's help an appropriately beautiful and splendid belt will be in place before we depart." Then she opened a box she was holding and pulled out a belt woven of the richest gold and silk and strands of hair that were so bright and shiny that one could hardly tell them apart from the gold threads. And in them were set rich and precious stones and two golden buckles so fine that their equal could not be found. "My dear lord," Perceval's sister continued, "here's the belt that should accompany this sword. Be assured that I made it from the most precious thing I had, that is to say, my hair. And it's no wonder that my hair was dear to me, for on Pentecost when you were dubbed a knight," she said to Galahad, "I had the finest head of hair that any woman has possessed. But as soon as I learned that this adventure awaited me and that I would have to undertake it, I had my head shaved and fashioned the tresses you see here."

"In God's name, lady," said Bors, "you are truly welcome here! You have saved us from the trials we would have endured without this news." She drew near the sword, removed the hemp belt and attached the new one as perfectly and effortlessly as if she had done this every day of her life. Then she asked the companions, "Do you know the sword's name?"

"Indeed not, lady," they replied. "You are the one to reveal it to us, as the inscription indicates."

"Be assured, then, that this sword is called the Sword of the Strange Straps, and the scabbard is called Memory of Blood, for no one with any sense can look at the scabbard, which was made from the Tree of Life, and not be reminded of Abel's blood."

Then the others said to Galahad, "We beg you, in the name of Jesus Christ and for the glorification of knighthood, to gird on the Sword of the Strange Straps, which has been desired in the kingdom of Logres more than Our Lord was desired by the apostles." The companions believed that the wonders of the Holy Grail and the perilous adventures that they encountered every day would be stemmed by this sword.

"Allow me to make good my right to the sword," said Galahad. "No one should have it who cannot grip the pommel. If I fail at this, you will know that the sword is not destined for me." The others agreed. Galahad placed his hand on the hilt, and as he grasped it, his thumb and fingers overlapped easily. The companions watching him said, "Now we are certain, sir, that the sword is yours. There can be no further argument that you should not gird it on." As Galahad withdrew the blade from its scabbard, it looked clear and bright enough to hold one's reflection. And he admired it as much as one can admire anything in the world. Galahad replaced the sword in its sheath.

Then the young woman removed the sword he was wearing and girded the belt of the other one around him. Once she had hung the sword by his side, she said, "Truly, sir, I no longer care when I might die, for I feel I am the most fortunate maid in the world to have dubbed into knighthood the world's most valiant knight. Know that you were not properly a knight when you carried the sword that you wore when you came to this land."

"Lady, you have done so much for me that I will forever be your knight. My heartiest thanks for everything you have told us."

"We can leave now," she replied, "and go about our business." So they left the ship and climbed onto the rocks, where Perceval said to Galahad, "I will thank the Lord every day of my life for allowing me to participate in such a lofty adventure; it was certainly the most extraordinary one I've ever witnessed."

[*A leprous woman was cured by the blood of Perceval's sister, who died from the bloodletting. Lancelot came to Corbenic Castle but was injured when he attempted to approach the Holy Grail. He returned to court.*]

22. Galahad Witnesses Mordrain's Death, Hears Simeon's Voice, and Rides to the Castle of the Maimed King.

Now the story says that when Galahad parted company with Lancelot, he wandered for many days, following the whim of chance, until he came to the abbey where King Mordrain lay.[19] He had heard about the king who was waiting for the Good Knight, and decided to pay him a visit. So the next day, after hearing Mass, Galahad went to see the king, who, by the will of God, had long before lost his sight and the strength of his body.

But as soon as Galahad drew near, the king was able to see clearly. He sat up immediately and said, "Galahad, servant of God and true knight whom I have awaited so long, hold me in your arms and let me rest against your chest, so that I can die in your embrace. You are more pure and chaste than all other knights, just as the lily of the valley, which signifies virginity, is whiter than all other flowers. You are like a lily in purity and like a rose in perfect virtue and in fiery color. The fire of the Holy Spirit burns so brightly within you that my flesh, which was wizened and old, is now thoroughly rejuvenated and revived."

Galahad sat at the head of the king's bed, wrapped his arms around him, and held him against his chest, as the old man had requested. The king bent forward, clasped Galahad tightly in his arms, and said, "Dear Lord Jesus Christ, now I have what I want! I ask You to come for me now, for I could not die in a more comfortable or pleasant state. In this bliss, which I have desired so long, there is nothing but lilies and roses."

It was immediately obvious that Our Lord had heard King Mordrain's prayer, for as soon as the words were uttered, the king gave up the ghost to Him whom he had served so long. King Mordrain died in Galahad's arms.

When the residents of the abbey learned of Mordrain's death, they examined the body and found, to their astonishment, that the wounds he had endured for so many years were now healed. The body was then given a funeral appropriate for a king and was buried in the abbey.

Galahad departed two days later and rode until he came to the Perilous Forest, where he found the fountain that boiled in great waves, as the story has told previously. But as soon as he plunged his hand into the water, the heat and fury subsided, because he had never been filled with the ardor of lust. When the people of that region heard that the water had cooled, they were amazed. From then on it was known as Galahad's Fountain.

After Galahad had completed this adventure, his wanderings brought him to the land of Gorre and to the abbey where Lancelot had discovered the

---

[19]The story of Mordrain (and of Simeon) was offered in a sequence not included in this volume.

tomb of Galahad, King of Hoselice[20] and son of Joseph of Arimathea. It was also there that Lancelot had encountered the tomb of Simeon and met with failure. As Galahad looked into the crypt beneath the chapel and discovered the tomb that burned so brightly, he asked the monks what it was.

"It's an extraordinary adventure, sir," they replied, "that can be undertaken only by a man who surpasses all the knights of the Round Table in virtue and valor."

"I would like you to take me to the door that leads inside, if you will." They readily agreed and led Galahad to the door of the crypt, where he began to descend the steps. But as soon as he drew near the tomb, the fire and flame that had burned vigorously for so many days began to wane and die. They were quenched by the arrival of a man in whom no base ardor burned.

Galahad then raised the tombstone and saw Simeon's dead body. And as soon as the heat had subsided, a voice spoke to him: "Galahad, Galahad, you should thank the Lord for bestowing such grace upon you. Because of the good life you have led, you can save souls from earthly suffering and give them the joy of paradise. I am your ancestor Simeon and have lived three hundred fifty-four years in this burning heat to expiate a sin I committed against Joseph of Arimathea. Along with the torment I have suffered, I would have been condemned to perdition. But the grace of the Holy Spirit, which has more of a foothold in you than does earthly knighthood, took pity on me thanks to your extreme humility. It has delivered me, in its mercy, from earthly torment, and has given me heavenly joy, simply by the grace of your arrival."

The monks, who had come down to the crypt as soon as the flame was extinguished, were amazed to hear these extraordinary words. Then Galahad took hold of the body, lifted it out of the tomb it had occupied so long, and transferred it to the chapel. The monks then shrouded the body in a manner befitting a knight, which Simeon had been, and held an appropriate service, interring the corpse in front of the high altar. Then they came to Galahad and paid him the greatest respect. When they asked who he was and from what country, he informed them fully.

The following day, after Galahad had heard Mass, he bade the monks farewell and departed, riding for five years until he came to the house of the Maimed King. During those five years, Perceval accompanied him wherever he went.[21] And Galahad completed all the adventures in the kingdom of

---

[20]Matarasso remarks that "Wales, if we are to believe the 'Lancelot-Grail,' was originally known as Hosselice." See Pauline Matarasso, trans., *The Quest of the Holy Grail* (Harmondsworth: Penguin, 1969), p. 303, n. 78.

[21]The text indicates that Galahad left alone, but was then accompanied by Perceval. How and why they met are not explained.

Logres, so that few were ever seen again except for certain miraculous revelations of Our Lord. Wherever they went and however numerous their enemies, the two knights could not be defeated, dismayed, or frightened.

One day as they were coming out of a vast and lush forest, they saw Bors riding alone across their path. There is no need to ask whether they were happy to see him; all the time they had been apart, Perceval and Galahad had looked forward to joining company again with Bors. They welcomed him warmly, wishing him honor and good fortune, and he did the same to them. Then they asked how he had been. He replied truthfully, explaining everything he had done. He said that in the last five years, he had not slept four times in a bed or human dwelling, but in distant forests and isolated mountains where he would have died one hundred times over if it had not been for the grace of the Holy Spirit, which comforted him and succored him in his distress.

"And did you find what we've been searching for?" asked Perceval.

"No, indeed," Bors replied, "but I don't think we will part company again before discovering the object of our quest."

"With God's help!" said Galahad. "But as God is my witness, nothing could make me happier than seeing you again. It delights me and fulfills my deepest wishes."

23. The Three Companions Witness the Wonders of Corbenic Castle.

Thus did chance bring the three companions together just as their unforeseen adventures had separated them before. They rode for a long time until they came one day to Corbenic Castle. As soon as the king recognized them, great rejoicing broke out, for the residents were well aware that the three companions would put an end to the adventures that had dominated their castle for so long. As the news of their arrival spread throughout the land, everyone came to see them. King Pelles wept at the sight of his nephew Galahad, as did the others who had known him as a child.

When the companions had removed their armor, King Pelles's son Elyezer carried in the Broken Sword, which the tale has already described: it is the one that wounded Joseph of Arimathea in the thigh.[22] When Elyezer had removed the sword from its scabbard and had told the companions how it had been broken, Bors held out his hand to join the two parts together, but he could not. He then handed it to Perceval and said, "See if you can put an end to this adventure, sir knight."

"Gladly," said Perceval. He grasped the sword, and aligned the two pieces, but he could in no way join them together. So he said to Galahad,

---

[22]See *The Quest for the Holy Grail,* Chapter 16; also included in *The History of the Holy Grail.*

"Since we have both failed to complete this adventure, you, sir, must try. And if you fail, I am certain it will never be completed by any man on earth." Then Galahad took hold of the sword's two parts and lined them up. The sections joined together so seamlessly that no one would ever be able to discern the break that had severed them, or to know that the sword had been broken.

When the companions saw this, they felt that God had given them a good beginning. They thought they would be able to complete the other adventures easily, since the initial feat had been achieved. When the castle residents saw that the sword had been joined, they rejoiced heartily. And they gave the sword to Bors, saying that it could not be put to better use, for he was a wonderfully good and valiant knight.

As the hour of vespers drew near, the skies darkened and the weather changed; an unusually strong wind came up. It struck the palace, causing such an intense heat to spread throughout that most of the residents thought they would be burned. Some even fainted out of fear. Then a voice said, "Let those who are not to sit at the table of Jesus Christ depart, for now the true knights will be fed with heavenly sustenance."

Everyone left the room except King Pelles, who had led a saintly life, his son Elyezer, and a young maiden, the king's niece, who was the holiest and most religious person anyone had ever known. The three companions remained along with these people to see what Our Lord was about to show them. After a brief delay, nine knights entered the room. They removed their helmets and armor and approached Galahad. Bowing, they said to him, "We have come in great haste to sit with you, sir, at the table where the heavenly food will be served."

Galahad told the knights that they had come in time and that he and his companions had only just arrived. Once everyone was seated in the middle of the hall, Galahad asked the knights where they were from. Three said they were from Gaul, three others were from Ireland, and three from Denmark.

As the knights conversed, they noticed a wooden bed being carried into the room by four young women. A man lay on the bed, apparently infirm; he had a gold crown on his head. When the women reached the center of the hall, they put the bed down and left. The man raised his head and said to Galahad, "Welcome, sir! I have been awaiting your arrival for a long time in a state of pain and anguish that others would not be able to endure. But the time has now come, God willing, for my suffering to be relieved; I will leave this world as I was promised long ago."

As he was uttering these words, a voice said, "Those who are not companions on the Quest for the Holy Grail must leave now; it is not fitting for them to stay." King Pelles, his son Elyezer, and the young maiden walked out. When the hall was empty, except for those who considered themselves companions on the quest, there descended from the sky, or so it seemed to those present, a man dressed in a bishop's vestments, with a crozier in his hand and a miter on his head. Four angels were carrying him on a lavish throne, which they placed next to the table that held the Holy Grail. The man had an inscription on his forehead that read, THIS IS JOSEPHUS, THE FIRST CHRISTIAN BISHOP, CONSE-CRATED BY OUR LORD AT THE HEAVENLY PALACE IN THE CITY OF SARRAS. The knights understood the words of the inscription, but they wondered how this could be, since Josephus had died more than three hundred years before.

Then he spoke to them, saying, "Knights of God, servants of Jesus Christ, don't be amazed to see me here with this Holy Vessel, for just as I was God's servant on earth, I now serve Him in heaven."

24. Josephus Performs the Grail Liturgy, and the Knights Witness the Mysteries of the Grail.

Josephus moved toward the silver table and prostrated himself on hands and knees in front of the altar. After a long while, he heard the door to the room open and slam loudly. When he looked up, all the doors were doing the same thing. Then he saw that the angels who had brought him into the room were leaving. Two held candles, the third a red silk cloth, and the fourth a Lance. The Lance was bleeding so profusely that the drops fell into a container held in the angel's other hand. The two angels carrying candles placed them on the table, the third put the cloth next to the Holy Vessel, and the fourth held the Lance straight up against the vessel so that it caught the blood running down the Lance's shaft. As soon as they had done this, Josephus rose and lifted the Lance a little higher above the Holy Vessel, and then covered it with the cloth.

Then Josephus appeared to begin the sacrament of the Mass. After a brief delay, he took from the vessel a host made in the form of bread. And when he raised it up, a figure in the form of a child descended from above; his red countenance seemed to burn like fire. As he entered the bread, those present saw clearly that the bread took on the form of human flesh. After he had held the host for a long time, Josephus returned it to the Holy Vessel.

When Josephus had finished celebrating the Mass, which is the task of a priest, he came to Galahad and kissed him, and told him to kiss the others. Then he said to them, "Servants of Jesus Christ, who have endured such suffering to witness part of the mysteries of the Holy Grail, sit at this table. You will be nourished with the most exquisite and most celestial food that a knight has ever tasted from the hand of your Savior. You can now say that your travail has not been in vain, for today you will receive the highest payment that a knight has ever received." With these words, Josephus disappeared, and those in attendance never knew what became of him. They sat at the table in great fear and wept softly as their faces were bathed in tears.

Then, as the three companions gazed upon the vessel, they saw an unclothed man issue from it. His hands were bleeding, as were his feet and his body, and he said to them, "My knights and servants and loyal sons, who from human beings have become spiritual creatures, you have searched for me so long that I can no longer conceal myself from you. It is appropriate for you to see part of my mysteries and my secrets. You have accomplished such feats that you now sit at my table, where no knight has eaten since the time of Joseph of Arimathea. The others have received the servant's due; that is, the knights living here and many others were fed by the grace of the Holy Vessel, but they have not occupied the place where you now sit. So partake of the heavenly food that you have desired so long, the very reason for your prolonged quest."

Then he took the Holy Grail to Galahad, who knelt down and received his Savior with a joyous heart and hands clasped. The others did the same, and they all concurred that Josephus had placed something like bread in their mouths. After each one had partaken of the heavenly food, which was so deliciously sweet that it seemed to have introduced all imaginable flavors into their bodies, He who had fed them said to Galahad, "My son, as clean and pure as a mortal man can be, do you know what I hold in my hands?"

"Indeed not," Galahad replied, "unless You tell me."

"It is the platter from which Jesus Christ ate the lamb with his disciples on Easter. And it is the platter that has generously fed all those in my service. It is the platter that no faithless man has beheld without suffering for it. Since it has proved so agreeable to so many people, it should rightly be called the Holy Grail.[23]

"Now you have seen what you most desired and have coveted so long. But you have not yet seen it as fully as you will. Do you know where this event will take place? In the city of Sarras, in the spiritual palace. So you must journey there in the company of the Holy Vessel, which will leave the kingdom of Logres tonight, never to be seen here again. Nor will the adventures associated with it take place here any longer. And do you know why it is leaving? Because it is not respected or rightfully served by the people of this land. They have turned to a dismal, worldly life, despite having once been nourished by the grace of this Holy Vessel. Because they have so poorly repaid the favor, I divest them of the honor I had conferred upon them.

"For this reason, I want you to leave in the morning for the sea, where you will find the ship from which you took the Sword of the Strange Straps. So that you will not go alone, I want you to take Perceval and Bors with you. And since I do not want you to leave this country before healing the Maimed

---

[23]The Old French is *a . . . servi a gré* ("has served to their hearts' content" or "in agreeable manner). The form *graal* or *greal* for "grail" permitted the etymological connection, which has great symbolic value, although no philological basis. This connection was first made by Robert de Boron in his verse *Romance of the History of the Grail.*

King, take the blood from this lance and use it to anoint his legs. This is the only way he will be healed; nothing else will work."

"Why will You not allow all the others to come with me, Sir?" inquired Galahad.

"Because that is not My wish. I prefer that you resemble My apostles. For just as they ate with Me the day of the Last Supper, now you will eat with Me at the Table of the Holy Grail. You are twelve, as they were twelve apostles. I am the thirteenth member, who will be your master and pastor. Just as I dispersed them throughout the world to preach the true law, so too will I disperse your group, some here and others there. And all but one of you will die in performing this service." He blessed them and disappeared without a trace. All they saw was His figure ascending toward heaven.

Galahad went to the Lance that lay on the table, and touched the blood. Then he went to the Maimed King and anointed the wounds on his legs. The king dressed himself and rose from his bed, strong and healthy. He thanked Our Lord for having cared for him so promptly; and he lived a long while after that, but not in this world. He immediately joined a community of white monks, and Our Lord performed many miracles out of love for him. But the story does not recount those tales, because they are not essential to its purpose.

25. The Ship Departs with the Three Companions and the Holy Grail.

Around midnight, after the knights had prayed to Our Lord for a long time, asking safe conduct for their souls wherever they might go, a voice came to them and said, "You who are my sons and not my stepsons, my friends and not my enemies, leave this place and go, as chance may lead you, to the place where you think you can do the most good. They responded in unison, "Heavenly Father, blessed are You who deign to consider us Your sons and Your friends! We can see that in truth our labors have not been in vain."

They left the palace and descended to the courtyard, where they found their horses and armor. Once suitably equipped, they mounted their horses and rode out of the castle, asking one another where each one was from. They discovered that of the three from Gaul, one was Claudin, son of Claudas, and that the others, no matter what their country of origin, were noble men of distinguished lineage. When it was time to leave, they kissed one another like brothers, weeping tenderly as they said to Galahad, "Be assured, sir, that nothing ever pleased us more than to know that we would be in your company, and nothing ever made us so sad as having to leave you so soon. Yet we realize that Our Lord wants this separation; and for that reason we should depart without grieving."

"Dear sirs," said Galahad, "I enjoyed your company as much as you did mine. But you realize that we cannot stay together. So I commend you to God

God and beg you, if you go to King Arthur's court, to give my greetings to my father, Sir Lancelot, and to the members of the Round Table." They agreed that if they went that way, they would not forget his request.

So they parted company. Galahad left with his two companions, and the three of them rode to the sea in less than four days. They would have arrived sooner, but they did not take the most direct route, since they were not familiar with the roads.

When they came to the sea, they found the ship on the shore, the one in which the Sword of the Strange Straps had been discovered. And they saw the inscription on the side of the ship, which warned that no one could enter there if he did not firmly believe in Jesus Christ. When they approached the side of the ship and looked in, they saw, on the bed that had been built aboard the ship, the silver table that they had left behind at the Maimed King's palace. The Holy Grail sat on the table, veiled with a red silk cloth.

The companions discussed this extraordinary event with one another, observing how fortunate they were that the very thing they most wanted to see would accompany them for the duration of their voyage. They crossed themselves, commended themselves to Our Lord, and stepped onto the ship. No sooner were they on board than the wind, which had been calm and serene up to that point, slammed against the sail so forcefully that it pushed the ship away from the shore and out into the open sea. The ship was soon speeding through the water, propelled by increasingly violent winds.

26. The Companions Come to Sarras, Where Galahad Performs a Miracle and Perceval's Sister Is Buried.

The three companions drifted at sea for a long time without knowing where God was taking them. Every morning and evening, Galahad prayed, asking Our Lord to allow him to leave this world at the moment he might request it. He repeated this prayer every morning and evening, until a heavenly voice said to him, "Do not worry, Galahad; Our Lord will grant your request. Whenever you ask for bodily death, you will receive the life of the soul and eternal joy."

Perceval had overheard the prayer that Galahad repeated so often and was puzzled by it. So he asked Galahad in the name of their friendship and the loyalty they shared, to explain why he asked for such a thing.

"I will gladly tell you," Galahad replied. "The day before yesterday, when we witnessed some of the mysteries of the Holy Grail, thanks to Our Lord's divine mercy, I saw hidden things that are visible only to the ministers of Jesus Christ. And when I saw these things that are unimaginable to the heart of a mortal man and indescribable by a human tongue, I felt in my heart such an intense sweetness and joy that if I had left this world at that moment, I am certain I would have died in a state of bliss unmatched by any man on earth. I was surrounded by so many angels and other spiritual beings that I was transported from the earthly life into heavenly existence: into the joy of glorious martyrs and the friends of Our Lord. It is because I think I will be able to experience that same joy again, if not a superior one, that I make the request that you overheard. I plan to leave this world, God willing, while contemplating the mysteries of the Holy Grail."

Thus did Galahad tell Perceval about his impending death, as the divine voice had revealed it to him. And thus did the sin of the people of the kingdom of Logres, as I have explained previously, cause them to lose the Holy Grail that had so often nourished and sated them. Just as Our Lord had sent the Grail to Galahad[24] and Joseph and their descendants because of their virtue, so too did he deprive the wicked heirs of it, because of their mean-spiritedness and the baseness he found in them. This shows clearly how the wicked lost through their perversity what the worthy maintained through their virtue.

The companions had been at sea a long while when one day they said to Galahad, "You have never lain upon this bed that, according to the inscription,[25] was prepared for you, sir. Yet you must lie down here, for the words designate this to be your resting place. So Galahad lay upon the bed and slept for a long while. When he awoke, he saw before him the city of Sarras and heard a voice, which said to the companions, "You must now leave the ship, knights of Jesus Christ, and carry this silver table into the city, but do not put it down until you come to the spiritual palace where Our Lord first consecrated Josephus as bishop."

When they were about to remove the table, they looked across the water and saw the ship in which they had long ago placed the body of Perceval's sister. As the ship approached, they said to one another, "In God's name, this young lady has kept her word and has followed us here."

With Bors and Perceval holding the silver table in front and Galahad behind, they carried it off the ship and headed toward the city. But by the time they came to the gate, Galahad was beginning to tire from the table's excessive weight. Near the gate he saw a mendicant on crutches who was soliciting alms from passersby, who often gave him something out of love for Jesus Christ. As Galahad drew near, he called to the man, saying, "Come and help us carry this table up to the palace."

"What are you saying, sir, in the name of God? I have not been able to walk unaided for more than ten years."

---

[24]Baumgartner notes that the reference is to Galahad of Hoselice, son of Joseph of Arimathea, mentioned in *Quest,* Chapter 22. See Emmanuèle Baumgartner, *La Queste del saint Graal* (Paris: Champion, 1979), 247, n. 3.

[25]Refers to *Quest,*Chapter 21, which describes a letter explaining the Tree of Life and the building of the ship.

"Don't worry about that," replied Galahad. "Just stand up and don't be afraid, for you are cured." Once Galahad had uttered these words, the man tried to stand and found that he was strong and healthy, as if he had never been ill. Then he ran to the table and helped Galahad hold it. As he entered the city, he told everyone he met about the miracle that God had worked for him.

When they came to the palace, they saw the throne that Our Lord had prepared for Josephus. The awestruck residents of the city rushed forward to see the maimed man who could now stand. When the companions had accomplished their task, they returned to the water and entered the ship where Perceval's sister was. They carried her, bed and all, to the palace and gave her an elegant burial befitting the daughter of a king.

When the king of the city, who was called Escorant, saw the three companions, he asked where they were from and what they had brought on the silver table. They gave truthful answers to all his questions, explaining the wonders of the Grail and the force God had placed within it. But the king was treacherous and cruel, like all those who descend from the wicked lineage of pagans. He believed nothing of what they said and claimed they were guileful deceivers. As soon as the knights had removed their armor, King Escorant had them seized and thrown into prison for a year, though they felt that they would be there forever. But as soon as the companions were taken captive, Our Lord remembered them and sent the Holy Grail to keep them company. They were nourished by its grace throughout their prison stay.

27. Galahad Dies.

One day, after a year had passed, Galahad complained to Our Lord, saying, "It seems to me, Sir, that I have lived in this world long enough. If You agree, please release me from it now." It happened that King Escorant lay ill on his death bed. He summoned the three companions and asked their forgiveness for having so mistreated them. They pardoned him readily, and he died.

When King Escorant was buried, the residents of the city were very concerned; they did not know who could be their king. They deliberated for a long time, and during their discussion a voice said to them, "Choose the youngest of the three companions. He will protect you from harm and give sound advice while he is with you." They did as the voice had directed and chose Galahad to be their lord, despite his reluctance. When they placed the crown on his head, he was dismayed. But he realized he must accede to their wishes; otherwise they would kill him.

When Galahad had become lord of the land, he built an ark of gold and precious stones to cover the Holy Vessel, which sat on the silver table. Every morning, as soon as he awoke, he and his companions came before the Holy Vessel to say their prayers.

At the end of a year, on the very day that Galahad had been crowned, he and his companions rose early in the morning. When they came to the palace that was called the heavenly palace, they looked in the direction of the Holy Vessel and saw a noble-looking man, dressed in a bishop's garb. He was kneeling in front of the table and saying confession. He was surrounded by as many angels as if he had been Jesus Christ himself. After kneeling for a long while, he rose and began to say the Mass of the glorious Mother of God. And when he came to the solemn part of the Mass, he lifted the platen from the Holy Vessel and called to Galahad, saying, "Come forward, servant of Jesus Christ, and you will see what you have wanted to see for so long." Galahad drew near and looked into the Holy Vessel. As soon as he did, he began to tremble violently, for his mortal flesh had caught sight of spiritual mysteries.

Raising his hands toward heaven, Galahad said, "I worship You and give thanks that You have granted my desire. Now I see clearly what no tongue could describe and no heart could imagine. I see here the source of great deeds and the cause of all prowess. I see mysteries that surpass all other mysteries! And since, Dear Lord, You have allowed me to see what I have always hoped to see, I ask that You now permit me, in this state of bliss, to pass from earthly life into eternal life."

As soon as Galahad had made this request, the worthy man standing in front of the altar in priestly dress took the host from the table and offered it to Galahad. He received the body of Our Lord with humility and great devotion. And when he had partaken of it, the good man asked, "Do you know who I am?"

"No, indeed," replied Galahad, "not unless you tell me."

"Know that I am Josephus, son of Joseph of Arimathea, sent by Our Lord to be your companion. And do you know why He sent me rather than another? Because you are like me in two ways: you witnessed the mysteries of the Holy Grail, as I did, and you are a virgin, as I am. It is thus fitting that we be together."

Galahad went to Perceval and kissed him, and then he kissed Bors, and said to him, "Bors, give my greetings to Sir Lancelot, my father, when you see him." Then Galahad returned to the table and prostrated himself on hands and knees in front of it. He held that position only a short while before falling forward on the palace floor. His soul had already left his body and was being carried away by jubilant angels who blessed the name of the Lord.

At the moment of Galahad's death, an extraordinary thing took place. The two companions saw a hand reach down from heaven, though they could not see the body to which the hand belonged. The hand moved straight toward the Holy Vessel, seized it along with the Lance, and carried them both up to heaven. Since that time, no man has been bold enough to claim that he has seen the Holy Grail.

Galahad's death provoked an intense sadness in Perceval and Bors. If they had not been such valiant and virtuous men, they would have succumbed to despair over the loss of such a beloved friend. The people of the region mourned him deeply and were very distraught. They dug his grave there where he died, and as soon as he was buried, Perceval withdrew into a hermitage outside the city walls and began to wear the religious habit. Bors accompanied him but retained his secular clothing, for he intended to return to King Arthur's court. Perceval spent a year and three days at the hermitage before he died. He had Bors bury him with his sister and Galahad in the heavenly palace.

When Bors saw that he remained alone in the distant lands of the kingdom of Babylon, he left Sarras in full armor, went to the sea, and boarded a ship. After a short voyage, he arrived at the kingdom of Logres and rode as far as Camelot, where he found King Arthur. Never has there been such a joyous welcome as the one he received. Bors had been away from court so long that the others thought they had lost him forever.

After they had eaten, the king summoned the clerks who were putting into writing the adventures of the knights at court. When Bors had recounted the adventures of the Holy Grail, as he had seen them, they were recorded and kept in the archive at Salisbury. Master Walter Map withdrew them to write his book about the Holy Grail, for the love of his lord King Henry, who had the story translated from Latin into French.[26] But here the story stops, and tells no more about the adventures of the Holy Grail.

---

[26]The historical Walter Map was a jurist and a man of letters at the court of King Henry II of England. But Map died (in 1209) before the *Quest* was composed and could not have been its actual author.

The Death of Arthur

TRANSLATED BY NORRIS J. LACY

1. Aftermath of Grail Quest; The Tournament at Winchester.

After Walter Map[1] had put into writing the *Adventures of the Holy Grail* as fully as he thought proper, his lord King Henry was of the opinion that his work would be left unfinished if he did not recount the rest of the lives of those about whom he had earlier spoken and the deaths of those whose feats of prowess he had recorded in his book. And for that reason he began this last part, and when he had composed it, he called it *The Death of King Arthur,* for the end tells how King Arthur was wounded in the battle at Salisbury and how he was separated from Girflet,[2] who stayed with him so long that he was the last one to see Arthur alive. And in that way Master Walter begins this final part.

When Bors had arrived at court in the city of Camelot from lands as far away as the area around Jerusalem, he found much there that pleased him, for everyone there wanted to see him. And when he had recounted the passing of Galahad and the death of Perceval, all those at court were grief-stricken at the news, but they consoled themselves as best they could. Then the king commanded that all the adventures recounted by the companions of the quest for the Holy Grail be set down in writing, and after that he said, "Lords, look around among yourselves and see how many of your companions we have lost in this quest." And they looked around and found that precisely thirty-two of them were missing, and of that number there was not one who had not died in battle.

The king, having heard it said that Gawain had killed many of them, had him brought before him, and he said, "Gawain, I ask you, by the oath that you swore to me when I made you a knight, that you tell me what I ask you."

"Sir," said Sir Gawain, "because you have asked me that way, I would be obliged to respond even if the answer showed me to be more shameful than any knight of your court."

"Now I ask you," said the king, "how many knights you think you killed by your own hand during this quest."

Sir Gawain thought about it for a moment, and the king asked him again: "Upon my word, I want to know, for some are saying that you killed a great number of them."

"Sir," replied Gawain, "you're asking me to reveal my disgrace; and I'll tell you, for I see that I have no choice. I tell you truly that I myself killed eighteen, not because I was a better knight than any other, but because misfortune afflicted me more than any of my companions. And you may be as-

---

[1]For Walter Map, see note 26 of *The Quest for the Holy Grail*. King Henry, mentioned later in the sentence, is Henry II Plantagenet, at whose court Walter held a comparatively prominent position as jurist and man of letters.
[2]See Chapter 7 of *The Death of Arthur.*

sured that it was not a feat of prowess, but rather the consequence of my sin. Now you have made me confess my shame."

"Indeed, dear nephew," said the king, "this was a true misfortune, and I know that it befell you because of your sin, but in spite of that, tell me whether you think you killed King Bademagu."

"Sir," he answered, "there is no doubt that I killed him. And I have never done anything that has caused me as much grief as that."

"Surely, fair nephew," said the king, "if that causes you pain, it's only natural, and, so help me God, it brings me terrible grief as well, for my household is more impoverished by his loss than by that of the four best knights who were killed in this quest."

When King Arthur spoke that way of King Bademagu, Sir Gawain was much more aggrieved than he had been before. And the king, seeing that the adventures of the kingdom of Logres had been brought to a close, so that scarcely anything more could occur, had a tournament cried on the fields at Winchester, because he did not want his companions to give up bearing arms.

Until now, Lancelot had remained chaste, following the counsel of the holy man to whom he had confessed during the Quest for the Holy Grail, and had renounced Queen Guenevere, as the story has told earlier.[3] Yet when he returned to court, not a month passed before he was as enamored and inflamed as he had ever been before, so that he again lapsed into sin with the queen just as he had done formerly. But whereas he had previously indulged his sinful passion so prudently and so discreetly that no one knew of it, now he behaved so foolishly that it became apparent to Sir Gawain's brother Agravain, who had never liked him and who watched his comings and goings more attentively than any of the others. He watched so intently that soon he knew beyond any doubt that Lancelot and the queen shared an illicit love.

The queen was so beautiful that everyone marveled, for at that time, although she was a good fifty years old, she was such a beautiful lady that her equal could not be found in the world. For this reason—that her beauty had never faded—certain knights said that she was the fount of all beauties.

When Agravain was certain about the queen and Lancelot, he was very happy, more for the harm that might befall Lancelot than for the possibility of avenging the offense to the king.

[*Guenevere became convinced that Lancelot was unfaithful to her, after he served as the champion of another woman, the Maiden of Escalot, in a tournament.*]

---

[3]In *The Quest for the Holy Grail,* just prior to our Chapter 10.

2. Arthur's Discovery of Paintings Depicting Lancelot's Love for the Queen.

[Arthur took lodging in the castle of his sister Morgan.]

That day was very beautiful, and the sun, which had risen bright and clear, streamed into all parts of the room, so that it was brighter than before; and the two of them were alone with each other, for they took pleasure in talking together. And when each had asked all about the other, it happened that the king began to look around him and saw the pictures and the images that Lancelot had painted while he was imprisoned there.[4] King Arthur could read well enough to decipher a text; and when he saw the letters and images that explained the meaning of the paintings, he began to read them, and he realized that they depicted Lancelot's deeds and the exploits he had performed since the time he first became a knight. And he saw nothing that he did not recognize as true, because news of Lancelot's deeds was regularly brought to court as soon as he accomplished them.

Thus the king began to read about Lancelot's deeds in the paintings he saw; and when he saw the images depicting the meeting arranged by Galehaut, he was astonished and became pensive. He began to look at that and said quietly to himself, "My word, if these letters are telling the truth, Lancelot has dishonored me with the queen, for I see clearly that he was having an affair with her. And if that's true, as these letters suggest, this causes me more grief than I've ever known. Lancelot could not shame me worse than by dishonoring me with my wife." Then he said to Morgan, "Fair sister, I want you to tell me the truth about what I'm going to ask you."

She answered that she would gladly do so if she could. "Swear it to me," said the king, and she swore it. "Now I demand," said the king, "by the faith you owe me and have pledged to me, that you tell me without fail who painted these images, if you know the truth about it."

"Oh, sir," said Morgan, "what are you saying? What are you asking me? I'm sure that if I told you the truth about this and if he who did the paintings found it out, no one but God could prevent him from killing me."

"In God's name," said the king, "you must tell me, and I swear as king that I'll never betray you."

"Sir," she said, "is there no way you'll permit me to avoid telling this?"

"None," said the king, "you must tell me."

"Then I'll tell you, and every word will be the truth. It's true," said Morgan, "and perhaps you already know it, that Lancelot has loved Queen Guenevere from the day he first became a knight, and it was for love of the queen

---

[4]See *Lancelot,* Chapter 37.

that he did all the feats of prowess he performed as a new knight. And you could have known about it when you first came to the castle of Dolorous Guard but could not enter it, for you were stopped at the river. And when you sometimes sent a knight there, he too was unable to enter. But as soon as Kay, who was the queen's knight, came there, he entered; but you weren't aware of this, as some were."

"To be sure," said the king, "I didn't realize that; but nonetheless it did happen as you say. Yet, I don't know if it was for love of the queen or on my account."

"Sir," she said, "there is more."

"Tell me," said the king.

"Sir," she said, "he loved my lady the queen more than any man could love a lady; but he never revealed it to her, either directly or through an intermediary, and his love for her drove him to perform all the feats you see depicted here. For a long time he was in such a state that he did nothing but languish, as men often do who are in love but are not loved in return, for he dared not declare his love.

"He was in that state until he met Galehaut, the son of the Giantess, the day he bore black arms and won the tournament organized by the two of you, as you see by the painting before you.[5] And when he had made peace with you and Galehaut so that you received all the honor, and when Galehaut saw that his state was worsening day by day and that he had stopped eating and drinking—so desperately did he love the queen—he pressed and urged him until Lancelot revealed that he loved the queen and was dying for her. Galehaut urged him not to despair, for he would see to it that Lancelot would have his will with the queen. And he did just what he had promised, for he implored the queen until she yielded to Lancelot and granted her love to him with a kiss."[6]

The king said, "You've told me more than enough, for I see depicted there my obvious dishonor and Lancelot's treason. But tell me who painted these pictures."

"Certainly, sir," she said; "Lancelot did them, and I'll tell you when. Do you remember two tournaments that were held at Camelot, when the knights of the Round Table said they wouldn't attend if Lancelot fought on their side, because he always won the prize? And when Lancelot learned of that, he turned on them and made them leave the field and forced them to retreat into Camelot. Do you remember that?"

"Of course," said the king, "it seems to me that I can see the tournament

---

[5]The meeting of Lancelot and Galehaut is recounted in *Lancelot,* Chapter 7.
[6]See *Lancelot,* Chapter 7.

even now, for never since that time have I seen any knight perform such feats of arms as he did there. But why did you mention that?"

"Because," she said, "when he left court on that occasion, he was away for more than a year and a half, and no one knew where he was."

"To be sure," said the king, "that's true."

"I tell you," she said, "that at that time I kept him in prison for two winters and a summer; and during that time he painted the images that you see here. And I would still have him in prison, so that he would never get out, had he not done the greatest sorcery that any man ever performed."

"What was that?" asked the king.

"On my word," she said, "he broke the bars of that window with his bare hands."[7] And she showed him the bars, which she had had repaired. The king said that was not the work of a man, but of a devil.

For a long time the king looked at the paintings in the room and pondered these matters without ever saying a word. And at long last he said, "Agravain himself told me this same thing the other day, but I didn't believe him; instead, I thought he was lying. But what I see here makes me more certain than I ever was, and I tell you that I'll never rest until I know the complete truth about it. And if it's true, as these images indicate, that Lancelot has shamed me by dishonoring me with my wife, I'll pursue this until they are caught together in the act. And then, if I fail to impose a punishment that will be remembered forever, I agree never to wear a crown again."

"Certainly," said Morgan, "if you don't do so, you'll be disgraced before God and everyone, for no king or any other man would tolerate being shamed that way."

The king and his sister discussed this matter in detail during the morning, and Morgan repeatedly urged him to avenge his shame quickly, and he swore to her that as king he would do it so cruelly that people would never stop talking about it, if he managed to surprise them together.

"It won't take long," said Morgan, "to catch them together, provided people are vigilant."

"I'll take steps," said the king, "to ensure that, if they love each other sinfully, as you tell me, they're found together before the month has passed, provided Lancelot comes to court during that time."

The king stayed with his sister that day and the next and the entire week. She hated Lancelot more than anyone in the world, because she knew the queen loved him. And while the king was there with her, she did not stop urging him to avenge his shame when he returned to Camelot, if he had the opportunity. "Dear sister," said the king, "you don't need to urge me, for I wouldn't fail for half of all my kingdom to finish what I've begun." The king

---

[7]See *Lancelot,* Chapter 38.

stayed there for the full week, for the place was beautiful and pleasant and full of game, which he spent his time and effort hunting.

But now the story ceases speaking of him and of Morgan, except to say that he did not want anyone other than Morgan to enter the room as long as he was there, because of the paintings that so openly depicted his shame; and he certainly did not want anyone other than himself to know the truth, for he greatly feared dishonor and was afraid that news of it might be spread everywhere. And now the story leaves that subject and speaks of Lancelot and Bors and their company.

[*The queen accidentally poisoned a knight and was accused of murder. A boat arrived at Camelot, bearing the body of the Maiden of Escalot and a letter stating that she had died of unrequited love for Lancelot; the queen then knew that she had not been betrayed by her lover. Lancelot returned to court and defended the queen against the murder charge, killing her accuser. She was declared innocent.*]

3. Entrapment of Lancelot and the Queen by Agravain.

One day it happened that the queen was alone with Lancelot, and they began to speak of many things, whereupon the queen said, "Sir, I was wrong to doubt you concerning the Maiden of Escalot, for I know beyond a doubt that if you loved her as much as many people led me to think, she wouldn't be dead now."

"What, lady!" said Lancelot. "Is that maiden dead?"

"Yes, indeed," the queen answered. "She's buried in Saint Stephen's Church."

"In God's name," he said, "that's a pity, for she was very beautiful; and may God help me, I grieve for her."

The two of them exchanged those words and many others. And if Lancelot had loved the queen before, he now loved her much more, and she him; and they conducted themselves so indiscreetly that many of the people there knew the truth beyond any doubt, and Sir Gawain himself realized it clearly, as did all four of his brothers.

One day it happened that all five of them were in the palace and were talking about this matter privately; and Agravain was much more concerned about it than any of the others. While they were speaking about this, it happened that the king came out of the queen's chamber. And when Sir Gawain saw him, he said to his brothers, "Be quiet: here's my lord the king."

Agravain answered that he would not stop speaking on the king's account. The king heard that and said to Agravain, "Dear nephew, tell me what you were talking about so loudly."

"Oh, pay no attention, in God's name," said Sir Gawain. "Agravain is unusually bothersome, and you have no need to know what it concerns, for it would be of no use to you or to anyone else."

"In God's name," said the king, "I want to know."

"Please, sir," said Gaheriet, "that can't be, for he's telling the worst gossip and lies imaginable; and for that reason I urge you as my liege lord to stop asking."

"On my word," said the king, "I won't do that; instead I ask you, by the oath you have sworn to me, to tell me immediately what you were arguing about just now."

Sir Gawain said, "I'm astonished at how eager and curious you are to hear news; I assure you that, even if you became angry with me and drove me, poor and ruined, from your land, I wouldn't tell you; for if you should believe it, even if it were the greatest lie in the world, the result would be the greatest evil that ever befell your land."

Then the king was much more astonished than before, and he said that he would either know it or have them all put to death.

"On my word," said Sir Gawain, "never, God willing, will you learn it from me; for you would eventually hate me as a result. And neither I nor anyone else could fail to regret it." Then he left the hall, and Gaheriet did likewise; and the king called after them repeatedly, but they did not wish to return. Instead, they went away, as sad as could be, saying to each other how unfortunate it was that that word had been spoken. For if the king learned the truth and took action against Lancelot, the court would be destroyed and dishonored, since Lancelot would have on his side all the power of Gaul and of many another country.

Thus the two brothers rode on, so sad that they did not know what to do. And the king, who had remained with his other nephews, led them into a room beside a garden; and when they were there, he closed the door behind them, and he spoke to them and urged them by the faith they owed him to tell him what he would ask them. First of all he asked Agravain, who answered that he would not tell him, that he should ask the others. And they said that they would not talk about it.

"If you refuse to tell me," said the king, "either you'll have to kill me or I you." And he ran immediately to a sword that was on a bed, and he drew it from the scabbard and came to Agravain and said that he would surely kill him if he did not tell him what he was so eager to know; and he lifted the sword high in order to strike him on the head.

When Agravain saw that he was so furious, he cried, "Oh, sir, don't kill me! I'll tell you. I was telling my brother Sir Gawain and Gaheriet and my other brothers, whom you see here, that they were disloyal and traitorous to have so long permitted Sir Lancelot of the Lake to cause you such shame and dishonor."

"What!" said the king. "Is Lancelot dishonoring me? What is this about?

Tell me, for I never suspected him of seeking my dishonor, and I've always honored and cherished him so much that he should never shame me in any way."

"Sir," said Agravain, "he is so faithful to you that he's betraying you with your wife the queen, with whom he has committed adultery."

When the king heard these words, he changed color and became pale and said, "I can't believe this!" Then he became pensive and said nothing more for a long time.

"Sir," said Mordred, "we've concealed this from you as long as we could; but now the truth must be known, and we must tell it; and by hiding it from you for so long, we've been deceitful and disloyal to you. Now we're doing our duty. And we assure you that it's the truth; now consider carefully how this shame will be avenged."

The king was so pensive and sad and disturbed by this that he did not know what to do. Nevertheless, when he spoke, he said, "If you ever loved me, do whatever you must to catch them in the act; and if I don't take revenge as one should with a traitor, I'll never again wish to wear the crown."

"Advise us, sir," said Guerrehet, "for it's a very fearsome thing to bring about the death of a man as valiant as Lancelot, for he's strong and brave, and his kinsmen are very powerful. Therefore, as you well know, if Lancelot dies, the kinsmen of King Ban will launch against you a war so fierce and marvelous that the most powerful men of your kingdom will find it difficult to withstand it. And even you, unless God himself takes a hand in it, might well be killed, for they'll be more intent on avenging Lancelot than on saving themselves."

"Don't despair on my account," said the king, "but do what I've told you, and see that they are captured together, if you can; and I command you to do so by the oath you swore to me when you became knights of the Round Table."

And they promised him that they would do so, since he was so eager; all three swore it, and then they left the chamber and went to the palace.

That day the king was more pensive than usual, and he appeared to be angry. At the hour of nones Sir Gawain and Gaheriet arrived, and when they saw the king, they understood by his expression that he had had news of Lancelot. For that reason they did not join him, but went to the windows of the palace. The room was quiet and subdued, and no one there dared say a word, for they saw that the king was angry. Thereupon, an armed knight arrived and said to the king, "Sir, I can tell you news of the tournament of Carhaix: the men of the kingdom of Sorelois and of the Land Laid Waste have lost completely."

The king asked, "Were there any knights from here?"

"Yes, sir; Lancelot was there and won on every hand."

When he heard this news, the king frowned and became pensive. When he had thought about it, he rose and said loudly enough for many to hear him, "Oh, God! What a pity and shame that treason ever took root in such a noble man!" The king went into his chamber and lay down, lost in thought, for he knew for certain that if Lancelot were caught in adultery and put to death, never would there have been in that land such bitter grief over the death of a single knight. And nonetheless, he would have preferred to die rather than see his shame go unavenged. Then he sent word asking his three nephews to come to him; and when they were there, he said to them, "Lords, Lancelot will be coming back from the tournament; now tell me how he might be caught in the act that you revealed to me."

"My word," said Guerrehet, "I don't know."

"In God's name," said Agravain, "I'll tell you: announce to all your servants that you'll be going hunting in the morning, and tell all your knights except Lancelot to go with you; he'll willingly stay behind, whereupon I'm sure that, as soon as you have left, he'll come to sleep with the queen; and we'll stay here to learn the truth for you. And we'll be hidden here in a room and will capture him and hold him until you return."

The king eagerly agreed to this plan. "But take care," he said, "that no one should know about this before what you have proposed is done."

Sir Gawain arrived during this discussion, and when he saw them speaking so confidentially, he said to the king, "Sir, may God grant that only good may come from this conversation; for I expect that more harm may come to you than to anyone else. Agravain, dear brother, I urge you not to begin anything you can't finish; and say nothing about Lancelot unless you know it for a fact, for he is the best knight you've ever seen."

The king said, "Gawain, leave here; I'll never trust you, for you treated me badly when you knew about my dishonor but tolerated it and didn't inform me."

"I assure you," said Sir Gawain, "that I never betrayed you." Then he left the room and saw Gaheriet and said to him, "In spite of everything, Agravain has told the king what we didn't dare tell him, and you can be sure that no good will come from this."

"Then I'll have nothing to do with it," said Gaheriet. "Never will such a noble man as Lancelot be accused of this crime by me. So let Agravain do what he has undertaken, and if any good should come from this, he may have the credit; but if harm comes from it, he can't say that we were responsible."

Then they left there and went to Gaheriet's lodging; and as they were going down through the city, they met Lancelot and his companions, and as soon as they saw one another, they were overjoyed. Gaheriet said, "Sir Lancelot, I ask a boon from you." Lancelot granted it willingly, provided that it should be within his power. "Thank you," said Gaheriet. "Now I want you and your entourage to take lodging with me today. And you can be sure that I ask it in order to benefit rather than harm you."

When Lancelot heard that, he agreed willingly; they turned back and went to Gaheriet's lodging just as they were. Squires and servants rushed forward to disarm Lancelot and the others who had returned from the tournament. At supper time, they all went to court together, for they very much loved Lancelot. But when Lancelot arrived at court, he was very surprised to see that the king, who customarily welcomed him warmly, did not say a word to him, but instead turned his face away from him when he saw him arrive. He did not realize that the king was angry with him, for he had no idea of the damning news that had been told about him. Then he sat down with the other knights and began to enjoy himself, but not as much as he customarily did, for he saw that the king was pensive. After supper, when the tablecloths were taken away, the king invited his knights to go hunting in the forest of Camelot the next morning.

Then Lancelot said to the king, "Sir, you'll have me as a companion on the way."

"Good sir," the king said to Lancelot, "you can stay behind this time, for I have so many other knights that I can do without your company." Then Lancelot realized that the king was angry with him, although he had no idea why; and it pained him greatly.

That night, when it was bedtime, Lancelot left, accompanied by a great many knights; and when they were at their lodging, Lancelot said to Bors, "Did you see how King Arthur looked at me? I think he's angry with me for some reason."

"Sir," said Bors, "you should know that he has been told about you and the queen. Now be careful what you do, for we're facing the war that will have no end."

"Oh!" said Lancelot. "Who was the person who dared to mention it?"

"Sir," said Bors, "if a knight did it, it was Agravain; and if it was a woman, it was Morgan, the sister of King Arthur." That night the two cousins discussed the matter at length.

The following day, at dawn, Sir Gawain said to Lancelot, "Sir, Gaheriet and I are going hunting; will you come?"

"No," said Lancelot, "I'll stay here, for I'm not free to go where my will would take me."

Sir Gawain and Gaheriet followed the king into the forest. And as soon as the king had set out, the queen sent a messenger to Lancelot, who was still in bed; she asked him to come to her without fail. And when Sir Lancelot saw the messenger, he was very happy; he told him to return and he would follow him. Then he dressed and prepared himself and considered how he could join her so discreetly that no one would know. He asked Bors for advice, and Bors urged him not to go. "And if you do go, harm will befall you; for my heart, which never feared for you until now, assures me of that." And Lancelot answered that he was determined to go. "Sir," said Bors, "since it pleases you to go to her, I'll tell you the path to take. There's a garden that stretches from here to the queen's room. Enter the garden, and you'll find the quietest and most deserted path I know. And I ask you in God's name not to fail to take your sword with you."

Lancelot did as Bors had advised him; he set out on the garden path that led to the lodging of King Arthur. When Lancelot neared the tower, Agravain, who had set his spies everywhere, knew he was coming, for a youth had told him, "Sir, there comes Sir Lancelot." Agravain told the young man to be quiet; then he went immediately to a window that looked out onto the garden and saw Lancelot, who was hurrying toward the tower. Agravain, who had many knights with him, took them to the window, pointed Lancelot out to them, and said, "There he is. Now make certain, when he's in the room, that he doesn't escape from you." They answered that he could not possibly escape, since they would surprise him when he was undressed.

Lancelot, who did not realize that he was being watched, came to the door that opened out from the room toward the garden; he opened it and entered and went from room to room until he came to the one in which the queen was waiting for him.

Once Lancelot was in the room, he closed the door behind him, as it was not his lot to be killed there. He undressed and went to bed with the queen. But he had not been there long before those who were lying in wait to capture him came to the door of the room; and when they found it closed, all of them were taken aback, and they knew that their plan had been foiled. They asked Agravain how they could get in, and he advised them to break down the door, for otherwise they could not enter the room.

They knocked and beat on the door until the queen heard it; she said to Lancelot, "Dear friend, we're betrayed!"

"How, lady?" he said. "What is it?" Then he listened and heard a great noise outside, made by people trying in vain to break down the door.

"Oh, dear friend," said the queen, "now we're disgraced and doomed; now the king will know all about you and me. Agravain set this trap for us."

Lancelot said, "Lady, don't worry about that; he has arranged his own death, for he'll be the first to die." Then they both leapt out of bed and dressed as well as they could. "Oh, lady," said Lancelot, "do you have here a hauberk or some other armor with which I can protect my body?"

"None at all," said the queen. "Instead, our misfortune is so great that both of us are condemned to die here. And may God help me, that pains me more for your sake than for mine, for your death would be a much greater tragedy than mine. And yet, if God should grant that you escape from here safe and sound, I know that no man in the world would dare condemn me to death for this crime while he knew you were still alive."

When Lancelot heard that, he went fearlessly to the door and called to those who were beating on it, "Evil, cowardly knights, wait for me; I'm going to open the door and see who will enter first!"

Then he drew his sword and opened the door and told them to come in. A knight named Tanaguin, who mortally hated Lancelot, stepped forward before the others. Lancelot raised his sword and, with all his power, struck him so hard that neither his helmet nor his iron coif could prevent him from being split down to his shoulders. Lancelot pulled out the sword and struck him dead. When the others saw what had happened to him, they all drew back so that the doorway was left empty.

When Lancelot saw that, he said to the queen, "Lady, this battle is finished; I'll leave when it pleases you, but I won't be kept here by any man."

The queen said that she wanted him to be safe, regardless of what might happen to her. Lancelot looked at the knight he had killed. The man had fallen inside the door; Lancelot pulled the body toward him and closed the door. Then he took his armor and armed himself as well as he could, and he said to the queen, "Lady, since I'm armed, I should be able to leave safely, may it please God."

She told him to go if he could. He went to the door, opened it, and said that they would not keep him there. Then he rushed into the middle of them, his sword drawn, and struck the first one he met so hard that he knocked him flat on the ground so that he was unable to rise. When the others saw that, they retreated, and even the boldest of them made way for him.

When he saw that they were leaving him alone, he went into the garden and set out for his lodging. There he found Bors, who greatly feared that he might not be able to return as he wished; for he had realized that the kinsmen of King Arthur had somehow spied on Lancelot in order to capture him. When Bors saw his lord approaching fully armed, whereas he had left unarmed, he understood that there had been a fight. He approached Lancelot and asked, "Sir, what made you arm yourself?"

Lancelot told him how Agravain and his two brothers had spied on him, wanting to catch him red-handed with the queen, and how they had brought a great many knights. "And they almost caught me, since I wasn't on my guard; but I defended myself vigorously, and I fought well enough, with God's help, that I escaped."

"Oh, sir," said Bors, "now matters are worse than before, for what we had hidden so long is now known! Now you'll see the war begin that will never end in our lifetime. For if the king has loved you more than any other man until now, he'll hate you all the more when he knows that you have offended him by shaming him with his wife. Now you must consider what we'll do, for I know that the king will henceforth be our mortal enemy. But, God help me, I'm most distressed about my lady the queen, who will be condemned to death on your account. And I would like for plans to be made, if possible, so that she might be rescued unharmed from her plight."

While they were discussing this, Hector arrived. When he learned where matters stood, he was exceedingly sad, and he said, "In my opinion, it would be best for us to leave here and go into the forest, but to take care that the

king, who is there now, can't find us. And when the time comes for my lady
the queen to be judged, I assure you that she'll be taken out there to be put to
death. Then we'll rescue her despite the efforts of those who thought they
were leading her to her death. And when we have her with us, we can leave
the country and go to the kingdom of Benoic or Gaunes; and if we could manage to lead her there safely, we would have nothing to fear from King Arthur
and all his power."

Lancelot and Bors agreed to this plan; they ordered their knights and servants—there were thirty-eight of them—to mount, and they rode until they
were outside the city and in the thickest edge of the forest, so that they would
be less visible until evening. Then Lancelot said to one of his squires, "Go directly to Camelot and stay until you hear news about my lady the queen and
about what they intend to do to her; and if she has been condemned to death,
come back and tell us immediately, for whatever pain and difficulty her rescue may cost us, we won't fail to do everything in our power to save her from
death."

Then the youth left Lancelot, mounted his horse, and set out on the most
direct road for Camelot, and he rode until he arrived at King Arthur's court.
But now the story ceases to speak of him and returns to the three brothers of
Sir Gawain, when Lancelot had left them after they had found him in the
queen's room.

4. The Queen Condemned to Death but Rescued by Lancelot.

Now the story says that, when Lancelot had left the queen and had escaped
from those who wanted to capture him, his enemies, seeing that he had left,
entered the room and seized the queen. They treated her much more shamefully and disgracefully than they should have, and said that her guilt was now
established and that she could not escape death. They covered her with in-
sults, and she listened, grief-stricken, and wept so bitterly that the evil knights
should have felt pity for her.

At the hour of nones, the king returned from the hunt. When he had
dismounted in the courtyard, he was immediately informed that the queen
had been found with Lancelot. The king was greatly saddened and asked if
Lancelot had been captured.

"No, sir," they said, "for he defended himself so ferociously that no other
man could have done what he did."

"Since he isn't here," said King Arthur, "we'll find him at his lodging.
Now have a large company of knights arm themselves, and go capture him,
and when you have him, come back to me, and I'll have him and the queen
tried together." Then as many as forty knights went in to arm themselves, not
by choice, but because they were required to do so, since the king had person-
ally commanded it.

When they came to Lancelot's lodging, he was not to be found. They were all overjoyed at that, because they knew that if they had found him and wanted to take him by force, they could not have avoided a great and terrible battle. Then they returned to the king and told him that they had missed Lancelot, because he had left earlier and had taken all his knights with him. When the king heard that, he said that he was most displeased by it; and since he was unable to avenge himself on Lancelot, he would take vengeance on the queen in such a way that people would never cease to talk about it.

"Good sir," said King Yon, "what do you want to do?"

The king answered, "I want her to be severely punished for her crime. And I command you first of all, since you are a king, and then the other barons who are here—and I make this request by the oath you've sworn to me—that all of you consider how she should die. For she won't escape with her life, and she would die even if you sided with her and said she should be spared."

"Sir," said King Yon, "it isn't customary in this country that any man or woman be condemned to death after the hour of nones; but in the morning, if we're required to pass judgment, we'll do so."

Then King Arthur fell silent and was grieving so much that he neither drank nor ate that night, nor did he want the queen to be brought before him. The next morning, at prime, when the barons were assembled in the palace, the king said, "Lords, what would be a just punishment for the queen?"

The barons went aside to discuss this, and they asked Agravain and his two brothers what should be done. They said they thought it proper that she should die a shameful death, for she had committed a very disloyal act when she let a knight other than the most noble king sleep with her. "And it is our judgment that, for that alone, she deserves to die."

All of them agreed by necessity, since they saw that it was the king's wish. When Sir Gawain saw that deliberations had proceeded to the point that the queen's death was decided, he said that, if it pleased God, his sorrow would not allow him to see the one woman die who had accorded him the greatest honor. Then he came to the king and said to him, "Sir, I'm returning to you whatever I have received from you, and never again will I serve you if you permit this outrage." The king did not respond to what he had said, because his mind was on something else. Then Sir Gawain left the court and went directly to his lodging, grieving as much as if he saw everyone around him dead.

The king ordered his servants to go to the field at Camelot and to prepare a great and wondrous fire, in which the queen would be burned; for since queens have been consecrated, that is the only appropriate death for one who has committed a traitorous act. Then cries and lamentations arose throughout Camelot, and people grieved as bitterly as if the queen were their mother. Those who were ordered to prepare the fire made it so large and so marvelous that everyone in the city could see it.

The king ordered them to bring the queen before him, and she came there weeping bitterly. She was wearing a robe of red silk, a tunic and a mantle, and she was more beautiful and attractive than any woman of her age in the world. When the king saw her, he felt so much pity that he was unable to look at her; rather, he commanded that she be removed from his sight and that the court's sentence be carried out. They led her out of the palace and escorted her down through the streets.

When the queen had left court and the residents of the city saw her coming, then people could be heard crying from all sides, "Oh, lady, you who are more gracious and noble than any other woman, where will poor people ever be able to find pity again? Oh, King Arthur, whose disloyalty has brought about her death, you can still repent, and the traitors responsible for this can die in shame!" That is what the people of the city said as they followed the queen, and they were weeping and wailing as if out of their minds.

The king commanded Agravain to take forty knights and go to guard the field in which the fire was lit, so that, if Lancelot came there, he would be able to do nothing. Agravain asked, "Sir, do you want me to go?"

"Yes," replied the king.

"Then command my brother Gaheriet to come with us."

The king ordered him to do so, but he said he would not. However, the king threatened him until he agreed to go. Then he and all the others went to arm themselves. When they had done so and had left the city, they saw that there were a good eighty of them.

"Now, Agravain," said Gaheriet, "do you really think I would be willing to do battle with Lancelot if he wanted to rescue the queen? You can be sure that I would not! Rather than see her die here, I would prefer instead that he keep her for the rest of his life."

Thus did Agravain and Gaheriet talk as they rode along, until they came to the pyre. And when Lancelot, who lay in ambush with all his men at the edge of the forest, saw his messenger returning, he asked him what news he was bringing from King Arthur's court.

"Sir," he said, "bad news, for my lady the queen is condemned to death, and there's the fire being prepared to burn her."

"Sir," said Lancelot, "let's mount, for someone who intends to kill her may himself die instead. May God, if He ever heard a sinner's prayer, grant that I first find Agravain, for all of this is his doing."

Then they looked around to see how many of them there were, and they found that they numbered thirty-two. They all mounted their horses and took up shields and lances and set out in the direction of the fire. When those who were in the field saw them coming, they all cried together, "There is Lancelot! Flee! Flee!"

Lancelot, who was riding ahead of all the others, charged at Agravain and called to him: "Villain! Traitor! You are about to meet your death!" Then Lancelot struck him so hard that no armor could prevent the spear from penetrating his body; the blow was powerful, for he was a man of great courage and strength. Agravain fell from his horse, and the spear broke when he struck the ground.

Bors, who rode up at full speed, called to Guerrehet to be on guard, for he was threatening him with death. He spurred his horse toward Guerrehet and struck him with such force that no armor could prevent him from thrusting the steel through his opponent's chest; and he knocked Guerrehet off his horse to the ground, in such condition that he had no need of a doctor.

The others drew their swords and entered the fray. But when Gaheriet saw his two brothers struck down, there is no need to ask if he was enraged, for he realized that they were dead. He charged Meliaduc the Black, who was doing all he could to help Lancelot and to avenge the queen's disgrace. Gaheriet struck him so hard that he knocked him into the fire. Then he drew his sword, like the valiant man he was, and attacked another knight, striking him down in the middle of the field, at Lancelot's feet.

Hector, who was watching everything carefully, saw Gaheriet and said to himself, "If that man goes on living, he can do us great harm, for he's a man of great valor. It's better that I kill him before he can do us any more harm."

Then Hector spurred his horse and charged at Gaheriet with his sword drawn. He struck him so hard that he knocked the helmet off his head. Gaheriet was astonished to find his head unprotected. Lancelot, who was riding through the ranks, did not recognize him and struck him on his head with such force that he split it right down to the teeth.

When King Arthur's men saw Gaheriet fall, they became dispirited; but those who were pursuing them pressed them so hard that of the eighty knights, only three remained. Mordred was one of them, and the two others were knights of the Round Table. When Lancelot saw that there was no one from the king's household to resist him, he came to the queen and said to her, "Lady, what shall we do with you?"

Overjoyed at the salvation God had sent her, she replied, "Sir, I'd like for you to put me safely in a place beyond King Arthur's control."

"Lady," said Lancelot, "you will mount a palfrey and come with us into the forest, and there we'll decide what is best."

She agreed to this. Then they put her on a palfrey and rode into the thickest part of the forest they could find. When they were concealed in the forest, they counted to see if all of them were there, and they learned that they had lost three of their companions. They all asked one another what had become of them.

"By my faith," said Hector, "I saw three knights killed by Gaheriet."

"What!" said Lancelot. "Was Gaheriet there?"

"Sir," said Bors, "why are you asking that? You yourself killed him."

"In God's name," agreed Hector, "you did kill him."

"Now we can be sure," said Lancelot, "that we'll never have peace with

King Arthur or with Gawain, because of their love for Gaheriet; and this is the beginning of the war that will have no end."

[Arthur declared war on Lancelot. In one of the ensuing battles, Arthur himself attacked Lancelot, but the latter refused to fight the king. The pope demanded that Arthur take back the queen, and Lancelot returned her to him. Lancelot left Arthur's land and went to Joyous Guard. Leaving to attack him, Arthur left the queen in Mordred's keeping. The war against Lancelot was fierce but indecisive. Mordred began to win the allegiance of Arthur's barons. He also fell in love with Guenevere and wanted to marry her. She took refuge in a fortified tower. Meanwhile, Lancelot met Gawain in single combat; before the battle was stopped, both knights were injured, Gawain suffering a very serious head wound. The Romans invaded and were routed by Arthur.]

5. Arthur's March on Mordred; The Queen's Flight to a Convent.

Now the story tells us that on the very day when the Romans were defeated, as the story has recounted it, the youth sent by Queen Guenevere from the kingdom of Logres to Gaunes, with news about Mordred, came before the king, who was very pleased and happy about the fine adventure God had sent him. However, he was not happy about Sir Gawain, who was so gravely wounded that it was obvious he would not survive. Sir Gawain complained of none of his wounds as much as he did of the head wound inflicted by Lancelot. The Romans had renewed his pain that day by the great blows they had rained on his helmet, and he bled profusely, because he had performed great feats in the battle that day; and if he had not been so valiant, the Romans would not have been beaten by the army opposing them.

Then the queen's messenger came before the king and said to him, "Sir, I've been sent to you by Queen Guenevere, your wife, who wants me to inform you that you have betrayed and deceived her, and you have done nothing to prevent her and her entire lineage from being disgraced." Then he related Mordred's actions: how he had been crowned king of Logres and how all the high-ranking barons who held land from King Arthur had paid homage to Mordred, so that, if King Arthur came there, he would be received not as their lord, but as their mortal enemy.

Then he told him how Mordred had besieged the queen in the Tower of London and had pressed the siege every day. "And because my lady fears that he'll destroy her, she implores you in God's name to come to her aid as soon as possible, because if you delay, she'll surely be captured. And he hates her so desperately that he will defile her body, and you'll be disgraced by that."

When the king heard that, he was so taken aback that at first he could say nothing. Then he said to the young man that he would set matters right, God willing, and he began to weep bitterly. When he was eventually able to speak, he said, "Oh, Mordred, now you've convinced me that you are the serpent I once saw issue from my belly, the serpent who burned my land and attacked me.[8] But never has a father done to a son what I'll do to you, for I'll kill you with my own two hands; let the whole world know that, and God forbid that you die at the hands of anyone but me."

A good many nobles heard what he said, and they were amazed by it, because they knew from the king's words that Mordred was his son. And many of them marveled greatly at that.

The king told those around him to give orders for the army to be ready to leave the following morning, because he would ride to the sea and cross to the kingdom of Logres. When the army learned of that, you could have seen tents and pavilions being struck all around. The king ordered them to prepare a horsedrawn litter to carry Sir Gawain; he would not leave Gawain far from him, because he wanted to be there if his nephew had to die; and if he lived, Arthur would be that much happier. And they did everything just as the king had ordered.

The next morning, as soon as it was light, the army set out. Once on the road, they traveled until they came to the sea. Then Sir Gawain spoke very gently to those around him, saying, "Oh, God, where am I?"

"Sir," said one of the knights, "we're at the seashore."

"Where do you plan to go?" he asked.

"Sir, we intend to cross to the kingdom of Logres."

"Oh, God," said Sir Gawain, "bless you for allowing me to die in my land, which I've missed so much."

"Sir," said the knight who had spoken to him, "do you therefore think you're going to die?"

"Yes," he said, "I know without a doubt that I won't live another two weeks; and my death distresses me less than the fact that I can't see Lancelot before I die. If I could see the man whom I know to be the best and most generous knight in the world, and if I could ask his forgiveness for my cruel treatment of him at the end, I believe my soul would be more at peace after my death."

The king approached then and heard the words spoken by Sir Gawain; he said, "Dear nephew, your treachery has done me great harm, because it deprived me both of you, whom I loved more than anyone else, and also of Lancelot, who is feared so much that, if it were known that he was on good terms with me, as he once was, then Mordred would never have been so bold as to commit the treason he conceived. Now I believe I'll be wanting for

---

[8]This vision was revealed to Mordred in *Lancelot,* in a passage not included in this volume.

valiant men, not only you but others whom I most trusted in times of need, for the disloyal traitor has assembled all the forces of my land to oppose me. Oh, God! If only I had in my company those I used to have, I wouldn't be afraid to have the whole world against me."

Sir Gawain was saddened by those words from King Arthur; he spoke with great effort and said, "Sir, if my foolishness has made you lose Lancelot, you'll regain him by your wisdom. You can easily bring him back to you, if you wish, because he's the most valiant and generous man I've ever seen; and he loves you so much that I know he'll come back to you if you send for him. I certainly think you need him, and you shouldn't let your allegiance to me stop you, because it's obvious that no one will ever see me bear arms again."

When King Arthur heard Sir Gawain say that he was certainly going to die, he was so distraught by that and he grieved so bitterly that everyone there felt great pity for him. "Dear nephew," said the king, "is what you say true, that you'll leave us now?"

"Yes, sir," he said. "I'm sure that I won't live another four days."

"Then I should indeed grieve," said the king, "for the greatest loss is mine."

"Sir," said Sir Gawain, "I nevertheless advise you to summon Lancelot to help you, and I know without a doubt that he'll come as soon as he receives your message, because he loves you much more than you think."

"I'm sure," said the king, "that I've offended him so much that my request would be to no avail, and therefore I won't send for him."

Then the king's sailors came to him and said, "Sir, whenever you wish, you can board your ship, because we have made all necessary preparations, and the wind is good and strong and swift. It would be foolish to wait any longer."

The king then had Sir Gawain placed in the ship, and those caring for him made him as comfortable as possible. Then the most powerful barons boarded, taking with them their armor and their horses; and the other barons and their men boarded other ships. Thus King Arthur came back, angry about Mordred's betrayal of him; but he was more grief-stricken still about Sir Gawain, whom he saw growing weaker and closer to death with every passing day. It was that grief, more than any other, that struck at his heart; it was that grief that denied him rest night and day; it was that grief that prevented him from eating and drinking. But now the story stops talking about him and returns to Mordred.

Here the story says that Mordred continued the siege of the Tower of London until it was damaged and battered, for he had repeatedly used catapults against it, and those within could not have held out as long as they did if they had not defended themselves so tenaciously. And while the siege continued around the tower, Mordred never ceased to summon those nobles of Ireland and Scotland and other countries who held land from him. And when they came, he gave them such fine gifts that they were astonished; he won them over that way, so shrewdly that they agreed to everything and announced openly that nothing could prevent them from helping him against anyone, even against King Arthur, should chance bring him back to that land.

Thus Mordred won over to his side all the noblemen who held land from King Arthur, and he kept them with him for a long time. He was able to do that because, before leaving, King Arthur had left him all his wealth, wherever it might be located. In addition, everyone brought more and gave it to him; they thought that a good investment, considering his great generosity.

One day, when he had attacked the tower, it happened that one of his messengers came to him and gave him information in private: "Sir, I can give you momentous news. King Arthur has landed in this country with all his forces and is advancing on you with a great army. If you want to wait for him here, you'll see him within two days, and you won't be wanting for a battle, because that's his only reason for coming. Now consider what you'll do, because if you don't receive good advice, you could lose everything."

When Mordred heard that, he became confused and dismayed, because he greatly feared King Arthur and his forces. He was especially afraid that he would be punished for his disloyalty. He discussed this situation with those whom he trusted most; he asked what he should do, and they said, "Sir, the only advice we can give you is to gather your men and march against him and demand that he leave this land, which has been given to you by the nobles. And if he won't leave, you have more men than he, and they truly love you, so you can do battle with him confidently. You can be sure that his men won't be able to hold out against you, because they are exhausted and weak, whereas we are fresh and rested, for we haven't done battle recently. And before you leave here, ask your barons if they are in agreement about the battle: we believe the result will be just what we've said."

Mordred said that he would do that. He summoned all his barons and all the country's nobles who were in the city. They assembled, and when they were there, he told them that King Arthur was marching against them with all his forces and that he would be in London within three days. Those who were there said to Mordred, "Sir, what do we care if he comes? You have more men than he; meet him confidently, because we'll risk our lives in order to protect the lands we've given you, and we'll never fail you as long as we can bear arms."

When Mordred heard them urging one another on to battle, he was delighted; he thanked all of them and ordered them to take up arms, because there was no reason to delay, and he wanted to meet King Arthur before any harm had been done to the land.

Soon the news was known throughout the country, and they all said they would leave the following morning to meet King Arthur. That night, they busily made preparations. The next day, as soon as it was light, they set out from London, and they estimated that there were more than ten thousand of them. And here the story ceases to speak of them and returns to Queen Guenevere, the wife of King Arthur.

Here the story says that when Mordred and his army had left London, those in the tower heard that King Arthur was coming and that Mordred's men were going to meet him; they told the queen, who was both happy and sad about it: happy because she would be rescued, and sad about the king, for she feared that he would die in battle. She began to think about that and was so miserable that she did not know what to do. While she was thinking about it, her cousin happened to come to her. When he saw her crying, he was very unhappy, and he said to her, "Oh, my lady, what's wrong? In God's name, tell me, and I'll advise you as well as I can."

"Then I'll tell you," said the queen. "Two things have made me feel this way: first, the fact that I see that my lord the king has entered this battle and, if he is defeated, Mordred will then kill me. But if my lord is victorious in the battle, he'll never believe that Mordred didn't sleep with me, considering all the force he used in trying to get me, and so I know the king will kill me as soon as he gets his hands on me. Because of these two threats, you can clearly see that I can't avoid dying one way or the other. Now tell me whether there's any way I can be at peace."

He did not know how to advise her, because he saw her threatened with death on every hand. He said to her, "Lady, may it please God, my lord the king will be more merciful to you than you think. Don't be so dismayed, but pray to our Lord God Jesus Christ that he give your lord honor and victory in this battle and that Arthur will no longer be angry with you, if he ever was." That night, the queen rested very little, for she was not at peace, but instead very frightened, because she truly thought she was lost.

The next morning, as soon as it was light, she woke two young women whom she trusted completely. When they were dressed and ready, she had each one mount a horse. She took two squires with her and had them lead from the tower two packhorses loaded with gold and silver. Thus the queen left London; she went to a nearby forest, where there was a convent which her ancestors had established.

When she arrived there, they received her in a manner befitting such a lady. She had the squires unload all the treasure she had brought with her; then she said to the young women who had come with her, "Young ladies, you may leave or stay, as you wish, and as for me, I will stay here and join the nuns; for my mother, who was queen of Carmelide and was considered a good lady, came here and spent the end of her life."

When the young women heard the queen's words, they wept profusely and said, "Lady, you won't receive this honor without us." And the queen said she was very happy to have their company. Then the abbess came forward, and as soon as she saw the queen, she greeted her with great joy. The queen asked to join the order. "Lady," said the abbess, "if my lord the king had left this world, we would gladly take you as our lady and companion. But since he is alive, we wouldn't dare receive you, because he would surely kill us as soon as he learned of it. But there's also something else, lady: even if we accepted you, you wouldn't be able to live in accordance with our rule, for it is too painful, especially to you who have enjoyed all the comforts of the world."

"Lady," said the queen, "if you don't accept me, it will be the worse for me and for you, because if I leave here and by chance some disaster befalls me, I will suffer for it, but since the disaster would be your fault, you can be sure that the king would take revenge on you." The queen continued to talk to the abbess, who did not know how to answer her. The queen took her aside and told her of the anguish and fear that made her want to join the order.

"Lady," said the abbess, "I'll give you good advice: you'll stay here with us, and if by chance Mordred defeats King Arthur and wins the battle, then there will still be time for you to take our habit and join the order. And if God in glory permits your lord to win the battle and return safe and sound, I'll see to it that the two of you are reconciled and on better terms than ever before."

The queen answered the abbess: "Lady, I think you've given me good and faithful advice, and I'll do as you've suggested." Thus the queen stayed there with the nuns, taking refuge because of her fear of both King Arthur and Mordred. But now the story stops speaking of her and returns to King Arthur.

6. The Death of Gawain.

Here the story says that, when King Arthur put to sea to go to Logres and destroy and ruin Mordred, he had a good and strong wind, which soon took him and his army across the sea, and they landed beneath the castle of Dover. When they had landed and had taken their armor off the ships, the king instructed the people of Dover to open the gate and receive him, and they did so with great joy; and they said that they thought he was dead. "You can be sure that Mordred is responsible for this betrayal," said King Arthur, "and if I have any power over it, he'll pay for that with his life, as a traitor and a perjurer against God and against his liege lord."

That day, around the hour of vespers, Sir Gawain said to those who were with him, "Go ask my uncle to come and speak with me." One of the knights went to the king and said that Sir Gawain was asking for him. When the king came to him, he found Sir Gawain in such a grave state that no one could get a word from him. The king began to weep and lament bitterly; and when Gawain heard his uncle grieving so for him, he opened his eyes and said with great effort, "Sir, I'm dying; in God's name, if you can avoid doing battle with Mordred, do so, because I tell you truly that if you die at the hand of any man, it will be his. And greet my lady the queen on my behalf; and you, lords, if any of you, God willing, should see Lancelot, tell him that I send more sincere greetings to him than to anyone I've ever known and that I ask his forgiveness. And I pray that God will keep him as I left him. And I ask that he not fail to come and see my tomb as soon as he knows that I'm dead; that way, he can't fail to take pity on me."

Then he said to the king, "Sir, I ask you to have me buried at Camelot with my brothers, and I want to be placed in the same tomb where Gaheriet was buried, because he was the man I loved most in the world. And have the tomb inscribed, "Here lie Gaheriet and Gawain, whom Lancelot killed through Gawain's folly." I want those words written there so that I will be blamed for my death, as I deserve to be."

When the king, who was grieving bitterly, heard Sir Gawain say that, he asked him, "What, dear nephew? Have you met your death through Lancelot?"

"Yes, sir, by the head wound he caused; and it would have healed, except that the Romans reopened it in the battle." After that, no one heard Gawain say anything else except, "Jesus Christ, Father, do not judge me by my faults." And then he left this world, his hands folded on his chest.

The king wept and lamented loudly and fainted repeatedly over the body, proclaiming himself miserable, distraught, and grief-stricken. He said, "Oh, hostile and perverse Fortune, the most perfidious thing in the world, why were you once so generous and kind to me, only to make me pay so dearly in the end? You once were my mother, but now you have become a cruel step-mother; and to make me die from grief, you've brought Death here with you, and you've dishonored me in two ways: with my friends and with my land. Oh, villainous Death, you should never have taken such a man as my nephew, who surpassed everyone in goodness!"

King Arthur was very distraught over this death, and he felt so much anguish that he did not know what to say. He fainted from grief so often that his barons were afraid he would die in their arms. They therefore carried him into a room, because they did not want him to see the body, for as long as he saw it, his grief would never end.

All that day, the grief in the castle was so great that God's thunder could not have been heard; and they all wept just as if Gawain were cousin to each of them. That was not surprising, because, to a great many people, Sir Gawain had been the most beloved of knights. They paid all possible respects to the body, draping it in silken cloths worked with gold and precious stones. That night there was so much light in the room that you would have thought the castle was burning.

The next morning, as soon as it was light, King Arthur, who was weighed down by many burdens, took a hundred knights and had them armed, and he had a horsedrawn litter prepared, and he had the body of Sir Gawain placed in it. And he said to them, "Take my nephew to Camelot for me, and have him buried there, as he requested, and placed in Gaheriet's tomb."

As he was saying that, he was weeping so hard that those who were there were scarcely less moved by his grief than they had been by the death of Sir

Gawain. Then the hundred knights mounted, and as they set out they were accompanied by a thousand others, who followed the body, wailing and crying and saying, "Oh, good and true, courteous and kind knight, may Death be cursed for depriving us of your companionship!"

Thus all the people wept over the body of Sir Gawain. When they had accompanied the body for some time, the king stopped and said to those who were to take the body back to Camelot, "I can go no farther; go on to Camelot and do as I have directed." Then the king, more distraught than anyone could be, came back and said to his men, "Oh, my lords, now we'll see how you do from here on, for you've lost the man who was your father and a shield to you in every need! Oh, God! I think we will miss him greatly!" That is what the king said as he left. [. . .]

The next morning [. . .] they rode until they came to Camelot, and when the people of Camelot learned that the body they were bringing was that of Sir Gawain, they were very distressed and downcast, and they said that they had now lost everything. They accompanied the procession and placed the body in the center of the main church. When the masses learned that the body of Sir Gawain had been brought there, so many people came to the church that they could not be counted.

The body remained there, as was proper, until the hour of tierce; and then they placed it in the tomb with his brother Gaheriet, and they wrote on the tomb, HERE LIE TWO BROTHERS, SIR GAWAIN AND GAHERIET, WHOM LANCELOT OF THE LAKE KILLED THROUGH GAWAIN'S FOLLY.

Thus was Gawain buried with his brother Gaheriet. The people of that land grieved bitterly over the death of Sir Gawain. But now the story stops speaking of Sir Gawain and the lady of Beloé and turns once again to King Arthur and his company.

7. The Battle of Salisbury Plain.

Now the story says that, when King Arthur had left Sir Gawain's body, which he had sent to Camelot, he returned to the castle of Dover and remained there all that day. The next day, he left and rode with his full army to meet Mordred in battle. That night he lay at the edge of a forest. When he had retired and was asleep in his bed, he dreamed that Sir Gawain came to him, more handsome than he had ever seen him, and after him came a crowd of poor people, all saying, "King Arthur, we have won the house of God for Sir Gawain, your nephew, because of the great good he has done for us; do as he did and you'll be acting wisely."

The king answered that he would certainly do so. Then he ran to his nephew and embraced him; and Sir Gawain said to him, weeping, "Sir, don't do battle with Mordred; if you do, you'll die or will be mortally wounded."

The king answered, "I most certainly will fight him, even if I must die as a result; for I'd be a coward not to defend my land against a traitor."

Then Sir Gawain left, grieving very bitterly and saying to his uncle the king, "Oh, sir, what a tragedy and a pity that you are rushing to your death!" Then he came back to the king and said to him, "Sir, send for Lancelot, for you can be sure that if you have him in your company, Mordred will never be able to hold out against you. But if you don't send for him in your need, you won't be able to escape death."

The king said that he would not summon him for this reason, because Lancelot had so wronged him that he did not think he would come if sent for. And Sir Gawain then turned away, weeping and saying, "Sir, you can be sure that this will be a pity for all good men." Such was the dream that King Arthur had.

In the morning, when he woke up, he crossed himself and said, "Oh, fair Lord God Jesus Christ, who have bestowed on me so many honors since I first became king and began to hold lands, fair dear Lord, by Your mercy, let me not lose honor in this battle, but instead give me victory over my enemies who have deceived and betrayed me."

When the king had said that, he rose and went to hear the Mass of the Holy Ghost, and after that, he had all his men eat a light breakfast, because he did not know when he might meet Mordred's men. When they had eaten, they set out and rode easily and in leisurely fashion all day, so that their horses would not be too tired whenever they had to do battle. That night they camped undisturbed on the plain of Lovedon. The king retired in his tent, all alone except for his chamberlains.

When he had fallen asleep, it seemed to him that the most beautiful lady in the world appeared before him and lifted him up from the earth and took him up onto the highest mountain he had ever seen; and there she set him upon a wheel. The wheel had seats, some of which rose as others sank. The lady asked him, "Arthur, where are you?"

"Lady," he said, "I'm on a large wheel, but I don't know what wheel it is."

She said, "It's the Wheel of Fortune." Then she asked him, "Arthur, what do you see?"

"Lady, it seems to me that I see the whole world."

"Indeed," she said, "you do see it, and in it there is little that you have not been lord of until now, and of all you see, you have been the most powerful king who ever was. But such are the effects of earthly pride that no one is so highly placed that he can avoid falling from worldly power." And then she took him and dashed him to earth so cruelly that it seemed to King Arthur that he was crushed and that he lost all the strength of his body and its members.

Thus did King Arthur see the misfortunes that were to befall him. In the morning, when he had risen, he heard Mass before taking up arms, and to an archbishop he confessed, to the best of his knowledge, all the sins he thought he had committed against his Creator. And when he had confessed and had asked for forgiveness, he revealed to the archbishop the two visions that had come to him during the two preceding nights. And when the wise man heard them, he said to the king, "Oh, sir, for the salvation of your soul and body and kingdom, turn back to Dover with all your army, and ask Lancelot to come to your aid, and he'll willingly come. For if you attack Mordred now, you'll be either mortally wounded or killed, and the tragedy that befalls us will last as long as the world. King Arthur, all this will happen if you do battle with Mordred."

"Sir," said the king, "I'm amazed that you are forbidding me to do what I can't avoid doing."

"You must do as I asked," said the good man, "if you don't want to bring shame upon yourself." Thus did the man speak to King Arthur in an attempt to make him reconsider, but that was not to be, for the king swore on the soul of his father Uther Pendragon that he would not turn back but would instead attack Mordred. "Sir," said the good man, "it's a pity that I can't change your mind." But the king told him say nothing more about it, for nothing in the world could prevent him from doing his will.

That day the king rode directly to Salisbury Plain, knowing that on that plain would take place the great deadly battle of which Merlin and the other diviners had talked. When King Arthur arrived at the plain, he told his people to make camp there, for there he would wait for Mordred. They did as he ordered, setting up camp quickly and making preparations as best they could.

That night, after supper, King Arthur and the archbishop walked out onto the plain to get some air. They came to a high, hard rock, and the king looked up at the rock and saw that letters were engraved on it. He looked at the archbishop and said to him, "Sir, you can see a wondrous thing here; on this rock are letters that were carved long ago; look at what they say."

He looked at the letters, which said, THIS PLAIN WILL BE THE SITE OF THE TERRIBLE BATTLE BY WHICH THE KINGDOM OF LOGRES WILL BE ORPHANED.

"Sir," he said to the king, "now you can understand their meaning: if you do battle with Mordred, the kingdom will be an orphan, for you will die or be mortally wounded there; you cannot escape that. And so that you may be certain that this message is entirely true, I tell you that Merlin himself wrote these words, and everything he has ever said has been true, for he knows what will happen in the future."

"Sir," said King Arthur, "I see enough that, if I hadn't come so far, I would be convinced to turn back, however eager I had been until now. But now may Jesus Christ come to our aid, for I will never leave until Our Lord has given victory to me or to Mordred; and if I come to harm, it will be because of my sin and my own failure, for I have far more good knights than does Mordred."

King Arthur spoke this way, far more dismayed and frightened than was his custom, for he had seen a great many things that portended his death. The archbishop wept tenderly, unable to persuade Arthur to leave.

The king returned to his tent, and there a young man came to him and said to him, "King Arthur, I don't salute you, for I serve your mortal enemy, Mordred, king of the land of Logres. He has sent me to inform you that it was foolish for you to enter his land; but if you give your word as a king that tomorrow you and your army will return to the land you came from, he will permit it and will do you no harm. But if you won't do so, he warns you that there will be a battle tomorrow. Now send him word of your response to this message, for he doesn't seek your death, provided you leave his land."

The king, hearing this message, said to the youth, "Go and tell your lord that I will certainly not leave this land, which is mine by inheritance; rather, I'll stay in it as in my own, to defend it and drive him out as a traitor. And Mordred the traitor can rest assured that he'll die at my hand; inform him of that for me. I'd much prefer to fight him, rather than give up, even if he should kill me."

When he heard that, the young man did not linger, but instead departed without taking leave. He traveled until he came to Mordred, and he delivered King Arthur's message word for word, saying, "Sir, you can be sure that you cannot fail to have battle, if you dare wait for him tomorrow."

Mordred said, "I'll most assuredly await him, for there's nothing I desire so much as a pitched battle against him."

Thus was set the battle in which many valiant men died without deserving it. That night King Arthur's men were very fearful, for they knew well that they had far fewer soldiers than Mordred had on his side. For that reason they greatly feared to do battle with Mordred's army. Mordred had repeatedly requested help from the Saxons, and they came to his assistance; they were a great and strong army, and although they were less experienced in battle than King Arthur's army, they had a mortal hatred for the king. Thus, they had taken Mordred's side, and the most noble men of Saxony had paid homage to him, so eager were they to avenge many wrongs done them by King Arthur.

Thus were great armies gathered on both sides. And as soon as day broke, King Arthur rose and heard Mass, then armed himself and commanded his men to do the same.

[*Then the battle of Salisbury Plain began. The fighting claimed many of Arthur's best knights, and when Sir Yvain was killed, Arthur grieved, only to be told by Sagremor that Fortune was making the king pay for the honors he had had. Yet, Mordred's army suffered terribly as well.*]

King Arthur's men, who were guarding the standard, performed so well in this encounter that all except twenty of Mordred's four hundred knights were killed and hacked to pieces before the hour of nones. If you had been on the battlefield then, you would have seen the ground littered with the dead and a great many wounded.

A little after the hour of nones, the battle had been concluded in such fashion that of all those who were gathered on the plain—and there had been more than one hundred thousand—no more than three hundred now remained alive. All the knights of the Round Table had been killed except four, for they had thrown caution to the wind when they saw how desperate matters were.

Of the four who remained, one was King Arthur, the second Lucan the Wine Steward, the third Girflet; the last was Sagremor the Unruly, but he was so gravely wounded that he could scarcely stay in the saddle. They assembled their men and said that they would rather die than fight an indecisive battle.

Mordred charged at Sagremor and struck him so hard, within sight of the king, that he sent his head flying across the field. When the king saw that, he said in great sorrow, "Oh, God, why do You permit my prowess to be so abased? For the sake of that blow, I vow to God that either Mordred or I must die!"

He grasped a thick and strong lance and spurred as fast as his horse could carry him; and Mordred, who saw that the king sought only to kill him, did not retreat, but instead turned toward him. The king, bearing down on him with all his force, struck him so hard that he ripped apart the links of Mordred's hauberk and thrust the steel of his lance through his body. And the story says that when the lance was withdrawn, a ray of sunlight shone through the wound, so clearly that Girflet saw it; and the people of that country say that it was a sign of Our Lord's wrath.

When Mordred saw the seriousness of his wound, he realized that it would be fatal; and he struck King Arthur so powerfully on the helmet that nothing could protect his head, and the sword cut away part of his skull. This blow so stunned King Arthur that he fell from his horse, just as Mordred did. They were both so seriously wounded that neither had the strength to rise, and they both lay there, one beside the other.

Thus did the father kill the son, and the son mortally wounded the father.

When Arthur's men saw the king on the ground, they were so enraged that the human heart could not comprehend their pain. They said, "Oh, God, why do you permit this battle?" Then they charged at Mordred's men, and they at them, and the deadly struggle resumed. As a result, before the hour of vespers, all of them were killed except Lucan the Wine Steward and Girflet.

8. The Death of King Arthur.

When those who were left saw how the battle had ended, they began to weep bitterly, and they said, "Oh, God, did any mortal man ever witness such great sorrow? Oh, cursed be this battle, which has created so many orphans and widows in this country and others! Oh, cursed be this day, which dawned only to reduce to poverty the kingdom of Great Britain, whose heirs, famed for their prowess, lie here dead and grievously slaughtered! Oh, God, what more can You take from us? We see here all our friends dead."

When they had grieved for a long while, they came to where King Arthur lay and asked him, "Sir, how are you faring?" He said to them, "There's nothing to do but mount and leave this place, for it's clear that my end is near, and I don't want to die among my enemies."

Then he gingerly mounted a horse, and all three of them left the field and rode toward the sea until they came to a chapel called the Black Chapel. A hermit, who had his lodging nearby in a grove, sang Mass there every day. The king dismounted, and the others did so as well, and they removed the bridles and saddles from their horses. The king entered and knelt before the altar and began to recite his prayers. He remained there until morning without moving, and he did not complete his prayers until he had invoked mercy for his men who had been killed that day. And while he was praying thus, he was weeping so openly that his lamentations were obvious to those who were with him.

King Arthur continued to pray throughout the night. The next morning it happened that Lucan the Wine Steward was behind him and had seen that the king was not moving; and he said, weeping, "Oh, King Arthur, what great sorrow is ours on account of you!"

When the king heard these words, he raised himself up slowly, for he was weighed down by his armor. He seized Lucan, who was wearing no armor, and embraced and clutched him so strongly that he crushed his heart within his chest. And Lucan had no time to say anything as his soul left his body.

And when the king had remained in that position for a long while, he released Lucan, not realizing that he was dead. When Girflet looked at him intently and saw that he was not moving, he knew that he was dead and that the king had killed him. He began to grieve again and said, "Oh, sir, what a horrible thing you've done: you have killed Lucan."

And when the king heard him, he shuddered and looked around and saw his wine steward lying dead on the ground. Then his grief increased, and, enraged, he answered Girflet: "Girflet, Fortune, who has always been a mother to me but has now become a cruel stepmother, makes me spend the remainder of my life in pain and rage and grief."

Then he ordered Girflet to saddle and bridle the horses, and he did so. The king mounted and rode toward the sea until it was noon. He dismounted at the shore and ungirded his sword and drew it from the sheath. And after looking at it for a long time, he said, "Oh, Excalibur, good and powerful sword, the best in the world except for the Sword of the Strange Hangings,[9] you will now lose your master! Where will you find any man who will use you as well as I have, unless you fall into the hands of Lancelot? Oh! Lancelot, most worthy man and best knight in the world, may it please Jesus Christ that you have this sword and that I know you have it! Then my soul would surely be at peace forever."

Then the king called Girflet and said to him, "Go to that hill, where you will find a lake; and throw my sword into it, for I want it to disappear from this kingdom, so that it won't fall into evil hands."[10]

"Sir," he replied, "I'll do your bidding, but I would much prefer, if it please you, that you give it to me instead."

"I won't do that," said the king, "for you would not use it properly."

Then Girflet climbed the hill, and when he came to the lake, he drew the sword from the sheath and began to look at it. And it seemed to him so good and so beautiful that he thought it would be a great pity to throw it into the lake as the king had commanded, for thus it would be lost. It would be better to throw his own into the water and tell the king that he threw Excalibur in. He then ungirded his sword and threw it into the lake, and hid the other one in the grass, and he returned to the king and told him, "Sir, I have followed your order and have thrown your sword into the lake."

"And what did you see?" asked the king.

"Sir, I saw nothing unusual."

"Ah!" replied the king. "You're tormenting me. Go back again and throw it in, for you have not yet done so."

Girflet then returned to the lake and drew the sword from the sheath and began to lament its fate bitterly, saying that it would be too great a pity if it were lost. He decided to throw the sheath into the water and keep the sword, for it could yet be used by him or by someone else. He took the sheath and threw it immediately into the lake, and then hid the sword again under a tree. And he returned to the king and said, "Sir, now I have carried out your order."

"And what did you see?" asked the king.

"Sir, I saw nothing that I shouldn't have seen."

"Ah!" exclaimed the king. "You haven't yet thrown it in! Why do you continue to torment me? Go and throw it into the water, and you'll then know what will happen, for the sword won't be lost without some marvelous occurrence."

---

[9]The Sword of the Strange Hangings is presented, and its history recounted, in *The Quest for the Holy Grail,* Chapters 16, 21.

[10]In the English-language tradition, from Malory on, this task is generally given to Sir Bedivere rather than to Girflet.

When Girflet saw that he had no choice, he returned to the place where he had left the sword, and he took it and began to look at it intently and to lament, and he said, "Good and beautiful sword, it's such a pity that you cannot be possessed by some valiant man!"

Then he threw it into the deepest part of the lake, as far from him as possible. And as it neared the water, he saw a hand emerge from the water, and he saw the arm up to the elbow, but not the body to which the hand belonged; and the hand caught the sword by the hilt and brandished it three or four times in the air.

Girflet saw this clearly. Then the hand disappeared into the water with the sword. He waited there for some time to see whether it would reappear, and when he saw that it was to no avail, he left the lake and returned to the king. He told him that he had thrown the sword into the lake and recounted what he had seen.

"In God's name," said the king, "I was right to think that my death was fast approaching." Then he became pensive, and tears came to his eyes; and when he had been lost in thought for a long time, he said to Girflet, "Now you must go from here and leave me, and you will never see me again."

"If that's the case, I'll never leave you," said Girflet.

"Yes, you will," replied the king, "or else I will have nothing but hatred for you."

"Sir," said Girflet, "how could I possibly leave you here all alone and go away, when you tell me that I'll never see you again?"

The king said, "You must do as I tell you. Leave here quickly, for you can't remain. And I ask this of you in the name of the love that you and I have had for each other."

When Girflet heard the king ask him so tenderly, he answered, "Sir, I'll do what you command, despite my terrible grief. But tell me, if you please, whether it's possible that I might see you again."

"No," said the king, "you may be assured of that."

"And where is it you are going, good sir?"

"I won't tell you that," answered the king.

When Girflet saw that he would learn nothing more, he mounted his horse and left the king. And as soon as he departed, a strong and wondrous rain began to fall, and it continued until he reached a hill half a league from the king. And when he came to the hill, he paused beneath a tree to wait for the rain to stop, and he began to look back toward the place where he had left the king. He saw coming across the water a ship with many ladies on board, and when the ship neared the shore where the king was, they gathered on that side of the ship. The first among them held Morgan, the sister of King Arthur, by the hand and began to beckon to the king. And the king, as soon as he saw his sister Morgan, immediately rose from the ground where he was sitting and went aboard the ship, leading his horse after him and taking his arms and armor with him.

When Girflet, who was on the hill, had seen all this, he returned as fast as his horse could run. When he arrived at the shore, he saw King Arthur among the ladies, and he recognized Morgan the Fay, for he had seen her many times. In a very short time, the ship had gone farther from the shore than eight crossbow shots would have carried. When Girflet saw that the king was thus lost to him, he dismounted on the shore and mourned bitterly; and he stayed there all day and all night with neither food nor drink; nor had he had any the day before.

The next morning, after daybreak, when the sun had risen and the birds had begun to sing, Girflet was still suffering mightily from grief and pain. Sorrowful as he was, he mounted and left there and rode until he arrived at a nearby grove. In that grove lived a hermit whom he knew well. He went to him and remained with him two days, because he was ill from the grief he had suffered, and he told the holy man what he had seen happen to King Arthur.

On the third day, he left there and decided to go to the Black Chapel to see whether Lucan the Wine Steward had been buried. When he arrived there about noon, he dismounted at the entrance and tied his horse to a tree and went in. Before the altar he found two tombs, both of them very beautiful and rich, but one of them much more so than the other.

On the less beautiful was written the following: HERE LIES LUCAN THE WINE STEWARD, WHOM KING ARTHUR CRUSHED IN HIS ARMS. And on the tomb that was marvelous and rich were letters that said, HERE LIES KING ARTHUR, WHO BY HIS VALOR CONQUERED TWELVE KINGDOMS. And when Girflet saw that, he fainted upon the tomb; and when he regained consciousness, he very gently kissed the tomb and began to grieve bitterly, and he remained there until evening, when the holy man came who was to serve at the altar. Upon his arrival, Girflet asked him immediately, "Sir, is it true that King Arthur lies here?"

"Yes, my friend, truly he does; some ladies whom I don't know brought him here."

Girflet understood that they were the ones who put Arthur on the ship. He said that since his lord had left this world, he would no longer remain in it, and he so entreated the hermit that he accepted him into his company. Thus Girflet became a hermit and served at the Black Chapel, but that was not to be for long, for after King Arthur's death he lived only eighteen days.

9. Battle with Mordred's Sons; Deaths of the Queen and of Lancelot.

[*The queen learned of Arthur's death, after which she entered a convent. Lancelot too heard about Arthur's death; he was very distraught, because he had loved King Arthur greatly.*]

Lancelot and his company were approaching, and no one could have been more enraged and grief-stricken than he, for on the very day when the battle was to take place, he had received the news that his lady the queen had died and departed this world three days before. And it had happened just as he was told, for the queen had recently left the world. But never had a lady met a finer death or repented more nobly, nor had any lady more fittingly asked our Lord's mercy than had she.

Lancelot was stricken with pain and grief when he learned of her death.

[Lancelot and his army defeated the forces of Mordred's sons but suffered great losses themselves. At the end of the battle, Lancelot was separated from his men.]

Lancelot rode throughout the night wherever chance led him, never in a direct line. In the morning he happened upon a rocky hill where there was an isolated hermitage; he started in that direction, thinking he would go there to see who lived in that place. He went up a steep path until he came to the hermitage, which was very poor; and there was a small ancient chapel there.

At the entrance he dismounted and took off his helmet; he entered and found in front of the altar two holy men dressed in white robes; they appeared to be priests, and they were. He greeted them, and when they heard him they returned the greetings; and when they turned toward him, they ran to him with their arms outstretched and kissed him and expressed great joy at seeing him. Lancelot asked who they were, and they answered, "Don't you recognize us?"

He looked at them and realized that one was the Archbishop of Canterbury, who had tried for a long time to make peace between King Arthur and the queen; the other one was Blioberis, Lancelot's cousin. He was very happy, and he asked them, "Good sirs, when did you come to this place? I am very pleased to have found you."

They answered that they had come there right after the sad day when the battle took place on Salisbury Plain. "And we must tell you that, to our knowledge, none of our companions survived except King Arthur and Girflet and Lucan the Wine Steward, but we don't know what became of them. Chance brought us here, and we found a hermit here who took us in; he has since died, and we have stayed on here. And may it please God, we'll devote the rest of our lives to the service of Our Lord Jesus Christ and will pray that He forgive our sins. And what will you do, sir, you who have until now been the best knight in the world?"

"I'll tell you what I'll do," he said. "You have been my companions in the pleasures of the world; now I'll join you in this place and in this life, and for as long as I may live I won't leave here; and if you won't accept me, I'll do it somewhere else."

When they heard that, they were overjoyed, and they gave heartfelt thanks to God, raising their hands toward heaven. Thus Lancelot stayed there with the holy men. But now the story ceases speaking of them and returns to his cousins.

Now the story says that when the battle of Winchester was ended and the soldiers of Mordred's sons had fled, if they could, or had been killed, King Bors entered Winchester with the full force of his army, despite the resistance of those within. When he learned that his brother Lionel was in fact dead, his grief was indescribable. He had the body buried in the city of Winchester, as was befitting the body of a king; after the burial, he ordered that Lancelot be sought far and wide, but no one could find him. When Bors saw that Lancelot could not be found, he said to Hector, "Hector, dear cousin, since my lord is hopelessly lost, I want to return to our country; come with me, and when we're there, take either of the two kingdoms, for you may have whichever you wish."

Hector said that he did not want to leave the kingdom of Logres at that time, but that he preferred to stay there awhile, "but when I leave, I'll return directly to you, for in all the world you are the man I should and do love most."

Thus Bors and his men left the kingdom of Logres and returned to his country; and Hector rode here and there throughout the land until by chance he came to the hermitage where Lancelot was staying. The archbishop had instructed Lancelot so well that he had taken priestly orders, and he sang Mass every day and abstained from all nourishment except bread and water and roots that he gathered in the brush. When the two brothers saw each other, they both sobbed and shed many tears, for they loved each other dearly; and Hector said to Lancelot, "Sir, since I have found you engaged in such a noble cause—the service of Christ—and I see that you wish to remain here, I'll never leave, but instead I'll stay with you for the rest of my days."

When those who were there heard that, they rejoiced that such a fine knight had offered himself to the service of Our Lord, and they accepted him as their companion. Thus the two brothers were together at the hermitage and were ever vigilant in the service of Jesus Christ. For four years Lancelot lived a life of fasting and vigils and constant prayers and rising at dawn—a life such as no other man could have endured. During the fourth year, Hector died and departed this world and was buried right in the hermitage.

On the fifteenth day before May, Lancelot took to bed ill; and when he felt that he was going to die, he asked the archbishop and Blioberis to convey his body to Joyous Guard immediately after his death and to place it in the tomb containing the body of Galehaut, the lord of the Distant Isles. They promised him as his brothers that they would do so. Lancelot lived four days after that request and died on the fifth day. At the moment when his soul departed his body, the archbishop and Blioberis were not with him but were sleeping outside beneath a tree. It happened that Blioberis awoke first and saw the archbishop sleeping beside him. And in his sleep the archbishop saw a vision and rejoiced greatly and said, "Oh, God, blessed are You! For now I see what I wanted to see."

When Blioberis saw that he was laughing and talking in his sleep, he marveled greatly, and he feared that the enemy had entered him; for that reason he awoke him gently. When he opened his eyes and saw Blioberis, he said to him, "Oh, brother, why have you torn me away from the great joy I was experiencing?" Blioberis asked him what that joy was. He said, "I had such great joy and was in the company of so many angels that never have I seen so many people in one place, and they were taking the soul of our brother Lancelot up into heaven. Let's go then and see if he has really died."

"Yes, let's go," said Blioberis. They came to the place where Lancelot was and found that his soul had departed. "Oh, God!" said the archbishop. "Blessed are You. Now I know truly that the angels whom I saw rejoice so were celebrating for the soul of this man. Now I know well that penitence is more important than anything else, and never will I give it up as long as I live. Now we must take his body to Joyous Guard, for we promised him that before he died."

"That's true," said Blioberis. Then they prepared a bier, and when it was ready, they placed Lancelot's body in it. Then they took it, one on each side, and walked for many days, in hardship and pain, until they reached Joyous Guard. When the people of Joyous Guard learned that it was Lancelot's body, they rushed to it and received it with lamentations and tears; and around the body you could have heard such grieving and sobbing that scarcely could one have heard God's thunder. They went into the main church of the castle and did the body all honor, as was befitting a man as noble as Lancelot had been.

On the same day that the body was brought there, King Bors arrived at the castle accompanied by only a single knight and a squire. When he learned that the body was in the church, he went there and had the body uncovered and looked at it until he knew that it was his lord. When he recognized it, he immediately collapsed on the body and began to grieve more intensely than anyone has ever seen and to lament bitterly. That day there was a great deal of grief expressed in the castle, and that night they ordered that the rich and sumptuous tomb of Galehaut be opened. The following day they placed the body of Lancelot in the tomb, which they then had inscribed as follows: HERE LIES THE BODY OF GALEHAUT, THE LORD OF THE DISTANT ISLES, AND WITH HIM RESTS LANCELOT OF THE LAKE, WHO, WITH THE EXCEPTION OF HIS SON GALAHAD, WAS THE BEST KNIGHT WHO EVER ENTERED THE KINGDOM OF LOGRES.

When the body was buried, all the people in the castle kissed the tomb; and then they asked King Bors how he had happened to arrive just in time for the burial of Lancelot. King Bors answered, "In fact, a holy hermit, who lives in the kingdom of Gaunes, told me that if I came to this castle at this time today I would find Lancelot, dead or alive; and it has happened just as he said. But in God's name, if you know where he lived since I last saw him, tell me."

And the archbishop immediately told him all about Lancelot's life and about his death, and when King Bors had heard it all, he said, "Sir, since he was with you until the end, I'll stay here with you in his place for as long as I live; and I'll go away with you and spend the rest of my life in the hermitage." And the archbishop very tenderly gave thanks to Our Lord for that.

The next day King Bors left Joyous Guard and sent away his knight and squire, and sent word to tell his men to choose as king whomever they wished, for he would never return. Thus King Bors went away with the archbishop and with Blioberis and spent the rest of his life with them for the love of Our Lord. And now Master Walter Map has no more to say about the *Story of Lancelot,* for he has brought it to an end and has told everything that happened; his book ends here, and anything else that might be added would be a lie.

Appendix:
The Post-Vulgate Cycle

TRANSLATED BY MARTHA ASHER

Limitations of space make it impossible to include full chapters or extended excerpts of the Post-Vulgate Cycle. However, we offer here the segments that constitute four of the Cycle's distinctive themes; some, like the Questing Beast, have been chosen because they are not present in the Lancelot-Grail Cycle, others, such as the death of Merlin, because they offer accounts of events that are at variance with their counterparts in the preceding cycle. The four sequences presented here are (1) The Adventurous Kingdom, from the Dolorous Stroke to the Healing of Pellehan; (2) The Questing Beast; (3) The Death of Merlin; and (4) From Arthur's Sin to the Fall of the Kingdom.

The Adventurous Kingdom, from the Dolorous Stroke to the Healing of Pellehan

From Chapter 20. The Dolorous Stroke.

When the Knight with Two Swords saw the king coming, he did not refuse him but raised his sword. The king surprised him from one side and struck against the sword so hard that he broke it just below the hilt, so that the blade fell to the ground and the hilt remained in his hand. When the Knight with Two Swords saw this, he was more than a little frightened. He sprang quickly into a room, for he thought he would find a weapon there. But when he got there he found nothing at all, and then he was more frightened than before, for he saw that the king was after him with his club raised. He ran into another room, which was longer, but he found no more there than in the first, except that he saw that the rooms were the most beautiful in the world and the richest he had ever seen. He looked and saw the open door of a third room, which was longer yet, and he headed that way to go inside, for he thought all the while to find some weapon there with which to defend himself against the man who pursued him so closely.

When he wanted to enter the room, he heard a voice, which cried to him, "Woe to you if you enter, for you are not worthy to enter such a noble place."

He heard the voice clearly but did not, for that, leave his path but dashed into the room and found that it was so beautiful and rich that he did not think the whole world held its equal for beauty. The room was square and marvelously large and sweet smelling, as if all the spices in the world had been brought there. In one part of the room was a silver table, broad and tall, supported on three silver legs. On the table, right in the middle, was a vessel of silver and gold, and standing in this vessel was a lance, the point up and the shaft down.[1] And whoever looked long at the lance wondered how it stood upright, for it was not supported on any side.

---

[1] When the Grail knights finally find it in the Grail Castle, it has been reversed.

The Knight with Two Swords looked at the lance, but he did not recognize it. He headed that way and heard another voice, which cried loudly to him, "Do not touch it! You will sin!"

In spite of this warning, he took the lance in both hands and struck King Pellehan, who was behind him, so hard that he pierced both his thighs. The king fell to the ground, severely wounded. The knight drew the lance back to himself and put it back in the vessel from which he had taken it. As soon as it was back there, it held itself as erect as it had before. When he had done this, he turned quickly toward the palace, for it seemed to him that he was well avenged, but before he got there the whole palace began to shake; all the rooms did the same, and all the walls shook as if they would instantly fall down and disintegrate. Everyone in the palace was so dumbfounded at this marvel that there was no one brave enough to remain standing, but they began to fall, one here, the other there, just as if they were all dead. They all had their eyes closed, so as not to see the hour they would all fall into the abyss. Because they saw that the palace shook and trembled as hard as if it would fall down at once, they thought that the end of the world had come and that they must now die.

Then came among them a voice as loud as a wild man's, which said clearly, "Now begin the adventures and marvels of the Kingdom of Adventures, which will not cease until a high price is paid for soiled, befouled hands having touched the Holy Lance and wounded the most honored of princes, and the High Master will avenge it on those who have not deserved it."

From Chapter 75. The Perilous Seat.

How Galahad entered the palace and accomplished the Perilous Seat.[2]

While they were speaking of this, they looked and saw that all the doors and windows of the palace had closed; however, it did not become dark in the palace because of that, for a ray of light entered and extended through the whole building. Then a great marvel took place, for everyone in the palace lost the power of speech; they looked at one another and could say nothing. There was no one there so brave that he was not frightened, but no one left his seat while this lasted. Then Galahad entered, armed in hauberk, armpieces, and helmet, with two insignia in red silk. After him came the hermit who had asked to accompany him, and he carried a mantle and a robe of red silk on his arm.

But this much I tell you, that no one in the palace could see where Galahad had entered, for the doors did not open at his coming, nor did they hear

---

[2]Here and below, these italicized titles are contained in the original, not supplied by the translator or editor.

door or window open, but I cannot say as much of the hermit, for they saw him enter by the great door.

As soon as Galahad was in the middle of the hall, he said so that they all heard, "Peace be with you."

The good man put the clothes he carried on a red woolen cloth, went to King Arthur, and said to him, "King Arthur, I bring you the desired knight, the one who comes of the high lineage of King David and Joseph of Arimathea, by whom the marvels of this land and others will come to an end."

The king was happy at what the good man said; he answered, "If that is true, you are welcome, and the knight is welcome, for if he's the one who is to bring to an end the adventures of the Holy Grail, never was mortal man so honored in this court as he will be by us. Whoever he may be, I wish him well, since he comes from such a high lineage as you say."

"My lord," said the hermit, "soon you will see him make a good beginning." Then he had Galahad put on the robes he carried and sit in the Perilous Seat, and he said, "Son, now I see what I have greatly desired, when I see the Perilous Seat filled."

When they saw Galahad in the seat, all the knights suddenly regained the power of speech, and they cried out all with one voice, "Sir Galahad, you are welcome!" They already knew his name, for the hermit had spoken it.

From Chapter 148. Galahad at Corbenic; The Quest Is Accomplished.

As he was thus on his knees, he heard a voice, which said to him, "Galahad, get up. Take that basin from under the lance. Go to King Pellehan and spread it on his wounds, for thus is he to be healed by your coming."

But when Galahad took the basin, he saw that the lance went away toward heaven, and it mounted up so that neither he nor anyone else ever saw it again in Britain. When he took the basin, he saw nothing inside it; nevertheless, he was sure that there was a great deal of blood in it, as he had seen the drops falling thickly.

He said then, "Oh, My Lord God, how marvelous are Your powers!"

The room was wonderfully large, made in the form of a square, and so beautiful that one could hardly find its equal. King Pellehan, for whom God had performed many miracles, had not emerged from that room for a good four years and had never had anything else to eat but was sustained by the grace of the Holy Vessel; he was so badly hurt that he had no strength to rise but remained always lying down.

When he saw Galahad, who was bringing the basin from the lance, he cried out to him, "Son Galahad, come here and see to healing me, since God wills me to be healed at your coming."

When Galahad heard what the king was saying, he knew at once that this was King Pellehan, for whose injury everyone mourned. Then he went directly to him, the basin in his hands.

The king held up his clasped hands toward the basin, uncovered his thighs, and said, "You see here the Dolorous Blow that the Knight with the Two Swords struck. Much harm came from this blow, and I'm grieved by it."

And know that the wounds were as fresh as on the day he was stricken. Galahad tipped the basin, in which he thought there was nothing, over Pellehan's thighs, and when he tipped it he saw three drops of blood fall onto the thighs, and just as quickly the basin went out from between his hands, so that he had no power to hold it, and went off toward heaven. It happened just as I have told you with the Lance of Vengeance and the basin that stood under it, for they departed from the kingdom of Logres, with Galahad watching, and went off to heaven, just as the true history testifies. We do not know for sure if that holy lance and basin went to heaven, but it was God's will that nobody in England after that time could say he had seen them.

King Pellehan was immediately healed of the wounds he had had for so long, and he went to Galahad, embraced him, and said, "Son, holy knight, holy creature, filled with great righteousness, truly you seem to me true rose and lily, because you are clean of all sensuality. A rose you truly seem to me because you're more beautiful than any other knight, better and of better grace, filled with all good powers and all the good habits in the world. You are Jesus Christ's new tree, which He has filled with all the good fruits man may have."

The Questing Beast[3]

From Chapter 1. The Bizarre Beast.

The king listened and heard a great barking of dogs, who were making as much noise as if they were thirty or forty and seemed to be coming toward him; he thought they were his greyhounds, so he raised his head and began to look in the direction from which he heard them coming. In a short time he saw coming a very large beast, the most bizarre of form ever seen, as strange of body as of conformation and as strange inside as outside.[4] The beast came at great speed to the spring and had a strong desire to drink.

When the king had got a good look at it, he crossed himself and said to himself, "Now I see the greatest wonder I have ever seen. For I have never heard of such a bizarre beast as this one. If it is marvelous on the outside, it is even more marvelous on the inside. For I can hear and recognize quite clearly that it has in its body living hounds who are barking. Never before in the kingdom of Logres were such strange things found or seen."

This the king said of the beast. As soon as it had begun to drink, the animals who were barking inside it fell silent. When it had drunk and emerged from the spring, they began again to yelp just as they had done before. And they made as much noise as twenty hounds after a wild animal. So the beast left the spring with great noise and barking.

All the while the king stared at the strange thing he saw, so amazed that he did not know if he slept or waked. It went away at full speed, so that the king had soon lost sound and sight of it. When it was gone, he began to think harder than before.

While he was deep in thought, a knight approached him on foot and said, "Listen, you knight brooding there, answer the question I'll ask you."

The king raised his head and heard the knight; he answered, "Sir knight, what do you ask?"

"I ask you," said the knight, "if you saw pass by here the Bizarre Beast, the one which has inside it the barking of hounds?"

"Indeed," said the king, "I have truly seen it; it was here just now. It cannot be two leagues away."

"Oh, God!" said the knight, "how unfortunate I am! If my horse had not

---

[3]The strange story of the Questing Beast (or Bizarre Beast) will be familiar to readers of the works of Sir Thomas Malory. It is included here for that reason and also because it is lacking from the Lancelot-Grail Cycle.

[4]Paris and Ulrich (editors of this text) note that something is missing from the text and quote Malory I:17: "The noise was in the beast's belly like unto the questing of thirty couple of hounds."

died just now, I could have caught up with it, and my quest would be over. Oh, God! I've followed this beast a whole year and more to learn the truth about it."

"What, sir knight," said the king, "have you followed it that long?"

"Yes, my lord."

"And why, good sir? I beg you to tell me that, if you please."

"Certainly," said the knight, "I'll tell you. The truth is, and we know it well, that this beast is fated to die at the hand of a man of my line, but he must be the best knight to come from our kindred and the kingdom. Now, as things stand, they consider me the best knight of our land and of all our country. And because I wanted to know if I was the best of our line, I have followed it so long. I've said this not to brag but to learn the truth about myself."

"Indeed," said the king, "you have said enough about it, sir knight. Now you may go on when you please."

"On foot?" said the knight. "Rather I'll await the chance coming of some knight or man-at-arms, whom God may bring here, who will give me his horse."

While he was talking to the king this way, a squire came along mounted on a great horse, strong and fast; he was seeking the king as fast as he could go.

When the king saw him coming, he said to him, "Dismount, and let me mount that horse; I want to go after a beast who went by here."

"My lord," said the knight, "you won't do something so ignoble as to rush off after my beast which I have chased so long. Instead, have the courtesy to give me this horse, and I'll take up my quest again, for I have no reason to stay. If I lose it by your fault, the shame will be yours and the loss mine."

"Sir knight," said the king, "you have pursued the quest so long that you should leave it. Stay, then, and I'll carry it on for you until God gives me the honor of it, if He pleases."

"What!" said the other. "Discourteous knight, do you want to take on by force my quest which has so tormented and wearied me? Indeed, you shall not!" Then he went to the squire, threw him down off the horse, and mounted before the king could get there. Then he said to the king, "Discourteous knight, now I owe you no gratitude if I go after my beast. Stay, now, and I will go. And be sure that if I get the chance, I'll reward you richly for what you have done to me, wanting to take my quest from me. Because you wanted to interfere in such a noble quest as this, for that alone I think you a fool and a knave. For certainly you are not a knight who should interfere in such a high matter."

"Knight," said the king, "you will say what you like to me, and I will listen, but you know that if I hoped to find you, today or tomorrow, near or far, I would go after you and show you with a steel blade that I am, I hope, as good a knight as you and as worthy of a great quest."

"You will not have far to ride," said the knight, "if you want to find me, for I always stay in this forest in order to follow this beast."

"Then I promise you," said the king, "that I will never be at ease until I have shown which of us two is the better knight."

"When you want to find me," said the knight, "come to this spring. And know that, if you want to designate a day, you will find me here, for there is no day that I don't come here."

"Now you may go," said the king, "for I do not seek to know more of your affairs."

From Chapter 85. Yvain the Bastard and Girflet Wounded by the Knight of the Questing Beast.

Yvain said [to the hermit], "I'll tell you the truth. I've been following the Questing Beast, and I'll follow it until I know where the barking comes from; once I know what cries they are that issue from it, I won't follow it any more."

When the good man heard this, he bowed his head, and tears ran down his cheeks. When he had brooded sadly for some time, he said, "Oh, my lord, you are going to your death, for that beast you seek is a beast of the devil. That beast has done me so much harm that I will always lament it, for I had five handsome sons, the best knights in this land, and as soon as they saw the beast, just as you did, they longed to know what you want to know about it, and they set out to seek it, just as you are now doing. I was then a knight errant, just as you are now, and I went with them."

How the hermit told Yvain about the marvel of the beast.

"One day it happened that we were beside a body of water, and we saw the beast totally surrounded, so that there was no way it could escape.

"The oldest of my sons was holding a lance, standing nearer to the beast than his brothers, and the youngest of my sons called to him, 'Strike! strike! And we'll see what it carries in its body, from which these cries emerge.'

"He heeded his brother and the others, who were saying the same thing, and he struck the beast through the left thigh, for he couldn't strike it anywhere else. When it felt itself stricken, it gave a frightful cry, after which there came out of the water a man blacker than pitch, with eyes red as live coals, who took the lance with which the beast had been stricken and struck the one of my sons who had stricken it with such a great blow that he killed him. And the second, then the third, then the fourth, then the fifth. And then he went into the water, so that I never saw him again. This affliction about which I've told you happened to me in one hour because of that beast you are following. After I saw that there was nothing more I could do about it, I had my sons brought here and had them all five laid in one grave in a chapel that stands here. For love of them I stayed here, leaving the pleasures of the world's riches, and I want to serve God forevermore for their sake and for my own. I tell you this," said the hermit, "because I would advise you not to seek the beast. If you started the quest in folly, free yourself of it in wisdom, for, so help me God, I expect you to die in it rather than to live, for this is a thing not of God but of the devil."

"Indeed," said Yvain the Bastard, "since I've begun it, I won't abandon it, for those who knew about it would criticize me, and I'd rather die than abandon it thus."

"Do as you like, " said the good man. "I don't think good will come of it for you."

How Yvain was wounded by the Knight of the Beast.

When Yvain heard this, he was very happy, and he went to the top of the mountain. When he reached the tree, he saw a knight under it, fully armed and riding a good horse, and he had with him thirty beautiful dogs, good to all appearances.

"Friend," said Yvain the Bastard, "can you give me news of the Questing Beast that often comes here?"

The knight asked him, "Why do you ask about it, and what do you want with it?"

"I would gladly find it," said Yvain the Bastard, "for I'm going about looking for it, and I'm not going to leave off until I know why it is so strange."

"Indeed," said the knight, "you're mad and foolish to involve yourself in such a quest, for such a quest as this is not for you. A much better knight than you is needed here, and I, who am the most famous knight in this land, have been following the beast more than twelve years, with all the dogs you see here, and have never been able to catch it or kill it or know more about it than you do. And you're a stranger and hope to catch it alone? Indeed, you're chasing folly."

From Chapter 97. Perceval and the Knight of the Questing Beast.

How Perceval found the Questing Beast.

The next day at noon, Perceval found the Questing Beast in a valley, and when he saw it and knew that it bore within itself the source of the barking, he marveled more than at anything he had ever seen and said, "Truly this is the beast that my father followed so long and for which he labored so hard.[5] Indeed, I want to follow it to know if God will give me better luck with it than He gave my father."

---

[5]Perceval's father, King Pellinor, was hunting the beast in earlier chapters.

Then he left the road and went after it. He had not gone far when he lost sight of it, for the beast was fleet and went at a great pace, as if chased by lightning. Perceval followed it at a walk, for he did not want to tire his horse. While he was riding like that, there suddenly appeared the pagan knight who had been hunting the beast so long;[6] he was armed all in black and rode on a good horse, also all black, from which he had knocked down Gaheriet, Gawain's brother.

*How Perceval met the pagan knight, who forbade him to follow
the Questing Beast any more.*

As soon as the knight reached Perceval, he asked without greeting, "Did you see the Bizarre Beast pass by here, and thirty dogs after it?"

"I didn't see any of the dogs," said Perceval, "but truly I saw the beast, and it was going so fast that nothing could have caught it; by now it's probably a full league from here."

The knight answered, "May the beast and the dogs go to the devil, for that beast will make me die of grief!"

Then the knight who had inquired after the beast asked Perceval, "Who are you?"

He said, "I'm a knight errant of the house of King Arthur and a companion of the Round Table."

"What's your name?"

"Perceval of Wales," he answered.

"In the name of God," said the knight, "I've often heard men good at chivalry speak of you and praise you highly. But tell me this, as God may help you: what are you seeking alone in this country?"

"Indeed," said Perceval, "I take no companion with me because it isn't the custom of the knight errant to take company, unless he finds it by chance, for men would think it cowardice in him."

"And what are you seeking?" asked the knight.

Perceval said, "I ride in the quest for the Holy Grail, like the other knights of the Round Table, and I've been working at it for a long time now and haven't done anything by which I'm worth more or less. But now truly I left the road to go after this beast you are seeking."

"And what do you want with it?" asked the knight. "Why were you following it?"

"I followed it," said Perceval, "because my father, King Pellinor, hunted it a long time and couldn't catch it, and he was such a good knight that still today they speak of him throughout the whole world. And I, who am not of such great reputation, wanted to see if I could accomplish that at which he failed."

---

[6]That is. Palamedes.

"Indeed, Perceval," said the knight, "you've labored at folly; you're a good knight but not so good that you should concern yourself with such a great thing as this, and I ask you, as you value your life, to meddle in it no more but keep to your great quest for the Holy Grail, for you may be sure that if I find out that you're hunting this beast again, we'll have a fight."

From Chapter 147. Palamedes Kills the Questing Beast.

After Galahad had gone about the kingdom of Logres so much that he had accomplished more adventures and caused himself to be widely talked about throughout the land, one day it happened, where he was going through the Deserted Forest, that he met the Questing Beast, and fully twenty pairs of dogs were chasing it. The beast was moving fast, but it seemed tired.

When Galahad saw it before him, he said in his heart, "Now it will be wrong of me if I fail at least to accomplish this adventure, since so many good men have labored at it and not been able to do anything."

Then he went after the beast, but he had not gone far when he saw two other knights chasing it; one was Palamedes and the other Perceval. When they saw Galahad, they knew him by his shield, but he did not recognize them, for it was a long time since he had seen them, and they had changed their arms. As soon as they reached him, they made themselves known to him. He was very glad and embraced them, and they him.

"Sir Galahad," they said, "how have you been since you left us?"

"Very well," he said, "thanks to God. I've found many marvels in the kingdom of Logres, and, thanks to Our Lord, I haven't yet found an adventure so difficult that I couldn't accomplish it except this one of the Questing Beast. I met this beast long ago and have never been able to do anything about it. Therefore, I'm following it, for it seems tired to me."

"By God, my lord," they said, "we've been chasing it for more than a month. Nevertheless, since you've taken on the quest for it, we'll leave it to you, if you like."

"Don't do that," he said. "I'd rather you bear me company and I you."

Then they promised one another that they would never leave that quest as long as they could keep to it.

That day the three knights started hunting the Questing Beast, and they followed it wherever they thought it was going, but they could not find it that day or see it, so far distant from them had it gone. They slept that night in the forest in a hut they found there; they neither ate nor drank, but they saw to their horses as well as they could.

The next day they started out again, and Galahad said to the others, "I think we're nearing the end of our quest."

"How do you know, my lord?" they asked.

"I believe it to be so." he said.

"May God make it so," they said.

They rode thus until midday, and they found a good twenty dogs dead.

"The beast is going this way," they said, "and it killed these dogs here."

As they were speaking of this, they met a squire on foot, and they asked him if he had seen the beast.

"Yes," he said, "in an evil hour for me, for it killed my horse, and I have to walk."

"Which way is it going?" asked Galahad.

And he showed him the path it was following.

After they had left the squire, they went in the direction he had shown them. They had not gone far when they entered a deep valley, and in the middle of that valley there was a small, deep lake. In that lake was the beast, who had just arrived, weary and breathless, and had entered the water to drink, for it was very thirsty. On the bank were the greyhounds; they encircled the lake on all sides, and they were barking in such a way that the knights who were following the beast heard the barking.

Galahad said to Perceval, "Do you hear the cries of those dogs?"

"Yes," he said, "it's the beast. Let's go there."

Then they rode as fast as they could. When they reached the lake, they saw the beast in it, but it was not so far from the bank that they could not hit it if they wished by throwing a lance. As soon as they saw it there, they went toward it as quickly as they could. Palamedes was very brave; he had a mind to kill it and had already taken great pains to that end. He went into the lake just as he was, on his horse, and struck the beast in such a way that the lance passed through both its sides, and the point, with a great deal of the shaft, appeared on its other side. The beast gave a cry so loud and frightful that it frightened Palamedes's horse and those of the others so that they could hardly hold them. But when the beast felt itself wounded, it went under the water and began to make such a great tumult all through the lake that it seemed that all the devils of hell were there in the lake, and it began to throw and shoot forth such flames on all sides that anyone who saw it would have thought it one of the greatest marvels in the world. That fire did not last long, but a marvel resulted from it that still endures there now: that lake began to grow hot and to boil in such a way that it never stopped boiling, but it boils still and will boil as long as the world lasts, or so men believe. That lake, which got its heat from such a marvel as I have told you, is still called "the Lake of the Beast."

The Death of Merlin

From Chapter 37. The Death of Merlin.

Merlin loved the Lady of the Lake so much that he was dying of it, and he did not dare ask her to do anything for him, because he knew well that she was still a virgin. Nevertheless, he did not much want to be with her without knowing her carnally and doing with her all that man does with woman. He had taught her so much magic that she knew hardly less than he did. She knew well that he wanted nothing but her virginity, and she hated him mortally for it and sought his death by any means she could. As I told you on another occasion, she had so changed him by her magic that he could know nothing of what she did. She had already revealed to one of her cousins, a knight who was traveling with her, that she would wait no longer but would kill Merlin as soon as she saw her chance, "for I could not have the heart to love him, if he made me mistress of all the wealth under the throne,[7] because I know he is the son of the devil and not like other men."

Such things the Lady of the Lake said many times about Merlin, for she hated him excessively because he was the son of the devil. One day it happened that they were riding through the Perilous Forest, and night came on them in a deep valley, full of stones and rocks and far from city and castle and from all people. The night was so dark that they couldn't go forward but had to stay there. They made themselves comfortable and, gathering some of the driest bushes and lighting them to make a large fire, ate food they had brought from a castle where they had been that day.

When they had eaten their evening meal, Merlin said to the maiden, "My lady, near here among these rocks I could show you the loveliest little room I know; it was all made with a chisel, and its doors are of iron, so strong that I don't think anyone inside would ever get out."

"You tell me of marvels," said the maiden, "telling me that among these rocks there is a lovely, elegant room, and I believed that nothing ever came here but devils and wild animals."

"You were right," said Merlin. "Not a hundred years ago there was in this country a king named Assen, an honorable man and a good knight, and he had a son, a good man and a valiant knight, named Anasteu. Anasteu loved the daughter of a poor knight with such a great love that mortal man could not love a woman more.

"When King Assen knew that his son loved a woman so low-born, he criticized and rebuked him, but never because of this did Anasteu love her less, staying with her always. When the king saw that his son would not respond to his pleas, he berated him, saying, 'If you don't leave her immedi-

---

[7]I.e., God's throne, the sky.

ately, I'll kill you.' The son said, 'I'll never leave her but will love her all my life.' 'Indeed,' said the king, 'know then that I'll separate you from her, for I will kill her in front of you.' When the knight heard this, he had the woman taken away and hidden, so his father could not find her. He thought he would seek out a place, strange and far from all people, where no one went, and take her there so that they would be there the rest of their lives. He had hunted in this forest many times, so that he knew this valley well. He came here, bringing with him those of his companions whom he most loved and men who knew something of making rooms and houses, and with a chisel he had a room and a beautiful hall made in the living rock. When he had made it just as he wanted it, so rich that you could hardly believe it unless you saw it, he went to where he had left his love. He brought her here and, equipping the rock with everything he thought would be necessary, lived here all the rest of his life in great joy and happiness with his love. And it's true that they both died on the same day and were buried together in the room itself, and their bodies are still there; they won't decay in my lifetime, because they were embalmed."

When the maiden heard this story, she was full of joy, and she thought then that she would put Merlin there, if she could, and if magic and the power of words could help a woman, she thought she could accomplish it.

Then she said to Merlin, "Indeed, Merlin, these two lovers you have told me about loved each other most faithfully here, for they left all people and the world to enjoy their happiness and festivity together."

Then Merlin told her, "So have I, my lady, for I have left, for your company, King Arthur and all the noblemen of the kingdom of Logres, of which I was a lord, and I have had no profit out of following you."

Then she answered, "Merlin, if you could get all your desires at the first try, perhaps you would consider yourself rich and fortunate. Certainly, I would, if I could get mine."

"Indeed, my lady," said Merlin, "there's nothing in the world so difficult that I wouldn't do it, if you wanted it done. I entreat you to tell me what it is that you cannot do."

"I won't tell it to you now," she said, "but you will know it in time. I want to see this room you have told me about, which those two lovers made, and you and I will rest there tonight, for certainly, I like the place better because of their faithful love."

Then Merlin was very happy and said that she would see the room, since she wanted to, for they were very near it. He had two boys take torches and went along a narrow path that turned aside from the road. He had not gone far when he came out on top of a big rock, and there they found a narrow iron door. He opened it and went it, with the others after him. When they were inside, they found a room all covered in gold mosaic worked as richly as if the best artisan in all the world had studied there twenty years.

"Certainly," said the maiden, "this is a rich and beautiful place, and it's obvious that this place was made for great voluptuousness and for pleasure-seeking people."

"This is not yet the room where they lay," said Merlin. "Here they often ate, but I'll take you where they lay."

Then he went forward a little, found an iron door, opened it, and went in, calling for the candles. When he was inside, he said to those who came after him, "Now you may see the two lovers' room and the place where their bodies are."

Then they went in and began to look all around. When they had looked at the room and the works there, they said that never under the throne had there been a house as beautiful as this was.

"Indeed," said Merlin, "it is beautiful, and they were beautiful who had it made like this."

Then he showed the maiden a rich, beautiful tomb, which stood at the end of the room and was covered with red silk, worked very elegantly with animals in gold.

"My lady," said Merlin, "under this stone are the bodies of the two lovers I have been telling you about all night."

Then she lifted the covering and saw the stone that was over the tomb. When she had looked at it closely, she knew it was of red marble.

"Indeed, Merlin," she said, "this place is very beautiful and rich. It certainly seems that it was planned and constructed for pleasure-loving, happy people and for games, feats, and delights."

"So it was, truly," said Merlin. "If you knew with what great care and planning it was made, you would be totally amazed."

"Can this stone be raised by human hand?" she asked.

"No," said Merlin, "but I will raise it. Nevertheless, I don't advise you to view the bodies, because no bodies that have lain in the earth as long as these have would be beautiful to see, but ugly and horrible."

"Still," she said, "I want the stone raised."

"Willingly," he said. He took it at once by the larger end and raised it up. It was so heavy that ten men would have had enough to do to move it, because of which one should believe that his mind served him better than his strength there. Indeed, so it was in everything he did.

When he had raised the stone, he laid it on the ground beside the sarcophagus. The maiden looked and saw that the two bodies were shrouded in white silk, but she could not see either their limbs or their forms, only the bodies all shrouded.

When she realized that she would see no more of them, she said to Merlin, "Merlin, you've told me so much about these two people that, if I were God for one hour a day, I tell you that I would put their souls together in everlasting joy. Indeed, I delight so much in the remembrance of their deeds and their life that for love of them I won't leave here tonight but will stay here all night."

"And I with you," said Merlin, "to keep you company."

Thus the maiden said what she would do, and in truth she did it, for she ordered her bed to be made there. Those she commanded made it, and she went to bed at once, and so did Merlin, but in another bed.

That night Merlin was troubled, and he was not as happy and joyful as usual. As soon as he went to bed, he fell asleep, for he was already completely enchanted and had lost all the knowledge and memory with which he had been furnished. The maiden, who knew this, rose from her bed, went to where he slept, and began to enchant him still more. When she had reduced him to such a state that if someone had tried to cut off his head he would not have had the power to move, she opened the door of the room and called all her retainers. She made them come forward to Merlin's bed, where he lay, and began to turn him back and forth and upside down like a clod of earth, and he never moved, any more than if his soul had left his body.

She said quickly to those who were with her, "Say, now, my lords, is he, who used to enchant others, thoroughly enchanted?"

They crossed themselves in amazement and said they did not think the whole world could reduce him to such a state.

"Now tell me," she said, "what one should do. He comes with me and follows me, not for my honor but to degrade and deflower me. I would rather he were hanged than touch me in this manner, for he is the son of the devil, and I couldn't love a son of the devil for anything in the world. Therefore, I must take counsel how I may be free of him. For if I don't act now so that I am freed from him forever, I'll never again have such a good chance as I have now."

"My lady," said a page, "why are you always seeking and planning? I'm ready to free you from him right now."

"How would you free me from him?" she asked.

"I'd kill him," he said. "What else would I do?"

"God help me, he may not die in front of me," she said, "for I haven't the heart to see him killed. But I'll avenge myself on him better than you suggest."

Then she had him taken by the feet and the head and thrown upside down into the hole where the two lovers lay. Then she had the stone put on top. When with some difficulty they had replaced it, she began to work her spells and so joined and sealed the stone to the sarcophagus by magic and strength of words that there was never afterwards anyone who could move or open it or see Merlin, dead or alive, until she herself came there because of Tristan's entreaty, as the true history of Tristan tells, and the very Branch of the Cry[8] speaks of it, but

---

[8]In Old French, *Le contes del brait*. Concerning the theory that there was a lost French *Conte du brait,* see Fanni Bogdanow, "The Spanish *Baladro* and the *Conte du Brait*," *Romania* 82 (1962), 383–399. Bogdanow concludes that there was no *Conte du Brait,*

not much. Nor was there ever after anyone who heard Merlin speak, except Bademagu, who came there four days after Merlin had been put there. Merlin was still alive at that point and spoke to him when Bademagu tried to raise the stone, for Bademagu wanted to know who it was who complained so hard in the tomb.

Then Merlin said to him, "Bademagu, don't strain to raise this stone, for neither you nor any other man will raise it until she herself who shut me in here raises it, and no strength or ingenuity will be effective, for I am so strongly shut in by words and spells that no one could get me out but she herself who put me here."[9]

Of this adventure which I tell you here this book does not speak, because the Tale of the Cry tells it clearly. Know that the cry about which Master Helye is making his book was the last cry that Merlin uttered in the hole where he was, of the great sorrow he had when he perceived he was given over to death by a woman's wiles and that a woman's mind had defeated his. The sound of the cry of which I speak to you was heard throughout all the kingdom of Logres, wide and long as it was, and many marvels came of it, as the branch tells, word for word. But in this book we will not speak of it because it is narrated there, but I will tell you what pertains to us.

When the maiden had put Merlin in the hole, as I have told, she went to the door of the room and closed it the best she knew how, but she used no magic, and thus she and her retainers lay the night in the outer room of the house. In the morning when daylight appeared, she departed, shutting the door after her, but not in such a way that those whom chance would bring there could not open it.

---

that the Post-Vulgate author followed a common practice of the time in referring his audience to another "branch" for episodes he did not want to relate, and that the term "Contes del Brait" is probably a confused memory of the prose *Tristan*, called in several manuscripts "li Bret."

[9]Elsewhere, Merlin also tells Bademagu how Gawain may be saved from the Rock of Maidens. There are various versions of Merlin's end. In the prose *Perceval* he retires to a forest where, alive, he will await the last judgment (*The Romance of Perceval in Prose: A Translation of the Didot Perceval,* trans. Dell Skeels, Seattle: University of Washington Press, 1966, p. 94). In the Vulgate *Merlin,* Ninianne, who returns his love and wants him all to herself, enchants him so that he thinks he is in the loveliest tower in the world; he cannot leave, but she comes to him often. Malory condenses the post-Vulgate version to the bare bones: Merlin is "assoted"; Nenyve is "wery of hym" and "aferde . . . and so . . . by hir subtyle worchyng she made Merlyon to go undir that stone to latte hir wete of the marvayles there, but she wrought so there for hym that he came never oute for all the craufte he coude do." In Welsh tales he frequently winds up in a house of glass (Patrick K. Ford, "The Death of Merlin in the Chronicle of Elis Gruffydd," *Viator,* 7 [1976], 379–390).

From Arthur's Sin to the Fall of the Kingdom

From Chapter 1. The Conception of Mordred.[10]

Here the story says that one month after King Arthur's coronation there came to a great court, which the king convened at Carduel in Wales, the wife of King Lot of Orkney, the king's sister. But she did not know that she was his sister. The lady came to court in great luxury, with a large company of ladies and maidens. She had with her many knights, and she brought the four sons she had borne to King Lot, handsome boys and of such an age that the eldest was only ten. The eldest was called Gawain, the second Gaheriet, the third Agravain, and the fourth Guerrehet.

So the lady came to court with her children, whom she loved dearly. She was so beautiful that there was hardly her equal for beauty.

The king paid her great honor, because she was a crowned queen and of high lineage, kin to King Uther Pendragon.[11] King Arthur received the lady and her children with rejoicing and feasting. He saw that the lady was beautiful and loved her passionately and kept her at his court for two whole months, until finally he lay with her and begot on her Mordred, by whom such great wrongs were later done in the land of Logres and in all the world.

Thus the brother knew his sister carnally, and the lady carried the one who later betrayed and killed his father and put the land to torture and destruction, about which you may hear toward the end of the book.

From Chapter 7. Arthur Sets the Children of Logres Adrift at Sea.

One day the king said to Merlin, "Merlin, soon the time will come when you said he would be born by whose deeds this kingdom would be destroyed. Now know that I will arrange for every child born in the kingdom in that month to be taken and put in a tower, or two or three, if it takes that many. And there I'll have them cared for until I have had counsel on what you told me."

"King," said Merlin, "you are worried for nothing. Know that you will not find him, but it will come about just as I told you, for so it must be."

The king said he would do just as he wanted.

So the king waited until near the time that had been foretold. Then he had men search throughout the kingdom of Logres so that all the children of the

---

[10]The Post-Vulgate incorporated the Vulgate's version of the *Merlin* and, apparently, the *History of the Holy Grail*. Only with the anonymous *Suite du Merlin* (*The Continuation of the Merlin*) did the second cycle diverge to any significant degree. The material translated from Chapter 1 represents the beginning of the *Suite*.

[11]She is kin to Uther only by marriage, being Ygraine's daughter. Though not named here, this woman, the mother of Gawain and his brothers, is traditionally identified as Morgause.

kingdom of Logres were brought to him. The people of the country did not suspect that the king wanted to do with them such a strange thing as he did, and each one sent his child. They brought him so many, before the day came when the child Mordred was born, that he had more than five hundred and fifty put in one tower, and the oldest was not more than three weeks old.

Thus did the poor and the rich alike: as soon as their children were born, when they had christened them, they had them brought to the king, and he commanded at once that they be put in his towers. King Lot, who knew that his wife was pregnant and ready to lie in, asked the king many times what he wanted to do with all these children he was having gathered this way, but the king concealed his purpose and would not tell him. When King Lot knew that his wife had delivered and saw that the child had been born, he had him baptized, and in baptism he was named Mordred.

Lot said to the queen his wife, "My lady, I want to send your son to your brother the king, for everyone is sending infants to him."

"Since it pleases you," said the lady, "I also wish it."

Then the king had the child put in a cradle which was very rich and beautiful. When the mother was putting the child into the cradle, it happened that he struck his head, so that he had a great wound in the middle of his forehead which left a scar that was visible all his life. The king was angry over the injury, and so were all the others, but they did not give up putting him in the cradle because of that.

Then they put him in a ship with a large company of ladies and knights, and the king said that they would go thus by sea and escort the child to the king his uncle. "And when you are there, tell him that I send him his nephew."

They said they would deliver this message faithfully, if God let them come to the right place.

In this way King Lot's men left the city of Orkney. The wind filled the sail of their ship and in a little while had taken them so far from the port that they could see land nowhere.

So they sailed that day and that night as well, and such a large storm blew up at sea that all those on the ship began to cry out, "Oh, Jesus Christ, let us not perish here! Have pity on us and on this tiny creature, the king's son." So each one cried out and called on the saints, male and female, and made vows and acts of contrition. The sea was so roiled and the wind so violent that the ship struck a rock and was quickly broken into more than ten pieces. All those on the ship perished except the child who lay in the cradle.

It happened that the cradle was floating near the shore, after the others had all drowned. A fisherman in a little boat came to the place, seeking fish. When he found the cradle and the child near shore, he was marvelously glad and took them both and put everything in his boat. But when he saw the child was so richly dressed, swathed all in sheets and garments of silk, he thought at once that he was the scion of a noble line and was gladder of him than before.

He went back quickly, put cradle and child and all on his shoulder, and returned in haste to the town; he went by a side street to his house, taking care not to be seen, and showed his wife, who was there, what God had sent them.

"Indeed," said the lady, "this is a fine adventure, and God has sent it for our betterment. For we can live well and nobly twenty years on the wealth of this cradle, and I think God has done this to send us help."

"My lady," said the good man, "this child is of high birth; we can see that. He will have to be raised as well as possible. For if God let those o whom he is born recognize him, it would be better for us, and they would do well by us for it. It will be a long time before he is recognized. I rather suggest that we carry him, just as we found him, to the lord from whom we hold this land. For if he found out by some chance that we had found the child and had not brought him at once, he would have us destroyed, us and our children."

The woman said that this was the best advice and the most wholesome that he had given.

"Let us go, then," he said, "you and I, and we will make the lord a present of this child." She agreed completely.

So they took Mordred and left their home and went straight to the castle that ruled all the country. There they found the lord, who was called Nabur the Unruly and had a small son five weeks old called Sagremor; later he was a companion of the Round Table and a marvelously good knight, and his true name was Sagremor the Unruly, as the story will tell clearly later.

Nabur was very glad of the child they brought him, for he thought him the son of good people, high and powerful, from the fine garments he had around him. He gave the fisherman such a reward for his present that he was well satisfied. The lord had the child kept with Sagremor his son and had them raised together, and he said that, if God prospered them until they came of age to be knights, he would have them knighted together.

So Mordred escaped from danger, and all the others were drowned, for so the adventure went. Duke Nabur had Mordred healed of the wound he had in his forehead. He found a note in the cradle explaining that he was called Mordred, but he found nothing in the note of his birth or parentage. So Mordred found help and comfort after the peril of the sea. But now the story stops speaking of this and returns to King Arthur.

King Arthur, the story says, had had the children who were born in his country gathered in these towers, as I have told you. When the time of which Merlin had spoken had passed, the king thought he would have all the children killed, for he truly believed that the one through whom such evil was destined to come was there in that company.

One night while the king slept in his bed, it seemed to him that a man came to him, the largest he had ever seen, and four beasts bore him, but the king could not tell what they were.

The man said to the king, "King, why are you preparing to do such a great wrong, to destroy such holy and innocent creatures who are yet pure and clean of the world's corruption? The Creator of earth and sky would rather not have given you the grace He has. He established you to be shepherd of these people, and you have become a treacherous enemy to them. What wrong can these creatures have done you that you want to put them to death? Certainly, if you do it, the High Master who gave you the power you have will take such vengeance on you that it will be talked about forever after."

The king looked at the good man and was thoroughly abashed at what he said, and he began to think about the matter. The good man said to him, "I'll tell you what to do in order to think yourself well avenged in this. Have them all put into a ship on the sea, and let the ship be without a master, and let the sail be raised. Then have the ship launched in the sea and let it go where the wind will take it. Then if they can escape from such danger, Jesus Christ will have shown clearly that He loves them and that He does not wish the destruction of children. And this should suffice you, if you are not the falsest king who ever lived on earth."

The king said to the good man, "Certainly, you have shown me a marvelous vengeance. I'll carry it out exactly as you have said."

"It is not vengeance that you will do, for they have done no wrong to you or to anyone else, but this is to fulfill your wish and because you think that by this act you can turn destruction from the kingdom of Logres; but you will not do it, for it will happen just as the devil's son told you."

At that the king woke up, and it seemed to him that the good man who had spoken to him was still before him. When he saw it was a dream, he commended himself to Our Lord and made the sign of the cross on his face. And he said he would do with the children just as he had dreamed.

That day he had a large ship prepared, but even those who prepared it did not then know why he was having it done. In the evening, as soon as it was dark, the king had all the children, who were seven hundred and twelve by count, taken and put in the ship. When they had been put inside, the king had the ship's sail raised, and the wind, which had risen, filled the sail so that in a short time the ship was launched on the high seas.

Thus the children were put in danger of death. But it did not please Our Lord that they be thus endangered, for He saw creatures who had not deserved to perish in this manner. He gave such aid by His divine mercy that the ship arrived at a castle called Amalvi. The castle was beautiful and well situated, and its lord was a king who had long been a pagan, but he had recently become a Christian and greatly loved and feared Our Lord. He had just recently had of his wife a son, and he called the child Acanor, but later his name was changed in King Arthur's court, and because he was not a handsome knight but black and sunburned like his father, yet more valiant and bolder than anyone else, they called him everywhere the Ugly Hero. The story speaks much of him in the time when he engaged in the quest for the Grail and before.

When the ship came to the shore by the castle I told you about, it happened that King Orians had come out, and with him a large company of knights, and he had come by chance to amuse himself at the port.

When he saw the ship that had arrived, he said to those with him, "Let's go see this ship and find out what is inside, for it seems to me that it comes from far away."

They went there quickly, because they saw it pleased the king. When they had come to the ship and gone inside and found such a great number of children there, they crossed themselves in wonder.

The king said to his companions, "God's mercy! Where can these children have come from, and who can have gathered so many and put them together? For I did not think there were so many in all the world."

"On my soul, my lord," said an old knight to the king, "I'll tell you what it is, and I won't lie. The fact is that I happened to be wandering in the kingdom of Logres, and I came to King Arthur's court. There, without fail, before I left, I saw that King Arthur was having all the children of the kingdom of Logres gathered up, just as they were born, and put in the king's towers, but no one knew why the king did this. Now I think the truth is that the barons of the kingdom have put them to sea this way, perhaps because of some evil destined to come to them from the children, and they could not bear to have the children die in their presence. Therefore, they had them put to sea in the guidance of Our Lord and the care of Fortune. And everyone can see that if the barons had wanted them alive more than dead, they would not have let the vessel go without a pilot."

To this the king replied, "What you say seems to me the truth. But let us consider what we can do with the children. For since God has sent them to us, I would have them put where few people would know about them. For I know that since the king had them put in danger of death, if he knew I had them, he wouldn't thank me, but perhaps might hate me, and I would not have his hatred for anything, for evil would come of it to me and my land."

"My lord," said the old knight, "I'll tell you what you can do with them. Put men on this ship who know the sea, and then send these children to a retreat on some sea island. Certainly we can keep them so secretly that King Arthur will never hear of them."

The king had it done just as he had said, and he had them put in one of his retreats and put nurses with them, as many as were necessary. Afterwards, he had a good, strong castle built, and when it was made the king called it, for love of them, the Castle of Boys.

But now the story leaves them and returns to King Arthur.

Now the story says that when the barons of the kingdom of Logres knew what the king had done with their children, they were as sad as they could be.

They went to Merlin because they knew he stood well with the king and said to him, "Merlin, what can we do about this treachery the king has committed? No king ever committed one so great."

"Good lords, for God's sake," said Merlin, "don't be so angry. For he did this for the general good of the kingdom of Logres. For know truly that in this month in which we are now, a child has been born in this country by whose deeds and undertakings the kingdom of Logres is destined to be so devastated that after him there will be no good man but will meet his death in a pitched battle. Thus will this country be orphaned and stripped of both a good king and good knights. And know that this is no tale but as true as that you see me talking to you. Because the king wanted this sorrow to be averted and never come in his time either to him or to you, he has done what he has with the children."

When the barons heard these words, they said to Merlin, "Are you telling us the truth, that he did it with this intention?"

"Yes, God help me," said Merlin. "And I'll tell you more about your children. Know truly that they are all safe and sound and have escaped death, for Our Lord did not want them to die. Before ten years are up, you will see the healthiest of them."

When they heard this, they were much happier than they had been before, and they curbed their anger, for they believed everything Merlin told them, and they forgave the king for what he had done and said they would never hold it against him. Thus Merlin reconciled the barons to the king, and great evil would have resulted to the country if Merlin had not brought about this reconciliation.

From Chapter 11: Arthur Learns of Lot's Enmity.

[Merlin said to Arthur,] "I tell you that you have to deal with one who can do scarcely less harm than King Rion. Do you know who that is? It is King Lot of Orkney, your brother-in-law, who is the best knight you know in your kingdom, especially of those who wear crowns. He is at odds with you and hates you mortally. And do you know why? You well know the crime you committed with the children you commanded be brought to you from all over your land. It was when you had the children taken that your sister, King Lot's wife, had a child. They put him on a ship to send him to you. Whatever became of the child, whether he's dead or alive, King Lot believes firmly that they brought him to you and that you sent him out to sea like the others. From this they have conceived for you such a great hatred, your sister as well as the king, that they've gathered all the valiant men and good knights of the kingdom of Orkney and made them come to Camelot, as if to your aid, but this is not true; rather it is wholly for your harm."

From Chapter 13. The Death of King Lot.

"Merlin," said King Lot, "if I hate Arthur, it's not surprising. For he has recently committed the greatest treachery a king ever committed and has hurt by it all the noble men of this kingdom. He has deprived me myself of a child whom God had sent me; he never considered that the child was my son—and I the highest ranking man in his kingdom and so much his friend that I married his sister, so that my child was his nephew. Speaking of treachery, see what his crime was!" [. . .]

King Lot . . . charged with his sword drawn, as if seeking death. When King Arthur saw him coming, he was not prepared to meet him, and he reined back and threw up his shield against the blow. King Lot, who had aimed his blow, missed the king and struck the horse right on the front of the saddle. The sword was good and sharp, the blow came from above, and King Lot was full of strength; he struck the horse so hard that he cut it right through the withers, so that the horse fell dead to the ground, and King Arthur fell over his neck. Then the Knight of the Bizarre Beast[12] thought King Arthur was dead; he was very sad and said it was a great pity, for the people of the kingdom of Logres would not get as king another man as valiant as he was.

"So I'll avenge him if I can."

Then he charged at King Lot with drawn sword. When Lot saw him coming, he did not refuse him but awaited him undaunted, without a shield, for he had just dropped his on the field. The other struck him so hard that neither his helmet nor his iron headpiece kept him from being split to the shoulders. The knight carried his blow through and knocked King Lot to the ground. [. . .]

They were defeated, and Pellinor killed King Lot of Orkney. All King Lot's sons, when they came to knighthood, wanted to avenge the shaming of their father and of all their kin; among them Gawain later killed Pellinor and his eldest son Melodiam, and he killed Agloval on the quest for the Holy Grail . . . .

From Chapter 66. Lamorat's Last Adventures and Death at the Hands of Gawain, Agravain, and Mordred.

However, since this business was begun on Sir Gawain's advice, he would come out on top, if he could. He charged at Drian with considerable misgiving, because he knew Drian to be a good and valiant knight, and he struck him with all his force, so that he pierced his shield and hauberk and drove the point of his lance into his body. He struck him so hard that he knocked him from his horse to the ground, and at the fall Drian fainted from the anguish he felt, for he was mortally wounded. [. . .]

---

[12] Pellinor. not Palamedes.

When Lamorat[13] came to where Drian lay wounded to death and he recognized him, he let himself fall on him from his full height, embracing him and lamenting over him. Drian, who was not yet dead, opened his eyes when he felt himself thus embraced.

When he saw Lamorat, the one of his brothers he loved best and thought the best knight, he had enough strength to say, "Brother, I'm dying. Avenge me, if you please."

Lamorat replied with great sorrow, "Tell me, brother, who has killed you, and I'll avenge you if I can. I'd rather put life back into your body."

Drian, who was on the point of death, summoned the strength to say, "By my faith, those who have killed me are going away by this road." He told him what armor they were wearing.

When Lamorat heard what armor the man wore who had killed Drian with his own hands, he replied in great anger, "Brother, I'll avenge you, if God gives me the strength."

Then he went to his horse and mounted. He had been so sorely grieved by this encounter that he saw that his wounds had opened and begun to bleed again, although he had previously stanched the bleeding. When he had started on his way, so sorrowful that tears ran from his eyes under his helmet all across his face, he rode along the way his brother had showed him until he caught up with Sir Gawain and his brothers in a valley. As soon as he saw them, he recognized them by their armor, for he had seen them previously in the same or similar armor.

Then he cried to Sir Gawain, "Sir Gawain, you've dishonored me without challenging me except a long time ago. Now defend yourself against me, for, if I can, I'll avenge your killing of my brother."

At this Sir Gawain looked around, as did the other brothers. When they saw that it was Lamorat behind them, they said, "Now we're in a good position to avenge ourselves, for here's Lamorat, through whom all our sorrows began, all alone."

Sir Gawain, who respected his chivalry, replied, "Just because he's alone doesn't mean you've won. So help me God, he alone is worth more and can do more than twenty such knights, I know. I don't know any knight of his age in the world whom I would less like to attack than he. But since I see that I have to defend myself against him, there's nothing for it but to charge."

Then he lowered the lance he carried and struck his horse with his spurs. Lamorat, who hated him mortally and for many reasons, struck him angrily and so hard that he pierced his shield and hauberk and gave him a large, deep wound, bearing him from his horse to the ground. When the other two saw their brother on the ground, they charged at Lamorat, and both struck him on his shield. They were both of great strength and found Lamorat wounded and

---

[13] Pellinor's son.

tired, and they knocked him to the ground in such bad condition that he had no strength to get up. When Sir Gawain saw him fall, he feared that he would get up again and vanquish them all three, and he ran there quickly and seized him by the helmet while he lay unconscious; he pulled the helmet so hard toward himself that he broke the laces and wrenched it off his head, throwing it as far away as he could. When he had knocked off his iron cap, he cried to Lamorat to yield himself defeated or he would kill him, and with the pommel of his sword he gave him the greatest blows on the head, so that he made the blood spurt out in more than ten places. Lamorat regained consciousness and opened his eyes when he felt himself being so badly treated.

Sir Gawain said to him, "Unless you admit defeat, you're dead. May God never help me if I don't do as much to you as I did to your father."

Then Lamorat realized that Sir Gawain had killed his father, and he replied as he could, in anger and sorrow, "Oh, Sir Gawain, since you took my father from me when I was still a small child and you have killed my brother today, may God never help me if I ask you for mercy. Kill me after the others, for I wish it, and, God willing, there will yet come forward a man of my lineage or another who will avenge this great wrong. Indeed, if I lived long enough, I'd avenge it, but I won't, in my opinion, for it doesn't please God that this be accomplished by me."

As soon as he had said this, he fell back in great pain and lost consciousness. Sir Gawain, who had been very cruel to him and who feared that he might kill him, raised his sword, cut off his head, and threw his head away; then he said that it now seemed to him that he had avenged his father's death.

When he had thrown away the head and wanted to mount his horse, suddenly there was coming through the wood on foot a man of religion, dressed in a white robe. When he saw the dead knight, he went there, thoughtful and sad over this adventure.

When he saw Sir Gawain, he said to him, "My lord, for the sake of God and the faith you owe to all knights, tell me who is this knight you've killed?"

Gawain was too proud to conceal it from him and said, "Know that it's Lamorat, son of King Pellinor, the best knight of his lineage."

From Chapter 158. The Death of King Arthur.

When King Arthur left the Ancient Chapel, just as I have already told you, he went with Girflet toward the sea, full of grief over the adventures he had seen and the misfortunes that had recently come to him, one after another.

When he reached the sea—this was at midday—he dismounted and seated himself at the edge of the sea. He unbelted his sword, drew it from its scabbard, and saw the blade red with the blood of those he had killed.

After he had looked at it a long time, he said, sighing, "Oh, Excalibur, good and honored sword, the best that ever entered the kingdom of Logres except for the one with the strange straps, now you'll lose your lord, but where will you ever find a man by whom you'll be as well employed as you have been by me, unless you come into Lancelot's hands? Oh, Lancelot, the best man and the best knight I ever saw, except for Galahad, who was the best of the best! Now would that it pleased Our Lord for you to have this sword and for me to know it! Indeed, my soul would be more joyful forever."

Then he called Girflet and said to him, "Take this sword, and go up there to that knoll, and there you'll find a lake; throw it in, for I don't want the evil men who'll live after us to have such a sword."

"My lord," he said, "I'll obey your command, but I'd rather, if it pleased you, that you gave it to me."

"I won't," he said, "for by you it wouldn't be used as I wish, for you haven't long to live."

Then Girflet took the sword, went to the knoll, and found the lake. He drew the sword from the scabbard and looked at it, and he saw it so good and rich that it seemed to him a terrible waste to throw it in the lake and better to throw in his own, take this one for himself, and tell the king he had thrown it in the lake. Then he took his own sword and threw it in the lake; he concealed the king's sword among the weeds, returned to the king, and told him that he had thrown it in the lake.

"What did you see then?" asked the king.

"My lord, I saw nothing."

"Oh," said the king, "you're tormenting me. Go back there and throw it in, for you haven't yet thrown it in."

Girflet went back and took the sword; he looked at it, mourning, and said it would be a great pity if it were thus lost. He thought he would throw the scabbard in and keep the sword, for it could yet be useful to him or to someone else. He took the scabbard and threw it into the lake, and he returned to the king and said he had thrown the sword in. The king asked him again what he had seen.

"My lord," he said, "I saw nothing. What was I to see?"

"What were you to see?" said the king. "You haven't yet thrown it in. Why do you wrong me so? Go and throw it in. Then you'll see what happens to it, for it can't be lost without a great marvel."

When Girflet saw that he had to do it, he returned to the lake and took the sword, saying, "Oh, good and rich sword, what a great pity it is that no good man holds you in his hand!"

Then he threw it as hard as he could, and when it got near the water, he saw a hand come out of the lake, appearing as far as the elbow, but of the body he saw nothing. The hand received the sword by the pommel and brandished it three or four times. After it had brandished the sword, it withdrew with it into the water. Girflet waited a long time to see if it would appear again.

After that, he left the lake and returned to the king. He told him how he had thrown the sword in and what had happened.

"By God," said the king, "I knew all this would happen. Now I know well that my death is fast approaching."

Then tears came to his eyes; he thought a long while and said, "Oh, Girflet, long have you served me and kept me company. But now the time has arrived when you must leave me. You may well boast that you are the companion of the Round Table who bore me company the longest. But now I tell you to go; I don't want you to stay with me after this, for my end is approaching, and it isn't fitting that anyone know the truth of my end, for just as I became king here by adventure, so shall I pass from this kingdom by adventure, and after this, no one will be able to boast that he knows for certain what has become of me. For this reason I want you to go, and after you've left me, if they ask you for news of me, answer them that King Arthur came through God's adventure, and by God's adventure he departed, and he alone was the King of Adventures."